HISTORY OF
Sikh Gurus Retold

VOLUME – II
(1606 – 1708 C.E.)

Surjit Singh Gandhi

ATLANTIC
PUBLISHERS & DISTRIBUTORS (P) LTD

Published by

ATLANTIC

PUBLISHERS & DISTRIBUTORS (P) LTD

B-2, Vishal Enclave, Opp. Rajouri Garden,
New Delhi-110027
Phones : 25413460, 25429987, 25466842

Sales Office
7/22, Ansari Road, Darya Ganj,
New Delhi-110002
Phones : 23273880, 23275880, 23280451
Fax : 91-11-23285873
web : www.atlanticbooks.com
e-mail : info@atlanticbooks.com

ISBN 978-81-269-0857-8 (Vol. I)
ISBN 978-81-269-0858-5 (Vol. II)
ISBN 978-81-269-0859-2 (Set)

Printed in India
at Nice Printing Press, Delhi

PREFACE

The first volume of this work deals with Guru Nanak's vision which was revealed to him at Sultanpur Lodhi: its metaphysical spiritual, social and political aspects. How were Guru Nanak's formulations a creative resonse to the contemporary challenges as well as the ones likely to come up in future? What were Guru Nanak's concepts regarding God, cosmology, world, society and polity? Which institutions were set up by Guru Nanak and his successors upto Guru Arjan Dev? What was the organizational structure of early Sikhism? What was the exact connotation and importance of 'Shabad, Guru, Hukam and Nām?' What is the place of *Adi Granth* in Sikhism? Why was it compiled and made final in the sense that utterances embodied in it were unalterable? All these questions are adequately answered in the first volume.

In addition, the emergence of a new Sikh community was based on distinct belief system, ethics and world-view, absolutely unshackled from age-long unnecessary rituals, superstitious, totems, fetishes, esoteric practices and obsolete and irrelevant notions, ever-aspiring for building a fresh and novel society and man on fresh bases, such as equality, dignity of labour, freedom of conscience and freedom from fears of all kinds.

Such a society and religion were bound to cause friction/clash with the stereotypes and people with steno mentality both at social and political levels. The Sikhs showed remarkable resilience, firmness and steadfastness even when they were to face the wrath of the state which under Jahangir had leaned towards Islamic orthodoxy, especially of *Naqshbandi* variety.

Jahangir had a special dislike for the Sikhs atleast in the initial phase of his rule, and did not feel any compunction while ordering the execution of Guru Arjan Dev, the fifth Guru in succession to Guru Nanak.

The execution of the Guru was deemed by the Sikhs as no ordinary or a normal death. It was treated a martyrdom, an act in defence of a righteous cause or a witness to the Inscrubtale Truth of the Guru's dispensation. On a community level it was taken to signal that death courted or embraced in the cause of Truth is to be blessed with beatification and a share in the happiness of heaven. In a way, the Guru by courting martyrdom conveyed a distinct message that death courted in the noble cause in the spirit of humility and love for all is an instrument to give a fillip to the process of regeneration of man and society as a whole.

In this Volume (second volume), further growth of Sikhism and Sikh society has been traced. Aside profiling of the Gurus from Guru Hargobind to Guru Gobind Singh, certain aspects of Sikhism which were hitheto implicit are made explicit. The structural bonding of religion and politics, and concepts such as Sri Akal Takht and *Miri* and *Piri* have also been deliberated upon.

The volume also takes cognizance of the challenges posed by Islamic Imperialism led by Mughal state and Muslim orthodoxy. Besides, it deals with disintegrative forces unleashed by dissentient sects and '*Masands*' *et al.* The nexus between Hindu orthodoxy and Muslim orthodoxy to smudge and distort Sikh dispensation has also been spotlighted. How and why did Guru Gobind Singh bring into being the order of the Khalsa? Such questions and many more have adequately been answered in this study.

How did the Khalsa add new vistas to human history? How did the concepts and institutions which the Guru inherited from his predecessors culminate and what was their final shape? What were the new social formulations the Gurus wanted to be pursued? Was the Khalsa a mere organization in the sense, the communist party of Lenin was or something else? Arnold Toynbee, the world famous historian and philosopher of history, in his *magnum opus* 'Study of History' refers to Sikhism as the forerunner of the true élan of the communist party. But the Khalsa, the apotheosis of the Sikhism, has affinity and kinship of élan with communist party of Lenin in so far as it is essentially an organization of committed elites for furthering the cause of social transformation, but in aims and content, it is poles apart from communism as it is irrevocably committed to social pluralism and freedom of conscience. Tolerance and recognition of human individual is an end in itself and not an expendable limb in the beehive society of communism. This aspect has also been adequately deliberated. The Khalsa being a fresh ambience taking all aspects of life into its orbit, progonosticated a new civilization to be better designated as a challenger one more particularly in the context of two contemporary Hindu and Muslim civilizations capable enough to kindle hope in the human mind and affairs in the Indian subcontinent.

The upshot was that both the civilizations which were otherwise antagonistic to each other, sometime in conjunction with, sometime individually, organised onslaughts on the Khalsa model. A long drawn-out battle started and in the process many new milestones in the course of history were pitched. The Khalsa hegomonised politically for some time but as a civilization it could tread only a little onward. How all this happened? One will find rumblings and reflections in this volume.

SURJIT SINGH GANDHI

CONTENTS

VOLUME 2

PIRI-MIRI—STRUCTURAL BONDING OF SPIRITUAL AND TEMPORAL CONCERNS

MASTERLY INACTIVITY—A STRATEGIC RESPONSE TO ISLAMIC IMPERIALISM

CULMINATION

Guru Hargobind. A perception of an eighteenth century artist

(Twentieth Century Painting. *Courtesy:* Central Sikh Museum, Golden Temple, Amritsar)

At Srinagar in Uttarakhand, Guru Hargobind met Ram Samrath, the spiritual guide of Shivaji Maratha. The Saint was wonderstruck at the sight of the Guru with swords dangling on his both sides, a white hawk on his wrist and an aigrette attached to his turban. He asked the Guru "What kind of Guru are you? You are successor of Guru Nanak who had renounced the world, while you wear swords, keep horses and an army." The Guru replied, "Saintliness within, worldliness without. Arms for poor man's protection and the wickeds' destruction. Guru Nanak gave up not the world but the worldliness."

The Darbar of Guru Gobind Singh. This rare painting shows the Guru in regal dress. The Sikhs in the background are paying their respect and showing humility in the presence of their true King.

Guru Gobind Singh on the horseback with attendants 1830 CE

Esteemed Bhag Kaur in the battle of Khidrana – a Symbol of Khalsa Ladyhood. (Twentieth Century Painting, *Courtesy* Central Sikh Museum, Golden Temple)

Bhai Kanhaiya, a devout Khalsa, serving water to a wounded soldier of the enemy's camp in 1704. He emerged as a progenitor of *Seva Panth*—Path of Services. (Twentieth Century Painting by Kirpal Singh)

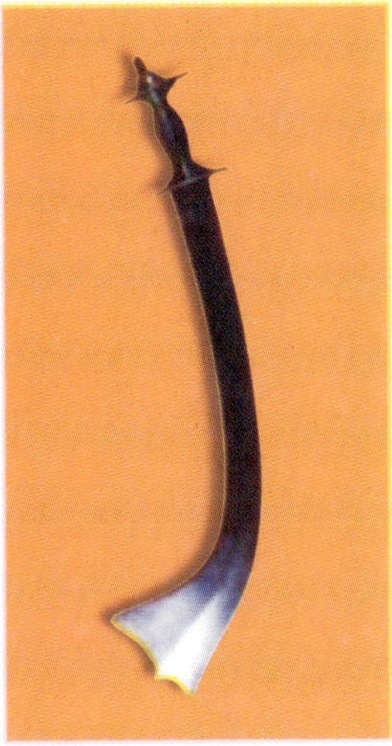

Shamsheer-e-Tegha
– *scimitar* of Guru Gobind Singh

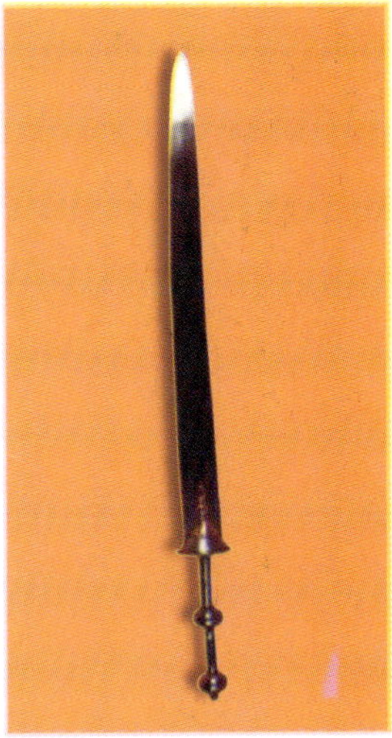

Saif, presented to Guru Gobind Singh by Mughal Emperor Bahadur Shah

Nihang Singh

PIRI-MIRI—STRUCTURAL BONDING OF SPIRITUAL AND TEMPORAL CONCERNS

7

GURU HARGOBIND

(b. 1595 C.E.; d. 1644 C.E.)

Guru Hargobind was born to Guru Arjan Dev on June 7, 1595 C.E.[1] at Vadali, a village near Amritsar. His birth caused a lot of heart-burning on the part of Prithi Chand who intensely desired that Guru Arjan Dev should die issueless and his Gaddi be inherited by his son, Manohar Das Meharban. Unfavoured by God, he began to test his own ill nature to succeed in his object. He hatched conspiracies to put an end to the life of child Hargobind; but all his designs met with utter failure. As Hargobind came of age, appropriate arrangements were made for his education. Bhai Budha educated him in theology, Sikh ethics and Sikh polity while Bhai Pairaga[2] a devout Sikh of village Katiala in Jehlum district of Western Punjab (now in Pakistan) gave him weapon training. Ganga Sehgal[3] made the Guru adept in horsemanship. The Guru learnt art of warfare from Bhai Jaitha and acquired knowledge of music from Bhai Mukand. The Guru also studied astrology and medicines, and scriptures of different religions. The Sikh tradition is unanimous in its assertion that the Guru grew to be an expert in military tactics and highly proficient in different fields of knowledge.

Guru Hargobind was extremely handsome, his feet resembling the pink lotus, his nails shedding luster like the diamonds arrayed on line. Both his legs were straight and muscular like the plant of *supari* and the joints of ankles and knees were stout and broad. He possessed broad chest and strong shoulders. The fingers of his both hands were like the luminous stone, whilst his face was as lustrous as moon. The milk-white teeth, pouting lips and eyes as sharp as the edges of the petal of the lotus, were adding to his beauty.[4] Bhai Gurdas says beautifully about the Guru, "The Guru was a mighty hero, a great benefactor and a powerful enemy-smasher."[5]

Guru Hargobind effected three marriages and had five sons and one daughter. Out of the five sons, the four, Baba Gurdita (b. 1613), Suraj Mal (b. 1617), Ani Rai (b. 1618) and Atal Rai (b. 1620) passed away during the lifetime of the Guru and his fifth son Guru Tegh Bahadur became Guru in C.E. 1664.[6]

He married his daughter Bibi Veero with Sadhu, son of Dharma in C.E. 1629. She begot five sons—Gulab Chand, Jit Mal, Ganga Ram, Shah Sahgoo and Hari Chand, who were all very bold and became skilled warriors under the guidance of Guru Gobind Singh. They played their part well in the battle of Bhangani (1688 C.E).

LAUNCH OF PIRI-MIRI

In 1606 C.E., Murtaza Khan at the instance of Jahangir sent a message to Guru Arjan Dev to come to Lahore to explain why he had helped prince Khusro.

The Guru was fully aware of the implications of Jahangir's summon but still he resolved to go to Lahore. On the verge of his departure, he placed five paisa and a coconut before Hargobind as an emblem of having nominated him as his successor. This happened on Jeth Vadi 25 Bk/25 May, 1606.[7] On this occasion, Baba Budha put a saffron mark on Guru Hargobind's forehead.

On Har 26, Samvat 1663[8] (June 24, 1606 C.E.) the recitation of *Sri Adi Granth* was completed and huge gathering offered prayer. At the conclusion of congregational prayer, Baba Budha brought him a seli, a woolen cord worn as a necklace or twisted around the head by former gurus and a turban as '*appurtenances*' of his calling. Guru Hargobind very politely laid it aside. He then addressed Baba Budha "My *seli* will be my sword belt and I shall wear turban with a royal aigrette. He wore two swords—one symbolizing Piri, spiritual power and the other signifying Miri, the temporal power. He told his follower that "in the Guru's house spiritual and mundane powers shall be combined". *There deg or meals for friends and teg or punishment for foes would always be ready.* "My rosary shall be the sword belt and on my turban, I shall wear the emblem of royalty." Guru Hargobind lit the torch as it was lit by Guru Nanak; but added to it the luster of the sword. He gave the same message as that of Guru Nanak; but he added to it the challenge of a hero.

By doing so, the Guru demonstrated that in Sikhism, the spiritual and temporal powers were not exclusive to each other, rather these existed side by side as parts of the one and the same whole. Their mutual relationship was that of the nature of correlationship, not of subordination of one to the other. This implied that only that temporal authority would be acceptable to the Sikhs and finds validity in Sikhism, which was not antagonistic and repugnant to the social structure as envisaged by his predecessors. The true guide in religious and a socio-political affairs would be the Guru himself.

No doubt, the Guru echoed what the Gurus preceding him had propounded but in terms of emphasis the Guru's pronouncement had its own uniqueness. Before Guru Nanak, the main tradition of religious thought was individualistic, other-worldly and static in character. Now the Sikhs were articulated to believe that the world here and now (*Halt*) and the world thereafter (*Palt*) would be seen in a new relationship. Similarly body and soul should not be considered mutually exclusive. Religion should be conceived as an ideology covering man's relationship to society along with the relation of soul to God.

In Sikhism God is conceived as one, the only one, permanent, eternal, beyond time, unborn, constant, deathless, beyond birth, self-existent, creator-person, considered as absolute, unconditioned and attributeless. He is also considered as all love, Guide, Enlightenment, Merciful, Benevolent, Extirpator of tyrants. Since He is Creator-Person, His creation including this world cannot be a mere illusion or *mithia,* rather a reality and something permanent within time and space. And this being so, God, being love, guide and enlightener operates the world/universe with his Will (*Hukam*) and with care and love, certainly altruistically. By doing so, He does not make a division between *Miri* and *Piri*, Halt and Palt, rather he guides both the *Piri* and *Miri* aspects of the universe/world. Being Creator-Person (*Akal Purakh*), he has created it and is always in it to improve upon it. This thing gives spiritual sanction to moral life of a man, because the basic Reality is the fount of all virtues and values.

Thus, in Guru Nanak's perceptions, for a Sikh to be a disinterested onlooker of the world and life is just out of question.

This being so, monasticism and asceticism stood rejected, and instead, the householder's life was accepted in Sikh system. Guru Nanak condemned the Yogis for being idlers, not ashamed of begging alms at the door of a householder whose life they otherwise hated. Most of the Indian systems accepted monasticism and asceticism or *Sanyas*. In fact, asceticism was considered to be the Indian contribution to the world culture. But Guru Nanak straightway rejected all such world-views which directly and indirectly gave credence to these concepts, institutions or practices. In fact, there was nothing like half-life-affirmation or half-life-negation. Life is one composite whole. It has no non-essential compartments. God is the Gracious Master of the entire universe and life. And, for that matter, faith in Him leaves the seeker no choice to select some aspects and leave others. In Granthic hymns, it is stressed again and again that in ultimate analysis, all spirituality has to be lived in the form of human conduct. The *Bani* says "Man's assessment in His court is done on the basis of his deeds. It is by one's deeds that we get nearer or away from God." It is in this context that Guru Nanak held: "Everything is lower than truth, higher still is truthful living."

One of the attributes of God is that He is the extirpator of tyrants. Guru Nanak says *ASUR SANGARAN RAM HAMARA* (Our God kills the demons). Logically man who accepts His will would not tolerate tyranny of any kind, whether it is spiritual, social, economic or political and would always be willing to take upon himself the responsibility to resist, confront and combat injustice and oppression or cruelty. Against this backdrop, Guru Nanak criticized trenchantly the faults in social, administrative, religious and political set-ups of his times. He deprecated hypocrisy, greed and evil ways of *Pandits and Mullahs,* the social discriminations, practices of pollution and caste inhibitions.

It was again against this backdrop that Guru Nanak set up organisations such as *Sangat* and institution of appointing a successor so that his mission could be carried on and responsibility was discharged adequately and appropriately.

From the above it is evident that the Piri-Miri thesis was not only a part of the spiritual experience of Guru Nanak, but it was also he who in own lifetime took all the necessary basic steps, theoretical as well as organisational, to implement and continue his spiritual mission.

The subsequent Gurus made no addition or alteration in the thesis of Guru Nanak. Their role can thus be understood primarily as a development, demonstration, and implementation of Guru Nanak's mission in socio-spiritual context.

Guru Angad and Guru Amar Dass strengthened the institutions of *Langer and Sangat* implying that Guru had a mission to develop solidarity and equality among the Sikhs as also to provide food to the needy, the indigent and the poor. They also made it clear that Udasis and recluses were not welcome to the Sikh society, since their out-worldly ideology was incongruous with Guru Nanak's system of *Piri-Miri.*

The role of Guru Arjan Dev also was an epitome of *Piri-Miri.* He constructed Hari Mandir, to provide a divine and social adhesive to the Sikhs. He introduced the system of *Daswandh,* according to which every Sikh was to contribute one tenth of his earnings towards the cause of the Sikh society. Besides, he accomplished the momentous work of compiling Sikh Central Scripture thereby enabling the Sikhs to be in touch with the real instructions of the Gurus. Not only this, he took steps to make the city of Amritsar financially viable apart from being the a locale of Harimandir. He founded new cities, namely Tarn Taran, Hargobindpur and Kartarpur where he tried to create ethos of mutual harmony on the basis of respect for one another. The Guru also constructed a number of tanks at various places which suffered from scarcity of rains and famine conditions frequently. The Guru persuaded Emperor Akbar to remit or reduce the revenue demand as a relief to the famished peasants of the area. Further, providing free food at every Sikh centre has always been a Sikh social practice since Guru Nanak.

From all this, it can safely be surmised that in the Sikh concept of *Piri-Miri*, adequate care of secular needs of the people was essential and was considered its integral part. Even the personal stance of the Guru was manifestation of the *Piri-Miri* concept. The Guru procured horses from central Asia, kept elephants and engaged retainers for them. He also dressed himself splendidly like the Maharajas of his times and people called him 'Sacha Padshah', the honorific expressive of the spirit of *Piri-Miri*.

From the time of the sixth Guru, the *Piri-Miri* complexion of the Sikh society became tangibly visible. On the very first day of his guruship, the Guru's wearing of two swords as symbols of *Piri-Miri* aspects of Sikh religion was a vivid demonstration of the fact that in Sikh scheme of things, worldly affairs were not an isolated phenomenon. The very significant fact is that in Sikh symbolism even for the *Piri* sword is the requisite insignia and not a rosary; for, it clearly defines and stresses that in Sikh ideology, *Miri* is an essential component of Sikh religious system, and not that two separate concepts have been combined. In fact there is a structural bondage between *Piri* and *Miri*.

In this context a question arises as to which factors were responsible for making *Piri-Miri* concept explicit, and more tangible during the pontificate of Guru Hargobind. The answer to this question can easily be found if we focus on the contemporary scenario.

The martyrdom of Guru Arjan Dev led the Sikhs to ponder upon the question. Was it right to knuckle under the evil instead of combating it? Masands who had become corrupt and selfish pleaded inadvisability to adopt the latter course because it would involve the Sikhs in a war against the Mughals. Many people were simply stunned at the sudden change of circumstances and were in utter confusion. Mother Ganga, a bold and sensible lady indeed, although opposed to the views of *masands*, felt totally confused. Bhai Budha and many other prominent Sikhs of the time were also not very clear as to the course to be adopted at that juncture.

Under such circumstances, definite guidelines were the need of the hour because a little laxity or mistake could entail incalculable harm. Psychologically, the moment was crucial. Danger there was that the Sikhs might feel exasperated and revert to escapism and asceticism thus abjuring faith in Guru's philosophy of energizing the people to struggle for truth and righteousness. It was feared that the Sikhs might become inactive and start believing in 'Let things move on as they are'. What fun to take part in the drama of life! The struggle between virtue and evil is always there and it is always safe not to take either side.

Moreover, there were people who were gasping at taking revenge of Guru's execution. They were also to be taken cognizance of before framing and ushering in a fresh programme. The traditional dislike of the Jats for passivity who had entered the fold of Sikhism in large numbers and the adventurous spirit of the nascent mercantile class also warranted due attention while configuring and launching any fresh initiative. The interest of hitherto neglected classes and social groups namely the so-called *Shudras* who had come into the embrace of Sikhism in quite a large number would have to be taken care of. Dialectically, the interests of the plebians (peasantry and *Shudras*) ran counter to those of the mercantile class whose natural tendency was to be capitalists and to establish capitalism. The overall jagirdari system of the Mughal administration did not allow this inherent contradiction to sharpen itself and in the face of the mightier enemy that is to say, jagirdari system, the likely conflict did not surface, but there was every possibility that natural antagonism between mercantile class on one hand and the plebians on the other might assume dangerous proportion levelling a stunning blow to the solidarity of the Sikh community. Besides, there was a challenge from Minas, now spearheaded by Manohar Das Meharban, who staked their claim to guruship and did not recognize Guru Hargobind as the legitimate successor of the fifth Guru.

To buttress his cause, he did not hesitate to connive at with the son of Chandu and certain Mughal officials. Quite a number of Bhalla families of Goindwal also sulked at the elevation of Hargobind.

The activities of Naqshbandis under the active leadership of Sheikh Ahmad Sirhindi had not yet abated even after the martyrdom of Guru Arjan Dev. They were hell-bent to convert especially the whole of Punjab, Kashmir and Sind to Islam and in the process, they scorned the Sikh movement which, in their reckoning, had the potentiality to foil their designs.

The whole scenario was carefully observed and analyzed. How should the Guru react to that? *Piri-Miri* concept of Sikhism which the Guru had demonstrated nudged the Guru to forge a suitable response according to which the Sikhs were enjoined upon to combat the evil and never to knuckle under it. In Guru's views, the meaning of the evil was quite comprehensive: it included economic, social, political and religious exploitation. Since in the context of the obtaining situation, the political evil was more pronounced and more quick in its effects, it was but natural that the refrain of the response should be to fight vigorously against the Mughal fanatical imperialism. Lest the Sikhs should divorce the spiritual matters from mundane affairs, the Guru set the norm of being a saint-soldier for every Sikh.

The response suited all interests. In it Jats found hope for their energies to have full play, the mercantile class the fulfilment of their latent desire to see the fall of Jagirdari-based Mughal administration, and the masses the hope of the dawn of an era wherein they would attain dignified social status. The policy also secured the position of the Guru. Since response touched bigger issues, the small ones sparked by the Guru's opponents and detractors could not gather strength. The schismatic move of the *Minas* which revolved around, more or less, the personal factor instead of doctrinal one, weakened and ultimately vanished.

On 26th Har Sudi Dasmi Sri Guru Hargobind Sahib seated himself on Sri Akal Takht Sahib which at that time was specially bedecked. The Guru attired himself in royal dress consisting of *Churidar Pyjama,* saffron coloured gown, a beautiful turban with aigrette affixed on it, a precious necklace around his neck, two swords hanging on his left and right sides. Masands and sangats from far and near reached. Bhai Gurdas and Baba Budha accompanied by a host of other celebrities also came to pay homage to the Guru. The Guru ordained that he would prefer offerings of arms and horses instead of money. According to M.A. Macauliffe, encyclical letters to Sangats and Masands at different places had already been sent to this affect.[9] The devotees including Masands lost no time to come forward to make their obeisance and present their offerings of arms and horses, swords and arrows. The Guru explained that the one sword symbolized his will that he would guide the Sikhs in spiritual domain and the second epitomized that he would guide his disciples in secular affairs. His followers, therefore, were required to seek guidance both in spiritual and temporal affairs, because in Sikh religion since its inception there was no dichotomy between both these domains and it envisaged people functioning as 'saint soldiers' and world totally spiritualized and socialized entity, fragrant with love and harmony basing itself on dignity and social equality.

The Guru's words seemed to be striking a fresh note besides sounding sublime message. No wonder, the people were transported into the realm of wonder. Nathmal and Abdullah who belonged to village Sur Singhwala (District Amritsar) and had enjoyed the beatitude of Guru Arjan Dev's teachings and of his beneficent personality composed and sang a 'Var', a kind of poem meant for relating heroic deeds or some other topics which were particularly significant and striking. They composed "Two swords the Guru wore on his either side, one to represent spiritual power, the other to symbolise temporal power, one to indicate his spiritual splendour and other to epitomize Guru's lofty will". Strong he is like a fortress, and is determined to smash the tyrants and the wicked.

In moral efflorescence, balladeers did not hesitate to utter that the Guru's turban emitted splendour hundred times more than Jahangir's.

As it is clear from 'Var'[10] of Natha and Abdullah as also from perceptions of the authors of *Gurbilas Padshahi 6* and *Sikhan di Bhagat Mala* and 'Vars' by Bhai Gurdas, the Sikhs highly venerated the Guru and called him, *Sacha Padshah*—a True king vicariously implying that all other kings including the Mughal one could not claim equality to the Guru in terms of delivering justice and welfare to the people.

The decision to adopt a new course necessitated some alterations and fresh emphases in the prevalent Sikh customs and institutions. It also required appropriate infrastructure to sustain and promote it. Besides, the message of the Guru was also to be delivered in tones and tunes warranted by the new policy. Conscious of all this, the Guru addressed the problems with his characteristic forthrightness. He dressed himself in a marital style and asked his followers to bear arms not only to defend themselves but also to extend protective coverage even *suo motu* to all those who stood in need of. He made it clear that a Sikh imbued with Sikh ideology must strive for all-round development with his eyes fixed on ameliorating the lot of the people irrespective of any prejudice and bias both at social and spiritual levels.

Offerings of Weapons and Horses

Foreseeing that *Piri-Miri* concept could result in far-reaching ramifications—even clashes with those forces which were opposed to it out of some ulterior design or mere ignorance, the Guru thought it prudent to take recourse to certain steps which looked peculiar in the then obtaining circumstances. He issued '*Hukamnamas*'—encyclical letters[11] to his Masands to the effect that they should inform the Sikhs that he would be happy if they brought arms and horses instead of money. The call of the Guru was responded with fervour and offerings of arms and horses arrived in abundance.[12] According to the celebrated author of *Gurpartap Suraj Granth*, these *Hukamnamas* also carried the contents of Guru's future programme.

Raising of Army of Saint Soldiers

The Guru also resolved to raise the army of his disciples to defend his dispensation from internal and external saboteurs. It was in this context that the Sikh soldier was given the epithet of *Sant Sipahi*—saint-soldier, a saint ready to make any sacrifice for the cause of goodness. The Guru enrolled as his bodyguard fifty-two impassioned soldiers, ever agog to measure their swords in the performance of their duties. This formed the nucleus of Guru's future army. Soon after the number of recruits increased. Five hundred youths came from Majha, Doaba and Malwa regions of the Punjab.

They told the Guru that they had no offerings to make except their lives. So far as their pay was concerned, they only required instructions in his religion and two meals a day. They professed that they would be highly pleased to die in his service. The Guru gave them each a horse and weapons of war and gladly enlisted them in his army. He made Bidhi Chand, Pirana, Jetha, Paira and Langha, each a captain of a troop of one hundred horses.[13] The exact strength of the army of the Guru is not known. Mohsin Fani states 'The Guru had seven hundred cavaliers and sixty artillery men who were always in his service.[14] This force as Cunningham suggests[15], possibly served as the Guru's bodyguard and secured the safety of his person. In addition there were bands of Pathan mercenaries. A Pathan chief named Painda Khan became one of his able and trusted adherents. The army was committed to the cause of combating the evil in whatever form it might be. Since the Guru's cause was progressive and in consonance with the ethos of the Sikh movement, his followers extended to him their whole-hearted co-operation. The Guru's kitchen never ran short of provisions.[16] According to Kavi Sohan, people of all castes such as *Jats, Chhimbas, Jhiwars,* Barbers and Carpenters *et al.* were members of Guru's army proving thereby that the Guru never subscribed to the age-long belief that only Kshatrias had the capability to fight. Some scholars have criticized the Guru on the ground that the Guru recruited in his army the worst type of criminals, highway men and confirmed plunderers.[17] A careful study of the Guru's soldiers and their subsequent achievements would help us a lot to determine the true character of the people. The soldiers of the Guru were devoted to the cause and were clear in their minds that their devotion to the Guru might cost them their heads.[18] Moreover, the scholars ignored the effect of the Guru's word on the people; it transformed them into the militia to remain in the vanguard to strike the satanic forces. Bidhi Chand who was a noted dacoit in his early life was transmuted by the alchemy of the Guru's word into a beau ideal of a saint-soldier.

The Pathans did come with mercenary motives, but that was quite well-known. The Guru in fact had recruited them with specific purpose of getting his followers trained in the art of warfare. The Guru did not find any difficulty in providing meals to his soldiers. The provisions flowed into the Guru's kitchen in abundance and never any shortage of anything was experienced by him. Some people, however, were skeptical with regard to the success of the Guru in maintaining such on army, but the Guru's resourcefulness and force of character removed their fear after some time. Bhai Gurdas's testimony in regard to the demeanour of Sikh soldiers is pertinent in his Var 15 Pauri 4. He highly praised the selfless devotion of the Sikh soldiers and their concern for the lacerated humanity. He also bespoke their excellent transformation from mere soldiers to saint-soldiers.

Engendering of Martial Spirit

In order that the Sikhs in general and Sikh soldiers in particular should imbibe martial spirit and acquire physical fitness, the Guru considered it appropriate to take certain tangible steps. He made daily exercise an important part of the daily routine of the Sikhs. He marked a piece of land just facing Sri Akal Takht to serve as *Akhara* (wrestling ground) where wrestling and other physical exercises were done. For the recruits of the Guru's army, rigorous training in different arts of war-archery, horsemanship, swordsmanship, throwing of lances *et al.* was arranged under the direct supervision of the Guru's commanders such as Bhai Bidhi Chand, Bhai Jetha, Bhai Pairana, Bhai Langa and Bhai Paira. The game of hunting was also resorted to as it was considered very useful in building up stamina, capacity to fashion quick responses to even sudden and unexpected challenges.

The Guru himself took special interest in this game which he made an important part of his daily routine. Accompanied by an army of forest beaters, hounds, tame leopards and hawks of different varieties, he used to sally forth and traversed long distances. The Guru relished the most the hunting of tigers, lions and leopards.

His mastery in this game exacted praise from one and all, even from Emperor Jahangir with whom he went on hunting campaigns in the sanctuary near Agra. Equally well-known were his feats in Chhanga Mangha forests, in Kashmir valley, and in the wastes of the Malwa region. According to Giani Gian Singh, hunting had become a favourite pastime for the Guru who was always anxious to seize time out of his busy schedule to enjoy this sport.[19] This being so, it can be legitimately surmised that the Guru did not harbour any prejudice against meat diet, although his primary motivation had always been to make his followers spirited and fearless.

In this context Mohsin Fani narrates a story, which imports credibility to our conclusion. Partab Mal Giani admonished a Hindu youth who was inclined to become a Musalman because he was averse to restriction on meat eating, thus "If you want to get full freedom in eating, you may become a Sikh of the Guru and then eat whatever you like.[20] Dr. Hari Ram Gupta's findings are also supportive of our conclusion. He says that at nightfall the Guru would return home with the carcasses of animals he had killed. These he distributed among his disciples and the poor people living near the place.[21]

The Guru also trained his soldiers in war-crafts *viz.* selection of ground for positioning forces, formation of forces according to enemy positions, determining frontage, patrolling, intelligence, organising sorties and camouflage, communication, psychological warfare *et al.* As for Guru Nanak, life without dignity was not worth living (*G.G.S.*, pp. 94, 142, 223) and for Guru Arjan Dev, fearlessness is a divine gift to be equated with liberation itself (*G.G.S.*, pp. 498, 702, 820, 1299). Guru Hargobind, not only laid added emphasis on this theme but also tried hard to make it a part and parcel of the psyche of soldier-saints.

Fortification of Amritsar

Apart from the raising of the army to combat the forces, be constructed a wall around the city of Amritsar. A fort named Lohgarh was also built in the city[22] in 1667 Bk (C.E. 1660). These were the times when a fort occupied a place of great importance in war strategy and the Marathas called it 'mother'. No wonder the fort imparted to them a new confidence, besides symbolising the determination of the Sikhs to pursue their ideals fearlessly.

Singing of *Vars* By *Dhadis*[23]

Under Guru Hargobind's direction, martial music was employed to energise the spirit of the people. *Dhad,* a special instrument to produce martial tunes was said to have been harnessed and made use of extensively by the Guru to sing 'Var', a special form of Epic whose unfailing effect is the raising of the drooping spirit of the people as it dealt with heroic deeds of heroes, both religious and secular. Some scholars have averred that the 'Dhad had been invented by the Guru'; but this is not correct. In the *Dasam Granth* (*Charitra Pokhyan* 405), ancestors of Dhadis (players of Dhad) could be traced back to mythological combat between Makkal and Suasvirva, the first ancestor of Dhadis being born of the sweat of the former. The fact that Guru Nanak called himself Dhadi[24] also indicates that the institution of Dhadis was very old. Certainly, it existed prior to Guru Hargobind. Even then, in Sikh tradition, Dhadis flourished since the days of Guru Hargobind who engaged some leading exponents of this art to recite balladry at Sikh assemblies. Abdullah and Natha of the village Sur Singhwala in the district of Amritsar were the chief Dhad players of Guru Hargobind's court. *Asa Di Var* began to be sung two times every morning by the rebeck players inside Harmandir and by Dhadis at Sri Akal Takht. The Guru set heroic tunes (*Dhunis*) to the nine out of twenty Vars in *Guru Granth Sahib*.[25] The singing of Var by balladeers in accompaniment with Dhads went a long way to inspire the Sikhs to feel spirited and courageous. According to Giani Gian Singh, the Dhad players set ablaze the latent war-like emotions of the people of Punjab.[26]

Nagara

According to the author of *Gurbilas Padshahi Chhevin*, the Guru introduced two innovations: one, the beating of *Nagara*—big drum to call the people instead of calling by voice, and second, the hoisting of saffron flag in front of Sri Akal Takht.

Both these innovations were innocuous, apparently having no political undertones or overtones. These were, at best, the adjuncts to Sikh religious organisation. But the Mughal government and the Muslim religious elites drew their own inferences. They reckoned that they were emblems of Sikh sovereignty as also a challenge to the Mughal authority. Their perception obviously was based on their own parochial vision, came into being partly under the influence of Naqshbandis and partly because of their narrow self-interests. The reformist thrust of Sikh dispensation which was universalistic and transcended cultural and political affiliations was altogether misinterpreted with the consequence that Guru Hargobind and his ideology were not received well by the ruling elites.

Congregational Prayer

The Guru laid added emphasis on the organisation of congregation-Sangats and congregational prayer. He was sure that this practice would enable the Sikhs to transcend idiosyncrasies, parochialism and particularistic propensities, born out of local, racial, religious or narrow national affiliations thereby facilitating and accelerating the growth of the sense of unity and mutual cooperation. The impact of Guru's strivings was so deep and wide that the Sikhs started looking upon Sangat as divine bodies, akin to Guru or God or both.

According to Mohsin Fani, 'when a Sikh wished for God's benefaction, he would come to an assembly of the Sikhs called Sangat in Sikh religious parlance and beseech it to pray for him, so much so even the Guru himself asked the Sikh congregation (Anjuman-I-Sikhan) to pray for him.'

Sri Akal Takht

As a concomitant to the Guru's design to articulate *Piri-Miri* aspect of Sikhism, he felt obligated that the concept should be institutionalized and the requisite infrastructure raised to practise it. He, therefore, planned to erect Sri Akal Takht just a few yards away in the west of Darshni Deori of Sri Harmandir Sahib. The Guru along with Bhai Budha and Bhai Gurdas reached the spot adjoining Kotha Sahib which had already been built by Guru Arjan Dev to serve as a resting place of *Adi Granth* at night. After making obeisance at Sri Harmandir Sahib, the Guru laid the foundation of Sri Akal Takht on Har Sudi Panchmi 1663 Bk. (15th June, 1606) and the rest of the work was assigned to Bhai Budha and Bhai Gurdas who jointly completed the construction which then consisted only of a platform which was seven feet in height, eight feet in breadth and fourteen feet in length.[27] The construction was given the name 'Akal Takht'—Timeless throne or throne of the timeless one.[28] The Guru seated himself on the throne daily, when he was at Amritsar and conducted both religious and temporal affairs of the Sikhs in the light of the Divine Word as it was enshrined in *Adi Granth*. The temporal affairs included the religious questions/issues so far their application, propagation and interpretation were concerned. The Guru, however, did not pontificate spiritual matters which he did only at Sri Harmandir Sahib.

The construction of Sri Akal Takht held out a distinct message that temporal life would have to be led as envisaged in Gurbani, Guru's Word as lived by the Guru themselves. This thing by itself had far-reaching implications. Firstly, it brought forth for the first time in the history of religious thought, the concept of God-in-history, God's descent into time, that is, history, is through the vehicle of the Guru who as such partook of the temporal and spiritual sovereignty and authority.

Secondly, it betokened that Sikhism projected a distinctive moral and socio-political code, which in its roots and structure, depended upon 'Word'.

Thirdly, for guidance and right type of orders, the Sikhs should look towards Sri Akal Takht, embodying supreme authority in '*Halt*' literally meaning in this world and '*Palt*' literally meaning in the world beyond.

Fourthly, state or any other agency had no right to interfere, flout or tamper, with politico-religio-social world-view as postulated and propounded by the Gurus.

Sardar Kapur Singh says: "The step was the starting point of double sovereignty. Here the peculiar Sikh doctrine as Double Sovereignty took birth essence of which is that a man of religion should never submit to the exclusive claim of the secular State to govern bodies and minds of men."

From this, it should not be deduced that the Guru had some political motive in the sense that he was in quest of a territory, or any temporal gains. In fact he had no such intentions, although he wished that the Sikhs should pattern their lives both at individual and communitarian levels in the design and cast as recommended by the Gurus or Divine Word. He deliberately chose to build Sri Akal Takht very close to Sri Harmandir to signify that both the words, one *Miri* and the other *Piri*, were not exclusive to each other, they are mutually complementary. The physical and institutional separation of Sri Harmandir and Sri Akal Takht implied that the religious and the political-social concerns were different from each other but never mutually antagonistic, temporality always endeavouring to get spiritualised ultimately eliminating dichotomy between spirituality and temporality. The Guru strongly believed that in this spiritualised temporality lay the genuine progress of the Sikhs, nay of the whole global community. It was in this context that the Guru held courts, heard temporal cases but the decisions which he made always reflected Sikh/spiritual and moral content as posited in the compositions of the Gurus.

Sri Akal Takht right from the beginning was considered the throne brought into being by God himself and was thus indestructible and hallowed. The poetic compositions of Natha and Abdullah of the village Sur Singhwala (Distt. Amritsar) as are recorded in *Gurbilas Padshahi Chhevin* by Sohan bear eloquent testimony to the veracity of our statement. They together sang:

> The throne everlasting
> Has by the holy Guru's presence become hallowed
> Indescribable is its splendour
> How many sing its glory
> Seeing the Guru, both the sun and the moon were shamed
> So sat on the throne, the Holy Guru.

The Guru in Gurbani had been regarded synonym of God/Word. This thing naturally engendered the belief that whatever is said or done at Sri Akal Takht has got the sanction of God/Guru and is, therefore, conducive to the welfare of the whole people.

The Guru sat on the throne and delivered advice and guidance to. the Sikhs as well as non-Sikhs. Here besides preaching and praying, talks were held on questions concerning the relationship of man with God and between Sikhs and Society/State, the position of Sikh ideology *vis-à-vis* other religious ideologies, the Sikh code of discipline *et al.* It was while sitting on the throne that the Guru would watch the wrestling bouts and military feats of his disciples performed in the open space opposite to Sri Akal Takht Sahib. At times, the Guru issued *Hukamnamas*—commandments from Sri Akal Takht which were mandatory for the Sikhs. These *Hukamnamas* were never expediency-oriented: these were always value-based trend-setters and posited high moral principles. The Guru also sent envoys to the ruling princes and received their agents in his *Darbar* which was held at Sri Akal Takht.

Besides the throne, the Guru adopted other emblems of royalty, the umbrella, the swords, the aigrette and the hawk. No wonder, the Sikhs called him a true King—*Sacha Padshah,* a king to all appearances and in deeds and in purity as holy and great as any of his predecessors.

As the Guru constantly through his personal stance and his sermons impressed upon the Sikhs that the Guru's house stood a guarantee for their integrated elevation instead of developing their temporal or spiritual side alone, the Sikhs started looking towards Sri Akal Takht instead of Lahore or Delhi or any other centre of power. This attitude later on contributed a lot towards their solidarity which stood them in good stead when they had to wage a struggle first against the Mughals and then against the Afghans for their survival as well as for the remodelling of society on the principles of Sikhism.

In a way, the throne started functioning independent of the throne in Delhi as it was perceived by the disciples of the Guru. The functioning, however, was always on the path of righteousness dispensing justice, defending the weak and serving the needy and the helpless. Not in the quest of a territory, temporal gains, gold or kingdom, the throne was exclusively the seat of *Sacha Padshah* blending together Bhakti and Shakti.

It is not difficult to surmise that Sri Akal Takht from its very inception came to possess a multidimensional status, a supreme social-religious authority, a supreme court to dispense justice, a symbol of new political dispensation, a divine agency, not only to heighten Sikhs' awareness in regard to the Guru's Gospel but also to steel the hearts of the Sikhs to hold fast to the Sikh values. The Takht also engendered the feeling that the Sikhs had entered a covenant with Akal/Guru to establish the rule of Akal/Eternal God which implied the rule committed to build society based on righteousness, perfect harmony and social equality, liberty of conscience, perfect justice, non-exploitation and freedom from fear and oppression.

Sri Akal Takht played very important role both as a concept and as an institution. It moulded Sikhs into saint-soldiers, a balanced amalgam of Shakti and Bhakti. It awarded Sikhs a corporate identity, religious and political at one and the same time. It enabled the Sikhs to develop and put premium on macro-approach.

The prerogative of *Miri* (temporal sovereignty) and *Piri* (Spiritual sovereignty) remained with the Gurus up to Sri Guru Gobind Singh who on the verge of his immersion in the Eternal Light conferred the spiritual authority on *Adi Granth* and the temporal authority on the Panth. The *Adi Granth* became *Guru Granth* and the Sikh Panth was raised to the status of Guru Panth or Khalsa Panth. The spiritual sovereignty of God having become embodied in the Word, Harmandir with *Guru Granth Sahib* installed therein came to be deemed as the highest seat of spiritual authority while Sri Akal Takht was envisaged as the symbolic seat of the secular and religious authority vested in the Sikh people.

A building subsequently raised over the Takht was called Akal Bunga (house of Akal). The Takht is now officially known as Takht Sri Akal Bunga, although its popular nomenclature Sri Akal Takht is more in common use.

A Critique Of 'New Policy'

The Guru's innovations caused great misgivings not only among the people but also among a number of Sikhs. It is said that some of the Sikhs went to Mata Ganga, the Guru's mother and appealed to her to use her good offices to prevail upon the Guru that he should desist from following the wrong path, he had adopted or else the Guru would incur the displeasure of the Mughals and invite trouble. Although Mata Ganga replied that they should have no anxiety and tried to keep up courageous face, she remonstrated with the young Guru and told him to follow in the footsteps of his father and grandfather. Similar representations were made to Bhai Gurdas and Bhai Budha to the effect that they should put pressure on the Guru so that he might not follow the new policy. As a matter of fact, the Guru, immediately after assumption of the guruship began to live away from Amritsar and the Sikhs records often speak of the anxiety and concern that the Guru's people felt for him. Indeed, there is evidence to show that the Guru had been leading, more or less, a wandering life, and this, together with his other innovations, led to a good deal of misunderstanding.

Bhai Gurdas's reactions to the inability of the Sikhs to appreciate Guru's policy in right perspective are contained in the following verses:

> People say the former Gurus used to sit in the Temple;
> The former Emperors used to visit the former Gurus;
> The present Guru was sent into the fortress by the Emperor.
> Earlier Gurus were accessible in Durbar.
> The present Guru leadeth a roving life and feareth nobody.
> The former Guru's sitting on their thrones used to console the Sikhs;
> The present Guru keepeth dogs and hunteth.
> The former Gurus used to compose hymns, listen to them and sing them;
> The present Guru composeth not hymns, nor listeneth to them.

He keeps not his Sikh followers with him, but taketh enemies of faith and wicked persons as his guides. I say the truth within him cannot possibly be concealed; the Sikhs like the bumble bees, crave his lotus feet. He supported a burden intolerable to others and asserteth not his self[29] (*Var* 26 Pauri 24).

From this it is clear that the Guru's new mode of life was not well understood even by some of the devout Sikhs, at least in the beginning although very soon realisation dawned upon them that the Guru's doings did not mark any deviation from the faith chosen by his predecessors. Bhai Gurdas informs that the faith of the Sikhs in their Guru and his policies did not suffer in any way and they like humble bees were enamoured of his lotus feet.

Bhai Gurdas in order to justify the Guru's change in the policy under peculiar circumstances writes in thirty-fourth *Var*, Pauri 13:

Just as one has to tie pail's neck while taking out water.
Just as to get *Mani* snake is to be killed.
Just as to *get Kasturi* from deer's neck, deer is to be killed.
Just as to get oil, oil seeds are to be crushed.
To get Juicy seeds, pomegranate is to be broken.

Similarly to correct senseless people, sword has to be taken up.[30]

Some critics have not done full justice to Guru Hargobind while assessing the new policy inaugurated by him. They think that "lure of politics and glamour of arms led him away from the true path of a religious and spiritual leader". The judgement is altogether unfounded for two reasons: firstly, Guru Hargobind had no political motive, secondly, he did not swerve from the path of spirituality. His daily routine was to listen to *Asa-di-Var* early in the morning and then to give religious instructions to his followers. He appointed preachers in various regions of the country. He himself went on tours to various places in the Doaba and Malwa regions of the Punjab and the rest of India. All these activities go to prove that he did not cease to be religious leader. Besides this, the policy of the Guru symbolized in itself the response to the challenge of times. There were many solid reasons which led to its formulation.

I.B. Bannerjee says: "Both externally and internally, the situation was changing and the policy of the Guru had perforce to be adjusted to the new environment. The organisational development of Sikhism had mostly taken place during the tolerant days of Akbar who had, on the contrary, even helped the Gurus in various ways. But the execution of Guru Arjan Dev and Guru Hargobind's imprisonment definitely showed that sterner days were ahead and that the old policy of the mere peaceful organisation no longer sufficed.... Guru Arjan Dev had foreseen and Guru Hargobind also clearly saw that it would no longer be possible to protect the Sikh community and its organisation without the aid of arms; and the way in which he proceeded to achieve this end speaks a good deal of his sagacity and his shrewd political sense."[31]

As a matter of fact, the emphasis on the policy based on *Piri-Miri* was the only course left for the Guru. But for it, the community of pious householders would have either not survived or at the most relapsed into the limited merit or community of monks and mendicants.

ARNOLD TOYNBEE'S MISCONCEPTION

Arnold Toynbee, a world famous historian, remarks "Sikhism fell from its religious height in a political trough because, the Sikh Guru, Hargobind Sahib...succumbed to the temptation to use force." And further he comments that "this downfall of Sikhism was used by a clever militant Hindu reaction against the Mughal Empire as its instrument". Toynbee's assessment is unwarranted. The Sikh Guru did not succumb to the temptation of using force but regarded it legitimate to use force as the last resort to protect righteousness. Guru Nanak says, "It is the privilege and right of the true man to fight for righteousness." Guru Arjan also in his speech made on the eve of his departure to Lahore expressed similar views. By doing this, Sikhism did not fall from religious heights. The Guru even in the thick of battles remained in tune with the Reality and this was the reason that he did everything to protect the righteousness even when he made use of the force. And certainly there was no harm in using it as a last resort, and that too for smashing the tyrants. To use violent method to combat the evil is certainly not falling from religious heights, rather it affirms one's faith in a virtuous cause. And into which political trough, the Guru fell? Toynbee is mum on this point.

The view that the downfall of Sikhism was used by the militant Hindu reaction against the Mughal Empire as its instrument is also far from truth. Sikh religion had its own stance. It is wrong to observe that the downfall of Sikhism was made use of by the militant Hindu reaction for the furtherance of their vested interests. The development that took place among the Sikhs was not a degeneration but culmination of the ideals set forth by the founder of their religion. There is no denying the fact that the Sikhs embraced and espoused the cause of the Hindus, but they did it not because they were the Hindus but because they were victimized and persecuted. And to take cudgels against injustice and tyranny is the core of the message of Sikhism and this certainly provided rallying point for the diverse elements of India to integrate and to harmonise.

THE NEW POLICY WAS NOT NEW, RATHER A PHASE OF THE CONTINUUM

Many scholars regard the *Piri-Miri* policy of Guru Hargobind as new one but this conclusion is unwarranted. The policy followed by Hargobind was the same as it was pursued by his predecessors; only it flowered and became more known under the stress of circumstances. When Guru Nanak began his work, he observed the political and social degradation of the people around him. He wanted to see them free in every way, from the foreign yoke as well as from the trammels of the priestly class. According to him "Only fools or idiots try to rule over others" (Basant). He condemned the Lodhis for their cowardice and upbraided the Mughal invaders for their tyranny. He lashed up the ebbing patriotism of his people who abjectly offered loyalty to the alien rulers and would mimic their fashions and manners in order to be acceptable to them (Var Asa). All this was not spiritual yet it issued from the heart of a Bhakta who saw that the earthly freedom was rooted in spiritual freedom, and could not be separated from it. This may sound strange to those who regard saint as a recluse muttering *mantars* in a far-flung corner. The Sikh Gurus, however, were of different mould. They thought it not inconsistent with their religious ideals to take active measures to serve mankind as much through advancement of trade, art and learning as through holy communion, high thinking and noble living.

No doubt they were humble, gentle and sweet, yet when their self-respect was at stake, they knew how to be firm as Guru Angad did when he was threatened by Humayun. Under the third and the fourth Gurus, the number of the Sikhs had increased considerably and the Sikh movement had become an arena of opposing forces, wherein the Guru had to fight heroically against the odds. Guru Arjan Dev talked of his struggle in terms of wrestling matches (Sri Rag). Under the stimulating leadership, the Sikhs had acquired an intensity of character which pitched them against all tyranny. After doing the work of organisation among his Sikhs, the Guru declares, "Now the Order of the Merciful has gone forth that no one shall molest another. The Sikhs had been sufficiently prepared to comprehend what that Order meant." Birbal threatened to punish the Guru if he did not pay to him a stipulated amount. The Guru refused to do so. But just at that time Birbal was called upon to quell the rebellion of the Yusufzais. Nothing happened and the prospective conflict was averted. But it is clear that the war which broke out during the time of Guru Hargobind could start earlier. Only Providence postponed it. As the coming events cast their shadows before, Guru Arjan Dev before leaving for Lahore in response to the summons of Murtaza Khan, clearly spelled the policy to be pursued by his son.

The unjust execution of Guru Arjan Dev convinced the Sikhs that they should not knuckle under evil but combat it. Guru Hargobind, on the occasion of his assumption of guruship, wore two swords: one representing spiritual interests and the other temporal interests.

Some scholars, especially Dr. McLeod, have averred that the Guru adopted "New policy" under the impact of the entry of Jats into the Sikh fold on a large scale. His exact words were that "the growth of militancy within the Panth was "primarily due to the impact of Jat culture patterns". Dr. I.B. Bannerjee also expressed similar views albeit in different words and a little less emphatically. But their assessment is incorrect as it is based on the assumptions which were fallacious and betrays incomprehensibility of the Sikh ideology and its concomitant social actions.

In the first place there is no reliable data to infer that the Jats were preponderant element among the Sikhs when the Guru made prevalent the so-called 'New Policy'. Rather all the available evidence points to the contrary. Bhai Gurdas in his eleventh VAR provides a list of individual Sikhs beginning with the followers of Guru Nanak and terminating with the sixth Guru Hargobind. In most of the cases, the caste name is given and we are thus provided with the evidence concerning the constituency of the Panth. It becomes clear that the early Panth incorporated in itself a broad spectrum of castes. Of those castes in absolute majority were *Khatris,* others such as Jats, there being in minority.

Secondly, the contention that the Jats were the only people who bore arms is also unsubstantiable because it could not be possible that Khatris counted superior to them in social status did not possess the arms unless they were disarmed by the state. Nor can it be said with certainty that the castes or classes including Jats considered inferior in social status did not bear arms. Therefore, it is fallacious to say that since the Jats bore weapons and were the only people to do so, they affected the course of Sikh movement and were responsible for the rise of militancy.

Equally illogical is the contention that the Jat cultural patterns determined the course of Sikh movement under Guru Hargobind Sahib. Which cultural pattern? The learned McLeod has failed to expound. The only distinctive Jat cultural patterns in the contemporary world were tribal. Among the Hindus and Sikh Jats, especially in the north-central districts, a form of ancestor-worship called 'Jathera' was common. It passes one's comprehension how this ancestor-worship gave rise to the new course adopted by the Guru which was clearly revolutionary as it aimed at radical changes in spirito-social and political systems at micro and macro levels. Nor could the Jat social egalitarianism be equated with the Sikh idea of brotherhood. Jat partook some of the traits of both a tribe and a caste. Their social equality was tribal confined to Jat brotherhood and did not extend to castes lower than them. They, whether Hindu, Muslim or Sikh, dominated and exploited the Sudras and the 'outcasts in their own villages'. How could such tribal equality square with or lead to the emergence of the society as conceived by the Guru where the spirit of equality was a vital principle and even a Brahmin had no higher claim than the lowest Sudra who swept his house. Hence the influx of Jats into the Sikh society had got nothing to do with the emergence of Sikh militancy which in effect was a concomitant of 'New Policy' which in turn had its roots in Sikh ideology which aimed at restructuring society on new bases namely Fatherhood of God. Brotherhood of humankind, non-recognition of differences on the basis of caste, creed, status, birth or wealth *et al.*, mutual equality, dignified living, righteousness and non-exploitation. In order that the ideology might prevail, it was imperative that proper social actions should be followed.

In the process, the Sikhs of the Guru were sure to come into clash with all those who did not like change and were champions of *status quo*. The rise of Sikh militancy was in fact a response to such situations and hence it found recognition in Sikhism with the consideration that it would confine to itself, within the parameters of Sikh ethics. In the Guru's compositions, God has also been conceived as "Extirpator of the wicked" (ASUR SINGHARAN—*G.G.S.*, p. 1028) and 'God, the Extirpator' (Guru Ram Das). Such expressions of Guru was in a way a sort of exhortations to the Sikhs to emulate the example of God and feel no hesitation to oppose unrighteousness and their sponsors. This type of motivation led the people to develop spirit of resistance to unjust happenings. This made them shed the old hackneyed and out-of-tune notions, and take to Sikh ideology which provided them fresh goals, the right type of social actions and motivations.

The Imprisonment

Soon after the formulation of the above-mentioned policy, the Guru was imprisoned in the Gwalior Fort. Various reasons have been ascribed to his imprisonment. Most of Sikh accounts assert that after the Guru's pontification, Chandu once again requested the Guru to accept the hand of his daughter. The Guru refused and Chandu began to plan for his destruction. As chance would have it, Jahangir fell ill and called some astrologer to suggest him some way how he could recuperate. Chandu bribed the astrologer and made him say that he could be cured if some holy man would undergo penance in the fort of Gwalior and vicariously Guru Hargobind was recommended for the purpose. Accordingly, the Guru was shut up in the fort.

Obviously, this account is more a fable than history. The story suffers from many improbabilities. Firstly, nowhere in the contemporary Mughal records, the name of Chandu as Dewan has been mentioned and secondly even if we believe that penance of some holy man can cure disease, the imprisonment and subsequent ill-treatment meted to the Guru could have not ensured the penance for the cure of the Emperor. According to M. Akbar, the Guru was imprisoned on charge of embezzlement of some money.[32] Cunningham also says that the Guru was involved in difficulties with the Emperor for retaining for himself that money which he should have disbursed to his troops. From the account of Cunningham, it appears that the Guru was in the service of the Emperor. Both these authorities base their conclusion on a passage in *Debistan-i-Mazahib* and we are sure that the passage makes no reference whatsoever to the effect that the Guru was in Imperial service. Hence the view of Muhammad Akbar and Cunningham is unfounded. The correct translation of the passage is as under:

> "He had many difficulties to contend with. One of them was, that he adopted the style of a soldier, wore a sword contrary to the custom of his father, maintained a retinue and began to follow the chase. The emperor in order to extort from him the balance of the fine which had been imposed on Arjan Mal, sent him to Gwalior fort."

Archer also gives a very funny story regarding the cause of the imprisonment of the Guru. He says 'there is some evidence that the Guru himself was once captured by a band of irregulars whether they were Sikhs or Rajputs and was detained by them in Gwalior fortress until a fine was paid for his release'.[33] No evidence supports Archer's view. He should have known that the fort was neither in possession of the Rajputs nor of the Sikhs during the time of Guru. Moreover, Bhai Gurdas himself in one of his Vars says that the Guru was imprisoned by the Mughal Emperor.

The true cause is that Jahangir, alarmed at the royal state and military preparation of the Guru, wanted to retard the growth of the Sikh movement or to secure orderliness of the

Sikhs in general. Natha Mal and Abdullah 'In Coronation Ode' compared the turban of the Guru with that of Jahangir and extolled his qualities which far surpassed those of the contemporary Mughal Emperor. Mohsin Fani[34] also seems to support this view. Bhai Gurdas also seems to suggest the same 'The former Guru used to sit in the temple; the present Guru was sent into the fortress by the Emperor'?

Closely connected with all this, a question can legitimately be asked. "Were the military preparation of the Guru who was still in his teens on such a grand scale that they could pose a threat to the Mughal Empire"?

There is no doubt that the military preparations were insignificant and negligible but its potentialities could not be denied. At the same time, what the Sikh records say about the intrigues of the enemies of the Guru and his family should not be entirely ignored. As Prof. Beni Prasad suggests "The Emperor's own remark in the Tuzuk make it more or less clear that even in the more serious matter of Guru Arjan's execution he had been goaded into action by others and it is not at all improbable that these very same men now procured Guru Hargobind's imprisonment. Historical facts also lend some substance to the whole affair. Jahangir, on his way to Kabul and back, had twice halted at Lahore for some days in 1607 and beginning of 1608 and it may well be that it was on these occasions that Hargobind's enemies procured the Emperor's audience and made their representations against the young Guru. Possibly Siad Khan Chagtai and Quily Khan both governors of Punjab played their roles in this respect.

Period of Detention

Mohsin Fani[35] states that Guru Hargobind had to remain a prisoner in the fort of Gwalior for a period of twelve years. Gordon also follows him.

According to *Panth Parkash* the period of imprisonment covered a little over two months. Some Sikh records hint that the period of internment lasted for only forty days. Teja Singh and Ganda Singh say that the period of the detention of the Guru was only two years. Because of the divergent opinions, we cannot reach any conclusion without conducting a thorough probe into the problem.

Let us examine, first of all, the statement of Mohsin Fani who was contemporary and a friend of Guru Hargobind. If we assume that this is correct, the period of 12 years must be fitted in somewhere between 1606 and 1627, the latter year being the year of Jahangir's death; but it is impossible to fit it in this period. All accounts, Sikh or non-Sikh agree that Guru Hargobind was imprisoned and released during the time of Jahangir as towards the close of Jahangir's Period, the Guru had turned to be the friend of Jahangir. It shows that in C.E. 1627 the Guru was not in the prison and he could have not been imprisoned later than 1614, the period of his imprisonment being twelve years. The Guru could not have been in the prison for the period between 1614 to 1626 on account of the following:

(1) Kaula, the daughter of the qazi was brought to Amritsar in 1620.

(2) Guru Hargobind excavated the famous tank Kaulsar in her honour and we are told that this was done in 1621.

(3) Baba Atal Rai, the Guru's second son by his wife Nanki, was born in 1620.

(4) Guru's son Ani Rai was born in 1618, his second son Suraj Mal in 1617 and his eldest son Baba Gurditta towards the close of 1613.

Thus, it is clear that it is impossible to find a period of 12 years which can be fitted in between 1606 to 1627 during which the Guru might have been in the jail.

M.A. Macauliffe states that the Guru was summoned to Delhi in 1612 and when his mother saw that he did not return in time, she became very anxious and sent Bhai Jetha to Delhi who succeeded in curing Emperor who had been troubled with fearful visions, and as a reward, the Emperor ordered the release of the Guru. The period of the detention is hinted as only 40 days. But this seems improbable because the matter was not so easy as the Sikhs chroniclers would have us believe.

Frantic efforts were made to secure the release of the Guru; and it is quite probable that the intercession of the saint Mian Mir had to be requisitioned for that purpose. Moreover, the stories connected with the Guru in jail could be true only if the Guru had been detained in the jail longer than 40 days or so.

Some Sikh scholars, however, opine that the Guru was summoned to Delhi in 1612; but this view also does not stand the test of historical analysis. Jahangir was not available at Delhi or Agra from 1613 to 1619. Nor was he at Mewar, and from November of 1616 to March 1617, he was at Mandu (Beni Prasad: *History of Jahangir*, pp. 237, 277, 300). There is, however, a period of about five years from C.E. 1607 to C.E. 1612 during which the Guru could have been in the fort. The facts relating to the marriage of the Guru with Nanki also throws a flood of light on the subject. Nanki was married to the Guru just before the birth of Bhai Gurditta in 1613. Question arises as to why the marriage was postponed till that time. The argument that Nanki was too young may not perhaps carry any weight in view of the fact that the child marriage was the much-honoured custom during those days. Moreover, even if Nanki was young, it was not essential that the bride should go and live with bridegroom immediately after her marriage. Obviously, there were some serious reasons which deterred the mother of the Guru from marrying him to Nanki. According to I.B. Bannerjee, the serious reasons must have been his internment in the Gwalior fort where he probably remained for five years from 1607 to 1612. Even this period of five years does not seem to be a correct assessment. It is a well-known fact that the Guru was interned on account of his war-like activities, and it was but natural that such activities must have taken some time before they posed a threat to the Mughal rule. We must, therefore, allow at least two or even three years, for his preparations. Thus if we make allowance of two years for the military preparations, the period of imprisonment would come out to be three years *i.e.* from 1609 to 1612.

Life of the Guru in the Fort

The Gwalior Jail did not unnerve the Guru, rather it provided him an opportunity to influence the Rajput princes and others and explain to them his point of view. Though the life in the fort was arduous, yet he never lost balance or equipoise.

He got up in the early hours of morning. Having taken a bath he would recite *Japji* and other compositions. The Guru had to live on scanty ration. More often than not even that he distributed among the needy prisoners. According to Prof. Satbir Singh, the Guru had to safeguard himself from the poison which was often administered in veiled form to the enemies whom the emperor considered very dangerous. The Guru, perhaps, because of this, lived on the food supplied by one grass-cutter, who became his devout disciple. The Guru's demeanour impressed the jail superintendent so much that he offered to serve food to the Guru from his own house. According to Bhai Gurdas, he was Hari Das who always admired the Guru. The Guru was at last released probably in 1612.

Factors Responsible for Guru's Release

According to Mohsin Fani[36] many Sikhs during the period of the Guru's confinement in Gwalior used to go there and bow before the walls of the fort. The Emperor was moved by pity and ordered Guru's release. According to Macauliffe, Jahangir fell ill and had been troubled by fearful dreams and visions. Bhai Jetha, a pious Sikh went to Delhi. He succeeded in soothing the Emperor and thus in return obtained the orders for the Guru's release.

Both the aforesaid views do not seem to be correct. The release of the Guru was a political decision and it is unlikely that it was made under the force of pity or superstitions or some emotional outburst.

With the lapse of time, Jahangir's attitude underwent a change. The reasons are not far to seek. Firstly, after some time, political sagacity dawned on Jahangir and he realised that without recourse to the liberal religious policy, it was not possible for him to maintain stability and tranquility in his vast empire, and secondly, Nur Jahan imbued with Sufi ideology had her affect on Jahangir. Mian Mir began to be respected in the royal house, especially because Nur Jahan was her devotee. Incidentally, Mian Mir was the friend of Guru Arjan who occupied a very high place in his regard. Guru Arjan Dev's remarkable calmness even in the face of torture of the worst kind on the part of the Mughal Empire raised him still more in Mian Mir's estimation. No wonder Mian Mir had great love for Guru Hargobind and the ideology he was championing. He along with Wazir Khan -and Nizamuddin approached Jahangir with the request that the Guru, being innocent, should be released. Jahangir, who was already made aware of the innocence of the Guru and who, by this time, had emancipated himself from the orthodox section of the nobles responded to their request and ordered for his release. Thus efforts of Mian Mir, Wazir Khan and Nizamuddin brought about a change in Jahangir's heart and henceforward there were established cordial relations between Jahangir and the Guru.

The news of the Guru's release struck consternation among the Rajas who were imprisoned in the fort as hostages for millions of rupees because in Guru's release they were losing a spiritual mentor and a moral elixir. The Guru requested Jahangir to set the Rajas at liberty along with him. To make the task easy for the government, he stood surety for their loyal behaviour. Jahangir who by this time had revised his opinion about the Guru granted that request and ordered the release of these rulers as well. It was for this reason the Guru Hargobind was respectfully called '*Bandi Chhor Baba*' (Revered Emancipator). According to Sikh tradition, the Rajas who were released were fifty-two in number. The Guru got a special gown stitched which had 52 hems (*Kalis*). As Guru Hargobind Sahib left the fort, the captive kings caught the hems of the cloak and came out of the jail along with the Guru.

With the Guru's release opens a new epoch in the life of the Guru—the epoch of friendly relations between the Guru and Jahangir, which lasted till the death of the Emperor.

According to Sikh tradition, Jahangir paid a visit to Amritsar and offered to bear the whole expenses of the construction of 'Akal Takht'. The Guru, however, refused to avail of the offer and uttered 'I and my Sikhs would build this edifice with the money earned by the sweat of their brow. Never will it be memorial to any King's charity rather I would like it to be the symbol of the sacrifice and service of the Sikhs.' Likewise, the Guru accompanied the Imperial camp during the Emperor's tour of Rajputana and also subdued Tara Chand of Nalagarh who had continued for a long time in open rebellion and all efforts to subdue him had failed (C.E. 1618). But what exactly the position of the Guru *vis-à-vis* Jahangir was, it is not clear.

Nature of Relationship

Mohsin Fani says 'Hargobind was always attached to the stirrup of the victorious Jahangir'[37] meaning thereby that Guru Hargobind was attached to the Mughal government in some capacity or the other.

Two later Sikh works *Panth Parkash* and *Itehas Guru Khalsa* assert that "he (the Guru) was appointed a sort of supervisor over the Punjab officials and was placed in command of 700 horses and five guns".[38] This, on the face of it, seems absurd and is positively disapproved by the almost decisive negative evidence of the *Tuzuk-i-Jahangiri*. In *Jahangir's Memoir* wherein minutest details have been given in respect of Jahangir's life and achievements, even the name of Guru Hargobind does not occur.[39]

Dr. I.B. Bannerjee opines that Guru Hargobind was holding a very minor position in the administration and for some period at least he was a mere assistant of a Faujdar.[40]

Some Sikh writers, however, believe that the Guru was not at all in the employ of the Mughal Emperor. He had purely friendly relations with Jahangir. Even while he accompanied Jahangir to Kashmir or Rajputana, he did it out of sheer friendship.

Though we do not come across any positive historical evidence, yet it is difficult for us to believe that the Guru entered Mughal Imperial service. If the Guru accompanied Jahangir in his military campaign in Rajputana, it was not because of the fact that he was in Mughal employ but he did so, because firstly Jahangir had developed respect for the Guru, and had started following in the footsteps of Akbar and secondly, he might have thought of gathering first-hand knowledge of the military strength and strategy of the Mughal armed forces.

Whatever the nature of the relationship of the Guru with Jahangir, friendship there was and to enter into friendship with Jahangir was the need of the hour. The incarceration of the Guru made no difference to his plans of strengthening the defence potential of his community. His relations with the Emperor Jahangir were now better, and obviously there was no immediate danger to the Sikhs from the side of government. The Guru took a long range view of the problem and did not allow his personal relations with the Emperor to come in the way of his programme. The Guru also used the period of peace following upon his release from imprisonment to consolidate the ranks of his community. During the period he was in prison, the strings of discipline had greatly loosened and several selfish Masands had arrogated to themselves powers that were never vested in them. They had become corrupt and strayed from the sphere of their proper functions. Some of them had begun to pose as Guru in their own right and had each raised a body of followers or devotees called Shehlang. Guru Hargobind thought it high time to penalize the corrupt missionaries and made a lesson of them to impress upon other functionaries. But this was not enough. So long as the institutions of *charanamrit* remained unchanged, the individual Masands would continue to enjoy the privilege of initiation of new Sikhs by virtue of having been so authorized by the central authority of the Guru. Guru Hargobind realized the defect in this system and declared that in future any five good Sikhs could also prepare and administer *charanamrit* and initiate people into the fold of Sikhism. The measure did not end the Order of the Masands. But the initiating of an alternative arrangement for the admission of new members into the community did, to a great extent, erode the authority of the Masands.

After his release from Gwalior fort, the Guru proceeded to Delhi—the purpose being to see Jahangir and to organise Sikh congregations. He halted outside the Imperial city at a site known as *Majnu ka Tilla* on the bank of Jamuna river. Here he gave instructions to his followers who thronged to him in hoards. The disciples of the Muslim Faqir named Majnu also benefited from the Guru's presence. The Guru is said to have accompanied Jahangir on a chase and saved Jahangir from the sudden attack of a fierce tiger whom he killed with one stroke. Sikh tradition avers that Jahangir very patiently listened to the Guru on various religious issues and was fully convinced that the Guru's dispensation did not pose any threat to the state or Islam or any other religion and is palpably in the interest of the people.

Some Muslim saints including Sikandar Pir, possibly at the instance of the Emperor, also discussed with Guru on various topics concerning spirituality. They were fully convinced that the Guru was aware of mysteries of God and His creation. (*Debistan-i-Mazahib* English tr. by Shia and Troy) and is an accomplished personality.

After sojourning for some time at Delhi, the Guru started his homeward journey. On the way he halted at Kurukshetra where now a beautiful gurdwara stands in memory of Guru's visit. Travelling through Beas, Goindwal, Tarn Taran and Khadur, he reached Amritsar where he was accorded a hearty welcome and the whole city including Darbar Sahib Complex was tastefully illuminated. The anniversary of the event is still celebrated at Harmandir with lights and fireworks.

PREACHING TOURS

The Guru's interest in preaching his mission has always been keen and he seized every opportunity that came his way to pass on his message to the people. In the first three years of his pontificate, the Mughal government was under the influence of Naqshbandis and rival claimants of guruship were very actively opposed to the Guru. Even then the Guru did not relent in his attempts to spread his mission. His preachings forays into the areas around Amritsar and in Doaba and Malwa regions were conspicuous as these won over many converts to Sikhism. Many Sikhs from Majha, Malwa and Doaba offered themselves for enrolment in the Guru's army of saint-soldiers.

During the Guru's imprisonment in Gwalior Fort for about three years, the job of preaching did not sag, obviously under the instructions of the Guru. Baba Budha and Bhai Gurdas organised the bands of the Sikhs who proselytized among the people of rural areas. Such bands did such a wonderful job that even in the long absence of the Guru, people could not detached from the Guru by the Naqshbandis and their cohorts in the government. At the instance of Bhai Budha and Bhai Gurdas, the esteem of Harmandir and Sri Akal Takht as central shrines of the Sikhs was kept up and the Sikhs were impressed upon that it was their sacred duty to defend and honour these institutions. On their own part, both the Sikh sages worked hard to set up bodies of vigilantes called Chowkies to perform three-fold duties: (1) to go around Harmandir Sahib to see that no mischievous element caused any disturbances, (2) to watch that proper decorum was maintained in Darbar Sahib Complex, and (3) to stimulate the people including devotees to feel attached with the Guru and his programmes by always reciting sacred hymns (*shabads*) from *Adi Granth*. Even in the fort, the Guru spared no efforts to preach Sikhism. The conversion of Haridas, the superintendent of the fort, and many others in the city of Gwalior amply testified to the success story of the Guru as regards preaching. The empathy between the Hill Rajas and the Guru is one such example, out of many, to illustrate this point.

TRAVELS OF THE GURU

After his release from the fort the Guru put in more vigour in his task of proselytisation. He traversed long distances in different regions and in different climates and met people of different shades of opinion, of ethnicities, of different religions and of different castes and psyches. Apart from travelling at different places in Punjab, he visited Uttar Pradesh, Kashmir,

Pothohar and Haryana. He travelled the area only less than that of Guru Nanak; no other Guru travelled so extensively.

Recently SGPC has got prepared a list of gurdwaras raised in memory of the visits of Guru Hargobind. The list referred to only those gurdwaras which exist in the Punjab of India. According to the list, there are over four hundred gurdwaras. Out of these majority of them exist in the Malwa followed in terms of numbers in Majha and Doaba. The places which were visited by the Guru in Kashmir and Uttar Pardesh were also identified by Giani Gian Singh and Tara Singh Narotam. These are far less in numbers as compared to the number of gurdwaras in Malwa and other regions of the Punjab. From the locations of the gurdwaras, certain conclusions can safely be drawn:

(1) The Guru made concentrated and focalized efforts in Malwa region. A large number of converts were won over by the Guru. Out of these, the Jats were preponderant, numerically speaking.

(2) The Jats were attracted to Sikhism because of certain factors. Firstly, most of them were unclaimed by Hinduism or Islam. Many of them were *Sultanias* and *Sakhi Savarias*—followers of Sakhi Savars. A chunk of them were worshippers of Devi (goddess), or folk deities such as Gugga *et al.* Almost all of them were steeped in superstitions, totems, esoteric practices *et al.* Their social structure was mainly tribal having faith in ancestor-worship. Even caste system had crept into their social structures. Such people when came face to face with Sikh ideology and its proponent Guru Hargobind, a man of myriad virtues and charismatic personality, they were simply swayed. They found in the words of the Guru a new hope, a new confidence and a fresh direction. In the Guru's metaphysical thoughts and in his social philosophy which was a concomitant of his metaphysical philosophy, they found chance of their regeneration and rejuvenation.

(3) The said region attracted very little attention of the Mughal rulers as it was not productive, being arid and sandy, for which it was called a waste-land. The Mughal Faujdar of Sirhind in whose jurisdiction most of Malwa region fell paid only scanty attention to the areas of Bhatinda and Sangrur and confined his administrative attention mostly to the areas now comprising Ropar, Fateh Garh and Patiala. This being so, the Guru's proselytizing activities went unnoticed, especially in the above alluded neglected areas with the result Sikhism reaped a rich harvest of converts.

(4) Except in Sirhind and its environs, no religious centre of Muslims existed in Malwa region. Naqshbandis' activities revolved around the royal court at Sirhind or in urban areas near it. They did not establish any centre anywhere between Patiala and Bhatinda. This fact also facilitated the proselytizing job of the Guru.

(5) The success of Guru's preaching was at once marked and fruitful. Many families of note embraced Sikhism and placed their resources at the disposal of the Guru.

(6) The Guru while preaching and travelling always took care of the compelling needs of the people. He tried, wherever it was feasible, to get the wells dug to mitigate water-scarcity. Such wells can still be identified in a large number in the region. It was at the instance of the Guru that wells were laid out around Kiratpur, Nanakiana Sahib near Sangrur *et al.* The Guru also persuaded the people to sink their mutual differences and finish quarrels born out of tribal or family pride. A large number of cases of reconciliation can be identified to support this contention.

(7) The density of gurdwaras in the Malwa region is the highest especially in the areas starting from Sangrur to Mandi Phul including the area of Barnala, proving thereby that the people of this area were the lot most attracted towards the Guru. It was because of this

that the largest number of recruits belonged to this area and uptill now their regard for the Guru seems to be the highest and the deepest.

In Majha region too, the Guru travelled a lot. The historical gurdwaras bear ample testimony to this conclusion. The Guru did achieve a lot of success in converting the people to his ideology and undoubtedly the number of the Sikhs in this area swelled manifold, but in its entirety, the Guru cannot lay claim to the whole credit. A huge share of the same goes to Guru Arjan Dev. The greatest contribution of the Guru is that he fired his disciples with new zeal to work for the evolution of a new man, a Gursikh and a new society embodying Miri & Piri. In this area, apart from preaching Sikh metaphysical principles, the Guru suffused into his followers the social values on which Sikh society was to be structured. The Guru also organised social actions for the benefit of the common man. He also gave them lessons in fearlessness and truth. This area too provided the Guru with good Sikh soldiers, generals and sages and savants. Bhai Budha, Bhai Gurdas, Bhai Pirana and many others were the shining stars belonging to this area.

Doaba also responded fervently to the Guru's proselytizing attempts. Sri Guru Hargobindpur and Kartarpur were two important radiating centres of Sikhism among many. At Hargobindpur, the Guru built a mosque for Muslims and a temple for the Hindus holding out that the Gurus believed in multiculturalism as well. Besides, the Guru tried to alleviate the sufferings of the people whether these resulted from physical ailments or oppression of the government.

In Kashmir, Uttar Pradesh and Himachal Pradesh, the Guru preaching sallies were also successful but not to the extent these were in the Punjab. The reasons were clear. Islam was deeply entrenched in Kashmir valley and the Hindus were so myopic in their vision that they required continuous and sustained efforts which the Guru could not put in because of his preoccupations elsewhere. Even then, quite a number of Kashmiri Hindus including Pandits entered into the fold of Sikhism.

In Uttar Pradesh, the Guru's influence was considerable but confined to only the area visited by him. The area being in stranglehold of Brahmanism could not be easily converted to Sikhism, although the Guru's itinerary aroused a lot of sympathy for Sikhism.

In Himachal Pradesh, the Guru did his preaching mostly after he settled at Kiratpur. Before that, his eldest son, Baba Gurditta proselytized albeit on a small scale. The thrust of the Guru's preaching had always been towards emancipating people both from shackles of Brahmanical religion and Imperial Islam along with their social theories and structures as also towards evolving a corporate life based on Sikh ideology. According to Sikh chroniclers, the Rajas of several states—Mandi, Kulu, Saket, Haripur and Chamba became followers of Guru Arjan Dev and the Rajas of Kangra and Pilibhit were converted by Guru Hargobind. It is also believed that hill people in large numbers entered the fold of Sikh religion under Guru Hargobind. Probably the chroniclers made no distinction between actual converts and followers who without ceasing to be Hindus paid personal homage to the saintly Gurus. In any case, it seems certain that Sikhism was acquiring influence in the hills. The process was accelerated during Hargobind's stay at Kiratpur. *The Debistan-i-Mazahib* says that "disciples of the Guru (in the hills) increased considerably". The results however appear to have been temporary, for Guru Gobind Singh had to face the hostility of the Hill Rajas.

It is not possible, at least for the present, to profile the itineraries of Guru Hargobind chronologically because of the non-availability of the source material, but certain rough conclusions can be hazarded. Firstly, most of the Guru's visits to places in Malwa region were undertaken after Guru's visit to Kashmir, probably because the Guru at that point of time could foresee for the coming events, especially the intensification of the antipathy of the Mughals towards the Sikh movement. Secondly, the Majha and Doaba areas were visited before the Guru's departure to Kashmir in or about 1620. Thirdly, the order of visits to different places in different areas cannot be determined correctly because, as it seems, the Guru preferably responded to the calls of his disciples or devotees and in the process he did not care for the distance and direction, even normal routes.

Notwithstanding all these predicaments, we have ventured to give a connected account of the different itineraries of Guru Hargobind Sahib touching upon only the important sojourns of the Guru.

The Guru started his preaching campaigns from Amritsar. Thereafter, he reached Kartarpur where he stayed for seven months and made it the centre of Sikhism in Doab area. Many people of this city and of the area around embraced Sikhism. The people of the village Bara Mir not only entered into the fold of Sikhism but also offered themselves to serve in the Guru's army. It was here that Painda Khan was brought by his mother, the widow of Fateh Khan of village Alampur to the presence of the Guru who out of compassion for him took him in his charge. At that time Painda Khan was in his boyhood. The Guru brought him up so well that he grew to be a sturdy soldier and a capable general. He took part in different battles fought by the Guru against the Mughal government. As the time lapsed, he became too ego-centric and did not hesitate even to be perfidious towards the Guru. He was arrogant enough even to induce the Mughal authorities to harm the Guru. Ultimately, in the battle of Kartarpur, he was killed by the Guru himself while he was arrayed on the Mughal side.

The Guru's preaching covered a wide spectrum of people—Hindus, Muslims, high castes, low castes and *Sakhisarwarias et al.* He went to Jalandhar city and preached among Muslims of Basti Sheikhan, presently a ward of the city. It is said that many Muslims became attached to the Guru's cause. Occasionally he toured various places in the Malwa region such as Sudhar, Gujjar Khan, Sidhwa Kalan, Bara Sahib, Sirhind, Takhtpura, Dorili Bhai, Nathana, Samadh Bhai Kaonke, Raikot, Lopo and Bhoonder *et al.* People flocked to him to listen to his message. At Daroli, Sain Das, the husband of Ramo, the elder sister of the revered Damodari, the spouse of Guru Hargobind lived. He was a Sakhi Sarwaria to begin with but soon he changed over to Sikhism.

In 1617, Murtza Khan, the Subedar of Punjab died and Gias Beg father-in-law of Jahangir was appointed to his place. The Guru who had been away from Amritsar for the last two and half years thought it advisable to return to Amritsar to take care of his flock in the altered administrative set-up.

Jahangir had never visited Punjab since 1608 because of his preoccupations in Rajputana and at other places. In 1919, he found time to pay his visit to Punjab to have on the spot feel of the affairs specially when Gias Beg had taken over as the subedar of the province in 1617. On his way to Lahore, he sojourned for some time at Gumtala now a suburb of Amritsar. According to the author of *Gurbilas Padshahi Chhevin*, the Guru made fine lodging and boarding arrangement for Jahangir and his entourage. Jahangir praised the Guru for his hospitality and went to Harmandir Sahib and Sri Akal Takht Sahib to offer his homage. Bhai Jetha accompanied Jahangir to Sri Akal Takht where he made his offerings. Thereafter he made his obeisance at Harmandir Sahib. The Guru then met Manohar Das Meharban personally to conciliate him; but he continued to blaze ire. No argument could carry weight with him. The Guru opened his conversation "Thy father and mine are in Heaven. We are both brothers now, so we ought not to bear each other enmity from which happiness can never result." The Guru added, "Lord of the world, the supreme Being will not be pleased to bestow happiness or prosperity on those who harbour evil in their hearts while on the contrary the Creator will make him happy who is pleased with the happiness of others." The Guru then quoted the following from Kabir's compositions:

"Indulge not in enmity and bickering, O, my soul
Do good deal and gain reward."

Meharban far from being won over became all the more enraged and scornfully blurted "The enmity that has subsisted between us, I will never forget."

The Guru then met Mian Mir, originally named as Mohammed Mir who was born in Sivastan in Sind (Pakistan) in A.D. 1550 and like many other distinguished Mohammedans found his way to Punjab and settled in a barren plain about five miles away from Lahore. He had gained a high reputation for sanctity and devotion. According to Dara Shikoh, he was considered the path-finder for all the *aulias* of the age, a man of deep illumined understanding and wisdom. Mian Mir welcomed the Guru at his place. Both the Guru and Mian Mir conversed on various topics. Then the Guru returned to his camp. Later on when some one connected with the government asked about the Guru, Mian Mir told that the "Guru is a sincere believer in God. His heart is pure and his words leave impression on the mind."[41]

After this, the Guru returned to Amritsar. Soon after, the Guru visited Mukerian and villages in its neighbourhood.

From there he reached the bank of river Beas on the Majha side where the fifth Guru had selected a spot near village Rohilla, for he could envisage that this place would one day become a great trade centre apart from being an important strategic point from military point of view.

The author of *Mahan Kosh* contends that Guru Arjan founded a city on this spot in celebration of the birth of his son. He named the city as Gobindpur which later on changed into Hargobindpur during the period of Sri Hargobind. But this view is erroneous because firstly, except *Mahan Kosh* no other historical source makes a mention of it. Nor there is any monument in or around connected with this event. Tradition however preserves that village Rohilla one kilometre away from the present site of Sri Hargobindpur had association with Guru Amar Das who established a Manji (a religious centre) there.

When Guru Hargobind encamped on the above said spot, a bigoted Hindu Bhagwan Das alias Gharar (Gharar is a misconstruction of the word 'Karar' which literally means unscrupulous or acutely miser) who held a small Jagir close by picked up quarrel with the Guru by putting up a false claim to the ownership of the land in C.E. 1629. He along with a few ruffians attacked the Guru's camp. In the fight he was killed. The infuriated Ratan Chand who was his son and agonised

Karam Chand, son of Chand Shah, lodged a complaint with Abdullah Khan, the Faujdar of Jalandhar against the Guru, painting him a great disturber of peace and an inveterate enemy of the Mughal rule. The faujdar in his characteristic rashness did not care to ascertain the truth and attacked the Guru. After three days of hard fighting, Jalandhar forces had to eat the humble pie at Rohilla *ghat* at the Beas river. Abdullah Khan, Ratan Chand and Karam Chand, all the three were slain. On the Guru's side among the killed was Mathura Bhatt who was the son of Baba Bika. Having stayed there for some time, the Guru founded a city known as Sri Hargobindpur.

He then addressed the Masands to take steps to complete the construction at Hargobindpur which was carefully planned. A wall around the city was raised. It had five gates for the ingress and outgress of the people. Streets and market place were carved out meticulously. The city reflected Sikh spirit and Sikh social ideas. No separate wards for different communities were created as the Guru abhored any segmentation of people on grounds of caste, creed and wealth *et al.* Whereas a gurdwara for the Sikhs was constructed, a mosque for the Muslims and a temple for the Hindus[42] were also built thereby beckoning that Sikh ideology favoured multiculturalism and pluralism based on belief that every one on this earth partook of the Divine and hence he or she is honourable. The Guru built his home there and chose to stay for some time along with his family members. He took steps to set up a missionary centre for the spread of his mission in Doaba in particular. He encouraged expert Granthis (scripture-reciters) to inhabit the city to train Granthis (scripture reciters).[43] Such people prepared copies of Guru Granth Sahib and gutkas, literally meaning small-sized books containing chosen hymns from *Adi Granth*, for distribution among the Sikhs. The *Gurdwara Dharam, Asthan Granthis* is the place where scripture-reciters did their job of preparing copies of the compositions of the Gurus. The city in due course of time became an important market of sugar. In the eighteenth century Jassa Singh Ramgarhia made it capital of his *Misl.* After this the Guru reached[44] Amritsar.

Even amidst multiple engagements, the Guru had made it a point to tender spiritual instructions to his disciples. One day, as he was discoursing as to how one should study scriptures, he remarked "Everyone who reads the Word of the Guru should do so with understanding and try to live it in his own life. But how many are there who could even utter correctly and with faith the first composition in *Granth Sahib*, the *Japuji* of Guru Nanak. A Sikh named Gopal came forth and very humbly offered to undertake the task if the Guru blessed him. The Guru welcomed the self-confidence of this devotee and allowed him to exhibit his performance. So perfect was his delivery and his utterance so much charged with devotion that the Guru seriously intended to transfer him the Guruship. But when he reached the end of his performance, his eyes fell on horses brought by a devotee and he wished in his heart that if the Guru be merciful, he should reward him with one of the horses. The Guru reading his mind granted him his wish and said, "But for your Haumei (egocentricity) which bred in you the greed to possess an earthly object, I would have surrendered my apostolate to you. Indeed it is hard to concentrate on God dismissing out of account the pleasure of life. A Khwaja from Kashmir, Jani, a Sayyad and Nitya Nand, a proud Brahmin of Batala and a great scholar of Sanskrit were some of the celebrities who waited upon the Guru and admired him. Nitya Nand embraced Sikhism and turned a zealous preacher.

Baba Atal, one of the Guru's sons, started performing miracles. He is said to have revived his dead playmate, Mohan. The Guru showed his utter displeasure, because in Sikh religion, miracles had no room. The angered Guru uttered: "My son has started dissipating his spiritual powers without discrimination. Shall our occupation now be to revive everyone's dead son and interfere ever in God's Will. We who are enjoined to accept whatever good or bad comes to us in His Pleasure."[45] *Karamat kaihar hei* (Miracle making is violence). None should attempt to intervene in the Will of God.

Baba Atal took the reproof so much to heart that he gave up the ghost thereafter while yet he was only in his ninth year. This led to great sorrow and lamentation in the family but the

Guru said "Atal has become like his name. 'Atal' literally meaning immortal, for he has obeyed the Will of God willingly. He will be the guardian angel of the city of Amritsar and no one will turn away from his door hungry and empty-handed. Later on a nine storeyed structure called the Bunga of Baba Atal was raised in memory of this wonderful child. To this day the poor are constantly fed, night and day, at this beautiful shrine. There is a popular adage *Baba Atal Pakki Pakai Ghal* (Revered Atal ji, provide food cooked and palatable).

It appears that the Guru visited Hargobindpur quite often—the purpose being supervision of construction and the organisation of proselytizing activities. In C.E. 1630 when he was sojourning there, Baba Budha, Bhai Gurdas, Bhai Jiwan, Ajitta and Jodha came to make obeisance. They were struck with astonishment at the Guru's splendour that the Guru's work reflected. Baba Budha in all humility requested the Guru that he should be spared from active duty and allowed to go to Jhanda Ram Das, the village which his son Bhana had founded. The Guru granted his request and he retired to Jhanda Ram Das.

Shortly after, the Guru rushed to Jhanda Ram Das when the news reached him that Baba Budha was nearing his final end and ardently wished to have a glimpse of his Guru. The Guru put his hands on the forehead of the Baba and blessed him. Soon Baba ji went into eternal sleep (C.E. 16 November, 1631). According to *Gurbilas Padshahi Chhevin*, the Guru gave his shoulder to his bier. Bhai Gurdas recited Kirtan Sohila. The Guru presented a turban to Baba Budha's son Bhai Bhana. Two shrines stand at Ram Das, in memory of Baba Budha—one Gurdwara Tap Asthan Baba Budha ji where Baba ji meditated and the second gurdwara Samadhan where Baba ji was cremated on 16 November, 1631. Kaulan another dedicated Guru's disciple too left for heavenly abode in the same year, just before the death of Baba Budha. A beautiful gurdwara stands at Kartarpur as a tribute to her ideal of remaining pure and firm in the midst of impurities like the lotus which remains untouched even in dirty water.

From Jhanda Ram Das the Guru visited Kartarpur, the city founded and raised by Guru Nanak where he lived for about thirty years of his later life. The Guru met Bedi Dharam Chand and his sons, Mehar Chand and Nanak Chand who felt happy at the visit of the Guru. Thereafter, the Guru proceeded to the village Barth in the Pargana of Gurdaspur to pay respect to Sri Chand, the ascetic son of Guru Nanak. The latter complimented the Guru for his chivalry and piety. The Guru replied with profound humility that "It is all the result of your blessings." While engaged in exchange of pleasantries, Baba's eyes fell on Guru's son Gurditta and Suraj Mal. He spontaneously asked "which of your five sons you would like to give to him (Baba Sri Chand). The Guru very humbly uttered "All my sons belong to Baba." Sri Chand then gave away his Persian Cap to Gurditta and put on his neck a string of lotus seeds as if to transfer his gaddi to him. Baba Sri Chand then made very meaningful remarks "Baba Gurditta henceforth would be a successor not only to you but to me as well." He in a way signalled that from now onward he and his followers would serve the main-stream Sikhism. His Udasi organisation would function to extend the cause of Sikh religion instead of professing and flaunting their own separate identity. This event was a momentous one because Udasies instead of being a challenge to Sikhism turned its supporters—the fact which accrued a lot of benefit to Sikhs in the eighteenth century when they were engaged in life and death struggle first against the Mughals and then against Afghans and found little time to attend to their religious chores. After this the Guru is said to have returned to Amritsar.

The Guru in Uttar Pradesh

Now the Guru planned to visit different places in Uttar Pradesh. His visit to this area was prompted by the news that Almast, who had been preaching the Sikh religion at Nanak Mata had been expelled from the shrine by the Jogis who thereafter assumed control of the same. Not only this, they displayed the audacity to set fire to the *peepal* tree under which Guru Nanak Dev had seated and in discourse with the Yogis defeated the latter. The place earlier known as Gorakh

Mata assumed another name *i.e.* to say, Nanak Mata. Guru Hargobind reached the place in C.E. 1627 corresponding to Bk. 1684, 13 Har. He had with him two hundred horsemen. The Yogis got frightened and instigated Baj Bahadur, a local chieftain to chastise the Guru whom they painted as a menace to his authority as well as to their spiritual hegemony. When he glimpsed the Guru he was so much overwhelmed that he simply took a U-turn. Instead of championing the cause of the Yogis, he entered into discipleship of the Guru. According to Giani Gian Singh, he granted four villages as Inami Jagir to the shrine which still exists.[46]

The Guru, thereafter restored the shrine to Almast who made it a headquarter wherefrom preaching forays were conducted into the whole region and whereto different Sangats looked for guidance.[47]

M.A. Macauliffe records that it is believed the Guru sprinkled water mingled with saffron on the burnt roots of the *peepal* tree which at once sprouted and ultimately the whole tree made its appearance.[48]

After this, the Guru took up homeward journey. On the way, he made halts and preached. He enjoyed himself at Garh Mukteshwar. He sojourned at Kurukshetra, the religious centre of the Hindus in North-Western India, understandably to interact with the Hindu religious leaders. From this he proceeded to Darauli where he had left his family members with his disciple and relative Sain Das, the husband of Ramo, the sister of his wife. Then the Guru left for Amritsar.

The Guru in Kashmir

In 1621, the Guru went northwards into Kashmir. Since the visit of Guru Nanak, Brahman Das and his descendants had been looking after congregations in the Kashmir valley. Guru Arjan had deputed Madho Das Sodhi (see Bhai Gurdas Var II, *Mehma Parkash* and *Bhagat Ratnavali*). Guru Hargobind proceeded thither through Wazirabad, Mirpur, Bhimpur, Behram and Sialkot. According to Teja Singh and Dr. Ganda Singh, the Guru converted thousands who had gone over to Islam.

En-route to Kashmir, the Guru halted at Gillotin, 16 kms from Wazirabad. From there he reached Wazirabad. After that the Guru reached Sialkot, then the abode of some renowned Sufis. He conversed with many of them and tried to convert them to his viewpoint. At Chaper Nala near Sialkot, the Guru advised a Brahmin to shed his caste-pride and egocentricity. As the soil of the place was sandy, the people faced acute shortage of potable water. The Guru identified a spot which would yield water only if a little effort was made. The Sikhs lost no time and constructed a tank, later to be called 'Gurusar'—literally meaning Guru's tank.

Next important sojourn of the Guru was at Mirpur. People flocked to him to receive instructions. Bairam Dutt and Jhaigar both Brahmins by caste, embraced Sikhism.

According to Mohsin Fani (1614-1670) a Sikh named Bhai Jhanda met the Guru and was simply won over by the Guru's charismatic personality.

From Mirpur, the Guru went to Rajouri via Poonch. A gurdwara constructed on the site marks the visit of the Guru. After passing through towns such as Sukih Salai, the Guru reached Shahji Marg now in Palyma district of Jammu and Kashmir. Guru's horse stood under a sapless Chinar tree, which according to local tradition, is still standing near the gurdwara raised in memory of Guru's visit. On the way to Shahji Marg, the Guru came across a child on the road, forlorn and wrapped in dirty clothes crying and shrieking. The Guru got down his horse instantly and picked up the child. Some of the Sikhs who happened to be nearby remarked that the child was *Kuthra* (dirty). The Guru washed the child with his own hands, dressed him neatly and caressed him uttering at the same time that "He is not Kuthra he is ever 'Suthra' literally meaning clean betokening that the innocent are always clean, dirty are only the ignorant. The Sikhs felt ashamed and begged Guru's pardon. The next sojourn of the Guru was Supian. A devoted Sikh named Kathu Shah along with people met the Guru for blessings. From Supian, the Guru proceeded to Srinagar. Sewa Das who had embraced Sikh religion at the behest of Bhai Madho whom Guru Arjan Dev had deputed in the Kashmir Valley welcomed the Guru and took him to his home near Kathi Darwaza. Sewa Das's mother, Bhag Bhari, was immensely delighted to have Guru's glimpse for which she had been cherishing since long. She offered him the robe which she had prepared with the yarn she had spun herself. The Guru accepted the same and blessed her. The Guru's benedictory utterances transported her to the realm of ecstasy and she spoke aloud about the greatness of the Guru and his illuminating words. She thanked the Guru for his condescension to her place and uttered:

> Who but thee, my jewel, could do such a thing
> Cherisher of the Poor, Lord of the Earth
> Thou has put over my head the umbrella of spiritual sovereignty. (*Maru Rag*)

Both Sewa Das and his mother served the Guru with utmost devotion as long as he lived in their house. While still at Srinagar, the Guru raised a gurdwara at Hari Parbat where Sewa Das was ordained to stay and conduct his proselytizing activities. According to Jasbir Singh Sarna "the Guru during his stay at Srinagar met Sangats regularly. Devotees gathered in large numbers to listen to his message. The Guru familiarized them with concept of *Piri-Miri* and Sikh way of life. Lots of people from the Valley of Kashmir including the city of Srinagar thronged to the Guru and were illumined. Many of them embraced Sikhism.

A very remarkable event is said to have occurred during the Guru's stay in Srinagar. A party of Sikhs came to the Guru from some distant villages. They requested him to taste the honey which they had brought very lovingly. The Guru declined to oblige them. On being asked the reason, the Guru told that on the way they refused to give it to Kattu Shah who had an attack of asthma and needed it for his treatment. The Guru then dwelt on the nature of relations between the Guru and a Sikh and told that by refusing to respond to the needs of Kattu Shah, they had simply shown their insensitivity and intransigence to one of the cardinal instructions of the Guru. The Guru emphasised that they should never forget "The Guru's treasure chest is the mouth of the needy."

Shortly after Mata Bhag Bhari breathed her last. Babak recited the sacred hymns on the occasion and the Guru presented a turban to Sewa Das. The Sikhs later on converted her home into a gurdwara to serve as a monument to the dedication of Mata Bhag Bhari for the Guru.

While the Guru was in last leg of his itinerary in Kashmir Valley, a disease in epidemic form overtook the people of Srinagar and of its surrounding areas. People suffered a lot of hardships. The Guru forthwith harnessed his resources to provide relief for which he earned heartfelt gratitude of the people. The Guru paid personal visits to many of those who were affected. It is said that the Guru also met Jahangir who at that time happened to be in Srinagar on his royal visit.

Shortly after, the Guru returned towards Punjab via Baramula where he camped on the right bank of the river Jhelum at the foot of rocky hill near Kot Tirath and Varah Ganga. The famous stone cutters of Baramula presented a beautifully designed stone throne to King Jahangir which he gave to the Guru who in turn blessed the stone cutter. While still in Baramula, a number of devotees presented a Chinar sapling to plant it as a sign of their devotion to him. The Guru planted the same before proceeding further. After this, the Guru visited village Kamalpur (Singhpura) which is hardly one kilometre from Baramula-Srinagar highway.[49] The villagers were in great difficulty due to the scarcity of water. The Guru realizing the acuteness of their problem identified the spot where a well could be struck. After this, he asked his followers to accomplish the job which was done forthwith, to the joy of the whole population of the village.

Here a faqir named Bahlol entered into religious discussion with the Guru. He was so much impressed that he decided to become Guru's devotee. Later on the Sikhs constructed gurdwara Tharah Sahib[50] at the hallowed place where the Guru met the faqir. When the Guru left Kashmir, Bahlol and his disciples started candling a flame near the spot.

The next halt was at Uri. A gurdwara constructed on the right side of the river marks the Guru's visit and the place is called Panj Peernia. The place is seven kilometres away from Uri on the Baramula road. A local tradition would have as believe, that the Guru held discussion with the five Muslim Pirs named Gulsher, Rangi Imam, Nurmihal, Bhor Sultan and Abdul Gafoor in the presence of Jahangir. The three Pirs admired the Guru's higher spiritual knowledge, while the two, namely Abdul Gafoor[51] and Rangi Imam[52] flaunted their stubbornness.

Travelling through Muzaffarabad[53], and Abbotabad the Guru reached Hasan Abdal (Panja Sahib). The next halt of the Guru was at Rawalpindi[54], then an agglomeration of a few huts. After this, he visited the village known as Nirali. There he met his disciple Guzar Khan. From there the Guru reached Gujrat.

At Gujrat he met Shah Daula, a much revered Sufi saint for his keen interest in the welfare of the unprivileged and the helpless.[55] Shah Daula was astonished at the sight of the Guru with swords hanging on his both sides, aigrette attached to his turban and a hawk perched on his wrist. In his discussion with the Guru, Shah Daula raised a point: how can you (the Guru) be a religious man when you have a wife and children and possess worldly wealth and have arms. The Guru retorted "A wife is man's conscience, his children perpetuate his memory, wealth enables them to live, arms are needed to extirpate the tyrants."

At Wazirabad, the Guru met his devotee Khan Chand Khatri in whose house he stayed. The place is now called Guru Kotha. From Wazirabad the Guru reached Hafizabad, in the district of Gujranwala where he explained the meaning of 'Japuji', to one Karam Chand. Before proceeding from the place the Guru enjoined upon Bhai Karam Chand to preach Sikhism in the area around Hafizabad.

From Hafizabad, the Guru went to a village called Matto Bhai. After staying there for some time, the Guru reached Mandiali.

While still at Mandiali, the Guru was informed by Langha of the sustained efforts of some of the Mughal officials and ulemas to poison the mind of the Emperor Jahangir to destroy the sacred buildings of the Sikhs, especially those at Lahore and Amritsar. The Guru took only a casual notice and proceeded to Talwandi, the birth place of Guru Nanak. The Guru imparted instructions to the people who had gathered there in connection with the *Nimani* fair.[56] The descendants of Lalo[57] and Rai Bular felt extremely excited at the sacred sight of the Guru. From that place, the Guru proceeded to Madar—the place already rendered sacrosanct by the visits of Guru Amar Das and Guru Arjan Dev and which preserved one *slipper*[58] of Guru Amar Das and a stick of Guru Arjan Dev. Guru Hargobind met Bhai Manak and enthused him to take up the preaching work with more vigour. From that place the Guru proceeded to Manga in the Lahore district wherefrom he went to Amritsar, where as usual there were rejoicings on a large scale.

Guru in Malwa

Soon the Guru visited Zira, Rode Lande, Gill, Kotra and Mari. The last two villages were inhabited by the Bhullar Jats who were at the time of the visit of the Guru had gathered together to pay homage to their first ancestor and had prepared a grand feast to be offered to the priests. The Guru laughed at them and made them realize their folly. At this juncture, the Sidhu Jats who claimed their descent from their ancestor Marajh, driven by the Pachadas from their villages, came to the Guru and requested him to help them secure a piece of land from the Bhullars for habitation. The Guru asked the Bhullars to part with some of their land to enable the Sidhus to settle. The Bhullars flew into rage whereupon the Guru advised the Sidhus to found their village away from this place. The Sidhus founded a village in 1627 about three miles from Mari and named it Marajh after the name of their ancestor. The Bhullars were piqued and they attacked the Sidhus of Marajh. The Guru sent his brave soldiers such as Bhai Bidhi Chand, Jaita, Jetha, Parana, Saktu, Apira and Mala for their help and the Bhullars could not oust them.

After that the Guru having visited Marajh, Dabwali, Mahal, Ded Maluke, Demru en-route, reached Darauli. After staying for some time at Darauli, the Guru decided to move in the Malwa region again. Having sent Baba Gurditta, Baba Tegh Bahadur and his mother, Nanaki to Kartarpur and Suraj Mal and his mother to Kiratpur, he proceeded to Bara Ghar, a village situated at a distance of five miles from Darauli. Before his departure, the Guru blessed the Darauli people and gave them a *Pothi* and a *Katar* (small sword) as mementos. Rai Bhag Mal and many others of the village of Bara Ghar accorded him hearty welcome and provided all possible facilities. After staying here for 5 days the Guru proceeded further. Having visited Mado, Lopo and Sidhwan etc. Guru reached Sidhar. Rai Jodh, a big zamindar of Kangar, inspired by his wife Bhagan who was the daughter of Bhag Mal Gill, a devotee of the Guru, waited upon the Guru and was impressed by him so much that he desired to embrace Sikh religion. Giani Gian Singh says that Mai Bhagan requested the Guru to initiate them to his faith. The Guru blessed them and said: "The torch of Sikhism will ever give light in your house." The impact of the Guru's message was at once deep and widespread. After some days, Umar Shah, the brother of Rai Jodh and many others belonging to or having relation with his family became Sikhs.

Shortly before, a party of Sikhs from Peshawar and Kabul departed from their abodes to benefit from the message of the Guru. Masands such as Bakht Mal and Tara Chand accompanied them. They had many things to offer to the Guru including two horses, named Dil Bagh and Gul Bagh of unsurpassing beauty and fleetness. On the way, the animals were forcibly seized by the Emperor's officials who desired to present them to Shah Jahan. On reaching Sidhwan, they made obeisance to the Guru and laid before the Guru the offerings they had brought with them except the horses. The Guru blessed them but was pained at the high-handedness of the Mughal government. The party after a brief sojourn returned home except Bakht Mal, Tara Chand and Dayal Chand who remained with the Guru at the village named Bhai Rupa.

A PERIOD OF OPEN HOSTILITY WITH SHAH JAHAN

Within a few years of the succession of Shah Jahan, the Sikh-Mughal relations became strained. The ties of cordial relations as there had been since C.E. 1611 were snapped and a period of open hostility started. Many factors were responsible for this big change.

Shah Jahan's Fanaticism

The foremost factor was the religious policy of Shah Jahan. During his period orthodoxy and religious fanaticism was at considerable height. According to Sri Ram Sharma "He (Shah Jahan) took keen interest in the welfare of new converts to Muslim faith and appointed special officers to look after them. In accordance with one of his orders, if any Muslim gave up his religion, he was severely dealt with. *Badshah Nama*, a contemporary work, tells us that Shah Jahan ordered the destruction of all temples which were under construction or were still incomplete." Three temples were demolished in Punjab and mosques were raised in their places. The *Baoli* of Guru Arjan Dev, situated in Dabbi Bazaar, Lahore, was filled up with rubbish and the kitchen (*langar*) building attached to it was converted into a mosque. In 1632, when he was returning from Kashmir, he found that some Hindus of Rajauri, Bhimber and Gujrat accepted Muslim girls as wives and converted them to their faith. The Emperor stopped such marriages and Muslim women already married were seized from their husbands who were fined, and in certain cases they were executed. They could retain their wives only on their embracing Islam. As many as 4500 such women were recovered. In 1635[59], it was reported to the Emperor that a Muslim girl Zinab had been converted and was taken as a wife by Dalpat, a Hindu of Sirhind. The woman, along with her seven children, one son and six daughters, was taken away and the man was executed.[60]

Naqshbandi Order

The propaganda of Naqshbandis was having its affect. In Jahangir's time, they could affect the people in a limited way but now they started their activities with redoubled zeal.

Masud, the son of Shaikh Ahmad Sirhindi, spared no pains to spread his views. The high officials of the government came under his influence. Aurangzeb often listened to his lectures when he was in Gujrat as a Viceroy. Masud was also enamoured of the prince and prayed for his success in unambiguous terms in the impending struggle for the throne. The activities of the Naqshbandis were more marked in the Punjab. They established many *madarsas* (schools of learning), obviously to influence the men through education. The cumulative effect of all these activities was that a big segment of the Muslim population became vibrantly conscious of their communal interests. Undoubtedly such people would not like such movements that might enlighten the people to awaken to new realization of resisting any attempt to exploit them for a particular social or religious group.

Some Sikh scholars, as for instance Professor Satbir Singh, aver that Manohar Das Meharban, the son of Prithi Chand, was also responsible for the strained relations between the Guru and Shah Jahan. He says "He (Meharban) entered into alliance with Karam Chand, the son of Dewan Chandu and with Jamil Khan, the son of late Sulhi Khan. All these persons did their worst to poison the mind of Jahangir, but they failed, although they succeeded in dinning some fabricated facts about the Guru into the ears of the heir-apparent and no wonder he remembered many forged stories."[61] Similarly, it is said that Dhir Mal did his best to bring about snapping of the ties of friendship between the Guru and the Emperor. We do not subscribe to the aforesaid views. We do not know any reliable historical source assigning responsibility of the strained relations between the Guru and Emperor to Meharban. Nowhere do we find any hint of the meeting of Meharban with Khurram. No doubt, Meharban bore enmity towards the Guru, but to regard him as a determining factor *vis-à-vis* the relations between the Guru and the Emperor is such a case which is totally unacceptable.

Similarly, Dhir Mal has been blamed for the change in the policy of Shah Jahan towards the state. This is also incorrect.

The protagonists of this view quote Macauliffe in their support. Macauliffe says:

> "Dhir Mal, the Guru's grandson, accepted the evil forebodings of the Masands who said that the Guru would certainly be defeated. The imperial army had arrived like a flight of locusts. The Guru's army was insignificant. It did not even bear the same ratio to the Imperial army as condiment to the viands of a feast 'The Guru, knoweth not the enemy's prowess and strategy.' I shall, therefore, probably attain my object and succeed him in his holy office."

Dhir Mal's mind having been thus perverted, he sat down and wrote the following letter:

> "Brother Painda Khan, my grandfather hath expelled and disgraced thee without cause, but I know thee to be my friend, and I will do the best for their interests. If thou come tonight and make a sudden attack, the fort and its treasure will fall into your hands for here there is no preparation made. I will render thee every assistance."

From the above account, it becomes clear that Dhir Mal was not true to the Guru but it does not lend support to the view that Dhir Mal's machinations were responsible for the change in the policy of Shah Jahan towards the Guru.

Kaulan's Episode

Kaulan's episode also contributed to embitter the relations of the Guru with Shah Jahan. Who was Kaulan? The author of *Umda-tul-Twarikh* states that Kaulan was the maid-slave of Qazi Rustam Khan. His view is endorsed by some of the later writers including J.D. Cunningham and G.C. Narang. We, however, do not subscribe to this view.

Kaulan was the daughter of the Qazi Rustam Khan. Sikh tradition unanimously affirms it. Giani Gian Singh in his *Twarikh Guru Khalsa* and Sadhu Govind Singh in his *Itihas Guru Khalsa*, also give her father's name as Rustam Khan. All the Sufi sources including those relating to Qaidirya order adulate her piety and spiritual illumination. Not even an oblique reference to her being a maid-servant of the Qazi exists in any of the contemporary records.

Deeply religious from childhood, Kaulan came under the influence of Sant Mian Mir, a famous saint of Qaidirya Order of the Sufis who was deeply respected alike by elites and people in general. He was a great admirer of Guru Arjan Dev. He had special affinity for Hari Mandir whose cornerstone he himself had laid. It was he who saw to it that Emperor's order to confiscate the property of Guru Arjan Dev and to imprison his family at Lahore was not implemented.

According to Dr. Trilochan Singh, whenever Guru Hargobind visited Lahore, he stayed close by the *Khanqa* of Sant Mian Mir which stood in the vicinity of Qazi Rustam Khan's house.

Once Kaulan watched Guru Hargobind discussing spiritual matters with Mian Mir.[62] She was impressed by the Guru's demeanour and spoke high of him. Her father who was a Sunni fanatic did not like her daughter admiring Sikh Guru whom he rated as the leader of infidels. Already an altercation had taken place between him and the Guru's disciples about the transaction of some horses. He now could not brook his daughter in a frame of mind to venerate the Guru.

Kaulan lived most of the time at *Khanqa* of Mian Mir whom he called *Bala Pir* (high priest). She imbibed from him the spirit of true Islam. She also learnt from him spiritual practices of Qaidirya Sufi faith. She was so much inspired that she decided to stay permanently at the Khanqa to lead a life of a Sufi giving up all thoughts of worldly life.

As per convention at the Khanqa, she could not be allowed to stay after attaining the age of puberty. However, she could be permitted to go to some householder's religious teacher with the consent of her Master if she was determined to lead a life of prayer and meditation. Kaulan took a decision to live in the protection of Guru Hargobind. Mian Mir permitted her and advised that she should seek the permission of her parents. Her mother agreed but his bigoted father threatened to kill her. With the help of her mother, she quietly escaped to Mian Mir's *Khanqa.* The saint sent her to Amritsar along with one of his disciples. According to another version, Guru Hargobind personally went to Lahore along with five Sikhs to escort her safely to Amritsar.

Kaulan was provided a separate house and some attendants. Complete arrangements were made for her comforts.

There she enjoyed the calm, the peace and the security of Mian Mir's *Khanqa.* She was now free to pursue her spiritual pursuits undisturbed by any fanatic or bigot. Kaulan's poised mind and her radiant soul shed light on all who came near her. Guru Hargobind admired her spirituality, sublimity, nobility and piety and thought it appropriate to excavate a tank, named Kaulsar as a memorial to her greatness in C.E. 1621.[63]

The incident caused much uproar among the Muslims. Rustam Khan was highly incensed. He lodged a complaint against the Guru for abducting her daughter. Jahangir refused to listen to him, for, he had full faith in the Guru's moral integrity. Possibly Jahangir took this decision under the influence of Mian Mir for whom he had utmost regard.

There are some *Sakhi Kars* who set the matter in a different setting. M.A. Macauliffe also could not escape their influence. According to them, Sajjan, a devout Masand, was bringing a handsome steed from Kabul. The horse was forcibly captured by a Mughal officer who in turn gave it to the Qazi. The Guru recovered the horse forcibly and along with it abducted his daughter.

The story of abduction at best is the creation of a befuddled mind. No contemporary record has even alluded to it. Even Mohsin Fani who makes as close an observation as to see whether the Guru while discharging his arrows brings some feeling of anger on his face does not even hint at this episode.

Jahangir died in 1927 at Rajauri. Shah Jahan, then in Deccan, hurried to Agra and made a state entry into the capital on January 24, 1628. He ascended the throne on February, 1628. Khidmat Prasat Khan was appointed Viceroy of Lahore. Since Shah Jahan was not as liberal as his father in his later years, it was feared that the Hindu reactionaries and the bigoted Mullahs and Qazis might incite the new Viceroy against the Guru on the issue of Kaulan. Already the enemies of the Guru had started spreading scandalous rumours. The situation became so alarming that some prominent Sikhs of Lahore and Amritsar requested Bhai Gurdas and Bhai Budha to persuade the Guru not to keep Kaulan at Amritsar. The Guru accepted the advice and sent Kaulan to Kartarpur holding out assurance. 'In history of her devotion for him and God would be remembered as the love of gypsy girl (Bhilni) for Lord Rama.' Kaulan passed away at Kartarpur in 1631 C.E.

The case of Kaulan was taken up again by his father who lodged a fresh complaint against the Guru. Since Shah Jahan had already issued the proclamation that the Muslims converted to other faiths would be severely punished, Kaulan's case which being a simple case of teacher-disciple relationship was blown out of context and was labelled a case of forcible conversion by an infidel. The fanatics among the Muslims spared no pains to poison the mind of the Emperor against the Guru.

Battle of Amritsar, C.E. 1634

Sensing the change in the temper of the government, the Guru intensified his activities. Apart from undertaking preaching tours and forging emotional contacts with the people, he stepped up his activities of training his people in the technique of fighting by organising regular training exercises and rousing them to a sense of fervent heroism by precept as well as example. The followers of the Guru responded to his call willingly and the Guru became rallying point of disaffection, a potential source of danger to the established order. According to Dr. I.B. Bannerjee "It should not be forgotten that behind all this was a, more or less, compact organisation and religious ideals of a highly intense fervour.[64] Thus, the situation, which had arisen immediately after the close of Guru Arjan's pontificate was aggravated further and though it might seem that compared with the mighty resources of the Mughal Empire all this was insignificant and hardly worth of serious notice, its potentiality could not be underestimated. The fact that the Guru seated himself on Sri Akal Takht (the Timeless Throne), heard the complaints of his followers, decided their cases, issued ordainments and was acclaimed with the appellation of 'Sacha Padshah' (True King) caused a lot of estrangement between state and the Guru. As a matter of fact, both the parties were primed for a clash and the slightest cause was sufficient to make them go at each other. The moment came in C.E. 1634.[65] In that year Shah Jahan's soldiers happened to be hunting in the sanctuary of Gumtala, a place in the neighbourhood of Amritsar. Chance so conspired that the Guru along with his retainers was also similarly occupied nearby. According to Prof. Satbir Singh, it was not the Guru but the Sikhs gathered at Amritsar on the Baisakhi day who were engaged in the game of hunting. Whatever be the truth, a clash took place between the Sikhs and the royal soldiers over the issue of a royal hawk. One of the royal hawks of the Mughals who was flying after a victim strayed away and fell into the hands of a hunting party of the Sikhs. Moved by compassion or for the sake of the fun of the game, the Sikhs set their own hawk on it and the royal hawk was brought down. The royal soldiers came to recover it but because of their impudence, arrogance and their abusive language, the Sikhs refused to part with the bird. And thus started the trouble. Altercation led to blows. According to I.B. Bannerjee the Imperialists were driven out with a slaughter. This was too great an offence to be lightly passed over and the enemies of the Guru including Naqshbandis thought it a good opportunity to revive the charges against the Guru and reminded the Emperor of his alleged misdeeds. The Emperor who according to B.P. Saxena was sojourning at Lahore while en route to Kashmir nodded in agreement. An expedition consisting of 7000 soldiers under Mukhlis Khan was sent against Guru Hargobind. The attack was unexpected, for the Guru was then busy with preparations for his daughter's marriage and had no idea of war with the Mughals.

The battle lasted for two days and it was fought at two places *viz.* Lohgarh and at the site where now the Khalsa

College stands. On the first day, the Mughal detachments attacked Lohgarh, a mini mud fortress just outside the city of Amritsar. Since the Guru had received the news of the impending attack a day earlier, the fort had, to all intents and purposes, been evacuated and had nothing except the sweets prepared for the groom's party which was scheduled to reach the next day. Even then a few brave Sikhs opposed the enemy. Their number being very small as compared to the number of enemy, they were soon overcome and destroyed. The Mohammedans proceeded to the Guru's palace in search of him, but they were disappointed to find nothing.

The second day, however, saw a fierce fighting. The Sikhs fought under the supreme command of Bhai Bannia, although after his death, the command was assumed by the Guru himself. The Guru's army consisted of archers, horsemen and footmen. A small contingent equipped with muskets also appeared to be there. There was virtually no artillery, because the manufacture of guns was the prerogative of the government alone. According to Macauliffe, the Sikhs had only to discharge stones and in no case the balls. The weapons of the Guru's soldiers were spears, swords, muskets, arrows *et al.* The details of the formation of the Sikhs soldiers are not clear; but so far as we know each unit was commanded by its own leader. The Sikhs, as need arose, resorted to retreats even; but only as one of the tactics of the broad strategy. The renowned warriors of the army of the Guru were Bhai Jeta, Nihalu, Tilok, Anant and Niral, Nand, Piraga, Bhir and Bhikhan, Bidhi Chand, Bhai Jati Mal, Gulab, Gokal, Babek and Painda Khan. The seven thousand Mughal soldiers had their supreme command in Mukhlis Khan and were divided into units, each to be commanded by its own commander. Shams Khan, Anwar Khan, Sayyad Mohammad Ali, Sultan Beg were some of the brave Muslim soldiers in the army of Mukhlis Khan.

Both sides fought valiantly and with determination. Many brave soldiers perished in the battlefield, but at long last, with Mukhlis Khan's head cleft in twain by the blow of Guru, the Mughal pressure decreased and they retracted their steps to Lahore. After nine hours of fighting the Guru's victory was complete. The Guru went to inspect the field of the battle and visited Lohgarh. He collected all the corpses, wrapped them in shrouds and cremated them with due honour.

Dr. I.B. Bannerjee does not agree with the conclusion that the 'Guru came out victorious in this battle'. He in his support quotes from Mohsin Fani's book "Debistan-i-Mazahib" that the baggage and property of the Guru was plundered. Moreover, in order to lend additional strength to his stand, he subjects the clear-cut facts to new interpretation. He says "It is stated that the Sikh detachment at Lohgarh (a small mud fortress outside the city of Amritsar) was too small to cope with the invaders. The Mohammedans made short work of them and took possession of the Guru's place. As the coming day had been fixed for the marriage of the Guru's daughter, Viro, sweets had been stored in the house for the marriage feast. The Mohammedans gorged themselves to repletion and surfeited by the Guru's sweets could not help sleeping and when they were surprised by the Guru's men, they were entirely routed, Mukhlis Khan was killed in the fray.

It is needless to discuss the merits of the story. Suffice it is to say that clearly the Guru's house was plundered by the Mohammedans on this occasion and that his so-called victory could not prevent his hasty retreat from Amritsar.

We have examined the Sikh accounts carefully and we have reached the following conclusions:

(1) That the Guru's house was certainly plundered on the first day of the war.

(2) That Mukhlis Khan was killed and the Guru had an upper hand in the battle on the second or the last day of the war.

Thus Dr. Bannerjee's version as given above is to read the Sikh tradition in parts. Nowhere does the Sikh account connect the plunder of Guru's property with the death of Mukhlis Khan. In fact Mohsin Fani's account does not make mention of the victory attained by the Guru—especially when Mohsin Fani seems to be a great admirer of the Guru. Possibly Mohsin Fani did not regard Guru's victory a decisive one which certainly it was not because the Mughal Government had not yielded to the Guru nor did it feel frightened in any way, rather it was piqued to take action against the Guru with redoubled vigour. The battle though not important from the military view-point because neither party showed any military acumen, but it was undoubtedly significant in the history of the Punjab. Apart from the fact that it was the first combat in the annals of the Punjab which was fought between the Great Mughals and the Sikhs; it epitomized the consummation of the efforts of the Guru to lend militancy to the Sikh movement so as to enable it to stand against all types of oppression. Moreover, this battle broke the spell of the much trumpeted invincible might of the Mughal government. Besides this, it made explicit the hitherto implicit aspect of Sikh ideology that the oppressors should be given hot welcome. Sir J.N. Sarkar writes: "Many men came to enlist under the Guru's banner. They said that none else had power to contend with the Emperor."[66]

The success, however, did not elate the Guru with pride. As he was fully aware of the strength and resources of Shah Jahan, he retired to the semi-desert waste-land of Bhatinda. Another tussle with the Imperial forces began, this time over the possession of two horses. Guru's fondness for horses and the almost incurable habit of the officials to seize these whenever one of a good breed and fleetness could be found, involved him in conflict with the government. It is said that two Masands named Bakht Mal and Tara Chand had brought two beautiful horses for the Guru. They were seized on the way by a Mughal official and sent to the royal stable at Lahore. The seizure of the horses by the officials was taken very seriously by the Sikhs who regarded this as a challenge to their ideology which was very dear to them. It was against this background that Bidhi Chand was determined to recover the horses at all costs. The task was, no doubt, difficult, but still more difficult was to compromise with the wanton high-handedness of the Mughal officials. Some writers have narrated the story of the recovery of the horses in such a way that Bidhi

Chand seemed to have been motivated by the marauding instinct, but this conclusion is preposterous.

Bidhi Chand went to Lahore to achieve his mission of recovering the horses. He contacted Jiwan, who was Sikh by faith and carpenter by profession and was equally interested in getting the horses back. Jiwan provided him a *Khurpa,* an iron instrument for grubbing up grass and Bidhi Chand posed as a grass-cutter. Soon, he gained access to Sondha Khan, the stable-keeper and so managed that he was appointed a grass-cutter to the Emperor's favourite steed at a wage of one rupee per day. Bidhi Chand worked as such for some days during which he won over the admiration of the officials. One night finding the official watchmen lying in Bacchanalian slumber, he placed the saddle on Dilbagh and whipped him. The horse which had never previously been struck even by the stalk of a flower, on receiving a cut with the whip, roused himself at the unusual summons, gathered his strength, set his limbs and on Bidhi Chand lifting the reins cleared without hesitation the high battlement and plunged with his rider into the deep water of the ditch around the fort. Bidhi Chand, well-skilled in horsemanship, steadied the animal in the water and guided him safely to shore and then to the village, Bhai Rupa where Guru resided at that time. In the morning when Sondha Khan, the incharge of the royal stable came to know of the missing of one of the favourite two steeds of the Emperor, he felt much perturbed. The trackers were sent all-around, but no clue could be found.

But Bidhi Chand was not fully satisfied. He resolved to recover the second horse also, this time the additional factor was the compassion for Dilbagh who, it was thought, would not be able to survive the pangs of separation for his companion, Gulbagh. Accordingly, he went to Lahore and declared that he was an experienced tracker and astrologer and could trace any thing that had been lost. Soon, he attracted the attention of the stable-keeper who entreated him to locate where the horse was. Bidhi Chand, who passed himself under the pseudo name of Ganak, very cleverly got ingress in the fort. According to Sikh tradition Bidhi Chand was presented to the Emperor and told him that he had the skill to interpret omens, discover tracks, and read the stars and planets. The Emperor promised him lakhs of rupees if he pointed out where the stolen horse was concealed. Bidhi Chand, holding magician's chain, put his hand on the ground and raised it three times to his forehead. He then ostentatiously bowed to his supposed patron saint and preceptor. He began to count by the aid of the thumb the joints of his fingers so that all might think, he was interpreting omens. He then said to the Emperor "I know where the horse is, but I want to have one look at the place whence he was stolen, and then I will give them all information. I will tell thee the chief's name and how he effected the theft. It is then for thyself to consider whether thou canst recover the animal peaceably or go to war for him." Upon this, the Emperor, the stable-keeper, Bidhi Chand and a few others went to the stable. Some tried to dissuade the Emperor from trusting the stranger, but the advice was disregarded.

When the Emperor, in reply to Bidhi Chand, said that the horse which had been stolen had his saddle on. Bidhi said that, if it had been otherwise, he could by the calculation he had already made discover the tracks. If, however, the remaining horses were saddled and bridled, he could consider what could be done without the delay which would be necessary to recast his calculations.

Bidhi Chand's suggestion was adopted. Bidhi Chand assured the Emperor for information regarding the horse by the morning. The impatient Emperor pressed Bidhi Chand not to wait till morning and in consonance with the desire of him ordered that perfect solitude and tranquility might be maintained and to this effect caused all the inhabitants to close the doors and go to sleep and put embargo on the ingress and egress of the inhabitants of the fort. In this way when everybody had retired to rest, Bidhi Chand undid the ropes that tethered the horse to the peg and galloped it to Bhai Rupa where the Guru lay encamped. It is said that Bidhi Chand, on the eve of his flight to his Guru, thundered aloud:

> "Hear everything, consider not the thief a person to be forgotten. Thy father, by the power of his army, formerly

took possession of an excellent horse, intended for the holy and worshipful Guru Hargobind, whose fame is like that of the sun and thou hast now in imitation of the unjust father seized these noble steeds specially intended by the pious Sikhs for their beloved Guru. I have made reprisal and taken the first horse by my ingenuity. My name is Bidhi Chand, I am Guru's servant. It was I who took home Dilbagh the horse thou are in search of. On account of separation from his mate, he wept copiously on his arrival, and we could only induce him to eat and drink with difficulty. Wherefore, in the guise of a tracker and with love for dumb animals, I have come to take his companion to join him. I am thief, the true king is my master. Thou hast now given me Gulbagh ready saddled. I have thoroughly gauged the wisdom of the court. I will tell where the horse is, and in so doing remove all the blame from myself. The Guru hath pitched his tent in the new village of Bhai Rupa. Know that Dilbagh is standing there. Gulbagh shall now go to join him." (Macauliffe, *The Sikh Religion*, IV, p. 177)

According to Sikh chroniclers, Dilbagh and Gulbagh were renamed as Jan Bhai—as dear as life and Suhela—dear companion respectively.

Obviously, the Sikh tradition is partially true. It seems to have preserved the exaggerated account of the way the horses were recovered. Certainly Shah Jahan did not meet Bidhi Chand as he was not at Lahore at that time.

At best, the services of Bidhi Chand were requisitioned by certain officials connected with the royal stable at Lahore. However, some of the things implicit in the tradition such as the daring of Bidhi Chand, the penchant of the Sikhs to recover the horses and the focalised notice, the Sikh Movement had attracted of the high-handedness of the government are undoubtedly historical.

BATTLE OF LAHIRA IN 1634 C.E.

Military preparations were, therefore, made on a large scale and the command of the Mughal forces was entrusted to

Qumar Beg and Lala Beg. The royal forces moved towards the barren country of Bhatinda to chastise the Guru. It seems that the Guru had the inkling of the Mughal designs. Accordingly, he had chosen strategically sound ground at Lehra Beg at Bhatinda-Barnala road. The Guru had three thousand soldiers plus one thousand men under the command of Rai Jodh. He had stored necessary provisions for the army and established control over the solitary well at that place.

The stationing of troops was so designed that it was not easy for the Mughal forces to gain access to water in particular. The climate of Bhatinda was also insalubrious for the Mughal army. No wonder, when both the forces met each other in 1634 C.E. (17th Poh, 1691) at the place cited above, the Guru had not much difficulty in beating his adversaries. The Mughal commanders were slain in the combat and remnants of the army rushed back to Lahore. More than 1200 Sikhs were killed or wounded. Casualties on the other side including those of the commanders were much more numerous. The Guru to commemorate his victory built a tank called *Guru Sar* on the spot. It lies near the village of Nathana about three miles from Rampura Phul railway station. The bravery shown by Jati Mal, Bidhi Chand and Rai Jodh during the battle was highly admired by the Guru.[67]

Mohammad Latif, commenting upon the factors, which led to the defeat of the Mughal army, says "Lack of provision and the difficulties of the march had a disastrous effect on the Mughal forces. They were reduced to great straits and being defeated by the Sikhs fled to Lahore, leaving commanders slain in the battlefield."

BATTLE OF KARTARPUR IN 1635 C.E.

After this, the Guru went for repose at Kangar and soon turned to Kartarpur. Soon after, war again broke out between the Sikhs and the Mughals. This time the cause was Painda Khan[68], the Afghan ex-general of the Sikh troops who had been dismissed on account of his haughty demeanour. He went over to the governor of Lahore,[69] Wazir Khan (1632-1639) and induced him to despatch a strong force against the Guru. Another expedition was sent against the Guru under the command of Kale Khan, the brother of Mukhlis Khan who had been killed in the battle of Amritsar. Painda Khan, and Qutab Khan, the faujdar of Jalandhar, assisted him. The Guru was besieged in Kartarpur in 1635.[70] The Sikhs bore the brunt of the attack under the able command of Bidhi Chand, and Baba Gurditta, the eldest son of the Guru. Even Guru Tegh Bahadur who was about 14 years old is said to have shown feats of valour in war. As the battle was going on, a man rushed with his sword upon the Guru and wielded it against him. The Guru, however, parried it and with another stroke severed his head saying, "Not so, but thus, is the sword used." In a hand to hand fight, Painda Khan fell upon his Master Guru Hargobind, but receiving a mortal blow fell at the latter's feet. The Guru cried, "You are a Musalman. Now is the time for you to repeat Kalma." It is said that the Guru shaded him with his shield from the scorching rays of the sun and with tears rolling down his eyes bade him final farewell.[71]

Painda Khan's death was followed by that of Kale Khan and consequent upon it, the Imperial army was disheartened and a general stampede followed. Mohsin Fani seems to corroborate the Sikh chroniclers because he too says that on this occasion, Mir Baderati and Painda Khan met their death.[72] We however, do not know who this Baderati was; most probably he was an imperial officer who had accompanied the expedition but there is no doubt that Mohsan Fani's Painda Khan is the same person whom we have discussed above.

According to Mohsin Fani, the Guru retired from the war at Kartarpur to Bhagwarati (Phagwara) and because, there, in the vicinity of Lahore, he met with difficulties he betook himself thence in haste to Geractpur (Kiratpur), which lies in the mountainous district of the Punjab.[73] The Sikh records also state that after the battle of Kartarpur, which is said to have taken place in 1635, the Guru left the place, and in the course of his journey reached Bhagwarati (Phagwara). As the town was on the road to Lahore, whence reinforcement could easily be sent against him, he continued his march to Kiratpur. Near Phagwara in the village of Palahi a contingent of royal forces made a sudden and unexpected attack on the Guru under the command of Ahmad Khan, the son of late Ahdallat Khan and inflicted considerable loss on the Guru's soldiers. In this battle, Bhai Desa and Sohela, sons of Balu Bhat, grandsons of Mula Bhat fell martyrs.[74] This battle was fought on the 1st of Jeth Bk 1692 (C.E. 1635).[75]

Guru Hargobind had won four battles and through these effected a great change in the character of the Sikhs who, side by side their rosaries, buckled on the sword in defence of their faith. The fighting spirit of the Sikhs having been roused and their mettle proved, they became a power to be reckoned with. Guru Hargobind was looked upon by the Sikhs not only a divine messenger but as an accomplished swordsman, a hero, and a thorough master of war.

But what did Guru aim at by doing all this? Since Guru's purpose had always been defensive, he did not acquire even an inch of territory as a result of these victories. There was something far significant involved in this warfare than mere dispute over a hawk or a horse. A new heroism was rising in the land. The objective then dimly seen was to create the will to resist the mighty power of the Mughal government who had embarked upon the policy of religious discrimination *vis-à-vis* the non-Muslims.

Guru's Activities at Kiratpur

After this, Guru proceeded to Kiratpur and continued to stay there till his death. Why did the Guru proceed to Kiratpur, a city in the foothill of the Himalayas. Three factors seem to have affected the decision of the Guru: Firstly, the Guru was shrewd enough to see that his limited means would not last long, being no match in the long run, to well-nigh inexhaustible resources of the Mughal Emperor and therefore he thought it advisable to beat his retreat to Kiratpur, which was not so easily accessible during those days of undeveloped and scanty means of transportation and communication and, secondly, the constant pressure which Mughals exerted on the rising power of the Sikhs brought to a virtual standstill the work of religious propaganda, and, accordingly, he decided to give some time to the hitherto neglected job of proselytisation. Thirdly since some of the Rajput Hill Rajas were great admirers of the Guru because he was instrumental in getting them released from the fort of Gwalior and some of them had developed veneration for Sikhism and in token thereof had paid visit to Guru Amar Das, he made up his mind to make Kiratpur as a permanent residence.

Towards the middle of the year C.E. 1634, Guru Hargobind received the sad news of the death of his friend Wazir Khan at Agra. It was he who always pleaded the cause of the Guru in the court and mellowed the Emperor in his attitude towards the Guru. Next year, in the year C.E. 1635, he received further the sad news of the departure of the great saint, Mian Mir. Both Mian Mir and Wazir Khan were the golden bonds bridging the gulf between the progressive and resurgent forces of Sikh faith and aggressive bigoted forces of Mughal Imperialism. Even when Mughal Imperialism was at daggers drawn with the revolutionary ideals of Sikh faith, Wazir Khan and Mian Mir established that there was eternal unity and an unbreakable spiritual and cultural bond between Sikhism and true Islam. The exit of both these persons from this world who were well-wishers of the Guru and his cause was sure to prove a great factor to influence the Guru to stay at Kiratpur. The Guru lived in the city from 1635 to 1644 C.E. During those days, the Guru was not disturbed by any extraneous power. Even the Mughal Emperor seemed to have turned genial probably under the influence of Dara Shikoh.

We do not know much of Guru Hargobind's life at Kiratpur. It, however, appears that the Guru laid more emphasis on the work of Sikh organisation and proselytisation. During his preoccupation with his wars, he had appointed Baba Gurditta, his eldest son to look at that. In fact, Baba Gurditta was the most suitable for the job. He was a married man and a soldier. He was looked upon by the people as an exact replica of Baba Nanak. Besides, he had been accredited as successor of Sri Chand and was in a position of vintage to harness Udasi order to escalate proselytising activities. This being so, the preaching was done studiously, but it received additional impetus when Guru Hargobind found time to attend to. The Guru was fully aware that the *masands* or missionaries appointed by earlier Gurus had become corrupt, profligate and exploiters, by and large. He was also in the know of the fact that his long absence from the plains of Majha had encouraged his opponents and rivals to flaunt their hostility as well as their sectarian and cultish ideologies. Ram Das Pur had been taken over by Manohar Das Meharban, the son of Prithi Chand who wrote his own 'BANI' under the pen name of Nanak and claimed to be the seventh Guru. He wrote a Janamsakhi of Guru Nanak to buttress his claim. His son Harji succeeded to his position at Ramdaspur in 1640 as eighth Nanak. Despite all this, Minas and others could not influence the people only marginally because of marrow-deep effect of Sikhism which the Gurus right from Guru Nanak through Guru Hargobind had accomplished. In fact, the Guru's esteem increased instead of suffering erosion. He had numerous devout followers in Punjab and at far off places such as Delhi, Ujjain, Burhanpur, Lucknow, Prayag, Jaunpur, Patna, Raj Mahal and Dacca which signified very clearly that the import of the Guru's dispensation was fully grasped and admired as the legitimate recipe for the advancement of the Sikhs and non-Sikhs. Even then in the Guru's understanding it was only proper that a fresh organisation might be set up to put new life into the preaching work. In 1636, he asked Baba Gurditta to appoint four head preachers: Almast, Phul, Gonda and Balu Hasna which he did investing them with his own peculiar dress in which he had symbolized himself as Guru Nanak before Pir Budhan Shah, the great simeon of Sikh History.

Almast was made as the chief organiser for the proselytising activities in East India and it goes to his credit that he did commendable work and raised gurdwaras in commemoration of Guru Nanak's visits at different places. There were a number of places in Bengal, Bihar and Orissa where he raised Sangats. Balu Hasna[76] who was the younger brother of Almast, established himself among the people of Pothohar, Kashmir, Chuchh and Hazara. Phul and Gonda were assigned the area of Doab to carry on the proselytising work. Both were allotted their duties in C.E. 1636. Both were successful missionaries. Phul also preached in Malwa region of Punjab besides his allotted area of Doaba.

All these four Udasis established in their allotted territories the preaching centres which were named as Dhuan or Hearths, symbolizing the flame of Sikhism.

The Guru sent Bhai Garia to Kashmir with twin purposes to preach Sikhism among Kashmiris[77] and to collect tithe offered by Sikh Sangats. He was also given a Hukamnama[78] for the Sangat of Kashmir. En route to Sri Nagar, Garia met Shah Daula who had turned Guru's admirer since his meeting with him. He stayed at Gujrat for some time and then proceeded to Kashmir Valley. His preaching was so effective that many Kashmiris embraced Sikhism and many became its admirers.

Bhai Sunder was another zealous preacher who spread Guru's dispensation at Ayodhya and Agra. Bhai Nawal of Patna and Bhai Mohan of Dacca were other important preachers who disseminated Guru's message.

Besides this, the Guru sent Bidhi Chand[79] first to Bengal and then to Ayodhya. Bhai Gurdas was assigned preaching work first in Kabul and then in Benaras. He reached Bengal through Devnagar in Uttar Pradesh. At Devnagar he held religious discourses with a well-known saint Sundar Shah[80] who was a disciple of Pir Buddhan Shah. Khwaja[81] along with Jani, a Sayyad, and Nand Lal both of whom embraced Sikh religion under his impact and harnessed their energies and resources to mould the lives of the people in the light of the instructions of the Guru. In appreciation of the conduct of Nand Lal, Guru called him Sohina—the beautiful.

It speaks volumes for an all-round development of Sikh character that a warrior at such a short notice could be sent out as a missionary and a scholar as a trader. In the course of time, Guru Har Rai, Guru Teg Bahadur and Guru Gobind Singh instituted many other similar centres of missionary work, called Bakhshishs or Bounties. Suthra Shah, a great humorist, had also a commission to carry on the mission of Guru Nanak in his own way. A question may be asked as to how Udasis could propagate Sikhism whose canons did not fit in their ideology of renunciation. The answer can be found in various developments of Udasis. Guru Ram Das had mellowed Baba Sri Chand considerably and it appears that with the passage of time, the soundness of the Sikh Guru's stand which became more visible, affected Sri Chand deeply and a man of conscience as he was, he decided to wind up his business and to lend helping hand to strengthen the movement as set afloat by the Gurus. During his wanderings, he happened to come face to face with Guru Hargobind probably in 1629. He asked Guru Hargobind to give him one of his sons for adoption. The Guru gave him Gurditta who got Sri Chand's mitre and necklace. The words of Sri Chand addressed to the Guru on that occasion were: "The Guruship was already with you. I had only the Fakir's mitre and now that too is given over to your family." This event instead of laying the foundation of a new schism marks the closing scene of reconciliation between the two estranged families and confirms the unity of Sikh organisation for which the previous Gurus had worked so hard. Henceforward Udasis ceased to be a separate creed, and they placed their services at the disposal of the Guru to be used any way he liked. Since by virtue of their training, they could reduce their demands to the minimum, they proved vigorous preachers. They undoubtedly did not preach Udasism but they certainly preached with stoic indifference to handicaps which were the natural concomitants of the task.

The Guru's arrangements worked nicely and produced remarkable results. The Guru acquired a great influence over the hill people and the Rajas alike. The Sikh chroniclers state that in the days of Guru Amar Das, the Raja of Haripur had accepted Sikhism, and that the Hill Rajas of Kulu, Suket, Haripur and Chamba visited Guru Arjan Dev and became his followers as the Raja of Mandi had previously done. Similarly, Guru Hargobind is said to have converted the Rajas of Kangra and Pilibhit. The Guru's religious propaganda was gaining ground among the people also. In this connection Mohsin

Fani narrates an interesting story. A Sikh called Bhairo cut off the nose of the goddess, Naina Devi, at the place nearly ten miles distant from Kiratpur. This was reported to the neighbouring Raja who lodged a complaint with the Guru regarding the outrage. Bhairo was summoned. He pleaded that he would admit the charge, if the goddess herself attested it. One of the Raja's counsellers said in reply, "O blockhead, how can the goddess speak"? Bhairo smiled and said "We now know who the blockhead is. If the goddess cannot repel her assailant and give evidence against him, how can you hope for any advantage from her."[82] Bhairo's answer is said to have had a tremendous effect and Mohsin Fani says that "from this time the disciples of the Guru increased considerably, and in this mountainous country as far as the frontiers of Tibet and China there is no trace of Islam".[83] Subsequent events, however, give us a wholly different picture because the Hill Rajas remained to the last the most implacable enemies of Guru Gobind Singh and his cause. Thus, it is evident that the movement in favour of Sikhism in the hill states was a temporary one and it did not survive for a long time. "However, the Guru had friendly or cordial relations with the Hill Rajas and that he had gained a considerable reputation is proved by the fact that Perrah Kaivan Yazadani was moved by the name of the Guru and came to pay him visit as also Fazal Irani and Pir Hasan Ali from Saudi Arabia came to have the sacred glimpse of the Guru.[84]

The Guru undertook occasional preaching tours in hill territories. In one of his tours, he met the great Maratha saint Samrath Ram Das at Srinagar (Garhwal) in 1634. The saint was struck with astonishment at the sight of the Guru with two swords hanging on his both sides, a white hawk perched on his wrist and an aigrette attached to his turban. Ram Das asked the Guru, "I hear that you are the successor of Guru Nanak. Guru Nanak had renounced the world, while you wear the swords, keep horses and an army and people call you 'The True King'. What kind of a Sadhu are you?" Guru Hargobind replied:

'Saintliness within, worldliness without; Arms poor man's protection and enemy's destruction; Nanak gave up not world, He gave up worldliness.'

(Batan Faqiri, Zahir Amiri, Shastar Gareeb Ki Rachhia Jarvane Ki Bhakkhia).

In the Sikh tradition this incident is traced to an old Punjabi manuscript entitled *Punjab Sakhian.* Interestingly Samrath Ram Das meeting with Guru Hargobind is corroborated in a Marathi source *Ram Das Swami's Bakhar* by Hanumant Swami in 1793. Though the details of the meeting are an apparent distortion.

These words found a ready response in the heart of Samrath Ram Das who spontaneously said, "This appeals to my mind—*Yeh Hamre Man Bhavti Hai.*"

It is believed, as Dr. Charanjit Singh Udasi, a renowned Sikh theologian suggests that Guru Hargobind's reply deeply impacted Samrath Ram Das who refurbished his socio-political philosophy which he imparted to his disciple Shivaji Chhatarpati who later made it the *modus operandi* of his political career.

Side by side preaching, the Guru laid appropriate emphasis on the right type of social action rooted in and reflective of Sikh ideology. He himself set up example and wished his followers to emulate him. In the region outside Kiratpur, there was scarcity of water and the people had to fetch water from distant places. The Guru got sunk four wells in the neighbourhood of Kiratpur, first in village Paval situated on the road that reached Guru Ka Lahore, second in village Kotla, third on the spot between Kiratpur and Anandpur Sahib and the fourth in village Kalaynapur. The last one was washed away by flood sometime later.

The Guru avoided involvement in the mutual disputes of the hill Rajas, generally speaking. But at times he did perform some role, to effect rapprochement or to moderate the belligerence of the rival powers. Nasir Khan, the Faujdar of Ropar, seized some territory of the Raja Dharam Chand of Hadur across the Sirsa river. The Guru on the Raja's request despatched one hundred chosen warriors under the command of Baba Gurditta on Asu Sammat 1692 Bk., C.E. 1635. A pitched battle took place, Mahammad Beg a nephew of Nasir Khan had to withdraw having been severely wounded. The Sikh forces pursued the enemy up to the village Malikpur Rangran from where Baba Gurditta came back to Kiratpur. Immediately after, reconciliation was brought about through the mediation of the Guru between Dharam Chand and the Nawab. In the process, Shams Khan of the Kotla Nihang who had always admired the Guru also played his part. Later on, the Nawab invited the Guru to Ropar. The Guru immediately responded. The Nawab and his family accorded the Guru a warm and affectionate welcome. The Guru stayed at Ropar for two days after which he reached Kotla Nihang to stay with Shams Khan for two days.[85] After that the Guru reached Lakhimpur village from where he went to Kiratpur.[86]

Because of the presence of the Guru, Kiratpur grew up a city reflecting Sikh religious ethos. Congregations were held in morning and evening reciting and deliberating upon Shabad and enjoying the splendour that Guru was. Every one tried to mould his/her life in the light of Guru's instructions. It was on this account that the people of the city, by and large, became guru-oriented and service-oriented. Exuberance and buoyancy were the dominant elements of their lifestyle. Differences on bases of caste, creed, wealth and birth were almost non-existent. Superstitions and empty rituals were not given recognition. People were vibrant with faith in oneness of God, His fatherhood of mankind and altruistic service to the needy. *Guru ka Langar* (Guru's Free Mess) ran in every house and sweet harmony existed among the people. The city's construction plan did not reflect any prejudice or bias, and there was no segmentation of the city on the basis of caste or religion as it was common in most of the cities of the medieval period. The people had developed healthy recreations such as water splashing in the river, hunting, horse-racing, swords plying, and wrestling *et al.* instead of drinking bouts and vulgar and indecent parties.

In such an atmosphere it was but natural that people grew to be a healthy society, always agog to achieve excellence in every field. The people coming to the city imbibed and admired Sikh religion including its cultural and social projections.

The last days of the Guru's life were saddened by a series of domestic tragedies. Within a few years five members of his family, including three of his sons, died one after another. Bhai Gurdas left for heavenly abode in 1632 (according of Bhat Vahi Talaude Pargana). Bidhi Chand passed away in 1640 at Dev Nagar. The most gravest death was that of Gurditta in C.E. 1638. To add to his sorrow, Gurditta's elder son Dhir Mal turned refractory. He even refused to come to Kiratpur to perform the last rites of his father, not to speak of his point blank refusal to send the copy of Granth Sahib which was in his possession. He very arrogantly declared that since he had entered into an alliance with the Mughal Emperor and had conveyed to him that he held no parleys with the Guru, it was not proper for him to come to Kiratpur (Macauliffe: *The Sikh Religion*, IV, p. 222).

The Guru had two sons living: Suraj Mal, who showed little interest in Sikh affairs and Tegh Bahadur, who was too withdrawn within himself to be entrusted with the leadership of a rapidly growing community. After deliberating a good deal over the issue of succession, the Guru appointed the younger son of Gurditta, Har Rai, to succeed him in preference to Gurditta's elder son Dhir Mal.

Guru Hargobind then sent for Bhai Bhana, the High Priest and Bibi Viro and her husband. Early in the last week of February, 1644 C.E. when all the disciples were assembled, Guru Hargobind seated his grandson, Har Rai, on the pontific throne and circumambulating him three times, placed five pice and a coconut and then bowed before young Har Rai declaring from that day onwards 'Har Rai would be the seventh Guru on the spiritual throne of Guru Nanak.' He then asked his sons to acknowledge Har Rai as the Guru by bowing before him. Baba Tegh Bahadur was the first to do so, and he was followed by Suraj Mal.

Guru Hargobind then turned to Guru Har Rai and said, "Live in peace and as you are quite young, avoid armed clash with the Mughal armies as far as possible. The Hindu states around this place keep on quarrelling and fighting. Do not get involved in their internecine warfare, but as the Mughal rulers are quite untrustworthy, be prepared for all eventualities. For any emergency that may arise, always keep at least 2200 soldiers fully armed with you. But not for first to provoke fighting. For the sake of protecting the poor, the helpless and the oppressed, do not hesitate to use the arm" (Santokh Singh, *Gur Partap Suraj Granth*, Ras 8, Ansu 56).

On the 26th February a Yazdani named Parrai Kauvan came to see him. The Guru recognized in him the greatness of a seer and met him with great respect and reverence. After a long spiritual discourse which gladdened his heart and inspired his soul, he went away (*Dabistan-i-Mazahib*).

Early on 28th February, Guru Hargobind entered the room which he had specially constructed on the bank of the Sutlej. The door of the room was closed from outside by Guru Har Rai as Guru Hargobind had directed. For four days, the hymns of praise of God were sung, the free kitchen was kept open day and night and clothes were distributed among the poor. On the fifth evening accompanied by Baba Tegh Bahadur, Suraj Mal, Bhai Bhana and Bhai Sadhu, Guru Har Rai opened the door of the room. There sat in *Samadhi,* with his back resting against the wall, Guru Hargobind, his face still glowing with spiritual fervour. Everyone bowed before the Guru who seemed to be sitting in meditation. When they went closer, they found that he had left the body for heavenly abode.

According to Mohammad Latif the Guru's death was a natural calamity and the estimation in which he was held may be judged from the fact that a great many of them volunteered to burn themselves on his funeral pyre. Two of his followers one a Rajput Raja Ram Partap of Jasselmer[87] and the other a Jat[88] who served the Guru's son-in-law Bhai Sadhu Ram jumped into the flames of burning pyre, continued moving around the corpse and finally fell and expired at the Guru's feet. Others were agog to follow the example, but were forbidden by Guru Har Rai because self-immolation violated Sikh dispensation.

Most Misunderstood Guru

Even a cursory glance at the career of Guru Hargobind would convince one that he was a multi-splendoured personality. Yet it appears that he has been much misunderstood. No doubt, he framed a policy which not only formed a correct response to the challenge of times, but also to the ones likely to come up in future, yet it is held by some scholars that he fell short of the high ideals that had guided his predecessors. The points made against him are as under:

(1) The Guru abandoned the gentle and spiritual teachings of Guru Nanak for the use of arms and for the love of adventure.

(2) His predecessors were great men of religion and composed many hymns for the guidance of their Sikhs. Guru Hargobind did not compose even a single such hymn for the purpose.

(3) According to I.B. Bannerjee, it appears that many among his contemporaries came to think that the lure of politics and glamour of arms were leading him away from the true path of a religious leader.

(4) Guru Hargobind changed the character of the peaceful Nanak's disciples who now laid aside their rosaries and buckled on the sword in defence of their faith.

(5) The Guru recruited outlaws, renegades, plunderers, robbers and men of doubtful character in his army and gave refuge to some of the Muslims who did not repose faith in Sikh religion. The Guru was rather a mercenary soldier than a religious zealot and fought for and against the Mughals, as the prospect of gain dictated.

On analysis, it has been found that the objections raised above are lacking in solid foundations or smack of misunderstanding or incapability of grasping the full import of the policy pursued by the Guru and the challenge of which this policy was an answer to. Referring to points No. 1 and No. 4 our assertion is that the Guru did not abandon the policy of the Gurus preceding him. The use of arms was never prohibited or made blasphemous by the earlier Gurus; only they did not make use of it and who can give guarantee that they would have not used arms, had they been called upon by the environments. The days when liberalism was in the imperial saddle had gone with the death of Akbar; and with the accession of Jahangir and Shah Jahan, a new era in the religious policy had started. The non-Muslims began to be looked down upon as the non-desirables. Guru Arjan Dev had fallen victim to the parochial religious policy of Jahangir and many more Sikhs were likely to meet the same fate under Shah Jahan who was certainly less liberal than Jahangir. Under the circumstances, if the power of the government was to be used to cater to the religious whims of the Emperor blinded by fanaticism or wrong notions about religion, the use of arms on the part of the Guru was, in no way, a sin. Even Guru Nanak could have not disapproved of it. Guru Nanak's *Babar Vani* amply acquaints us with the attitude of the Guru *vis-à-vis* sufferings. Certainly it was the attitude of putting up resistance to the perpetrators of tyranny or to the authors of sufferings. Furthermore, the epithet 'Asur Singhar' used for God by Guru Nanak leaves us in no doubt that Guru Nanak's attitude towards oppressors was that of a revolutionary. Guru Angad laid emphasis on the physical exercises, and showed firmness when he was threatened by Humayun. By the time of the third and fourth Gurus, the Sikh community had become large enough to attract the attention and also the hostility of those whose interests were affected by its rise. Guru Ram Das in his Var Gauri describes the Sikh movement of his time as an arena of opposing forces, wherein the Guru had to fight heroically against the odds. Guru Arjan too had to talk of his struggles in terms of wrestling matches (Sri Rag). After describing the work of organisation he had effected among Sikhs he says, 'Now the Order of the Merciful has gone forth that no one shall molest another.' And the Sikhs have been sufficiently prepared to understand what that Order meant for them. Birbal, a minister of Akbar, imposed a capitation tax on the Khatries of Amritsar, who led by Guru Arjan Dev refused to pay it. He threatened to bring an army to punish the Guru but he was called away to the frontier where he was killed, and nothing happened. Thus war was averted; but it is clear from this incident that the clash which came in the time of Guru Hargobind could have occurred earlier; only an accident postponed it. Guru Arjan Dev in his parting message instructed Hargobind to take resort to arms. Hence Guru Hargobind was not doing something new or deviating from the path of his predecessors by taking up arms as a last resort—rather by doing this, he was affirming his faith in the ideology as propounded and practiced by the earlier Gurus. In view of all this, it seems that Joseph J.H. Gordon misunderstood the character of the Sikh movement under Guru Hargobind. The Sikhs did not lay aside rosary as the symbol of Bhakti. In fact, there are examples when even in the battlefields, prayers and regular services were held. But there is no doubt that the Sikhs began to yearn for Shakti (Power) with so much intensity as they did for Bhakti. Why scholars of the stature of Gordon and Trumpp could not understand the Sikh movement in true colour was, perhaps, due to the fact that they could not think of any religion which regarded force to be an important adjunct of religious programme. Since it fell to the lot of the Gurus to face the Muslim ruling class in their efforts to reconstruct society on new foundations, they did not deem the use of force illegitimate or improper if it was made as a last resort and for a good cause. From another point of view also, the stand of the Gurus was justified. Sikhism, in Arnold Toynbee's analysis, formed a response of Hindu civilisation to the challenge of Islam and was born in time of trouble of Indian civilization. There was but all justification that it should adopt the ways of Islam to meet it and there was nothing surprising if Sikhs adopted sword as necessary concomitant along with rosary.

The objection No. 2 is also unsustainable. It appears that Trumpp has equated greatness with the composing of verses for *Guru Granth Sahib*. Really a strange modality of judging!

Gautam Buddha has not composed even a single verse and yet he is great and so is the case of Mahavir. In view of all this how can greatness be denied to Guru Hargobind? Moreover, to live the spirit of verses and to propagate them is a work of no less importance. As regards point number 3, it may be said that lure of political or glamour of arms never dazzled the Guru. He did take interest in developing the military instincts in his followers but never at the cost of the spiritual development of the Sikhs. In fact the Guru desired, like his predecessors, that all the earthly task should be rooted in spirituality. This may be seen queer to those who are accustomed to think of saints as merely recluses uttering *Mantras* with hands folded and eyes upturned. The Sikh Guru was, however, cast in a different mould. He was a practical leader as also a meditating saint, and thought it not inconsistent with his religious ideals to take active measure to do service of mankind as much through advancement of trade, art of living, as through holy communion and high thinking. In fact, the bonding of the heroic and the spiritual was Guru Hargobind's distinctive contribution to the evolution of the Sikh people as also of mankind.

It is absolutely wrong to say that plunderers or robbers comprised his army. Some one of them, as for instance, Bidhi Chand might be a dacoit or a robber before entering into the fellowship of the Sikhs but once he embraced Sikhism, he never indulged in any anti-social activities. In view of this, the Guru should be given credit for bringing about a unique transformation even among indecent characters. The Guru never thought in terms of Hindus and Muslims and made friends with anybody irrespective of caste, creed and birth etc. provided he/she was prepared to repose faith in Sikh religion and was a true seeker of truth.

All said and done, the Guru's personality sparkles like a sun in the sky. He was at once a great spiritual and temporal leader. Under him the Sikh movement not only steered clear through difficulties but also progressed in all its dimensions. Bhai Gurdas has well said of him "The smasher of enemy's ranks, the brave, heroic Guru, yet a lover of mankind."

During the stormy career of thirty-eight years, the Guru carried the message of Guru Nanak from Srinagar to Pilibhit in Uttar Pradesh, he sent missionaries even to distant places like Bengal and Ceylon. He had made it clear to the world that worldly pursuits were quite compatible with the deeper religious spirit and highest piety, and to bear arms in defence of their homes and hearths was a paramount duty of Sikh faith. The successes of the Guru's army had made the Sikhs realise their own power and the weakness of the Mughal empire. He stirred people to feel free from fear, superstitions, the social and political burdens of the ages, shackles of tyranny and despotism, and from anarchy of thoughts and faiths. He gave them moral and spiritual courage, to laugh at death, to spurn tyranny and despotism, and to love and serve humanity without any prejudices of castes and creeds. He also taught them to face and fight the fanatic, the bigoted, the cruel and the barbaric, be he a Muslim, a Hindu or a Christian. He transformed the passive Indian mood of servility into one of confident defiance of autocratic rulers.

FOOTNOTES AND REFERENCES

1. According to *Bansavli Nama*, the date of birth Har Samvat 1647. According to *Gurbilas Padshahi Chhevin* it is 1652 Bk. *Panth Parkash* says it was Bk 1652. Gulab Singh fixes 1653 Bk as the date of birth.
2. Pairaga embraced Sikhism during the period of Guru Arjan Dev. He took part in battles fought by Sri Guru Hargobind. He had four sons namely Bhai Mati Das, Sati Das, Jati Das and Sakhi Das.
3. *Encyclopedia of Sikhism*, Vol. II, p. 50, Punjabi University, Patiala.
4. Refer to *Suraj Parkash* by Bhai Santokh Singh.
5. Dal Bhanjan Guru Surma, Wad Jodha Bahuy Par Upkari.
6. S.S. Gandhi: *History of the Sikh Gurus*, p. 276, Gurdas Kapur and Sons, New Delhi, 1978.
7. *Encyclopedia of Sikhism*, Vol. II, p. 233.
8. *Ibid.*, Vol. II, p. 233.
9. *Gurbilas Padshahi Chhevin*, Chapter 6; Macauliffe: *The Sikh Religion*, Vol. IV, p. 3.
10. *Gurbilas Padshahi Chhevin*, Chapter 8.
11. Sohan Kavi: *Gurbilas Padshahi Chhevin*, p. 150.
12. Macauliffe, M.A.: *The Sikh Religion*, Vol. IV, p. 31.
13. *Ibid.*, p. 4.
14. Nanak Panthis: *The Punjab—Past and Present*, Vol. I, Part-I, April 1967, p. 65. J.S. Grewal, Irfan Habib, *Sikh History from Persian Sources*, p. 69.

15. Cunningham, J.D.: *History of the Sikhs*, p. 56.
16. Macauliffe, M.A.: *Sikh Religion*, Vol. IV, pp. 52, 76.
17. Trumpp, Ernest: *Adi Granth*.
18. Bhai Gurdas: *Varan*, *Var 15*, Pauri 4.
19. Giani Gian Singh: *Twarikh Guru Khalsa*, p. 416.
20. Refer to the translation of the Nanak Panthis in *Debistan-i-Mazahib* by Irfan Habib found in "Sikh History from Persian Sources".
21. Hari Ram Gupta: *History of the Sikhs*, Vol. I, p. 157.
22. Bhai Gurdas, *Var* 15, Pauri 4.
23. Balladeers who sing Var in accompaniment with a drumlet held in the palm of one hand and played with fingers of the other hand.
24. A drumlet held in the palm of one hand and played with fingers of the other hand.
25. Sohan Kavi: *Gurbilas Padshahi Chhevin*, p. 58.
26. Giani Gian Singh: *Twarikh Guru Khalsa*, p. 416.
27. Principal Satbir Singh in his book *Bandi Chhor* gives the height of Sri Akal Takht as 12 feet.
28. The word Akal a negative of Kal (Time) is equivalent of timeless, beyond time, everlasting and Takht in Persian language means "Royal Throne".
29. *Var XXVI* of Bhai Gurdas.
30. Again Bhai Gurdas refers to the Guru's saying "Man is top creation of God, superior to animals and others; but he is no better than them. An animal does not beg from other animals. Similarly, the birds never indulge in flattery of one another. Man who is endowed with superior mind, intellect, power to think and feel and discriminate acts no better. He has selected a king to rule over himself and has made his life a hell.
31. Bannerjee, I.B.: *Evolution of the Khalsa*, Vol. II, p. 32.
32. Muhammad, Akbar: *The Punjab under the Mughals*, p. 194.
33. Archer John Olar: *The Sikhs*, p. 173.
34. Beni Prasad: *Jahangir*, p. 150.
35. *Debistan-i-Mazahib*, Vol. II, p. 74.
36. *Ibid.*, Vol. II, p. 247.
37. *Debistan-i-Mazahib*, Vol. II, pp. 273-74. The Guru attached himself to Yar Khan the accused who held the office of a faujdar in the Nawabi of the Punjab and in administration. However, no reference to this is indexed in M. Athar Ali: *Apparatus of the Empire*: Awards and Ranks.
38. *Panth Parkash*, p. 107, *Itihas Guru Khalsa*, p. 128.
39. Beni Prasad: *Jahangir*, p. 454.
40. Bannerjee, I.B.: *Evolution of the Khalsa*, Vol. II, p. 13.
41. Please refer to *Sri Hargobindpur Da Itihas Sarvekhan*. Punjab History Conference. Punjabi University Patiala, 1989, pp. 30-35.
42. *Ibid.*
43. *Ibid.*
44. Bakshi Singh Adil, *Maharaja Jasssa Singh Ramgarhia*, Literature House, Putlighar, Amritsar, p. 32.

45. Dardi, Gopal Singh: *A History of the Sikh People,* pp. 227-28, World Sikh University Press, 1979.
46. Giani Gian Singh: *Twarikh Guru Khalsa,* p. 43.
47. Almast, it is said, was deputed by the Guru to go to Shijatpur near Dacca and take charge of Sangats there. The Sangat was known after Natha Sahib third in succession to Almast. According to the inscription on the wall, its founding was ascribed to Almast and its priests were appointed and removed by the High priest of Nanak Mata (vide G.B. Singh's article 'Sikh Relics in Eastern Bengal').
48. Macaullife, M.A.: *The Sikh Religion,* Vol. IV, p. 53.
49. According to Brangish Rish's book *Vitasatha Mohatani*, the present Baramullah, up to Khatnavar is known as Kot Tirath.
50. Hari Singh Nalwa constructed a beautiful gurdwara near the Chinar tree. Baren Charles Hugel also visited this gurdwara.
51. *Gurdwara Gazette*, January, 1997.
52. Giani Gian Singh: *Twarikh Guru Khalsa*, p. 439.
53. *Ibid.*
54. Wal-I-ullah Khan: *op. cit.*, p. 38.
55. Shah Daula had passion to serve the people. His Khangah was a great attraction for the people who considered its visit a pilgrimage, an act of high spiritual merit. He built quite a number of bridges, roads and inns. The shrine of Shah Daula is still revered by thousands.
56. Nimani fair called by the Brahmans the Nirjala Ikadashi was held on the eleventh day of the light half of the month of Jeth. The Sikhs observe this fair in commemoration of Guru Nanak's visit.
57. Younger brother of Mehta Kalu. He was born in 1444 C.E. and dies in C.E. 1542 vide *Mahan Kosh*, p. 1065.
58. *Mahan Kosh*, p. 947. According to Mohan Kosh, the second slipper of Guru Amar Das is preserved in the village named Dhani, Tehsil Hafizabad, Gujranwala. It was given to Bhai Paro Mal by Guru Amar Das.
59. Abdul Hamid Lahori: *Badshahnama,* II, pp. 57-58. Muhammed Salen: *Amal-e-Salih*, II, p. 64. Khafi Khan, *Muntakhabduhal,* I, p. 510.
60. *Ibid.*
61. Satbir Singh: *Sada Itihas*, Vol. I, p. 275.
62. Trilochan Singh: *Guru Tegh Bahadur*, pp. 33-34, Gurdwara Parbandhak Committee, Delhi, 1967.
63. Gian Singh: *Itihas Khalsa*. Some scholars believe that the name Kaulsar was given to the tank because lotus (water lily) flourishes in it.
64. I.B. Bannerjee: *Evolution of the Khalsa*, Vol. II, p. 21.
65. Fauja Singh: *Chronology of the Battles of Guru Hargobind*, Punjab History Conference proceedings, 1971, Punjabi University Patiala. Also refer to Bhatvahi Multani Sadhi preserved in the department of Punjab Historical Studies. Our conclusion is that the battles of Amritsar, Lehra and Phagwara were fought on 17th Poh Bk 1691 (C.E. 1634) and 29th and 30th Baisakh, Bk 1692 (C.E. 1635) respectively. Thus the fighting started in April 1634 and ended in May 1635. During the period the Guru moved

rapidly from Amritsar to Mehraj, and then to Kartarpur. This looks more realistic far more typical of a war scene than the picture provided to us by some writers such as Macauliffe and others in which quite some years are shown to intervene between the battles.

66. J.N. Sarkar: *A Short History of Aurangzeb*, p. 156.
67. Fauja Singh: *Chronology of the Battles of Guru Hargobind*, Punjab History Conference Proceedings, p. 136.
68. Painda Khan was the son of the nurse of Guru Hargobind and the Guru always held his foster brother in high esteem.
69. Painda Khan did not approach the Emperor as some scholars would have us believe.
70. Fauja Singh: *Chronology of the Battles of Guru Hargobind.*
71. Macauliffe, M.A.: *The Sikh Religion*, Vol. IV, p. 209.
72. Refer to Nanak Panthis in *Debistan-i-Mazahib* by Mohsin Fani. Translated version in 'Sikh History from Persian Sources' edited by J.S. Grewal and Ifran Habib, Tulika, 2001.
73. *Ibid.*
74. Fauja Singh: *op. cit.*
75. Bhatvahi Multani Sindhi available in the Department of Punjab Historical Studies Punjabi University, Patiala. Macauliffe fixes C.E. 1628 for the battle of Lehira, C.E. 1634 for the battle of Kartarpur. These dates were accepted to be correct by later writers including Dr. Ganda Singh and Dr. I.B. Bannerjee. We, however, have based our inferences on Bhatvahis discovered recently.
76. Balu Hasna was born to Pandit Hardat and Mai Prabha of Srinagar (Kashmir) on November 13, 1564. He embraced Sikhism in C.E. 1604 under the influence of Guru Arjan Dev. He endeared himself to the sixth Guru for his dedication to the Sikh cause. His original name was Balu. He always had a smile on his face, and on this account, the Guru gave him the appellation of 'Hasna', the laughing one. *Encyclopedia of Sikhism*, Vol. I, p. 169.
77. Sarup Das Bhalla: *op. cit.*, p. 517.
78. *Ibid.*
79. Giani Gian Singh: *Twarikh Guru Khalsa*, pp. 578-79.
80. Khwaja was a domicile of Kashmir. He turned a devotee of Guru Hargobind when the latter visited Srinagar.
81. Macauliffe: *The Sikh Religion*, Vol. IV, pp. 121-23.
82. Nanak Panthis translated from the *Dabistan-i-Mazahib*. Refer to Punjab—Past and Present, April 1967.
83. *Ibid.*
84. *Ibid.*
85. *Guru Kian Sakhian*, Sakhi No. 3.
86. *Ibid.*, Sakhi No. 4.
87. *Dabistan-i-Mazahib*, pp. 178-93.
88. *Ibid.*

MASTERLY INACTIVITY—A STRATEGIC RESPONSE TO ISLAMIC IMPERIALISM

8

GURU HAR RAI

(b. 1630 C.E.; d. 1661 C.E.)

Guru Hargobind had five sons—Baba Gurditta, Suraj Mal, Ani Rai, Baba Attal and Tegh Bahadur. Baba Attal, Ani Rai and Gurditta died before their father. Suraj Mal being too worldly and Tegh Bahadur not yet up to the mark were thought not fit for carrying the burden of guruship. Baba Gurditta left two sons—Dhir Mal and Har Rai. Dhir Mal although being elder was disloyal and had been plotting with the enemy. Har Rai alone had proved himself capable enough to lead the community during those difficult times. Therefore, Guru Hargobind nominated him as his successor and himself left for heavenly abode on March 3, 1644.

He was born at Kiratpur on 30th January, 1630.[1] He was married to Sulakhni Kaur[2], the daughter of Daya Rai a Sillikhatri of Arup Shanker.[3]

Not much is known of his early life; but this much is certain that he was brought up in an atmosphere surcharged with Sikh ethos. He received best possible education; he was given fine martial training; he was a good horseman, a great hunter and terrifically adept in handling different weapons such as sword, lance, javelin. He was also well-versed in the art of warfare.

From the beginning, he had shown a fine amalgam of strength and tenderness. He was a mighty hunter and yet he was too kind-hearted to kill animals he had chased and captured. One day, as he was passing through a garden, his loose coat broke the stems of some flowers which fell to the ground. He felt much upset and tears rolled down his eyes. He loved singing Baba Farid's lines, "All men's hearts are jewels; it is wicked to agonize them. If you have the desire to see your beloved, hurt no man's heart." He hated to hurt any being. He often said, "You can repair or rebuild a temple or a mosque, but not a broken heart." Nothing pleased him better than to do good to others.

In the last week of February 1644 C.E. Guru Hargobind seated Har Rai on the pontific throne and circumambulating him three times, placed five *paise* and a coconut. He then bowed before Guru Har Rai declaring from the day onwards that he would be the seventh Guru. He then left for his heavenly abode.

Guru Har Rai kept the style that Guru Hargobind had introduced. He was attended by his armed followers, but no further conflict with ruling power occurred. Kiratpur in the hills was the Guru's permanent seat. Here the disciples and visitors came to seek blessings and instructions. The Guru kept the daily practice of his predecessors. *Guru Ka Langar* continued to be the key factor in the social change Sikhism had initiated. Early in the morning he rose and after oblation enjoyed reciting hymns from *Adi Granth*. Thereafter, he listened to the *Kirtan in Sangat*. He also discoursed to the *Sangat* and quoted copiously the hymns of his predecessors, although he did not compose any hymn. He often repeated to his followers the verses of Bhai Gurdas:

> A true Sikh rises before the night ends and turns his thought to God's Name
> To charity and to holy bathing
> He speaks humbly and humbly he walks
> He wishes everyone well and he is joyed to give away gifts
> He sleeps, but little
> And appropriately does he eat and talk
> Thus he receives Guru's instruction

He lives by the labour of his hands and he does good deeds
However eminent he might become
He demonstrates not himself
He sings God's praises in the company of holy men
Such company he seeks night and day
Upon Word is his mind fixed
And he delights in Guru's Will
Un-enticed he lives in this world of enticement.
(Var XXVIII.15)

Guru Har Rai's seventeen years ministry although not marked by any spectacular events, yet was not insignificant. The Sikhs had just passed through a stormy career and it was only logical and appropriate for the Guru to have respite and undertake the task of consolidation quietly and peacefully without any fanfare and clatter of arms. Yet the Guru was not passive; his was a calculated policy. In fact, he required time and peace to accomplish the work of peaceful organisation and arrest disintegration that has set in mainly owing to certain internal and external factors.

The Guru did not reverse or revise the policy of his father, rather he stuck fast to that. He kept a strong contingent of 2200 cavalry men ready to be employed whenever and wherever necessary. He reiterated his total commitment to *Piri-Miri* philosophy. He however took precaution to avoid as far as possible any intermeddling with politics.

Eventful change took place in Kahlur state in which Guru Har Rai was living. Kalyan Chand, the Raja of Kahlur, was killed in 1635 C.E. when he tried to invade the territory of Raja of Suket, whose daughter he had married. His son Tara Chand tried to avenge his father's death, but only with partial success.[4] Being rebellious in disposition, he refused to pay tribute to the Emperor Shah Jahan, who was so annoyed with his attitude that in 1645 C.E. he sent Najabat Khan, son of Mirza Sharuk, to attack his territory. Najabat Khan mobilized a large army and took Raja Tara Chand a prisoner. Guru Har Rai was only fourteen years old at that time. He thought it is advisable to move his army to Thapal near Sirhind.[5]

Raja Tara Chand was released and his kingdom was restored to him when he agreed to pay the tribute. Shortly after, the Guru came back to Kiratpur. The Guru avoided active involvement in political affairs as far as it was possible, but at times when circumstances crossed limits, he was quick to take action.

In 1656, when he was coming back to Goindwal, from the tour of Malwa, Muhammad Yar Beg Khan (son of Mukhlis Khan, who was killed by Guru Hargobind in the battle of Amritsar) who chanced to be on the way with 1000 men, attacked the baggage and the ladies who were following the Guru at some distance. The Guru's escort put up a stout resistance and ultimately drove the enemy with a considerable loss. Bhai Garro, the son of Bhai Bhagta (whose descendants later ruled at Kaithal state) who was eagerly looking forward to the opportunity to win over the Guru whom he had displeased by putting to sword a devoted Sikh of his, showed extraordinary courage and pluck in this encounter. The Guru was pleased and rewarded him. The Raja of Kahlur was also shown his place when he tried to pick up the quarrel with Guru over the *Prasadi* elephant which he demanded from the Guru on the plea that this being emblem of royalty should have been with him and not with the Guru who was not a ruler.

Peaceful Consolidation

Guru's task of consolidation was not a smooth sailing. It was beset with great difficulties. First, the *Masands* whose primary function was to spread Sikh faith had gone corrupt, immoral and recalcitrant. Secondly, the government of the day was not well-disposed towards the Sikhs. The Naqshbandis, an ultra orthodox element of the Muslims, were very active and were deadset to pressurize the Mughal government to fall in line with their thinking and take steps to convert the whole of India into *Dar-ul-Islam*. They aspired to see their design take practical shape especially in the north-western part of India. The continued absence of Guru Hargobind from Amritsar, Goindwal, Khadur Sahib gave rise to various misgivings and this thing seriously precluded the advancement of Sikh community. The hostility of the disappointed claimants was also a factor in impeding the progress of Sikhism. The Minas headed by Harji were also throwing a challenge by flaunting Harji as the legitimate Guru in Guru Nanak's line and by raising supportive infrastructures. Sri Harmandir Sahib had fallen to their control and several *Masands* had joined them. The tradition started by Guru Hargobind was to be developed to its logical end whereby the Sikhs should develop spiritually and militarily at one and the same time. Guru Arjan Dev had practically completed the organisation of his followers on peaceful lines. Under Guru Hargobind, Sikhism had added into itself an army, however small it might have been and had pronounced hitherto not so explicit a principle, that Sikhism was all-embracing religion committed to guide its followers both in temporal and spiritual fields. This thing created ripples in the political circles which considered the dispensation of the Guru a threat to their social and religious constructs. The situation, therefore, was intriguing and challenging. The Guru exerted hard to respond to it. He avoided open conflict with the government or with any other socio-religious organisation so that he might be able to pursue his agenda undisturbed and unhampered. The Guru proceeded cautiously but firmly. Apart from laying emphasis on *Guru Ka Langar*, altruistic service, faith in Word as incorporated in *Adi Granth, Sangat* and *Kirtan*, he undertook extensive tours in Malwa and Doaba regions of the Punjab.

Proselytising Tours

Guru Har Rai immediately after ascending pontific seat threw himself heart and soul into the task of proselytising as also that of revamping his contacts with *Sangats* at different places.[6] He visited Amritsar and made obeisance at Sri Harmandir Sahib and Sri Akal Takht. Manohar Das Meharban, the son of Prithi Chand, who taking advantage of the absence of the Guru Hargobind surreptitiously had assumed management of Darbar Sahib quietly withdrew to Hardwar, understandably to avoid open clash with Guru Har Rai who might expose the hollowness of his claim. The Guru appointed dedicated Sikhs to do religious services as also to conduct administrative affairs connected with Sri Darbar Sahib.

Having stayed for some time at Amritsar, the Guru proceeded to Goindwal Sahib, another center of Sikhism.

He took bath at Baoli and made obeisance at the place where Guru Amar Das dwelt. At that time, he interacted with devotees and all those who came to see him. He also met the descendants of Guru Amar Das.

From Goindwal, he reached Khadur Sahib, which had been the headquarter of Guru Angad Dev. He urged the people to form *Sangats* and be in regular touch with the Guru directly or through *Masands/Manjidars*. He specially enjoined upon them to run *Guru Ka Langar* at every *dharamsala* or *gurdwara*. He laid emphasis that *Sangat* and *Pangat* should operate together as one is integral part of the other. Guru also visited Tarn Taran, the city founded by Guru Arjan Dev in the heart of Majha region of the Punjab.

Guru's visit in Majha region was short in duration because he did not want to arouse suspicion among government circles. Yet it had a salutary effect. Sikhism received a boost. Administration of the central shrine of the Sikhs, *Sri Darbar Sahib* complex, was streamlined. Mina's influence abated. Religious service in Harmandir Sahib was rendered systematic under Guru's instructions. *Kirtan* began to be performed all the twenty-four hours. Bhallas got completely reconciled to the mainstream Sikhism.

Having stayed for some time at Kiratpur, the Guru again proceeded on tour. He first visited Ropar where he was accorded a hearty welcome by people led by Bhai Binju, Bhai Binda, Bhai Gajjar, Bhai Gharian. After this he reached Waddi Lehal. The people of this place won over the heart of Guru through their devotion—so much so that the Guru was pleased to bless them with the honorific "True savant of the Guru".

From Waddi Lehal, the Guru reached Harianwelan. He was accompanied by a contingent of twenty-two hundred warriors. The place is also the locale of another important event in Sikh history. A *Sangat* proceeding to Anandpur Sahib was plundered by Gujjar and Rangar marauders of Bajraur[7] (Harianwelan) in March, 1701. The Guru then reached Chautra Sahib wherefrom he proceeded to Kartarpur via Jalandhar. This city was founded by Guru Arjan Dev in 1594 on a tract of land donated by Emperor Akbar and it played a crucial role in the dissemination of Sikh faith in the Doaba region. Baba Gurditta, Guru Arjan Dev himself and his son and successor, Guru Hargobind came to stay here at different points of time. The marriages of latter's two sons, Suraj Mal and Tegh Bahadur were solemnised here. Guru Hargobind also fought a battle here in April 1635 C.E. against the Faujdar of Jalandhar. After the battle Guru Hargobind went to Kiratpur, but his grandson, Dhir Mal and after him his descendants continued to stay at Kartarpur. The Guru visited Kartarpur several times. This time the Guru met his uncle Dhir Mal and paid homage to 'Adi Granth' and got prepared its renditions. The well known Gangsar which had been sunk by Guru Arjan Dev in 1599 C.E. was bricklined.[8]

Bhai Bhagtu, a dedicated Sikh of the Guru, died here and Guru himself set fire to his pyre. Bhai Bhagtu's death took place in 1609 Bk (1552 C.E.).

Later on in 1658, the Guru encamped here along with his horsed warriors. The place where the Guru stayed now bears a Gurdwara named *Tahli Sahib*, after the name of *Shisham* tree under which Guru seated himself.

The next important halt of the Guru was at Nur Mahal. It is said that Guru came here in response to the invitation of his devoted Sikh Bhai Sukhia. Chaudhri Sood of this place waited upon the Guru. Tradition goes that Chaudhri Sood asked for an issue and the Guru advised him to pray to God who is Eternal-Giver and listens to sincere prayers. Here Bhai Fateh Shah, an important member of the Bakhshish led by Suthre Shah met the Guru and sought his blessings.

After Nurmahal the Guru visited Puandra Sahib and was overjoyed at the devotion of the people. He blessed them peace of mind and the will to be always righteous. From Puandra the Guru reached Drauli, now in Firozpur district. The place had a special niche in the Sikh history. Sain Das the husband of the sister of Mata Damodri lived here and Guru Hargobind often visited this place. Baba Gurditta was born here. The Guru raised memorials in honour of his grand-mother and his father. He also completed the construction of the well which had been started by Guru Hargobind.[9] Bhai Roop Chand Bhinder, Bhai Kirpal, Bhai Bidhi Chand and other devoted Sikhs came here to pay their homage and also to discuss their plans of proselytising with the Guru.[10] Bhai Gurdas and Bhai Tara, the grandsons of Bhai Behlo, Bhai Behari, the son of Bhai Bhundari served the Guru with so much devotion that the Guru was simply overjoyed. He blessed the whole of Malwa region where such people had taken birth. He awarded the land the honorific "The *Subhaga Malwa*—the Fortunate Malwa".

From Drauli, the Guru proceeded to the village Bhai Roopa, which the parents of Bhai Roopa, Sadhu and Surti founded at the instance of Guru Hargobind. They were the original residents of Akolani also known as Tukolani and were the followers of *Sakhi Sarvar*. Guru Hargobind's teachings so transmuted them that they became zealous devotees of the Guru and even left their village which then was the stronghold of Sakhi Sarvarias (the followers of Sakhi Sarvar). They raised a new village which they named it Roopa after the name of their son believed to be born in response of the blessing of Guru Hargobind.

Roopa grew to be an illumined Sikh seriously interested in the promotion of Sikhism in Malwa. According to Gian Singh he had a rare knack of converting the people to Sikhism. His impact was sudden and spontaneous and the people not only listened to him but also found comfort in his company. *Sakhi Sarvarias* in hordes shifted their faith to the Guru. Their *Pir Khanas*—worship houses to worship Sakhi Sarvar were closed.[11] The Guru in recognition to his services himself installed him as an overall in charge of the preaching work.[12]

From Bhai Roopa the Guru proceeded to visit different places and ultimately sojourned at village Mari, where he got sunk a well to provide potable water to the people.

Soon the Guru reached Nathana where Guru Hargobind had battled against the Mughal forces in 1534 C.E. Here the Kala and Karam Chand, two brothers and sons of Mohan, the leading most figures of Sidhus/Brars came to express their devotion to the Guru and to seek his blessings. They told their sordid story how they were maltreated by Kauras and Bhullars headed by Zaid Pirana who threatened them to evict even from the village Mehraj. They were sure that since Kauras and Bhullars were also Sikhs, they would listen to the Guru.

The Guru called Zaid Pirana and advised him to stop terrorising the Sidhus/Brars because it did not behove a Sikh fight against a Sikh and that too on the basis of tribal particularism which was against the very spirit of Sikhism. Zaid Pirana agreed, but soon the pride in him overwhelmed him and he backed out of his commitment. Being himself a warrior of renown possessed of Herculean strength even to handle a very heavy spear, he had the audacity to boast that "except a few stalks of grass, Brars would have nothing".

Finding the Bhullars/Kauras unreasonable and bloated with pride, the Sikhs of the area turned empathetic to the cause of Sidhus/Brars and rendered active help with the result that Zaid Pirana was defeated and killed by Kala.

Kauras and Bhullars could not but feel sullen and disappointed.[13] At this juncture, the Guru intervened and brought about harmony between Brars and Kauras/Bhullars saying that both of them should shed narrow affiliations and feel coequal and honourable members of the large Sikh fraternity.

Under the impact of teachings of the Guru, the caste and tribe-based marriages were considerably discouraged. Kauras and Bhullars also started entering into marital relationships with Sidhus/Brars. With the weakening of particularistic tendencies, Malwa Sikhs trudged towards wider fraternity based on the principle of the oneness of the human kind.

From Nathana the Guru reached Mehraj in response to the invitation of the people of Mehraj especially of Kala who was the *Chaudhri* of the village. The village owed its existence to the blessings of Guru Hargobind who inspired Mohan, the father of Kala, to found it.[14] Guru Har Rai, therefore, had special fascination for the village.

One day Kala took his nephews, Sandhali and Phul, whose father had been killed in a battle during the time of Guru Hargobind. Phul who was then five years old struck with his hands, of course at the instance of his uncle, his own naked belly like a drum in front of the Guru. When asked why he did so, Kala explained that he was hungry and wanted something to eat. The Guru took compassion and uttered "He shall become great, famous, wealthy. The steeds of his descendants shall drink water as far as Jamuna; they shall have sovereignty for many generations and be honoured in proportion as they serve the Guru." This may very well be a prophecy ex-eventful but at the same time, it seems clear that the obscure Phul first came into prominence under the patronage of Guru Har Rai and this led to the foundation of the future greatness of his family. Phul had six sons, from the eldest of whom namely Tilok Singh the Rajas of Nabha and Jind descended and Phul's second son Ram Singh bore the Maharaja Ala Singh of Patiala. These three were known as *Phul-ke Raja*, or Rajas of Phulkian States.

Having received blessings of the Guru, Chaudhri Kala returned home and related the story to his wife. She rebuked him because it would not benefit him or his progeny and remarked that if Phul's descendants became rulers of the country it would be better to be lorded by Muhammedans than their own agnates (*Shareek*). She advised him to seek Guru's blessings in favour of his own progeny. He, therefore, appeared again before the Guru with his own son. The Guru said that the lot of Phul's descendants was unalterable whereas Chaudhri's descendants would enjoy free grants of land. In the case of Kala's descendants also the prophecy came out to be true and they happened to be big Jagirdars.

Next important sojourn was at *Majhe-ki-Mari* in the Malwa region. Here the Guru initiated one Pharinda into Sikhism. Bhai Pharinda was a trader by profession and supplied *Ghee* to far off places. Finding that the Guru's *Langar* (Guru's

Mess) had run short of *Ghee*, he offered the same and refused to receive payment in spite of repeated requests of the in-charge of the Guru's Mess. The news reached the Guru who called him to his presence. Pharinda fell at Guru's feet and cherished the desire to be initiated into the house beautiful of Sikhism. The Guru fulfilled his desire and he dedicated his life to the cause of Sikhism. After initiation he was given a new name Bhai Pheru, implying thereby that he was a divine wanderer always delivering comfort to the comfortless and the desolate.

Pheru was blessed with an esteemed honorific "Lord of *Guru Ka Langar*".[15] Since then he took pains to establish *Guru Ka Langar* as necessary adjunct of Sangat. He was untiring in his efforts to enlighten the people on Sikhism. He established his *Dera* (abode) on Multan-Lahore road where *Guru Ka Langar* ran for all the twenty-four hours. He expired at sufficiently advanced age and was cremated near village Chunia on the outskirts of Lahore (now in Pakistan).

From Majhe Ki Mari, the Guru returned to Kiratpur. He built a fortress and a hospice at Dulowal (close to Makhowal). The fort had a spacious stable, a tank, a well and accommodation for a sufficient number of warriors. These constructions were undertaken and completed very speedily, understandably to cope with any eventuality in case politics took an adverse turn about which news·had started pouring.

Although the avowed policy of the Guru was that of non-involvement in the political affairs, yet the Guru was not in a mood to be a mute spectator of the things if these trespassed certain limits and adversely affected the Sikh affairs. He undertook rapid rounds of tours, his purpose being to forge and update his contacts with as many *Sangats* as it was possible and also to avoid contact with Dara or his forces at Talwan and Ropar where they had planned to cross the river Sutlej. The Guru left Kiratpur for Pehova and Thanesar. Then he staged a quick visit to Samrala, Bahnewal, Jaspal Bhai Ke and Dosanj Masandan. From the latter place he proceeded to Palahi about 5 Kilometres from Phagwara. Qasim Beg and Umar Hayat Khan, the grandsons of Mukhlis Beg who had been killed in the battle of Amritsar (1634 C.E.) launched a sudden and unprovoked attack on the Guru. At that crucial juncture, Gaura, the elder son of Bhai Bhagtu, who had earned the displeasure of the Guru because of his murder of a highly devoted Sikh who served the Guru as his personal attendant, and had been long waiting for some opportunity to redeem himself, rushed upon the Mughal forces along with his own troops. He fought so fiercely that the Mughal forces had to seek shelter in flight under cover of darkness.

When the Guru came to know of this, he at once sent for Gaura who presented himself before the Guru, all stained with blood. The Guru was moved and pardoned him for his unwarranted mortal attack on *Bhai* Jassa, one of the bodyguard of the Guru. The Guru learnt from Gaura the events of the battle and allowed him to return to his own territory.

After a very short stay at Palahi, the Guru paid visits to Hadiabad, Kartarpur, Baba Bakala, Amritsar, Goindwal. At the latter place, Dara Shikoh, the eldest son of Shahjahan, waited upon him and sought his blessings. He also asked for active help in his struggle to reoccupy the throne of Delhi. The Guru blessed him and also promised to join his camp at Lahore.

According to Bhat Vahi Talaunda Pargana Jind, the Guru reached Srinagar via Ghalotian, District Sialkot in 1660 C.E. and stayed in Hap Bazar, Srinagar. Mata Saraswati, the mother of Bhai Pera and Pairaga, did her best to make Guru's stay comfortable. Makhan Shah, the Lubana trader, Pelia Makho Chand and other devoted Sikhs came to the Guru to make obeisance. Among them was included Aru Ram, father of Kirpa Ram Dutt who later led to the presence of Guru Tegh Bahadur a group of Kashmiri Pandits driven to dire distress by state persecution.

The Guru blessed them and iterated that they must follow the Sikh discipline because that is the sure highway to attain *Gurmukh*-hood.

From Srinagar, the Guru went to Natan and Martand wherefrom he reached Mote Tanda to which his disciple

Makhan Shah hailed.[16] From there he visited Akhnur and after that he reached Jammu. At Jammu the local Masand Bhai Kahna waited on him with *Sangat*. From that place, the Guru proceeded to Ramgarh, Khirri and Samba. Then he left for Pathankot where he stayed for two days. After this he returned to Kiratpur.

The Guru concentrated more in the Malwa and Doaba regions. In doing so he had certain designs. The Guru had convinced himself fully that the Mughal government and Muslim elites were averse to Sikh ideology—especially its social and political aspects which in their reckoning went totally contrary to the world-view of Muhammedans in India. This being so, the Guru rightly understood that with the lapse of time as the contradictions would sharpen, clash was bound to occur. To meet such an eventuality, the Guru thought it essential that the coverage of Sikh ideology must be extended and in this context preaching was undertaken with all seriousness in Malwa and Doaba regions as Malwa was still unattended by Islamic and Hindu missionaries and Doaba only partially attended.[17] Further Malwa region being far away from Sirhind and Lahore and semi-desert in most of its parts was no attraction of the Mughal rulers, at least upto the Guru's time. People in large numbers including village *Choudharies* and heads of various tribes such as Kala and Jaita Piarana *et al.* embraced Sikhism. New *Sangats* were formed and the old ones were vitalised and placed under the direction of *Bakhshish* holders, *Masands/Manjidars*. The Guru took care that the *Masands* were not encouraged and the Sikhs were asked to have direct links with the Guru. The main thrust of the teaching of the Guru was that the Sikhs should establish perfect harmony among themselves and among the people who were non-Sikhs. The people were told to be fearless and firm in their faith in God who is Formless, Singular, All Compassion, and Eternal Enlightener. At individual and social levels, they should present themselves as role models of personal piety and well balanced social beings.

Raising of a New Missionary Organisation

But the most striking achievement in the field of proselytisation was the raising of a new organisation. Quite a number of *Manjidars* and *Masands* had earned notoriety for their dereliction of duties, self-aggrandizement, coercion and exploitation of the believer. Guru Hargobind appointed his eldest son, Bhai Gurditta to streamline the preaching work who established a network of missionary centres far and wide called *Dhuans*. These centres did remarkable job but still much more was to be done.

Guru Har Rai, therefore, raised a fresh complementary organisation to put more vigour and elan into the preaching work. He established three fresh missionary centres, each bearing a name Bakhshish—Grace. Eminent Sikhs under the leadership of Suthre Shah, Sangat, Bhagat Bhagwan, were appointed to function these missionary centres. In view of Bhagatgir's hundred per cent dedication to the cause of Guru whom he preached as God in visible form, people called him by the name of Bhagat Bhagwan. The Guru appointed him as the in-charge of preaching work in the East where he along with his followers established as many as 360 centres. Bhagat Mal[18] and his disciples chose to spread Sikhism in Bahawalpur and Multan and Sindh.[19] Suthra Shah[20] took upon himself to preach Sikhism in and around Delhi.

Another centre was established in the Lamma region between the Beas and the Ravi. *Bhai* Pheru was made the organiser of preaching work there. With his vigorous efforts a large number of people embraced Sikhism.

Bhai families of Kaithal and Bagrian were made responsible for missionary work in the land between Jamuna and Sutlej. The ancestors of the present day families of Bagrian and Kaithal preached in the Malwa region.

Upto the time of Guru Hargobind, Sikhism had become all-India religion. According to one reckoning in Guru Hargobind's time, there were twenty-nine Sikh centres outside Punjab in central, north-western and southern India.[21] Guru Hargobind had evolved a system to keep them attached with the headquarter and the personality of the Guru. In Punjab, it goes to his credit that he deepened the impact of Sikhism in Majha and Doaba regions. In the Punjab beyond the river Roja, the coverage of Sikhism was extended. In Malwa region too, a good start had been made and Sikh ideology began to affect the life-style of the people. Side by side the spread of Sikhism the organisational aspect was also given due consideration. In different regions of the Punjab, the dominant organisations to keep the Sikhs vibrant with Sikh fervour was that of *Masands/Manjidars* and *Dhuan* holders while the areas beyond Punjab, not un-often the notable Sikhs were asked to take care of *Sangats* as also to keep the Guru informed of what happened in their localities/regions. As the organisational network widened certain *Masands/Manjidars* began to act independently, and in quite a number of the cases took liberty to exploit instead of persuading them to lead their lives in the light of the Guru's teachings.

When Dhir Mal was not given guruship by Guru Hargobind, certain *Masands* went all-out to bolster Dhir Mal's claim to guruship, understandably to feel free from mainstream Sikhism in order to serve their own selfish ends. Much harm could not be done by them because of the strong personality of Guru Hargobind.

Guru Har Rai strove hard to preserve and enrich the legacy. He still more deepened the effect of Sikhism in the Punjab and so far as the state of Sikhism in Malwa was concerned, he culminated the work initiated by Guru Hargobind. The organisational aspect of the Sikh movement was also taken care of. The Guru tried to discipline *Masands/Manjidars*, although the success was not marked as for instance *Masands* of Lahore did not hesitate even to misread the instructions of the Guru in order to help Ram Rai against the wishes of the Guru. Besides, owing to political reasons the Guru could not have regular and systematic contacts with the *Sangats* outside Punjab. No organisation or system emerged to keep regular rapport with them, nor were any concerted efforts made in this directions. The Guru did not do all these things for three reasons: firstly, the government was not sympathetic to the progress of Sikhism, and secondly Dhir Mal and Ram Rai seemed to be bent upon starting heretical movements and thirdly quite a number of *Masands* had become self-seekers, self-centred, avaricious and had been bandying themselves to be apotheosis of the Divine.

The Guru and the Mughal Emperors

From 1634 onwards right through the period of Guru Har Rai, Shah Jahan, the Mughal Emperor, took casual notice of the Sikh activities, understandably under the influence of his dearest and eldest son, Dara Shikoh, who had Sufi propensities and was an ardent advocate of a liberal religious policy. The relations between the Guru and the Mughal Emperor further improved when the former readily supplied the rare medicine in response to Shah Jahan's request. The latter administered the medicine to Dara Shikoh who had fallen seriously ill because whiskers of a tiger in a dainty dish had been administered to him allegedly by Aurangzeb.

The medicine had a desired effect and Dara was completely cured. The Emperor naturally got mellowed. Just about this time, someone asked the Guru why he had saved the life of the son of Shah Jahan who was not well disposed towards his father. The Guru replied, "The man breaks flowers with one hand, offers them to the people with the other, but the flowers perfume both the hands alike. The axe cuts the *sandal* tree, yet the *sandal* perfumes the axe. The Guru ought, therefore, to return good for evil.[22]

Dara became highly respectful towards the Guru not only because of the medicine he supplied, but also because he loved his views which bore resemblance to those of his own. According to J.N. Sarkar, Dara paid the Guru visits of respect, as a part of his general devotion to saints and *Darveshes*[23], although the Guru was fifteen years younger than the Prince.

On September 6, 1657 C.E. Shah Jahan fell ill of strangury and constipation. The malady took so acute a turn that the daily *Durbar* was stopped. The Emperor ceased to show his face to the public from a balcony. A fratricidal struggle for the crown began in which Aurangzeb took a leading part.

Dara Shikoh managed the king's affairs and in so doing, he was within his rights, as eldest son and presumptive heir to the crown of Delhi. But he had to reckon with three brothers each in command of a province. Shuja was the governor of Bengal, Aurangzeb was down south in Deccan, Murad Bakhsh was the governor of Gujrat.[24] Shujah advanced from Bengal to force his claim but he was defeated and had to wheel back. Aurangzeb made Murad his ally and faced Dara's well equipped army in the battle of Samugarh. Both sides fought doggedly and heroically, but ultimately Dara was trounced and he was forced to flee. Raja Jaswant Singh and Raja Jai Singh, seemingly his trusted allies, turned back on him and transferred their fealty to Aurangzeb.

Aurangzeb imprisoned his father in the Agra fort. He connived at making his boorish brother Murad disgracefully drunk and threw him into Gwalior prison. Three years later he had him beheaded by two slaves in the prison.

Dara Shikoh moved to Delhi wherefrom he rushed to Lahore where his faithful deputy, Sayyed Ghairat Khan, helmed the affairs and where he himself was held in high esteem as a man and a commandant-administrator.

On the way to Lahore, Dara visited Goindwal on July 1st, 1658 and had a meeting with Guru Har Rai who had been there in response to the invitation of the descendants of Guru Amar Das. According to Dr. Trilochan Singh, Dara might have also waited upon Holy mother Nanki and Baba Tegh Bahadur on the way to Amritsar. In his meetings with the Guru, Dara asked for assistance. The Guru advised him to go to Lahore, collect an army and obtain allies. Next morning Dara was informed that Aurangzeb's army was pursuing him. Without loss of time he started for Lahore requesting the Guru to impede the progress of the pursuing army as long as it was possible. The Sikh sources do not tell us whether the Guru took any step in compliance with this request, but according to *Mehma Parkash*, he put a strong guard at the ferry to prevent Aurangzeb's forces from crossing the river. This story found confirmation by scholars such as Trumpp and

Cunningham. J.N. Sarkar also asserts that the Guru covered Dara's retreat by blocking Aurangzeb's troops on the Beas.

There are serious snags in the story. There arose no occasion immediately after Dara's departure from Goindwal to warrant the Guru to station his forces at river Beas near Goindwal. Dara left Goindwal on July 1, 1658, while Aurangzeb reached Sutlej full two months after the meeting of Dara and the Guru. Aurangzeb crowned himself on July 21, 1658 and made a move to the Punjab after that. Bahadur Khan was the first general of Aurangzeb to attack Dara's army at Ropar on August 6, 1658. While Dara's army fell back from Sutlej ferry to Goindwal ferry, Aurangzeb had reached the Sutlej by this time. It was now impossible for the Guru to send any help to Dara's army at Goindwal without coming into conflict with the huge army of Aurangzeb. Obviously, the statement of *Mehma Parkash* as also of those of Cunningham, Macauliffe and J.N. Sarkar is far from facts.

But this does not mean that the Guru did not render any help. As it has been earlier said the Guru had a lot of sympathy for Dara who implored for his help in his predicament. He readily came forward to bless him and also to help him, even militarily. J.N. Sarkar observes the Guru had blessed the Prince when a fugitive in the Punjab after battle of Samugarh[25] although he does not clarify the nature and form of help.

Dara reached Lahore on July 3, 1658. The Guru also reached there a little after to join Dara's camp. But Dara was so much terrified by the designs of his brother that he decided to flee to Multan and Qandhar. He confided his intentions to his associates. This spread panic in the camp of Dara. Finding the cause of Dara entirely hopeless and Dara altogether dispirited, the Guru as also many others including Raja Rajroop of Nurpur State left the Dara's camp.[26] Sujan Rai wrongly insinuates that the Guru left the Dara's camp giving false assurance that he would shortly rejoin the camp with a large number of soldiers. The Guru, in fact, did whatever was right and possible. He did not give any false promise, firstly, because that was not his nature and secondly, Dara himself had made up his mind not to fight. The evidence embodied in epitaphic inscription of Ram Rai's monument at Dehradun also confirms the view that the Guru rendered assistance to Dara.[27]

Dara Shikoh fled from Lahore on the August 18, 1658. On the next day, Aurangzeb took possession of Lahore as a strategic measure. Guru Har Rai retired to village Ghaloti[28] (district Sialkot), wherefrom he proceeded back to Kiratpur. A shrine in village Ghaloti still commemorates Guru Har Rai's stay in the village during the rainy season of the year 1659.

Having made his position secure on the throne of Delhi, Aurangzeb embarked upon his wretched enterprise of religious crusade against the non-Muslims, specially the Hindus. We learn from Khafi Khan that Aurangzeb ordered temples of the Sikhs to be destroyed and the Guru's agents (Masands) for collecting the tithe (*Daswandh*) and presents of the faithful to be expelled from the cities. In 1659 he ordered that the standing temples should not be destroyed but no new temple should be allowed to be built. This was a moderate beginning for a policy which acquired poignancy as time rolled on. Aurangzeb's religious policy was mainly actuated by the concept of Muslim polity which was very close to his heart, and the notion that this would turn majority of the Muslims in his favour many of whom had disliked his attitude towards Dara Shikoh and his own father, Shah Jahan. As a corollary to his biased plan, it is not difficult to surmise that he could not ignore the Guru's contact with Dara—whatever its exact nature might be, especially when he himself had the full knowledge of the Guru's popularity and his dispensation's potentiality. The reports of some bigoted Muslims and conservative Hindus that the Sikh scripture's teachings were an attempt to corrupt both Hinduism and Islam also contributed a lot in the final configuration of government's policy towards the Guru. No doubt, some of the closest advisors of the Emperor like Mirza Jai Singh spoke high of the Gurus and their teachings, yet the Emperor could not be inveighed upon to change his opinion *vis-à-vis* the Guru until he met the Guru.

To this effect the Emperor addressed a letter to the Guru summoning him to his presence at Delhi. The Guru foreseeing the intentions of the Emperor submitted on 7th Baisakh 1717 Bk (1660 C.E.) a mild petition to him representing that he had no business at the Imperial court and therefore his presence might be excused. Instead of going himself, the Guru sent his eldest son, Ram Rai along with his petition to explain Sikh philosophy as well as the conduct of his father during the war of succession. He was asked to maintain the integrity and veracity of the faith of Guru Nanak whom he was to represent. He was strictly advised not to be cowed down, or intimidated but to give exposition of Sikh scriptures without fear. He was asked to be loyal to his ideals, firm in his convictions, frank and truthful in his exposition. He was given a recently prepared copy of the *Adi Granth*[29], in which Mul Mantar had been written by Guru Har Rai in his own hand. Although Ram Rai was quite young, his intellectual and spiritual training was well-nigh complete. His assignment to the Emperor's court was a test of his ability and his spirituality.

Whenever Aurangzeb wanted to put a non-Muslim saint to test, he first gave him three days to perform a miracle. If he failed to perform the same, he was asked either to accept Islam or face death. In some rare cases he was spared if he proved to be politically useful. Ram Rai was an adept in occult powers. He showed nearly seventy-two miracles which impressed the Emperor very much. The Emperor, himself a great theologian, discussed Sikh philosophy and asked innumerable questions to probe whether there was anything un-Islamic in Sikhism. It goes to the credit of Ram Rai, who was only fourteen years old, that he made a spirited exposition of Sikhism and almost convinced the Emperor that there was nothing un-Islamic or anti-Muslim in Sikh philosophy. It was a universal faith grounded on the experience of Truth and Absolute God. But a courtier probably a Hindu able to read scriptures, mischievously pointed out two lines from a composition of Guru Nanak; which were apparently critical of Muslims. The question about these lines came as a surprise to Ram Rai and when Aurangzeb asked him to explain the following verses he quailed, fearing that the literal meaning of the first two lines might annoy the Emperor and he might refuse to bear the symbolic meaning and philosophical explanation might not be accepted. Anxious to maintain the excellent impression, he had already created on the Emperor, he told a lie. The hymn as read by the courtier was as follows in English translation:

> The clay of a Muslim's grave
> Falls into the hands of the potter
> Pots and bricks out of it he makes
> In the fire burns the poor clay
> As it burns it weeps and wails
> Shedding tears of cinders at its fate
> Says Nanak, God and Creator
> Who is the Cause of all the causes
> Knows where departs and what befalls
> The soul of man hereafter.
>
> (*Asa Di Var 2.6*)

The verse only gives Guru Nanak's theory that the soul of man leaves the body and does not remain in the grave as Semitic faiths believe till dooms-day. The graves of poor men are often dismantled by the potter who makes pots out of the clay, while the fate of the soul is known only to God. Out of cowardice Ram Rai said that the scribe had by mistake written the word Musalman in place of *Beiman*, literally meaning a wicked man. This explanation satisfied the Emperor and the *Ulemas* in Delhi, but it grievously offended the Guru when the matter was reported to him by the Sikhs from the capital. Not only did Ram Rai perform several miracles and earn a name at Delhi as a Thamaturge against the instructions of the Guru but also he felt no qualms in distorting a verse of Guru Nanak in order to flatter the Emperor. *Shabad* being eternal and being voice of God, its distortion or smudging was a sacrilege unpardonable. The Guru forthwith disinherited his son with perpetual injunction that no true Sikh should, on pain of ex-communication from Sikhism, maintain any social intercourse with him or his progeny.

'The *Guruship*', said the Guru, is like a tigress's milk which can be contained in a golden cup. Only he who is ready to dedicate his life thereto is worthy of it. The Guru even refused to see Ram Rai's face. The Guru loved his son intensely and had taken keen interest in his education and up-bringing, but he did not let his paternal sentiments sway his stern disapproval of his son's cowardice and disloyalty to Guru Nanak's faith and philosophy.

Ram Rai begged forgiveness and personally called upon his father at Kiratpur, but he could not re-win his father's confidence. He went to Lahore in the hope of persuading the Guru to accept him through the Sodhis and *Sangat* of Lahore. Guru Har Rai sent a *Hukam Nama* to the *Sangat* of Lahore to disown Ram Rai and not to make him any offering[30], Ram Rai even requested his uncle Dhir Mal to intercede on his behalf but the Guru could not be conciliated who was firm in his opinion that he did not deserve pardon for he could stoop to such cowardly acts of sacrilege as distorting a composition of Guru Nanak. He was certainly not fit to carry the burden of spiritual sovereignty of Guru Nanak.[31] About a month later he appointed his second son Harkrishan as his successor and passed away on October 6, 1661 C.E. As a sequel to it, Ram Rai turned hostile to him and the central church and in due course of time, like his uncle Dhir Mal, founded a rival sect and joined hands with the Mughal authorities in a bid to disrupt the Sikh authority.

Sayyed Muhammad Latif, the author of the *History of the Punjab* (1889), basing himself on Cunningham's *A History of the Sikhs* (1849), states that Guru Har Rai did not like Ram Rai on account of the latter's independence of character. He says that Ram Rai being in the habit of making his own disciples, his father invariably made it a rule to speak of Harkrishan his younger son in public as apostolic successor though, at that time, he was a minor about six years of age.

These scholars' difficulty was that they were ignorant of the fact that *guruship* among the Sikhs could be passed on to the most meritorious; law of primogeniture did not apply in this case. Further, *Shabad* being co-equal to God/Guru, could not be altered, extended or subtracted. Any one doing contrary to this was a committer of sacrilege, never to be pardoned. Had they been able to grasp the import of Sikh ideology, they would not have justified the cause of Ram Rai. Independence of character is a great quality, no doubt, but certainly Ram Rai was not disinherited because of this, rather his right of *guruship* was forfeited because he distorted the sacred 'Word' which the Guru regarded as the voice of God/Guru.

Even after this, Aurangzeb did not take any stringent action against the Guru, unlike his grandfather who passed orders for the execution of Guru Arjan Dev. Taking cue from this, Dr. A.C. Bannerjee rakes up a question, "Why did Aurangzeb not raise political issue with Ram Rai?"[32] and then draws the conclusion that Aurangzeb did not consider the Guru's offence serious enough to deserve punishment. This led the learned scholar to conclude that Har Rai's sympathy for Dara did not extend to military aid[33] and Aurangzeb was conciliatory towards the Sikhs.

There is no tangible evidence to testify that Aurangzeb did not ask for the explanation of the political issue. It is also almost certain that the Guru joined Dara's camp at Lahore and when he found that the Prince's case was hopeless and he himself had lost heart, he quietly withdrew. These facts were well-known to Aurangzeb through his reporters and therefore it is wrong to presume that the Guru did not want to render military aid to Dara. The fact has been certified by Sujan Mal and Jadu Nath Sarkar. Undoubtedly, Aurangzeb did not take any strong action but he had its own reasons. Aurangzeb was still in the process of consolidating his position and was averse to take stern action against the Guru who had a large following and had acquired a lot of influence in the Punjab. Further, being himself a great general, he could assess that the Guru's help to Dara was not substantial; it was at the most symbolic. The Guru's military strength was also not large enough to pose any threat, immediately or otherwise, to the Emperor. He, of course, did not like the Sikh movement neither its political philosophy, nor its social stance. He, therefore, took to diplomatic artifice. Instead of dealing with Guru with violence, he kept Ram Rai, understandably as a hostage, to put a check on the Guru's activities. When the Guru disinherited[34] him from *guruship*, he propped Ram Rai with a large Jagir of seven villages in Doon valley. He is said to have granted five hundred rupees daily for his public kitchen. The court helped him a lot in his moves to regain the *guruship*. Even after the ascension of Guru Har Krishan on apostolic seat, Aurangzeb continued to buttress Ram Rai's cause. In fact the wily Aurangzeb wanted to weaken the Sikh movement by encouraging schism among the Sikhs, whom he regarded as a serious threat to the stability of the state—the fact well-known to him from the time he had been the governor of Sind and Multan from 1648 to 1652. In Ram Rai, he found a pliant personality with good contacts among the Sikhs likely to be used any time for manipulating the Sikh affairs to his advantage.

On the fourteenth day after the installation of Guru Harkrishan, Guru Har Rai summoned all the ministers and missionary administrators of his *durbar* and addressed Dewan Durga Mal, the chief of the Guru's *Durbar* thus, "My noble Diwan, you have served the House of Baba Nanak for many years and now I leave my son under your administrative care. He is independent-minded and is illumined and blessed by Guru Nanak. He will perform great deeds but let the imposter gurus particularly Ram Rai, who is continuously being misguided by his *Masands* not harm him any way."[35] He then addressed his son Harkrishan, "Scrupulously avoid meeting the emperor Aurangzeb and never visit his court under any temptation. Fear not any earthly king, least of all Aurangzeb and consider only God as the True King of Kings."[36]

Thereafter, Guru Har Rai covered himself with white sheet and within a short time he immersed himself in the Divine Light. The day was Sunday, Kartik Vadi 9, 1718 (October 6, 1661 C.E.).[37] His body was cremated on the bank of Sutlej near Kiratpur where his father and grandfather had been consigned to flames.[38]

The Guru's charismatic personality, his disciplined demeanour, his equipoise and his enlightenment—all these things had wonderful effect on the people. Whoever came to the Guru, he/she felt his impact. He would pass by the hutments of the poor and accept their food and eat it in their company to their utmost pleasure, highlighting at the same that the Guru stood for all and did not recognize differences between man and man. Morning and evening, he would listen to the devotional music in the company of his followers and then discoursed on the Gurus' word.

He would miss no opportunity to inculcate in his disciples the noble sentiments of humility and altruistic service without which he said, mere knowledge of the Divine was of little avail. One day the Guru saw a wounded snake crawling with difficulty as it was tortured by worms. The snake's skin was sparkling in the warm sunshine of winter. Pointing it out the Guru said, "This serpent might as well have been a *pundit* in his previous life—beautiful to behold in his dress. But the only knowledge he has is to bite. Men also bite others through jealousy; even when they teach about God, it is not through love or humility but through the sharp wits and poisonous fangs of controversy and argument." The Guru always advised his followers to recite *Granth Sahib* and abandon the worship of any inanimate object.

The Guru had immense love for his devotees. *Bhai* Gonda was a devout Sikh whom Guru thought fit enough to send him to acquaint the people with the dispensation of Guru Nanak. Gonda touched excellence while performing his duty to gain converts. He raised a *Gurdwara* in Kabul and established a large *Sangat*. Once he went deep in meditation. The Guru through intuition could gauge the intensity of his attachment with him. And so attached to him the Guru himself became that when once he could not be awakened out of meditation for hours and the Sikhs became anxious for his life, he explained as he opened his eyes, "A devout Sikh of mine Gonda by name is meditating upon me at Kabul and much as I would like to shake myself off his sight, he would cling tenaciously to my feet. I had therefore no choice but to remain seated, unmoved and absorbed in his thought."

He very zealously spread the network of *Sangat* and *Guru Ka Langar*. The Guru never missed any opportunity when he did not highlight the importance of these institutions. *Sangat* and *Guru Ka Langar*, as he emphasized, were manufactories to produce *Gursikhs*—ideal human beings who always looked to the Guru for guidance. Similarly *Guru Ka Langar* embodied as well as reflected unity of mankind, equality among human beings.

Once some Sikhs boasted that they ran *Guru Ka Langar* (Guru's mess) and did not let anyone go hungry if he/she came to them at the meal time. The Guru quipped that this was not enough. They ought to keep additional food ready all the time. They should serve food in such a way that guests should not feel uncomfortable or awkward, he should rather have the feeling that he had come to Guru's home and not to any charitable institution. The Guru made a very meaningful utterance: "He who has more should consider it as God's trust and share it in the same spirit. Man is only an instrument of service; the giver of goods is God, the Guru of us all."

On one occasion, when some Sikhs singing hymns from *Granth Sahib* came to the Guru, who, then, was lying on the couch. The Guru forthwith got up in all humility in deference to the Holy Word. When asked, the Guru told his Sikhs that the *Adi Granth* embodied the voice of God and hence it was his duty to make obeisance by standing with folded hands. Reverence for the hymns is reverence for the Guru.

Impressed by the greatness of the Guru in the year 1657 C.E. Bhai Mai Das, son of Bhai Balu Ram, came from Alipur near Multan and presented to the Guru his three elder sons; Jet (later Bhai Jetha Singh), Dayal Das and Mani Ram (later Bhai Mani Singh) who were eighteen, fifteen and thirteen years old respectively. For two years all the three sons served Guru with great devotion. Mani Ram performed the duty of washing utensils in the community kitchen (*Guru Ka Langar*).[39] After two years Bhai Mai Das sought the permission of the Guru to go to Alipur to perform the marriage of Mani Ram who was now fifteen.[40] Mani Ram's marriage was performed with Sito Bai, daughter of an eminent Sikh Lakhi Rai (also known as Lakhi Shah) a Yadav Kshatriya, in Tahsil Alipur of Muzaffurpur district.[41] After the marriage, the three brothers Dayala, Jetha and Mani Ram remained in the service of Guru.[42]

During these years Bhai Hira Nand left for heavenly abode. He was a great warrior saint. Before leaving his body, he sought the Guru's blessings for his sons Mati Das and

Sati Das,[43] who were great Persian scholars. Guru Har Rai blessed them and they took a vow to lead their lives in complete dedication to the Guru's cause.

Hunting was a part of training during those days. Guru Har Rai had given strict instructions that only ferocious animals like tigers, wild beasts, prowling man-eaters on the hilly sub-areas of Kiratpur were to be killed. Other animals that could be tamed and birds were to be caught alive and kept in the zoological garden of the Guru. The zoo had been raised by his grandfather. We have a letter of Guru Hargobind asking the Patna Sikhs to acquire some rare birds.[44] There was also a botanical garden in which beautiful flowers and medicinal plants were planted and grown.

Among the precious possessions of the Guru was a white elephant which the neighbouring Hindu chiefs thought of taking by force. The white elephant was the symbol of royalty and political prestige of the Guru. He refused to give.[45]

While staying at Kiratpur, Guru Har Rai had a fixed programme of his daily meditation, prayer and apostolic duties. He took personal interest in the education and training of his children and the moral and spiritual progress of his devotees. The Sikhs, the Hindus, the Muslims, Parsees, Jews, Sages and political leaders—all sought his blessings and friendship. Prince Dara Shikoh, Sufi Saint Sarmad, the author of *Dabistan-i-Mazahib* (Z'ulfigar Ar Dastani, also known as Azar Sasani) poets and medicants *et al.* went all the way to Kiratpur to receive Guru's instructions and blessings.

Whoever visited the holy city of Kiratpur was greatly impressed by various elements of culture visibly emerging in the historical development of Sikhism. "It consisted of magnificence of architecture of the mansions and palaces, patronage of music, literature, poetry, decoration, elegance in dress and adornments and the aesthetic expression of beauty in the royal grandeur of the Guru's court which was enriched by a beautiful garden and zoo and collection of finest horses and elephants (including white elephant). The whole atmosphere was filled with fundamental of culture—teaching of scriptures, divine poetry, music, moral and spiritual discipline of the highest order. Divine life made its presence felt on every inch of the earthly existence of Kiratpur. The whole city was charged with the atmosphere of peace, hope, love in human brotherhood, and above all fearlessness and freedom from bigotry and terror of the rulers.

NOTES AND REFERENCES

1. We have followed *Gurbilas Padshahi Chhevin*. *Suraj Parkash* gives Magh 1683 (January 1627 C.E.) as the date of Guru's birth. We have preferred *Gurbilas* because that is an earlier composition than *Suraj Parkash*.

2. About Guru Har Rai's marriages, many peculiar stories have been given currency. Kesar Singh Chhibber, one of the eighteenth century chroniclers says, "Guru Har Rai married Kot Kalyani also named as Sunita. With her came a beautiful maid-servant, Punjab Kaur. As Punjab Kaur was more talented than Kot Kalyani, Guru Har Rai married her. Eight years after the marriage Ram Rai, the elder son was born to the maid-servant, Punjab Kaur. Five years later, Punjab Kaur gave birth to a daughter, Sarup Kaur. A year later, Kot Kalyani gave birth to Harkrishan, the youngest son of the 'Guru'.

   The statement is erroneous on the very face of it. Punjab Kaur was not the mother of Ram Rai but one of the four wives of Ram Rai, highly talented who controlled Ram Rai's Ashram after the tragic death of her husband.

   The *Gurparnalis* (chronological statements) of the Guru's family tree by different authors have made confusion worse confounded. An early nineteenth century *Gurparnali* published by S.G.P.C. says that Guru Har Rai married seven women such as Kishan Kaur, Toki, Anokhi, Ladiki, Chand Kaur, Prem Kaur and Ram Kaur. With Kishan Kaur came Kalyani, the maid-servant. Another *Gurparnali*, the manuscript of which is in Jind State Public Library also mentions that with the only difference that it includes Kot Kalyani (maid-servant) of Kishan Kaur and deletes the name of Ram Kaur from the list of women whom the Guru married. Gulab Singh's *Gurparnali* gives eight marriages. Four of these women the Guru married were of noble birth while four others were maid-servants. According to this Parnali, Guru Harkrishan was son of Kishan Kaur while Ram Rai was the son of maid-servant Kot Kalyani.

   An unbelievable fantastic thing about these marriages is that the most of chroniclers give 1690 C.E. as the date of these marriages when the Guru was only ten years old. Most of them even suggest that seven of these wives were sisters and all marriages took place on the same day. If the eldest of these sisters was as old the Guru that is 10 years then the youngest sister whom the Guru is alleged to have married could not be more than 2 years old.

   Kavi Santokh Singh is said to have mentioned eight marriages of Guru Har Rai in his Magnum Opus *Suraj Parkash* granth. On careful scrutiny it becomes clear that the pages bearing this information were later interpolation because these pages are unnumbered.

Recent researches have altogether rejected the story of seven/eight marriages on the basis of more authentic documents. Kavi Saundh an eighteenth century saint and poet writes "Guru Har Rai's father was Baba Gurditta and his mother was Raj Kaur. His wife's name was Sulakhni and from her he had two sons Harkrishan and Ram Rai." Sarup Das Bhalla, the celebrated author of *Mehma Parkash* vouchsafes "Baba Gurditta was the father of Har Rai, Raj Kaur was his mother. Sulakhni was his wife to whom were born two sons, Harkrishan and Ram Rai."

The Bhat Vahis and Panda Vahis of Hardwar and other places which give partly factual and partly hearsay stories, also give Sulakhni as the only wife of Guru Har Rai. Sarup Kaur is believed to be four years younger than Ram Rai while Harkrishan was nine years younger than Ram Rai. Ram Rai was born in the year 1647 C.E. and the year of birth of Sarup Kaur is given in some *Gurparnali* as 1652 C.E. Guru Harkrishan was born on Monday July 7, 1656 (Savan Vadi 10, Vikrami Samvat 1713).

3. *Suraj Prakash Ras & Ansu*, 53.
4. *Punjab State Gazetteer*, Vol. III, Bilaspur, 1910.
5. Guru Har Rai passed one year in Kiratpur, when in the year One Thousand Fifty-five, Hijri, Najabat Khan, son of Mirza Shah Rukh under the order from Emperor Shah Jahan mobilized his army and took possession of the country of Tara Chand and took the Raja prisoner, Guru Har Rai went to Thapal which is near one of the possessions of Raja Karam Parkash near Sirhind. The Sikhs call Har Rai the seventh Mahal. He is well-known to the author of *Dabistan-i-Mazahib*.
6. Since exact chronology of the Guru's visits is not available, only plausible chronological order has been followed.
7. To perpetuate the memory of Guru's visit a gurdwara exists. It is named as Harianwelan gurdwara. It is situated in the revenue limits of Bajraur village, 11 Kms southeast of Hoshiarpur.
8. The fact has been mentioned by Abdulla and Nath Mal in their 'Var', a type of poetic form.
9. Tara Chand Narotam: *Sri Guru Tirath Sangreh*, p. 62.
10. Gian Singh: *Twarikh Guru Khalsa*, Bhasha Vibhag, 1970.
11. *Itihas Riast Bagrian*, 33-36.
12. Gian Singh: *Twarikh Guru Khalsa*, p. 602, Bhasha Vibhag, 1970.
13. *Itihas Riast Bagrian*, p. 54.
14. The village was founded in *Bk Samvat* 1711 (1654 C.E.).
15. Bhai Vir Singh: *Guru Kirat Parkash*, pp. 28-29, Punjabi University Publications, *Itihas Riast Bagrian*, pp. 61-63.
16. Sarup Singh Kaushish: *Guru Kian Sakhian*, p. 44, Singh Brothers, 1995. The book has been edited by Piara Singh Padam.

17. *Ibid.*, p. 45.
18. Bhagat Mal belonged to Nakka region.
19. *Udasi Mat Darshan*: *Itihasik Pattar*, Sikh History Society, 1953-54.
20. Suthra was *Kshatriya* of Madware sub-caste. He was born at Bahrampur near Bara Mula. His parents threw him outside their house because they considered him omnivorous on account of his having born with teeth in his mouth. Guru Hargobind, while on tour in Jammu-Kashmir region, heard the cries of the child and inquired what had happened to him. On being told that he was a cast-off of his family and is extremely dirty being littered with refuse and dirt, the Guru called him Suthra—clean and took care of him. He grew to be a great savant of Sikhism. He died in the time of Guru Gobind Singh. He was a good poet and wrote folk-poetry full of affection and devotion to the Guru. *Dabistan-i-Mazahib* also made mention of him.
21. Balwant Singh Dhillon: *Parmukh Sikh Te Sikh Panth*.
22. Macauliffe, M.A.: *The Sikh Religion,* Vol. IV, p. 279.
23. Sarkar, J.N.: *History of Aurangzeb*, III, Calcutta, 1928, pp. 311-12.
24. Lane Pole: *Aurangzeb*, pp. 35-36.
25. Sarkar, J.N.: *Aurangzeb,* Vol. III, p. 311. The Guru blessed the Prince, a fugitive in the Punjab after the battle of Samugarh.
26. Sujan Rai, in his work, *Khulasat-ut-Twarikh*, states "Having been defeated, Dara Shikoh rushed to Lahore, where the impending designs of his brother gravely terrified him and accordingly he decided to flee to Multan and Kandhar. He confided his intentions to his associates. Raja Rajrup exclaimed that he would go home to improve arrangements for mustering troops, and leaving his son and emissary, he departed. The Guru also, who had come with his army, left the camp with assurance that he would collect more troops for him." Raja Rupraj was the ruler of Nurpur state, according to Irfan Habib in his book *Sikh History from Persian Sources*.
27. Epitaphic inscription as recorded by Ajit Singh Bagha in his book, *Banur Had Orders*.
28. Sarkar, J.N.: *Aurangzeb*, Vol. III, p. 312.
29. Recently this copy of *Adi Granth* was present at Dehradun up to the start of Akali movement. The date of completion of this copy was *Samvat* 1716 (1659 C.E.) *Vaisakh Mah* (March) *Vaisakh Vadi* 1. The copy was prepared only about a year and a half before Ram Rai left for Delhi.
30. Puran Singh: *The Ten Master*, p. 82.
31. *Suraj Parkash:* Ras 9, Ansu 58.
32. Bannerjee, A.C.: *The Sikh Gurus and the Sikh Religion,* p. 249. Munshi Ram and Manohar Lal, Delhi, 1983.
33. *Ibid.*

34. Macauliffe, M.A.: Vol. IV, p. 310: "The Guru passed in review the whole of Ram Rai's conduct since his arrival in Delhi. His long absence decided that he was not fit for Guruship."

35. *Suraj Parkash:* Ras 10, Ansu 28, 16-17.

36. *Ibid.,* 19-20.

37. Kanahiya Lal: *Twarikh-i-Punjab*, Punjabi Translation.

38. Ajit Singh Bagha basing his conclusion on the authority of some Tibetan sources and the epitaphic inscription in the premises of Ram Rai's monument at Dehradun, says that poison was administered to the Guru at the instance of Emperor Aurangzeb, who nursed a grudge against the former for his having aided Dara Shikoh in the struggle for succession. The evil deed was performed with the vicious aid of nefarious intriguer Ram Rai. The view does not find corroboration in any source. Dr. Bagha has not quoted what exactly Tibetan source is. So far as the epitaphic inscription is concerned, the author himself went through the same and found no clue leading to such conclusion.

39. *Sewa Singh Shahid Bilas*: ed. By Garja Singh, Punjabi Sahitya Academy, Ludhiana, p. 57.

40. *Ibid.,* p. 56.

41. *Ibid.,* p. 59.

42. *Ibid.,* p. 56.

43. *Mahan Kosh* says that Mati Das and Sati Das were four brothers and all were sons of Bhai Pairagh. Later researchers and newly found documents Bhat Vahis give the correct chronology as follows: "Mati Das and Sati Das were sons of Hira Nand, grandsons of Lakhi Das and great grandsons of Pairagh. Both of them were executed by Aurangzeb along with Guru Tegh Bahadur *Bhat Vahi Multani Sindhi.*

44. The letter (*Hukam Nama*) of Guru Hargobind is preserved in *Takht Patna Sahib*. The letter states, "Please acquire two young ones of Koil and when they grow up and start singing then send them here in a cage. Also send *Kuka Kabutar*. Search them and acquire them as soon as possible.

45. Sarup Das in his *Mehma Parkash* (p. 545) states that an exceptionally beautiful white elephant had been presented to Guru Har Rai by his disciples of Uttrakhand (Lower Himalaya Range). Heinrich Zimmer states, "In the Vedas the elephant was the symbol of Royal splendour. Hastyayur Veda is the standard encyclopedia on elephants. The owning of an elephant, it appears, was the prerogative of the kings. Elephants were hunted and captured in the wilderness and then kept in the forest reservations or in garrisons for the purpose of warfare. A special value is attached to the white elephants." (Heinrich Zimmer: *Myths and Symbols in Indian Art and Civilisation*, pp. 103-04.)

9

GURU HARKRISHAN

(b. 1656 C.E.; d. 1664 C.E.)

Harkrishan succeeded to the pontifical throne on September 23, 1661. At that time he was five years two months and sixteen days. The installation ceremony was performed by Guru Har Rai himself, in the *Shish Mahal*, a spacious building constructed by Guru Hargobind in which he gave audience and arranged congregational prayers.

Even before he was raised to the status of the Guru, he had given ample proof of his precocity, high class intellectual attainments, deep knowledge of Sikh scriptures and Sikh ideology, a penchant for illumining the people and devotees. Through education and training imparted to him by his father, he grew to be a great exegete of Sikh scriptures, and a cynosure of scholars and mystics present in the court of his father. He had a melodious voice and could recite sacred hymns in musical intonation. Even before the assumption of guruship and in spite of very young age, people were impressed by his splendid demeanour, so much so that they began to call him 'Baba', a word of Persian language which means sage, elder or enlightened one. He took care that the devotees who came to Kiratpur were properly looked after. He would visit ailing people and besides consoling them in their agony, he arranged medicines and appropriate nursing.

In Guru Harkrishan, the people, especially the deseased, found a great healer of their sorrows and a unique fulfiller of their innocent wishes. People came to him with pain and agony in their hearts, and returned with hearts full of joy and hope. Baba Harkrishan possessed an alert mind, full of calm confidence and peace of divine wisdom. For him, illuminative love and intense care and concern for the poor and the destitute was the leitmotif of religion.

After his assumption of guruship, Guru Harkrishan addressed himself to the multifold apostolic responsibilities which was no easy task. The clouds of bigotry and persecution were thickening. Aurangzeb, who had succeeded in occupying the Mughal throne after killing his brothers and imprisoning his father had launched the policy of religious persecution towards the non-Muslims, especially the Hindus and the liberal Muslims. He had so harassed Mullah Shah, a disciple of Mian Mir that he prayed to God to spare him the sufferings which Aurangzeb was planning to heap upon him and died of heart attack in the cell where his Master Mian Mir meditated. Muhammad Said of Sirhind was another liberal Muslim who fell victim to Aurangzeb's fanaticism and religious parochialism. Sarmad's only fault was that he championed liberalism and loved Dara who had a compassionate heart and did not believe in persecution of non-Muslims. Sarmad and Mulla Shah did not help Dara militarily or politically but even then they were persecuted to death. A host of other liberal and heretical Muslims also could not escape the persecution of the Emperor. In the case of the Hindus the persecution was undertaken with greater vigour—the fact which is vouchsafed by different edicts of the Emperor. The Sikhs also were not allowed a smooth sailing. The Emperor's asking of the Guru to attend his court at Delhi was obviously in line with his general policy of harassing and chastising the non-Muslims.

In the case of Sikhs, his concern was conspicuous because of two reasons. In the first place, the missionary activity of the Gurus had virtually halted the conversion of the people to Islam in the areas of the Punjab on the left of the Ravi. Secondly, the *Naqashbandis* whose headquarter was at Sirhind and had great influence over Aurangzeb were hell bent to check the progress of Sikhism which, as they reckoned, was a potent threat to their scheme of weeding out the heretical and non-Hindu elements in the whole of India, particularly in Kashmir, Punjab, Sindh—the areas contiguous to Muslim countries such as Kabul and other neighbouring countries of Middle East, to realise their dream of Pan-Islamism. The political atmosphere being murky and discriminatory, Guru Harkrishan's functioning could not be but smooth.

The Guru's difficulties enhanced still further because of the activities of Ram Rai and of the *Minas* (lit. mean, the followers of Prithi Chand contemptuously called as such by Sikhs). Ram Rai, who was disowned and disinherited by his father was not in a mood to acquiesce. His *Masands* threw themselves heart and soul into the campaign to convince the Sikhs that the rightful person to be invested with the guruship was Ram Rai. Supportive of their claim, they invented different alibies as for instance they gave currency to the idea that certain *Masands* had conspired to seat Guru Harkrishan on the pontific throne at the death of Guru Har Rai. They also vouchsafed that the guruship was in fact passed unto Ram Rai the day when Guru Har Rai sent him to Delhi in response to the summons of Aurangzeb. Guru Ram Rai on his part harnessed all his resources, his political influence, his social connections and his own personal ingenuity to make himself acceptable to the Sikhs as a legitimate Guru.

Similarly the *Minas* were quite active. Harji, son and successor of Manohar Das Meharban at this time did not openly challenge Guru Harkrishan but certainly he found a chance to consolidate influence on the people especially of Majha region. He came to Amritsar from Mahamadi Pur (now in Lahore district of Pakistan). He assumed the control of Darbar Sahib complex and ousted the officients who had been appointed by Guru Har Rai. He also bandied that it was he who alone was the rightful heir, being the eldest son of Manohar Das Meharban, who had inherited guruship from his father Prithi Chand, the eldest son of Guru Ram Das. Because of his erudition and softspokenness, he did succeed to some extent in creating confusion among the Sikhs who came to

Sri Darbar Sahib and made offerings.[1] Dhir Mal also did not relish the ascendance of Guru Harkrishan as the Guru.

At organisational level, many difficulties had cropped up to the time of Guru Hargobind. Sikhism had spread to far off places beyond the boundaries of the Punjab. Sikh *Sangats* had emerged in north, west, east and the south in the subcontinent of India. Even such places as Kabul, Ghazni, and Balkh had Sikh *Sangats*. Dr. Balwant Singh had identified twenty-nine Sikh centres outside Punjab.[2] In Punjab, in Majha region, the Sikhs had acquired considerable influence while in Malwa region their influence was also widespread and since Guru Hargobind it had been continuously upbeat vertically as well horizontally. The Doaba region also showed ever-mounting inclination towards Sikhism. Guru Harkrishan deeply perceptive to the calls of the Sikhs of the Punjab was very quick to cater to the spiritual and physical needs. He, however, could not be very fast in forging suitable responses to the Sikhs—living beyond Punjab—the plausible reason being not-so-pleasant relations with the Mughal government.

Guru Hargobind had taken full care that he should have some sort of rapport with the Sikhs living at far off places. He encouraged them to form *Sangats* which were asked to seek guidance from Sikh centres especially set up for the purpose or to seek the guidance from the Guru directly. In some cases, the Guru sent his special emissaries to forge linkages between the Guru and the *Sangats*. In addition to these, there were very devoted Sikhs who were asked to look after *Sangats* and individual Sikhs. In Punjab, *Sangats* were organised and put under the charge of *Masands/Manji* holders, whose duties were to link the people with the Guru on the stipulated occasions. The Guru tried hard to keep the Sikhs well-knit whose each unit (*Sangat*) had galvanised itself into a community, and he achieved a wonderful success, although certain self-seeking *Masands/Manji* holders did not relish what was happening to Sikhism and only bided time to fill in their coffers and pursue their selfish ends.

After Guru Hargobind, Guru Har Rai gave special attention to preaching work, its consolidation and extension. He successfully maintained and invigorated existing *Sangats* and established new ones. He took care that these were properly looked after by *Masands* or certain devoted Sikhs. He also established new organisation called 'Bakhshish' (lit. 'grace'). To put vigour into proselytising work, he encouraged Udasis, specially those who held charge of preaching centres known in Udasi parlance as *dhūān* (lit. flame). He sent *Hukam Namas* to far off *Sangats* reminding them of their duties towards their Guru. Sikhism did make significant progress under his able stewardship. People in large numbers embraced Sikhism. He in fact was largely responsible for organising the proselytising work especially in Malwa and Doaba regions. In the time of Guru Gobind Singh if the Sikhs swarmed to the Guru in his fight against the Mughals, the credit indisputably goes to Guru Har Rai.

Guru Har Rai partly because of political reasons and partly because of his preoccupation in the Punjab could not attend to the organisational as well as spiritual affairs of the Sikh *Sangats* outside Punjab. He could not build linkages with them or with the Sikhs in general with the result that their interest in Sikh affairs could not be stepped up. As the Mughal government turned hostile to Sikh movement because of Guru's predilection towards Dara Shikoh, certain *Masands* even in Punjab preferred their own interests to that of Sikhism.

The net effect of Guru Har Rai's efforts was that Sikhism at organisational level suffered a set back in Punjab as well as outside it, of course in varying degree. In Punjab, especially in Majha, Malwa and Doaba regions, its influence increased and it affected considerably the life-style of the people embracing it. The net loss in terms of its escalation and organisation was nevertheless not substantial but certainly not negligible.

Guru Harkrishan during his ministry struggled hard at least to arrest the downward trend of the Sikhs in terms of their organisation, expansion and intensity of faith; but because of the paucity of time at his disposal, he could not forge adequate response to challenges which the circumstances threw up.

Even then, he started well. He kept up his calm even against the heaviest of odds and extreme provocation. People came and informed Guru Harkrishan how his elder brother Ram Rai had sent out *Masands* to win over support of all the religious centres and how his *Masands* were using clandestine and deceitful means to promote the lie that Rai had been installed as the true successor. Guru Harkrishan's attitude to all these things was that of a sage mystic deeply immersed in the love and will of God. He said "I have no ill-will against my brother. The mischievous propaganda will ultimately loose its effect on true seekers of God's light. He is going from place to place even seeking the support of Mughal rulers. We shall stay in Kiratpur and we have taken a vow never to submit to the influence and temptations of the Mughal court. Guruship is the gift of God and not a religious or political position acquired by external influences."[3]

Some Sikh *Sangats* living in states outside Punjab appealed to Guru Harkrishan to remove corrupt and inefficient missionaries of their areas and appoint learned men. The Guru at once took the step and directed Diwan Durgah Mall to look into the matter and send saintly and dedicated missionaries to these areas.

One of the major activities of Guru Harkrishan was to get copies of *Adi Granth* and Prayer books prepared by excellent caligraphists and scribes. He autographed some of these copies. One of such copies is still preserved in the *Tosha Khana* of Sri Takht Patna Sahib. The handwriting of the young Guru shows remarkable fairness and clarity and a distinctly different and more accomplished style than that of his predecessor.

Another daily activity of Guru Harkrishan was to address individuals or groups of people who came to solve the problems of their search for a nobler and holier life. A disciple would come and say, 'Master, I am illiterate. I can't read the scriptures. I can't read them and memorise them. Does that mean I would be deprived of liberation?' Another Sikh would do obeisance and express, "I am employed in the Mughal army and administration. What should I do, Master?"[4]

Guru Harkrishan answered all such questions. To the illiterates, he advised that they should devote all their energy to service and love of those who were needy. A Sikh's first and foremost commitment should be to God, his faith and truth. He should avoid involvement in every such service which comes into serious conflict with his faith. Anything which destroys a person's innerself, causes injury to his conscience should be given up.

Soon the stories of Guru's wisdom, his charity and compassion spread far and wide. One day Guru Harkrishan went out on horse back to visit some neighbouring places. People came with simple and humble offerings. But apart from everyone stood a man as if he was afraid to come close to the Master. He was carrying on his body a deadly malady, the living death that eats away the joy of life and renders one horrible and loathsome. He was a leper. The Guru looked at him with compassion and sympathy. The Guru not only carried the burden of human sorrow in his heart but also had strength of action and power of healing. He placed his hand on his head, bent lowly and spoke to him with such deep concern and sympathy, that the leper was amazed at the gentleness and grandeur of the Master's compassion and concern for him. For the first time in his life, he heard any one having faith in the hidden dignity of his soul. The Guru's words awakened a new consciousness and a new power within him. He regained his inner strength, with his face turned away from darkness of life. He felt that he was only a wounded soldier who had allowed his wounds to become festering sore. He felt greatly relieved when the Guru assured him that he had a beautiful soul. Now the leper felt that many people who were dressed in glamorous clothes and were visibly attractive were plagued with unbelief, cowardice, selfishness, cruelty. With his awakened consciousness, he could see many people in robust health slowly dying with cancerous maladies in their souls. The new ferment of spiritual power unleashed a new healing energy with which leprosy began to heal and disappear.[5]

Bhai Santokh Singh writes:

> "Guru Harkrishan dispelled people's sorrows fulfilled their ambitions and imparted to them Light of True

> name of God. He erased evil from the mind of the people and inspired them with patience, righteousness and charity. Thus, Sikhism flowered and illumined the hearts of seekers. From distant lands devotees came to seek his benediction and healing touch. He cheered them up and removed their affliction.[6]

The Guru's Hukamnama (sacred edict) to the *Sangat* of Patna shows that within a year, he considerably consolidated his position even in distant *Sangats*. Ram Rai's following decreased and his influence greatly waned, especially in the Punjab. Ram Raiyas' main stronghold was Lahore where there still is building which continued to be Ram Rai's Ashram. All the successors of Ram Rai had to come to Lahore for missionary training and study of Sikh scriptures at the Lahore Ashram.[7] Its activities slackened, under the impact of Guru Harkrishan's efforts.

But still the road was long and there were many milestones to cross. The Guru was well poised to take further steps towards consolidation and expansion of his mission, he had to face a two momentous challenges: one of Aurangzeb's making and other was of God's call.

Ram Rai, the elder brother of Guru Harkrishan, had not reconciled himself to the succession of his younger brother to the apostleship. He made up his mind to contest the office with all the vehemence at his disposal. He attached a few Masands to his cause and called himself Guru. His *Masands* went in all directions to announce his accession but the Sikhs who knew of the late Guru's decision refused to accept him. He tried hard through his *Masands* but failed even to mislead far off *Sangats* of Patna, Benaras, Lucknow in the East, and Pak Pattan, Kabul and Kashmir in the West of India. Not to speak of Diwan Durgah Mal, Bhai Dayal Das and Bhai Gurditta (a scion of Baba Budha) who were close associates and advisors of Guru Harkrishan, the descendants of Guru Nanak, Guru Angad, Guru Amar Das and leading Sodhies as well as the descendants of Baba Budha—all had full knowledge that Guru Harkrishan was a true successor who had been installed by his father fourteen days before the latter passed away.

Having failed to win over the acceptance of the Sikhs as the Guru, he now resorted to another stratagem. He planned to seek Aurangzeb's patronage and help. He thought that once the Emperor acknowledged him as the legitimate heir of the Guru Nanak's pontific throne, he would force Guru Harkrishan to abdicate in his favour. To this purpose, he approached the Emperor in October 1663 at Lahore, two years after the assumption of guruship by Harkrishan. He hesitated to approach the Emperor earlier because he had reckoned that he would soon win over the acceptance of the Sikh community through the help of *Masands* and thus there was no need of seeking the help of the Emperor. Secondly, throughout the year Aurangzeb being seriously ill had gone to Kashmir on 8th December, 1662 and came back to Delhi on January 18, 1664. En route to Delhi, he stayed for some time at Lahore, Ram Rai tried to meet Aurangzeb at Lahore but Aurangzeb directed him to follow him at Delhi.

Aurangzeb reached Delhi on 18th January, 1664 and Ram Rai probably met him a couple of weeks later. The author of *Mehma Parkash* says that Aurangzeb (*Alam Patshah*) who was a strong supporter of Ram Rai felt quite upset and wondered why Guru Har Rai had ignored the legitimate claim to the leadership of the Sikhs to such an Arif (saint and philosopher) Kamal-I-Karamat Auliya (saint perfect in the gift of miracles).[8]

Ram Rai in his meeting with Aurangzeb insisted on his intervention. Aurangzeb agreed but for his own reasons. He saw in it a very good opportunity for realising his religious mission. If he could get Ram Rai the apostolate of the Sikhs, he would be a mere tool in his hand, and through him he would perhaps be able to spread Islamic faith in the Punjab or if he was able to set both brothers at variance[9] and they shall die by mutual slaughter, his purpose would be served. The ultimate objective was to put a strong check on the progress of Sikhism and to play a decisive role in the affairs of the Sikhs which by all means were the exclusive concern of the Sikhs.

Accordingly, the Emperor issued order to the Guru to repair to Delhi. Ram Rai and his chief *Masands*, Gurbakhsh, Tara and Gurdas son of Behlo were greatly elated on learning that Aurangzeb had at long last summoned Guru Harkrishan to Delhi. They considered it a great tactical victory for themselves, 'for, if the Guru presented himself to the Emperor, he would break his vow given to his father which in turn would lower his prestige among his followers, and if he came to Delhi and refused to meet the Emperor, the latter would surely order his arrest and the Guru would suffer humiliation. Further, his arrest would cut him off from the Sikh people. And if the Guru escaped to the inaccessible regions of Shivalik Hills and continued to remain beyond the reach of the Emperor, he would not only earn the wrath of the latter but also provide occasion to them to win over the Sikh community and install Ram Rai as the eighth Guru. They reckoned that they were sure to stand to gain from his coming to Delhi, as also from his refusal to obey Emperor's summons. But they did not gauge that the Mughal Emperor had his own plans and motives and he simply wanted to use them as just a pawn in his game plan.

The Sikhs of Delhi apprehending something ominous to happen to the Guru if he was invited, lobbied that nothing untoward happened to the Guru. They approached Mirza Raja Jai Singh who was looked upon by non-Muslims as having a lot of influence on the Emperor as also requisite potential to dilute the strictly communal and narrow approach of the latter. According to Dr. Trilochan Singh another factor that impelled the Sikhs to seek the help of Mirza Raja Jai Singh was Jaipur's Raja's close relation with the Sikh Guru whom they considered as one of them being the scion of Surya Vanshi dynasty to which they themselves belonged.[10] It is also said that Raja Bhagwan Das of Amber was instrumental in bringing Akbar and Guru Ram Das close to each other. What exactly was the response of Mirza Raja Jai Singh and his son Ram Singh is not well-known, but the later events conclusively indicate that the Raja became favourably inclined to the cause of the Sikhs.

Jai Singh at that time was sixty and ranked only immediately after the princes of the blood. The reckless cavalier had grown into a shrewd and cautious commander, a wise counsellor and skilful diplomat, employing four languages with equal ease.

With the name and prestige of a princely family, he brought to Mughal court the subtlety and exquisite address of an ancient culture. In diplomacy he had attained to a success surpassing even his victories in the field. Whenever there was a difficult or delicate work to be done, the Emperor had only to turn to Jai Singh. "His foresight, his polite and cultured tongue and coolly calculating policy were in striking contrast to the impulsive generosity, reckless daring, blunt straightforwardness and impolitic chivalry associated with Rajput character."

In view of seriousness of the task which if not done with a finesse could lead to turmoil in the Punjab—the thing most unwanted by the Emperor in his initial years of his rule, he assigned the task to Mirza Raja Jai Singh to pursue Guru Harkrishan to respond positively to the Emperor's summons. Mirza took upon himself the responsibility and also got assurance from the Emperor that as long as he was not satisfied with the succession issue, Guru Harkrishan would stay in one of his bungalows as his honoured guest. Aurangzeb[11] readily agreed as it did not clash with his game plan.

Raja Jai Singh sent a courtier named Diwan Pars Ram[12], aged, wise, calm, cautious and an extremely courteous man along with gifts and presents, requesting the Guru to come to Delhi. While delivering the *Parwana* (official letter) of the Emperor and presents from the Raja, he very humbly made a point that his presence in Delhi would dispel the ugly impression created by Ram Rai and his crafty *Masands*; the Sikhs' morale would be boosted and above all Aurangzeb would see for himself in what great esteem young Child-Guru was held by the Sikhs and what serious risks he would have to take by causing harm to him. The Guru gave affectionate hearing to him who on his part was much impressed by the Guru's self-confidence, his fearlessness, his equiableness and determination.

The Guru took counsel with his leading Sikhs. They said to him with clasped hands "We are thy servants, Lord. With thy knowledge of all the three worlds thou knowest best." Guru Harkrishan called Pars Ram (the emissary of Mirza Raja Jai Singh) and informed him that he would be in Delhi in about two or three weeks.

Jai Singh had taken full responsibility for the safety of the Guru even as he was aware that the Guru had given the pledge to his father that he would never allow himself and the Sikh religion to become a political tool in the hands of Delhi rulers and he would not only keep away from the Mughal court but never make a voluntary appearance before the king. Under such circumstances every one expected dramatic and unfortunate development in the triangular encounter between the Guru Harkrishan, Ram Rai and Aurangzeb.

But Guru Harkrishan remained unruffled and made preparations for his intended departure to Delhi. Holy mother Sulakhni expressed her desire to accompany him to Delhi. She thought that she could possibly dissuade Ram Rai from causing any further harm to his younger brother. In case she failed, her presence at Delhi would send a clear message that Guru Harkrishan was the rightful Guru, chosen and installed by her husband fourteen days before his death. There was also a possibility that Guru Harkrishan's refusal to present himself in the court of Aurangzeb might lead to imprisonment or severe punishment at the hands of the Emperor. Under such grim circumstances, Mother Sulakhni deemed it her duty to be with the Guru. In addition to her mother, he took with him about twenty to thirty leading Sikhs prominent among whom were Durgah Mal Chibber, the Diwan; his nephews Bhai Jetha (later Jetha Singh), Bhai Dayala (Dayal Das)[13], Bhai Mani Ram (later known as Bhai Mani Singh), Bhai Gurditta the High priest, *Masand* Gurbaksh Mal.[14]

The Guru left Kiratpur sometime in the second week of February, 1664. His first stoppage was at Dayalpur[15] near Banur. He met his dear sister, Sarup Kaur, who was to see her apostle brother for the last time. He proceeded further and as he reached Panjokhara, a Sikh spoke with humility, "*Sangats* are coming from Peshawar, Kabul and Kashmir. Stay here for a day so that they could have the chance of seeing you, Master." The Guru agreed and decided to encamp to meet the wishes of his devotees. The *Sangats* from the aforesaid places and devotees from far and near who were trekking their way to Kiratpur to attend the annual gathering on the Baisakhi day which was drawing near, converged on this place. The Guru met every one and doled out his blessings and instructions to them. He received humble offerings symbolic of their love, devotion, joy and exuberation. The Guru enjoined upon them to learn to live in the light of the Word—SHABAD.

In that village lived a *Pandit* Lal Chand by name who was proud of his caste as well as of his learning. He came to see the Guru and spoke tauntingly "It is said that you sit on a apostolic throne of Guru Nanak. But what do you know of the old religious books?" The Guru called Chhaju Ram, shabbily dressed and dark-skinned water carrier who happened to pass by at that moment. Chhaju came and was asked to explain to the haughty Pandit the gist of Bhagwat Gita. The seemingly illiterate Chhaju astonished every one by his cogent commentary on the sacred book. The point was brought home to the Pandit that knowledge was not the exclusive monopoly of a Brahmin; it could be gained by any person of any status at any time and place. For complete knowledge love is rated more important than perception and other epistemological sources. Since Chhaju had love within him, it was not difficult for him to recite and interpret Gita meticulously.

Pandit Lal Chand was so satisfied by this strange miraculous phenomenon, that his pride of being *Brahmin* and a scholar was shattered. He fell at the feet of the Guru.[16] He became Guru's disciple and travelled with him upto Kurukshetra. In the time of Guru Gobind Singh, he entered the fold of the Khalsa and took the name of Lal Singh. He met with a hero's death fighting in the battle of Chamkaur on December 7, 1705 C.E.

At this time, another messenger sent by Mirza Raja Jai Singh arrived. He urged the Guru to reach Delhi without delay to avoid any misunderstanding which was likely to create complications. The Guru assured the Raja's envoy that he would reach Delhi in the next few days.

Thousands of Sikhs who thought that the Guru was sent for by Aurangzeb to mete out the same sort of treatment as the Emperor was, at that time, doling to Hindu Faqirs and even to Muslim Divines less orthodox than him with a view to coerce them to embrace orthodox Islam, decided to accompany the Guru to give him physical protection in case any attempt was made to imprison or harm him.[17]

Guru Harkrishan, however, did not permit his devotees to follow him to Delhi for many reasons. In the first place, Raja Jai Singh had taken full responsibility for the security and safety of the Guru. Secondly, a large crowd following him would give the impression that the Guru was demonstrating man-power to overawe the government. Thirdly, Ram Rai would start propaganda that the Guru had managed the crowd from the Punjab because he had no following in Delhi. Fourthly, the Guru wanted to demonstrate that the House of Nanak's stability depended on the Will and Grace of God.

When a large number of the Sikhs insisted on going along with him, he ordered that only the important members would constitute his entourage destined for Delhi, all others were ordained to return to their homes.[18]

From Panjokhra the Guru reached Kurukshetra, the ancient place of pilgrimage which was visited earlier by Guru Nanak, Guru Amar Das, Guru Hargobind and Guru Har Rai. The people who had come to the city were wonderstruck at the knowledge and spiritual gifts of the Guru. The question that was apparent in their minds was 'How will the Guru react to the whims and fancies of bigoted Emperor? Will he show some miracles and please the Emperor as his brother Ram Rai did or will he suffer like Sarmad and many other saints who did not submit to Imperial commands against their conscience?

From Kurukshetra the Guru moved towards Delhi. On the way he made halts at Bani Badurpur, Karnal and Panipat reaching Delhi in about a week's time. Mirza Raja Jai Singh received the Guru. His son Ram Singh was also with him. As a mark of respect Raja made an offering of rich gifts and robes of honour. Guru Harkrishan blessed him and other dignitaries and presented the customary robe of honour to his host. Then the Raja received the prominent members of the entourage of the Guru. After that the Guru and his party were taken very reverentially to Raja's palace at Raisina. This was the area where Raja Jai Singh's armies encamped and was known as Jai Singh Pura. The shrewd Raja watched Guru Harkrishan's personality, his character and disposition to give the correct impression to the Emperor. He was found to be quite a contrast of his brother Ram Rai. While Ram Rai was ambitious, and at times, betrayed cowardice and sycophancy, Guru Harkrishan was majestically gentle in mien, humble but firm in his conviction, fearless and indifferent towards worldly rulers and princes. Guru Harkrishan entered Delhi like a prophet with an entirely different spirituality, different outlook from his magician brother. Guru Harkrishan was placid like an ocean, firm like a rock and creative like a spring, while his brother was self-centred, unprincipled and time server. The Guru's wisdom silenced his detractors, comforted the sick and agonised and enabled the weak to grow strong.

Guru Harkrishan unlike his brother avoided meeting the Emperor and disregarded all suggestions to meet and interact with Emperor.[19]

According to Khazan Singh "The Guru was treated with respect and Prince Muazzam paid him a visit as a mark of distinction. The Prince was highly pleased with what he saw of the Guru and praised him a good deal before his Majesty."

The Emperor wanted to test the Guru's intelligence of which everybody spoke very highly. The Guru was surrounded by the women of Jai Singh's house including maid-servants who were equally well dressed and was asked to identify the Rani, Anand Kaur.[20] The Guru looked at their faces and had no difficulty in recognising her. This thing convinced the Rani, his husband and other members of the family that the Guru was no ordinary person. Out of reverence, they began to address him 'Bala Mukand' an epithet of Lord Krishna, or Bala Guruji (child prophet).[21]

In about a week's time the Guru's influence in Delhi was visible. People of all shades and creeds flocked to him and listened to his enlightening discourses. Diwan Durgah Mal sent some of his trusted missionaries along with leading Sikhs of Delhi to counter the misleading propaganda being done by Ram Rai's *Masands* all over the city and the neighbouring regions. This step yielded rich dividends. One by one, the *Masands* of the neighbouring regions came and ignoring Ram Rai's claim to the guruship offered gifts to Guru Harkrishan. The Guru blessed them with robes of honour and letters of authority to carry on the missionary work on behalf of the Guru's *darbar*. Ram Rai also sent his own letters to neighbouring regions in Gangetic Doab some of which can still be found in the homes of traditional followers of Ram Rai, but without much success. Now Ram Rai and his *Masands* started using coercive methods. They threatened simple and innocent folks with curses and even extended physical threats.

In spite of Ram Rai's mischievous role, the Guru's popularity continued to increase. The reporters of Aurangzeb had already given very favourable and exciting reports about the magnetic personality of Guru Harkrishan. Raja Jai Singh explained to the Emperor that guruship in Sikh religion, right from the time of Guru Nanak, was never bestowed on a successor on the basis of the law of the primogeniture. It had been given to the most meritorious and deserving. Not only the eldest son, but in the selection of Guru Har Rai, all the sons were ignored and bypassed in favour of the fourteen years old grandson. Aurangzeb had known up to now that almost all missionaries and Sikh divines of the Punjab and neighbouring regions had unanimously accepted Guru Harkrishan as their legitimate heir and successor to Guru Har Rai because he was installed by his father during the latter's lifetime. The Sikhs of Delhi also gave this impression in the court of Aurangzeb. Impressed by good reports of government's intelligence and high opinion of Jai Singh and his wide acceptance of the Guru as the legitimate heir by the overwhelming majority of the Sikhs, Aurangzeb became convinced that the choice of Guru Harkrishan was not wrong and dismissed the claim of Ram Rai[22] but Aurangzeb did not announce his arbitration, for he wanted, as a matter of policy to keep both the claimants under his thumb.[23] He however, tried to satisfy Ram Rai by giving him a Jagir (fief without fee) of seven villages: Khurvedi, Dhamalal, Chamasari, Dhartanwali, Pundiwari, Mianwal, and Rejpura in Doon valley where Ram Rai later built a religious centre of his own called Ram Rai's Dehra[24]. With passage of time the city of Dehradun developed around it.

The Guru at Delhi remained always unruffled and spared no efforts to animate the helpless, destitute and the poor. He would not hesitate to move among such people to apply balm to their lacerated hearts. He was always friendly and compassionate to the poor. His gracious blessing which inspired faith in God gave them inner power and hope.

Suddenly, cholera broke in some parts of the city. Sufferings and death brought in its trail were alarming. The Mughal administration in spite of high intentions was helpless in the face of this epidemic.

Guru Harkrishan forthwith asked his prominent physicians to accompany him to the affected areas. They delivered medicines made from medicinal herbs. He spoke compassionately to every sick person. His very presence and sight brought inner healing and hope to otherwise disappointed victims of the disease. The Guru's touch gave them joy and pulled them out of their despondency. There was certainly something peculiarly wonderful in the personality of this Child-prophet who had brought to this disease-stricken city the sacramental spring of new life, a new bliss and a new dawn.

Soon, the Guru began to be acclaimed as 'A Great Healer'. The people in hordes thronged to the bungalow of Raja Jai Singh to have the blessing of the Guru. Raja Jai Singh got a reservoir built and the water in it was sanctified by prayers and by the divine touch of the Guru.[25] People with faith and devotion sought the water and felt inwardly changed.

The people of Delhi who were still in the grip of the menace of Cholera had to face another menace of small pox.

The disease being contagious, people hesitated to even come close to the victims. The Guru was undeterred and moved among them like a messenger of hope and peace. When the bards of the Guru sang soul-elevating hymns from the *Adi Granth*, the sick and the dying felt a peculiar relief. Even death looked sweet to them. He made everyone feel that the miracle of healing through the blessings of the Master was a gracious miracle of God. He urged the people to shed the fear of earthly Kings and Emperors, the rich and the powerful. The Guru often said, "No one is great for his wealth alone. He alone is great who loves the Lord with a single minded devotion. Truth makes us free, Truth destroys doubts and Truth eliminates every sickness of the soul."

Guru Harkrishan who gave food to the hungry, medicine to the sick, clothes to the naked, peace to the agonised minds, and light to the ignorant won more adherents than any other religious leader in the city. Whosoever came to him, experienced peace. This fact was recorded later by Guru Gobind Singh.

'Contemplate the Spirit of Harkrishan.'

The sight of whom depelleth all sorrow and sufferings.[26]

The informers of Aurangzeb gave very impressive reports about the welfare-oriented activities of the Guru with the result that his long-cherished desire to see the Guru personally became poignant.

He summoned Raja Jai Singh and Diwan Durgah Mal and firmly ordered that Guru Harkrishan must present himself in the Imperial Darbar.

Without any firm assurance, both of them promised that they would pass on the Emperor's order to the Guru who was busy helping the victims of epidemic and other sundry calamities. They informed the Guru about the Emperor's wish. The Guru remained silent for a moment and then said, "The will of God will prevail." He along with his whole entourage moved out of bungalow of the Raja so that Raja might not have to face the wrath of Aurangzeb on account of his refusal to meet him. He encamped at a place on the bank of the river Jamuna, now known as the shrine of Bala Sahib.[27] The Raja at once went to the Guru and prevailed upon him to retract from his resolve and stay at his bungalow. The Guru agreed only partially. He made out that he would remain outside during the day instructing his people and stay at his bungalow for the night. Now Aurangzeb fixed March 28, 1664 C.E. as the date of his meeting with the Guru and asked Jai Singh to make requisite arrangement.

Early next morning, on Friday March 25, 1664, Guru delivered his last sermon and calmly declared that for the next five days he would remain in quiet retreat in the inner apartment of the palace. He would come to the audience hall just to give his blessings.

The decision was momentous and a sort of open declaration that he refused to meet Aurangzeb—the step obviously fraught with dangerous ramifications. Raja Jai Singh immediately put a strong guard of his loyal Rajput soldiers outside his palace instructing them to protect the Guru in case a hasty arrest was ordered. The whole entourage of the Guru also got prepared for sacrificing their lives to save the Guru from any physical harm that might be caused by Aurangzeb.

The Guru was placid as he was ever. He had resolved never to compromise with sovereignty of his faith, his ideology and his independence, nor was he prepared to allow any government much less imperial forces of Aurangzeb to utilise Sikh religion or him as a tool for the advancement of the interest of Mughal state.

By noon on the same day, Guru Harkrishan had higher fever to be followed by small pox the next morning. To those who had difficulty to comprehend as to why should the Great Healer suffer from the same disease, the Guru uttered, "The suffering or the martyrdom of the Guru is in the redemptive spirit. The Guru is one with God's light and Presence. His body, and soul never suffer any pain and sorrow, but he was to take upon himself the suffering of the human world in a human way. To lessen other people's sufferings is an act of compassion and charity but to suffer for fulfilment of God's will is an apostolic responsibility to the supreme love of God."

As soon as the Emperor was told by Durgah Mal and Raja Jai Singh about the illness of the Guru, he cancelled the appointment with him. On the sixth day of illness the night of 30th March, 1664 the light of Guru Harkrishan blended with the light of God (Chaitra Sudi 14, Vikrami Samvat 1721).[28]

The body of the Guru was bathed and dressed in austere robes and covered with fragrant flowers. After prayers, it was placed on the bier. Bhai Gurditta, Diwan Durga Mal, Raja Jai Singh, Kanwar Ram Singh were his pall bearers. As the funeral procession marched in slow measured steps towards Barapula, people followed in hordes to pay their last respect to the Child-Prophet from the Punjab. A funeral pyre of sandalwood was prepared on the bank of Jamuna on the exact spot where the Guru had pitched his tent earlier. The last prayers were offered by Bhai Gurditta, master of ceremonies. Then the pyre was lighted. There were the flames of the Light and Love. On the third day, the ashes were collected and taken from Delhi to Kiratpur where they were immersed in the waters of the Sutlej. According to *Guru Kian Sakhian*, Mata Bassi, the grandmother, asked Gurdas of the family of Bhai Bahilo to start reading the Holy Granth in his memory. Durgah Mal and Munshi Kalayan Das were sent to Punjab with the mournful news. They first went to Kiratpur to inform the Guru's sister, Bibi Rup Kaur. The next day, they sent out for Bakala to inform Guru Tegh Bahadur who consoled them and told them to abide by God's Will.

While on the threshold of death, the Sikhs asked the Guru who should be their Guru after him. Ram Rai was plotting at the Mughal court and Dhir Mal and other Sodhis were planning to put forward their claims. The Guru looked at the High priest, Bhai Gurditta and asked him to bring the articles of spiritual regalia (coconut, five paise, rosary and sword) which were immediately brought to the presence of the Guru. He placed them on the ground offered silent prayers and uttered 'Baba Bakala' "The baba is at bakala." Within a month, the young prophet scored a moral victory both over his brother and Aurangzeb. Fearlessly he came to Delhi, fearlessly he lived, fearlessly he protected his integrity and ideals and fearlessly he died remaining all the time unruffled emitting spiritual light illumining the people. Fearlessly he chose his successor, giving a stunning blow to the hopes of Ram Rai and long cherished desire of Aurangzeb to place his own man on the pontific throne. Juxtaposed in this context Prof. Puran Singh says, "The illness of Guru Harkrishan to us, his disciples, is in the nature of protest. The Mughal Emperor had every political and military weapon to finish Guru Harkrishan for his disobedience. Guru Harkrishan's illness ordained by the Will of God had drawn him away from the tyrant's den and made tyrant's power and authority useless and ineffective.

Reflecting upon the ministry of the Guru, we can safely strike certain conclusions. By his own example, he bought many into Sikh fold. At Delhi his demeanour was so impressive that within a very short span he became the cynosure of the people. His focalised attention to prepare copies of Gurus' hymns and their wide distribution in spite of the fact that he was yet a child spoke very high of his concern for the spread of Guru Nanak's religion. His immediate response to the Patna as well as other *Sangats* even at far off places testifies his keenness to consolidate Sikhism. How fast he acted in dispelling misunderstanding among the Sikhs about legitimate guruship was indeed admirable and fore-portended the progress of Sikh religion. At Delhi he showed remarkable forbearance and firmness and notwithstanding the machinations of Ram Rai and crafty Aurangzeb, he stuck to his stand of upholding the sovereignty and independence of the Guru's House. He neither displayed miracles nor submitted to Aurangzeb. His last act of nominating Guru Tegh Bahadur as his successor was in a way symbolic of the Guru's rejection of the stand bolstered up by Aurangzeb and his protege, Ram Rai.

In spite of all his splendid achievements, the Sikh movement and Sikh religion did not take rapid strides on the road to progress. Organisationally, the pace of Sikh movement suffered a decline. The *Masands*, *Bakhshish* holders and even *Sangats* could not be kept in touch with the central church. Ram Rai's *Masands* became defiant of the Guru, although they did not float a separate cult with separate objects of worship and ceremonies. *Minas* got activated and similarly Dhir Mal's dormant desire of assuming guruship of the Sikhs awakened. *Sangats* also did not function properly as they could not get regular directions of the Guru which they often got either through *Masands* or through the Guru himself or through his special messengers. The policy of the Mughal Emperor to engender schism among the Sikhs could not be countered with the requisite velocity and force. No special social templates were evolved to allow the Sikhs' ideology express itself in all its aspects. In this perspective, the progress of Sikhism as also of Sikh society was marginal, if not negative during the period of Guru Harkrishan.

NOTES AND REFERENCES

1. Sewa Singh: *Shahid Bilas*, ed. Giani Garja Singh and published by Punjabi Sahitya Academy, Ludhiana, p. 69.
2. Dhillon, Balwant Singh: *Parmukh Sikh Te Sikh Panth,* pp. 118, 119, Singh Brothers, Amritsar, 1997.
3. Trilochan Singh: *Life of Guru Harkrishan*, p. 92, Delhi Sikh Gurdwara Prabandhak Committee, 1991.
4. Duncan Greenless: *The Gospel of Guru Granth,* p. xci.
5. Kanahiya Lal: *Twarikh-i-Punjab,* p. 35.
6. Santokh Singh: *Suraj Parkash Ras* 10, Ansu 5-7.
7. Kanahiya Lal, *Twarikh-i-Punjab,* p. 35. The place is known as Ram Rai Da Chabucha.
8. Sarup Das Bhalla: *Mehma Parkash*, p. 633.
9. Macauliffe: *The Sikhs Religion,* IV, p. 318.
10. Trilochan Singh: *Life of Guru Harkrishan,* p. 105, D.G.P.C., Delhi, 1991.
11. Jadu Nath Sarkar: *Aurangzeb*, Vol. III, p. 207.
12. Giani Gian Singh: *Tawarikh Guru Khalsa*, p. 201.
13. *Shahid Bilas* ed. by Sewa Singh and published by Punjabi Sahitya Academy, Ludhiana, 1991.
14. Santokh Singh: *Suraj Parkash*, Ras 9.
15. Bibi Sarup Kaur's husband had settled here after the death of Guru Har Rai.
16. Giani Gian Singh: *Twarikh Guru Khalsa,* p. 267, Bhasha Vibhag, Patiala.
17. Santokh Singh: *Suraj Parkash*, Ras 10, Ansu 39.
18. Giani Gian Singh: *Twarikh Guru Khalsa*, p. 268.

19. Kesar Singh: *Bansavali Nama*; Khazan Singh, *History and Philosophy of Sikh Religion,* p. 144.
20. The Principal Rani prepared some dresses for the Guru including turban and shirt. She marked one which she desired the Guru pick up as a proof of his spiritual height. She also decided to dress like a maid-servant. If the Guru recognised her and embraced her as an Avtar of Krishan then she would have full faith in the Guru's greatness (*Bansavali Nama,* p. 77).
21. Giani Gian Singh: *Twarikh Guru Khalsa,* p. 269. Raja Jai Singh had five wives: (1) Anand Kaur Chauhan daughter of Sham Das of Harnauli State and mother of Raja Ram Singh, (2) Rani Nodhi ji daughter of Jai Singh of Indergarh, (3) Rani Raj Kaur d/o Keshav Das, (4) Rani Rup Kaur from Sasodia family, (5) Rani Bakirati d/o Kirat Singh (Family records of Jai Singh in Sanskrit preserved in Pathi Khana of Jaipur).
22. Forster George: *Travels in India*, Bhasha Vibhag Punjab, Patiala, 1970, Vol. I, p. 260. "The cause it is said, terminated in a permission being granted to the Sikhs to nominate their priest (Guru). When adjudging the contest they elected Harkrishan."
23. The dispute between Harkrishan and Ram Rai was referred to Delhi where both the parties went and by an imperial decree of Aurangzeb, the Sikhs were allowed to elect their own priest (Guru). They chose Harkrishan. Malcolm Sir John: *Sketch of the Sikhs*.
24. The followers of Ram Rai are called Ram Rayyas and they are socially bycotted by the Sikhs as per the injunctions of Guru Gobind Singh.
25. Giani Gian Singh: *Twarikh Guru Khalsa* (Urdu), p. 236. Raja Jai Singh got a reservoir constructed and filled it with water sanctified by the Guru's feet (Charanamrit).
26. Guru Gobind Singh: Sri Harkrishan Dhiyaei Jis Dithian Sabh Dukh Jaei.
27. Macauliffe: *The Sikh Religion,* Vol. IV, p. 326, S. Chand and Company, Delhi.
28. The time varies between midnight and dawn in different records, but all historical records e.g., *Bansavali Nama*, *Mehma Parkash*, *Twarikh-i-Punjab*, etc. are unanimous on date.

10

GURU TEGH BAHADUR

(b. 1621 C.E.; d. 1675 C.E.)

EARLY PHASE

Fifth and the youngest son of the sixth Guru, Guru Tegh Bahadur was born at Amritsar on April 1, 1621 C.E. On the auspicious occasion of Tegh Bahadur's birth, Guru Hargobind invoked Akal Purkh (Timeless Master) to bestow on the new child unflinching courage to fight forces of evil and to work for the establishment of Truth and Dharma to the last breath of life. As we shall see later, the father's aspirations and expectations of little son were subsequently realised in full measure. Guru Hargobind named him as Tyag Mal.

As a child, Tegh Bahadur was brought up with utmost care and attention. He lived and grew in the atmosphere of religious discipline. During childhood Tegh Bahadur was aloof but always active. He was silent and meditative but very energetic and quick to learn everything his teachers taught him.[1]

At the age of four and a half, Baba Tegh Bahadur was entrusted to Bhai Budha and Bhai Gurdas for his education who, apart from imparting education themselves, arranged other teachers also to make the child knowledgeable in different subjects. The Guru studied languages, History, Arithmetic, Metaphysics, Logic, Theology. Six systems of philosophy and classics like the Bhagvat Gita, Mahabharata, Ramayana,

Elementary Islamic Philosophy, Koranic Lore and Sufi Texts were also taught.[2] Guru Tegh Bahadur also learnt military tactics and made himself adept in horsemanship, swordsmanship and the science of looking after the horses. He also became well-versed in music in which his interest was deep—the fact which is amply borne out by his poetic compositions set to different musical measures.

Guru Tegh Bahadur owed not a little to the general environment and to his parents and teachers. From his mother Nanaki, he imbibed tenderness of his heart, love of solitude and charitableness. From his warrior father, he learnt the noble qualities of fearlessness and courageous will to fight tyranny, love of travels, skill in the use of arms and above all the urge to uphold dharma. Baba Budha so affected his sensitive mind that there grew proclivities of mysticism which he himself had imbibed from Guru Nanak, the founder of Sikh religion. Under the influence of Bhai Gurdas, Tegh Bahadur developed philosophic and poetic bent of mind. The general atmosphere also contributed a lot towards the growth of the psyche of Guru Tegh Bahadur. Amritsar, the place of Guru Tegh Bahadur's birth, had already assumed the role of the capital town of Sikhism. The holy tank, the revered Hari Mandir rising in its pristine beauty in its midst, the Akal Takht, recently constructed to serve as the Supreme temporal authority of the Sikhs, and above all the charismatic presence of Guru Hargobind had lent a rare grace and charm to the place. Devotees from far and near, sometime in groups and sometime severally, rallied to this Mecca of theirs from all sides. Everyday both morning and evening, assemblies were held where prayers were offered, hymns were sung often to martial tunes and talks given on Sikh tenets. From the rise of the day, the Guru was busy receiving gifts of weapons, horses *et al.* from his faithful visitors, underscoring the virtues of martial valour and heroism, watching feats of physical strength, such as wrestling bouts, *gatka* play and supervising lessons in horsemanship and swordsmanship. In between, he would find time occasionally to organise hunting excursions, then considered the best mode of imparting training in war manoeuvres.[3] All this left a deep imprint on the impressionable mind of young Tegh Bahadur. No wonder, he showed keen interest in learning the military arts and developed fondness for hunting.

During these early years of his life, Tegh Bahadur did not always stay at Amritsar. He did a lot of travelling in company with his father and other members of family. In course of these travels, he paid visits to Tarn Taran, Khadur Sahib, Goindwal and Kartarpur. At Goindwal and Kartarpur, his education suffered no interruption because his teachers Bhai Budha, Bhai Gurdas and others were mostly staying with him.[4]

Tegh Bahadur was married to Gujri, the daughter of Lal Chand, a Subhikhi Khatri of Lakhnaur near Ambala who had migrated and settled at Kartarpur. His brother-in-law, Kirpal Chand, who rose to prominence under Guru Gobind Singh, also migrated with his father while his elder brother-in-law Mehar Chand, continued living at his ancestral place. Family links were thus maintained with Lakhnaur. Sahibzada Tegh Bahadur was an eye-witness to the battles, if not all of them, which his father had to fight against the Mughals. His physical presence at Amritsar, Kartarpur and Phagwara at the time of fighting was undoubted, though about the battle of Lehira, it is not possible to say anything definitely. This shows that Tegh Bahadur, along with other members of his family had to pass through arduous times.

In the battle of Kartarpur (26th April, 1635) when the Mughal forces under the overall command of Kale Khan and Painda Khan attacked Guru Hargobind, Tegh Bahadur fought valiantly in the rearguard of the Guru's army. Fearlessly he rode into the thick of the battle and using lance and sword worked havoc with the enemy ranks. The father, Guru Hargobind, was so much pleased with his heroic performance that according to a popular Sikh tradition, in a thrill of exuberance of joy, he changed his name from Tyag Mal to Tegh Bahadur meaning 'Hero of the sword'.

Ever since the battle of Kartarpur, Guru Hargobind had lived at Kiratpur. During all these years he continued his programme of training his people in the art of warfare, horsemanship and organising hunting expeditions. Occasionally, he would go out in the hills as well as in the plains on missionary tours. Sahibzada Tegh Bahadur took deep interest in all this and would often accompany his father in his hunting expeditions and missionary tours. According to Dr. Fauja Singh, "In 1638, the death of Baba Gurditta left a deep impress on the mind of young Tegh Bahadur. It was for the second time that a son of the sixth Guru had earned his displeasure by indulgence in occult powers." Atal Rai had done it many years earlier at Amritsar and had been severally reprimanded for this act of indiscretion. He took his father's displeasure to heart and met an early and premature end. Bhai Gurditta now committed a similar indiscretion for which he got an equally severe reprobation from his father. His end, too, was similar to that of his younger brother Atal Rai. The lesson of these two incidents was too strong for Tegh Bahadur to forget. That he could never be unmindful of this fact is amply evidenced by the resoluteness with which during his incarceration at Delhi, he resisted the insistent demand of the authorities for the display of a miracle.

In the last week of February, 1644, Guru Hargobind invested Har Rai with guruship and asked his sons to show reverence due to the pontificate. Guru Tegh Bahadur was the first to bow to Guru Har Rai. Sikh records state that a change occurred in Guru Tegh Bahadur's disposition even during the life of Guru Hargobind and he grew indifferent to the world and its matters. Taking into consideration these tendencies, Guru Hargobind considered him unfit for the guruship and bestowed it on Har Rai.

The aforesaid logic leading to the non-bestowal of the pontificate on Tegh Bahadur is not convincing. Firstly, because Guru Tegh Bahadur never turned recluse, hesitant of doing work or taking interest in the affairs around him; his was only a contemplative silence and secondly if Tegh Bahadur had really turned a recluse, Guru Hargobind had not told his wife, Nanaki, on her anxiety to know as to why his noble son had been by-passed that he will live long enough to shoulder his responsibility and do great deeds. It appears that Guru

Hargobind had to ignore the claim of the Guru Tegh Bahadur not because of he was a renouncer of the world but because the people mistook his contemplative silence. Immediately after the passing away of his father, Tegh Bahadur along with his wife and mother Nanaki went to Bakala, an historic village in Amritsar district about two miles and a half north of the Beas Railway station, which was a flourishing business centre in the seventeenth century. The possible reason for retiring to Bakala was that his stay at Kiratpur might not create an in-group of his followers.

For nearly twenty years (1644-64) the Guru lived at Bakala in the house built by Bhai Mehra[5] specially for the Guru. He was amply provided by income from Hargobindpur[6] and the whole of Amritsar district which was considered as his diocese. It is wrong to presume that the Guru confined himself in the underground cell of his residence and had got no social intercourse with the world. The Guru did meditate but to conquer the senses in the clear sight of the Insight; but at the same time he did maintain contacts with the world outside. He was deeply concerned and took keen interest in social and political changes that were taking place, as an artist watches a drama in which he is to play a hero's part. His brother-in-law, Kirpal Chand, who was a soldier in Guru Har Rai's army came twice a year and informed him of all the small and great things that were happening at Kiratpur. Baba Dwarka Das, the descendant of Guru Amar Das and the eminent Sikhs of Amritsar district like Bhai Gurhia and Baba Gurditta came to pay him homage and brought with them the news of Lahore.[7] Now and then he even went out for hunting. He did not practise any self-mortification; nor did he undergo any monastic penance of an ascetic.[8] He attended to household affairs as other people did.

After staying at Bakala for about twelve long years, Tegh Bahadur along with his family decided to visit some of the principal holy places of the country. With that end in view, he proceeded to Kiratpur,[9] wherefrom he vended his way through Kurukshetra around the middle of C.E. 1657.[10] Having stayed there for three months, the party left for Prayag via Garh

Mukteshwar, Mathura and Agra. The Guru along with his party reached Prayag[11] in the beginning of C.E. 1661.[12] After a month's stay there, the onward journey was resumed. The party reached Kashi (Benaras) on 21st June, 1661 A.D. From Benaras the Guru reached Sasaram and then Gaya where he met Bhai Jetha Seth, a devoted Sikh of Guru Hargobind who took him to Patna. It was here that the news of the passing away of Guru Har Rai (Katik Vadi 9, 1718 Bk.—6th October, 1661 A.D.) reached him and he decided to return to Kiratpur to mourn the death of the seventh Guru. On the way back, he along with his party, arrived at Prayag[13] on 5th Magh 1719 Bk (3rd January, 1663 C.E.). When he was approaching Delhi, he learnt that the late Guru Har Rai's son and successor Guru Harkrishan had arrived in Delhi. The actual date of his arrival at Delhi was 21st March, 1664.[14] The Guru stayed at Dharamsala Bhai Kalayan for some time where a large number of devout Sikhs paid their respects to him. Baba Ram Rai also called upon him at this place and informed him in detail about the visit of Guru Harkrishan to Delhi. Shortly after, Tegh Bahadur accompanied by his mother and other people waited upon Guru Harkrishan and his mother Sulakhni at the residence of Mirza Raja Jai Singh and expressed profound sense of sorrow and sympathy in their bereavement. Immediately after this, Tegh Bahadur left for Bakala.

On March 30, 1664, Guru Harkrishan on the verge of his passing away declared that his successor would be Baba Bakala meaning thereby that his successor would be his 'Baba' living at Bakala and, in token thereof, he entrusted the spiritual regalia (five pice and a piece of Naryal) to Diwan Durga Mal. According to *Bhat Vahi Talauda Pargana Jind* and *Guru Kian Sakhian* by Sarup Singh Kaushish, the Guru did not leave any vagueness[15] in his statement and actually mentioned the name of Tegh Bahadur to be the Guru and Diwan Durga Mal to take the articles of spiritual regalia to Bakala and personally offer them to the new Guru. The news of the passing away of Guru Harkrishan spread far and wide but somehow the information that reached Bakala and the country around regarding the nomination of the successor was incomplete and vague with the result that many false pretenders had become self-appointed successors of Guru Harkrishan and the problem of finding the true Baba which at first seemed simple and logically conclusive had now become complicated. There were twenty-two[16] pretenders who set themselves up as successors to Guru Harkrishan at Bakala.[17] The Sodhis of Lahore, the Mina Sodhis of Amritsar, the descendants of Suraj Mal and many impostor-Sodhis who acquired certificates from Pandas to declare that they were Sodhi Babas set up tents and employed agents to do propaganda for them, and win supporters even on payment. All material means of inducement including bribery and enticement were used by the paid advocates and propagandists of each impostor Guru.[18] The most vociferous and conspicuous claimant, however, was Dhir Mal, who was the first to pitch his camp at Bakala. There were two attractive features of his claim to guruship. One was that he was the only direct descendant of the eldest son (crown prince) Baba Gurditta whose son and grandson had so far reigned as the seventh and eighth guru respectively, and secondly, he possessed the first compiled copy of *Adi Granth* prepared by Guru Arjan Dev.

A few months were passed in this state of confusion and then in the month of August on 11th, 1664, a Sikh *Sangat* from Delhi arrived at Bakala in obedience to the late Guru's command for the installation ceremony of Guru Tegh Bahadur. The *Sangat* was led by Diwan Durga Mal, the son of Dwarka Das Chhiber, a prominent devotee of Guru Harkrishan. The *sangat* included several other prominent Sikhs[19], such as Chaupat Rai, son of Pera and grandson of Ballu and great grandson of Mulu Mani Ram son of Mai Das and grandson of Ballu; Jammu, son of Padma and grandson of Kaula, Gurbaksh son of Baba, Nanu son of Baba and grandson of Unaida and Mata Sulakhni, mother of Guru Harkrishan. Baba Gurditta son of Bhai Budha and Dwarka Das[20] son of Arjani Sahib and grandson of Baba Mohri Bhalla were also there at the installation ceremony. It appears that they were specially invited to the occasion. The installation ceremony was held in open Diwan. The Tikka ceremony (affixing of Safron mark on the forehead) was performed by Baba Gurditta. Diwan Durga Mal informed the assemblage about the late Guru's decision of appointing Tegh Bahadur as his successor.

Even after the formal anointing ceremony, a few months passed in confusion. During this period, unworried by what Dhir Mal and other impostors were doing and confident that truth would ultimately prevail, Guru Tegh Bahadur went about his work in the normal way. Ten days later his succession (August 21, 1664)[21], he accompanied by Dwarka Das, Diwan Durga Mal and Jaggan went to Kiratpur to condole with Bibi Roop Kaur over the deaths of her father Guru Har Rai and her brother Guru Harkrishan. The visit synchronized with the holy ceremony of the immersion of the late Guru's ashes in the waters of the Sutlej on 22nd August. On Diwali day[22] (9th October, 1664) Makhan Shah[23], a Lubana trader, came to Bakala from Tanda, a village in Srinagar Territory. According to Sikh tradition he had come to offer 101 Gold *Muhars*, which he had promised when his ship, laden with merchandise, had been saved from sinking by a prayer to the Guru. But on reaching Bakala, he was taken aback to find many of the Sodhi pretenders setting themselves up as gurus. According to Sikh tradition, Makhan Shah hit upon a plan for detecting the Guru. He started offering two *Muhars* to each instead of 101 *Muhars*. He thought that the real Guru would himself ask for the remaining 99 *Muhars*. When he was convinced of the falsity of the pretenders, he enquired if there was any other Sodhi. Someone informed him of Tegh Bahadur who was living in solitude and had no truck with the people outside.

Makhan Shah went to Guru Tegh Bahadur. He made obeisance before him by placing two *Muhars*. Guru Tegh Bahadur said, "O Sikh! you promised an offering of 101 *Muhars*, when the ship was on the point of sinking, why do then, hesitate to pay the remaining 99 *Muhars*?"[24] Thereupon Makhan Shah ascended a house-top and waving his flag proclaimed from there, "I have found the Guru; I have found the Guru." On hearing this, the Sikhs assembled from every quarter and paid their homage to the Guru.

From this tradition, it appears that Makhan Shah did not know Guru Tegh Bahadur. But it does not sound correct. Makhan Shah had been the follower of Sikhism since long. When Guru Hargobind visited Kashmir, he waited upon him, and at his request, the Guru visited Tanda, a village founded and developed by Makhan Shah himself on the bank of the river Jhelum. Guru Har Rai too was accorded hearty welcome by him. He also paid a visit to the eighth Guru at Delhi. He was a well-known Sikh and had acquaintance with almost all the important Sikhs of Kashmir or those who were permanently attached to the Guru's household. In the face of all this, it is rather unjust to assume that Makhan Shah did not know Guru Tegh Bahadur or what Guru Harkrishan meant by 'Baba Bakala'.

This being so, he ought not to have offered two *Muhars* to each Guru as a strategy to find out the real Guru. The truth seems to be that he visited Bakala to lay down his offering of 101 gold *Muhars* with his men; but on finding that the impostors were creating confusion, he and his men took up the cause of the Guru so vigorously that the impostors were completely exposed. When Makhan Shah visited the Guru, his two sons, Lal Chand and Chandu Lal and his wife Solji were with him.[25]

In this way, the Guru could assume the undisputed charge of the Sikhs after nearly six months and a half. The Guru appointed Mati Das and Sati Das[26] as Dewan and minister and Bhai Dayal as the household minister.

The discovery of the genuine Guru put an end to the pretensions of the false Gurus. But Dhir Mal did not reconcile with the turn of tide; on the other hand, he was determined to snatch the guruship by force. He felt that peace-loving pacifism of Guru Tegh Bahadur was no match for his armed might and money-power. He schemed to kill the Guru, and for this purpose he hatched a conspiracy with the help of his *Masand* Shihan, who with about a hundred armed ruffians attacked the house of Guru. Shihan aimed a bullet at Guru Tegh Bahadur and fired point blank. The bullet scratched the surface of his shoulder without causing any serious wound.

Guru Tegh Bahadur stood calm and composed as if nothing had happened. Diwan Durgah Mal, Bhai Mati Das, Bhai Dayal Das and Kirpal Chand gave physical covering to the Guru, hitting anyone that came near them. Before Shihan could load another bullet, Kirpal attacked him and wrenched the match-lock from Shihan's hand. At this, the rogues ran back, carrying with them all that they could get hold of. The whole operation was conducted under the very eye of the wicked Dhir Mal.

When the Sikhs learnt all this, they attacked the house of Dhir Mal[27] under the leadership of Makhan Shah and Kirpal. They not only retrieved the things plundered from the Guru's house but also carried away some of Dhir Mal's belongings. Besides this, they took possession of the copy of the *Adi Granth* lying with Dhir Mal. Both Dhirmal and Shihan were handcuffed. The Guru forgave them considering forgiveness to be the greatest virtue and ordered the Sikhs to return the articles looted from Dhir Mal's house. The Sikhs returned everything but the copy of *Adi Granth*, which they considered to be the property of the Sikhs and not a private belonging of Dhir Mal. Later on when Guru Tegh Bahadur came to know of it, he persuaded the Sikhs to return even that.

On November 22, 1664, Guru Tegh Bahadur left for his birth place, Amritsar, to pay homage to the sacred place. He bathed in the sacred tank but the ministers of Hari Mandir shut its doors against him, and he was not allowed to enter the holy precincts.[28] According to Trilochan Singh[29] the whole of Amritsar was under the control of Harji Mina and the priests of Hari Mandir also belonged to the Minas. This being so the Minas feared that once Guru Tegh Bahadur and his adherents entered Hari Mandir, they would never leave it and drive the *Masands* of the Mina-Guru out of it. Dr. Ganda Singh, however, says that the doors of the Golden Temple were slammed fearing that they would have to submit to a central control. In our opinion the view expressed by Trilochan Singh seems to be correct; firstly because the necessary evidence is available and secondly, because it looks more probable.

Whatever the merit of the story, it is evident that the organisational cohesion which had been the glory of Sikhism up to Guru Hargobind was becoming a thing of the past and the movement was losing the strength that Guru's undisputed leadership had given to it.

Under the circumstances, the Guru thought it advisable to return to Kiratpur. On way back in view of the sincere devotion of Mata Hariyan, he stayed at village Walla near Amritsar.

Leaving Amritsar the Guru decided to spend some time touring the Majha and Malwa regions of the Punjab before proceedings to Kiratpur. The Guru with all his entourage wended his way through the heartland of Majha; and on the way probably made a brief visit to Khadur Sahib, Goindwal and Tarn Taran. Last of all, he reached Khem Karan, a town now in the extreme west of Amritsar district. At this place, one Kamboj Chaudhari Raghupat Rai, out of devotion, presented a mare to the Guru. During his sojourns at different places, large numbers of country people rallied to him to benefit from his teachings. After travelling across the Majha, Guru Tegh Bahadur crossed the river Sutlej and entered the Malwa region from the side of Ferozepur. He was soon in the midst of Lakhi jungle—the name by which the entire sparsely populated tract of land now covering roughly the district of Bathinda and Faridkot was called. There in this area a large number of villages had the honour of Guru's holy visit. Talwandi Saboke (Damdama Sahib), Maur and Maisarkhana are but a few of the many such places which were sanctified by the Guru's presence, but for want of evidence it is difficult for us to ascertain which place was visited at this time and which on subsequent occasions.

Next to the Malwa, Bangar area (which is, in fact an extension of Malwa) was hallowed by the Guru who reached Dhamdhan on the occasion of Baisakhi (1665). Guru Tegh Bahadur liked the place and thought of developing it into a centre of Sikhism. With this view, the Guru gave some money to Bhai Doggo, a devoted *masand* of this place and gave instructions to him to raise a building with a well for water supply and to dig the tank nearby to be named as 'Gurusar'. Having spent a few days here, the Guru reached Kiratpur in May, 1665 (around 9 Jeth, 1772 Bk). On May 13, 1665, the Guru attended the *Satarvin* (a ceremony performed on the 17th day from death) of Raja Dip Chand of Bilaspur. Mata Nanaki, Mata Hari (Baba Suraj Mal's wife), Dip Chand and Nand Chand (sons of Baba Suraj Mal). Diwan Durga Mal, Jetha, Dayal Das, Durga Das (sons of Padma Rai Hajabat), and Dariya Khan (son of Mula Jalhan) were with the Guru.

The Guru was received with utmost respect by Rani Champa who did all she could to make the Guru's three days stay as comfortable as possible. During his stay, the Guru expressed that he would like to build a new settlement somewhere near Kiratpur and offered to buy a suitable piece of land for the purpose. The Rani consulted her ministers and offered to donate the site of Makhowal, Mathaur and Lodipur.[30] The Guru highly appreciated the spirit of devotion in which the offer was made but he preferred to buy it.[31] The Rani was not willing to receive anything, but ultimately the Guru succeeded in prevailing upon her to accept a token amount of Rs. 500.[32] On returning to Kiratpur, the Guru instructed Diwan Durga Mal to make a careful survey of the land. This done, the foundation stone of the new settlement was laid by Baba Gurditta, the son of Baba Budha on June 19, 1665 (Harh 21, 1722 Bk). This new settlement was named Chak Nanaki, after the revered name of the Guru's mother. The humble beginning served as nucleus for the beautiful town of Anandpur which subsequently grew around it.

Eastern Tours

The Guru did not have a prolonged stay at Chak Nanaki. He appointed his trustworthy followers to supervise the construction work at that place and himself left for travels (August 1665). What were the factors which prompted him to go on tours hurriedly while it was expected that Guru would stay at Chak Nanaki for sometime to watch the growth of the new settlement. Various explanations have been put forward in this connection. One explanation is that the Guru did so with a view to getting away from the scene of the Sodhis' rivalries and machinations. But this explanation is inadequate because except Dhir Mal at Kartarpur and Harji at Amritsar, there was none actively hostile to him, rather the sons of Suraj Mal (Dip Chand and Nand Chand) were favourably inclined towards him and they had attended installation ceremony at Bakala and later in May, 1665 had accompanied him to Bilaspur to attend the *satarvin* function of the late Raja Dip Chand of that state.

According to another explanation, the Guru went to Dhamdhan (Bangar) to fetch some of his luggage he had left there during his earlier visit to the place. There he was arrested by the Mughals and taken to Delhi and produced before the Emperor Aurangzeb. Then, through the intercession of Raja Ram Singh of Amber with the Emperor, he was released after which he proceeded towards the east on the advice of Raja Ram Singh. This explanation too appears inadequate because it implies that the Guru had no set programme of his own and travelled as demanded by the circumstances. Moreover the underlying idea here is the belief that Punjab was not a safe place for the Guru to stay in, which does not seem to be correct.

The plausible view seems to be that the Guru undertook tours to further strengthen the links with the *sangats* functioning in the eastern regions of the country whom he had personally observed during his earlier tour in Uttar Pradesh and Bihar as also to remove their general grouse that much attention was not paid to them. According to Dr. Trilochan Singh, the Guru undertook tours in response to the invitation of some Sikhs from the east, namely Bhai Bulaki Das and Bhai Hulas Chand from Dacca and Bhai Darbara and Bhai Chain Sukh from Patna, who met the Guru at Kiratpur and begged him to come with his family and major portion of the Darbar.[33]

The date when the Guru left Anandpur for undertaking tour of the east was about August, 1665 C.E. From Anandpur, the first important halt was at Saifabad. The Guru had many of staunch devotees accompanying him, such as Sati Das, Mati

Das, Gawal Das, Gurdas, Sangata, Jetha and Dayal Das. Nawab Saif Khan[34] who had been governor of Agra and of Kashmir under Aurangzeb and had a religious disposition accorded a hearty welcome to the Guru and served him with devotion. On the Guru's departure from Saifabad, Saif Khan made presents of a horse, camels, a tent and a chariot. He held the stirrup in reverence as the Guru mounted his horse to resume the journey.

From this, the Guru proceeded to Dhamdhan in the Bangar area. This was the second visit of the Guru to this place. The purpose of the Guru seems to be to see for himself the progress of his projects at the place whose care he had assigned to the local *Masand*, Bhai Doggo when he visited this place for the first time. Besides this, the Guru wanted to reinvigorate the *Masand* to follow the Guru's teachings with sincerity and devotion. In fact, the Guru was interested in developing it into a major centre of Sikh faith.

Guru Tegh Bahadur's arrival at Dhamdhan must be sometime prior to Diwali because the day was celebrated by organising a fair which was attended by large crowds of people. The Guru prolonged his stay here to celebrate Guru Nanak's Birth Anniversary.

However, four days before the great occasion came, Alam Khan Rohilla suddenly appeared with imperial order from Delhi and arrested him along with Bhai Sati Das, Bhai Mati Das, Bhai Gawal Das.[35]

According to one of the Buranjis[36], the orthodox Ulemas the Brahmins were much upset at the deep impact of the teachings and they complained to the Emperor that the whole atmosphere was being vitiated by the Guru. The Emperor, after examining the complaint, issued orders that the Guru should appear before him.

The Guru, however, did not pay heed to this and continued his work as usual. Thereupon the Emperor commissioned Alam Khan to effect the arrest of the Guru which he did on the day as mentioned in the preceding paragraph. Forster Malcolm, Cunningham and Latif state that discomfited in his efforts to attain pontific seat for himself, Dhir Mal began to conspire with Ram Rai to devise some ways to bring about the ruin of Guru Tegh Bahadur and as a result of that, the Guru was summoned to Delhi—the view which is not supported by any sound evidence.

On being produced before Alamgir Aurangzeb at Delhi, the Guru was thoroughly interrogated and then handed over to Raja Ram Singh of Amber for custody and surveillance. Aurangzeb wanted to execute the Guru; but through the successful intercession of Ram Singh, who took full responsibility of the Guru's good conduct, the Guru escaped punishment. According to Bhat Vahi Jado Bansian, Guru Tegh Bahadur remained in custody of Raja Ram Singh for a period of about one month. On December 13, 1665 (Poh 1, 1722 Bk), the Guru was released and allowed to go anywhere. The Guru thereupon resumed his travel to different places in the East. The news of the Guru's release angered Aurangzeb who disapproved of this act of Raja Ram Singh which he considered as the violation of the terms of the custody.

The next important halt was Mathura, wherefore he betook to Agra where there was already a very important Sikh centre built in memory of Guru Nanak's visit to the place. Here he stayed in the house of one old pious lady Mai Jassi, in Mai Than Mohalla of the city where now a gurdwara exists in memory of the Guru's visit. From there, the Guru and his entourage moved on to Etawah, Kanpur, Fatehpur and reached Allahabad early in March, 1666 C.E. At Kora Manakpur, 65 Kms northwest of Prayag (modern Allahabad) Guru Tegh Bahadur converted a vaishnava Sadhu, Maluka Das. He was surprised to see Guru Tegh Bahadur accompanied by armed disciples who hunted animals. But on beholding the Guru and listening to his sermons, his doubts disappeared as clouds disperse before high winds. He fell at the Guru's feet. The Guru blessed him and honoured him by visiting his hut. It was at Allahabad that Mata Gujri got conceived. Next important halts were Mirzapur and Benaras. At Benaras the Guru stayed for many days. According to Dr. Fauja Singh 'Like the other places, he had visited Benaras before more than once and felt quite at home among his devotees, chief among whom was Bhai Jawahri Mal. As the local tradition goes, the white horse, Sri Dhar, gifted to him by Saif Khan of Saifabad, fell ill and subsequently met his death at this place. Then the Guru moved to Sasaram where he met important Sikh missionary Phagu Shah who lodged the Guru in a beautiful new house which has since become a holy shrine.[37] Having visited Bodh Gaya, Rai Garh, the Guru reached Patna towards the end of May, 1666 C.E.

The heads of the Patna diocese, Ram Rai and Bhai Durbari made an excellent arrangement for the stay of Guru Tegh Bahadur and his family. A devout lady known as Mata Paidi looked after holy mother Nanaki, and Maṭa Gujri who was expecting a child. The Guru spent the early months of the rainy season (*Chamasa*) at Patna. During this period, he organised the missionary work in Bengal, Bihar, Uttar Pradesh and other neighbouring areas by placing all *sangats* of these areas under the unified command of Bhai Dayal Das who by his sincerity in the Sikh cause had risen very high in the estimation of the Guru. Sometime around the Dussehra festival, a few prominent Sikhs of Dacca waited upon the Guru and entreated him to visit and bless them and their city.

The Guru agreed to go with them at once entrusting his family to the care of Patna *Sangat* (congregation). The Guru proceeded to Dacca via Monghyr, Colgong, Sahibganj and Kant Nagar. The last named place was subsequently wiped out by the floods and the inhabitants moved to a new site towards the north, now known as Lackmirpur. Many people in this area still profess Sikh faith.[38] The prominent disciples who accompanied him were Bhai Mati Das, Bhai Sati Das and Baba Gurditta son of Bhai Budha. From Kant Nagar, the Guru reached Malda,[39] a great Sufi centre. Here the Guru is believed to have stayed for more than a month during which he had exchange of ideas on many religious problems. The Muslim saints were much impressed by the piety and spiritual splendour of Guru Tegh Bahadur. From Malda, the Guru reached Dacca passing through among other such places as Godagari, Gopalpur and Pabna.

Guru Tegh Bahadur reached Dacca at the end of October, 1665 C.E. According to Teja Singh, Ganda Singh "There flourished quite a network of prosperous Sikh *Sangats* and ministries all over. From Raj Mehal in the west of Sylhet in the east, from Dhubri in the north to Bansbhali and Fateh Kachehri in the south, there was hardly a place of importance during the days of Mughal viceroyalty where some Sikh temple did not exist or some Sikh ascetic (Udasi) had not established himself and gathered a number of followers around him. The movement had spread even to some islands like Sondip, as early as Shah Jahan's time. These *Sangats* were not only places of worship but as usual served the useful purpose of wayside inns where food and shelter were given free to the poor and the indigent way-farers.[40] These *Sangats* had been well-organised by Almast and Natha Sahib.[41] Dacca was the *Hazuri Sangat* or the head *Sangat* of these parts with a number of others seeking guidance from it and in turn was controlled by the Guru from Anandpur. Besides local *Sangats*, there were always a number of Sikh merchants from the Punjab and Sind, who were always anxious to keep themselves connected with their spiritual guide. No wonder, the Guru received great respect from the people of Dacca whose association with the Sikh faith was as old as its founder, Guru Nanak. Bhai Bulaki, the local *masand* and Bhai Natha the disciple of Almast did all whatever they could do to make the stay of the Guru comfortable. The place where the Guru used to hold *Darbar* to give audience to the people is marked by a gurdwara called *Sangat* Tola Gurdwara. Tradition has it that a big *Jagir* was later assigned to it by Nawab Shaista Khan, the then Mughal governor of Bengal in token of his goodwill towards the Sikh *Sangat*. However, there is no reliable record of this *jagir*. It was here that he received the welcome news of the birth of his son at Patna on December 26, 1666. He wrote a letter of thanks to the *sangat* of that place for looking after his child. From this letter, it appears that there was no prospect of his return in near future because he hoped that his family would continue to be looked after as usual.

From Dacca the Guru left for Jantia Hills and Sylhet early in the year 1667 where he established a missionary centre known as the Sylhet *Sangat*.[42] After spending the rainy season at Sylhet, Guru Tegh Bahadur moved south towards Chittagong and Sondip. He passed through Shairganj and stopped at Agartala, the capital of independent Tripura state. From here, he went to Chittagong, where he stayed towards the end of the year 1667 C.E.[43] During his stay at Chittagong, he established a large religious centre of his faith (*Sangat*) which flourished so much that during the times of Guru Gobind Singh it provided weapons and war material for the saint soldiers engaged in struggle for upholding righteousness. Passing through Noakhali, Chandpur and Narayan Ganj, Guru Tegh Bahadur reached back Dacca in 1668 C.E. Around the middle of 1668, the Guru completed his visit and set out on homeward journey. Probably he reached Patna and spent some time with his family before moving out again but we are not sure of this. Anyhow, he was out travelling and preaching somewhere in the neighbourhood of Monghyr when the Amber Rajput Chief, Raja Ram Singh met him.

Meeting with Raja Ram Singh—Guru's Tour in Assam

In December, 1667 C.E., the Ahoms captured Gauhati and Aurangzeb, in order to retrieve the lost prestige, resolved to despatch a strong contingent to oust the Assamese. Accordingly, Raja Ram Singh son of Mirza Raja Jai Singh was issued formal orders on January 6 to achieve the task, which was obviously very difficult, first, because the climate of Assam was not congenial for the soldiers to keep fit; and secondly, the Assamese were feared because of their command over black magic. To enthuse the soldiers and to build their morale, Raja Ram Singh took with him five pirs (Muslim saints) of Malda.[44] While reaching Monghyr, the Raja,[45] who had deep reverence for the House of Guru Nanak and regarded Guru Tegh Bahadur a rich repository of spiritual power, resolved to take Guru Tegh Bahadur who had already wished to have a tour of Assam. The Guru accepted the request.[46] Raja Ram Singh and Guru left Dacca sometime in the middle of December, 1668 C.E. and reached Dhubri in February, 1669. Guru Tegh

Bahadur camped at Dhubri while Raja Ram Singh camped at Rangmati, the Mughal outpost near the frontier of Assam.

Soon after, the war between the Mughal forces and Assamese forces ensued. Raja Indra Daman Singh was in command of Assam army of the Ahom King Chakradvaj (Raja Surg Dev of Guru ki Sakhian).[47] The Mughals pressed their opponents hard but the decisive victory was not easy to get because of the difficult mountainous terrain, insalubrious climate, and heavy torrents during the rainy season which impeded the rapid movements of the Mughal forces unacclimatised to the climate and the hurdles of the terrain. Moreover, the Assamese were determined to fight to the last drop of their blood to keep Gauhati, the seat of their culture and government, under their control. However, as the Sikh tradition goes, the witchcraft, or sorcery of Kamrup women could not have any effect on the Mughal[48] soldiers because of the presence of the Guru in their camp. But the Guru and his Sikhs did not participate in the battle. The assertion of Cunningham that the Guru was fighting for Ram Singh or was employed by him is a pure fiction. Guru Tegh Bahadur's own letters give us no clue about his movements.[49]

In the meanwhile, certain factors operated to bring about change in the moods of both the parties engaged in warfare. The reverses which the Ahom King had suffered mellowed down his enthusiasm. Similarly, by now the realities of situation had dawned on the Mughals also. Ram Singh was convinced that the attempt to have clear victory would mean a long drawn-out and desultory warfare which was neither advisable nor practicable. Moreover, Ram Singh received a letter[50] from his widowed mother to the effect that the Padshah (Aurangzeb) contrived the death of his son Kishan Singh by making him fight with the tiger, which naturally dampened his spirit.

Sensing the change in the mood of the contending parties, Guru Tegh Bahadur strived for peace between them. His attempt brought fruit and a negotiated settlement was arrived at. According to the agreed terms of peace, the old boundaries were to be maintained.

As a mark of complete harmony that now prevailed, the Guru invited the soldiers of both armies to join together and filling their shields with earth to raise a mound at Dhubri in memory of Guru Nanak, a great unifier of human kind. At the top of mound, there stands a Sikh Temple known as Damdama. It was here that a local chieftain Raja Ram came to seek blessing for a son. His wish was fulfilled and according to Sikh sources the Raja's son Rattan Rai became a follower of the Guru and visited Anandpur with presents in Guru Gobind Singh's time.[51] While in Assam, the Guru also visited Cooch Behar, Chander Bhanga, Kishen Ganj and Purnea.

The Guru left Assam early in the year 1670 C.E. The Guru took a route different from the one he had travelled in the direction of Patna via Bongaigaon, Siliguri and Katihar. Though it was a different route that the Guru took on the backward journey, he revisited places as Sasaram and Banters. A Persian document, lately discovered, evidences the grant by the local authority of fifty-two *bighas* of land to Sasaram for the establishment of *Sangat* and for building a *dharamsala* and planting a garden for the comfort of faqirs, travellers and visitors. There is still in Sasaram a place called Bagh Guruji.[52]

The Guru was in hot haste to reach Punjab. The reason was that during this period, there was a marked change in the socio-religious policy of Emperor Aurangzeb who adopted a much stiffer attitude towards the Hindus. On April 8, 1669, the Emperor, according to *Ma-a-Sar-i-Alamgiri*, issued orders to all the governors of provinces "to destroy with a violent hand the schools and temples of the infidels, and they were strictly enjoined to put an entire stop to the teachings and practising of idolatrous forms of worship". According to De Graff "In the month of January 1670, all the governors and native officers received the order from the Great Mughal prohibiting the practice of pagan religion throughout the country and bring down all the temples and sanctuaries of idol-worshippers in the hope that some pagans would embrace the Muslim religion.[53] While this general order of the Emperor was having its effect in the country, the Sikhs also, according to Mohammed Hashim Khafi Khan's *Mutakhab-ul-lubab*, "had their share that is Emperor Aurangzeb having received information about them had ordered their deputies to be turned out and places of worship to be destroyed". As it has been told by Mirza Inayatulla Ismi, in the *Ahkam-i-Alamgiri* "the Sikh temple in the town of Burya, in the parganah of Khizrabad of the Sarkar of Sirhind, had been demolished and a mosque had been raised on its site.[54]

The Guru did not consider it wise to stay at Patna for a longtime because he wanted to avoid delay. Instead, he asked Bhai Mati Das and Kirpal Chand to take the family straight to Lakhnaur via Ayudhya, Lucknow, Nanakmata and Hardwar, while he would join them at Lakhnaur after seeing Rani Pushpa Devi, mother of Raja Ram Singh at Delhi. Immediately all the family members of Guru Tegh Bahadur including child Gobind Rai left for Lakhnaur and according to Bhat Vahi Multani Sindhi, they arrived at the place on the 13th September, 1670[55] (Asu Sudi 9, 1727 Bk). The Guru reached Delhi on 20th June, 1670[56] (22 Harh, 1727 Bk) and sojourned at Jaunpur, Ayudhya, Lucknow, Shahjahanpur, Muradabad en route. At Delhi, the Guru was waited upon by Rani Pushpa Devi and her daughter-in-law (wife of Raja Ram Singh) who made their obeisance. The Guru informed that Raja Ram Singh had gained initial victories and would return shortly. On the way back to Delhi, the Guru was arrested by the Kotwal of Agra but was soon released when it was made clear that earlier order for the arrest no longer stood valid and applicable.

Soon after, the Guru left for Lakhnaur via Rohtak, Kurukshetra and Pahewa. The Guru at this time was accompanied by Nawab Saif Khan who had been leading hermit's life since C.E. 1669 and had met the Guru either in Assam or somewhere on the way back. The exact date of the Guru's arrival at Lakhnaur is not available, but it is almost certain that on the day of Dussehra, he was at Lakhnaur. It was on this auspicious day that the hallowed child Gobind Rai was seated on a cot and his elder maternal uncle Mehar Chand Subhikhi performed *Sirvana* and *Dastar* (turban) ceremonies, and fixed *Tikka* mark of sandalwood on his forehead. Gobind Rai was ceremoniously dressed for this special occasion. Then followed the offerings. First of all Jhanda, the *Masand* of Lakhnaur presented 101 *Mohurs*. Many others followed suit. After that, every day people would flock from the neighbouring areas and present their offerings to him by way of homage.

After a short sojourn at Lakhnaur, the Guru along with Bhai Dayal Das and Bhai Sadhu Ram left for village Malla to meet his elder sister Bibi Viro. The family, however, was instructed to stay at Lakhnaur till they were sent a message. From Malla, the Guru proceeded to Bakala. Shortly afterwards, he was joined by his family there. It is not possible for us to determine when the Guru arrived at Chak Nanaki but this much we can say on the evidence of Shahid Bilas of Sewa Singh that on March 29, 1672, Guru Tegh Bahadur was definitely present at Chak Nanaki where Bhai Mani Das had the good fortune of paying his homage to the Guru. The Guru during his eventful and long missionary tours practically covered the whole of north India from Punjab in the west to Bengal and Assam in the east. No Sikh Guru after Guru Nanak had travelled so extensively as did Guru Tegh Bahadur.

Second Tour of Malwa and Bangar

About the middle of 1673 C.E. the Guru left for extensive tour of Malwa and Bangar Desh. Details of the tour are not available but according to Sakhi Pothi, the Guru spent nearly one and a half years on this tour. According to Santokh Singh, Gian Singh of *Twarikh Guru Khalsa* and Sakhi Pothi, the Guru visited thirty places but our findings are that he visited 104 places in Malwa and 24 places in Bangar. Exact account of anecdotes of his visits to different places is not known, yet a few have been recorded in Sakhi Pothi, Suraj Parkash and *Twarikh Guru Khalsa*. Guru Tegh Bahadur's important halts were Dukhnivaran, Mulowal Sekha, Hadiaya, Sohiwal, Dhilwan, Dikhi, Saifabad, Maisar Khana, Ponderian, Alisher, Goga and Bhaupali, Khkiwa, Samaon Bhikhi, Khayala Maur, Talhi Sahib and Talwandi, Bathinda, Sulisar, Bara, Bachhoana, Gobindpura, Gaga, Gurne and Makorar.

At Saifabad, the Guru stayed for about four months to honour the wishes of the chief of the place, Nawab Saif Khan.

At Mulowal, the Guru made arrangements for the supply of potable water by getting wells sunk. According to local tradition, the brackish water of the well that was there before the Guru was made fresh and potable as if by a miracle. Triloka, the Chowdhary of Sekha, did not pay heed to the Guru who advised the Chowdhary that ego-centricity was a disease and it should be got rid of. At Hadiaya, the Guru was accorded a hearty welcome. During his stay there, the Guru found that the village was in the grip of a terrific epidemic causing mortality by suffocation through the swelling of neck. They were asked to have a dip in the small pond[57] closeby the water of which had some medicinal qualities for the cure of that epidemic. Subsequently, the Guru helped the people in deepening and widening the tank which has now become the holy tank bearing the name 'Gurusar', where every year a big fair is held.[58] The people of Dhilwan received the Guru with great reverence. The Guru liked the place and stayed there for several months, and as the tradition goes, the Guru made arrangement for the supply of 101 cows to the people to enable them to alleviate the shortage of the milk. In the village Dikhi, Ali Sher and Bhupali, the local panchayats accorded hearty welcome to the Guru and made offerings to him. One of the persons who came to pay homage to the Guru was Chaudhari Jagraj with whom the Guru was specially pleased and to whom the Guru asked to found a new village on a particular mound.[59] After Bhupali, the Guru camped at Khiwa.[60] A person named Singha served the Guru so much and with such devotion that the Guru blessed him. His fellow-villagers, in token of the appreciation of his service to the Guru, doubled his share of water in the customary distributory of the village community.

The next important place of sojourn was Samon. It was here that the Guru was informed of the arrival of Sikh *Sangat* from Kabul. In honour of the visit of the *Sangat*, a special Diwan was held where they offered to the Guru their precious presents. The meeting of the *Sangat* and the Guru was so soul-stirring that a peasant who was working in his fields nearby was deeply moved and he could find satisfaction only in offering all his cooked food, which he had just received from home, to the Guru and the Sikh *Sangat*. At the village Bhikhi, a local zamindar Des Raj (nicknamed Desu) waited upon the Guru. The Guru advised him to remove the symbol around his neck which showed that he was a follower of *Sakhi Sarvar*. Des Raj promised to abide by the advice, but when he was taunted by his brothers-in-faith, he threw to winds the advice of the Guru and reverted to the old faith. He threw away the arrows given by the Guru.

The Khayala and Maur villages were visited next. The people of both the villages gave warm reception to the Guru. At a small distance from Maur at a place now called Talhi Sahib, a huge function was organised in celebration of the Sikh Guru's birth anniversary.

The next stoppage of the Guru was at Talwandi Sabo, now known as Damdama Sahib. The Guru was attended by a large number of people. This place was sanctified by the Guru in getting a tank dug. The Guru prophesied that this place would become a great religious centre in due course of time.

From Talwandi, the Guru reached Bathinda. The Guru stayed there for a period of nine days during which he enjoyed hunting in the thickly forest nearby. From Bathinda, the Guru marched to a place called Sulisar where a few rascals made an abortive attempt to steal horses. According to Sakhi 22 of Sakhi Pothi, the thieves were caught and hanged by the Sikhs. This thing struck terror into the hearts of those people who made light of the Sikhs' presence.

Next important places to which the Guru paid visits were Bara and Bachhoana. At the former place, the Guru stayed for the whole of the rainy season. The people of the village served the Guru with devotion. They placed a number of their fields at the disposal of the Guru for the supply of green fodder to the animals in the Guru's camp. At Bachhoana too the Rangar inhabitants spared no pains to make the Guru's stay comfortable. A most significant feature of the Sakhi Pothi account pertaining to the place is the reference to the vast numbers of people attending upon the Guru during the journey.

From Bachhoana, the Guru proceeded to Gobindpura and after a short stay there moved on to Gaga, Gurne and Makorar. The Rangars of Gaga misbehaved towards the Sikhs but they soon regretted and asked for Guru's pardon. According to Dr. Fauja Singh "to begin with, the Guru paid no heed to them but when they still followed him begging for forgiveness, he excused them saying that their identity would ever remain un-impaired though they would never be an adequate match for the local Sidhu *jats*, who had always seen respectful towards the Sikhs. As a mark of their deep reverence for him the Sidhus made offerings of potfuls of ghee and cotton sheets. They also fell under the spell of Guru's personality and entered into the fold of Sikhism.

Shortly after, the Guru entered Bangar, which is just an extension of the Malwa Desh. The Guru had toured this area previously also and therefore he did not face much difficulty while treading his way through the region. The most important of the places visited by the Guru in this part of the country was Dhamdhan and he must have stayed here for quite some time. The Guru did his best to minimise the sufferings of the people of this area. He caused many wells sunk which were really a boon to the people of that parched region.

During all his travels, the Guru identified himself with the people and their sorrows and sufferings and he did whatever he could do to provide relief to them. He felt that only those minds which are strong in moral fervour and spirit were capable of struggling against tyranny and injustice. Accordingly, Guru exhorted the people to imbibe spiritual and ethical values, sink differences on the bases of caste or birth, give up all fear and face tyranny with resolute calmness. The Guru's motto was 'frighten not, and fear not' (*G.G. Sahib*, p. 1427).

From the foregoing account of the travels of the Guru, some important inference can be drawn. First, Guru's long journeys in the northeast, Malwa and Bangar were a great success as these left a deep imprint on the people. Secondly, the Guru took care to make personal contacts with the panchayats, Chaudharies and elders of different villages. Thirdly, he organised big functions to bring together people from far and near to discuss problems of common interest from common platform. He also made arrangements to keep himself in touch with them.... At some places he asked *Sangats* to consider themselves as his 'Khalsa' implying that they needed no intermediary to contact or communicate with him as they were directly under his guidance. Fourthly, he established centres of Sikhism at various places to impart continuity and strength to his mission. Fifthly, the Guru gave special attention to the zamindars of the area. May it to be, he had come to realise that they were the natural leaders of the people and their conversion to his faith would facilitate his work of awakening and articulating the people so as to enable them to achieve higher standard of culture and civilisation. Sixthly, during the greater part of his travels, the Guru moved with a large following and received the homage of the people along with many offerings. This was particularly true during the later phase of his travels. This caused misgivings and panic among the official circle and the local news-reporters made exaggerated, even distorted reports, to the government regarding the movements and activities of Guru Tegh Bahadur. The fact that in the course of his tour the Guru conducted himself with dignity and authority lent some plausibility to these reports with the result that subsequently the Guru was martyred on their basis.

As regards the duration of the tour, nothing definitely can be said probably the tour lasted for a year and a half. It appears that start was made about the middle of 1673 C.E. and it was not till the end of 1674 C.E. or the beginning of 1675 C.E. that the Guru with his large train of followers returned home.

Martyrdom of Guru Tegh Bahadur

Guru Tegh Bahadur's martyrdom is such an event that did not take place suddenly; it was, in fact, the result of the contradictions that lay at the root of the conceptual frameworks and operational activities of the Sunni section of the Muslims and those of Guru Tegh Bahadur, besides the hyper-sensitivity which was partly the product of over-zeal for the implementation of the Sunni policies and partly the psychological hurt which was caused by Emperor's inability to prop up the tottering jagirdari-based polity.

The part played by Ram Rai, if at all there was any, was insignificant and certainly it was not the determining factor *vis-à-vis* the Guru's execution. As a matter of fact, Ram Rai played into Aurangzeb's hands whose influence on him was so deep that he felt pleasure in defecting from the Sikh rank. When the decision of Guru's execution was to be taken, Ram Rai was not at all consulted. Aurangzeb took the decision in keeping with his own policy and mission. There is no historical evidence that Ram Rai[61] had discussion with the Emperor on this matter before or after leaving Delhi for Pathan region in the northwest region of India.

However, to be clear about the factors which were responsible for the execution of the Guru, we will have to examine all relevant facts carefully.

The period of the Great Mughals was a period of religious stresses. As a matter of fact, the orthodox Muslim religious unity suffered its greatest stress during the period from 1605 C.E. Many forces, some political and more religious, were conspiring to weaken the hold over Indian Muslims of Sunni orthodoxy.

The Mughals were, by ancestry, taste and conviction, eclectic in religious-characteristics which their political necessities and ambitions tended to conform. Taimur showed greater respect to Sufi thinkers than to the Sunni Ulemas. Babar and his son were no religious bigots and accepted Shi-ism although outwardly while negotiating for the support of the Persian Shiite Safarids. Moreover, during the sixteenth and seventeenth centuries, Shi-ism in India enjoyed political patronage. In the Deccan, Yusuf Adil Shah of Bijapur (1469-1510) pronounced himself a Shia as did Burhan-ud-Din of Ahmednagar and Qutab Shah of Golcunda. In North India, Bairam Khan, the guardian and minister of young Akbar, was Shia with a large Persian Shia following who settled down in India.

Furthermore, significant religious developments within the penumbra dividing Muslim from Hindu had softened religious acerbities in India. If from within Islam the mystics had appeared to reach out towards Hinduism, from within Hinduism, Kabir, Nanak and Chaitanya with their condemnation of caste, Hindu rituals and idolatory appeared to be reaching out towards Islam.

Important changes also occurred in the character of Muslim mysticism. From Persia—The Shattri whose Shaikh Muhammad Ghawth was Humayun's spiritual preceptor, the Qaidiri whose Shaikh Mir Muhammed was tutor to the Mughal prince, Dara Shikoh, and the Naqshbandi order, whose greatest luminary was Shaikh Ahmed of Sirhind. Members of the first two orders in particular were deeply influenced by the pantheistic doctrines of the Spanish Muslim mystic, Ibn 'Arabi (1164-1240); they observed few of the restraints in expression characteristic of the earlier Chisti and Suharwardhi Orders. What is more, their adherents were often intimately acquainted with Hindu mysticism.

Besides this, the Hindu revival which had been ushered in by the dawn of Bhakti movement had been gaining strength and the Hindus relieved of the initial shock of the Muslim conquest had started asserting once again.

None of such challenges were exactly new to Sunni orthodoxy, what was new was the political climate in India in which they had to be met. Until Aurangzeb's time, the Sunnis could not be confident of the exclusive support and patronage of the ruling power.

Akbar came to an understanding with the Hindu Rajputs, who served to underpin his empire, and with policy reinforcing his own personal religious inclinations, set his face against Muslim orthodoxy. The orthodox were scandalised not so much by the presence of Islamic ideas and practices in the Indian Muslim community as by the absence of political support in resisting them. Nonetheless, they did not relent and were always intent upon establishing their hegemony and eliminating all the factors which did not allow their notions to be consummated in practice. In 1580 C.E., their sympathies were with Mirza Hakim and they spared no effort to instigate Jahangir to rise against Akbar's religious policy. A critical examination of the factors that led to the revolt of Jahangir against his father would show how the Sunni Muslims formed the backbone of it. Sayyads of Burha helped him only when they exacted promise from Jahangir that when he ascended the throne, he would revise the liberal religious policy, at least for some time.

The cause of orthodoxy had been continually buttressed by the great traditionalist Abdul-Huqq-al-Dehlvi and others. However, the greatest figure in the reaction against Akbar's religious policy and mystics' religious syncretism was Shaikh Ahmed of Sirhind (1564-1624) who, arguing from mystic experience itself against the pantheism of Ibn 'Arabi exhorted Muslims to a fresh realisation of the religious value of traditional observance. His followers were known as Naqshbandis. Shaikh Ahmed laid emphasis on two things: (1) Submission to laws, precepts and traditions, (2) distance from innovations (Rafi-i-Bidat). He reproved the use of reason in matters of faith and held the opinion that if reason was sufficient, then great philosophers who had adopted reason as their guide should not have fallen in the melting pot of error. His thesis was 'as the mode or reason transcends the mode of sense, and, therefore, whatever is not perceived through the senses is apprehended by reason, in the same way the mode of prophecy transcends the mode of rational devotion that does not demonstrate the divine truth and is a denial of the mode of prophecy'. According to him he who wants to be a philosopher must belong to the company of Satan and therefore he will be a loser and will be disappointed. He believed "God sends his message through prophets in regard to his essence and attribute and in regard to actions whether they were in agreement with or against His will." As the prophet is the vehicle of God's commands, obedience to him is equivalent to obedience to God. It follows that the true believers must conform in thought, word and deed to the injunctions or practices of the prophet. It was on this ground that he condemned all types of innovations. Shaikh's condemnation of innovation was all-comprehensive and knew no exception. Shi-ism was an innovation which was worse than infidelity. It was, therefore, necessary to refrain from associating with the Shias. Shaikh Ahamed was fiercely hostile towards the Hindus whom he regarded as infidels and considered nothing more pleasing to God than their humiliation and disgrace. He looked upon "the realisation of the poll tax (jazia) as a means of heaping calumny and scorn upon infidels". He was unhappy over the Muslims adopting Hindu manners and customs—marriage ceremonies, funeral observance etc. Shaikh Ahmed declared them wholly reprehensible and worthy of rejection. He desired that the Muslims should live like the Arabs of the time of the prophet and should refuse to assimilate any of the way of the vast majority of the non-Muslim inhabitants of India. In short, according to him, purification of faith through Quran and Hedith, as interpreted by the just and right-minded Ulemas, a strict adherence to law and abandonment of all innovations, were the main principles of Islam which it was the bounden duty of all Muslims to follow. The Shaikh worked hard to propagate his views. He corresponded extensively with many prominent men and influential nobles belonging to different walks of life, and made every effort to propagate his views among them. His correspondents included Khan-i-Khanan Sikandar Lodi, Mahabat Khan, Murtaza Khan, Shaikh Farid Bukhari, Qulich Khan, *et al.* Evidently, he, through these great personalities, acquired influence in the court of Jahangir, and, small wonder, his influence played a great part in building the psyche of Jahangir and then propelling him to order the execution of Guru Arjan Dev, the fifth Guru of the Sikhs. Murtaza Khan, the governor of the Punjab, who put into execution the order of Jahangir was a devout follower of the Shaikh Ahmed Sirhindi.

The waxing influence of the Sunni party on the court waned to a great extent when Jahangir was awakened to the political imperative of keeping the non-Muslims particularly the Hindus with them. The influence of Nurjahan who was a votary of Mian Mir, the Sufi saint of Qadirya Order having full belief in liberal attitude towards the Hindus and other non-Muslims was also no less important for the dawn of the new awareness on Jahangir. But the Shaikh did not relent and according to Dr. Tara Chand, despite the action taken against him by Jahangir, Shaikh Ahmed's mission spread. The Shaikh died in C.E. 1624-25. The work was taken by his son, Masum, who took upon himself the work of the dissemination of the views of his father. He achieved wonderful success in his mission.

On Shah Jahan's accession to the throne, Masum redoubled his activities probably because he was aware of the religious propensities of Shah Jahan. He was very successful in his mission and through his vigorous propaganda reaped a rich harvest of converts. Among his adherents was Aurangzeb who attended his lecturers while he was the governor of Multan. Masum also grew fond of the prince and on the eve of his pilgrimage to Mecca predicted that in the struggle for the throne Aurangzeb would be victorious. He addressed a letter to Aurangzeb when he was appointed to lead the Imperial forces against Balkh, in which he expatiated upon the virtues of holy war (jehad).

Muhammad Masum's son, Shaikh Saif-ud-din (b. 1639-40) was adopted by Aurangzeb as his preceptor and guide.

In this way, the orthodox mode of thinking had its full play during Aurangzeb's reign who under its influence tried hard to translate Shaikh Ahmed Sirhindi's ideas into action. Incidentally, these actions seemed to serve the political purpose as well. Aurangzeb could justify the murder of his brothers and the imprisonment of his father on ground of his plans to promote the cause of Islam. Moreover, by stopping the entry of the Hindus into government service, he could oblige the Muslims on a large scale—which fact secured the purpose of creating Muslim vested interest and of encouraging the Muslim orthodox reaction.

The remarks of A.N. Ikram and S.A. Rashid are very pertinent in this respect. They say "Shaikh Ahmed Sirhindi contributed largely to the swing of the pendulum from Akbar's heterodoxy to Aurangzeb's vigorous ultra-orthodoxy rather than a return to Babar and Humayun's policy of laissez faire. The rhetoric and appeal of Shaikh's letters kindled religious fervour and resulted in a religious revival which took some time to bear fruit which completely altered the history of this subcontinent."

Aurangzeb, after ascending the throne, hastened to convince the orthodox Muslims in the empire of their having backed the right horse. He began with puritanic measures. In the second year of his reign he discontinued the celebration of Naurauz (first day of the Solar year). A few years later, music and dancing were prohibited. *Jharokha Darshan* was discontinued on the ground that it smacked of human worship. Severe punishments were awarded for anything that was construed by the theologians as violating the spirit and even letter of Islam. Permissible length of the beard was fixed at four fingers and offenders against this order were penalised.

But most of these restrictions were of a general nature and covered all communities. Non-Muslims were singled out for discriminatory treatment in four specified fields; public services, construction and repair of temples, conversion and taxation. Regarding the discrimination of the Government towards the Hindus in services, the remarks of Shri Ram Sharma are pertinent. He says that "towards the end of Aurangzeb's reign there was a smaller number of Hindus occupying the Mansabs of 1000 and above, than the number of similar mansabdars towards the end of Shah Jahan's reign. But the decrease in number becomes still more significant when we take into account the increase in the total number of mansabdars which rose enormously in the reign of Aurangzeb. In 1657 under Shah Jahan there were 8000 Mansabdars in all, whereas in 1690, the number of mansabdars had risen to 14556...the percentage of the Hindus in the higher ranks of the services could not have been more than 50 per cent of what it was towards the end of Shah Jahan's reign."

Besides this, a careful planned attack was launched prohibiting the construction and repair of temples. Even before Aurangzeb, in the reign of Jahangir and Shah Jahan, there were several instances of destruction of temples, but then these occurrences were generally part of military operations. In 1659 the year of his coronation, he ordered that "no new temple should be allowed to be built although it was decided 'according to our common law' the standing temples should not be demolished".

The Emperor became more and more aggressive with the passage of time. In C.E. 1666, the stone railing of the famous Keshav Rai temple of Mathura was razed to the ground by Imperial orders. In April 1669, he issued a general order for the destruction of all schools and temples of Hindus. "Orders were now sent to the governors of all the provinces that they should destroy the schools and temples of the infidels and put an end to their educational activities as well as the practices of the religion of Kafirs.[62] It was followed by the demolition of the temples on a large scale. In August, 1669, the temple of Vishvanath at Benaras was demolished. The temple of Gopinath in Benaras too was destroyed about the same time. A plan was also made to destroy the Shiva temple of Janganwari in Benaras, but it was somehow given up for the time being.

Similar destructions were ordered in the various Rajput States, Ajmer, Ujjain, Bengal and other provinces of the Empire.

Lest the order should go amiss, strict administrative measures were taken. He appointed officers in all the sub-divisions and the cities of the Empire to enforce the regulations of Islam with the destruction of Hindu places of worships one of their chief duties. The Qazis were actively associated with the new policy.[63] The officers were told that reports of destruction of temples would be looked upon as authentic only if they bore their seal and attestation.[64]

Like other non-Muslims particularly the Hindus, the Sikhs too, according to Khafi Khan, came in for their share; their temples were being destroyed and their leaders externed (Muntakhab-ul-Lubab ii 651-52). Mirza Inayat Ullah Ismi tells us in *Ahkam-i-Jahangiri* that in compliance with the orders of the Emperor and with the consent of the local Qazi the Sikh Temple in the town of Buriya in the parganah of Khizrabad of the Sarkar of Sirhind had been demolished and a mosque had been raised on the site.[65] Sayyad Zafar Darvesh was appointed in-charge of that mosque to guide prayers and say benedictions. Some Sikhs attacked the mosque and killed the Darvesh. The Emperor rebuked the Qazi and his father who was the head of the police. According to Hari Ram Gupta, this sort of incidents had become a common occurrence.[66]

In the field of taxation, the policy of discrimination was launched with great vigour. *Jazia* and pilgrimage taxes were re-levied. Custom duties on the Muslims were fixed 2.5 per cent and in the case of the Hindus at 5 per cent. It was ordered that in the lunar year the Muslims should pay 2.5 per cent and the Hindus 5 per cent on the price of their cattle.

Another important factor which formed an important part of the texture of the mood and policies of Aurangzeb was that the economic foundation of the Empire was shaking. Jagirdari system on which the whole Mughal administration was built was suffering a serious crisis. According to the mansabdari system, each mansabdar was a public servant and in his case appointment carried military obligations. He was required to keep a contingent of troops to be requisitioned by the Central Government if and when necessary. For his own maintenance as well as for the maintenance of his contingent, he was granted a jagir which was in fact an assignment of revenue accruing from a particular piece of land as per assessment regulations of the Central Government. The system worked well for some time, possibly because of the moderation and sagacity of the mansabdars and of those at the helm of affairs. But some time later, it began to suffer from cracks and the condition of the peasants became very deplorable. The reasons were not far to seek. The assessment of land being related to military obligations, the centre, in its anxiety to make the mansabdars keep large contingents, was often prone to over assessment of land.

The jagirdars would pass on the incidence of over-assessment to the cultivators. Added to this, was the practice of frequent transfers of the assignees. This introduced an element of contradiction between the interests of the Imperial administration and the individual jagirdars. A jagirdar whose assignment was liable to be transferred any moment and who never held the same jagir for more than three or four years at the most, could never follow a far-sighted policy of agricultural development. On the other hand, his personal interest would sanction any act of oppression that conferred an immediate benefit upon him even if it ruined the peasantry and so destroyed the revenue-paying capacity of that area for all time.

The peasants suffered in another way also. It was the general law in the Mughal Empire that if any robbery occurred within the area of a jagirdar or a faujdar, he was obliged either to trace the culprits and recover the loot or to restore the lost property himself. It offered the officials an excuse to sack any village they chose to suspect resulting in untold misery for its people.[67]

To such circumstances as these, the peasant reacted differently. Some of them left their lands and migrated to fresh areas. Some migrated to the estates of some neighbouring zamindars where condition of service was comparatively better—not because they were not exploited by the zamindars but because they were welcomed by the zamindar for his own selfish ends; some, the more daring among them, made common cause with men of similar persuasions and took to loot and rapine. The village and the areas which refused to pay taxes were known as *Zortalab*.[68] Such villages were often protected by fortresses or forests of hills. In the case of such peasants' rising assuming large proportion, community of faith or caste acted as major rallying forces. This being so, it was but natural on the part of the government to be sensitive to the stirring of peasants, and the rallying forces.[69]

In this connection, the role of zamindars was significant. These people were different from jagirdars. The *jagirdars* were appointed by the imperial orders but the zamindars by custom had emerged as the leaders of villages and had small armies of their own. Moreover, the zamindar unlike *jagirdars* were often the leaders of caste or tribal groups, and, as such, they yielded considerable influence. Not unoften, their influence was utilised for the collection of the revenue, but with the lapse of time and especially during Aurangzeb when the seams appeared in the agrarian structure, the zamindars gained in stature and reputation with the result that the government and *jagirdars* began to apprehend danger that they might defy their authorities. The zamindars, on their part, were fully aware of the predicament the authorities were faced with as also the psychosis of the men in power. They spared no pains to pose themselves as the protectors and defenders of the peasants against official tyranny. According to Irfan Habib, "as the number of stirrings of homeless peasants grew and peasants took to arms themselves, it became possible for the zamindars to organise them into a still larger bandits' armies for the dismantling the Mughal Empire and expanding their Chiefship".[70]

The government committed to the Sunni views of Islam and determined to perpetuate tottering jagirdari-based economic structure even in face of serious contradictions could ill-brook Guru Tegh Bahadur who was committed to refashion the society on Sikh principles and whose followers who were largely the peasants and in some cases zamindars were seething with discontent for the reasons enumerated above.

Recently, authors like Athar Ali have tried to prove that Aurangzeb's religious policy was motivated by certain political imperatives; it did not spring out of his religious convictions. He says "Aurangzeb having killed his brothers and imprisoned his father, justified the seizure of the throne on the ground that he was more competent than his father. This he tried to prove through military successes but in or about 1666, it was clear that the reckless policy of expansion begun in 1659 had proved to be a complete failure. A new post-facto justification had to be found for his crime of 1658-59." And this justification was provided by an emphasis on the Islamic character of the Empire apart from the desire to resume his prestige on a new basis. Other issues were also involved which impelled the Emperor to pursue the discriminatory policy in religious sphere. This policy was pursued to overcome the difficulties. So long as the empire was expanding, the nobility, as a whole, could satisfy its ambition by looking forward. Once, however, it became clear as it did in 1667, that any rapid expansion was not to be expected, the urge for promotions among the mansabdars could not be easily satisfied. In such a situation it must have been tempting for the Emperor to enlarge the avenues of income for them and gratify the nobility by progressively ousting the Hindus including Rajputs from the jagirs.[71]

But our study leads us to conclude that the views of Athar Ali are not convincing. We understand as we have spelled above, that Aurangzeb did act under the influence of the Sunnis' reaction to which he himself subscribed and the chief exponent of which was the Shaikh Sirhindi.

It is not correct to say that after his failure to prove that he was superior to his father, he followed the Sunni line to justify his stand and resurrect his impaired image. Aurangzeb's stance from the very outset was that of a Sunni Musalman, and most of his actions *vis-à-vis* the non-Muslims particularly the Hindus were rooted in the conceptual framework of the Sunnis. That he justified the murder of his brothers and the imprisonment of his father through the instrument of Sunni policies does not prove anything except that he was politically sagacious and shrewd.

A few scholars obsessed with the idea of finding secularism in everything aver that Aurangzeb was extremely selfish and power-hungry and had no qualms for Islam and his policy, therefore, was to promote his own self-interest. He killed Sarmad and a dozen of other Sufis who were certainly Muslims. A careful study of the executions of these Muslims during his reign will show that all such Muslims were either liberal Muslims or the supporters of Dara. Hence the conclusion is inevitable that Aurangzeb's policies towards the non-Muslims was what Sunni thought warranted.

The Guru, on the other hand, was against such a policy as it did not conform to the dharma ideology of the Sikhs according to which all human activities are legitimate, provided they are based on and governed by Dharma. Such actions as do not answer the demands of the test of Dharma are wrong and lead to evil results. Dharma ideology in the context of social and political reconstruction meant social responsibility or imbibing of moral values, social equality, transcendence of narrow or exclusive considerations of creed, caste, clime, sex and colour, rejection of hereditary principles as the basis of social order or ethics. The precept of justice formed important fact of Dharma ideology which figured prominently in the thinking of the Gurus. The scientific socialism as it developed in the West in the 19th century and as we understand was not known then, but justice as a principle of human relations was known and was vehemently advocated by Guru Nanak and his successors. As a matter of fact their close identification with the lower and down-trodden classes and their constant endeavours for their welfare and upliftment were conceived in a desire to plead for social justice. Similarly, the exploitation of the poor by the rich was held inhuman and unjust. The concept of justice propounded by Gurus extended to the political sphere as well, where it was regarded as the very basis of government and administration, while the actions of perpetrators of exploitation, injustice and tyranny were exposed and criticised and appeals made to their good sense and reason to mend themselves and the sufferers at their hands were exhorted to conduct themselves with self-respect and fearlessness. The cheap and senseless imitation on their part of their rulers' ways with no other object than that of placating them was exposed as an act of passive submission to a tyrant and was dubbed an act of shameful cowardice. Compromise with injustice or tyranny was thus shown as a great evil and fearlessness and heroism a great virtue. In the fight between good and evil, God's support, it was assured, would be always on the side of good, for he is verily the smiter of the evil and the wicked and since time immemorial has been the unfailing protector of the good as against their enemies. In all Jugas (aeons) He has been creating saints and in all Jugas they have been protected by Him. Harnakash, the tyrant, was smashed by Him and Prehlad the victim saved. Moreover, the ethical principle involved in the fights of the famous Hindu heroes like Rama and Krishna was accepted. Each one of them had to fight against evil and each one of them gained victory through the help of God. The Sikh devotees themselves were presented as '*Mall*' or *Pehalwanra* (wrestler) in the wrestling bouts between good and evil by Guru Arjan Dev ji.

The ideas of the Gurus held great attraction for the Hindu trading class who found in them an adequate answer to the Brahmanical exclusiveness and rigidity as well as a Catholicity of outlook which could enable it to build up harmonious relations with the Muslim rulers in the interest of their economic benefit. These ideas also presented opportunities to the lower classes like Jats to improve their social status. The result was that the Sikh movement grew rapidly in both number and resources. The growing popularity of the movement alarmed both the Muslim rulers and orthodox Brahmans. The former being the ruling community, their hostility mattered most. The Mughal government prompted by the Muslim orthodox section, began to view the Sikh movement with deep suspicion and resorted to strong measures to stifle it. It did not hesitate even to execute Guru Arjan Dev as per law of Yāsa.

Guru Hargobind reacted to this situation in the manner of a hero determined to hold aloft the banner of Dharma. His war with the Mughals was in the true spirit of Dharamyudh. His successor, Guru Har Rai was similarly inspired when he led his troops to the bank of river Sutlej in order to block the passage across the river of Aurangzeb's troops marching in hot pursuit of Dara Shikoh. The moral issue was very clear. Dara symbolised the forces of good where his adversary Aurangzeb unleashed tyrannical policy of religious intoleration, Guru Tegh Bahadur felt called upon to denounce it and to campaign against it in the true spirit of Dharamyudh tradition coming down to him from his illustrious predecessors. Guru Gobind Singh in his famous writing 'Bachittar Natak' has beautifully depicted the Dharam character of Guru Tegh Bahadur's martyrdom.

"The Lord (Guru Tegh Bahadur) protected their paste mark and sacred thread.
And performed a mighty deed in the Kali age.
To protect the good, he spared no pains.
Gave his head but uttered not a groan,
For the protection of righteousness he did his noble deed,
Gave his head but not his ideal." (*Bachittar Natak*)

Moreover, what Guru Gobind Singh meant by the word Dharma comes out very clearly from what he said about his own mission in the same work.

For this purpose am I born into the world,
For Dharma's sake I am sent here by Lord,
Ordained to promote Dharma here and there
And to demolish the wicked and the evil-minded
Let all good people understand that I am born for this purpose;
To promote Dharma, to protect the good, to extirpate the evil. (*Bachittar Natak*)

In view of this, it is wrong to presume that Guru courted martyrdom in order to protect Hindu religion alone. The special mention of *Janeu* (sacred thread) and *Tilak* (paste-mark) the distinguishing marks of the Hindus has been made only to highlight the point that the Hindus were the main target of the tyranny of the government of the time and in no case the conclusion can be drawn that the Guru's main or sole objective was to protect the Hindu religion.

In fact, the Guru Tegh Bahadur's struggle was against '*Adharma*' the greatest epitome of which was Aurangzeb and the Sunni character of his government. To achieve his purpose the Guru propagated his mission among the people. During his tour in eastern parts of the country, in the Bangar and in the Malwa region of the Punjab, the Guru's message brought new awakening among them who began to rally round the Gurus. The conceptual framework and methods of operation conforming to that were sharply different from those of Aurangzeb. The clash was inherent in the situation.

But how did the matter come to head? Knowing the mind and the official orders of Emperor Aurangzeb, the imperial intelligence seem to have been closely watching the movements and proceedings of Guru Tegh Bahadur since his return to the Punjab. The Sikh movement, as history knows it, had been looked upon with suspicion and disfavour ever since the accession of Emperor Jahangir to Mughal throne. In 1665 C.E., the Guru was hauled up at Dhamdhan and was allowed to proceed on his tours to the east and north-east only after Raja Ram Singh had given surety for the Guru's conduct. As it is well-known that the Emperor's attitude towards the leaders of non-Muslim faiths, especially after 1669, became very hostile, the royal intelligence and news-reporters were encouraged to interpret the large gatherings and money-offerings at the congregation of the Guru as a dangerous augmentation to his influence and resources like those of Hafiz Adam of Banoor—a religious leader of the Pathans—whom Emperor Shah Jahan had in 1632 banished from India on account of his activities.

How far misrepresentation could go may be evident from what the author of *Siyar-ul-Mutakhirin*, Ghulam Hussain, has written on the subject.[72] "This man (Guru Tegh Bahadur) finding himself at the head of so many thousands of people, became aspiring and he united his concerns with one Hafiz Adam[73], a Muhammadan faqir. These two men no sooner saw themselves followed by multitudes implicitly addicted to their chief's will then forsaking every lowest calling, they fell to subsisting by means of coercion and extortion, laying waste the whole province of the Punjab."

Malcolm and Cunningham basing their conclusions on the information supplied by the author of *Siyar-ul-Mutakhirin* have written: "Choosing for his haunts the waste between Hansi and Sutlej, he subsisted himself and his disciples by plunder."

It has also been alleged by some scholars that the Guru encouraged the refractory elements of the country to enter his service and prepared the people in general for a rising against the government. But before anything substantial could be achieved, he was overpowered, taken captive and brought to Delhi under a strong military escort. The statement has been rejected. Macauliffe and I.B. Bannerjee and many other scholars have said that Guru being just a Tyagi—renuncient, a lover of meditation and solitude, could not have done all this. We do not approve of their approach as it ignores the heroic aspect of Guru's personality. As a matter of fact, the Guru was a supreme embodiment of both *Bhakti* and *Shakti* in the manner of his great father.

The most effective manner of repudiating the views of Ghulam Hussain is on the basis of historical facts and the tenor of Dharam-ideology of the Guru. The statement of Ghulam Hussain suffers from serious factual inaccuracies. The Guru did not make common cause with Adam as he could not do it because the faqir had since long left India for Medina and passed away (1642). The Guru even on his own did not raise any special army to come into clash with the Mughal government.

In fact the Guru had neither the intention nor the means of leading any insurrection against Emperor Aurangzeb. The author of the *Siyar-ul-Mutakhirin* admits in unambiguous words that "the companions of Tegh Bahadur moved about like mendicants. The wearing of swords and arms was not customary among them." And the rebellion could not be expected to succeed against the great Mughal Empire without a strong trained army equipped with necessary arms.

It is possible that the Guru had a few of the persons from the army of Guru Hargobind. But certainly these persons did not insist on extortion or coercion of the people. Guru Hargobind and Guru Har Rai maintained their armies out of their devotees' offerings, could Guru Tegh Bahadur not do so? Besides this, 'coercion and extortion' even in special circumstances and as a means to righteous ends did not fit in with the essentials of Dharma as understood by the Sikhs. Coercion and extortion imply unprovoked aggression on less strong people. Could we be justified in believing that the author of the slogan 'fear not, frighten not' aggressed against un-offending people to secure subsistence for his militia even assuming that there was no other evidence in the form of his own writing and Sikh traditions to prove that he did not. Apart from the substantial body of his poetry incorporated in the *Guru Granth Sahib*, large number of *Hukamnamas* are available with us which deal with secular matters but nowhere the Guru had betrayed the compromises for worldly requirements if he had made any.

Dr. Fauja Singh's remarks in this connection are very pertinent. "In situation such as this where the cause had such a wide appeal, there was and should be no need resorting to coercion and extortion as a means of subsistence; in fact voluntary offerings were mistaken as forcible collection." There is no doubt that thousands of people, when he travelled in Malwa and Bangar, swarmed round the Guru but they cannot be taken as soldiers of revolt. No contemporary record shows that there was any outbreak of revolt on the part of the Sikhs, although under the impact of the Guru's preaching, the process of mass awakening had set in. The Guru's motif in doing so against the Mughal government was neither personal nor political power nor subsistence by coercion and extortion as stated by *Siyar-ul-Mutakhirin*, rather it was to prepare the people for the protection of righteousness (Dharma) against the tyrannical (Adharmic) policies of Aurangzeb.

The Story of Kashmiri Pandits

On May 25, 1675[74], a deputation of sixteen Brahmans headed by Kirpa Ram son of Arhu Ram reached Anandpur Sahib. They waited upon the Guru and told him how keen Aurangzeb was to convert the land of Kashmir into the land of Muslims, and in obedience of the *firman* of Aurangzeb how cruelly Iftikhar Khan, the governor of Kashmir, was implementing the contents.

There is a strong tradition that Guru Tegh Bahadur, on hearing the heart-rending tale of Kashmiri Pandits, was deeply absorbed in pondering over the problem. Suddenly, the young Gobind Rai entered the Darbar and was astonished at the complete silence reigning everywhere. After a brief pause, he quietly enquired from his father as to the cause of this silence.

The Guru explained to the boy the agony of the Pandits and significantly remarked that the only way was that some great person should make supreme sacrifice. Instantaneously, the boy asked his father whether there was anybody more worthy of this sacrifice than he himself. The hint was very clear. The Guru appreciated the bold and courageous reply of his son and forthwith decided to offer himself for the sacrifice. He told the Brahmans to go to their homes and tell the authorities that they would have no objection to changing their religion if Guru Tegh Bahadur was first prevailed upon to embrace Islam.

From this, the conclusion was drawn by some historians, that the Guru made up his mind to suffer martyrdom for them or for the Hindu religion alone. The protagonists of this view quote Guru Gobind Singh in their support. "Guru Tegh Bahadur did a miracle in the Kali Age by protecting the frontal mark and sacred thread of the Sikhs." But this view is unfounded. To regard the appeal of the Brahmans as the sole cause of the Guru's execution is to misjudge the real cause of the Guru's execution as also to circumscribe the width of the Dharamyudh ideology. The truth appears to be that the advice of the Guru to Kashmiri Brahmans brought the matter to the fore. The process of spreading Sunni ideas and converting the people to it, particularly at the places contiguous to north-western frontier and Punjab where the orthodox section of the Muslims was the strongest, received a severe jolt and setback at the hands of the Guru.

The intelligence reported all this to the Emperor. Busy as he was in quelling the Pathan rebellion in north-western frontier[75], he had neither the time nor perhaps the inclination to make extensive enquiries about the activities of the Guru. He was, as we know, already suspicious of the Sikh movement, which his grandfather, Emperor Jahangir, wished to put an end to at one stroke and which it was in keeping with his policy and orders "to put down the teachings and public practice of the religion of these mis-believers". He, therefore, readily believed all the intelligence reports and wrote to the governor of Lahore to arrest Guru Tegh Bahadur and ordered that he might be fettered and detained in prison.[76] The Lahore governor passed on the imperial order for compliance to Abdul Aziz Dilawar Khan, the faujdar of Sirhind, who in turn asked the circle Kotwal of Ropar, Nur Muhammad Khan Mirza, in whose police jurisdiction lay Anandpur to arrest the Guru. The order, however, was kept secret.[77]

The Guru, apprehending all this, conferred guruship on his son on 8th July, 1675. According to *Bhat Vahi Talauda Pargana Jind* and *Guru Kian Sakhian* the Guru performed the installation ceremony by offering the usual marks of guruship: a tilak on the forehead, 5 pice and one coconut. Having done, the Guru voluntarily left Chak Nanaki on 10/11th July, 1675. He was accompanied by Bhai Mati Das, Bhai Sati Das son of Hira Nand Chhibbar and Bhai Dayal Das son of Mai Das of Jalhana Balaut. It is not precisely known as to what prompted the Guru to leave Chak Nanaki. Irvine basing his inference on the information furnished by *Ferukh-Sayyar Nama* says that the Guru intended to proceed to the Ganges to bathe. However, the probable view is this that the Guru intended to see Emperor at Delhi to plead the case of the non-Muslims with him, and in the event of the Emperor's unfavourable reaction suffer the consequences.[78]

As the Guru arrived at a Muslim village, Malikpur Rangharan near Ropar on his way to cross the Sutlej for his onward journey, he was arrested by Mirza Nur Muhammad Khan, the Kotwal of Ropar, on July 12, 1675 (Sawan 12, 1732 Bk) and sent to the faujdar's headquarter at Sirhind where he was detained in prison. This was done deliberately, possibly at the behest of Aurangzeb, because it was reckoned wrongly though that the influence of Naqshbandis especially of their suave and charismatic leader, Shaikh Saifuddin would persuade the Guru to change his stand and cease to take up the case of the non-Muslims. Guru Tegh Bahadur's determination never to relent from his chosen path utterly disappointed them.

The Guru was kept in prison in Sirhind Fort[79] for about four months by faujdar Dilawar Khan waiting for further orders from the Emperor who was at Hasan Abdal at that time or from the governor at Delhi. According to Sarup Singh, the author of *Guru Kian Sakhian* (Sakhi No. 26) Guru Tegh Bahadur was taken to Delhi in an iron cage on receipt of a *parvana* (letter containing order) from the imperial headquarters. The Guru reached Delhi on Maghar Vadi, 1732 Bk. The Guru was kept in the Kotwali of the city under the instructions of the Subedar of Shahjahanabad who had acted as per instructions from Aurangzeb at Hasan Abdal.[80]

Our writers have narrated many interesting anecdotes about this period many of which cannot stand the test of historical scrutiny. One of the writers refers to the meeting between Aurangzeb and the Guru and narrates graphically what transpired between them. But the whole story cannot be authenticated because Aurangzeb, at that time was at Hasan Abdal. All the same, the tradition has a sure basis, but relates to the earlier occasion when in 1665 C.E., the Guru was arrested from Dhamdhan[81] and produced in the Imperial Darbar at Delhi.

Another story is narrated regarding the escape of the Sikhs, particularly Bhai Uda from the prison. "On witnessing the martyrdom of Mati Das, the Guru's other Sikhs were terrified. They went to him at night and represented their danger. He told them that they were free to leave them. They pointed to the chains of their feet and asked how their release could be effected. Through the Guru's miraculous interception, their fetters fell off, the prison doors all stood open and the guards snored in the sleep of neglect."[82]

It is said that at this juncture, Bhai Gurditta and Bhai Uda escaped. According to still another version, the Guru helped in the escape of some of his Sikhs because he wanted to send through them a message to his son at Chak Nanaki. As the account goes, they were instructed to carry the insignia of guruship to Chak Nanaki to offer on his behalf to his son.

All these accounts do not stand the test of historical scrutiny. There were only three men arrested along with the Guru and they were all executed and hence the question of helping others including Bhai Gurditta and Bhai Uda does not arise. Again the content of the story suffers from serious drawbacks and is un-Sikh like. To give credence to the display of miracle by breaking the fetters of the Sikhs in prison is positively against the Sikh ethos. Similarly, the story that the Sikhs were sent to Chak Nanaki to offer the insignia of guruship falls to the ground, because the Guru had performed the nomination ceremony of his son, Gobind Rai, as his successor prior to his departure from Chak Nanaki.

However, it is agreed that there was some communication between the Guru and his son, although it was extremely difficult. One such example was the exchange of two Slokas Guru Tegh Bahadur wrote to Guru Gobind Singh:

> All power shattered, humanity in fetters, availeth nothing at all. Nanak prays, 'O save all' as thou saved elephant while it made a call on the verge of drowning.

Guru Gobind Singh, in reply, uttered:

> "With power, fetters break, availeth all in grace Divine.
> All is in Thy hand, O Lord, Nanak seeks aid Divine."

Almost all Sikh writings on Guru Tegh Bahadur make a reference to these Slokas and give different interpretation of them. Of those Dr. Trilochan Singh's interpretation which is based on Bhai Mani Singh's evidence, seems nearest to truth. According to him Guru Tegh Bahadur in his Sloka expressed his deep concern over the helplessness of the people, whereas Guru Gobind Singh in his reply expressed his confidence to handle the situation with God's Grace.

During the eight days in Delhi Kotwali tortures of different types were inflicted on the Guru. On the first day of the Guru's arrival that is to say, on Thursday, Qazi Abdul Waab Vora offered the Guru three alternatives *viz*: (i) to show miracles, or (ii) to embrace Islam, or (iii) to prepare himself to court death. He refused to show miracles as it was contrary to Sikh faith. He also refused to accept Islam. He, however, chose the last alternative. On Friday and Saturday, the attempts were made to persuade the Guru to show miracles or accept Islam. Persuasions having failed, coercion was employed to make the Guru agree to one of the two alternatives. During the next four days, the Guru was subjected to severest tortures: burning sand was poured on his body; he was not allowed to drink water. Thursday, the 11th of November, 1676 was the fateful day. The Guru's three dearest disciples and companions Mati Das, Dayal Das and Sati Das were persecuted to death. Bhai Mati Das was tied to two poles and sawn asunder. Bhai Dayal Das was boiled alive to death in a cauldron of hot water and Sati Das was roasted alive with cotton-wool wrapped round his body. Even this could not shake the Guru.

When the authorities saw that the Guru was adamant, they ordered the executioner Jalal-ud-Din of Samana to sever the head from his body as according to Muslim law or *Shariat* person formally invited to embrace Islam becomes liable to death if he refuses to accept invitation. In a split second, it was done. According to Muhammad Ahsan Ijad, "When brought to the court (at Delhi), he (Guru Tegh Bahadur) refused to become Muhammedan and was executed." In the words of the contemporary scholar Munshi Sujan Rai Bhandari of Batala, the author of the *Khulasat-ut-Twarikh*, completed in 1697 "within twenty-two years of the great event, Guru Tegh Bahadur having been kept in prison by the Ameers of the kingdom, was executed under the orders of the Emperor Alamgir in 1086 al Hijri, corresponding to the 27th Alamgiri" (November 11, 1675 C.E.). The Guru allowed himself to be be-headed without uttering a groan. He remained wholly composed in the face of the executioner's blow. His was no stoic fortitude, but a decided gesture to force a moral issue. It was no passive submission but a positive decision to confront the tyrannous rule of Aurangzeb.

As per order of the government the Guru's body was to be quartered and exposed to public view, obviously to impart stern warning to all such people as dared to go against the wishes and order of the Emperor. But because of prompt and timely action of Sikhs, this could not be done. According to *Bansavali Nama*, a furious storm raged immediately after this brutal deed was accomplished.[83] In the confusion caused by it, a man, named Jaita (later Jiwan Singh) the resident of Dilwali Gate, Delhi, dashed out of the crowd and instantaneously disappeared with the holy head of the Guru. He shared his secret with his neighbour Bhai Nanu, the son of Bhai Bagha. Bhai Uda, the resident of Ladwa was also taken into confidence. All three decided to take the Guru's head to Anandpur.[84] They placed the holy head in a basket which was covered over carefully and started their journey to their destination. They made five halts on the way. Their first halt was at Bagpat, the second at Karnal, the third at Anaj Mandi (Sis Ganj Ambala), the fourth at Nadha Sahib (Near Chandigarh) and the fifth at Kiratpur. They left Delhi early in the morning of 13th November and reached Kiratpur on the 15th November, 1675. From there the holy head was taken to Anandpur with full honour and cremated there with proper ceremonies on the 16th November, 1675. Gurdwara Sis Ganj marks the place where the holy head was cremated. Guru Gobind Singh performed the obsequies with dignity and reverence. A pyre of *sandalwood* was constructed and *Atar* (scent) of red roses sprinkled on the head which the young Guru solemnly placed on the pyre. He then repeated the preamble of the Japji and ignited the pyre with his own hand. While the head was being cremated, the Sikhs in congregation sang hymns of the Guru. They called to memory and spoke of Guru Tegh Bahadur's philanthropic and self-sacrificing deeds. The Sohila (the last of Sikhs' five daily prayers) was then read with a concluding benediction and sacred food distributed. When Guru Gobind Rai reached home, the reading of the Guru's hymns from Adi Granth started, and this was continued for ten days. He consoled his mother and the Sikhs and greeted Bhai Jaita affectionately, exalting the whole tribe by conferring on it the blessing "Rangrete Guru Ke Bete *i.e.* Ranghretas are the Guru's own sons." The Guru bestowed the same affection on Nanu and Uda.

When Lakhi Shah Lubana who was a famous contractor of Delhi and had a deep faith in the Guru was informed of the martyrdom of the Guru by Uda, he felt much concerned. Bhai Uda and Lakhi Shah made a plan to get hold of the sacred headless body. Lakhi Shah, being a renowned contractor, was well-known among Muslim officials and did not arouse suspicion of any kind. He emptied his carts laden with lime near the Red fort and went in retreat to his home in village Rakabganj.

On the way, taking advantage of the darkness and the carelessness of the Mughal guards, Lakhi Shah, helped by his sons, Nagahia, Hema and Harhi, and Dhuma son of Kanha whisked the sacred body away on Maghar Sudi 6, 1732 Bk. (November 12, 1675) in one of their carts to their home.[85]

Apprehensive of the governmental reprisal, Lakhi Shah and his sons built up a pyre inside their house and set fire to it the same evening. A little after dark, it is said, that a police party arrived at the scene in search of the body, but finding the house consigned to flames and the inmates weeping bitterly, returned. After the cremation was over, the ashes were collected and put in a metal vessel called 'gagar' in Punjabi parlance and buried the same on the spot.

Lakhi Shah along with a few other Sikhs came to Anandpur with a part of sacred remains. Guru Gobind Singh received them with honour, and as says *Guru Kian Sakhian*, he hugged Lakhi Shah. Lakhi Shah narrated the Delhi events. The entire *Sangat* was overwhelmed with emotion. Guru Gobind comforted the Sikhs and bade them not to give way to grief. He said, "My father accepted what was God's will as the course most agreeable. The event will be remembered as long as the sun and the moon continue to shine.[86]

Importance of Martyrdom

The ninth Guru's martyrdom had far-reaching consequences. The Guru's was a bid, more conscious than powerful, which was made to instil among the aggrieved the spirit of manliness to rise against their oppressors. No doubt, no immediate success was possible, but the heroic manner the Guru sacrificed his life, blazed a new trail in so far as it was a commitment to an open struggle against the organised oppression of the state. The execution eliminated, possibility, if any, of an honourable settlement with the Imperial government. After that, it was clear that unless the Sikhs were prepared to go under, they had to wage a struggle against the aggressive fanaticism and oppressive administration of the Mughals under Aurangzeb.

The first course of going under was ruled out, almost instinctively, by the kind of training the community had received in the past. Selecting the second course as the only one compatible with the honour and mission of Nanak and his successors, Guru Gobind Singh plunged himself into the preparatory measures for the inevitable struggle of the future. In this context, various vital concepts were streamlined, elaborated and concretised. The organisation of the Sikhs too underwent great changes. The idea of Dharamyudh which was so far implicit became prominents and a complete theory of struggle (Dharamyudh) was evolved with a view to explaining its aims and boosting the morale of the participants.

Whereas, Guru Tegh Bahadur's martyrdom marks the high water mark of determination of the Guru to suffer for one's lofty aims, it exposed the barbarous character of the Sunni state headed by Sunni Mohammedans. Its immediate result was that it inflamed all right-thinking people. The Imperial Darogha or Superintendent, Khwaja Abdulla who had held Guru Tegh Bahadur in custody in Delhi was overwhelmed by remorse. He gave up his position and came to Anandpur to live in Guru Gobind Rai's company. As says a historian quoted by Indu Bhushan Bannerjee in his *Evolution of the Khalsa*, the whole Punjab began to burn with indignation and revenge. A most daring demonstration of this temper was an attack on Emperor Aurangzeb himself. This is how, the incident is reported in the *Ma-Asir-i-Alamgiri*: "On Friday, 27th October, 1676 while the Emperor was returning from Jama Mosque and had alighted from the boat in order to mount the movable throne (Takhti Rawan), an ill-fated disciple of Guru Tegh Bahadur (Sic) threw two bricks, one of which reached the throne. He was seized by royal retinue and ordered to be made over to Kotwal." Sikhism became the symbol of resistance. With Guru Tegh Bahadur's martyrdom, it acquired a new consciousness of its strength and self-sufficiency. It had inevitably entered upon the final stage of its evolution.

As the execution of the Guru Tegh Bahadur strengthened the resistance against Aurangzeb's policy, it prepared the way for the final stage in the evolution of the Khalsa. This event convinced Guru Gobind Rai that the tyranny had myriad layers and in order to combat it, all-out effort would have to be made. He had to forge instrument to achieve this purpose. With this end in view, he inaugurated the Order of the Khalsa a brotherhood of the persons committed to ending the tyranny of all kinds even by employing force as a last resort. But certainly, the permission to the Khalsa to use force should not be confused with imbibing the spirit of militarism. In militarism, force is employed for the sake of force, aggression or self-aggrandisement, but in Sikhism it was made subject to some major qualifications *viz.* (i) it must be for a cause, legitimate and noble, (ii) it must be a remedy of the last resort.

The martyrdom of the Guru had another effect. It kindled a new spirit among the Hindus, especially of the northern India for whom the Guru apparently made sacrifice. They became poignant in their criticism of the religious policy of Aurangzeb and the most potent among them began to think in terms of resisting the tyranny of the government. The hardened attitude of the Hindus served two-fold purpose. Firstly, it saved the Hindu religion and culture from total annihilation, and secondly, it contributed a lot so far as the downfall of the Mughal empire was concerned.

Nature of the Guru Tegh Bahadur's Struggle. Did the Guru have any political objective?

Regarding the true nature of Guru Tegh Bahadur's struggle, different opinions have been expressed. But before we draw our conclusion, it would be advisable to discuss all the questions connected with the struggle. Was it for the protection of religion? If so, which religion—the Hindu or the Sikh religion or for the religion in general? Could the struggle be viewed as one for the protection of civil rights like freedom of conscience or as one for the freedom of the country from the foreign yoke? Was there any political motive involved in it?

No communal considerations seem to have weighed with the Guru in his struggle. The fact that many important Muslims suffered executions at the hands of the Mughal Emperor and many Muslims such as Saif Khan offered support to the Guru in his mission shows that the struggle was not confined to the non-Muslims alone. The ordinary Musalman was also not happy. It is true that he had no difficulties like those of non-Muslims but socially, politically and economically, his lot was no better than that of the Hindus or the Sikhs. Guru Tegh Bahadur seems to be well-cognizant of this fact. Therefore, it would be a rather narrow view if it is argued, as it is often done, that the Guru's struggle was inspired only by the desire to protect Hindu religion. That such a thing was not absent from his mind may be conceded, because his son and immediate successor Guru Gobind Rai had made reference to it in his autobiography. But that it was an independent sole aim with the Guru is open to question. Guru Gobind Singh himself, lest his reference to Tilak and Janju should be taken in narrow sense, had added at the same place that the sacrifice of his father was for dharma. Here the significance lies in the absence of any prefix, Hindu or Sikh. The truth seems to be that the Guru's lofty object of building up a popular resistance to the tyranny of the government automatically covered the protection of Hindu religion or even Sikh religion; which too, had been dealt with severely. Moreover, the Dharma in the context of our culture, covers almost every aspect of life where the principle of justice or righteousness is involved. Anything done for a noble or righteous cause is something done for Dharma. When we say that the struggle of Guru Tegh Bahadur was for Dharma, it does not mean a struggle for religion much less a struggle for Hindu or Sikh religion. It was called so because the cause involved in it, the fight against tyranny, was a noble and righteous cause.

It is stated, sometimes, that the attempt of Guru Tegh Bahadur was for the protection of civil rights, particularly the freedom of conscience. To a modern mind saturated in consciousness of his rights such a statement would be only right and acceptable; but the consciousness of rights is comparatively a recent development in our country. In our civilisation till the advent of the British, emphasis used to be more on duties than on rights. And it is this thing which determined our concept of tyranny. Tyranny, then, was no infringement of rights but a departure from duties. The ruler was believed to owe certain duties to his subjects. If he departed from them the result was tyranny. It was in this sense that the word tyranny was understood by the Gurus in those days.[87]

Nor is it correct that the freedom of the struggle of Guru Tegh Bahadur was for the freedom of the country from a foreign yoke. Perhaps, nothing will be farther from truth than this, for, neither the concept of Hindustan as we understand it today was there, nor was the government of the Mughals considered a foreign yoke. The people who were born and died here who looked upon this land as their native land and who had been here for several generations, could not, in fairness, be regarded as foreigners.

Did Guru Tegh Bahadur have any political object? If arousing the people to resist against tyranny is a political objective, then the answer may be 'yes'. The Guru emphasised the Dharma character of his approach again and again when he was charged with sedition. His repeated statement[88] that he was a *darvesh* (recluse) having nothing to do with the overthrow of the government brings into relief the same dharma aspect. But as it had been made clear earlier that by 'dharma' the Guru meant anything done for a noble or righteous cause, no other cause was as righteous as the resistance to the tyranny of the Mughals.

The approach as well as the struggle of Guru Tegh Bahadur exactly fits in with the spirit and general tendency of the Sikh Movement in the past. The movement had already committed itself to resistance to all forms of tyranny including the political. What is more, the employment of force for a purpose like this had been recognised as legitimate. Guru Hargobind and Guru Har Rai had maintained troops and encouraged training in the use of weapons. Hence we can say that the aimed struggle of Guru Tegh Bahadur was a continuation and no distortion of the character of the Sikh movement.

VISION AND TEACHINGS

Guru Tegh Bahadur stood for the same system of metaphysical, moral, social and spiritual values as had been underscored by his predecessor Gurus. Still his writings which are incorporated in the holy *Guru Granth Sahib* have an identity of their own for the manner in which certain elements in the Sikh philosophy are expressed and highlighted.

The Guru composed 59 *Padas* and fifty-seven *Slokas*. The *shabads* are distributed over fifteen Ragas or musical measures. The Slokas or couplet's form the concluding portion of *Guru Granth*. As such, these are ceremonially intoned as part of epilogue when concluding an open congregational reading of the scripture on a religious or social occasion and are thus more familiar hymns of *Guru Granth Sahib*.

From the perusal of his compositions it is not difficult to surmise that the most striking element was Guru's unflinching faith in God, Omnipotent, Omniscient, Omnipresent, most-High and most Gracious, the ultimate ground of all that exists, and his desire that people should at once realise Him. The stage of realisation is a stage of perfect peace and happiness. The Guru calls this stage, as *NIRVAN PAD* also called *AMAR PAD, ACHAL PAD* and *MUKAT PAD*.

Nirvan in Sikhism is not extinction of flame called life (as it is understood in Jainism), it is a sublime experience, an exaltation of self and perfect communion with God. With this realisation the seeker of truth not only attains illumination of the highest wisdom but also complete freedom from fear and mundane authority and identity of the self with all human beings. It is the mysticism of action which instead of turning inwards and closing the soul could open wide its gates to the universal love.

Among Sikhs, the state of *Nirvana* is an all-absorbing state of boundless joy. "God is there and the soul is in God. Mystery is no more. Problems vanish and darkness is dispelled, everything is flooded with light. The man who attains *Nirvana* state feels truth flowing into the soul from the fountain-head like an active force. He can no more help spreading it abroad than the sun can help diffusing its light. For the love, which consumes him is no longer simply the love of man for God, it is the love of God for all men. Through God, in the strength of God, he loves all mankind that impelled Guru Tegh Bahadur to sacrifice his life for the freedom of worship of the Brahmans, although he did not agree with their mode of worship of the Deity. But how to attain *Nirvan Pad*? In order to charter steps to reach that stage the Guru makes a few important observations. He notices that life is short, it is hastening away. It is transient, yet man could make it worthwhile, but he has not. The transience of human existence is highlighted in many of his verses. It is compared to a hill of smoke, a mirage, shadow of a cloud, a wall made of sand. It is but a bubble on water, a night's dream. Human connections of wife, friend, son are tentative, temporary and they forsake when misfortunes over power. But man perceives not the Reality and continues to be engrossed in Maya—delusion. He is swayed by worldly attachments and passions. He is a victim and prisoner of his vanity, conceit and wilful ego.

He runs after physical pleasures. Even in old age, he is not amenable to the effect of the Divine Light. All through life, such a person walks in darkness. The worldly pleasures keep him/her in bondage and he/she is prevented from cultivating higher elements in his nature. The real pity is this emphasis on transitoriness of world and men and their mutual attachments have led some scholars to conclude that the Guru was a prophet of gloom. But this is absolutely wrong. The Guru nowhere applauds the hermit's life; nor does he belittle human life. On the contrary, he calls life a priceless gift which is obtained after countless wanderings. The human body is preciously obtained. The life is an opportunity. It is meant for good-doing for acquiring merit for getting liberation. Undoubtedly, there is repeated mention of death and stress has been laid on its inevitability but that is done, not to instil fear, but to make man alert to harness his resources and powers to find what Reality is and what is perennial and vital as also to prompt him to be pro-active in his quest for Reality and to take practical recourses to reach the stage of feeling union with

Him. According to Dr. Harbans Singh, "Guru Tegh Bahadur's perspective is life-offering not life-denying." The imagery of transience in his BANI does not create a static effect. Nor does it encourage quietistic withdrawal or retreat from the world. It arouses man to an awareness of what he is capable of achieving in spite of the limitations of his earthly existence. He is made conscious of his negative propensities and of the lusts and illusions of his personal life. He is reminded of how he is wasting away his opportunity and how he can yet make a fresh start. He is challenged for verdict, challenged to make his decision. He is under no determinist fate. The choice is his. The life should be lived for a purpose for an ideal. It is impermanent but not false. Man should participate in it, but not allow himself to be entangled in it. It is never too late for him to turn to the spiritual path. Nothing is yet lost, says Guru Tegh Bahadur (*Ajhun Kachhu Bigrio Nahi)*, there is still time for man to rescue himself.[89]

When the Guru refers to the people indulging in acts to satisfy their lowselves, he is pained and he pours out warnings prodding him/her, not to be enmeshed in material things and look beyond these. He should not be a victim of Maya, which in reality is a delusion, certainly a wall interposing between God and man. Maya is a reality but in the sense that it is also an activity of God but it cannot be the desideratum. It is certainly an obstacle on the path of Moksha which according to the Guru meant liberation. Certain scholars instead of seeing through the compositions of the Guru, have jumped to the conclusion that Guru's Bani was a lamentation. An absurdity indeed! Guru Tegh Bahadur's *Bani* is a call to man to transcend his given state, attachments with relations and friends whose devotion was merely a show and certainly not something to eternally go along with him/her, and keeps him/her to the higher levels of consciousness and insight. In this life itself, man can achieve the final goal of liberation. Guru Tegh Bahadur's approach to problems is unique. He looks at life from the point of view of death. He looks at the eternal reality of human existence from the point of view of transience of the material world. He points to the horizon of joy and peace from the valley of sorrow and suffering. He belittles our petty human relations to awaken in us everlasting bonds of human and divine love. He asks us to live in submission and humility before God, to attach the state of fearlessness and communion with God to serve society as an inspired fighter for freedom and human dignity. In wistful compassionate and moving words, he brings forth with vivid subjective reality, our selfishness, cowardice shamelessness, vanity and crazy discontent. From the Elysian heights on which he stands, he contemplates the sorrows of man and with a clear and serene vision proclaims the great truth to men of all ages.

What exactly causes man's malaise and bondage. The Guru clarifies that primarily it is the human ego (Haumei) that is the root cause of the melody. It separates man from Reality and beclouds the divine spark within him. This leads to spiritual blindness or nescience (Agyān). This alienates one from universal will and mistakes what is unreal from the real. An ego-centred person is ruled by passion and instincts and is unable to free himself/herself from the stranglehold of the five impulses—*Kama* (sensuality), *Karodh* (anger), *Lobh* (avarice), *Moh* (attachment) and *Ahankar* (pride). Guru Tegh Bahadur very artistically brings out this point in the following hymn where he says[90]:

> Ensnared in greed the mind drifts and drifts,
> Craving more and more for wealth
> In seeking worldly pleasure.
> My mind comes to acute grief,
> As it craves before everyone.
> Going like a dog from door to door,
> Blind to the devotion to God,
> Man wastes a precious human life,
> He is shamelessly heedless,
> Even when people chide. (*G.G.S.*, p. 41)

How can this ego or self-love be overcome? Fasts or pilgrimages are of no avail, as these are mere externals, mere forms. One involved in them remains unaffected like a rock in water.

Equally unavailing are the wearing of ochre robes as how a dress can be a substitute for enlightenment. Guru remarks:

Bear this in mind,
Wasted is the life of the man,
Who is devoid of devotion to God.
He who keeps fasts and goes to pilgrimages
And performs acts of piety,
Without purity of mind and self-control
Useless are all his pious acts
Believe me, I speak the truth.
Place a stone in water,
It remains hard and unsensible.
Such is the lot of a man,
Who is devoid of love of God.[91]

(*G.G.S., Rag Balawal,* p. 831)

The course to get rid of ego or self-love is to be enlightened and the first step towards it is the awakening that Transcendent is the only ultimate Truth. The awakening must be accompanied by an intense love of God, utter surrender to him and living one's life in accordance with *Hukam* or God's will. Personal fervour and purity are admired. By devotion and absorption in *Nām*, one gains control of the mind and evolves a one-pointed awareness of the absolute Being. True knowledge then dawns, ego is dissolved, one feels union with God and then he/she operates in this world to improve upon it like Bodhisatvas of yore. The will of God is not a challenge to the conceited and darkminded will of man, it is a voice from the unknown strong enough to shake the soul out of the wildness and shed light on his path. The end of man's material world and being is dust, but the goal of the spirit is not the graveyard but the realisation of Truth and Light. An enlightened man thus never sits idle (cross-legged but works on and on in this world shouldering social responsibilities and operating in the light of Spirit/Light within him/her. The closer a person is to the spirit, the nobler he/she is and such a person would ever be eager to collaborate in transcendent task. Being close to the Almighty, the Sole Creator and All powerful, such a person is beyond fear, the salient quality of God Himself.

God responds to devotion of such a person who works in the will of God (Hukam) and even engages himself/herself in the long remembrance of God's name. One need not go out anywhere seeking for Him. "He resideth within you as fragrance resideth in the flower or reflection in the mirror."[92] Guru Tegh Bahadur refers to God by various names such as Ram, Hari, Gobind, Gosain, Prabhu, Murari and Brahma. He is recalled by beneficent names. But he does not conceive Him as an anthropomorphic entity.

Repeatedly and constantly, the Guru exhorts one to turn to God. Loving devotion to God is the basic for one seeking spiritual realisation. The Guru assures that God responds to the prayers and appeals of the people who are sincere, unselfish, humble and genuine seekers of Truth. He cites as a proof the legendary story of the elephant which has taken strong roots in Indian tradition. The incident is said to have taken place on the banks of Brahmaputra. It is quite possible that the hymns having reference to this elephant were addressed to the people of this region. Reference to this legendary story is found in the composition of other medieval saints also. An annual fair is held in the place on the day.

According to this legend, an alligator once caught hold of an elephant and tried to drown it by taking it into deep water. In this difficulty, the elephant remembered God and was saved. Guru Tegh Bahadur seems to suggest that even this animal who concentrated his mind on his Creator and sought His help was blessed with the state of fearlessness, which enabled him to free itself from the clutches of the alligator. If human beings remember God sincerely and inwardly, His light descends on them as grace and illumination and under this inspired state of soul, they can work wonders.[93] The thought and remembrance of God inspired the elephant with the state of fearlessness and he freed himself from the alligator and was saved from drowning. Guru Tegh Bahadur identifies liberation (Mukti) with the state of fearlessness and this state is achieved by sincere souls through the love, devotion and Grace of God. Bhakti in a way vitalises one to live in consonance with the will of God and *ipso facto* in a stage of fearlessness because hundred per cent surrender to God is just like absorbing oneself in Him to feel union with Him, the state of close identity with God and of fearlessness. Bhakti thus becomes a sort of Shakti. Shakti in Sikhism is thus a part and parcel of Bhakti because the user of Shakti was required to work—even sacrifice, to see the will of God operating without any let and hindrance. In this sense Sikh Shakti is suffused with devotion to God because if it is not so, the Shakti (power) would turn out to be a power of a tyrant and not of God. A true Gurmukh or Gyani is the embodiment of Bhakti and Shakti. Guru Tegh Bahadur was one such example. In this context he was inspired by his inheritance. As he was rightly fed on Gurbani, the compositions, of the Gurus, he had noticed for himself that this theme was at the heart of the teachings of his predecessor Gurus.

According to Bhatt Kalsar, all the Gurus right from Guru Nanak to Guru Arjan Dev had lived the life of Raj Jogi.[94] Guru Hargobind underscored this point by wearing two swords representing Miri (temporal) and Piri (spiritual) aspect of Guru's office, which were the same as *Bhakti* and *Shakti*. Guru Tegh Bahadur, therefore, besides remembrance of God received military training. After he was elevated to guruship, he travelled widely and in course of his travels conducted himself in the manner of a chief, fond of horse-riding, wearing arms with the Kalghi on his turban, followed by a large retinue, just as his warrior father used to do.[95] According to Dr. Fauja Singh, "Bhakti was to be continued with Shakti to offer full view of the Guru's philosophy of life."

Guru Tegh Bahadur uses two terms for those who have perceived the Reality—Gurmukh and Giani. The Gurmukh as distinguished from the Manmukh is one who is committed to the Divine, is a God in flesh to use Marcus Aurelas' term, makes full use of that indwelling power which can keep a man unsullied by pleasures, untouched by insults and impervious to evil. He is a competitor in the greatest of all contests, the struggle against passion's mastery. He is imbued through and through with uprightness, welcoming whole-heartedly whatever falls to his lot and rarely asking himself what others may be saying or doing or thinking except when the public interest requires it. He confirms, having his attention fed on his own particular thread of universal web seeing to it that what falls him must be for the best—for his own directing fate is itself under higher direction. He does not forget the brotherhood of all rational beings.

According to Dr. Trilochan Singh, "The Gurmukh is marked for self-control, fixity of purpose and cheerfulness under ill-health or other misfortunes. His character is an admirable combination of dignity and charm, and all duties of his station are performed quietly and without much ado. He gives everyone the conviction that he speaks as he believes. He indulges neither in despondency nor is puffed up gaiety, nor has anger and jealousy. His kindliness, sympathy and sincerity all contribute to give the impression of rectitude that is innate and calculated."

Guru Tegh Bahadur's own description of Gurmukh is the aptest. He utters:

He who grieves not in grief,
From avarice, pleasures and fear is free,
And considers gold as good as dust,
Who indulges not in slander or flattery,
And is immune to greed, attachment and vanity,
Who in happiness and sorrow, self-poised remains,
Who discards all hopes and desires
Who lives detached from the world,
And is not affected by lust and wrath.
In such a one shines the Light of God
The man who receives the Guru's grace,
Discovers the secret of spiritual life,
Sayeth Nanak, the soul of such a man blends,
With God, as water mingles with water.

(*G.G.S.*, p. 1427)

NOTES AND REFERENCES

1. Trilochan Singh (Dr.): *Guru Tegh Bahadur*, p. 7.
2. *Ibid.*, p. 19.

3. Dr. Fauja Singh: *Guru Tegh Bahadur—Martyr and Teacher*, p. 12, Punjabi University, Patiala, 1996.
4. *Ibid.*, pp. 13-14.
5. Bhai Mehra was a devout Sikh of Guru Hargobind.
6. Gian Singh: *Twarikh Guru Khalsa* , p. 264.
7. Trilochan Singh: *Guru Tegh Bahadur*, pp. 94-95.
8. *Ibid.*, p. 93.
9. Sarup Singh Kaushish: *Guru Kian Sakhian*, Sakhi 13, Singh Brothers, Amritsar I.
10. Bhat Vahi Talauda.
11. According to Bhat Vahi Purbi Dakhni, Tegh Bahadur and his family were present at Prayag on the fullmoon of the day of Baisakhi, 1719 Bk (19 April 1661).
12. *Bhat Vahi Purbi Dakhni.*
13. *Bhat Vahi Purbi Dakhni*, Khata Barhton ka.
14. *Bhat Vahi Purbi Dakhni*, and *Guru Kian Sakhian.*
15. Till the discovery of *Bhat Vahis* it was generally thought that the Guru Harkrishan made only a vague hint regarding the succession of Guru Tegh Bahadur.
16. Kesar Singh: *Gur Bilas Padshahi* 10, p. 22. According to the author many Guruships were set up.
17. Kesar Singh Chhibber: *Bansavli Nama.*

    "Agon sunia bai manjian; Guru ban baithe han bahutere"

    Sukhbir Singh: *Gurbilas Patshahi* 10, p. 11.

    Sabas Guru nij kahave; bai baithe manjian lai

    Sikh Sakha je kochal aavai; bai thavar su bhet chadhavei.
18. Trilochan Singh: *Guru Tegh Bahadur*, p. 121, Delhi Gurdwara Parbandhak Committee, Delhi, 1967.
19. *Bhat Vahi Talauda*, Pargana Jind.
20. Sarup Singh Kaushish: *Guru Kian Sakhian.*
21. *Bhat Vahi Multani Sindhi.* Also refer to *Bhat Vahi Talauda Pargana Jind.*
22. According to *Guru Kian Sakhian* by Sarup Singh Kaushish. Makhan Shah along with his son Lal Das and his wife visited Bakala in 1721 Bk on the Diwali Day (Bhata Vahian).
23. Karam Singh Historian says that Labanas or Van were never traders or vanjaras. From this negative arguments that Makhan Shah was not a trader, Karam Singh draws another conclusion that Makhan Shah must have been a Masand who had brought the money of his diocese on the Baisakhi day as it was the custom then obtaining among the Masands to do so on the Baisakhi day or Diwali day. According to Dr. Trilochan Singh "Had Makhan Shah been a Masand of Gujrat, he would have certainly

waited till the dispute was settled. Sewa Das in his Parchian calls him both a Lubana trader and *Masand*. Garja Singh in *Shahid Bilas* by Sewa Singh calls him 'a trader', having deep faith in Sikhism. We agree with Garja Singh.

24. Makhan Shah vowed to donate 500 dinars. *Guru Kian Sakhian* mentions only 101 gold muhars. Bhat Vahi Bijlauton Ki gives same figure. We however attach more weight to the evidence of Bhat Vahis because firstly these are the earliest available record and secondly the Bhatts were the persons who had the intimate knowledge of the Sikhs and their history.
25. *Bhat Vahi Khata Bijlauton Ka*. Makhan Shah Beta Dase Ka Pota Arthe Ka ...Lal Chand, Makhan Ka Chandu Lal Makhan Shah ka Solji Istri Makhan Shah ki...Sal Satrai Ikis ki Diwali Shanivar Ke Din Bakala Gaon Maye Aya. Guru Tegh Bahadur Ji Mehal Durbar Ikotar Sau Mohar Bheta ki. Seth Dhuma Nai Aaya beta Kahna Ka.
26. Macauliffe, M.A.: *Sikh Religion,* Vol. IV, p. 334. Dewan Durga Mal requested the Guru that he, being too old to carry the heavy responsibilities of the post, be relieved and in his place, his nephews Mati Das and Sati Das be appointed as Dewan and minister of the Darbar respectively. He further recommended the appointment of Dayal Das, the son of Bhai Bula, who fell martyr in Guru Hargobind's battle of Amritsar as the household minister.
27. According to *Suraj Parkash*, Dhir Mal was attacked before he left for Kiratpur. According to Gian Singh he had already left for Kartarpur and was overtaken by hot chase.
28. Trilochan Singh: *Guru Teg Bahadur,* p. 168. 'Prithi Chand Guru Bansavli' and the writings of Harji Mina and Meharban clearly indicate that they had a complete control over the Hari Mandir and the people of Amritsar. Even the author of *Dabistan-i-Mazahib* first came into the contact with Meharban before he met Guru Hargobind and Guru Har Rai.
29. Opposition to the Guru was organized which clearly indicates that it was the work of some rival sect.
30. *Bhat Vahi Purbi Dakhni*. Khata Jalhana—Punjabi University, Patiala.
31. According to Kesar Singh Chhibber and a few other records, Guru Tegh Bahadur bought three villages: Makhowal, Mathar and Lodhipur, originally founded by two Pathan brothers, Makhe Khan and Kate Khan. The Guru selected Makhowal village for the temple, and his residence. It was named Nanaki Chak—the name which has come down in revenue records as 'Nanaki Chak'. The habitation of the city which was extended towards the southeast was named Anandpur either by the Guru Tegh Bahadur or by Guru Gobind Singh. According to *Guru ki Sakhian* by Sarup Singh Kaushish, Guru Tegh Bahadur founded the Chak Nanaki on Harh 21, 1722 Bk.
32. The statement of Bhat Vahi is not clear regarding this point. It may even mean free gift. The general view, however, is that this land was purchased from the Raja of Bilaspur (*Hoshiarpur Distt. Gazetteer*, Bhai Santokh Singh, Bhai Sukha Singh, Bhai Gian Singh), Teja Singh and Ganda Singh in

their *A Short History of the Sikhs*, p. 52, say that Guru Tegh Bahadur paid Rs. 500/- for it. But they have not given their source of information. Hence, we may conclude that some payment was made though we cannot say what exactly it was.

33. Trilochan Singh: *Guru Tegh Bahadur*, p. 178.
34. The place is about half a mile from Punjabi University, Patiala. The place was named so after the name of its founder Saif Khan. The place is now called Bahadurgarh after the name of the fort which was named after Guru Tegh Bahadur.
35. Bhat Vahi Jadobansian Khata Bartian as quoted by Dr. Fauja Singh in his book *Guru Tegh Bahadur Martyr and Teacher.*
36. S.K. Bhuyan: *Badshah Buranji*, Sakhi, 116.
37. The shrine is known by the name of Chacha Phagu Sangat.
38. The memory of the Guru is still fresh in the minds of people.
39. Harbans Singh: *Guru Tegh Bahadur*, p. 57, Manohar, 1994.
40. "Sikh Relics in East Bengal" by G.B. Singh in the *Sikh Review*, July 1965.
41. Natha was the third in succession to Almast.
42. Sylhet provided war elephants to Guru Gobind Singh.
43. Trilochan Singh: *Guru Tegh Bahadur*, p. 230.
44. Shah Akbar, Shah Bagmar, Shah Saran, Shah Safi and Shah Kamal.
45. "From a manuscript document in possession of Mahant Bachitar Singh of Gurdwara at Dhubri, it is learnt that Ram Singh counted upon the Guru's ability to undo the effects of the black arts for which Kamrup had a reputation all over India and which in the estimation of the Raja were sure to be against himself and his army." Quoted from *Guru Tegh Bahadur* by Trilochan Singh.
46. *Hukum Nama* 15, 16 in the book *Hukum Namas Sri Guru Tegh Bahadur Sahib* by Dr. Fauja Singh, Punjabi University, Patiala, 1967.
47. *History of Assam* by Sir E.A. Gait, p. 155.
48. *Anglo Assamese* Relations, by S.K. Bhuyan.
49. Assamese Records are very clear about it.
50. Letter of Raja Singh's widow as quoted by Dr. S.K. Bhuyan.
51. E.A. Gait: *History of Assam*, p. 155.
52. Ved Parkash: *The Sikhs in Bihar*, unpublished doctoral thesis submitted to Patna University, p. 85.
53. Refer to the Religious Policy of the Mughal Emperors by Sri Ram Sharma.
54. Refer to the Research Paper entitled *The Martyrdom of Guru Tegh Bahadur* by Dr. Ganda Singh.
55. *Bhat Vahi Multani Sindhi Karta Jallanon Baluton Ka.*
56. *Bhat Vahi Talauda Pargana, Jind.*

57. The tank has been deepened and widened and a big fair is held every year.
58. *Sakhi Pothi*, Sakhi 5, p. 10.
59. *Ibid.*, Sakhi 11, p. 14.
60. *Ibid.*, Sakhi 13.
61. Mian Ahmad Shah, author of *Twarikh-i-Hind* (1823) was the first historian who held Ram Rai alone responsible for the whole tragedy. Mufti Ali-ud-Din, author of *Ibrat Nama* and Bute Shah, author of *Twarikh-i-Punjab* also subscribed to this view. Bute Shah particularly tried to wash Aurangzeb's hands off the crime showing him filled with excessive remorse after the execution (Badshah of degar kasan tasaf namadaid). The view is totally wrong in face of the positive evidence to the contrary. Ram Rai had openly expressed his suspicions of the Emperor's intentions in summoning the child Guru Harkrishan to Delhi. He offered condolence to Guru Harkrishan's mother on her son's death. He met Guru Tegh Bahadur at Delhi on his return from his eastern tour.
62. Muraqat-e-Abul Hasan 202 as cited and translated by Sri Ram Sharma in the *Religious Policy of the Mughal Emperors* (New York, 1962, p. 30).
63. S.S. Bal: *Awakening the Oppressed.* Guru Tegh Bahadur's role and its reasons. Article published in *Sikh Review*. Guru Tegh Bahadur's Martyrdom Tercentenary Number.
64. *Muraat-e-Abul Hasan* 202, by Sri Ram Sharma *op. cit.*, p. 130.
65. *Kalimat-i-Taiyyabat*, p. 115.
66. Rumbling of Imperial wrath and back to Makhowal—Dr. Hari Ram Gupta. *Sikh Review*, Guru Tegh Bahadur's Martyrdom Tercentenary Number.
67. Fauja Singh and Gurbachan Singh Talib ed.: *Guru Tegh Bahadur*, p. 57, Punjabi University Publication, 1996.
68. *Ibid.*
69. *Ibid.*
70. Irfan Habib: *The Agrariana System of Mughal India*, Asia Publishing House (1963), p. 193.
71. M. Athar Ali: *The Mughal Nobility under Aurangzeb*, pp. 98-99.
72. *Siyar-ul-Mutakhirin*, English Translation by Dr. Raymond, R. Combroy and Co., p. 85.
73. Hafiz Adam (Banoori) left Hindustan and died at Medina in 1643 C.E. Therefore his making a common cause with Guru Tegh Bahadur is historically wrong. For details refer to Nazeer Ahmed Deobandi, *Tazkar-at-ul-Abdin*, pp. 124-25, Mirza Muhammad Akhtar's *Tazkar-i-Auliya-i-Hind Wa Pakistan*, p. 401. Even otherwise too being a disciple of Mujadid Alf Sani, there was no possibility of his joining the Guru.
74. The information regarding this date is obtained from *Bhat Vahi Talaudi Pargana Jind*. The evidence of Bhat Vahi is corroborated by *Guru Kian Sakhian* by Sarup Singh Kaushish.

75. On the 17th April, 1674, Aurangzeb had to leave Delhi for Hasan Abdal where he reached on the 26th June, 1674. The purpose of the Emperor was to restore Imperial prestige in the Pathan land from Qandhar to Attock where the different tribes had defied the Mughal authority, and had risen in open revolt against it. Aurangzeb stayed there from June 1674 to December 1675.

76. *Siyar-ul-Mutakhirin.*

77. Irvine: *Later Mughals,* p. 79: Mohammad Ahsaba Ijad's *Ferukh Siyar Nama*, f.13.a.

78. The Emperor at the time was in the north-west frontier. Considering the difficulty of communication in that age, it is not surprising that Guru had no idea about the exact whereabouts of the Emperor. The normal expectation was that he would be in his capital, Delhi.

79. Sarup Singh Kaushish: *Guru Kian Sakhian*—Sakhi 26. The Guru was kept in prison for about over three months.

80. That the Emperor was not physically present at the time of Guru Tegh Bahadur's martyrdom has been proved by the positive evidence of *Ma-a-Sir-i-Alamgiri* written by Saqi Mastan Khan serving in the administration of Aurangzeb. This was the best primary source for the study, other contemporary sources being not very useful as *Alamgiri Nama* covers only ten years of the reign of Aurangzeb and *Muntakhaab-ul-Lubab* contains no reference to the Guru. *Khulasat-ul-Twarikh* makes a very brief reference to the Guru's martyrdom. *Ma-a-Sir-i-Alamgiri* gives the dates on which the Emperor left Delhi for Hasan Abdal and returned from there.

    (i) The Emperor started on 7th April, 1674, 11 Muharrani for Hasan Abdal on Friday, the 26th June, he reached Hasan Abdal. (ii) On Thursday the 23rd December 1675, 15th Shawaal began the return journey from Hasan Abdal. The first stage was Kala Bagh... The Emperor reached the garden of Lahore on Friday, the 21st January, 1676. (iii) On Thursday the 24th February, 1676, the Emperor left Lahore.... On Monday, the 27th March 1676, the Emperor arrived at Delhi, original text, 153 and English Translation J.N. Sarkar, p. 94.

81. There are different views regarding the place of arrest. According to *Mehma Parkash*, the arrest was effected at Dhamdhan; according to *Bansavli Nama* at Malikpur, according to Koer Singh Kalal and Sukha Singh at Delhi and according to Santokh Singh's *Gurpartap Suraj Granth* and Gian Singh's *Path Parkash* and *Twarikh Guru Khalsa* and Macauliffe's *Sikh Religion at Agra*. We hold that the Guru was arrested at Dhamdhan for the first time, at Agra for the second time and at Malikpur finally. Refer to *Bhatwahi Joda Bansian Khata Bartian*, and *Bhat Vahi Talauda Pargana, Jind*. Regarding the arrest at Agra, it was effected while Guru sojourned at Agra on his return from eastern tour by the local Kotwal under the wrong impression that the earlier order of Aurangzeb to arrest the Guru at Dhamdhan still stood, and that was the reason that Guru was set at liberty (See *Guru Tegh Bahadur—Teacher and Martyr*). The story that the Guru sent a shepherd-boy to the bazaar with gold coins to make purchases

on his behalf so that he might arouse suspicion among the people and on inquiry might disclose identity of the Guru to the Kotwal of the city is not true: firstly, because the Guru was not such a person as to need such stratagem to disclose his identity, and secondly, the Guru was well aware that the seat of government was Delhi and not Agra during Aurangzeb's time. Besides, in the presence of the solid evidence that the Guru was arrested at Malikpur, the afore-referred story stands nowhere.

82. Macauliffe's *Sikh Religion,* V, p. 383. The account is essentially based on Bhai Santokh Singh's *Suraj Parkash*. Ras xi.
83. Kesar Singh Chhibber: *Bansavli Nama* "Tis Din Andheri, gardh gubari rahi".
84. *Bhat Vahi Multani Sindhi* (Punjabi University, Patiala).
85. Bhat Vahi Jadobansian Khata Barhton Kanoton Ka. Lakhiya beta Godhuka, Nagahiya Mema Harhi bete Lakhiya ke Barhtiya kanaunt, Naik Dhuma beta Kanhe Ke Bijlaut Guru Tegh Bahadur ji Mehl Naven Ki loth uthae lae, Sal Satraj Sai Battis Manghsar Sudi Chhat Shukarwar Ko Dag Diya Adh Ghari Rat Gai.
86. Sarup Singh Kaushish, *Guru Kian Sakhian,* Sakhi 28.
87. Dr. Fauja Singh: *Execution of Guru Tegh Bahadur*: A New Look, a research paper.
88. Sohan Lal: *Umdat-ul-Twarikh, daftar I*, pp. 48-49.
89. *Guru Granth Sahib*, Dhanasari, p. 726.
90. *Guru Granth Sahib*, p. 411.
91. Trilochan Singh: *Hymns of Guru Tegh Bahadur*, p. 32.
92. *Ibid.*, p. 105.
93. *Guru Granth Sahib*, Jai Jai Vanti, p. 1352.
94. Sahib Singh: *Steek Bhattan De Swayyai*, p. 121, Singh Brothers, Amritsar, 1987.
95. Recently a painting of Guru Tegh Bahadur has been discovered from the Sangat Tola Gurdwara, Dacca. In this painting, the Guru has been depicted as warrior with a Kalghi on the head and a falcon perched on the hand. Besides, there are several references with regard to his hunting expeditions on the course of his travels.

CULMINATION

11

GURU GOBIND SINGH

(b. 1666 C.E.; d. 1708 C.E.)

PRE-KHALSA PHASE

Guru Gobind Singh, the tenth pontiff of the Sikhs, was born on December 22, 1666[1] at Patna. He was the only son of Guru Tegh Bahadur, and Mata Gujri. At the time of his birth, Guru Tegh Bahadur was at Dacca engaged in missionary and organisational activities. Bhai Dayal Das, the chief of the *sangat* at Patna, immediately despatched a letter to Dacca giving the happy news which was carried post-haste by Bhai Mehar Chand and Bhai Kalyan Chand. There was a great rejoicing at Dacca.[2] Gobind Rai passed his early years at Patna under the care of his mother, grandmother and maternal uncle, Kirpal Chand. Not much is known about the Guru's childhood but this is certain that he was a prodigy and he created the impression in the minds of the people that he was destined to be a great man. His unassuming, yet assertive utterances, his amiable and affectionate manners made him the cynosure of all. Pandit Shiv Dutt,[3] an erudite scholar, Raja Fateh Chand Maini and his wife Kishori Devi,[4] Nawab Rahim Bux and Nawab Karim Bux (Muslim Zamindars) were the first few persons who recognised the child and turned to be his admirers.[5] Sikh tradition says that both the Nawabs admired and venerated the child so much that they went to the extent of offering a garden and a village for the comfort of Gobind Rai and his people.[6]

He indulged in child-like pranks like the breaking with pellets the earthen pitchers of women, who came to draw water from a well situated in the arena of his house. He would gather round himself a happy band of frolicsome playmates, run about on the banks of the placid Ganges, pull out boats, splash water, swim, wrestle, box and fight. He would then bring his contingent back home, give them presents and feed them. His mimic battles at the head of his bands evoked memories of Nanaki, his grandmother, of the grand old days of her husband, the sixth Guru who had challenged the might of the Mughals. To her particularly it looked as if her grand-child was rehearsing the role, he might be called upon to play in times to come. No constraints were, therefore, applied on him so that he might develop his lithe and lissomeness without let and hindrance. He often played the commander, loved bows, arrows, swords, lances *et al.* His favourite games were sham fights, military exercises and manoeuvres, raising of troops, holding of courts to settle the disputes among his playmates.[7] All what he did portended high profile role which he was destined to play.

In 1670, he was summoned by his father to reach Nanaki Chak, a city founded by him in the Shivalik Hills in the Punjab.

He then set out for Nanaki Chak along with his mother, grandmother, maternal uncle, Kirpal, and quite a number of attendants. En route he stayed at Danapur, Kanshi, Prayag, Lucknow, Chandausi, Mathura, Brindaban, Hardwar, Saharanpur, Buria, Lakhanpur.[8] According to *Bhat Vahi Multani Sindhi*, they arrived at Lakhnaur on the 13th September, 1670 (Asu Sudi 9, 1727 Bk). At Kanshi, Ayodhya and Mathura, he discoursed with Brahmans who were amazed at his brilliance and sharp intellect. At Lakhnaur, his formal education started. Bhai Sahib Chand taught him Gurmukhi and Sati Das gave him lessons in Persian. It was here that he received homage from a Muslim Pir, Arif-ud-Din, to the surprise of the latter's followers whom the Pir, later told that the sight of Gobind Rai had revealed to him the secrets of Infinite.

Sayyed Bhikhan Shah of Thaska, a pious Muslim saint, is also said to have made obeisance to the Guru at this place. As the story goes, he held upon his palms two earthen vessels when he saw the child. The latter touched both. By this, Bhikhan Shah judged that he would treat all, Hindus and Muslims alike.

Child Gobind Rai reached Nanaki Chak in February 1671 along with his father. He was received affectionately by the Sikhs.

Bhai Bajjar Singh and Bhai Sahib Singh continued to impart training in martial art and Punjabi respectively. Qazi Pir Muhammad replaced Bhai Sati Das whose services Guru utilised elsewhere and a fresh teacher Bhai Harji Das was appointed to teach Sanskrit.

Soon he acquired proficiency in languages such as Persian, Sanskrit, Punjabi, Hindi and Arabic. Besides, he learnt the art of warfare, horsemanship and swordsmanship and handling of weapons such as lance, bow and arrow, musket and matchlock. His interaction with Hindu poets and bards who had been there at Anandpur, either to seek refuge or to feel free to develop their art engendered in him a sensitive response to literature. After finishing his lessons, he would ride into forests with Kirpal Chand and his other associates for hunting.

When he was nine, a group of[9] Kashmiri Pandits under the leadership of Kirpa Ram Dutt of Mattan, who were ordered to embrace Islam, came to Anandpur to seek Guru's help (25th May, 1675). Guru Tegh Bahadur was pained to hear of the atrocities committed on them. After days of cogitation, Tegh Bahadur told the Pandits that if a man of piety was prepared to defy the government at the risk of his life, the Hindus could be saved. Gobind Rai asked, "Who could be more pious than the Guru?" Guru Tegh Bahadur made up his mind and told the Pandits to inform the governor of Kashmir, Iftikhar Khan that if he could convert the Guru to his creed, the Hindus of Kashmir would offer no further resistance. All this was conveyed to the Emperor Aurangzeb at Hassan Abdal, who passed order for the arrest of Guru Tegh Bahadur.

Guru Tegh Bahadur being apprehensive of his immediate arrest, installed his son Gobind Rai as his successor and conferred on him the traditional marks of Guruship on 8th July, 1675.[10] Guru Tegh Bahadur was arrested at Malikpur and taken to Delhi[11] where he was asked either to accept Islam or to perform a miracle and give evidence of his divine powers. The Guru would not renounce his faith and he was beheaded publicly in Chandni Chowk on November 11, 1675. The Guru's severed head was brought by Bhai Jaita to Anandpur. Gobind Rai was deeply moved by Jaita's courage and allegiance. When he heard how his devoted Sikh had defied the Mohammedan guards, he embraced Jaita and exclaimed "Rangreta Guru Ka Beta" (Rangretas are Guru's own sons).

The martyrdom of Guru Tegh Bahadur as it symbolised his resistance to the tyranny of Muslim rule as also to build a society, egalitarian and bound by faith in the oneness of God and guaranteeing freedom of worship, had a deep effect on the young Guru. A question arose, if evil is holding its head high, should a good man knuckle under or take up arms to combat and destroy it? The Guru decided in favour of the latter course *i.e.* to combat evil and to uphold righteousness. He, at numerous places in his compositions, expressed the ideal of a crusader on the path of God, yearning to attain the qualities which went a long way to forge such a character.

Though the task was stupendous, yet he addressed it with zeal. The process had been started by the earlier Gurus. Guru Nanak did not hesitate in condemning the atrocities perpetuated by Babar on the people of India. Guru Angad too did not acquiesce when Humayun threatened him with the naked sword. Guru Arjan Dev suffered execution but did not submit. Guru Hargobind took up arms to defend himself and his followers from the persecution of the Mughal imperialists. But it fell to Guru Gobind Singh to enjoin upon his followers to make use of the sword if all other means failed to liquidate the wicked and their wickedness.

To achieve his objective, he initiated schemes to orientate the Sikh psyche to fresh targets and to the fulfilment of teachings of Guru Nanak. He issued *Hukam Namas* (religious fiats) asking the Sikhs to bring him arms of different designs and makes. The Guru's orders were obeyed with zeal and fervour. His foundaries also supplied a large number of weapons. He himself bore arms and induced others to emulate his example. Many of his followers with martial instincts including those who had served in the army of his grandfather or had been members of the bodyguard of Guru Har Rai, flocked to him. He welcomed them and drilled them in martial exercises.[12] The Guru *Darbar* hummed with activities of inspired, energised and determined people.[13]

The Guru encouraged various martial and strenuous games as a part of his programme to impart physical fitness to his people. The Guru's preferred games were splashing of water in a flowing stream, hunting and sham fights. The Guru's principal companions of this time were, Sango Shah, Jit Mal, Gopal Chand, Ganga Ram, Mohri Chand, Gopal Rai, Sham Das, Bhai Daya Ram, and Bhai Nand Chand, an upright and favourite Masand. Alongside these concerns, the Guru took steps for their self-improvement. He enjoined upon his followers to lead a disciplined life.[14] Later on in one of his writings, he very tersely expressed, "I am not enamoured of a Sikh, what is dear to my heart is his disciplined life." He would rise well before dawn and sit in contemplation of the Eternal One. He would then come to assembly and listen to the holy hymns being sung by the musicians after which he would attend the lectures of the explicators of the sacred Word. The rest of the day was spent in recitation of heroic poetry, drills and athletic competitions and in administering to the needs and problems of disciples. The evening assembly was followed by common board and concourses far into the night at which general news would be discussed and stories narrated of the preceding Gurus and the Sikhs of their time.

Not only this, the Guru harnessed literature and the services of literary luminaries. According to the author of *Bansavli Nama*, the Guru issued *Hukam Nama* to the Sikhs in 1677 that poets, writers, painters and scholars might be persuaded to attend his court. A large number of eminent literary figures reached the court of the Guru and rendered into

Braj (varying round Sanskrit on one extreme and colloquial Hindi on the other), the stories of Ram and Krishna and the deeds of Chandi. The Guru himself had a natural genius for poetic composition. He bore highly artistic and elegant hand at Gurmukhi calligraphy specimens of which are preserved on the leaves of some copies of the Holy Granth of his time and in the form of inscriptions on several of his *Hukamnamas* which have come down to us.

The Guru composed 227 *Chhands* of *Debi Path* in 1683 and 1106 *Chhands* of *Dasam Katha Bhagwat ki* in 1685 C.E. The former composition deal with the ventures of *Chandi* in the process of extirpating the tyrants, while the latter composition relates to the story of Lord Krishna in *Duapar*, stated in *Daswan Skand*.

Another composition of the Guru which belonged to this period was 'Jaap'. In this composition the Guru revealed his mastery over the Sikh Philosophy.

The first eleven verses which set the theme could make that clear. They look upon God as follows:

Chakr Chihan ar(u) baran jat(i) pat(i) nahin Jeh.
Rūp rang ar(u) rekh bhekh kou kahe na sakat keh.
Achal murat(i) anubhav prakas(h) amitoj kahijai.
Kot(i) Indra indran sāh(u) sāhān(i) ganijai.
Tribhavan mahīp sur nar asur net(i) net(i) ban trin Kahat.
Tav sarab nām kathai kavan karam nām barnat sumat(i).

> Cantour and countenance, caste, class or lineage, He has none
> None can describe His form, figure, shape and semblance, whatever
> Immovable and self poised in His being without fear,
> He is the Sovereign of three worlds, the demon the mortals and the angelic beings
> Nay, even the grass blades in the forest proclaim him to be boundless, endless and infinite.
> O, who can count all the names that are Thy Glory.
> Through Thy enlightenment, I will count all Thy attributive names.[15]

Gobind Rai then passed on to give the names, personal and impersonal, transcendental and immanent, and metaphysical and mysterious. It is suggested that Gobind Rai wrote the *Jaap* on the model of *Vishnu Sahsarnama*. That might well be true but it should be remembered that Gobind Singh's *Jaap* was in complete consonance with Guru Nanak's *Japji* and very appropriately both now constitute the morning prayer of the Sikhs. The overall impact of all this was that a process was set in to articulate the people to think/react different from gross apathy to active involvement and action, always adhering to the cause of righteousness and universal brotherhood of humankind. Besides taking steps for fostering self-improvement and physical fitness, the Guru got prepared a drum under the supervision of Nand Chand, his trusted Dewan. The underlying objective of the Guru was to make use of it as an aid in military training as well as in generating a sense of discipline among his followers, although it caused a lot of misgivings among the hill chiefs as well as Mughal officials who looked upon the drum as a symbol of Guru's assertion of sovereignty, as in the current political parlance the beating of the drum was considered the prerogative of an independent chieftain. The name of the Drum—'Ranjit Nagara', a herald of victory, was also deemed to be suggestive of the Guru's political ambition. The Sikhs called the Guru 'Sacha Padshah' and his *Darbar* as *Sacha Darbar* (True Court). The implications of Ranjit Nagara and the title such as *Sacha Padshah* were misunderstood by the hill chieftains and the Mughal government. These were interpreted in temporal sense and appeared to them emblems of Guru's political ambitions.

The Guru *vis-a-vis* Hill States

While at Anandpur, the Guru had to take notice of hill states, their perception of the Sikh movement, their reactions to the Mughal Emperor's policies, their polity and their socio-religious beliefs.

Between the Sutlej and the Jamuna lay Kahlur (Bilaspur), Sirmour (Nahan) and Hindur (Nalagarh). Kahlur lay on both sides of Sutlej. On the east of Jamuna lay Garhwal which was not really a part of the Punjab. Between the Ravi and the Sutlej lay very important hill principalities of Kangra, Kulu, Mandi, Suket, Chamba, Nurpur, Guler, Datarpur, Siba Jaswan and Kutlehr. Between the Ravi and Jehlum several hill principalities such as Jammu, Basohli and Jasrota existed.

All the Hill states right from the ancient times were ruled by Rajput princes, who governed their principalities on the principles of feudal polity and of Brahmanical orthodoxy. In the early medieval period, when the Sultans established their hegemony in the Punjab, these states were only marginally touched.

In the later medieval period, situation changed and the Mughal Imperial system extended to the hill states more or less effectively during the reign of Akbar. The rulers of principalities officially designated as Zamindars were required to pay tribute. They were subject to the supervision and control of local Faujdars of Jammu and Kangra.

The Mughal Emperors employed force, cunning and diplomacy to keep their political hold strong on the hill rulers. They often resorted to the policy of divide and rule as for instance Nurpur and Guler were brought into prominence at the cost of Kangra. Even then the Mughals were only partially successful in keeping them politically subservient to them. This was because of their traditional love of independence which they had developed over past few centuries because of the inaccessibility of their locales which were hilly and difficult to traverse and their never-failing pride in their social system, which otherwise was unprogressive and ultra-conservative. The economy was sustained by the agricultural *Rathies* and semi-nomadic *Gujjars* who formed a large portion of the population. Social life was dominated by the Brahmans who were numerically stronger than the Rajputs whose support they utilized for the rigid enforcement of caste rules and preservation of the traditional caste hierarchy. Religion, often regarded the most important element to refine minds, had not crossed even primitive stages of animism and idol worship. The principal deities worshipped by the people were Siva, Mahadeva and his consort—Uma, Shyama, Shakti, Bhawani, Chandi and

Kali. Tantric ideas and practices in debased form were quite popular. Vaishnavism had made only marginal inroads into the hill areas. Quite a few hill chieftains patronised Vaishnavism. At people's level it was not welcome.

Belief in monotheism or monism was a far cry as also a universal society based on social equality, non-discrimination, non-exploitation and dignity of labour which formed the basics of certain religious dispensations in contemporary world.

Such being the broad parameters of the polity, society and religion in hill states, the entry of Sikhism into them could hardly be welcomed, rather it was bound to provoke opposition. Sikhism stood for equalitarian society based on principles of social equality, honest, hard labour, freedom from fear and respect for individuals, irrespective of caste, creed, birth and status *et al.* having full faith in the oneness and singularity of God and universal brotherhood. The political formulations to which Sikhism lent validity was democracy where the people were free to participate and spurn the aristocratic exclusiveness as it was associated with the Rajputs. The economic structure vouched by Sikhism was anti-feudal, democratic and equalitarian in spirit and social action.

To sum up, the politico-social model in the hill states was quite different from the model the Gurus envisaged, championed and sponsored.

The Rajput rulers hand in glove with socio-religious elites of the hill states resented in particular the social equality which Sikhism offered to the so-called low caste people and the Jats whom they treated as social inferiors because in their reckoning it not only ran counter to their long upheld religious notions but also levelled a stunning blow to their whole social fabric. Thus, in the face of the stout opposition of the hill states and their allies, the progress of Sikhism in the hill states was bound to be slow. Chronologically speaking, the contact of Sikhism with hilly region was peripheral upto the time of Guru Hargobind. In times of Guru Angad and Guru Amar Das, there were occasional visits of certain devoted Sikhs to this region as also of certain seekers of this region to the Guru's court as for instance the Raja of Haripur visited Goindwal to pay obeisance to Guru Amar Das. The impression of the Guru as also of Sikhism which the people from the hill areas carried was that of reverence. In Guler, one of the Punjab hill states, Sikh *Sangat* had been established through a *Manjidar*. Bhai Gurdas avers that there were Sikh *Sangats* at Sirhind and Kashmir from which it can be safely drawn that Sikhism at least had crawled into the hill states.[16]

In the time of Guru Hargobind, the penetration of Sikhism was marked and significant. This happened in spite of the fact that the Guru had to undergo incarceration, wage wars against the Mughal Islamic imperialism, and face the opposition of *Minas* and recalcitrance of certain *Masands*. The city of Hargobindpur was situated at the route adjoining Shivalik hills and leading to Kashmir. Its proximity understandably provided a chance for interaction between the hill states and the Sikhs in the plains of the Punjab.

At least the fame of the Guru and his work travelled to hill states. In 1618, the Guru came to Hindur to help Dharam Chand in a military engagement which the latter undertook to oust his father, Sansar Chand, who nominated his brother as successor to him, the fact which Dharam Chand did not like. Most probably Dharam Chand won over the heart of the Guru in Gwalior Fort, where the Guru and he had been imprisoned and stayed together. The Guru returned to his headquarter at Amritsar after Dharam Chand ascended the throne of Hindur after the death of his father in 1618. The Guru's help to Dharam Chand was significant in as much as it sent signals at least among the hill Rajas that the Guru was a military force as well. Since the Guru entourage consisted of scholars, preachers and devoted Sikhs, besides soldiers, people in general must have had the opportunity to interact with the Sikhs with the result their understanding of Sikhism improved. The Guru must have also experienced that the hill region needed Guru's dispensation for the elevation of its population steeped deep in ignorance and suffering worst type of conservatism. For almost seven years no special effort seemed to have been made by the Guru to advance Sikhism in that region. In 1627, when Jahangir died, the Guru sent his son Gurditta to Hindur to establish a Sikh Centre in the territory of Dharam Chand. Apart from the general impulse of introducing Sikhism in far off areas, the impending profile of political landscape also urged him to take this step. He gauged that Shahjahan, the son and successor of Jahangir, would not be as considerate towards him as Jahangir had been in the past few years and in that case a new centre outside the administrative jurisdiction of the Mughals could be useful in several ways. Baba Gurditta was well received in Hindur (Nalagarh) and he was helped to establish a centre at the present side of Kiratpur which lay close to the border of Kahlur.

In the thirties of the seventeenth century, Guru Hargobind fell out with the Mughal officials in the Punjab, and having fought different battles shifted his headquarter to the already flourishing city of Kiratpur which thrived still more. Kiratpur began to radiate the light of Sikhism to the neighbouring and far off places.

This caused commotion, even convulsion among the people and the elite, some appreciating and some deprecating the Guru's ideas and constructs. In short Sikhism started influencing the people, quite a big segment of whom became empathetic towards it. The ruling elite including Brahmans and the upper caste viewed Sikhism with reservation.

In 1642, the Nawab of Ropar attacked Hindur. Dharam Chand sought Guru's help and defeated him. Even in the time of Guru Harkrishan in 1656, the Sikhs rendered help to Dharam Chand in his war with the Chief of Kahlur. The Guru's sustained help to Dharam Chand seemed to have been actuated by his devotion to the Guru, the Sikh's concern for the security and stability of their headquarter, the righteousness of the cause of the ruler of Hindur and the benevolence with which Dharam Chand ruled the state.

As the time rolled on, Dip Chand (1650-1667), the ruler of Kahlur developed devotion for the Guru.[17] Guru Tegh Bahadur's arrival at Kiratpur in 1665 was considered a great event in the sense that whereas it instilled a new confidence into the devouts, it ushered in new era in the relationship between Dip Chand of Kahlur and the Sikhs. Dip Chand invited Guru to settle at Makhowal within his territory not far from Kiratpur (which was in the territory of Hindur). The Guru accepted the offer. Possibly the Guru wanted to be away from jealous Sodhis of Kiratpur and to give impression of being a common friend of Kahlur and Hindur who were rival to each other.

The existence of Guru's headquarters in two principalities did not create any immediate complication for various reasons. Bhim Chand who had succeeded to the Kahlur's throne after Dip Chand's death in 1667, was a minor and he could not assert himself in any way. Also, there was a general stir in the hills against the Mughals in the first half of the 1670's which overshadowed the mutual difference of the Chiefs of Kahlur and Hindur.

Within a few years after the assumption of the pontifical throne, Guru Gobind Singh intensified his activities. Following in the footsteps of his grandfather, Guru Hargobind, whereas he spared no pains to disseminate Guru's message, he also raised an army and made it publicly known that he would now particularly be pleased if the gifts were of use to his soldiers.[18] He followed it up by selecting a place strategically better situated than Makhowal, and set up a small establishment there.[19] The change was reflected in the appearance of the Guru's *Darbar*. The young Guru would now meet his daily congregation in a costly tent with elephants and horses as a part of the establishment. He would wear aigrette and sit on a raised platform. The Sikhs called him 'Sacha Padshah' and far off princes visited Anandpur.[20] The whole setting was that of a regal court.[21]

The scenario at Anandpur reflecting exuberance, vigour and a constructive dynamism was looked upon with suspicion by Bhim Chand, the ruler of Bilaspur, who succeeded his father after he was poisoned to death in 1667 by the ruler of Kangra and was determined to play a dominant role in hill affairs.

Up to the eighties, Bhim Chand had set himself on the road to realise his cherished goal. He had successfully beaten back the invasion of Mughal Faujdar of Kangra who intended to replace him with his uncle, Manak. Similarly, his new Wazir Parmanand had inflicted a defeat on the Faujdar of Sirhind and brought laurels to his young master.

It was at this stage when his reputation stood high, he took notice of the Guru's activities and appraised them not in the context of the Guru's vision and his grand design, but from his own perspective or at best from the perspective of the hill states. It was not difficult for him to surmise that Guru's activities not only did not fit in the long established social and political order in the hill states, but also could pose a serious threat to his authority. Ranjit Nagara, the maintenance of the army, infusing of new ideology into the minds of the people—all these things were regarded an affront to him and a prelude to establishing a state within state. Nevertheless, Bhim Chand decided to visit the Guru to see things for himself. The Guru received the Raja in the famous woolen tent which had been presented to him by a disciple Duni Chand from Kabul. Other gifts presented to the Guru were also displayed. Bhim Chand was surprised at the richness and splendour of the young Guru, at his confidence and at the devotion of his Sikhs to him. When he returned to Bilaspur, he decided to make it clear to the Guru that since Makhowal fell in his territory, he was within his rights as an overlord to levy tribute. From the Guru's point of view the question of overlordship was irrelevant because none of the Gurus had paid tribute either to Hindur or to Kahlur till then. Bhim Chand also insisted on being presented with things of his choice as for instance Prasadi elephant, and the unique weapon which could be used as a sword, a lance or a club, which were a gift from Raja Rattan Rai of Assam. He also demanded the embroidered *Shamiana* (Canopy) presented by Duni Chand.

Considering the Guru's refusal to oblige him as a challenge to his authority, he attacked the Guru in 1682[22] but was beaten back. Fearing the states on his north and north-eastern border might take advantage of his discomfiture, he hurriedly packed up and went back. In contemplating attack on Guru Gobind Singh, he had also been incited by the governors of Sirhind, Lahore and Jammu.[23] The unexpected conflict, perhaps because it was not followed by any understanding between the victorious and the defeated, began period of tension both for Bhim Chand and the Guru. In this stage of suspended hostilities, constant clashes between Sikhs and Bhim Chand's soldiers were inevitable. At this juncture, a large majority of *Masands* tried to dissuade the Guru from proceeding with war-like activities. The Guru declined to oblige them. Nand Chand, his maternal uncle Kirpal and all others supported the Guru in his stand. Masand's point-of-view obviously was actuated by the fear factor and certainly it did not take into consideration the far-reaching implications of Guru's acquiescence. In case the Guru had submitted, Anandpur would have lost its independent character which it had maintained as a religious community and the Guru would have to surmount more difficulties in the process of consummating his design. In C.E. 1685, Raja Medni Parkash of Sirmour (later known as Nahan) invited the Guru to settle in his territory. The Guru accepted the offer and left for Sirmour. Guru himself says in *Bachittar Natak*, "After this I left Anandpur and reached Paonta (a place in the Nahan state situated on the bank of Kalandri (Jamuna) and partook of various activities."[24]

The great majority of the Sikhs in Guru's township in Bilaspur state accompanied the Guru. There is a strong Sikh tradition about Gulab Rai and Sham Das, the grandsons of Suraj Mal, being left by the Guru at Chak Nanaki deliberately to look after the Sikhs who did not accompany the Guru to Nahan.[25]

Why did the Guru leave Anandpur? The event as it involved shifting of headquarter and settlement in another state was not fortuitous or just a freak; it was the product of the interplay of different factors. The first among them, of course, was the animosity of Bhim Chand. The Guru needed a place where he could mature his plans undisturbed without any interference from any ruler or such other authority. Second, the Raja of Sirmour cordially invited the Guru to settle in his state, knowing full well that the relation between the Guru and Bhim Chand had gone sour. Besides devotion to the Guru, he had certain mundane motives as well. Sirmour and Garhwal were neighbouring states engaged in hostilities for several generations. Supported by the Mughal government, the former encroached successfully upon the territory of the latter. During the reign of Aurangzeb, Sirmour received Kala Garh (near Dehradun) and the Doon was conferred upon Garhwal. This put the two states in dangerous proximity. After Aurangzeb's departure from Delhi in 1679, two new Chiefs became rulers of the two states Medni Parkash (1684-1704) in Sirmour and Fateh Shah in Garhwal (1684-1717). The former desired to strengthen himself by accommodating the Guru in his own territories.[26] Thirdly, there was Mughal factor that prompted the Guru to shift to Sirmour. For about ten years since the martyrdom of Guru Tegh Bahadur, there was no move on the part of Mughals against the Guru. Between Guru Tegh Bahadur's execution in November 1675 and the death of Maharaja Jaswant Singh in December 1678, Aurangzeb's hands were comparatively free. The situation in the rebellious tribal areas in the northwest improved to a large extent by the end of the year 1675. Shivaji won successes in the South in 1676-77 but this did not prevent Aurangzeb from continuing religious persecutions and military aggression in the north. He revived Jazia in April 1674, the purpose being to spread Islam and put down the practice of infidelity. Then the Rajput war drew him away to Ajmer where he established his headquarter in September, 1679 to deal effectively with the rebellion of Akbar, who had found shelter at the court of Sambhaji. The Emperor arrived at Burhanpur in November 1681. He never returned to the north. The Deccan became the chief centre of his political and military activities from 1681 onwards and Imperial policy did not concern itself with Sikh affairs for quite a long time.

If Aurangzeb really intended to harm the Sikh community after November 1675, he had an excellent opportunity during the three-year period after the commencement of Rajput war. Guru Gobind Singh was a mere boy, too inexperienced and not so mature. Minas, Dhirmalias and Ram Rayyas—the dissentient sects were active in their opposition to him. But even at the height of his religious frenzy symbolised by the reimposition of Jazia, Aurangzeb is known to have not taken any steps particularly against the Sikhs and their religion—rather instead of creating difficulties for the Guru he is credited to have directed his potential rival Ram Rai to retire to his possessions in Dun Valley, thereby enabling him to dabble effectively into the Sikh affairs. Had he really changed his mind towards Sikhism and the Sikhs and was now favourably disposed towards the Sikhs? Readings into his religious policy towards non-Muslims lead us to conclude that he could not be soft. This soft peddling towards the Guru and his Sikhs for quite a long time was actuated firstly by his belief that the Guru was not in a position, at least for some time, to challenge Mughal authority both in respect of its religious and politica! policies, and secondly, he computed that the Guru was bound to evoke jealousy/enmity of the hill states and would soon be bogged down in hill affairs with the likely result that he would lose the intensity, even shine of his mission.

The Sikhs, however, had no reason to expect that Aurangzeb's hostility would cease with the death of Guru Tegh Bahadur. Khushwant Singh says, "...the leaders of the Sikh community were concerned about the safety of Gobind for the possibility of his being taken to Delhi as hostage could not be ruled out. To avoid this the young Guru and his entourage were shifted from Anandpur further into the mountains at Paonta[27] which not only was farther from Sirhind as compared to Anandpur but also provided the nearest Mughal centre of power, a natural fortress which because of its difficult terrain was well-nigh inaccessible...."

Dr. A.C. Bannerjee says in this connection "In the years following the Guru's martyrdom, the 'Turks' took no steps against the young Guru nor did he seek to destroy them. His migration to Paonta took place most probably in 1685 at the instance of Raja Medni Parkash of Sirmour. It has nothing to do with the 'dread' of the Mughal hostility which appears to have evaporated as a result of Mughal inactivity for about a decade."[28]

The assessment of the learned scholar is fallacious as it runs counter to very strong Sikh tradition reflecting constant lurking fear of the Aurangzeb's wrath, besides lacking in any solid supportive historical evidence.

Stay at Paonta—A Period of Introspection and Preparation

Having taken the decision to accept the invitation of Medni Parkash, the Guru left Anandpur in May, 1685. Along with him were many Sikhs, including 500 soldiers, a large number of poets, scholars and musicians. His baggage consisted of a large number of horses, oxen, camels and elephants. The whole caravan of the Guru passed through Ropar, Kharar, Ramgarh, Rani Ka Raipur and Bhurewal. The Guru encamped at Toka situated at foothills on the border of Sirmour state.[29]

At Bhurewal, the Chauhan Rajput landlords who after embracing Islam were generally known as Rangars and had *zamindari* of eighty-five[30] villages entertained the Guru and his cavalcade exactly as their ancestors had done forty years earlier in 1645 C.E. when Guru Har Rai went to Nahan by the same route.[31]

At Toka too, these people provide provisions, performed other ancillary services and prayed for Guru's benefaction. The Guru's Grace did descend and he blessed them with an honorific "Bhure Shah". A small Gurdwara commemorates Guru's stay at Toka (now in Himachal Pradesh). A fair is held every year on the tenth of Jeth (May).[32]

A couple of days later, the Raja of Nahan came to escort the Guru to his capital. After a short stay at Nahan, the Raja led the Guru to a spot on the eastern limits of Jamuna which formed the boundary between Garhwal and Sirmour.

The Guru liked the place which soon acquired the name of Paonta—*Paon Than*, footstool, resting place. On July 22, 1685[33] the Guru laid the foundation of a fortress. Diwan Nand Chand Sangha of Darauli performed the Ardas and Ram Koer, a descendant of Bhai Budha, broke the ground. The fortress was completed within a very short span of twelve days.[34] Soon a hutment arose around the fortress to accommodate the Sikhs. The place had idyllic surroundings and the Guru loved it the most because it not only catered to his aesthetic sense but also provided him requisite peace to contemplate and mature his plans.

The Raja of Sirmour was so much impressed by the Guru's bearing, valour and culture, the discipline and dedication of the Sikhs and their unswerving faith in God that he requested the Guru never ever to leave this place.

Meanwhile, Raja Fateh Chand of Sri Nagar (Garhwal) heard of the Guru's repute and paid him a visit. As it has been pointed out, he and the Raja of Nahan were not on good terms. The Guru mediated between the two and brought them close to each other.[35] The Guru hunted big game in the surrounding forest, and once killed a tiger with a sword and a shield. The Guru himself says in *Bachittar Natak*, "I hunted a lot of tigers, bears and antelopes in the forest of Paonta."[36] The Guru lived at Paonta fort about three years.[37]

Literary Activities

During this period he undertook multifarious activities of utmost importance. He went through the whole gamut of epic literature in Sanskrit and was deeply impressed by the idea which runs through the Puranic literature—the idea of a saviour appearing from time to time to uphold righteousness and destroy unrighteousness for good. The stories of Rama destroying the demon-king of Lanka, the son of Devki crushing Kansa, and especially the exploits of that personification of righteousness and divine power called Durga breaking skulls and drinking the blood of Mahikhasur and other demons were found by him as incorporating and upholding not only the themes of destroying the wicked but also a medium of stirring the people to bold action against evil. Guru Nanak in one of his hymns had named God as 'demon-killer'. Similar views were expressed by Guru Amar Das and Guru Ram Das. In consonance with the views of his predecessors, Gobind Rai regarded God as a demon-killer[38] with the difference that unlike prophets sent by God, he did not appropriate to himself any power. Therefore, while strongly believing in his heaven-ordained mission, he humbly declared that he was but a servant of the Supreme Being and anybody calling him God would be thrown into the cauldron of hell.[39]

Guru Gobind Singh himself was a prolific writer. In 1686, he is said to have completed the composition of *Shastra Nam Mala* in the conventional literary style of the time having its model the emblematical verses of the great Masters.[40] The true import of the composition lies in personifying the weapons and for the Guru they were the medium of worship. The weapons which had been used by gods and demons alike, had been used in defence and for promotion of Dharma—righteousness. The *chaupais* and *dohas* of adoration which Guru Gobind Singh composed were all reserved for the weapons only when they were used by the righteous[41] for the sake of righteousness.

Almost at the same time, the Guru composed *Var Sri Bhagauti ji ki*, popularly known as *Chandi Di Var*. In this first Var of its kind, complete and exhaustive and in blank verse, used for the first time in Punjabi literature[42], the Guru succeeded in making his composition a means to impart heroic spirit—an important salient of his ideology. Though the source of the composition as in *Chandi Charitra* was also the tenth Skanda of *Markand Puran*, he related in his composition only the battle of Chandi and Durga. Of the fifty-five stanzas in the Var, forty-nine described the battle scenes, the first five and twenty-first being purely narrative and informatory, helping to elucidate the situation. Chandi's battles were, in the eyes of Guru Gobind Singh, fought on the side of righteousness.

The story of Durga has been so bedded with sentences full of choicest words that it simply savoured marvellous. He pictured Durga as the one clad in armour from head to foot, while serpents coiled around her neck hissing dreadfully at the foe. Her hand-drum makes the sound of roaring tigress. She is riding a lion and fights valorously against the Rakhshasas—tyrants and slays Mahikhasur among others. "Her offspring, Kali, bursting forth from her forehead gulps down the demons and elephants alike. Durga herself is skilled in the use of a hundred arms and gives an astounding display of her martial prowess. Herself the bulwark of righteousness, she moves back and forth fearlessly. Guru Gobind Singh sees her battle as one against sin.[43]

The gods themselves revere Durga as 'Mother' and they look up to her for help in overcoming and destroying their enemy.

She in fact is represented as a moral power to challenge an oppressive system and to establish harmony, morality and justice. Her aggression is, therefore, healthy as her anger is purifying.

The Guru's specific choice of Durga out of millions of gods and goddesses was significant from another point of view. She was one goddess without husband, consort or lover. She is independent. She is her own mistress. She is autonomous, capable of taking her own decision, always acting as a positive force to activise the good to dare the wicked. By attributing such characteristics to Durga, the Guru purposely gave a fresh role model in the form of a woman. This was indeed something revolutionary and breath-taking. In most of the cultures, the image of woman has been degraded. In 'Ancient Mirrors of Womanhood' Merline Stone cites several instances from a wide variety of cultures which reveal how the patriarchal structures have attempted to suppress, alter and even erase the lustre of the female. The Sumerians, for example, replaced the ancient creator goddess Nammu with less effective Inana. Bill Debuda in Drawing from 'Mythology in Women's Quest For Selfhood' sums up this entire process "while ancient mythology affirmed woman's power, those stories through patriarchal influence over the years have come to be 'muted', contacted and even perverted".[44]

The Guru's treatment of Durga was completely exempt from such detraction. On the other hand her exploits had been fully described rather magnified. In this recalling, Durga did not lose even an iota of her shine and fire. She was represented as a paradigm of independence, sovereignty and wholeness of a person. The exalted image of Durga which the Guru created or presented went a long way to bring about a change in the psyche of the people, especially of women. Mai Bhago from the Amritsar district of Punjab was one such example. When she saw how some Sikhs of her area had fled Anandpur, the seat of Guru Gobind Singh, in the face of the privations brought on by prolonged siege, she charged them for their pusillanimity. She led them back to fight for the Guru, and she herself took part in the battle that was fought at Khidrana, now named as Muktsar.

After the completion of *Shastra Nama Mala* and the Var, the Guru is said to set himself to complete the unfinished composition *Krishan Avtar*. He picked up the old threads in July, 1687 and having added 1347 Chhands (340 Chhands forming the portion of Ras Mandal and 875 Chhands composing Yudh Prabandh) up to July, 1688 Bk (Samvat 1745) completed *Krishan Avtar*.[45] According to Dr. S.S. Bal, both because of theme and effect of his two earlier compositions, the part of the *Krishan Avtar* written during this period was exclusively devoted to heroic poetry. It was natural that in this part of *Krishan Avtar*, the author should use *Bir Ras* and not *Vat Sakaya* and *Shingar Rasas* which the Guru used in the earlier portions of the composition.[46] Significantly, the Guru in the last verse of the composition told that he had written *Krishna Avtar* to wage a holy war.

"The tenth story of the Bhagwat is rendered into the (popular) Bhakha with no other purpose than that of war for the sake of righteousness." We also find the Guru saying in this composition that he was not interested in riches which could come to him from all parts of the country at his bidding but wished to die the death of a martyr. Dr. Harbans Singh very aptly puts "His poetic intuition was notable for its sublimity of style, mystical ardour and energy. His object was two-fold: to sing praises of the Timeless and to infuse new vigour into the limp mass of people. His compositions were most appropriately adapted to these purposes. Rarely has poetry in any tongue recaptured the transcendent vision in such a spirit of courage and heroism. His own literary creations apart, the Guru had gathered around him a comity of literary luminaries."[47] Sikh tradition fixes the number as fifty-two which is wrong because the arrival at or departure from Guru Darbar depended on each individual's sweet will. Possibly the number fifty-two has come into vogue because in the historical consciousness it had acquired sanctity or some sort of respect because the number of Sidds also numbered fifty-two. According to our discovery the number of poets, writers and thinkers was one hundred twenty-five—one hundred poets and twenty-five thinkers or prose writers.[48] The number does not include the poets of various compositions which do not suggest the names of authors. Understandably, the number of poets and men of parts we have identified formed only the nucleus, in fact there was a larger number of such people. There is a strong tradition that vigorous drive was made to re-write, restate, translate parts of Puranic literature besides preparing fresh literature which had the potentiality to remodel the psyche of the people to enable them to uphold righteousness, resist tyranny and secure the fulfilment of divine justice.

Though the detailed account of literary compositions of different poets and writers is not known, yet some works are available. Sainapat rendered *Chanakya Niti* from Sanskrit to Brij Bhasha.[49] Nand Lal[50] composed *Bandgi Nama*, Amrit Rai, Hans Ram, Kavresh and Mangal translated *Sabha Parb, Karan Parb, Dharm Parb* and *Salya Parb* respectively and were honoured with the award of huge sums[51], besides costly gifts. Hans Ram felt exalted at the cash of sixty thousand *Takas* given to him. Mangal Kavresh and Amrit Rai also were joyed when they were given cash and gifts in recognition of their services.[52] Mangal was so excited that he called the Guru '*Puran Avtar*' Perfect Incarnate and Anandpur the Abode of Bliss. Pandit Jagan Nath[53] who originally embellished the court of Shah Jahan was also attracted to the Guru and came to Anandpur and wrote *Adhyatmik Parkash* saying forever good-bye to his earlier predilection of producing erotic literature. Even the avaricious and ego-bloated poet Chandan[54] was welcome to the court of the Guru. The Guru's personality changed him into a humble servant of Guru and he created literature of the type and tenor the Guru had desired. Obviously, the leitmotif of the literature created under the sponsorship and inspiration of the Guru was to bring about re-awakening through the process of animating and articulating the best in our cultural heritage. The Guru very wisely and aptly employed the medium of literature to impart a new orientation to the minds of the people given to passivity. For this latter purpose, the Guru did not hesitate even to pick up themes from the ancient epics and mythology of India to produce verse charged with martial fervour.

Missionary Activities

Side by side the Guru's preoccupation with the creation of appropriate literature, the Guru carried on missionary activities with zeal and zest. He built a shrine in 1685 where he daily held congregations in the morning as well in the evening. He took religious tours to villages such as Kapal Mochan, Kalsia, Siana and Thanesar. He also visited the village Dhankoli on his way to Anandpur from Paonta. The village Lohar was also hallowed by the Guru's visit. All these places have gurdwaras in memory of Guru's visit.

A renowned Sufi Saint Pir Badruddin (1647-1704), popularly known by his nick-name Pir Budhu Shah who resided at Sadhaura, was fascinated by the Guru's splendid personality and came to the Guru to feel for himself the Guru's greatness. He held a long discussion with the Guru and was simply captivated by the Guru's spiritual knowledge. He turned an ardent devotee of the Guru, who on his part, showered affection on him—so much so that on his recommendation he enlisted 500 Pathans in his army who had been dismissed from the Mughal army for petty offences. Significantly, this gesture of the Guru had signalled that in the struggle for upholding righteousness (Dharma) any one irrespective of religion, status, birth and caste *et al.* was free to take part.

The Guru decided to establish a special Order of his Sikhs particularly to make comparative study of religions and also to interpret classical Indian tradition in terms of the basic philosophy of Sikhism. The project thus conceived had incidental advantages as well. Since times immemorial, learning and teaching had been the monopoly of Brahmans, Sanyasis or Bairagis (ascetics), but the project of the Guru, accorded no recognition to caste or status, was sure to level a strong blow to the long-held custom of class learning. Since most of the classical Indian religious literature was available in Sanskrit, the Guru found it imperative to make arrangement for the teaching of Sanskrit to his followers. The Guru asked his court poet, and eminent Sanskrit scholar, Raghu Nath, to do the needful. He politely and diplomatically replied that he was prohibited by convention to teach the language of gods (Dev Bhasha) and holy scriptures to the *non-divyas i.e.* Shudras and women. The Guru admonished him for his sticking to outworn ideals and concepts. *Udasis* also showed reluctance to impart the knowledge of Sanskrit and of scriptures to the non-Brahmans and non-Sanyasis.

The Guru selected a dozen of Sikhs from different classes, castes and creeds and sent them to Benaras. Their names were (1) Karam Singh, (2) Pram Singh, (3) Ganda Singh, (4) Vir Singh, (5) Sobha Singh, (6) Dharam Singh, (7) Daya Singh, (8) Kesar Singh, (9) Mohkam Singh, (10) Gian Singh, (11) Gaja Singh, (12) Chanda Singh, (13) Saina Singh. All these chosen Sikhs studied under the guidance of Pandit Sada Manak. In the eleventh year they came back to the Guru who now had shifted to Anandpur. Guru Gobind Singh was much pleased to find that they had become really good scholars and allotted to them different duties. Pandit Karam Chand was asked to interpret hymns from *Guru Granth Sahib* in the Guru's court. Bhai Mani Singh received knowledge of six traditional schools of philosophy from him. Bhai Punjab Singh and his disciple Roucha Singh spread Sikhism in Jammu and Kashmir. In 1699, these scholars were administered 'Pahul' and entered the Order the Khalsa. They were called Nirmalas—Pure ones. They played a significant role in the dissemination of Sikhism as also in Sikh politics in the eighteenth century. Later on as the time rolled on and the number of the contemporary associates of the Guru or of his staunch followers like Bhai Mani Singh thinned, they began to evince more interest in bandying themselves more as vedantic scholars than humble interpreters of Sikh philosophy and hence they began to superimpose the vedantic point of view on the Sikh theological and philosophical structures. No doubt, they recited *Guru Granth Sahib* and encouraged others to do the same, yet they did not do all this as an expression of bringing into limelight the distinctiveness of Sikhism, rather they projected it as a part of Hindu tradition.[55] The trend is reflected in most of their literary compositions which came into being particularly after the mid-eighteenth century. This being so, the Nirmalas ceased to be right type of missionaries of Sikhism and thus their services to the cause of Sikhism in the last few days of the eighteenth century and onward were not such which were altogether admirable. (For details refer to the chapter 'Sikh Orders'.)

Ram Rai's Reclamation

Ram Rai, Guru Har Rai's eldest son, was born in 1646 C.E. At the age of fifteen he was sent to Aurangzeb to explain the position of Guru Har Rai and his teachings. The Guru on the departure of his son Ram Rai for Delhi, enjoined upon him to fix his thought on God and everything would be all right. He also impressed upon him the propriety of not countenancing any objection the Emperor might make to *Granth Sahib* but of replying to him patiently and to the purpose.[56] But Ram Rai began to curry favour with the Emperor by acting in the manner that was hardly in consonance with the teachings of Sikhism. Ram Rai displayed miraculous powers. But the climax of his delinquency was reached when he did not hesitate even to distort a word in a verse of Guru Nanak to please the Emperor. Doubtless, these things pleased Aurangzeb but Guru Har Rai got angry and superseding him, nominated Har Krishan as his successor. Ram Rai did not accept his father's decision without a struggle. He, with the help and instigation of a few corrupt and recalcitrant *Masands*, Tara and Goinda in particular, declared himself as the Guru. He invoked Aurangzeb's assistance. Aurangzeb readily agreed as he found in it an opportunity to intervene in a matter, which by all means, should have been kept away from him.

In fact the whole incident showed up the Sikhs in a light which was hardly dignified.[57] The Emperor summoned the child (Guru Harkrishan) to his presence and since he became convinced of his divinity, he recognised him as the legitimate Guru.

Ram Rai again tried for guruship after the death of Guru Harkrishan, but he could not succeed in his designs and Guru Tegh Bahadur was acknowledged as the leader of the Sikhs. Even after this, Ram Rai persisted in his claim that he was the real Guru. After the execution of Guru Tegh Bahadur, the Mughal Emperor did not need him at the court and consequently he was sent to Dun Valley where he was granted a *jagir* of seven villages namely Chamasari, Dhamaval, Dhartanwali, Pandit Wali and Rajpur Khurvadi and Mianwal. In this *jagir* was established a headquarter known as Dera Ram Rai. The whole valley (Dun) later on assumed the nomenclature of Dehradun. The present city of Dehradun has received its name from Ram Rai's Dera.[58]

With the lapse of time, Ram Rai's views changed; but being a willing tool in the hands of the Mughal Emperor, and having harmed the cause of the Sikhs, he was afraid of Guru Gobind Singh and could not muster courage to face him.

The Guru, sensing all this, sent Nand Chand and Daya Ram to reassure him. According to M.A. Macauliffe, Ram Rai received them well and was delighted. He invested them with robes of honour and resolved to remain friendly towards Guru. The Guru's polite and sweet message brought about a change in Ram Rai, who regretted his past sins and yearned for a meeting with the Guru.

The meeting took place on Sunday in a ferry in the middle of the stream. Ram Rai touched the Guru's feet in obeisance and said 'I am fortunate to have obtained a sight of thee when I am gone, protect my family...my father, Guru Har Rai used to say that someone would be born from our family who would restore and fit the vessel for the safe conveyance of soul.[59] Ram Rai also spoke about his corrupt, headstrong and recalcitrant Masands who were determined to destroy him.

Henceforward, Ram Rai ceased to be a separate entity and for the rest of his life lived as an admirer and follower of Guru Gobind Singh. He did not leave any injunction in any form that he should be regarded as a Guru of a separate sect. He had full faith in the institutions of the Sikhs and led life as a devotee of Guru Gobind Singh. In September 1687, Ram Rai who was in trance was made out to be dead by wily Masands and was cremated by them in spite of the entreaties of Punjab Kaur, Ram Rai's wife. Completely non-plussed, Punjab Kaur sent a message to Guru Gobind Singh for help. The Guru at once responded to the request of Punjab Kaur and meted out condign punishment to the guilty masands, and restored property to Punjab Kaur. This event testifies that the Guru and Ram Rai had cordial relations.

Ram Rai's reclamation by the Guru was really a significant event. The leader having been won over, the schismatic move of *Ram Rayyas* lost its vitality and direction with the result that Sikhism gained a lot. Many of Ram Rai's followers turned devotees of Guru Gobind Singh. Punjab Kaur, the wife of Ram Rai, threw heart and soul into the Sikh movement. The Guru sent a few *Udasis* of Sri Chand's Udasi establishment to manage the affairs of the Ashram.

Exactly a year after, the tragic death of Ram Rai, Punjab Kaur arranged a get-together at the first death anniversary of her husband. This was a critical period for Guru Gobind, for, he was expecting an invasion by the armies of the hill chiefs on Paonta. Thinking that Guru Gobind Singh would be too busy in his defensive preparations, Mahant Gurbakhsh Singh reached Dehradun on August 23, 1688 and set himself up as a successor to Ram Rai and captured Ashram. Guru Gobind Singh sent Bhai Mani Singh and Diwan Nand Chand along with his fifty choicest warriors to Dehradun. On August 23, 1688 C.E., they operated against Gurbakhsh Singh and his cohorts. Bhai Mani Singh was enraged at the indecent remarks of Gurbakhsh Singh about Guru Gobind Singh so much that he pushed his bulky body so forcefully that he rolled down his throne-like cot. All his followers were killed. Gurbakhsh Singh escaped to Lahore and with the assistance of the Mughal

Officers succeeded in capturing control of Ram Rai's Ashram at Lahore wherefrom his followers started working against the Sikh cause especially after the death of Guru Gobind Singh. It was because of this that the Khalsa Holy Order decided to socially boycott such *Ram Rayyas*.

Militarism and Military Organisation

Militarism implies martial valour, martial aptitude and commitment to military ideals. Guru Gobind Singh possessed all these qualities. He was at once a brave soldier, a seasoned general, a matchless military organiser, but his militarism was of a higher order. The common motifs underlying militarism are: (1) Political domination; (2) Urge for patriotic strife; (3) Acquisition of wealth. But the Guru entertained none of these. Nor did the Guru's militarism resemble that of the Spartans, who were militarised to do anything—good or bad, for the state. The Guru's militarism had two things implicit in it, *viz*. Shakti and Divine Power. The Guru adopted two symbols for the propagation of his militarism: the Goddess Chandi and the Sword, Chandi being symbol of divine power and sword that of power and dignity. *Kirpan* (sword) was, therefore, an active symbol, an instrument of offence and defence and not a charm to be tied among the turban ends or stowed away in the back of the comb. "It is to be kept in a sheath and worn in a belt. It can cut through armour, men, horses, even elephants. It is superior to all instruments[60], yet it is to be used for the holy cause."

Since *Kirpan* (sword), besides being a temporal weapon, is at the same time a source of divine beneficence, signifying the divine power and destruction. Hence Sikh Militarism is rooted in the Sikh core belief that God is both a Creator and a Destroyer at one and the same time.

Military Organisation

Side by side refining and redefining the new type of militarism the Guru developed a viable military apparatus the beginning of which had been made at Anandpur.

The Guru composed an administrative body for his army. The administrative commanders were the most efficient. In the early career of the Guru, Jit Mal, Gopal Chand, Sangho Shah and Mohri Chand held charges of Civil Defence problems of Anandpur, weapons and ammunition, war animals, food and civil supplies portfolios respectively.[61] Such departments and portfolios although in rudimentary form looked analogous to the present-day army service corps. Also, such an administrative body foreshadowed the war council of the modern times. As management techniques, every soldier was made to realise his duties towards the individuals and society as a whole. Ample care was taken that an individual soldier was not driven to shoddy substitute to bolster his ego. Ordnance Factories at Paonta and Anandpur Sahib also functioned under the military administrative set up.

The Guru took special care of the training of his soldiers. He held regular competitions in archery, sword-fighting, hand-to-hand combat, ambush and patrolling. Large scale hunting expeditions were organised where soldiers got training to use their weapons on live and fast moving targets. Training was also imparted as to how to use cavalry shock the enemy to be immediately followed by swift attack of the infantry to further shock and spread demoralisation. The basic concept is even today accepted, when armour and infantry in conjunction with each other are to be employed against enemy having an organised anti-tank defence.

The bulk of the Guru's army consisted of the Sikhs from Malwa and Majha regions of the Punjab. They took food from *Guru ka Langar*; uniforms, arms and horses were provided out of the Guru's Golak (treasury). The soldiers belonged to all castes. Muslims were also in the Guru's army. The composite character of Guru's army was a positive proof of the Guru's non-particularistic approach, ideal of attaining freedom of conscience, of belief and of raising a social order on the basis of principles of tolerance and acceptance of diversity of faith and practice.

The Guru had no fondness for mercenaries, but, at times, when he felt shortage of men, and instructors for imparting military training, he did not hesitate to recruit them on salary basis. He enlisted 500 Pathans at Paonta at the instance of Pir

Badruddin but his experience was not pleasant. Regarding the scale of pay, not much is known. However, the Guru paid Rs. 5/-[62] to the Officer and Re. l/- to the soldier, per day in the case of aforesaid Pathan soldiers. It is likely that some rough sort of registration of them was kept with the Guru. According to the author of *Suraj Parkash*, when the people gathered around the Guru, he asked them to join his army and their descriptive rolls were prepared. Sainapat also supports this view.

The maximum strength of the Guru's army at any time has been estimated to be 20,000 and at Paonta it did not exceed five thousand. The artillery men were very few in number, although matchlockmen's number was considerable. The horses were procured on payment as well as through offerings of the believers. The Guru's own blue horse had become a tradition on account of its agility, boldness, steadfastness and intelligence.

Forts formed salient feature of Guru's military organisation. He built the fort of Paonta and raised walls around the city of Paonta. He regarded forts as a very potent bulwarks against aggression. He took special care that the fort should be built on hill-tops or at such place wherefrom the garrison could be able to observe the movement of the enemy forces while the enemy should not be able to move easily towards the fort. In addition, fort should be spacious enough to accommodate enough soldiers, war animals and foundries. It should have holes in the parapet and in the rampart for the cannon to fire.

The battle array of the Guru consisted of centre, right flank, left flank, reserve and vanguard. The Guru while advancing always took into consideration the terrain, the enemy's strength and the quality of fighting equipment. Ambuscade was a popular tactic employed by the Guru. Elephants were also valued much as a vehicle for the advance of the army. The Prasadi elephant was donated by Raja Rattan Chand, Zamindar of Assam and another was sent by *Sangat* of Dacca. The Prasadi elephant was harnessed in the battle.

The Guru did have spies to collect information regarding enemy's forces, their deployment, their weapons and their nature of organisation. How did he train the spies is not known but it is certain that they were efficient. On the eve of the battle of Bhangani, it was their information which led the Guru to select the elevated place a few miles away from Paonta wherefrom the battle could be controlled more effectively.

In the organisational vision of the Guru, weapons were also given requisite attention. In addition to the weapons he procured from his disciples, he got them manufactured in his own foundries at Paonta and Anandpur. The weapons used by the Guru were of four kinds: (1) Mukat. (2) Amukat. (3) Mukta Mukat. (4) Yantar Mukat. Mukat weapons were those weapons which parted company of the users as for instance arrows. Amukat were those weapons which remained with the users such as sword or Katar. Mukta Mukat weapons could be used while keeping them in the hands and throwing them on the enemy. The weapons such as spears and javelins fall in this category. Weapons of the fourth kind were used with the help of mechanical devices.

The Guru's varied activities entailed a lot of expenditure and needed strong support at least from his own disciples. In this context, the *Masand/Manjidars* who preferred to watch their own interest to that of the Sikh movement. They not only kept for themselves the whole or a large part of *Daswandh*, but also tried to make the Sikhs skeptical about the designs of the Guru. This being the perspective, the Guru got convinced that some alternative would have to be found to make the people informed of the latest activities of the Guru and what Sikhism really aimed at.

The Guru's period at Paonta marked a watershed in the Guru's life. He matured his ideas and fashioned his concepts. He evolved suitable strategies to implement them. He was responsible for making available requisite literature and rallied round himself the most capable persons from different corners of India to harness their wisdom in the service of his mission which he refined and defined with absolute clarity and lucidity. He gave new metaphors, new symbols and new slogans to energise vitalise and rejuvenate the people given to mental and physical Inertia. He reclaimed Ram Rai and worked in such a way that his establishment ceased to be separate entity and functioned as if it were the Udasi establishment of Baba Sri Chand. He organised his internal affairs diligently and made proper arrangement for carrying on correspondence with *Sangats* and eminent Sikhs. It is likely that the letters from *Sangat*/disciples were received and registered.[63] Similarly, the Hukamnamas or letters from the Guru were registered before they were sent to different places. There is every possibility that the copies of the Hukamnamas were kept by the Guru's establishment and proper arrangements made to keep record of the amount of *Daswandh* and other offerings. He organised appropriate war machine. Lest his militaristic organisation reduce itself to an organ of tyranny, the Guru reconstructed the concept of militarism. The Guru viewed and reviewed the policies of the contemporary governments both of the hill chieftains and the Mughals. He also observed the objectives, the policies and the extent of the influence of *Naqshbandis* who had their centres at important places such as Sirhind, Lahore, Delhi, Agra and Jaunpur *et al.* He carefully studied their theology, their social ideas and their attitude towards Sikhs and non-Muslims and liberal Muslims. He also took note of different faiths and their impact on society and made bold to denounce what he considered contrary to his vision. He fine-tuned the Sikh ideology left in legacy by his predecessors. He forged a theory of Dharam Yudh—struggle for righteousness which was different from Muhammedan concept of Jehad and Christian concept of crusade in as much as its causative factor was injustice, tyranny and unrighteousness and its goal was the establishment of Global Order based on righteousness which was defined not in terms of any specific group or race or religion but in terms at once universalistic and humanistic.

BATTLE OF BHANGANI

A Violent Reaction of Hindu Orthodoxy

On September 18, 1688[64], the Guru fought the battle of Bhangani against Fateh Shah and his allies. As to the circumstances which led to the battle, different versions are in vogue. The Sikh records state that Bhim Chand asked the Guru for the loan of Parsadi elephant, both to assert his suzerainty and to use it on the occasion of the betrothal ceremony of his son. The Guru refused to oblige him which embittered Bhim Chand who vowed to take revenge from the Guru. Bhim Chand consulted some of his brother chieftains, Raja Kirpal of Katoch among others, as to the course he should pursue to punish the Guru. It was ultimately decided that this question should be finally taken up as soon as the ensuing marriage of Bhim Chand's son with the daughter of Fateh Shah was over. Fateh Shah himself had been consulted about it. In the meantime, the Guru had retired to Paonta and became a great friend of Fateh Shah by amicably settling the disputes between him and the Raja of Nahan.

As the day of the marriage approached, the groom's marriage party started for Srinagar, the capital of Garhwal state. The shortest route to Srinagar passed through Paonta, but the Guru refused to give them the passage apprehending trouble from Bhim Chand who was accompanied by a large number of soldiers. After a lot of negotiations the Guru agreed to allow bridegroom and a small number of his guests to cross the ferry near Paonta. The rest of the party was constrained to follow a circuitous route to reach Srinagar in the present province of Uttaranchal.

This made Bhim Chand desperate who waited for the opportunity to give vent to his anger, which came when the Guru sent Dewan Nand Chand[65] to present rich presents at the *Tambol* ceremony.[66] Bhim Chand openly threatened that he would sever all connections with Fateh Shah and return without marrying his son if the presents were accepted. Nand Chand was attacked by Bhim Chand's men, but he escaped unharmed. No sooner was the marriage accomplished, than Bhim Chand held a conference with Fateh Shah and some other hill chiefs, such as Kirpal of Katoch, Gopal of Guler, Hari Chand of Hadur and the Raja of Jaswal, who were there. They all decided to attack the Guru at Paonta.

From the above account, three points emerge: firstly, the sole or the main cause was the estrangement between Bhim

Chand and the Guru. Secondly, it was caused because of the Guru's refusal to oblige the Raja and then to disallow passage to the marriage party through Paonta. Thirdly, Fateh Shah was forced to wage a war under the pain of threat by Bhim Chand that the latter would sever his relations with Fateh Shah.

Let us examine first two points in the first instance. If we accept the authenticity of these points, the Guru's stay in Nahan territory must have been minimal, for he left Makhowal when the marriage of Bhim Chand's son with the daughter of Fateh Shah was impending and he came back immediately after the marriage ceremony was over. The view is upheld by the Sikh records unanimously. The Sikh Chroniclers' view that Bhim Chand asked for a temporary loan of the animal on the occasion of his son's marriage also points to the conclusion that even when Bhim Chand was making preparations to proceed to Srinagar to celebrate his son's wedding, the Guru was still at Makhowal. From the Guru's own account, we learnt that the Guru left Paonta immediately after the battle of Bhangani.[67] This being so, we have very good reason to believe that the Guru made somewhat protracted stay at Paonta. From this, it follows that the Guru must have not gone to Paonta immediately before the marriage of Bhim Chand's son. And if this is so, the entire story that the bitterness between the Guru and Bhim Chand grew as a result of the Guru's refusal to loan out elephant on the marriage of his son falls to the ground. But it does not mean that Bhim Chand was well-disposed to the Guru. In fact, when Bhim Chand grew to his adulthood and took upon himself the responsibility of running the state, he took note of the activities of the Guru at Makhowal and became keen in asserting his authority on the establishment of the Guru. In his youthful pride, he threw all caution to the winds and made an unsuccessful attack on the Guru. It is possible that Bhim Chand might have played his nefarious role so far as the instigation of Fateh Chand was concerned. But to attribute the outbreak of hostility between the Guru and Fateh Shah solely to the enmity of Bhim Chand

and to consider it the major cause of the war is too much for the historical analysis to justify.

Another thing which fortifies our assumption is that in *Bachittar Natak*, practically the only reliable evidence regarding the battle of Bhangani, there is no mention of Bhim Chand in connection with the battle. This fact in itself is significant particularly when the Sikh tradition asserts that Bhim Chand's enmity was the main cause of the clash. If Bhim Chand had been the sole or main cause of the battle, it was improbable that the Guru would so readily return to Kahlur immediately after the battle was over.

Closely connected with this is the question: If Bhim Chand's enmity towards the Guru was not the cause or the major cause, what else then was responsible for the battle? J.D. Cunningham[68] says that the "Guru seems to have endeavoured to mix himself up with the affairs of the half independent chiefs and to obtain a commanding influence over them, so as by degrees to establish a virtual independent principality, amid mountainous fastnesses to serve as the basis of his operation against the Mughal Government." Cunningham's statement is only partially true. It is doubtful whether the view of the Guru had advanced to the extent of establishing an independent principality[69] but there are definite indications in the Sikh records that the Guru was interested in the affairs of the Hill Chieftain and we feel that was exactly this in which the genesis of the battle of Bhangani can be found. The invitation of Medni Parkash to the Guru to settle down in Sirmour was an act born not only out of his admiration of the Guru's personality or adoration of his mission, but was also a measure against any evil designs of his enemies which was a proof of his political sagacity and foresight. Medni Parkash did so, because he was convinced that the Guru and his armed followers would prove beneficial for his state. In close proximity to the Sirmour state on the western side of Jamuna was the state of Garhwal. These two neighbouring states had borne enmity towards each other for about four generations if not more.

The Rajas of Garhwal had some tangible reasons to hate the Sirmour Royal House for its being an instrument in the hands of the Mughals who had been keen on depriving the rulers of Garhwal of their independent status. Moreover, the Sirmour Rajas who were then basking in the sunshine of the Mughal favour had seldom missed the opportunity of territorial gain at the expense of Garhwal.

The Kangra and Simla Hills had been brought under the sovereignty of the Mughals by the time of Jahangir. During the time of Shah Jahan, attempts were made to bring Garhwal under the influence of the Mughal Rule.[70] In 1635, Najabat Khan, the Faujdar of the country at the foot of the Kangra Hills, was entrusted with the task of maintaining Mughal hegemony over Garhwal. Mandhatta, the grandfather of Medni Parkash, helped him. The campaign failed, in spite of a few initial successes. Najabat's failure cost him his position and his *Jagir* although Sirmour ruler was allowed to retain the territory conquered in the initial stage.[71] In 1654, Shah Jahan sent another expedition. Mandhata expired before the campaign was actually launched and his son and successor honoured the promise made by his father. The campaign, being a grand success, the Raja of Sirmour was given the title 'Subhag Parkash' and was given the territory of Kotaha[72], which he occupied after expelling the Zamindar of the area.

To Aurangzeb Raja Subhag Parkash rendered important services. He intercepted the correspondence between Dara who was in Punjab making frantic efforts to gain the Mughal throne and Suleiman, who was at that time a guest of Prithvi Shah, the Garhwal ruler.

With the twin purpose of bringing the ruler of Garhwal within the ambit of the Mughal influence and persuading him to hand over Sulaiman to the Mughals. Aurangzeb commissioned Ra'd Khan to undertake the expedition.[73] Subhag Parkash got the area named Kala Khar identified in the Sirmour state with the modern area of Kalagarh[74], which lies near Dehradun.[75]

Subhag Parkash expired in 1664 and Budh Parkash succeeded him. During his reign (1664-1684) the Mughal government stopped meting out preferential treatment to Budh Parkash.[76] This was because Medini Shah (he was different from Medni Parkash of Sirmour) the heir-apparent to the Garhwal throne had handed over Sulaiman Shah to Aurangzeb in December 1660, and soon after when he became the Raja, he had recognised the Mughal Emperor as his suzerain.[77]

In appreciation of the submissive demeanour of Medini Shah, Aurangzeb handed back the Dun to the Garhwal state.

Now the situation as it stood during Aurangzeb's reign was that with Sirmour possessing Kala Khar and Garhwal owning the Dun, the boundaries of the two rival states got mixed up in such a way that Aurangzeb was able to exploit the situation to his own advantage. Though situation was explosive, yet no open conflict occurred. In 1684, Budh Parkash and Medini Shah died and they were succeeded by Jog Raj under the title of Medni Parkash in Sirmour and Fateh Shah in Garhwal.[78] Both the new chiefs were ambitious men of ability and for that very reason, they were afraid of each other. While watching each other's moves on the frontier, they had to be on guard against surprise attacks. It was in this background that Medni Parkash invited the Guru to Sirmour state and allowed him to build a fort at Paonta, a place guarding the only convenient route from one state to the other.

The Guru, whose relations with Bhim Chand of Kahlur were strained, welcomed the invitation and shifted his headquarters to Paonta.

There was every likelihood of the Guru being involved in the boundary dispute if it arose between two rival states. But he tackled the problem with a fitness worthy of a great statesman. He improved relations between Sirmour and Garhwal.[79] His success in accomplishing the task was indeed a miracle. It is said that the Guru also made use of Ram Rai in getting the things straightened.[80]

With the passage of time, the relations between Sirmour and Garhwal got strained once again. Fateh Shah decided to break the agreement and bring all the disputed territory between the two states under him by force. As a first step in breaking Sirmour resistance, the Garhwal ruler marched towards Paonta, which was so close to the border and so strategically placed that Fateh Shah felt it imperative to break the headquarter of the Guru at Paonta. In this project, Fateh Shah was helped by the chiefs of Dadhwar and Jaswal, Gaji Chand of Chandel, Gopal of Guler and Hari Chand of Kotiwal. According to later Sikh chroniclers the number of chiefs who joined Fateh Shah stood at fifteen.[81]

The Guru, however, forestalled Fateh Shah and checked the invading army at the point where it crossed the river Giri into the area of Sirmour state before marching.

The opposing forces met in the field of Bhangani about 6 miles to the north-east of Paonta on the plains between the Jamuna and the Giri (called Kalindri by Guru Gobind Singh in *Bachittar Natak*), not far from the city of Rajpur on the Mussoorie road. Just on the eve of the battle, the four hundred Pathan mercenaries under the leaders Hayat Khan, Najabat Khan, Bhikhan Khan and Jawahar Khan who had been on the Guru's pay were seduced by the hill chiefs by flaunting rich rewards and they deserted the Guru to join their forces.[82] Only Kale Khan with his one hundred men remained loyal to the Guru. One thousand Udasis with the exception of their leader Kirpal also left the Guru. The Guru's army, which comprised 2000 soldiers was thus reduced to 1000 soldiers, while the allies' forces numbered 10000—ten times more than the Guru's forces.

Even then, the Guru was unnerved. He correctly anticipated the route which the Garhwal troops would follow and occupied a hillock to check Fateh Shah's march on Paonta, and established himself on an elevation which was of an immense advantage to him. The bulk of the reserve, with the hillock in between, was not visible to the rival commanders, thereby enabling the Guru's troops to undertake manoeuvres without the knowledge of the enemy.

The Guru himself standing on an elevated ground could clearly watch the deployment and movement of the enemy forces on the other side.

From the contemporary or semi-contemporary records which throw light on the battle, it is difficult to comprehend clearly the way the two armies were deployed. However, the impression that emerges is that both the armies were divided into units with separate leaders making their moves under their respective supreme commanders, Fateh Shah and Guru Gobind Singh. No elaborate war strategy was followed; units moved simply or in groups as directed till the leader was killed or the force felt exhausted. Then the combatants would run to the supreme commanders who would commission fresh men to take up the task.

The battle commenced with great determination on both sides. Immediately after the five sons of Bibi Viro, Sango Shah, Jit Mal, Gopal Chand, Ganga Ram and Mohri Chand organised an attack. They were ably backed by Daya Ram, Dewan Chand and the two Kirpals: One, the Guru's maternal uncle and the other, an Udasi Mahant. Kirpal (Mahant) hit Hayat Khan on the head and killed the deserter. This was quickly followed by Sahib Chand's entry into the fray to kill the murderous Khan from Khorasan.[83] At this juncture Pir Budhu Shah along with his two brothers, seven sons and 500 men arrived to add to the small reserve that Guru Gobind Singh possessed. Upto this time Fateh Shah's side was on the defensive. Then Raja Gopal and Hari Chand launched vigorous offensive. The Guru ordered Jit Mal and his men to advance. For some time the Guru's prospects looked very bleak. At this juncture, Jit Mal with his spear struck Hari Chand who fell down senseless and had to be carried off the field. In the confusion that followed, Kesri Shah Jaswalia and Modhur Shah Dadwalia, two of the prominent chiefs on Fateh Shah's side escaped being killed only because the Guru's men desisted from hitting the fleeing army. At this moment, Hari Chand regained consciousness and immediately became alive to the duties of a leader. He recalled the hill troops and the Pathans and the last phase of the battle started. The Guru sent Sangho

Shah or Shah Sangram as the Guru would call him to foil the offensive of Hari Chand. He fought hard, led his men well killed Najabat Khan and many of his men, but only at the cost of his own life.[84] The Guru who had not taken actual part in the fray till then was now stung to action. He moved forward and struck Bhikhan Shah on the face. The blow was so hard that Bhikhan Shah could not survive. Now began the great duel with bows and arrows between the Guru and Hari Chand, who was famous for his valour and dash and had already killed hundreds of his adversaries in the battle. The Guru had a narrow escape three times, but ultimately took aim and killed Hari Chand.[85] The death of Hari Chand disarrayed the hill forces and they had a disorderly retreat. The Guru's victory was complete.[86] He attributed his success to the Grace of *Kāl* (God) (*Bachittar Natak*). Bhei Jit Merī Kirpā Kāl Terī.

Fateh Shah arrived back at Srinagar in ignominy, totally crest-fallen. The battle was fought for about nine hours. The Guru's Sikhs had vindicated themselves in the battlefield with honour. They had displayed great skill in swordsmanship, spearing, archery, horse-riding and hand-to-hand combat.

Just after the battle, the Guru went to the place where lay the dead bodies of Sangho Shah, Jit Mal and other Sikhs. He ordered the slain on both the sides to be disposed of with due honour: the bodies of Sikhs were cremated and of the Muslims buried with all solemnity. The wounded were properly tended. The dead bodies of Sangho Shah and Jit Mal, were brought to Paonta, where they were cremated with due honour the next day. The dead bodies of the sons of Pir Budhu Shah which had also been brought to Paonta were buried with due honour.

The recitation of *Guru Granth Sahib* started the same day and was concluded on Thursday Kartik Vadi Panchmi Bk 1745 corresponding to C.E. 1688.

On returning to the fort of Paonta, the Guru held a *Darbar* (Court), bestowed robes of honour and other gifts upon the valiant soldiers and generals.[87] Pir Budhu Shah was pleased to get the fallen hair of the Guru, a turban, a comb, and a Hukamnama admiring his services.[88] Those who deliberately kept themselves away from the battle were driven out of the place. Guru himself says, 'He fostered the faithful and rooted out all the wicked.'[89]

The battle of Bhangani brought into focus many points of importance. It bolstered up the morale of the Sikhs. It instilled new confidence among them. It demonstrated that the power of the ideology coupled with appropriate organisation was more than a match for the massed might of princes and potentates. The Guru got convinced that the mercenaries were no substitute for the persons imbibed with the spirit of mission.

The battle also highlighted that all was not well with internal organisation of the Sikhs. The *Masands* as a group had gone corrupt and were more interested in their selfish ends than responding to the call of the Guru. Instead of doing their duty of linking the people with the Guru's message, they exploited their gullibility. This thing sparked off a question: 'Whether Masand system should be scrapped or kept as such?' The battle was significant from another point of view. Nearly fifteen hill chieftains had combined their military strength to attack the Guru. The coming together of so many chiefs and that too within a record time was indeed astonishing for the Guru who had done little to provoke them. He was not a ruler and as such did not possess any principality. To organise such a massive attack on him was obviously uncalled-for and a clear-cut case of moral turpitude.

Under the circumstances, the Guru was constrained to think that the hill chieftains including Fateh Shah of Garhwal had been motivated by certain ulterior designs which could possibly be the annihilation of the Sikh religion and the Sikh movement which in their reckoning had the potential of destabilising their socio-political system in which they had been nursed and which they had loved for so long and which had given them prominence in society.

Dr. Hari Ram Gupta says that the hill chieftains were instigated by the Mughal authorities but this view seems to be far-fetched, at least at this stage. There is no concrete evidence that the Mughals encouraged the hill chieftains to organise and to lead expedition against the Guru. The Guru, therefore, had to be wary of them while formulating his plans, especially when even the ruler of Sirmour preferred to remain aloof from the battle, possibly because he did not wish to be out of step with his brother hill chieftains when they gave the expression that they were doing all this to safeguard their politico-socio cultural heritage which the Guru's dispensation sought to destroy.

Return to Anandpur (1688)

The Guru did not stay at Paonta for long. The Guru's stay at Paonta after the battle of Bhangani was very short—one month and ten days, according to Sarup Singh Kaushik.[90] He left Paonta Sahib on Kartik Sudi Trodsi, Bk 1745 for Kapal Mochan, an ancient pilgrimage centre of the Hindus 20 Kms. away from Jagadhri. The Guru delivered his instructions to a large number of people who had gathered there to celebrate the fair held annually in honour of Kapal Mochan. Since that was the fullmoon day in Kartak (28th October, 1688) the day which was believed to be the birthday of Guru Nanak, the Guru held a special congregation and honoured his Sikhs with *Siropas* (robes of honour) consisting of Saffron coloured pieces of coarse cloth.[91]

From there, the Guru went to Sadhaura to console Nasiran, Pir Budhu Shah's wife for the death of her two sons in the battle of Bhangani. The Pir was simply overwhelmed and in a spirit of utter surrender and thankfulness uttered, "How beneficent is God to me who enabled my sons to lay down their lives in His service."

After Sadhaura, the Guru pitched his camp at Laharpur[92], fifteen Kms. from Sadhaura. There he spent over two weeks. Pir Budhu Shah made it a point to visit him as often as he could. From Laharpur the Guru sent his armies to Anandpur and he himself proceeded[93] to Toda which he left shortly to enter Raigarh state. He encamped at Tabra for more than a week. From there he left for Raipur, the headquarter of the state in response to the invitation of the queen of that place[94], who was acting as regent for her minor son and had great reverence for the Guru. She offered a purse of eleven hundred rupees and a well-caparisoned horse. Ranghars of Toda village stole Guru's camels in the darkness of night and passed them on to their relatives at Laha, where under the pressure from people, they had to restore them to the Guru. Two gurdwaras stand at Raipur, one outside the fort of Raipur where the Guru encamped and the other inside the fort where the Guru dined as the Rani's guest.

Next stay of Guru was at Mani Majra[95] where Mata Raj Kaur accorded a hearty welcome (Maghar Sudi Dasmi Bk 1745). Therefrom he went to the village Dhakuli[96] and addressed the *Sangat* of the village and also met Ishar Das, the Masand of the place. After this, the Guru met Nihang Khan, the Zamindar of Kotla Nihang, a place in proximity to the present-day Ropar city. Nihang Khan was so moved that he decided to dedicate his all in the cause of the Guru. This happened on the Amavas of Maghar 1745 Bk 1688.[97]

A day after, the Guru visited the places such as Ropar, Ghanaula, Bunga *et al.* Then he arrived at Kiratpur and stayed with Mata Sulakhni. Bhai Amar Chand, the grandson of Har Rai, Deep Chand and Nand Chand, the sons of Suraj Mal, made their obeisance to the Guru.

In *Bachittar Natak*, while the Guru gives the details of the battle of Bhangani, he did not even allude to what made him leave for Anandpur immediately after the battle was over. According to Dr. Fauja Singh, 'Anandpur was strategically a much better place than Paonta in the state of Sirmour and that is why after about three years only, the Guru had returned to Anandpur.' But this does not explain the whole thing. It seems that the disappointing attitude of the ruler of Sirmour contributed a lot in arriving at the decision on the part of the Guru. Sandwiched between Fateh Shah as his avowed enemy on one side and Medni Parkash, an indifferent friend on the other, the Guru was bound to rethink and reshape his policies.

In the meanwhile Bhim Chand had also softened towards the Guru. He had seen for himself that the Guru has a force and it was not easy to dislodge him from Anandpur. He had also observed that the Guru was not a jingoist, taking sadistic pleasure in waging wars. Besides a member of the family of

Bhim Chand had developed devotion for the Guru and his causes. It is on record that Rani Champa Devi, mother of Bhim Chand, had high regards for the Guru and took pleasure in inviting him to her home or going to him to pay her respects. This thing also helped to bring about harmony between the Guru and Bhim Chand. Political ambition of Bhim Chand at this stage also played its role. During Guru Gobind Singh's absence from Chak Nanaki, Bhim Chand's position in the hill politics had changed for the better. Known chiefly as the head of an important state till 1685, he was now acknowledged as a great military leader. This was because in 1686, he had won a great victory over the combined forces of Bashahar, Mandi and Kothai who had attacked Bidhi Chand the Raja of Kulu, the maternal uncle of Bhim Chand.[98]

Among the hill Rajas the tradition of rebelling against the Mughals was an old one, because they considered them as political and cultural imposition. The first widespread rebellion had taken place in the reign of Akbar.[99] The Rajas of Nurpur and Basu, Suraj Mal and Jagar Singh had revolted in the later years of Jahangir and early in the reign of Shah Jahan. Perhaps believing that a concerted efforts would be better rewarded, the Hill Rajas formed a combination in the reign of Aurangzeb in 1675 C.E. and even defeated the then Mughal governor when he invaded the hills.[100] The Emperor's sudden return from the north-west had, however, discouraged the combination so much that it disintegrated soon after. There were much better prospects now, for, Aurangzeb had involved himself in the Maratha war in the far off Deccan and Imperial administration in the north India was fast losing its grip over the affairs in North India. The Hill Rajas hoped that they would liberate themselves from the Mughal yoke by concerted military action. Hence they felt encouraged to join a combination[101] which included states from all the three groups—Simla, Kangra and Jammu.

Bhim Chand saw in the victor of Bhangani a good ally, and he, therefore, sought rapprochement with the Guru which was reached through the mediation of the queen of Raipur. Both the Guru and Bhim Chand entered into an agreement at

Raipur.[102] The Guru now felt free to join his army which he had already sent to Makhowal. Bhim Chand was relieved of the fear of the Sikhs whom he considered a great threat to his sovereignty.

Guru Gobind Singh used the changed circumstances and the rapprochement with Bhim Chand to freely build up his headquarter. He renewed his contacts with his disciples in the Majha and Doaba regions of the Punjab. Many of its inhabitants who had accompanied him to Paonta came back. Anandpur began to bustle with new life. Many poets, scholars and thinkers came to pay their homage to the Guru. Many of them brought their families with them and made Anandpur as their home. He also called expert artisans, skilled-masons from far and wide and to this effect he even issued Hukamnama.[103] He rapidly increased the strength of the army. He fostered the faithful and rooted out all the wicked. He drove out of the place those who had kept themselves away from the battle of Bhangani and patronised those who had distinguished themselves there.[104] He had to put his own house in order, for there were people in the Guru's camp who cared little for his cause and who had followed him merely for the sake of personal profit.[105] He took many defensive measures.

He built a chain of forts Anandgarh, Keshgarh, Fatehgarh, Lohgarh, Agamgarh (also called Holgarh) and Taragarh, Keshgarh was in the centre and all the rest were around it. It would be rash to conclude that the Guru had only anti-Mughal projects in view while taking up the construction of the forts. Anandpur which he had made his headquarter was situated in potentially hostile territory. Bhim Chand's attitude could change any time and the political atmosphere of the region never portended stability always likely to cause flare-ups even on trivial issues among the hill Rajas or between the hill Rajas and the Guru. It was obviously necessary for a body of outsiders like the Sikhs to put themselves in a strong position. The Guru encouraged his people to train themselves in martial art. He himself led many expeditions in the surrounding forests which were rich in wildlife including leopards, bears and elephants. The area was then known as Hathout (abode of elephants).

FIGHTING IN THE FOOTHILLS OF THE HIMALAYAS

Alif Khan's Expedition—1790 C.E.

Two years after Guru Gobind Singh came back to Anandpur. The combination of the Rajas consisting of Gopal Chand of Guler, Ram Singh of Jaswan, Prithvi Chand of Dadowal, Kesri Chand Jaswal and Sukhdev Singh of Jasrota stopped paying their respective annual tributes. The Faujdars of Kangra and Jammu, who used to collect tributes, sought help from the government of Lahore to realise the arrears. A strong contingent under Mian Khan with Alif Khan as his deputy led expedition against the hill chiefs.[106]

The object of this expedition was to crush resistance simultaneously in the Jammu and Kangra regions. Mian Khan himself went to Jammu and sent Alif Khan to Kangra.[107]

Alif Khan moved to Nadaun instead of Kangra (30 Kms. south of Kangra) which seems to have been a *Naib Faujdari* with a small contingent to look after the eastern part of the Kangra state. His aim was to make Nadaun his base and therefrom to attack Bhim Chand to make a quick end of the challenge of Hill Rajas. His movement was brisk and he thought that he would not allow Bhim Chand to have any help from outside. He selected an elevated ground and raised a wooden fortress on it.[108] Besides, he asked the Faujdar of Kangra to prevail upon the Hill Rajas who had joined the rebels to come with their forces to Nadaun. Kirpal of Kangra and Dayal of Bijarwal joined Alif Khan.[109]

Bhim Chand, contrary to the expectations of Alif Khan, acted with speed and alacrity. Raj Singh[110] and Ram Singh Jaswal[111] immediately rushed to his help since their territories were very close to Nadaun. The Rajas of distant states also sent help, although they did not come themselves. Prithvi Chand[112] of Dhadwal sent his contingent. Sukhdev, a Gazi from Jasrota, also came to participate in the impending war. Bhim Chand specially invited the Guru on the occasion[113], who came in person at the head of a strong contingent equipped with bows, arrows, swords, spears and a few muskets.

Though Bhim Chand had mustered a strong force, yet it was not easy to wrest victory. The enemy was entrenched in the fortress which though not very strong, being made of wood, assured advantage to its occupants of a cover denied to Bhim Chand. Moreover Alif Khan's forces being arranged on an elevation held distinct advantage over Bhim Chand's forces. Bhim Chand opened the attack. The sharp arrow and the shots could make no impact on the enemy because of its position and struck only the wooden rafters of the fortress. Bhim Chand led two more attacks which too were ineffective. Now Bhim Chand became desperate and launched another attack invoking Hanuman[114] for help. Kirpal assisted by Dayal[115] of Bijarwal fought so vigorously that Bhim Chand got unnerved. At this critical juncture various tribes such as Nanglu, Panglu, Jaswal and Guleriei, who had rallied in favour of Bhim Chand, rushed upon Kirpal Chand's contingent. Bhim Chand also invoked the special help of the Guru, who uptil now had stationed his forces on a hillock nearby the improvised wooden fortress of Alif Khan. The Guru's forces lost no time to discharge arrows on the enemy in the fort and Bhim Chand's sagging morale got a shot and he and his allies rallied round their forces and made an assault. Kirpal and his ally Dayal stood their ground and were on the verge of repelling the attack. Now the Guru came out openly to play his part most effectively. He writes "Then this humble servant (of God) took up his gun and aimed at the heart of a Raja (Dayal). Fighting bravely he fell to the ground. Even when falling, the proud warrior in his rage shouted 'kill'. I put aside the gun and took up my bow, shot four arrows, with my right hand and three with my left. I could not see whether they struck any body. By that time, God turned the battle in our favour. The enemy was driven into the river. Arrows and bullets flew in abundance as if warriors were playing Holi.[116]

Alif Khan and his men fled.[117] They crossed the river Beas and Bhim Chand's victory was complete. The Rajas of Jaswal, Guler and other states hastened to their capitals for fear of

Mughal reprisal on their respective states. Guru Gobind Singh stayed there for eight days[118] and then marched with his followers to Anandpur. Bhim Chand along with his troops remained there behind at Nadaun[119] where soon after he reached an understanding with Alif Khan through Kirpal Chand Katoch who acted as intermediary. Bhim Chand and his associate Rajas settled terms of peace without consulting the Guru. The *Bachittar Natak* is completely silent about the scenario as it developed after Nadaun victory but from Bhim Chand's role in later years, it appears that Bhim Chand and his associate Rajas had agreed to pay tribute thereby recognising Mughal sovereignty. The Guru, however, was not at all apprised by Bhim Chand while contracting agreement, to the Guru's dismay and anguish.

The Guru and his followers while still on their way to Anandpur-Makhowal had to punish the inhabitants of the village Alsun who refused to sell supplies to them and displayed the audacity to ridicule Sikh religion, presumably at the instigation of the certain officials of Kahlur who harboured strong dislike for the new religio-cultural model outside the Hindu context and at least for the present found themselves very strong because of their rapprochement with the Mughals.

It is difficult to determine as to whether the village was plundered or only the slanderers were chastised. However, one thing is certain that the village being dominated by the Rajput caste and having ties of lineage with Bhim Chand had aversion for the Guru and his mission and in the case of the rapprochement of Bhim Chand with the Rajas and the Mughal government, the villagers thought it an appropriate occasion to pick up dispute with the Guru to please their master and to give vent to their own innate hatred. The Guru under such circumstances had no alternative but to punish the villagers.

The Guru, in spite of his help to Bhim Chand in the battle of Nadaun, gained nothing, not even the goodwill of Bhim Chand. The Guru, however, won over two friends in Raja Raj Singh and Raja Ram Singh. Raj Singh's state Jaswan lay to the north of Anandpur and watched the only route that the Mughal Faujdar at Kangra could take to harm the Guru at his headquarter. Guler lay towards the northwest of Anandpur linking the Guru with his devoted following in the present district of Hoshiarpur. He could not thus be easily threatened by Bhim Chand even with the Mughal support from Kangra. The Guru severed all connections with Bhim Chand.

The experience of the Guru at Nadaun convinced the Guru that he could not hope to depend for long on the friendship of his two neighbours and therefore, he stepped up his activities to build up his strength. He during the next three years and nine months when he had undisturbed peace planned his way to greater armed strength. He gave his army a strong social base by giving a call to his followers not only to come to Anandpur in greater numbers every year but also to make the city as their home. But the Guru's preoccupations in raising the army did not blind him to his religious duties. Once well-settled at Anandpur, he took up the completion of his work *Akal Ustat* in 1691, which he had started writing in 1684. The composition is considered to be one of the best works of the Guru and is divided into six parts. In the first part there is invocation to God who is looked upon Timeless, Omnipresent, All Steel and Supreme Nature. The second part deals with the futility of worldly pomp and power. The third part is a satire on the various penances and austerities. The fourth part relates to the popular theological queries on the spiritual aspects of life and philosophy of Hindu *Shastras*. The fifth part sings the praises of Chandi as Shakti of God. The last part is a hymn to God in all His splendour. Another composition *Pokhyan Triya Charitra* was composed in this period in September 1693[120] by some unknown poet, perhaps to expose the wiles of the perverse and unscrupulous.

Dilawar Khan's Attempt to Weaken Guru's Power

Large congregations at Anandpur and the Guru's rapidly increasing military strength unnerved the Kangra faujdar and possibly a few hill Rajas. Their nervousness was compounded when they pondered upon the influence which the Guru brought to bear upon the hill chiefs to take decision of stopping payment of tribute to the Mughal exchequer and the dangerous and wider ramifications which could result if Guru's influence was not checkmated. They, therefore, sought Aurangzeb's directions as to how to meet the menace.

The Emperor, in response to this representation, directed his Faujdars of Delhi, Sirhind, Lahore and Jammu to stop the Guru from collecting his Sikhs at Anandpur. A special order was issued in November, 1693 to the governor of Sirhind to admonish Gobind Rai[121] son of Tegh Bahadur, to make him follow the instructions of the Emperor.[122] Accordingly, Dilawar Khan, the Faujdar of Kangra began a series of attacks with intention of breaking the Guru's power at Anandpur.

Khanzada's Expedition—1694

He sent his son Rustam Khan called Khanzada in *Bachittar Natak* to curb the power of the Guru at Anandpur in November-December, 1694. He framed a plan to take the Guru by surprise. He crossed the river Sutlej with a thousand soldiers under the cover of darkness at about mid-night, but just then a Guru's *dheoridar* Alam Singh[123], informed the Guru. Immediately, Ranjit Nagara (war drum) was sounded. The Sikhs with alacrity and promptitude took up their arms and with the zeal of a crusader arrayed themselves in a battle-array to give a hot welcome to the enemy. The quick formations of the Sikhs bewildered the enemy and the guns of the Sikhs which began to discharge volleys of shots and emitted murderous fire altogether terrified the enemy and they were constrained to reel back with their weapons unused.[124] While going back, the soldiers of Khanzada plundered village Barwan, stayed for some time at Bhulan and then returned to Dilawar Khan crestfallen. Thus the Guru got the victory without a fight as he writes: "Through God's favour, the wretched fools could not even touch me, and they fled."

Hussain Khan's Expedition—1695

The failure of Khanzada piqued Dilawar Khan[125] to plan another expedition against the Guru. He chose Hussain Khan, perhaps the ablest general with the Kangra Faujdar for the purpose. Hussain Khan marched with fury and carried whatever came before him. He brought Madhukar Shah, the Raja of

Dhadwal to his knees and plundered Dūn. Kirpal Chand the brother of the Raja of Kangra joined him. Bhim Chand of Kahlur too cast his lot with Hussain, most probably with a view to achieving double-purpose: winning the favour of the Mughals and annihilating the Guru and the movement he was piloting.

All the three (Hussain, Kirpal and Bhim Chand) along with their armies made plans to proceed to Anandpur, but just then an incident occurred which changed the course of future developments. The Guru had assessed the design and made preparation to foil it. On hearing the submission of Ajmer Chand of Kahlur and Kirpal, Gopal, the Raja of Guler along with a powerful chief Ram Singh, proceeded to negotiate with Hussain Khan. Flattered and blinded by his successes, Hussain Khan did not deem it proper to take note of the difficulties of Gopal and threatened him with dire consequences if he did not pay ten thousand rupees as war levy. Gopal pleaded his inability to pay and came back.[126] Thereupon, Hussain besieged the town of Guler. Finding that the inhabitants of the town were incapable of withstanding the rigours of the siege, Gopal sued for peace but nothing less than ten thousand rupees could satisfy Hussain. The helpless Gopal approached the Guru who sent Sangatia along with seven other Sikhs to re-open the negotiations on his behalf. Sangatia on his own security brought the Gopal in Hussain's camp to negotiate but the two parties could not reach any settlement. Kirpal and Bhim Chand began to conspire to arrest Gopal but the latter escaped in time. Kirpal lost his temper and fulminated in fury. He together with his brave commando Kimat, Himmat, Hussain Khan and Ajmer Chand lost no time to attack the city. Fighting commenced with vengeance. Raja Gopal was helped by Guru's commanders, Lal Chand, Ganga Ram, Kirpa Ram and Agri Singh Brar along with 300 chosen soldiers and Raja Ram Singh of Jaswan. Hussain's bravery won a lot of applause but a sharp pointed arrow struck Hussain Khan dead. Raja Kirpal and several other brave officers such as Himmat and Kimat fell fighting. On the side of Gopal, there was a heavy loss. Sangatia and his seven comrades were killed. Agri Singh Brar also fell fighting.

Gopal came out victorious. The Guru felt jubilant and correctly appraised that "the rain of bullets that was originally intended for me was showered by the Almighty elsewhere".[127] The Guru calls this battle in *Bachittar Natak* as Hussaini Battle.[128]

Dilawar Khan sent yet another expedition in August, 1695. Jujhar Singh and Chandan Rai[129] were sent to Jaswan but they could not achieve the purpose. They undoubtedly recovered Bhalan[130] (14 Kms. away from Anandpur) a strategic place in the state, which had previously been captured by the hill chiefs and was now in the charge of Jaswan contingent. But before they could proceed further, Gaj Singh[131] of Jaswan with his contingent fell upon them. Jujhar Singh and Chandan Rai fought like lions but were soon over-powered. Jujhar Singh was killed in action[132] and Chandan Rai fled. The enemy failed to reach Anandpur and retired. The result of the defeat of the imperial forces was that the Mughal administration in the hill area fell in disarray, much to the chagrin of Aurangzeb, who was away in the southern India to extend his sovereignty to the Shia States and the Marathas. The hill Rajas took courage to withhold payment of their annual tributes in defiance of their agreement. The Sikhs were emboldened in their attitude towards the Imperial authority. The scenario being grave and disturbing, Aurangzeb realised that some drastic measures became absolutely necessary and accordingly sent one of his sons Prince Muazzam afterwards known as Bahadur Shah for the restoration of the order in hill area and for the recovery of unpaid tributes.[133] Prince Muazzam was born in September 1643. He was arrested by Aurangzeb in 1686 on the suspicion that he reached secret understanding with the Shia ruler of Golcunda to make use of his services later on certain occasions. He was set free in 1691. He remained viceroy of North West region including Punjab and Afghanistan from 1696 to 1699.[134] He resided at Kabul and occasionally visited other provinces.

The prince took up his position in August 1696 at Lahore[135] and from there he directed operations aimed at the hill Rajas. He deputed Mirza Beg to teach a lesson to hill Rajas. "He inflicted upon them defeat after defeat, plundered their country, set to fire villages, took hundreds of prisoners and in order to make an example of them had them shaven clean and their faces blackened, seated them on donkeys and made an exhibition of them throughout the disturbed area. Even those who deserted the Guru or turned apostates or grabbed the offerings collected for the House of Guru also suffered destruction, and humiliation. After Mirza Beg, the Prince sent four more high profile (*Ahdyas*) officers who also pursued the policy of Mirza Beg relentlessly and with severity.

Under the circumstances the Guru doubtlessly passed through turbulent time.[136] He, therefore, prepared himself to meet any contingency. He sent *Hukamnama*[137] dated 2nd August, 1696 directing some leading disciples such as Bhai Triloka and Bhai Rupa to rush to Anandpur along with their followers. He also wrote to the progenitors of the Phulkian house asking for assistance.[138] But the Prince while taking strong measures to humiliate and demoralise the hill Rajas left the Guru untouched presumably he did not find any justification to proceed against the Guru. The Guru had no principality nor did he flaunt sovereignty. The Guru took arms against the Mughals only twice, for the first time at Nadaun and for the second time at Guler. In both these cases, the Guru came to assist the hill Rajas with twin objectives that the Mughals did not find opportunity to financially squeeze and socially degrade the people and did not proceed against him under the influence of the smitten Mughal officers or local elements inimical to the Guru.

The Guru's power did not pose any threat to Mughal authority—the fact which had been amply brought home to him at Lahore by Mahabat Khan (1693-1696), the then governor of the Punjab. Besides, the Prince himself was open-minded, liberal and particularly considerate towards saints. Understandably, Guru Gobind Singh whom he called Darvesh—a saint (he mentioned him so in one of his royal prescripts) could not be a victim of anybody's whims or distorted thinking.

Nand Lal Goya who was a litterateur in the court of the Guru and had formerly been in the service of the Prince at Agra also seemed to have exercised his personal influence with the Prince in favour of the Guru.[139]

Real politik also warranted good behaviour towards the Guru. The Prince had seen for himself that the Guru had a following totally dedicated to him. That could be useful in case the struggle for the throne ensued after the death of his father who had grown very old and in view of the average longevity of life in India at that point of time could be expected to leave this world any time.

Certain other issues also demand answers before we close the account of the expedition of the Prince. One, how did the hill Rajas react to the Guru under the circumstances? Two, why did the Guru keep quiet? Three, what has the Guru to say regarding those persons who deserted him or turned apostates or made away with the offerings of the Sikhs deposited with them by the faithfuls.

The hill Rajas tried to involve the Guru on their side and against the Mughals, but the Guru did not respond because he had observed for himself that they were selfish and had always tried to cause demoralisation among the Sikhs. However, pressure tactics did have their effect on the internal cohesion of the Sikhs, many of whom left the Guru—some out of fear of the Mughal forces, some under the instigation of the hill Rajas, some prompted by the urge to grab the offerings, otherwise meant for the Guru. There is explicit mention of such people in *Bachittar Natak*. In *Chaupais* 5 to 8 Guru condemns those persons who proved treacherous to his cause.[140]

In Chapter 13, the Guru calls them opportunists, sure to become penniless and desperate. In that state they would come to the Guru for shelter and help but they would not be allowed soft corner.[141]

Regarding his own safety and that of his followers at Anandpur he says, "Providence Himself protected the saints as He could not see any pain being caused to them."

"He considered me as His own slave and saved me from all troubles by extending His Hand of Grace."[142]

According to Teja Singh and Ganda Singh, the Prince did not touch the Guru because of some kind of understanding between the Guru and the government. The learned scholars based their conclusion on the following statement of the Guru as recorded in *Bachittar Natak* (XIII, 90).

BABE KE BABAR KE DOU
AAP KARE PARMESHWAR SE AOU
DIN SHAH UN KO PEHCHANO
DUNI PAT UN KO ANUMANO
JO BABE KE DAM NO DE HAI
TIN TE GAIH BABAR KE LEI HEI

Sardar Kapur Singh has strongly criticised the statement of Teja Singh and Ganda Singh. Writing in 'The Baisakhi of Guru Gobind Singh' he says[143], "The learned authors make a most amazing statement about the Sikh doctrine of the Church and the state inter-relationship, which is wholly unwarranted and which is pernicious to the extreme. Neither the context hints at any such understanding, nor the text is susceptible of translation or interpretation which the learned authors have made it here. Nor, the whole Sikh history of Sikh doctrine lends any countenance to the doctrine of ultimate and mutual exclusive dichotomy of the church and the state." The learned Sardar then gives his version of the translation which in our view reflects correct sense of the original:

Those of Baba (Nanak)
    and those of Babur
God himself maketh them both
    Know the former thus:
As the king of religion
Understand the latter thus:
    As the secular king.
They who fail to render that
    What is due to the (House of) Baba
The minions of Babur seize them,
    And make exactions upon them

And inflict severe punishments
Upon such defaulters;
In addition, their worldly goods and property are looted and taken away.

The text nowhere says, explicitly or by implication, that the church and the state both derive their authority from God Himself. It clearly says "God maketh them both as the instruments of His will. The word in the text *Kare*, neither literally nor here can be interpreted to mean authorised; it simply means made by or maketh. Similarly the word '*Pehchano*' is not in the sense of a commandment: thou shalt recognise. It means know, identify, understand the term to mean thus as such. Likewise '*Anumano*' cannot and does not mean recognise and accept. It literally and here in the next stanza means, understand, see, take it as, infer that the House of Babur means the secular state."[144]

There is no doubt left by the Guru about the meaning of this text. "He says that there are two forces which claim allegiance of men's souls on earth, the truth and morality as religion, and the state as embodiment of mere utilitarianism and secular politics. The primary allegiance of man is to the truth and morality and those who fail in this allegiance suffer under the subjugation of the earthly state unnourished by the courage and hope which is born through unswerving adherence to their primary allegiance. In this perpetual struggle between the state and the church, for exclusive possession of the soul of a man, a man of culture and religion shall not lose sight ever of his primary allegiance and he who does so, does it at his own peril, for, by doing so, he helps give birth to times in which everything is force, politics, utility and labour, poverty and hardship, tyranny and slavery. The Guru does not assert that this perpetual dichotomy and antagonism of the Church and the state must be resolved or even that it is capable of being resolved, by the suppression or subjugatism of the one by the other; rather, he appears to recognise their eternal antagonism and in this antagonism sees the hope and glory of man, the social and political context in which the Sikh way of life is to be practised." "The church must perpetually correct and influence the state without aiming to destroy or absorb it, for, as the history shows, the attempt of the one to oust the other, meets with no lasting success, and each of the two antagonistic entities arises again after having been crushed in vain and both appear anew as if bound together. This is what the Guru means when he declares in the text that the House of Baba Nanak and the House of Babur, God maketh both of them and that 'those who repudiate their allegiance to the House of Nanak, suffer grievously without hope, at the hands of the state'."[145]

In the afore-alluded excerpt from chapter thirteen of *Bachittar Natak* as also in the whole corpus of chapter, the Guru nowhere mentions even in nuances that there was any understanding between him and the Mughal government, or that the Sikh doctrine is, in essence, the care of the other world, through non-interference with the world which should remain within the exclusive domain of the secular state.

The only established fact is that the Imperial expeditionary contingents inflicted severe punishment on the rulers of different hill states as also on their residents including those who deserted the Guru out of fear or for selfish motives or both. The Prince did not think it necessary or wise to attack the fortified town of Anandpur, the seat of the Guru. The Guru declares that the imperial forces decided not to join issues with him.

The decision of the Prince not to touch Guru was personal and had no connection with any directive from Emperor Aurangzeb. Nor was it the product of any understanding, tacit or avid, between the Guru and the Prince. It seemed that various factors, his understanding that the Guru was not a potential threat of Mughal kingdom, his innate respect for the sages, the Real Politiking, the pleas of Bhai Nand Lal, all combined impelled the Prince to arrive at the decision of leaving the Guru untouched.

The Guru on his part kept cool because the Prince did not distort or manipulate moral principles of the Sikhs, nor did he disturb the independent cultural and religious identities of the Sikhs.

The Guru did not come forward to help the hill Rajas, because firstly, the Rajas had always been unscrupulous in their conduct *vis-à-vis* him and his mission; and, secondly, they bandied claim of Almighty absolutism, professedly denying the right to the Sikhs to live and express independently, to act as per value-pattern set by their Guru. At times, they even threatened to oust him from Anandpur, if he and his Sikhs did not subscribe to their views regarding society and religion and did not pay annual tribute as a mark of recognition of the sovereignty of the Raja of Kahlur.

PHASE OF FEVERISH ACTIVITIES

Muazzam's departure from Lahore and his cowing down of hill rulers ended the Guru's anxiety and now he felt free to engage himself in peaceful pursuits. A phase of intense activity followed. He invited new entrants to his literary *darbar* already enriched with the return of the Sikhs who had been sent to Benaras in 1686.[146] He encouraged them to translate the relevant portions of *Ramayan* and *Mahabharat*.[147] To leave no room for any ambiguity and doubt in comprehending the *Avtars* not only in all their glory but also in their weaknesses such compositions as 'Vishnu De Chaubis Avtar' were completed. In 1696, 'Chritaro Pokhyan' was produced mainly to divert attention of his young disciples from sex thoughts to the noble cause, in the service of religion and nation. His own short biography, the *Bachittar Natak* was written in the first half of 1699. A perusal of his works would convince one that the Guru's literary activities had a purpose that the people should be energised to stand against injustice and, no wonder, the Guru took care to dish out from the classics that was vital and morale-building. He examined the conduct of *Avtars*, their strong points as well as their weaknesses, his purpose being that they were not God, all-powerful and infallible, rather personalities like others, liable to commit mistakes and prone to foibles. In *Bachittar Natak* he seemed to recapitulate and reaffirm the message conveyed to him directly by God. In congregations, the theme underlying his writings was deliberated upon frequently; and, as a result, the devout Sikhs as well as non-Sikhs who came to Anandpur felt its impact. This, in turn, infused into them fresh confidence and brought them face to face with new challenges.

Side by side, the Guru took care to expedite the process of acculturating his disciples. He exhorted them to attend '*Sangat*', listen to and participate in *Kirtan*, hold '*Guru ka Langar*'. The Sikhs consciousness expanded and was enlightened. Anandpur, therefore, fully reflected a new religio-social model. Every home functioned as if it were a 'Temple of Bread' (*Guru ka Langar*). Sometimes, the Guru tested his Sikhs. Very early in the morning of one day the Guru disguised as a common pilgrim went round in the streets of Anandpur for bread. The disciples were getting the bread ready so they could not promise any thing till they were fully prepared to receive guests. Then he reached Bhai Nand Lal's house and asked for food. He welcomed the guest with beaming face and placed at his disposal what was available in the kitchen: butter, half-kneaded flour, half-cooked pulse and sundry vegetables. He then very humbly said 'this is ready and is all for you, but if you permit me I will prepare them for you and serve you in the name of My Master'. Next morning the Guru told everyone that there was but one 'Guru Ka Langar' at Anandpur and that belonged to Bhai Nand Lal. The Guru's utterances were a sort of homily on 'Guru Ka Langar'. Every house of a Sikh should provide food to the needy in a spirit of thankfulness to God whom he/she should consider as the Primal provider of provisions.[148] While doing so, no consideration of caste and creed *et al.* should circumscribe the minds. Sikhs should never forget to offer thanks to the Almighty before taking or serving food. The Guru said "If a hungry person calls at your door and you turn him away, remember that you are turning out not him but me. He who serves the poor and the needy serves me. The mouths of the poor are the Guru's receptacles for all gifts."

Anandpur presented a spectacle of perfect harmony free from petty jealousies and parochialism. It bore the look of Heaven, where all castes, creeds and colours met in the joyous *Sangat*. The focal point of the people of Anandpur was the

Guru whom they looked upon as enlightener, sustainer and protector.

One day there came a *Kalal* or a wine distiller of Punjab, held in acute hatred by the society still clinging to the wrong belief that[149] avocation determined the status in society. Suffering from status complex in the society, he stood a little away from the Guru. But the Guru took him by hand and seated him in the congregation (*Sangat*). He hesitated and meekly said that he was a *Kalal*. The Guru proclaimed "You are not Kalal", but 'Guru Ka Lal' [a gem (son) of the Guru]. Such was the Guru's disposition towards so-called low castes. His mission was to uplift such people and give them a realisation that they were dignified as anyone else in this world. The Guru's baptism of love, indeed, articulated them to feel free, proud and self-confident.

On another occasion, the Guru called for a cup of water. That was brought to him by a handsome lad, a scion of a rich feudal lord. The hands fetching the cup were clean as also were water and the cup. The Guru held the cup in his hand for a while, but then returned the same to the young man without sipping, saying, "My son, it seems your hands have not yet laboured in the service of the people."[150] "No Sir, I have never worked with these hands as yet", said the boy. "Ah! My boy, go and make them pure first in the service of the people." The Guru's priorities were very clear that society based on caste should be discarded forthwith and it should be reorganised on bases of love for all, equal rights, divinity of individuals, dignity of labour and faith in the singularity and unicity of God with a commitment to improve the lot of the people.

Taboos, totems, superstitions, rituals, fastings, sacrifices, renunciation, yogism, pilgrimages, such things which had often been projected as the right tools to comprehend and realise God were simply rejected as irrelevance never to be owned and believed upon.

A group of Hindu Sanyasis visited Anandpur. They complainingly told the Master that he was not laying due emphasis on the virtue of renunciation. The Guru replied[151],

"My disciples are men of renunciation in joy, their bliss is infinite and no more is needed; all things come to their hands and they use them as they need. As long as they do not go under illusion (Maya), they are free and pure. If one has obtained self-realisation of what use, my friends, is renunciation."[152] They were for arguing further when he interrupted them, playfully bidding his Sikhs to put live charcoal on the lids of their coconut-bowls of renunciation. And as the lac cementing the joints melted under fire, the bowls were broken and gold coins dropped out exposing their hypocrisy and double-talk.[153]

Festivals, such as Baisakhi, Diwali and Holi were celebrated with gusto and care was taken that these occasions served as a means to suffuse the people with Guru's mission. Holi festival was so organised and celebrated that the Sikhs' perception of Holi altogether changed. They shed hollow belief that the festival was celebrated to express joy at the burning of Holka—the sister of Harnakash, who disliked his son Prahlad for not sharing his father's view that he was God. She, in order to please her brother, schemed to burn Prahlad. She took him in her lap, sat in the midst of a heap of easily combustible straw. She herself wore a sheet of cloth believed to be fire-proof made as such through incantation. But it so happened that the sheet moved aside uncovering a part of her body with the result that she was reduced to ashes. The boy escaped the furious fire because a part of that very sheet covered him. In the historical consciousness, the event has been considered triumph of goodness over evil; and on this account some people considered an appropriate occasion to celebrate.

The Sikhs, despite loving the theme, did not make this story the *mission-d'être* of their celebration of Holi festival. For them the festival symbolised loftiness of spirit and its assertiveness in the cause of humanity, very much akin to the nature of the spring blossoming forth amidst turnings and twistings. The Guru called Holi as 'Hola Mohalla' and not simply a festival of colours. Each celebration at Anandpur was a lesson in interpersonal socialisation and a rehearsal. In social actions he divided the gathering at Anandpur into two groups:

one part took up position in the Holgarh fort and dug in for defence against attack. The other under command of the Guru made the attack. In front of the attacking party were the standard bearers. Another flag was flying on the fort. Both the sides were divided into various battalions. It was a mock fight without arrows and bullets. The garrison was dressed in white, while the assailants wore yellow clothes. The fighting lasted four and a half hours. Eventually the fort was captured by the attacking force by employing many tactics of warfare. War drums were beaten. The soldiers on horseback from both sides rushed upon each other. A number of prisoners were taken by both parties. Afterwards a *darbar* was held and conventional Holi was played joyfully. Gulal, rosewater and saffron water were freely sprinkled on one another with pistons (pachkaris). Huge quantity of pudding worth Rs. 5000 would be prepared. Then it was laid on grassy ground in huge pans. It was plundered by the Sikhs under the order of the Guru. At once all would assault the *Karah Prasad* pans. Many pushed many to get at it. Some rolled on the ground to the laughter of all. In a moment the entire mass of *Karah Prasad* was gone. The Guru also participated in the game. He called it Mai Hola or a petty fight. Later on it became popular as Hola Mohalla[154] which according to Bhai Kahan Singh means 'attack and place to be attacked'. The occasion could not but attract the focalised attention of Bhai Nand Lal, a poet of Persian with Goya as pen name. He composed a poem. A free translation of the poem is reproduced here:

> "Many have written about the flower of Holi in the garden of the world. It made the lips beautiful like a flower bud. Rose water, amber, musk and saffron water fell like rain from all sides. The scattering of *Gulal* by the blessed hand (of the Guru) reddened the earth and the sky. The pistons filled with saffron-coloured water imparted lovely tinge to the uncoloured (Herr Be Rang Ra Khaehrang-o-Bu Kard). When my king (Shyam) wore the coloured neck cloth, both the worlds became happy through his kindness. One who happened to see his divine face achieved the objective of his life. Goya's

heart has only one desire that he should sacrifice himself on the dust over which the Guru's devotees pass."[155]

Despite Guru's enhanced attention to peaceful pursuits, he did not lose sight of the defence of his headquarter, for he could visualise the hardened attitude of the Hill Rajas towards him as also the thrust of the Mughal parochial approach. He, therefore, completed the construction (1699) of five forts all around the town: Keshgarh at Centre; Anandgarh (fort of bliss) 500 metres to the east; Lohgarh (fort of steel) one kilometre to the south; Holgarh one and a half metres to the north. Anandgarh and Keshgarh were built on Hill tops. All were located at strategic places. Fatehgarh, Holgarh and Lohgarh were situated on the banks of Charan Ganga. All the forts could face and house big guns. They were connected with each other through skilfully constructed earth works and underground tunnels. The strongest fort was Anandgarh which exists to date.

For water supply a huge well was dug up. It was worked by Persian wheel. The well and the wheel are still there.

The Guru repeatedly exhorted his followers to lead a life of discipline. The Guru declared:

> He is not a Sikh who does not observe discipline.
> Without discipline one is just a vagabond wandering aimlessly from door to door.
> Without discipline one falls into the hellish pit.
> One who does not observe discipline is a wild creature.
> One who does not observe discipline is a defaulter.
> One who does not observe discipline cannot be happy.

Therefore, hold fast to the disciplined way of life.[156]

FOOTNOTES AND REFERENCES

1. We have accepted 7 Poh Sudi, Samvat 1723, given in old Mss lying in Patna Gurdwara and inscribed on a commemoration tablet there, as Guru's exact date of birth. This date is also given in *Suraj Parkash* and *Gurbilas Padshahi Dasvin*.
2. Refer to Hukamnama of Guru Tegh Bahadur in the book *Hukamnama* edited by Dr. Fauja Singh: p. 52, Punjabi University, 1976.
3. The Sikh tradition has preserved the simple fact of Shiv Dutt's interest in the Guru Tegh Bahadur's family particularly the young son in the form of

Sakhi in which Gobind appears as a divine spirit and Shiv Dutt as an adoring disciple. Kartar Singh: *Life of Guru Gobind Singh*, p. 23.

4. *Ibid.*, p. 22.
5. *Ibid.*, p. 23.
6. J.S. Grewal and S.S. Bal: *Guru Gobind Singh,* p. 34, Panjab University, Chandigarh, 1967.
7. Khazan Singh: *History of Sikh Religion,* p. 166, Reprint, Department of Language, Punjab, 1977.
8. Giani Gian Singh: *Twarikh Guru Khalsa*, pp. 755-59.
9. Sarup Singh Kaushish: *Guru Kian Sakhian* (edited), pp. 78-79. Sakhi 28, Singh Brothers, 1995.
10. Bhat Vahi Talauda Pargana Jind. For corroboration see Sarup Singh Kaushish, *Guru Kian Sakhian*, Sakhi 28.
11. Sarup Singh Kaushish: *op. cit.,* 80, Sakhi 29, Kesar Singh Chhibber: *Bansavlinama, Nauwan, Charan Bhat Vani Multani Sindhi*, Khata Jalhane Balouton Ka.
12. Puran Singh: *Poet of Immorality*.
13. Gian Singh: *Twarikh Guru Khalsa,* pp. 755-59, Bhasha Vibhag, Punjab, 1967.
14. *Rehit Piyari Mujh Ko, Sikh Piyara Nahi.*
15. Guru Gobind Singh: *Jaap*.
16. Balwant Singh Dhillon: *Pramukh Sikh Te Sikh Panth*, pp. 131-33.
17. Dip Chand from C.E. 1650 to C.E. 1667 rule over the Kahlur state. According to Sarup Singh Kaushish, Dip Chand's wife Champa Devi was a great devotee of the Guru. Gradually Dip Chand also developed respect for the Guru. The facticity of this fact can be gleaned from the Sakhi No. 24 as incorporated in *Guru Kian Sakhian*, edited by Piara Singh Padam.
18. Grewal and Bal: *op. cit.*, p. 52.
19. The foundation of Anandpur was laid by Guru Tegh Bahadur (1621-1675) on 16th June, 1665 on a piece of land covering the ruined mound of an older village Makhowal, which the Guru had earlier purchased from the Rajput hill state of Kahlur. After the Battle of Bhangani (18th September, 1688) Guru Gobind Rai returned to Chak Nanki which he renamed Anandpur after one of a ring of forts (Anandgarh) which he now undertook to raise (*Encyclopaedia of Sikhism*, Vol. 1, p. 128). Rose, however says that Anandpur was founded in 1678 (*The Land of Five Rivers, Historical and Descriptive Sketches*, p. 213). The correct position seems to be that the piece of land of Anandgarh fort had been acquired in 1678, but Chak Nanki acquired the new name once the Guru returned to this place after the Battle of Bhangani.
20. According to Sikh tradition, Rattan Chand of Assam came to Makhowal in 1680. Though the Sikh tradition has preserved the memory of only this chief coming to Makhowal, others too must have visited.

21. The Persian writers tell us that Aurangzeb wanted his Faujdars on the North West to see that Guru Gobind Singh stopped practices that create the impression that the Guru was a Raja. Khushwant Rai, *Tarikh-i-Sikhan*, S.H.R. 116, pp. 632-33. *Gurbilas* by Bhai Sahib Singh, p. 104.
22. Rose, H.A.: *A Glossary of Tribes and Castes of the Punjab and North West Frontier Province,* III, 688. Rose puts Bhim Chand's defeat in C.E. 1682.
23. Hari Ram Gupta: *History of the Sikhs,* Vol. I, p. 227, Manohar, 1984. It was a challenge to the King's authority. The Guru followed the concept of Khalsa and if they paid any tribute that would mean 'serving man' whereas Khalsa serve only God.
24. *Bachittar Natak*, Steek p. 138, Singh Brothers, Amritsar, 1991.
25. Giani Gian Singh, *Shri Dashmesh Chamatkar*, p. 119.
26. Hutchinson and Vogel: *History of the Punjab Hill States*, II.
27. Khushwant Singh: *History of the Sikhs,* Vol. I, p. 76, Oxford University Press, Delhi, 1977.
28. A.C. Bannerjee: *From Guru Nanak to Guru Gobind Singh*, p. 230, Rajesh Publications, New Delhi, 1978.
29. Hari Ram Gupta: *History of the Sikhs,* Vol. I, p. 230, Manohar, Delhi, 1984.
30. Trilochan Singh: *Guru Tegh Bahadur*, p. 114.
31. Sirmour (later known as Nahan) was a mountainous tract with a steep rise from the north-west to the north-east with elevation of more than 11000 feet at its highest level. It was cut into two by Giri, a tributary of Jamuna.
32. *Sirmour State Gazetteer*, Lahore, 1907, p. 15. "The Sikhs have four gurdwaras in the state at Paonta, Bhangani and Nahan. The fourth gurdwara is at Tokah, but it only consists of a small platform near a well, built by Fateh Singh Ahluwalia when he held the Naraingarh Ilaqa in the later part of the 19th century (Bikrami). About 100 bighas are attached to the gurdwara, and it also enjoys a muafi in Naraingarh Tehsil and an annual grant of 100 Maunds of grain from Patiala. The income is appropriated by the descendant of the late Poujari.
33. Sainapat: *op. cit.*, p. 15, "Ketak Baras Bhat Eigh Bhail, Des Pawta Sat Guru Gaie, Jamma Mahal Banwai Karat Anand Prabhu Man Bhai." Macauliffe, M.A.: *The Sikh Religion*, V, pp. 16-17.
34. Macauliffe: *The Sikh Religion,* V, pp. 16-17.
35. Grewal, J.S. and Bal, S.S.: *op. cit.,* p. 71.
36. *Bachittar Natak*, Chapter 8, *Chaupai* 3.
37. *Sirmaur Gazetteer*. 112 as cited by Bannerjee, I.B., *Evolution of the Khalsa*, II, p. 69.
38. Asur Sangharan Ram Hamara.
39. *Bachittar Natak*, VI, *Chaupai* 33. "Mei Hoon Param Purakh Ko Dasa, Dekhan Aio Jagat Tamasha." "Jo Ham Ko Parmeshwar Uchreh Te Sabh Narak Kund Mein Pareh."

40. Astha, D.P.: *The Poetry of Dasam Granth Sahib,* Vol. I, p. 44.
41. Bal, S.S. and J.D. Grewal: *Guru Gobind Singh*, p. 75, Punjab University Publication.
42. Astha, D.P.: *The Poetry of Dasam Granth*. Arun Parkashan, Delhi, p. 147.
43. Akal Ustat in Shabdarth, *Dasam Granth Sahib,* Vol. I, p. 44.
44. Nikky Gurinder Kaur Singh: *The Faminine Principle of the Sikh Vision of the Transcendant*, p. 132, Cambridge University Press, 1993.
45. Bhai Randhir Singh: *Shabad Murat,* SGPC, Amritsar. *Itihasic Patrika* Vol. 5, *Sikh History Society*, SGPC, Amritsar.
46. Ashta, D.P.: *The Poetry of Dasam Granth*, p. 79.
47. Hukam Name Sikhan Wal, Likhe jo Likhari Sikh Hovei So Hazur Avei. (Rehat Nama Bhai Chaupa Singh).
Jo Brahmin Vidwan Hei Changa so Bhijwavna
Jo Khareb Lagei so Guru Ke Gharon Lana
(*Bansavli Nama*, Daswan Charan).
48. Piara Singh Padam: *Guru Gobind Singh De Darbari Ratan,* pp. 4-6, Kalam Mandir, Patiala, 1974.
49. *Ibid.,* pp. 25-32.
50. *Ibid.*
51. *Ibid.*
52. *Ibid.*
53. *Ibid.*
54. *Ibid.*
55. Gandhi, S.S.: *Struggle of the Sikhs for Sovereignty,* p. 571, Gurdas Kapur & Sons, Delhi, 1980. The veracity of the statement can be corroborated by examining the content of most of the books produced in this period. Gulab Singh Nirmala, who was initiated into the classical learning by Sant Man Singh wrote *Bhasha Vrit*, 1777 C.E., *Mokhsh Panth*, 1778, *Adhyatam Ramayan* 1782, *Prabodh Chander Natak* 1792. The general tenor of these books is vedantic.
56. Macauliffe: *The Sikh Religion*, p. 30, Vol. III and IV.
57. *Evolution of the Khalsa*, Vol. II.
58. Bhai Kahan Singh: *Mahan Kosh*.
59. Macauliffe, M.A.: *The Sikh Religion*, Vol. V, p. 21.
60. Sangat Singh, J.P.: *Bachittar Natak Steek*, p. 15, Chapter I.
61. Colonel Ravi Batra: *Leadership in its Finest Mould Guru Gobind Singh*, p. 31, SGPC, Amritsar.
62. *Hukamname*, edited by Ganda Singh, p. 131, Punjabi University, Patiala, 1967.
63. Ganda Singh: *Hukam Name*, p. 17, Punjabi University, Patiala, 1967. A large number of Hukam Namas were numbered. Besides they were written

in specific form as for instance on each Hukam Nama, there is Guru's sign or instruction on Guru's hand to be followed in the content of the Hukamnama to be scribed by a scribe who would start his writing with ੧ਓਁ ਸਤਿ (Ik Onkar Sat), ੧ਓਁ ਸਤਿ ਗੁਰੂ ਜੀਓ (Ik Onkar Sat Guru Jio).

64. Different dates regarding the war are given by different scholars. We have based our conclusion on the versions given by typed copy of Bhat Vahis (now preserved in Punjabi University, Patiala) and *Bansavli Nama* by Kesar Singh Chhibber (edited by Ratan Singh Jaggi, Parakh, Chandigarh, 1972, p. 124), *Shaheed Bilas* by Sewa Singh. We have rejected the dates given by Bhai Santokh Singh and *Gur Bilas Padshahi Dasvin* by Sukha Singh. Santokh Singh writes that the battle was fought in 1686 to 1689. *Mahan Kosh* fixed the date as April 16, 1686.
65. Dewan Nand Chand was the son of Suraj Mal.
66. Giani Gian Singh: *Panth Parkash*, Amritsar, 1973.
67. *Bachittar Natak,* VIII, 2.
68. Bannerjee, I.C.: *The Sikh Gurus and the Sikh Religion*, p. 286, Munshi Ram and Manohar Lal, Delhi, 1953.
69. The Guru's own account of battles in the hills discloses no desire either of the establishment of a virtual principality or for the commencement of anti-military operations. He faced hostilities only when these were forced upon him.
70. *Dehradun Gazetteer*, p. 171.
71. The territory gained by the Sirmour Raja included Shergarh Kalsi, and the fort of Boorat.
72. *Sirmour State Gazetteer*, 14.
73. *Sirmour State Gazetteer*, pp. 13-14.
74. *Ibid.*
75. *Ibid.*
76. Sarkar, J.N.: *Aurangzeb,* Vol. III, pp. 563-65.
77. *Ibid.*
78. J.S. Grewal and S.S. Bal: *Guru Gobind Singh,* p. 17, Pb. Uni., Chandigarh, 1967, *Sirmour Gazetteer*, p. 15, Jog Raj was the son of Budh Parkash who was the son of Subhag Parkash.
79. The Sikh tradition very significantly preserves the memory of both Fateh Singh and Medni Parkash visiting the Guru regularly. Sometimes they would visit the Guru at the same time and accompany the Guru for *Shikar* (hunting) in the Jungles around Paonta (*Gurbilas Padshahi Dasvin,* p. 120).
80. Prithvi Shah and Fateh Shah appear to have had considerable faith in the spiritual power of Ram Rai. This is clearly indicated by Prithvi Shah's Settling down Ram Rai at Khanabad and allowing him to build it as the

nucleus of Dehradun and Fateh Shah confirming the possession of several villages for the support of Mahant's retinue besides allowing him to build a small centre at Srinagar itself. *Dehradun Gazetteer*, p. 172.

81. According to Dr. Hari Ram Gupta, they were Fateh Shah of Garhwal, Bhim Chand of Kahlur, Kirpal Chand of Kangra, Sidh Sen of Mandi, Gopal Chand of Guler, Hari Chand of Hindur, Kesri Chand of Jaswal, Umed Chand of Jaswan, Dayal Chand of Kotgarh, Karam Chand of Bharmour, Daya Singh of Nurpur, Gurbhaj Singh of Indaurah, Bagh Singh of Talokpur, Hari Chand of Kotiwal, Lachhu Chand of Kot Khaai (Hari Ram Gupta: *History of the Sikhs*, Vol. 1, p. 236, Manohar, 1984).
82. Macauliffe: *op. cit.*, Vol. V, pp. 30, 34, 40.
83. According to Sainapat, Fateh Shah had so much confidence in his general and soldiers that he expected a walk over in the battle.
84. *Bachittar Natak,* VIII, 20.
85. *Bachittar Natak,* VIII, 25: "Hari Chand in his rage drew forth his arrow. He struck my steed with one and discharged another at me. God preserved me and it only grazed my ear in its flight. His third arrow penetrated the buckle of my waist belt and reached my body but wounded me not. It is only God who protected me knowing me his servant. When I felt the touch of the arrow, my anger was kindled. I took up my bow and began to discharge arrows in abundance. Upon this, my adversaries began to flee. I took aim at the young chief who fell dead" (Macauliffe's translation in *Sikh Religion*, V, p. 44).
86. *Bachittar Natak* "God in His grace bestowed victory on me."
87. *Gazetteer of Himachal Pradesh*, 1969.
88. *Mahan Kosh*.
89. *Bachittar Natak*, Chapter VIII.
90. Sarup Singh Kaushish: *Guru Kian Sakhian,* p. 102, ed. Piara Singh Padam, Singh Brothers, Amritsar, 1991.
91. *Ibid*.. pp. 102-03.
92. Kartar Singh: *Guru Gobind Singh,* p. 189, Singh Brothers, Amritsar, 1991.
93. *Ibid.*
94. *Ibid.*
95. Sarup Singh Kaushish: *op. cit.*
96. *Ibid.*
97. *Ibid.*
98. Hutchinson, J. and Vogel, J.P.: *History of Punjab Hill States,* I, pp. 388, 462, 582, *Mandi State Gazetteer*, p. 37.
99. *Ibid.*, 149-50, 225-26.
100. *Ibid.*, 205, 309.
101. *Journal of Indian History,* XXXI, pp. 140, 142, cited by Goswamy, B.N.: *Social Background of Kangra Valley and Painting.*

102. Bhai Vir Singh says that the agreement was signed at Paonta. We do not agree with this contention of his. He argues on the presumption that Bhim Chand led the attack on the Guru in the battle of Bhangani but this presumption is open to objection on the ground that the Guru makes no mention of Kahlur Raja's participation in the battle of Bhangani. We concur with J.S. Grewal and S.S. Bal in their view that the formality, if there was any, was effected at Anandpur, though a tacit understanding must have been reached through someone, when Guru Gobind Singh stayed with the Rani of Raipur.

103. Vir Singh, *Kalghidhar Chamatkar*, p. 165. Bhai Ji says that in a manuscript supplied to him by an *Udasi Sikh* it is written that the Guru sent messages to *Sangats* to send artisans and poets etc. to his *Darbar*.

104. *Bachittar Natak*, VIII, p. 37.

105. I.B. Bannerjee: *Evolution of Khalsa*, Vol. II, pp. 73-74.

106. *Bachittar Natak,* IX, 2.

107. *Ibid.*, I.

108. *Bachittar Natak,* IX, 2.

109. J.S. Grewal and S.S. Bal: *op. cit.*, p. 87.

110. Bannerjee, I.B.: *op. cit.*, II, 75. *Gurbilas*, 156, Hutchinson, J. and Vogel, J.P.: *History of Hill States,* I, p. 205.

111. Following the *Gurbilas*, I.B. Bannerjee rightly calls him the Raja of Jaswal. This gets confirmation from the name Ram Singh appearing in the list of the Rajas of Jaswal given by Hutchinson and Vogel. See Bannerjee, I.B.: *op. cit.*, II, p. 81 and Appendix A.

112. According to I.B. Bannerjee, he was the chief of Mudhwar, a hill state in the Jammu group. According to Hutchinson and Vogel, the later chiefs of Datarpur bore the titles of Dadwal. We feel that he was more likely to be the chief of Datarpur. *History of Punjab Hill States*, Vol. I, p. 212.

113. *Bachittar Natak,* IX, 3.

114. *Ibid.*, 6.

115. *Ibid.*, 16: (a) Naiglu is a sept of Rajputs descended from Chua Mian son of Sagar Chand, the sixth Raja of Kahlur. A glossary of the *Tribes and Castes of the Punjab and North West Frontier Province*, Vol. III, p. 156. Possibly the Panglu also is another Rajput sept. (b) It appears that Guler also supported Bhim Chand and this is confirmed by *Gur Bilas* (VII, 41). It seems that the Guru is referring to the clans of Jaswal and Guleria and not to the states of those names. Guleria and Jaswal were two of the six clans of Katoch. (Bannerjee, I.B.: *op. cit.*, II, p. 82. footnote.)

116. *Ibid.*, 18-20.

117. *Ibid.*, 22.

118. *Ibid.*, 23.

119. *Ibid.*

120. The date is given in the tale No. 405, in *Pokhyan Charittar*. The total number of tales is 404 but the last tale is numbered 405, showing thereby one tale is missing.

121. J.S. Grewal and S.S. Bal: *op. cit.*, p. 96. Akhbarat-i-Darbar-i-Mualla. An extract of a newsletter dated 20 November, 1693 in Akhbar runs as follows: News from Sirhind—Gobind declares himself to be Guru Nanak. Faujdars ordered to prevent him from assembling (his Sikhs).

122. Akhbarat-i-Durbar-i-Mualla (R.A.S.), 1677-79—An extract of the newsletter dated 20-11-93 in the Akhbar runs as follows: News from Sirhind—Gobind declares himself to be Guru Nanak. Faujdar ordered to prevent him from assembling (his Sikhs). Quoted by Teja Singh and Ganda Singh in *A Short History of the Sikhs*, p. 65.

123. According to Sunder Singh the author of the Battles of Guru Gobind Singh, Alam Khan was Guru's Deodhidar. According to I.B. Bannerjee he was Guru's attendant. Gian Singh calls him Alam Shah: *Twarikh Guru Khalsa,* p. 835 vide reference. *Evolution of the Khalsa,* II, p. 85.

124. *Bachittar Natak*, X, pp. 9-10.

125. *Ibid.*

126. The amount was exorbitant even if he was expected to share the burden with his friend, the Raja of Jaswan. It must have been compared with the annual tribute that they paid to the Mughal government which did not exceed a few hundred rupees for either Guler or Jaswan. For the amount demanded. See *Bachittar Natak*, XI, 13 and the annual tribute by the three Rajas to the Mughal government, see Goswami, B.N.: *op. cit.*, pp. 57-58.

127. *Bachittar Natak*, XI, p. 57.

128. *Ibid.*

129. Jujhar Singh was a certain Rajput prince whom Aurangzeb dispatched from Deccan. Chandan Rai was the deputy of Jujhar Singh (Hari Ram Gupta: *History of Sikhs,* I, p. 242, Munshi Ram Manohar Lal, Delhi, 1984.

130. I.B. Bannerjee: *op. cit.*, II, 86.

131. Guru Gobind Singh mentions this name in *Bachittar Natak*. He was the incharge of Jaswan contingent certainly not the ruler of Jaswan state who was Rai Singh.

132. *Bachittar Natak*, Section XIII, *Chaupais* 1-12.

133. *Bachittar Natak,* XIII, I, Bhai Santokh Singh: *op. cit.,* II, Ansu 48.

134. Irvine: *Later Mughal*, pp. 1-4.

135. Refer to Khafi Khan's account in Elliot and Dawson: Vol. VII, p. 153.

136. The statement is amply supported by different Hukamnamas. One of these letters is to the progenitors of the Phulikian house in which the Guru asks for assistance. In another Hukamnama addressed to the *Sangat* of Dacca the Guru acknowledges the receipt of swords, clothes and money and asks for more. Still in another letter asks for first class was elephants (Hukam Namas 35, 37 in the book *Hukum Name*).

137. *Bachittar Natak*, XIII, *Chaupais*, pp. 9-25.

138. Hukamnama dated 2nd August, 1696 (2nd Bhadon Samvat 1753 Bk) to Bhai Triloka and Rama and the entire congregation under them to come to him with a force. For English translation see *Patiala and East Punjab Historical Background*, p. 44. Also consult *Hukamname* by Dr. Ganda Singh, p. 147. Hukamnama No. 43, Punjabi University Publication, 1967. Also see Hukamnama 42, p. 145 of the same book.

139. According to *Gurbilas*, this was due to the pleas of Nand Lal 'Goya' who was sympathetic to the Sikhs and was in the employ of the Prince. Also refer to Bannerjee, I.B.: *op. cit.*, II, p. 116.

140. *Bachittar Natak,* XIII.

141. *Ibid.,* 12.

142. *Ibid.,* pp. 24-25.

143. Kapur Singh: *Parasara-Parprasna*, pp. 197-98, G.N.D. University, Amritsar, 1989.

144. Kapur Singh: *op. cit.,* pp. 197-99.

145. *Ibid.*

146. These later formed the nucleus of Nirmal Panth. They returned to Anandpur on 1692 according to Dr. S.S. Bal and 1697 according to Khazan Singh. We consider Bal's date as correct because there is a strong tradition that they lived at Benaras for seven years.

147. We observe some of the most talented poets in the Guru's *darbar* now beginning to translate portions of Mahabharat. Amrit Rai, Hans Ram, Kavresh and Mangal translated *Sabha Parb, Karan Parb, Daram Parb* and *Salya Parb* respectively. It is difficult to say something similar was done about Ramayana, but in all probability some poets did begin translation of Ramayana in this period. See Bhai Vir Singh's Tract, *Guru Gobind Singh Da Vidya Darbar*.

148. That is the Sikhs considered it their religious duty to feed and serve all who called at their door is confirmed by the testimony of Munshi Sujan Rai of Batala, who began his book, the *Khulasatut Twarikh* in 1695-96 C.E. and finished in 1697-98 or a year or two before the birth of the Khalsa. "If a person turns up at their door at mid-night and calls in the name of Baba Nanak, though he may be stranger, or even a thief, robber or scoundrel, they serve him according to his need, as they serve a brother or a friend." Sujan Rai Bhandari: *Khulastut Twarikh* (Pbi), p. 81, Punjabi University, 1972.

149. It was believed that merely stepping on the bone of a dead Kalal would condemn one to the fire of hell.

150. Puran Singh: *Ten Masters*, p. 102, Chief Khalsa Dewan, Amritsar.

151. Vir Singh: *Kalghidhar Chamatkar*. Puran Singh: *op. cit.,* p. 102.

152. Puran Singh: *op. cit.,* p. 101. Kartar Singh: *Life of Guru Gobind Singh*, p. 94, Lahore Book Shop, Ludhiana.

153. *Ibid.*
154. *Kalghidhar Chamatkar*—Nihangs have preserved the memory of that day by mock battle. They celebrate Hola Mohalla at Anandpur on the day following the Holi. They put on deep blue robes, tall conical yellow girdles and enact the mock battle. Riding on horses with sparkling spears and swords and shouting their war cries, they march in procession. On the way they stop for a while to display fencing and wrestling.
155. Sarup Singh Kaushish: *op. cit.*, p. 145, *Sakhi* No. 73.
156. Hari Ram Gupta: *History of the Sikhs*, Vol. I, pp. 244-45.

12

MANIFESTATION OF THE KHALSA

Behind feverish cultural and literary activities of the Tenth Guru as detailed in the preceding chapter, there could be discerned a peculiar restiveness in him which often one experiences before arriving at a momentous decision. To those who were intimately connected with the Guru it must have portended some great step. The Mughal government and the Hill rulers, however, could not have figured out what the Guru was thinking or aiming at. When they heard of the birth of Guru's third son Jorawar Singh early in 1797 and of another (Fateh Singh) two years later, they might have conjectured that the Guru was settling down and would pay more attention to family life than to his people and his mission. What was really in the offing none could figure out, and when at long last its configuration was visible, it was stunning striking, perplexing and storming besides heralding of a new era where hackneyed society would yield place to something novel, something unique. It was the setting up of the Khalsa. It was not a sudden or fortuitous happening; it was the logical outcome of the blue print of Guru Nanak. In order to put this unique event in its proper historical perspective, we need to understand the prevailing political, socio-religious scenario.

The Mughal state had assumed the form of a purely Islamic state under Aurangzeb. Earlier, especially in the times of Babar, Humayun and Akbar, the rule could be categorised as largely Islamic, but not totally Islamic. Babar and his sons were not religious bigots. Similarly, Akbar's religious propensities were those of a liberal ruler. He found no difficulty in reaching an understanding with the Hindu Rajputs and did not hesitate to set his face against religious orthodoxy. He strived to construct bridges of understanding between the two main religious communities of India *viz.* Hindu and Muslim. His Order, Din-i-Ilahi was an association of liberal people. He did not levy discriminatory taxes such as *Jazia* on the non-Muslims nor did he pass laws disfavourable to them. He did not interfere in religious affairs of any community. He was emphathetic even to Christianity and extended his patronage to Christian missionaries. Jahangir except for a few years in his early career when he was under the influence of the Naqshbandis and martyred Guru Arjan Dev followed, by and large, a liberal religious policy and did not allow state-power to serve the cause of Muslim orthodoxy exclusively and blatantly. Shahjahan was comparatively less liberal and took measures which buttressed orthodoxy, but even in his period the state cannot be designated as an Islamic state. In Aurangzeb's time, the state became Islamic, by and large, as the orthodoxy was in the Imperial saddle and ran the show.

J.N. Sarkar, a celebrated historian and an authority on the Mughal period, while explicating the nature of Muslim state in his book *History of Aurangzeb,* Vol. III says that in Islam "true king is God and earthly rulers are merely His agents, bound to enforce His law on land. Civil law is completely subordinated to religious law and, indeed, merges its existence in the latter. The civil authority exists solely to spread and enforce the true faith. In such a state, infidelity is logically equivalent to treason because the infidel repudiates the authority of the true king and pays homage to his rivals, the false gods and goddesses.... Therefore, the toleration of any sect outside the fold of orthodox Islam is no better than compounding with sin. And the worst form of sin is polytheism, the belief that the one true God has partners in the form of other deities."[1] Such a belief is the rankest ingratitude (*Kufr*).[2]

Islamic Theology, therefore, tells the true believers that his highest duty is to make exertion (*Jihad*) in the path of God by wagging war against infidels (Dar-ul-Harb) till they become a part of the realm of Islam (Dar-ul-Islam) and their populations are converted into true believers. After conquest the entire infidel population becomes theoretically reduced to the status of slaves of the conquering army.... The conversion of the entire population of Islam and the extinction of every form of dissent is the ideal of Muslim state. If any infidel is suffered to exist in the community, it is a necessary evil and for transitional period only. Political and social disability must be imposed upon him and bribes offered to him from the public funds to hasten the day of his spiritual enlightenment and addition of his name to the role of true believers.... A true Islamic king is bound to look on jubilantly when his infidel subjects cut each other's throats, for, whichever side may be slain, Islam is the gainer (Har Tarf Ke Sha Wwad Kushta Sud-i-Islam Ast).[3]

Aurangzeb was a believer in the Islamic theory of state, the view which continued to be buttressed and strengthened by the circumstances, Naqshbandis and the financial needs of the state. His reputation had suffered greatly in the Muslim world for executing his brothers and for imprisoning his father. The Naqshbandis who were then headed by Masum and Shaikh Saifuddin and had a wide network in the whole of Mughal empire had considerable influence on Aurangzeb's thinking who following them believed that it was his religious duty to help resurgence of Islam by eliminating infidelity and heterodoxy. He also needed finance to wage his wars for escalation of Islam as also for crushing infidelity which could easily be procured from the non-Muslims especially the Hindus including Sikhs. For all these reasons he adopted the policy of a bitter persecutor of non-Muslims as also of non-Sunni Muslims.

Aurangzeb, after ascending the throne, hastened to convince the orthodox Muslims in the empire that they had backed the right horse. He began with puritanic measures. In the second year of his reign, he discontinued the celebration of Nauroz (first day of the lunar year). A few years later music and dancing were prohibited. *Jharokha Darshan* was discontinued on the ground that it smacked of human worship. Several punishments were awarded for anything that was construed by the theologians as violating the spirit of Islam. Permissible length of the beard was fixed at four fingers and offenders against this order were penalised.

But most of these restrictions were of a general nature and covered all communities. Non-Muslims were singled out for discriminatory treatment in four specific fields; public services, construction and repair of temples conversion and taxation. Regarding the discrimination of the government towards the Hindus in services, the remarks of Sri Ram Sharma are pertinent. He says that towards the end of Aurangzeb's reign there was a small number of Hindus occupying the Mansabs of 1000 and above than the number of similar Mansabdars towards the end of Shah Jahan's reign. But the decrease in number becomes still more significant when we take into account the increase in the total number of Mansabdars which rose enormously in the reign of Aurangzeb. In 1657, under Shah Jahan there were 8000 Mansabdars in all whereas in 1690 the number of Mansabdars had risen to 14556. The percentage of Hindus in the higher rank of the state services could not have been more than 50 per cent of what it was towards the end of Shah Jahan's reign. Besides this, a carefully planned campaign was launched prohibiting the construction and repair of temples. In 1659, the year of coronation, Aurangzeb ordered that no new temple should be allowed to be built. In 1666 C.E., the stone railing of the famous Keshwa Rai Temple of Mathura was razed to the ground by imperial order.[4] In April, 1669, he issued a general order for the destruction of all schools and temples of Hindus. "Orders were now sent to the governors of all the provinces that they should destroy the schools and temples of the infidels and put an end to their educational activities as well as the places of the religion of Kafirs. In 1669, the temple of Vishwanath at Benaras was demolished. The temple of Gopinath in Benaras too was destroyed about the same time. Similar destructions were ordered in the various Rajput states such as Ajmer,

Ujjain, Bengal and other provinces of the empire. In 1678, Aurangzeb confiscated all lands held by Hindus as religious places.

Lest the orders go amiss strict administrative measures were taken. He appointed officers in all the sub-divisions and the cities of the empire to enforce the regulations of Islam with the directions that destruction of Hindu temples was one of their chief duties. The Qazis were actually associated with the new policy. The officers were told that the reports of destruction of the temples would be looked upon as authentic only if they bore their seal and attestation.

Like other non-Muslims, particularly the Hindus, the Sikhs too, according to Khafi Khan, came for their share. Their temples and their leaders externed.[5] Mirza Inayat Ulla tells us in the *Ahkam-i-Alamgiri* that in compliance with the orders of the Emperor and with the consent of the local Qazi, the Sikh temples in the town of Burya in the pargana of Khizrabad of the Sarkar of Sirhind had been demolished and a mosque had been raised on its site.[6] Sayyed Zafar Darvesh was appointed in-charge of that mosque to guide prayers and benedictions. Some Sikhs attacked the mosque and killed the Darvesh. The Emperor rebuked the Qazi and his father who was the head of the police. According to Dr. Hari Ram Gupta, such incidents had become a common occurrence.[7]

In the field of taxation the policy of discrimination was launched with great vigour. *Jazia* and pilgrimage taxes were re-levied, custom duties on the Muslims were fixed 2.5 per cent and in the case of the Hindus at 5 per cent. It was ordered that in the lunar year the Muslims should pay 2.5 per cent and the Hindus 5 per cent on the price of their cattle.

Islam being a missionary religion and the ruling Muslim community being in a minority, great importance was attached to conversion. Bakhtiawar Khan states that Aurangzeb himself administered Kalima to prominent persons and adorned them with Khilat (robe of honour) with his own hands.[8] In March 1695, all the Hindus except Rajputs were ordered not to ride on elephants, fine horses and in palanquins or to carry arms.[9]

Aurangzeb was equally bigotted towards Shia, Sufi saints and liberal minded people. In 1661, Mansur-e-Sani-Sufi Muhammad Sarmad was beheaded for believing in Sufi principles.[10] In 1678, Diwan Muhammad Tahir was put to death for liberal interpretation of Islam.[11] Qamir a famous theologian and a scholar of Sirhind was hanged on the same charge. In 1683, Mir Hussain was executed in Kashmir into tribal territory for breaking *Ramzan* fast a little before sunset.[12] In 1669, celebration of *Moharram* was banned. Many Shia Imams were executed.[13]

This policy of Aurangzeb had manifold implications one of which was that Mansabdars taking cue from Aurangzeb became highly zealous and vigorous in their dealings with the non-Muslims. They saw in this the fulfilment of their financial needs and greed apart from dislodging the non-Muslims from land they had occupied to be made available to the state to distribute among Muslims.

The second ancillary factor was the religio-social scenario. Islam and Hinduism were the two major religions in India, and were divided into sects and cults. Among the Muslims, the majority belonged to the Sunni variety, the *Qazi*, *Muftis* and the *Ulemas* were the exponents of their faith. The ultimate authority in their religious life was *Quran*. Besides this, Sunna, the sayings of the prophet also served the principal source. The books embodying interpretation of *Quran* (*Tafsir*) were also regarded by the Sunnis as the object of esteem. Collection of Hadis, prepared by Al-Ashri and Zama Khshari's commentary on *Quran*, called Kashshaf were very popular in the Punjab as also in India. Al-Ashri's (873-893 C.E.) book *Maqwalat* was also considered to be a good guide so far as Sunni's ideas and institutions were concerned. As a rule, a Sunni ought to have faith only in the oneness of God who is all-powerful, just, majestic, inscrutable, righteous and merciful and show no regard to idol worship, observe daily prayers (Salat), keep the daily fast during the month of Ramzan, go on pilgrimage to Mecca (Haj) and give charity to his Muslim brotherhood (Zakat). A mere external observance of these things was sufficient to be regarded as pious Muslims.

Next to Sunnis the most important sect of the Muslims in Punjab was that of Shias. The distinction between the Shias and Sunnis had its roots in the dispute between the Alids and Umayyads in the year which followed the Khalafat Utman's assassination (35 AH). In its origin, it had nothing to do with the religion founded by Muhammad, but rather it was occupied with the political question of the succession to the leadership of the Muslim community.[14] At first, the Alids on their side claimed that they were the legitimate Khalifas because they descended from the Prophet's daughter Fatima and his cousin and intimate companion, Ali. The Umayyads, on their part, claimed a nomination by the choice of the Muslims themselves and as a further title claimed kinship with the Prophet as being the Hashmite family. Later, the Alids stood for the claims of descent against all claims of right to office because of the popular choice. Besides this, among the Sunnis, the Khalifa is a political ruler essentially while the Alid party regards the prophet's successor as a religious guide and therefore preferred to designate him as a Imam of Muslim community. The Shias recognised twelve Imams in the line from Fatima and Ali. The last Imam Muhammad Ali Mahdi was believed to have disappeared from the world in 880 C.E. and was expected that he would reappear to restore justice and righteousness. Sunnis did not recognise them. The Shias recognised the authority of *Quran* and prophethood of Muhammad but had no faith in first three Khalifas.

Ismailis and Qarmathians were the other Muslim sects in the Punjab. The Ismailis reposed faith in seven prophets ending with Jafar-us-Sadiq and Ismail. They claimed to derive their teachings from the hidden source which must receive absolute obedience. The laws of Shariat according to Ismaili belief were not meant for those who possessed esoteric knowledge. *Quran* itself had inner meanings. They denied all divine attributes holding that the divine essence has given forth light by which various forms of intelligence and matter have been created which have no real individuality. The divine essence which was alone in the beginning will be alone in the end. The initiates were taught to use speculative philosophical reasoning as a result of which doubts were raised about the systems of religions including Islam. Besides Shias, Ismailis and Qarmathians were generally not liked by Sunnis. Aurangzeb also had no soft corner for them and so far as Shias were concerned, he was very bitter. There were various other sects of Islam but they had so small following that they were virtually incapable of playing any marked part in Islamic fraternity much less *vis-à-vis* Hinduism or its sects. Besides nursing inter-sects theological and doctrinal differences, they had also differences in social outlook and approach to different problems. They, however, had one thing common and that was they were steeped deep in formalism, particularism, obscurantism, esoteric practices, superstitions, demeaning rituals *et al.*

In the 16th and 17th centuries particularly, there emerged certain revivalist movements which created new religious groups, but even they did not hold any promise for the regeneration of Indian Muslims or of mankind as a whole. Mahadvis believed that Mahdi would reappear to restore original glory to Islam and it was the duty of the Muslims to believe and follow him. Sayyed Mohammad of Jaunpur (birth September, 1443) was a famous Mehdi in India. Naqshbandis was another religious group. Unlike Mahadvis, it wielded considerable influence among the Muslims even in Guru Gobind Singh's time. They believed that their *Qayyum* who had direct access to God and prophet Muhammad, was destined to usher in the revival and promotion of Islam, and in this process *Bidat* (innovation) and Kufar had to be erased by which they meant crusade (*Jehad*) should be launched against *Kafirs* who did not accept Islam of their concept to make them accept Islam or to finish them. In the case of Christianity and Judaism which were the religions of the Book, the crusade would not operate if their followers agreed to enter into agreement. The Sunnis which formed the majority of the Muslims were anxious that the Muslim *Shara* should be observed in totality and principle of Jehad should be pursued vigorously with the ultimate object of converting Dar-ul-Harb into Dar-ul-Islam. In the process, they supported and sponsored all such movements which in their reckoning could bring the goal nearer. Strangely enough, all those movements did not strive to shed unnecessary accretions to Islam, nor did they try to coalesce different sects of the Muslims into one unified whole with vision of seeking welfare of all. Regretfully, Religion was seen as an instrument to advance particularistic interests rather than to be considered a great artifice to reform individuals and corporate living. Even among Naqshbandis, there were groups having intra-group conflicts as for instance, Naqshbandis of Delhi had differences with their counterparts at Sirhind.

Sufism, another form of religious life of the Muslims in India, had also developed contradictions and according to one estimate there were Sufis and Sufis, some having faith in *Tahudi-i-Wajudi* and some in *Tahuhidi-Shuhadi*. In social outlook they were *Sulekul* (peace for all) but in Indian context they could not shed particularism and compromised with orthodox Islam, although they were hesitant to act as a fanatic and oppressive to other religions. Quite a number of Sufi saints such as Mian Shaikh Badruddin, Bhikhan Shah and Saif Khan had been in deep friendship with the Sikh Gurus and some of the Hindu saints. All the same, they did not throw up any programme for the uplift of mankind as a whole.

Hinduism too presented a sorry spectacle. Its main forms Vaishnavism, Jogism, Saivism were at the most half-baked attempts to regenerate society. These did not conceive Reality *in toto* nor did they project any social philosophy. The people brought up in these traditions grew to be good ascetics instead of being responsible citizens alive to the civic and social duties. Tantrism was another form of Hinduism that held the Hindus in tight grip. Regretfully this form also had debased itself to a few formulas to be muttered for attaining mundane advantages. The religious elite of both Hinduism and Islam had gone corrupt.

Corruption, immorality and vice were rampant among the *Qazis* as well as *Imams* of the mosques. They visited the *hamp* saloons without hesitation.[15] The theologians were shrewd enough to exploit the royal patronage to their utmost. They seemed to be following the maxim 'make hay while the sun shines'.[16] According to Shah Nawaz Khan, Aurangzeb himself bemoaned that in the reign of Timurids, not a single truth-loving person or an honest Qazi was heard of (with the exception of Murtza Khan).[17]

The Qazis of the cities and towns in concert with the governors and magistrates would sell out of greed the decrees of Qisas (retaliation on account of murders) for gold.[18]

The demeanour of Brahmans and other religious functionaries of various forms of Hinduism was no better. They had become extremely self-centred and had no moral qualms. There were certain movements as for instance Sufism, Baulism in Bengal, and Bhakti movement but their impact was marginal, and with the lapse of time, they had compromised with the orthodoxy either of the Hindu variety or that of Muslim.

About the approach and vision of different religions and sects the remarks of *Bachittar Natak* are illuminating and pertinent. In chapter 6th of *Bachittar Natak*, the Guru made it clear that Brahma, Vishnu, Mahesh, Dattatriya, Rishis, Siddhs, Prophet Mohammad did not improve upon this world, rather they began to present themselves as equals of God and enmeshed the people in rituals, formalism, meaningless practices as for instance Saint Dattatriya taught only how to beautify one's nails and hair and Prophet Muhammad began his own cult forcing people to call him as the sole spokesman of God.[19] "All of them were entangled in their own beliefs and could not see what the Reality was."[20]

The Guru was naturally upset at the sordidness of religious affairs. His anguish is amply visible in many of his poetic outpourings as for instance in *Bachittar Natak*, he says:

All those previously incarnated
Their own names having propagated
None showed the True Path.
Nor did they recognise the Almighty God.

Government and religious elites being altogether uncreative, partisan, greedy, tyrannous, ego-centred held no hope to the Guru in his wish to improve the lot of the people.

No less worrisome for the Guru were disintegrative forces that had been brewing in Sikh society and had the potential to disturb its internal organisation. The *Masands/Manjidars* who together with *Sangats* under their respective charges constituted the pivot of Sikh organisation and had served Sikhism creditably since the time of its inception. Upto the time of Guru Hargobind, Sikhism had crossed frontiers of Punjab and had won converts in far off regions such as Bengal, Uttar Pradesh, Madhya Pradesh, and certain parts of south India, Jammu, Kashmir *et al.* As a result *Sangats* had been formed on a large scale, sometime by the Sikhs themselves and sometime by the *Masands/Manjidars* deputed by different Gurus. These *Sangats* largely were connected to the Guru through *Masands* and their deputies (*Mewaras*) although examples of *Sangats* being guided and supervised by devoted Sikhs were not lacking. *Masands*, therefore, acquired a lot of influence over the *Sangats* as they were the medium through whom instructions of the Gurus to the people were transmitted. The offerings of the people were also collected and then remitted to the Guru by the *Masands*, although, at times, the *Sangats* sent them directly. The *Masands* kept a part of the offerings for performing their organisational, secular and episcopal duties. The system worked well for some time but as the time advanced, its functioning became shoddy and remissly. The office of a *Masand* which in the first instance was filled by men of piety and integrity, became hereditary in the families of the first incumbents, and in course of time, fell into the hands of those persons who were neither serious about their episcopal duties, nor possessed the requisite integrity in respect of financial matters. *Masands* not only took to jobbery and misappropriation of the offering on a large scale, but also claimed status equal to the Guru and did not hesitate to clone *Sangats*. Still they could not do much harm either to the solidarity of the Sikhs or the escalation of Sikhism, because they feared Guru Hargobind for his promptitude to take quick and strong actions.

After Guru Hargobind, because of no-so-good relations between the state and the Sikh Gurus and the provocative challenges of the rival claimants such as Dhirmal, Ram Rai,

Meharban and his successors to the guruship, the Gurus could not give much attention to the organisational as well as episcopal matters with the natural consequences that *Masands/ Manjidars* found opportunities to be more bold, more active in pursuing their petty designs instead of serving the cause of Sikhism. This tendency was clearly manifest during the pontificates of Guru Har Rai and Guru Harkrishan. It persisted even during Guru Teg Bahadur. The fact that quite a number of them sided with Dhirmal and one of them named Sihan did not hesitate even to fire at him was a brazen example of *Masands*' contumacy and recalcitrance.

Guru Gobind Singh had chartered a massive programme of rejuvenating and re-shaping the society, and in the process he had realised that he would have to face animosity of the Hill Rajas, conservative Hindu elements, ignorant masses, Mughal Islamic Imperialism, privileged classes, dissentient sects and his rival claimants of guruship. To steer clear through all this, he needed unflinching devotion of the Sikhs in general and whole-hearted co-operation of the *Masands* in particular, but the latter failed him utterly. They adopted many tactics to deflect him from his chosen path. They bred doubts in the minds of his family members, and the Sikhs in general regarding the soundness of his programmes and policies. When the Guru imparted military training and adopted assertive postures *vis-à-vis* Hill Rajas, they would at once go to revered mother of the Guru to prevail upon her to actively intervene to dissuade the Guru to stop such activities. Similarly, when the Guru decided to encounter the enemy at Bhangani, they were cynically critical. Not only this, they inveigled dissentients and rival claimants to the guruship to step up their nefarious activities. Many of them openly sided with them against the interest of the Guru. They also involved the *Sangats* under their impression in the issues, they championed and sponsored. Resultantly, *Masands* and the *Sangats* coalesced into different groups—each group under some *Masand/Manjidar* committed to the cause other than the cause of Sikhism/Guru. Many of *Masands* were bold enough to keep the offerings and *Daswandh* with themselves which they were enjoined upon to remit to the

Guru. These were the people who not only took away the offerings which the Sikhs had made to the Guru at Anandpur when there was cataclysm caused by the attack of Mirza Gias Beg and four Mughal *Ahdyas*. Such people wielded a considerable influence in the whole of Majha territory and most of the Doaba. They seemed to have co-operated in many cases with schismatic groups among the Sikhs. An indeterminate number of Sikhs were following the members of Guru Ram Das's descendants who had set up rival Guru lineages. Notable amongst them were the descendants of Prithi Chand and Dhirmal (the elder brother of Guru Har Rai). Ram Rai, the elder brother of Guru Harkrishan had also attracted considerable following contemptuously called Ram Rayyas but his strength lay in the hills where Aurangzeb had granted him seven villages in the Dun Valley.

Sikh chroniclers are galore with examples of *Masands*' utter perversity. It is said that one day, a company of mimes came to the Guru's court. The Guru asked them to imitate *Masands*. One of them accordingly dressed as a *Masand*, second as a Masand's servant and a third as a *Masand's* courtesan riding behind him on horse back as he went to collect offerings for the Guru. The mimes portrayed to life the villainies and oppression practised by the *Masands*. Again we are told that a *Masand* billeted himself on a poor Sikh and claimed sweets instead of the crushed pulses and unleavened bread which formed the staple food of the host. The *Masand* took the bread, threw it into the host's face and dashed the crushed pulse on the ground. He then abused the Sikh and would cease scolding him till the poor Sikh sold his wife's petty coat to provide him sweets.[21] The stories might not be wholly true but the truth implicit in them is certified by the Guru himself. He writes:

> If anyone goes the *Masands*, they will tell him to bring all his possessions at once and give it to them.
>
> If anyone serves the *Masands*, they will say 'Fateh' and give us all thine offerings.
>
> Go at once and make a present to us of whatever assets are in their house.

> Think on us night and day, and mention not others even by mistake.
>
> If they hear of anyone giving, they run to him even at night. They are not at all pleased at not receiving.
>
> They put oil into their eyes and make others believe that they are shedding tears.
>
> If they see any of their worshippers wealthy they serve him with sacred food and feed him with it.
>
> If they see him without wealth, they give him nothing, though he begs for it, they will not show him their faces.
>
> These beasts plunder men, and never sing the praises of the Supreme Being.[22]

Masands' shabby demeanour had been taken note of by the sixth Guru[23] and against this backdrop, he designated the Sikhs who had direct link with the Guru as 'Khalsa', the pure ones, or Guru's own like the Khalsa lands which were under the direct control of the Mughal sovereign. The Guru seemed to make use of this term deliberately so that the Sikhs might take note of the Guru's preference for the Sikhs with direct connection with the Guru. Guru Tegh Bahadur who used this term (Khalsa) for the Sikhs of Patna understandably to make known to them that they were preferred as they had direct linkage with him. Implicit in all this was that to be a Sikh directly of the Guru was dearer to the Guru than a Sikh linked with the Guru through the mediation of a *Masand*.

Guru Gobind Singh's perception about the Masands was no different from his father and grandfather, but he waited long before he took any decisive step against the *Masands*. The Guru's slow peddling in this regard seemed to have been actuated by practical considerations as for instance any drastic interference in their affairs was to put the whole Sikh organisation out of gear. But ultimately the Guru was roused to action. He exposed the misdeeds of *Masands* and issued Hukamnama to various *Sangats* that they should not only stop sending their offerings and the amount of *Daswandh* through *Masands* but also avoid having any social relations with them. They were asked to have direct link with the Guru. The story goes that the Guru was so much enraged at the misdemeanour of *Masands* that he had all the *Masands* captured and brought to Anandpur where he destroyed them to the number of 2200 in boiling oil and by other torments.[24] This does not seem to be believable as the Guru had hardly the means of laying his hands on all the *Masands*, particularly on those of outlying districts and it seems more probable that some of the *Masands* were punished, some were pardoned. The Guru, however, did not stop at that. He thought of abolishing *Masand* system altogether as he found it not only injurious as an organisation but also it was a great wedge between the Guru and the Sikhs. He naturally wanted to get rid of *Masands*.

Equally disruptive and inappropriate were the activities of dissentient sects such as the followers of Prithi Chand contemptuously called Minas by Bhai Gurdas, the followers of Dhirmal commonly known as Dhirmalias and the followers of Ram Rai, popularly called Ram Rayyas. Hardas the son of Meharban and grandson of Prithi Chand, was leading the Minas after his father and his grandfather in the time of Guru Gobind Singh. He called himself the seventh Guru in succession to Guru Nanak claiming to inherit his light and projected his sect as the mainstream Sikhism. He kept control of the central Sikh Shrine Sri Harmandir Sahib and Darbar Sahib complex including Sri Akal Takht and spared no pains to present the compositions of his father as well as his own as sacred texts.

His real purpose was to impress upon the Sikhs that guruship after Guru Ram Das vested in his father and grandfather and currently in his person. He made prevalent a code of conduct which like the writings of his father leaned towards Brahmanism.[25] Guru Har Rai's elder brother Dhirmal had already done his worst to gain guruship for himself and was still campaigning to attain his objective. The followers of Ram Rai had not ceased to present themselves as the representatives of Sikhism, although their progenitor, Ram Rai, had reconciled to Guruship of Guru Gobind Singh who had publicly proclaimed to this effect. They were particularly active at Lahore where their headquarter next in importance only to that of Dehradun was situated and at Srinagar (Garhwal) where some of the Ram Rayyas' *Masands* had decided to stay. At Dehradun they were wary of conducting vicious propaganda against the Guru because Punjab Kaur, the wife of Ram Rai, had converted to the Guru's mission. The example of these claimants of Sodhi family was not lost upon other members of the Sodhi family and twenty of them were audacious enough to simultaneously claim pontifical throne at the death of Guru Harkrishan. Many of the *Sodhis* began to consider themselves as entitled to the reverence of the Sikhs and appointed their own *Masands*. A great destructive force was thus let loose in Sikhism, of which *Masands* were not slow to take the fullest advantage. The greed of these aspirants for the guruship and recalcitrance of the *Masands* fed each other resulting in development of a serious threat to the solidarity of the Sikhs' loyalty to their Guru, as well as the immutability and sovereignty of the Sikh doctrine. The Guru, therefore, was obligated to take serious note of such development and therefore he denounced the Minas, Dhirmalias and Ram Rayyas as heretics projecting beliefs and opinions opposed to Sikhism. He also made the Sikhs aware of their nefarious activities and issued Hukamnamas to *Sangats* of different regions that they should not remit their offerings and amount of *Daswandh* to him through a *Masand* or any of his agent. These should be sent directly to him or through his specially appointed emissaries.[26] A Hukamnama to Sikhs not to have any social relationship with the followers of Prithi Chand, Dhirmal and Ram Rai was also issued.[27]

Equally irritating were the deliberate distortions of real concept of guruship. Guru Nanak was Guru because it was avowed that the guruship of Nanak derived directly from 'God'. With Guru Angad and his immediate successors, it would not have been direct and immediately. Indeed to them the words and message of the Guru as transmitted to them were considered as Guru, guruship being supposed to have been transmitted to them through Word. Guru Arjan also got guruship because he was transmitted the light that made his predecessors 'Guru', but he was at the same time the son of fourth Guru and it was from this cue that guruship began to be seen as something hereditary, a principle which conceptually speaking was against the concept and institution of Guru.

Since the hereditary principle and law of primogeniture were generally considered as adjuncts to each other by the people, Dhirmal, the eldest living son of Baba Gurditta and Ram Rai the eldest son of Guru Har Rai began to dispute the succession of the pontifical seat. They turned hostile to the central Sikh church and formed the rival sects and formed common cause with the Mughal authorities to disrupt/erode the Sikh authority. Besides this, the Guru realised that hereditary institution particularly of socio-religious nature in an expanding society was liable to deteriorate in character and to become authoritarian. There is evidence of Guru Gobind Singh himself to show that the *Masands* had actually turned authoritarian and used to indulge in corrupt practices that led to the exploitation of the poor Sikhs. All this convulsed the mind of the Guru and he had to give a serious thought to it. Accordingly he made up his mind to abolish personal guruship and vest it in something permanent and inviolate. The work had already been done in this direction. Now he resolved to take things to their logical end. There was revered Granth by then well established as the book enshrining Word of the Gurus and considered as sacred as the Gurus themselves.

On the matters other than spiritual, there was the institution of *Sangat* which had developed enough to take care of secular affairs as well. Between the two, the 'Word' and '*Sangat*' with the spiritual and secular functions of the Guru could be taken care of. Revered Granth could become the spiritual Guru, the Panth itself the secular Guru and the combination of the two as 'the mystic entity'. But how to translate these ideals into practice was the moot question?

The Guru had worked among the people of semi-independent states of Shivaliks. But he soon discovered that they were insensitive to any fresh calls including those of his own. Similarly, the Guru found hill Rajas holding fast to feudalistic values and totally reluctant to make efforts to introduce reforms with the result that the people had turned spineless bereft of vitality to play any worthwhile role in remoulding individuals and society.

The Rajputs of the present-day Rajasthan also did not hold any promise to the Guru. They had enmeshed themselves in feudal order and *Jati*-based structure. Not only this, they had succumbed to the Mughal hegemony and surrendered their political and social will. No doubt, in the time of Guru, Rathors of Marwars and Sisodias of Mewar had challenged the tyrannous Aurangzeb's religious policy of converting Dar-ul-Harb into Dar-ul-Islam, yet their cases were the product of vested interests and were not actuated by any higher motive or design. Such people obviously were not fit to be the vehicle of Guru's programme of rejuvenation and regeneration.

The case of the Marathas was no better. No doubt, they rose against the inequitable rule of Aurangzeb under their charismatic leaders first under Shivaji and then under his successors, Sambhaji, Raja Ram (Sambhaji's brother) and Tara Bai (Raja Ram's wife) and ultimately established Maratha sovereignty, yet they were not fit enough to reconstruct society on fresh bases of justice, equality, freedom and felt satisfied with *Varn*-based society clinging to feudalistic values. Their vision was circumscribed and their actions particularistic. Time needed persons with all-inclusive vision of society but they were too inelastic to expand beyond the parameters laid down by Dharam Shastras. They did not look beyond *Hindu Padshahi* or Maratha Swaraj at political level. No fresh concept either of polity or of governance or of society or of metaphysics was thrown up by them. Such people obviously could not be helpful to the Guru. Other people outside India were also taken cognisance of by the Guru. His compositions reveal that he surveyed at least mentally the people of Gazni, Banghshies (people from Kohat and Qurram valley), Nepalese, Machines (people from the regions of Burma adjoining China), Hingu (people from Sind), people of Arab, the French, the Portuguese. He also seemed to have critically appraised different sects including Rafzi, Imams, Naths *et al.* He found all of them ego-ridden[28] and unenthused in regard to participating of 'Guru's crusade against the perpetrators of 'Kubudh' (misdeeds)'.

Simultaneous to all this, the Guru seemed to have critically scrutinised social complexion of his disciples. The composition of the Sikhs had undergone a distinct change. The Jats of Majha and Malwa had entered into the fold of Sikhism in large numbers. They had brought along with them their tribal culture. Because of their profession of agriculture and their habitation amidst war-like people for quite a long time and difficult social and geographical environments, they had developed spirit of adventure and a sort of elasticity in their character and behaviours. They developed the natural tendency to be less rigid particularly in matters which needed adaptability. Sikhism threw no damper on all these qualities but they needed orientation towards Sikh values especially in relation to other components of Sikh society including the so-called low caste. Next to the Jats in number were the people designated so-called low castes in the Hindu caste hierarchy who embraced Sikhism. Their primary need was to have a dignified social status and an atmosphere which should enable them to keep their head high without any fear. Sikhism undoubtedly guaranteed dignified social status and condemned squarely any distinction on bases of caste *et al.*, yet they were to be assured.

Opposed to both these classes were Khatris and Brahmans who in spite of their entry into the fold of Sikhism had not been able to shed their caste affiliations and could ill-brook the Jats and the so-called low-caste people being raised in the social scale. Many of them did came forward to sarcastically comment on caste-system but beyond this they did nothing. Most of the Sikhs were still in the grip of various sectarian movements such as Nathism, Shaivism, Devism *et al.* in spite of professing faith in the Guru. They also needed a brainwash.

In sum, the sociological canvass bore only a confused picture of the Sikh society. The Guru must rub off some unrequired contours or draw new ones to ensure the success of his missions.[29]

The politico-socio-religious context being what it was, he pondered upon it in the context of his own experience, legacy which he inherited from his predecessors and the mission which was revealed to him directly from God. Guru Nanak, the first of his predecessors, came to this world to enlighten and improve upon it and this being so, he established *Tisra Panth* (the third Panth) the other two being Muslim and Hindu according to Bhai Gurdas.[30] Guru Nanak is said to have experienced direct encounter with God at Sultanpur on the bank of Bein rivulet and had a vision of Him. According to Guru Nanak, He was Transcendent, Formless, Infinite, Singular, a Unity as well as Unicity, Self-existent beyond time and space, beyond enmity and fear and the sole Creator. He was also Immanent. In his immanence, he pervaded everything, seen and unseen, who were related to him as rays are related to sun or sparks to fire. World also partook of his immanence. Man also emanated from Him. Since he was the source of all creations, He was not detached from it. He permeated it and regulated it just as a potter regulated his clay and in spirit form permeates his constructions. Hence, He had intimate relations with nature, man, world, universe, unmanifest and manifest things. He, therefore, was looked upon by Guru as attributive in His immanent aspect as for instance He was regarded merciful, saviour, sustainer, even destroyer, although Guru Nanak's expressions of God convey relatively sparsely the destructive attributes of God, probably because he reckoned that presenting God as saviour of people implied destruction of the wicked.

Guru Nanak's vision of God as delineated in the foregoing paragraphs led him to remodel Man and Society in the light of that. Since God was singular and sole Creator of the whole creation, this world being a part of creation, was not profane or irrelevant, rather it was a time-bound reality and a dwelling place of God. World being Sargun (immanent) aspect of God is to be held in veneration, not to be condemned as a varitable hell or an illusion. Also it is not to be exploited and squandered nor is it irrelevant to the process of ascent towards God. A love bond and an active association between God and world exists and are in-built. The world being reality and having infinite links with God as the immanent is a place to be lived upon to experience how God manifested Himself as also to struggle to experience the ultimate ineffable vision of God. Man's destiny is to endeavour to discover and realise himself/herself and then experience and operate as per spirit of the attributes of God which he could do by controlling evil impulses, eliminating Haumei (ego-centricity) and orientating his actions as per Will of God. In simple words, the Guru expected people to regenerate themselves through appropriate actions and meditate upon God in both His transcendent and immanent aspects. In this context, Guru Nanak propounded and preached the following triple precepts as the bases of an ideal society.

(i) Kirt Karnā

(ii) Waṅd Chhaknā

(iii) Nām Japnā.

Kirt Karnā means that one should earn one's livelihood by honest creative labour. *Waṅd Chhaknā* implies that one should share the fruits of one's labour with the fellow beings. *Nām Japnā* denotes meditating on Lord's Name, which means that one should not loose sight of the cosmic process and the Divine, permeating everything of the world. By imbiding Nām culture, one would not fall victim to *Haumei* which causes many evil impulses to emerge in a person. Society built on such precepts was bound to be healthy, egalitarion, non-exploitive, just, non-discriminatory, condemnatory of distinctions on the bases of caste, birth, status, creed and wealth *et al.* because these were the products of faulty perception of Reality/God and flawed notions regarding ultimate destiny of man, world and the nature of their relationship with God.

In the process of rejuvenation and regeneration of man and society, the Guru did not recommend any ascetic practices, pilgrimages, renunciation of the world because he rightly believed that imbibing *Nām* culture is a right type of pilgrimage. Eliminating of *Haumei* and other evil impulses should be considered as the right type of asceticism and renunciation instead of resorting to fasts, penance and shunning of world *et al.* The Guru set a fresh ideal before the people which was to seek union with God by which he meant that they should conform to different attributes of God which implied that they should be compassionate, kind, helpful and intolerant of injustice and oppressors or tyrants. Guru called such people Gurmukh (Guru-conscious), Nirmal (Pure), Khalsa (Immaculately Pure). In *Japji*, the Guru called such people as Panches and wished leadership to be comprised of them. In this context, the Guru expressed that only those should rule who are really competent, by which he meant that they should be ethical, enlightened and Guru-God conscious, never ever resorting to injustice and oppression and always remaining attuned to God.[31]

This mission of Guru Nanak was carried on by his successors who made it more lucid, clear and explicit through preaching, singing the compositions of the Guru, adding their own compositions to the already existing hymns of Guru Nanak. They contributed towards the development of Sikhism by adding concepts, institutions and symbols. The *Sangats* were established at far-flung regions, new cities such as Kartarpur, Amritsar, Tarn Taran reflecting and committed to Sikh ethos were founded. A system of *Daswandh* among the Sikhs was made prevalent, links with the Sikh *Sangats* were forged, central Sikh scripture, *Adi Granth* was prepared, central Sikh shrine, Sri Harmandir Sahib and fresh symbol of supreme Sikh authority both in religious and temporal affairs was created in the form of Sri Akal Takht Sahib. It was declared clearly and unequivocally that in Sikhism religious and temporal affairs were not exclusive to each other, rather these two are complementary and the Guru was to give guidance in both these spheres. Guru Hargobind flaunted this principal by wearing two swords: One symbolizing religious authority and the second symbolising temporal authority. This continued to be dinned into the ears of the Sikh people because there was apprehension that it was not easy to wean them away from their age-long belief that there existed dichotomy between spirituality and temporality, the belief continuously embedded in the psyche of the people by Indian religious tradition, generally speaking. All the Gurus were persistent in following the basic tenets as laid down by Guru

Nanak. To quote *Guru Granth Sahib* (p. 966): The same was the light and the methodology of all the Gurus, simply their bodies had changed *Jot Oha Jugat Sai Kaya Pher Platiay*. This factor was also testified by Guru Gobind Singh in *Bachittar Natak*. He said "Sri Nanak was accepted as Angad (Guru) and Guru Amar Das was identified as Angad, Guru Amar Das was called (Guru) Ram Das and this mystery was understood by the saints only. The stupid ones could not follow it, ordinary persons considered them in different forms but some rare ones understood them as one. Those who know them are bound to attain the high spiritual stages but without understanding (the mysteries) nothing could be procured."[32] Saying this, Guru Gobind Singh brings down the spiritual lineage of the Gurus to his own and thus proved in accordance with *Guru Granth Sahib* that all the Gurus were one, and their thought-frame was also one. At the same time, Guru Gobind Singh observed that in spite of hard efforts of his predecessors, people as individuals and as a social fraternity were intransigent, very slow to accept the proposed changes by the Gurus including himself. He in his compositions made no secret of his dissatisfaction with the concepts of state, sovereignty, God and His creations, the modalities of the reconstruction of society, demeanour of human beings both at individual and social levels. Even prevalent religions had ceased to function properly.

Face to face with such scenario, blatantly unhelpful to him in the fulfilment of his mission, the Guru seemed to be always in quest for some solution right from the day he assumed guruship. Whether he was at Anandpur or at Paonta or at any other place, he was persistent in his efforts to achieve his objective. He went through the whole gamut of ancient Indian literature, both religious and secular. He saw for himself the political apparatus of the Mughals and the hill-chiefs. He critically appraised the social and religious formations of the people along with their faiths and beliefs and himself wrote a number of compositions such as *Jāp* and *Akal Ustat*. In his compositions, the Guru addressed God by various names. He calls Him Attributeless, Formless, beyond death and time, Self-existent, Omniscient, etc. He also calls Him by various attributive names such as Sustainer, Giver of gifts, Merciful, Compassionate, Protector, Destroyer of oppressors, Extirpator of enemies and tyrants, Just, All-righteousness *et al.* He also calls Him by such names as Sarbloh (all steel), Mahan Loh (great steel), Sarb Kal (all death), Mahan Kal (great death), Asidhuj and Kharg Ketu (having sword in his hand).

From all this, it is clear that Guru's faith in God was unfathomable, as also in His potential to smash the wicked as well as to bless and elevate the virtuous. From this faith flowed his confidence that he was the arbiter of the destiny of the people—the task which He undertakes and accomplishes through His chosen people. It was against this background that he considered himself as the one commissioned by God to spread God's religion, to save the saints and to extirpate the tyrants. The veracity of the statement is vouchsafed by the Guru himself in his composition *Bachittar Natak*.[33] The Guru says:

> When God gave me the order,
> I assumed birth in this Kal age,
> I did not desire to come.
> ....
> Understand this, the holy men, in your souls
> I assumed birth for the purpose of spreading
> the Faith, saving the saints.
> And extirpating all tyrants. (*Bachittar Natak* Chapter VI)

From the reading of the above excerpts from *Bachittar Natak,* impression emerges that the Guru considered himself commissioned by God to spread religion, extirpate tyrants and restrain people from committing misdeeds. By considering himself as such, the Guru did not claim status of an incarnate of God, who according to Hindu belief assumed birth to save the saints and to destroy the tyrants. He was God's servant and slave; he was not to be guided by enmity to anyone or influenced by fear of mortals. His view of the problem resembled that of a judge punishing a criminal simply for the sake of protecting society against the unjust violator of justice who threatened its foundation.

In complete dedication to the mission of God, the Guru addressed the problems. He reappraised the whole of scenario as it existed or it was to exist in times to come. He computed his resources—historical, metaphysical, sociological and religious. He juxtaposed the results of his calculations with the ultimate configuration and destiny of people not only of India but of the world as a whole as envisaged by Sikhism and in the process realised that a timely adjustment between forces of evil and those of good through the use of force was an essential ingredient of the moral world. God could not tolerate the unhappiness of his saints (righteous people) who must be protected from the wicked. To this purpose, the use of force as a last resort in favour of the good was legitimate. It is in this context that Guru ascribed divinity to sword and raised it to the status of God and Guru named God as Bhagauti or *Kharag Ketu* (wielder of sword). By doing so, the Guru was carrying the mission of Guru Nanak and his successors to its culmination. Guru Nanak called God smasher of the evil (*Asur sanghar*) along with other attributive names of God and had not hesitated to denounce Babar for his excesses and Lodi rulers for abjuring righteous causes. This action-thinking-model continued to be followed by subsequent Gurus, of course with varying degree of emphasis depending upon circumstances and the intensity of challenges. Guru Gobind Singh, thus, did not plough a lonely furrow. He followed the path shown of his predecessors with this difference that he followed it with more vigour, and this he had to do because of the changed circumstances and the commission assigned to him by God himself (to extirpate the tyrants, save the saints and spread the religion), which implied that the Guru was obliged to improve upon the present as also to set the people on the road of Dharma through the leadership comprising of saints, lovers and crusaders for righteousness. Guru's mission was indeed a core impulsion, epitomic of what Sikhism stood in terms of doctrine, society, individuals and corporate living and ultimate destiny of mankind at global level. The praxis was the Khalsa.

Manifestation of Khalsa

The Guru decided to put his plan into operation on the first of Baishakh 1756 Bk (March 29, 1699 as per Nanak Shahi Calendar). He sent Hukamnamas to his followers inviting them to visit Anandpur in full strength on the Baisakh festival. He specially exhorted them to come with long hair and beards unshorn.

The Sikhs responded by gathering in very large number at Anandpur[34] on the day of the festival (March 29). Guru Gobind Singh rose early and sat in meditation. He then appeared before the *Sangat* who hailed him with shouts of greetings. Bhai Mani Singh gave exposition of a *Shabad* from the *Adi Granth*.[35] Guru Gobind Singh then stood before the assembly with his sword unsheathed and spoke: "Is there anyone here who would lay down his life for his Guru and *Dharma*? It was an amazing call and no wonder his words struck consternation among the gathering. They did not know what the Guru meant and gazed in awed silence until he spoke again. Now confusion turned into fear. For the third time, Guru Gobind Singh repeated his call. Daya Ram a Sobti Khatri of Lahore arose and said with humility 'My head is at thy disposal, my True Lord. There would be no greater gain than dying under Thy sword.' He walked by the Guru to an especially improvised enclosure close by. The Guru returned with sword dripping blood and waving it to the multitude asked for another head. This was more than any could endure. People started leaving the place. Some of them went to complain to the Guru's mother. But when the Guru had made a third call, Dharam Das, a Jat from Delhi came forward to sacrifice himself for the Guru. He too was taken to the enclosure. In the same way the Guru made three more calls. Mohkam Chand, washerman of Dwarka, Himmat, a cook of Jagannath and Sahib Chand a barber of Bidar, cheerfully responded one after another and advanced to offer their heads.

A while after, the Guru led the five Sikhs back from the enclosure into which he had taken one by one. In the enclosure confidentially guarded, he had kept sets of apparel especially designed and made. Decked in saffron-coloured gorgeous raiments topped over with neatly tied turbans of the same colour, the glorious five walked deferentially behind their Master, overwhelmed with thankfulness. The Guru was himself attired in the same manner as his chosen disciples. The gathering considerably thinned and still in shocked muteness was further puzzled to see those whom they had thought to have been sacrificed to the Guru's sword yet remain in flesh and blood.[36]

The Guru introduced these five to the audience as *Panj Piara*[37], the five devoted spirits, beloved of the Guru. He expressed his deep sense of gratitude for the culmination which had crowned Guru Nanak's revelation. He said that the five beloved had blessed themselves and brought glory to their faith. The Guru added that they (A Khatri, Jat and three from so-called low castes) would form the nucleus of the Order of the Khalsa, he was going to inaugurate.

Then the Guru proceeded to initiate them to his new Order by a new method. The method of initiation which Guru Nanak had introduced and which had hitherto been current in Sikhism was *Charan Pahul*, according to which the neophytes were asked to drink the water which had been touched by the Guru's toe. During Guru Arjan Dev, this initiation rite underwent a little change. The water was not touched by the toe, but simply placed under the cot of the Guru. Evidently the idea behind the rite was to develop the sense of surrender and humility. But in the context of the changed situation, this ideal alone was not required. Accordingly, the Guru introduced another method of initiation. The Guru put water in an iron bowl, stirred it with Khanda, a two-edged sword, along with the recitation of five compositions:[38] *Japji*, *Jaap Sahib*, *Swayyas*, *Chaupai* and *Anand Sahib*. Revered Jito did not relish that the five Sikhs who had offered heads to the Guru should be given plain water. She forthwith brought a plate full of sugar puffs (*Patashas*) and with the approval of the Guru put them into the water. This was considered to be propitiatory in the sense that the initiates would henceforth be blessed with the grace of womanly sweetness. *Amrit*—the nectar of Immortality—was now ready.

The nectar thus prepared was administered to the five beloveds from the same bowl to signify their initiation into the casteless and classless fraternity. They sat *Bir Asan*, *i.e.* in the heroic posture with the left knee up and the right knee on the ground. The Guru then gave them each five palmful of *Amrit* to drink. He sprinkled it five times on their hair, their face, and their eyes and caused them to call aloud *Waheguru Ji Ka Khalsa Waheguru Ji Ki Fateh*. At the end, all of them were given the steel bowl to quaff from it turn by turn the remaining 'Amrit' in token of having become brothers. The most striking thing in the process of the preparation of Amrit was the substitution of the two-edged sword in place of the Guru's toe. This thing heralded a new theme that henceforth the Khalsa would follow the ideal of self-assertion and self-reliance along with the ideal of humility and self-surrender. The baptism symbolised a rebirth by which the initiated were considered as having renounced their previous occupations—Kirt Nash—for serving the cause of righteousness, their earlier family ties—Kul Nash to become the family of Guru Gobind Singh, their earlier faiths—Dharam Nash for the creed of the Khalsa, all rituals—Karam Nash to feel unencumbered to treat the path shown by the Guru. The moment marked their complete break with the past. The baptised males and females were enjoined to affix 'Singh' (lion) and 'Kaur' respectively as suffix along with their names.

The baptism of the double-edged sword introduced on the day of the creation of the Khalsa required the initiate to live a virtuous life of morally responsible action under the discipline and code especially prescribed for him. For outward symbols, the Guru asked them to always wear long hair (*Kesh*), a comb (*Kangha*) in the hair knot, an iron bracelet (*Kara*) on the right wrist, a *Kirpan*—a sword on his person and *Kachha*—a pair of short breeches. These five K's (*Kesh*, *Kangha*, *Kara*, *Kirpan*, *Kachha*) are not mere external symbols.[39] A single and pervasive leitmotif discernible in these marks of investiture on the personality of a baptised Sikh (Singh), and this can be characterised as a sense of preparedness to uphold the ideals which the Guru had pin-pointed. These symbols the decision for which was announced more through profound deliberations upon the fragile moral complexities besetting human beings than through any mystically intuited wisdom gave the Sikhs their form and are symbolic of their conduct. The long unshorn hair besides being a symbol of manliness are also symbolic of the higher stage of consciousness of the wearer. The hair which the Sikhs maintain as a command of their Guru are also believed to imprint on the wearer, the investiture of spirituality, even of godliness. In Sikh scripture, an epithet used for God is Keshwa *i.e.* who wears long tresses. Let it be stressed here that God of Sikh perception is formless and it is personified only when the attributes with which He is remembered are to be explained. It is against this background, Professor Puran Singh calls hair 'a dear remembrance, an heirloom, a trust, a pledge, a love, a vow, an inspiration'. Guru Gobind Singh calls hair as the seal of Guru in one of his Hukamnamas.

Kara was necessarily made of iron and of no other metal. The Guru called Supreme Reality Sarb-Loh—All Iron. *Kara* therefore, was a constant reminder to the baptised Sikhs never to lose sight of this attribute of God as well. It had another symbolic significance. As a circle, it signified perfection. A circle is also said to represent *Dharma*. Thus *Kara* to a member of the Khalsa brotherhood represents a just, perfect and righteous life marked by self-discipline and self-control. The *Kara* served as a reminder to the Sikhs that they had promised to be true to the Guru and the Panth and that promise must be kept at all costs.

Kirpan is a synthesis of two words 'Kirpa' (mercy or kindness) and 'aan' (honour) which signify and highlight the purpose for which it is to be used. In Sikh religious parlance the sword conveys two dimensional meaning. One, sword (Bhagauti) is an attributive name of the Real one in the compositions of Guru Gobind Singh. Thus the wearer feels that he/she is ever under the protection of Bhagauti. Second, and which is in fact a derivative of the first, it symbolises manifestation of Shakti or divine power which is to be used in favour of the saints against the demonic powers as a last resort when all other means fail to impact.

The sword was never a symbol of aggression and it was never used for self-aggrandisement. It stands for righteousness and brave action for the protection of truth and virtue.[40] In *Akal Ustat*, the Guru addressed Timeless as All-steel. At the opening of *Bachittar Natak*, the sword is addressed as a synonym for the Timeless Being.

Namaskār Srī Kharag Kō
Karon su Hit Chit Lae

Honour to the Holy sword:
I bow to it with love and devotion.

It is also conceived as God's generative function:

Khanda Prithme Manai Kai
Jin Sab Sansār Upaiya.
"After the primal manifestation of the sword, the universe was created."

The sword was considered as synonym of God, Primal generative principle, supreme power to sustain moral order and to annihilate negative forces. In this way, the Guru conveyed to the Khalsa, as an individual as well as a corporate body that they, wielders of sword, should cast themselves in the mould of God, generator, sustainer, protector and annihilator of negative forces.

Unlike a dagger, which is associated with secret attack or hidden defence, the sword is associated with open combat, governed by certain principles. Thus, sword of the Khalsa, male or female, is the assertion of their right to freedom. To quote Kapur Singh "The Sword" is by ancient tradition and fascination is a typical weapon of offence and defence and hence a fundamental right to wear, of the free man and woman, a sovereign individual. All governments and rulers whether ancient or modern do insist to wear arms. Indeed in final analysis, a government or the state is sustained and supported by the organised might and exclusive right of possession of arms, a citizen's right to wear arms being conceded as only of a permissive and licensed character. It follows from this that the measure of freedom to possess and wear arms by an individual is the precise measure of his freedom and sovereignty. Since a member of the Khalsa brotherhood (or motherhood) is pledged not to accept any alien restrictions on his (or her) civic freedom, he (she) is enjoined upon and struggle for his (or her) unrestricted right to wear and possess arms of offence and defence.[41]

The Sikh stress on physical or bodily cleanliness along with inner purity warrants that hair should be kept tidy and obviously. Comb is the easiest means to realise this objective. Comb also symbolises the cleanliness of mind. As a divestural symbol it appears to repudiate the practice of tantric Yogis, the outward symbol of whose denominations is matted hair (*Jata*).

The last of the five Ks is the *Kachhehra* or *Kachha*—a pair of breeches, which must not come below the knee. It is a sartorial symbol signifying mainly reserve in the commitment of procreative functions. In this it stands to repudiate puritanical vows of chastity (of the Hindu *Sanyasi*) as also the Muslim practice of circumcision. It is also a garment well-suited to the eighteenth-century Khalsa, allowing their prowess as horsemen and as wielders of the sword.

The ceremonies that surrounded the event of the creation of the Khalsa are conspicuous for the absence of any mystic element. The Guru did not invoke any god or goddess, rather he tried to keep the entire ceremony human. He did so with the obvious aim of raising the human ingredients involved in the ceremony to the level of the Divine. According to Guru Gobind Singh, this can possibly be done not through the intervention of any deity but only through consecrating the human beings to be pure in thought and deed. If at all any mythological element is involved, it is demythologizing the myth of churning the ocean by gods and demons with a view to getting *Amrit* out of it. Guru prepared Amrit from pure clean water poured into a steel vessel and stirred by a double-edged sword (*Khanda*). *Patashas* (sugar puffs) were added to it. First Guru Gobind Singh stirred the water with *Khanda* while reciting hymns and thereafter the five baptised Singhs

(Khalsa) were declared eligible to perform this ceremony of preparing and giving Amrit.

The five symbols taken together signified that the Khalsa both as an individual and a corporate body should be strong in body, mind and develop an integrated personality. They not only gave a manly bearing to the Sikhs, but a distinct identity too. They also made it not possible for them in future to conceal their identity as some Sikhs of Delhi had done at the time of Guru Tegh Bahadur's execution in November, 1675.

Further they gave the Sikhs a distinguished appearance, different both from that the Hindus and the Muslims—the fact which imparted a semblance's of unity, close brotherhood and equality and group consciousness.

According to Dr. Hari Ram Gupta 'In those days Hindus of respectable families wore five ornaments: gold earrings, a necklace, gold and silver bangles, finger rings and a waist belt of gold or silver and a tragri. The wearer felt proud of displaying his superior social position. At the same time, he saw the risk of losing these articles as well as his life into the bargain. Guru Gobind Singh provided to his followers five jewels which were within reach of everybody down to the poorest peasant and the lowest labourer. Instead of creating fear in the mind of the wearer, his five jewels made his Singh bold, brave and awe-inspiring.[42] To quote from a report of the proceedings "Though several refused to accept Guru's religion, about twenty thousand men stood up and promised to obey him as they had the fullest faith in the divine message."[43] The novitiates came forward in batches to receive baptism. The first five among those who now volunteered were Ram Singh, Desa Singh, Tehal Singh, Ishar Singh and Fateh Singh. They were called by the Guru Panj Mukte, the five liberated ones.[44] According to *Guru Kian Sakhian*, in the next row stood Mani Ram, Diwan Bachittar Das, Ude Rai, Anik Das, Ajaib Das, Ajaib Chand, Chaupat Rai, Diwan Dharam Chand, Alam Chand Nachna and Sahib Ram Koer following by Rai Chand Multani, Gurbakhsh Rai, Pandit Kirpa Ram Dutt of Mattan, Subeg Chand, Gurmukh Das, Sanmukh Das, Amrik Chand, Purohit Daya Ram, Ratna, Gani Das, Lal Chand Peshauria,

Rup Chand, Sodhi Dip Chand, Nand Chand, Nanu Rai of Dilwali and Hazari, Bhandari and Darbari of Sirhind, countless more batches came, each one more eager than the other. Anandpur was seized with an uncanny fervour of the spirit.[45]

According to one estimate as many as 80000 men were baptised in a few days. The Guru called them the Khalsa[46], the pure and his own ideal (*Isht Suhird*). The Guru also sent instructions to those who called themselves Sikhs that they should get themselves confirmed by getting baptised in the manner as laid down by the Guru. In the Pre-Khalsa period, the term Khalsa was restricted to such privileged Sikhs as were virtually directly connected with the Gurus. In one sense all the Sikhs were made Khalsa, the privileged ones directly connected with the Guru without any intermediary such as *Masands*.

In addition to the five emblems, the initiated were to observe rules of conduct (*Rehat*). They were not to cut any hair on any part of their body.[47] They were disallowed to smoke[48], chew tobacco or take alcoholic drinks. They were not to eat meat (*Halal*) of the animal which had been slaughtered by being bled to death, as was customary with the Muslims. They could have only *Jhatka* meat where the animal had been dispatched with one blow. They were forbidden to molest Muslim women. They were to tie turban and not wear cap (*Joe Sikh Sar Topi Dharei, Sat Janam Kushti Hoe Mareh*). The Guru enjoined upon the Khalsa to be strictly monogamous. Regarding the sexual matters, the Guru said that his father Guru Teg Bahadur had given him these instructions which should serve as a guide to the Sikhs.

> "O Son! as long as there is life in the body, make this thy sacred duty ever to love thine own wife more and more. Approach not another woman's couch either by mistake or even in a dream. Know, that the love of another's wife is a sharp dagger. Believe me death entereth the body by making love to another's wife. They who think it great cleverness to enjoy another's wife, shall, in the end, die the death of a dog."

Again the Guru declared:

"Par Nari Ki Sej
Bhool Supne Hūn Na Jaiyo"

(Never enjoy, even in dream, the bed of a woman other than your own wife.[49])

The more remarkable episode of this connection was that the Guru having administered Amrit to the Five Sikhs stood up in supplication and with folded hands begged them to baptise him in the manner as he had baptised them. They were amazed at such a strange request, but he silenced them by saying that he too wanted to be one of them, that as he was their Guru, they collectively should be his Guru. The 'Five Beloved' initiated the Guru to the Order of the Khalsa according to the new rite. After this, there remained no difference between the baptised Sikhs and the Guru. They were to be his Khalsa, body of his body and soul of his soul, nay his otherself, his beloved ideals (*suhird*). The Guru thus merged himself in the Khalsa and the whole body of the Khalsa was invested with the dignity of guruship. Thenceforward the principle was established that five Sikhs could represent the Khalsa. The Guru also sent instructions that those who called themselves Sikhs should get themselves confirmed by receiving the new baptism. The baptised Sikhs were termed as the 'Khalsa'.[50] The use of the term was not without a precedent. In the pre-Khalsa period, the use of Khalsa was restricted to such privileged Sikhs as were virtually connected with the Gurus and whose subordination to the Guru was simply *de jure*. "The word 'Khalsa' in the sense of the privileged Sikhs occurs in the Hukamnamas (fiats) issued by Hargobind and Guru Tegh Bahadur."[51] But with Guru Gobind Singh anyone who is baptised by a new method and abides by the instructions of the Guru was the member of the Khalsa or Sikh brotherhood.

Apart from wearing five emblems and observing rules of conduct the Sikhs were expected not to pay homage to any external object except the sacred Granth, not to recognise caste prejudice, superstitions, empty rituals, esoteric and ascetic practices. They were to have faith that the Guru was always present in the general body of the Khalsa and that wherever even five Sikhs were assembled, Guru would be with them. They were free to marry themselves without any caste consideration.

But they were to have no social or matrimonial relations with smokers[52], with persons who shaved[53], with persons who killed their daughters and with the descendants or followers of Prithi Chand, Dhir Mal, Ram Rai and those *Masands*[54] who had fallen away from the tenets and principles of Guru Nanak. They were not to worship idols, cemeteries or cremation grounds.[55] They were to rise at dawn, bathe and recite the hymns of the Guru. They must have faith in the singularity and unicity of God.

According to a news-writer of the period, the Guru is reported to have said, "I wish you all to embrace one creed and obliterate differences of religion. Let the four Hindu castes who have different rules be abandoned by them.[56] The Sikhs were to live a truthful life and would never allow their attention to be deviated from Immortal God." The Guru, in fact, recommended an unqualified worship of One True Lord, as it was set out by him in his *Jaap*, and *Akal Ustat*. All beliefs, rituals or ceremonies that implied the recognition of anything but the one True Lord were categorically rejected as is evident from the following *Swayya* in which a direct reference is made to the Khalsa[57], his duties and beliefs:

> "He who repeateth night and day the name of Him
> Whose enduring light is unquenchable,
> Who bestoweth not a thought on any but the one God
> Who hath full love and confidence in God
> Who putteth not faith even by mistake in
> fasting, or worshipping cemeteries, places of
> cremation, or Jogis' places of sepulchre
> Who only recognizeth the one God and no
> pilgrimages, alms, the non-destruction of life,
> Hindu penances or austerities;
> And in whose heart the light of the perfect
> One shineth, he is recognised as a pure member of the
> Khalsa."

Significance

The creation of the new order of the Khalsa had manifold ramifications. It caused a great stir in the body-social of the Sikhs themselves. Some embraced the Order of the Khalsa, others reacted despondently. Some of the Sikhs cautioned against accepting the innovations till written orders from the Guru were received. Some others remarked that the code was extremely tough and also incompatible with our family traditions and customs. Many explained that the code was creation of the preceptors themselves. The situation led, at some places, to dissension[58] among the Sikhs while at others it resulted in tension between the Sikhs and the non-Sikhs. Khatries and Brahmans, by and large, remained aloof. Some of them professed that they had faith in the religion of Guru Nanak and other Gurus; but many out of them refused to renounce the teachings of the *Vedas* and *Shastras*. They had been quite willing to pay lip service to the ideal of the casteless society; but they loathed to embroil themselves to the task of the new order with the result that many of them reverted to Brahmanism. Some remained just Sikhs better known as 'Sehjdhari', and very few of them entered the Order of the Khalsa.

Sainapat mentions two events which amply depict the attitude of certain Sikhs, one concerns a Khatri who openly spoke against the fresh innovations of the Guru in a congregation at Delhi. The congregation turned him out. He then rushed to his like-minded friend named Pritam. The Sikhs warned Pritam for siding with the discarded person. Pritam ignored the warning and convened a special conclave at Darapur where the Sikhs had gathered in a large number to enjoy a fair. Pritam and his associates prevailed upon the Sikhs to keep the matter of adopting the innovations in abeyance pending receipt of written orders of the Guru. The dissentients did not stop at that. Some time after, they proclaimed at a get-together of the Sikhs arranged by them that there was nothing wrong in abiding by the religion of their ancestors and in this way, they persuaded many to ignore the innovations enjoyed by the Guru.[59] Meanwhile a Sikh passed away. His family members chose not to observe ceremony of *Bhadan* (shaving their heads). The matter evoked protests and caused a great commotion among those who did not like the innovations of the Guru. They arranged boycott of the adherents of the new Order of the Khalsa. Some of them occasioned a general strike in the main bazar of Delhi to show their solidarity. Quite a number of them approached the local government officials to instigate them to take action against such Sikhs who were determined to follow the path as chartered by Guru Gobind Singh. The Government officials however, issued orders that the shop should remain open.[60]

This thing had important social ramification since the Guru had invested the Khalsa with status equal to his own and projected them as limb of his limb; they *ipso facto* became the most esteemed personnel and it was but only logical that they assumed leadership of the Sikhs. Hitherto the leadership was in the hands of *Masands/Manjidars* or some ones considered to be held in high esteem by local *sangats* but now it passed to the Khalsa, self-sovereign and enjoying the status of the Guru itself. Expressed in ethnological term, the *Masands* or local leaders were mostly urban Khatris while the Khalsa consisted of the people bulk of whom were Jats and so-called menial classes such as artisans and scavengers *et al.*

The Khalsa leadership therefore came to be comprised of the latter mostly who from the time of Manu had been denied any respectable status in the *Varun*-based Hindu society. Since the Khalsa Order repudiated castes and other distinctions on the bases of wealth, profession, culture, and creed etc., Jats and other socially neglected classes rejoiced and the Khalsa movement became synonymous with the rise of hitherto neglected classes/groups/individuals.[61]

Ideologically, the Khalsa aimed at the balanced combination of the ideals of Bhakti and Shakti or to express it in the modern terminology the Khalsa was to be a brotherhood in faith and brotherhood in arms at one and the same time. The Guru's injunctions included that the Khalsa should bear arms, Kirpan, being one and the most important of them, that they should use double-edged sword in the preparation of Amrit, and use of the appellation of Singh at the end of each name as it signified the martial valour, the Khalsa was expected to inculcate. Sword became an object of worship with the Sikhs, for it symbolised power and safety. The sentiment of the Sikhs for the sword was so much that God was given the name of 'All Steel' by the Guru. This being so, those who worshipped sword were promised exemptions from every other kind of religious rites or ceremonies and he/she was to be regarded as the Khalsa who combats in the van, who mounts on the war horse, who is ever waging war and who is continuously armed[62] against the wicked, unrighteous and the tyrants.

The Guru himself says:

"I am the son of a brave man, not of a Brahman
How can I perform austerities?
How can I turn my attention to Thee
and, forsake of domestic affairs
Now be pleased to grant me the boon
I crave with clasped hands
That when the end of my life cometh,
I may die fighting in a mighty battle."[63]

As is evident from the utterances of the Guru in connection with the Khalsa, the soldiery qualities were given place of eminence. In fact, militarism was adopted as an article of faith. The Guru says:

"All Steel, I am Thy slave
Deeming me, Thy own, preserve me;
Think me Thine own, cherish me
Single out and destroy mine enemies
May both my kitchen and my sword
prevail in the world."[64]

The Guru's primary concern was thus with his kitchen (*Degh*) and his sword (*Tegh*), the one as the emblem of service to assist the weak, the helpless and the oppressed and the other the emblem of power to extirpate the tyrants, and the Khalsa was the instrument that he created to achieve his two-fold purpose.[65]

New awareness of social egalitarianism had a miraculous effect on the psyche of the disciples of the Guru. Teja Singh and Dr. Ganda Singh observed that, 'even those people who had been considered dregs of humanity were changed, as if by magic into something rich and strange. The sweepers, the barbers, and confectioners who had not even touched a sword and whose whole generations had lived as grovelling slaves of the so-called higher classes became under the stimulating leadership of Guru Gobind Singh doughty warriors who never shrank from fear and who were ready to rush into the jaws of death at the bidding of the Guru.[66] According to General John J.H. Gordon, "the dry bones of an oppressed peasantry were stirred into life, and the institution of the Sikh baptismal rite at the hands of a few disciples anywhere in a place of worship, in a house or by the roadside brought about the more full and widespread development of the new faith". In this way, within a few months, a new people were born, bearded and beturbaned, fully armed and with a crusaders' zeal to build a new commonwealth. They implicitly believed that "the Khalsa shall rule, their enemies will be scattered, only they that seek refuge will be saved" (General John J.H. Gordon, *The Sikhs*, London, 1904).

From sociological point of view, the Khalsa represented a new pattern wherein tribal or caste affiliations had no room, nor were the superstitions, demeaning ceremonies and empty rituals given any status. On the other hand, it stood for broad outlook transcending parochial prejudices. Even the differences on the basis of religion were considered irrelevant or the creations either of the ignorance or of opaque understanding. Exactly this impression emerges when the Guru dinned into the ears of his disciples that the four tribes of Hindus, the *Brahmans*, *Kshatryas*, *Vaishnavites* and *Sudras*, would like *Pān Pattā* (beetle leaf), *Chūna* (lime), *Supari* (betel-nut) and *Katha* become of one colour[67] when well-chewed. The Khalsa stood for righteousness, social equality, faith in *Nirgun* God, honest labour, and division of its fruit and repudiation of all types of exploitation. Evidently, this type of social pattern was more fit for arousing the dormant energies of the people and making them flow into the channel which fed the forces of righteousness in service of nation or the whole humankind.

It was significant from another respect also, as, for instance, it generated among the people the longing for social freedom and ascendancy. Evidently, this pattern of society was more congenial for the dormant energies to awaken with the result that the new confidence and new aspirations began to articulate the people, admittedly the precondition for progress. Moreover, as the accent of the programme of the Khalsa was to transcend the artificial barriers on the bases of caste, creed, race and region, the field was prepared for the sapling of nationalism and universalism to strike root.

Moreover, the Khalsa marked the culmination of the Sikh-Guru relationship. The Guru's regard for the Sikhs was an old thing but with a great difference. Guru Gobind Singh expressed his feelings about the Khalsa in one of his compositions in which his appreciation for them is juxtaposed with his decision to do his best for them.[68]

> "All the battles I have one against tyranny
> I have fought with the devoted backing of these people
> Through them only have I been able to bestow gifts
> By their kindness, the storehouses have been filled
> I owe my education to them
> By their kindness were the enemies killed
> I owe my glorious existence to them
> Otherwise ordinary men like me are found in millions
> Service to them is pleasing to me
> I do not enjoy serving any other people
> Giving gifts to them is meritorious
> Gifts to them prove fruitful in the next life
> Praiseworthy is this, all other gifts are futile
> My wealth, my body, my soul, my head,
> All that is in my house is dedicated to them."

The consideration of Guru for his Khalsa should not be interpreted as a personal affair; it should be interpreted in terms of mission of the Guru. Just as the Guru in his own eyes was the chosen instrument of God for restraining men from senseless acts[69], so his Khalsa were the willing agents for working out that mission. Thus, the Khalsa was the team of mankind always at war for destroying the evil and protecting righteousness.

In addition to it, the Khalsa marked the completion of the evolution of the Sikh *Sangat*. In the beginning, *Sangat* was merely a religious gathering of devotees functioning more or less in isolation. Gradually, there occurred an increase in its functions and the isolation of one from another was lessened by the forging of common links, such as the preparation of scriptures, the building up of certain religious centres, institutions of *Manjis* and *Masands* as the agencies of the central leadership and assertion of the principle of the supremacy of the Guru. With the foundation of the Khalsa, the network of semi-integrated *Sangats* was fully integrated. The investing of the Khalsa with supreme powers later on marked the completion of the historical process long underway.

Still from another point of view the Khalsa Order was significant. It marked the period of important beginnings. By the Guru's reforms, the Sikh community was not only strengthened but also converted into a great vehicle of revolution. New awareness dawned upon the Sikhs. They discovered that there was no dichotomy between man and God as man emanated from God. They shed age-long wrong notions about Reality (God) and His creations including this world. They realised that contemporary social and political constructs did not conform to the theological vision of God as experienced by the Gurus and its social reflections. As a result, they addressed themselves to build thinking-action praxis in the light of the Guru's personal examples and their utterances. The process was sure to lead to huge changes in all aspects of society.

Taking cue from the inevitable, the forces championing *status quo* rallied to crush the Khalsa. Consequently, the Khalsa had to launch a titanic struggle first against the Mughals and then against the Afghans who ruled over Punjab, the territory where the overwhelming majority of the Sikhs lived. The struggle continued till the Khalsa emancipated the land and established their sovereignty in 1765 after the conquest of Sirhind. A new form of polity replaced the old one and the concept of Kingship changed as also the nature of bureaucracy. Henceforth, the king would not be an absolutist monist, rather first among the equals, dedicated to exercise the sovereignty of God as his faithful agent, always caring his creations, seen and unseen, without any discrimination. This was the reason that in the Khalsa rule, the welfare and protection of the people were always at the centre stage. In social sphere too, the Sikhs tried to make radical changes. They always denounced casteist approach. Other approaches which smacked of religious/social particularism were also discarded. The Khalsa always put premium on harmony based on recognition of the divine in every one. It was because of this that in the eighteenth century the differences on bases of caste and creed *et al.* relegated to the background or ceased to operate as influential factors in the territories ruled over by the Khalsa.

With the creation of Khalsa, a few new doctrinal development took place. One, the Khalsa was united directly with the Guru or Akal Purkh (Guru in Sikhism had been equated with Akal Purkh Himself). The dissolution of the institution of *Masand*, and then of personal guruship signified that the Khalsa was as much of the Guru as of God. The Sikh salutation, *Waheguru Ji Ka Khalsa, Waheguru Ji Ki Fateh* literally meant that the Khalsa belonged to the Guru/Lord (Waheguru) and the Khalsa's achievements were in reality God's victories. Second, the Khalsa as a corporate body was equalitarian *inter se* as well as in terms of relation to the Guru himself. In 1699, Guru Gobind Singh first administered baptism to the select five and then himself received baptism from them. By doing so he underscored the point that there was a complete identification between the Guru and the Khalsa. The fact very clearly brought out in *Sarab Loh Granth* (a volume attributed to Guru Gobind Singh) as well as in a VAR by Bhai Gurdas II, who overwhelmed by sense of wonderment exclaimed, "Let all of us hail and greet Guru Gobind Singh who was Guru and Disciple at one and the same time". The

Khalsa therefore, being the image of Guru and God, became the body of spiritually and socially realised individuals committed and dedicated to the 'Word' as enshrined in *Guru Granth Sahib*, the *Joti* or spirit of the ten Gurus as also to work for the uplift of the whole mankind as a whole and was apotheosised as Guru in 1708. The latter point has been repeatedly emphasised by Guru Gobind Singh and his predecessors.

Since the constituents of the Khalsa Panth are realised selves, they realise the essential unity of mankind, and it is only the foolish (those who suffer from duality) who overlook the inner unity and wrangle over the outward difference.

Another doctrinal development was concept of true democracy whose constitution was built not on law books but on the law of love, law of truth and law of justice. In this constitution, the people inspired by the natural goodness of humanity, the spontaneous benediction of God and the Guru's mystic presence in all beings were made supreme. Its directive principle was the principle of happiness of all. A vital responsibility of the Khalsa was the maintenance of ethical values. However, the Khalsa democracy is different from the modern political democracy at least on two counts. One, the latter is essentially numerical or quantitative where the democracy of Guru Gobind Singh's vision is qualitative implying thereby that the source of sovereignty is God and this He exercises through his self-realised persons (Khalsa) who in turn get the job done through their representatives selected unanimously.

It is believed by some scholars that the Guru before initiating the Order invoked goddess Durga to bless him. Of all the scholars having such views, McLeod's remarks are the most striking because of their peculiarity. He states:

> Shivalik hills have long been a stronghold of the *devi* or *Sakti* cult.... The result of prolonged residence within the Shivaliks was that elements of the hill culture eventually penetrated the Jat Sikh culture of the plains and introduced yet another stage in the evolution of the *Panth*.[70]

> In his (Guru's) writings and in those which were produced at his court, we find constant reference to the mighty exploits of the Mother Goddess, one of the most notable being his own *Chandi ki Var*.[71]

He then hastens to add another work of *Chandi Charitar* (*Satasaya*) from *Markandeya Puran* to the list and ends with the explication that as a result of the fusion of the two cultures, a new and powerful synthesis took shape, one which prepared the *Panth* for determinative role in the chaotic circumstances of the eighteenth century.[72]

The remarks of McLeod can be split into three parts for purposes of understanding and analysis:

(i) That the Guru had full faith in *Sakti* cult.

(ii) That the influences of hill culture which in his perception was predominantly *Sakti* culture was so pervading that it influenced and permeated the Sikh culture which in his opinion was a Jat culture, pre-eminently.

(iii) Jat culture and hill culture when interacted with each other, a new synthesis came into being which unleashed powerful forces which helped the Sikhs to tide over difficulties that came in their way in the eighteenth century.

McLeod's remarks, or for that matter those of the scholars of his ilk, are frivolous. Religiously, empirically and ideologically, these cannot be justified.

The *Sakti* cult in different forms had been prevalent in India, especially in its north-western region since ancient times. The worship of Mother Goddess was probably widely practised in the Indus Valley region as well. During the Aryan period doubtlessly, male gods were predominant, but the traces of Devi cult can be found in *Vedic* literature. In this connection, references can be gleaned in ample measure from different texts of Aryans, as for instance, *Dehi Sukta in Rig Veda,* which provided the basis for the cult of *Chandi* in *Markandeya Puran and Sukta* in the *Atharveda* (VI, 38) in which Devi was worshipped as immanent in the entire creation. As Aryan settlements spread in different parts of India, the concept of *Sakti* received wider acceptance and assumed subtle ramifications. According to A.C. Bannerjee, "It developed in some of the *Upanishads* and *Puranas* and particularly in the *Tantras.*"[73] In the north-west, the Shakti cult found a prominent place in the Kashmir Saivism as also in the philosophy of Gorakh Nath which inspired the Yogis.

Although the Jogis were primarily devotees of Siva, they were subject to strong *Tantric* influence. The Aye-Panthis mentioned in a *Japji* canto (No. XXVIII) as also in a contemporary work, *Dabistan-i-Mazahib,* worshipped a female disciple of Gorakh Nath named Bimla Debi who was called Mai, later on corrupted into Aie.

In the hill region of the Punjab where Hinduism in its most archaic form existed, quite a few people were worshippers of Devi or Mother goddess. In Kangra alone there were numerous local *devis* (goddesses) and 360 of them are supposed to have assembled together at the founding of the Kangra temple.[74]

Guru Nanak's teachings had no scope for recognition of any deity, male or female, except the Transcendental Being, who is the only One, formless, Infinite, Self-existent, All-effulgence, and the sole Creator of this world and beyond. He is immanent in the sense that all creation emanated from Him. The goddesses or other deities do not have any separate entity, much less equality with or superiority over the Supreme Being. Hence, Guru Nanak and his successor Gurus, including Guru Gobind Singh, and their disciples worshipped and obeyed only the One God and no other deity. Nor did Guru Nanak or Guru Gobind Singh seek anything from any mortal or god/goddess. On the contrary, Guru Nanak saw himself on a mission to connect people to *Nām* in order to show them the way, to improve their lot.[75]

The attempt to associate Sikhism with *Tantra* becomes more pronounced in regard to Guru Gobind Singh. He has been described as a protagonist of *'Sakti'* cult whose interpretation of *Tantric* philosophy teaches man a new way of obtaining salvation through war. To appraise the Guru as such is to misinterpret and distort Guru's mission and approach. The *Sakti* cult has elaborate rituals. Guru Gobind Singh did not subscribe to that philosophy nor did he accept these rituals as necessary adjuncts of the spiritual discipline. He did not recognise pilgrimages, alms-giving, penances or austerities as legitimate means for spiritual elevation.

In this perspective, the Guru can only be described as opposed to the very basis of the *Sakti* cult. Salvation according to the Guru is full realisation of the unicity of God, which can be realised through proper discipline. War for the Guru was never an end in itself, rather it was a sacred duty in certain circumstances, the purpose being not to win salvation but elimination of injustice and oppression. The Guru uttered:

> Whoever decides to abide in the Khalsa shall not fear the clash of arms, but be ever ready for the combat and defence of his faith.[76]

Again:

> Take the broom of divine knowledge in thy hand and sweep away, the filth of timidity.[77]

Thus, the utterances of the tenth Nanak were in total conformity with those of his predecessors. Timidity in Sikh ideology has been considered as bar to spiritual advancement as also to the proper performance of temporal duties. In Guru Gobind Singh's scheme of regeneration, these two aspects of life are closely linked. The Guru prays: "May both my kitchen and sword prevail in this world."

The Guru's cardinal concern was with the kitchen and the sword, one the emblem of service to assist the poor and helpless, and the other, the emblem of power to resist and extirpate the tyrants.

From the above, it can be safely assumed that the Guru did not worship Durga or have any faith in *Sakti* cult. Nor is it correct that a synthesis of the Jat culture and the hill culture helped the *Panth* to play a determinative role in its affairs in the eighteenth century, for there is hardly anything that could be borrowed from the Jat and hill culture in the creation of the

Khalsa. While the former was largely tribal, the latter was based on caste and mired in feudal values and superstitions.

The most important work in Sikh annals pertaining to the times of the Tenth Master is *Sri Gursobha* by Sainapat, one of Guru Gobind Singh's court poets. The work gives a detailed and realistic account of the creation of the Khalsa on the *Vaisakhi* day and other events of the Guru. It does not make a mention of the worship of Durga. Had it been a part of the event, Sainapat would not have missed it, rather he would have flashed it. McLeod purposely states that the work was not contemporary even while accepting that it was completed in 1711 C.E. However, the date given on the manuscript is clearly 1701 C.E.[78] Whether the work was completed in 1701 C.E. or 1711 C.E., there is no doubt left that Sainapat was a contemporary and his was an eyewitness account.

Apart from negative evidence of the complete absence of the story of *devi* worship or *hom,* Sainapat gives positive statement indicating that "Devi like other *avtaars* only indulged in egoist self-praise for her own worship and not that of God, the Creator." At another place in *Sri Gursobha,* he avers "thousands like Dhruva, thousands like Vishnu, many like Rama, the king, many goddesses, many Gorakhs offer their lives at his (Guru Gobind Singh's) feet". The Mughal news-writer reporting on the occasion of the formation of Khalsa noted that the Guru urged his followers "not to adore incarnations such as Ram, Krishna, Brahma and Durga; but to believe in Guru Nanak and other Sikh Gurus" (Refer to Appendix IV).

The most decisive evidence in favour of total rejection of the *devi* story is found in the Guru's ideology as it is embodied in his own writings. He had total commitment to the concept of *Ik Onkar* and shared the vision of transcendence with Guru Nanak. He, therefore, could not worship any god or goddess. He says:

> O man, worship none but God, not a thing made by Him. Know that He who was in the beginning, unborn, invincible and indestructible is God.

Again:

> Without the support of the One Nām deem all religious ceremonies as superstitions.

Guru Gobind Singh was an uncompromising monotheist, so he cannot be said to have worshipped *devi,* much less on the occasion of the initiation of the Khalsa Order, for which he had been ordained by God Himself.

Some confusion had arisen from the Guru's use of the name 'Bhagauti', by which goddess Durga has often been called. But the Guru uses it in the sense of God or of sword, which is identified with God.

The brief discussion leads to the conclusion that the story of *hom/devi* has no historical basis.

Why did the Guru set up the Khalsa? Did he do so to avenge the unjust persecution of his father? Was he constrained by the contemporary politico-social scenario?

Cunningham says: "The Guru acted...under the mixed impulse of avenging his own and his country's wrongs."[79] He became an "irrepressible foe of the Mohammedan name". His aim was far-reaching, "In heart of the powerful empire, he set himself the task of subverting it." J.N. Sarkar observed that the Guru was "not the person to leave his father's death unavenged"[80] and so he began the policy of "open hostility to Islam". Gokul Chand Narang also endorsed the view of Cunningham, and concluded that the Guru's purpose was to avenge his father's death and strike a blow at the power of Aurangzeb.[81]

It is a pity that neither J.N. Sarkar nor G.C. Narang made an independent inquiry. They blindly followed Cunningham and took it for granted that it was but natural that the Guru should seek to avenge his father's cruel death and to punish the ruler who was responsible for it. These scholars attributed ordinary human motives to the Guru, neglecting absolutely the sublimity of his mission.

The story elaborated by Cunningham appears to have been based on *Ghulam Mohi-ud-Din's* version of the speech of

Guru Gobind Singh at Keshgarh on the *Vaisakhi* of 1699 C.E. as it is recorded in his work *Twarikh-i-Punjab*. According to him the Guru is reported to have uttered:

> You should remember that the Musalmans have maltreated us. They have killed our ancestors. Now in accordance with the mandatory wish of my father, Guru Tegh Bahadur, I cherish the desire of avenging myself upon my father's murderers.

Any such direction would have been entirely inconsistent with Guru Tegh Bahadur's tenor of life. He never lost an opportunity to emphasise that he/she who is unmoved by joy and sorrow, to whom friend and foe are alike, is a truly liberated soul. Also, it is an accepted fact that Guru Tegh Bahadur had voluntarily gone to Delhi, ready to sacrifice his life in order to stress the right of an individual to relate to God. Therefore, the question of "avenging" does not arise.

In view of this, the statement attributed to Guru Gobind Singh by Bute Shah (*Ghulam Mohi-ud-Din*) and believed by Cunningham or J.N. Sarkar is incorrect. There is another very cogent reason which renders the statement of Bute Shah redundant and superfluous. Bute Shah places the creation of the Khalsa soon after the execution of Guru Tegh Bahadur and before Guru Gobind Singh's battle with the hill *rajas* and the Mughals. This is a cut and dried case of faulty chronology that suggests a connection between the execution of the ninth Nanak and the creation of the Khalsa, which is not true.

From this two conclusions follow: One, Bute Shah did not verify the fact, and secondly, he did not take cognizance of the series of events that took place between 1675 C.E. and 1699 C.E. and which could provide him the right historical perspective. Similarly, the contention that the Guru was openly hostile towards Islam is entirely baseless. The Guru was never against Islam, or for that matter, against any religion. The Guru was a devoted votary of Love, raising it to the status of God. It was for this reason that both Hindus and Muslims were attracted towards him. Pir Budhu Shah of Sadhaura together with his sons and seven hundred followers fought hard on the Guru's side in the battle of Bhangani in 1688 in which he lost two of his sons and hundreds of his disciples. In the battle of 1702, Sayyid Beg and Maimon Khan commanded the Guru's forces in fighting against the Mughal troops. Nabi Khan and Ghani Khan in defiance of the wishes of Wazir Khan, the governor of Sirhind fearlessly and courageously helped the Guru out of his distress at Machhiwara. In *Akal Ustat* the Guru says:

> One man by shaving his head is accepted as a *sanyasi*, another a Jogi or a *brahmchari*, a third as *jati*.
> Some are Hindus while others are Muslims.
> Of the latter some are *Shias* and others are *Sunnis*.
> Man's caste should be considered as one.
> *Karta* (Creator) *Karim* (Beneficent) are the same.
> *Rajak* (Provider) *Raheem* (Merciful) are the same.
> Let no man even by mistake, suppose there is a difference.
> ...Temple and Mosque are the same,
> Hindu worship and Muslim prayer are the same.
> All men are alike, but they are under delusion.
> Deities, demons, heavenly dancers, singers, Muslims, Hindus wear different dresses under the conditions of their countries.
> But they possess eyes, ears, bodies, made of same elements composed of earth, air, fire, sky and water.
> *Allah* and *Alakh* (unknowable) are the same, the *Puranas* and the *Quran* are the same.
> They are all alike, it is the One God who created all.[82]

The Guru in his composition *Jaap* has given 735 names of God out of which thirty are from Islam. In another composition, *Akal Ustat,* the Guru is doubly forthright and remarks:

> Even in error deem not the God of the Hindus to be different from the God of the Muslims. Worship One God, recognise the Enlightener. All men have the same form, and the same divine light.[83]

Sujan Rai Bhandari wrote in 1698 C.E.:

> In their (Sikhs) eyes, their own people and others as well as friends and foes are alike.
>
> They love their friends but they do not ill-treat their enemies.[84]

In the presence of such a plethora of evidence, it is only appropriate to reject the view that the Guru entertained hostility towards Islam or created the Khalsa to avenge his father's execution.

The Khalsa was created as per will of Waheguru as revealed to Guru Nanak and his successors from Guru Angad to Guru Gobind Singh. Its foundation was laid on the principle that the whole creation including the whole human owes its existence to God who is permeating and pervading it and therefore all parts of it are complementary to each other and none is despicable or abominable. The inherent harmony is distorted only by 'Manmukhs', the people who do not understand this immutable truth. The Khalsa was to restore this harmony and through this to put the whole humanity on the road to progress. In the process the Khalsa was expected to be bold enough to overcome even the fear of death. In fact conquest of death and ego-centricity were the prerequisites of a Sikh to seek Amrit-initiation. Thus emergence of Khalsa heralded a new dawn in the upward evolution of the whole mankind.

FOOTNOTES

1. The Arabic term for polytheism is shirk meaning 'associating other (false gods) with God'. Hughs: *Dictionary of Islam*, 579.
2. Kafir means literally covering up the truth (Regarding God) and secondarily ingratitude.
3. Sirkar, J.N.: *History of Aurangzeb*, Vol. III, pp. 163-64, Orient Longman, 1972.
4. *Ibid.*, p. 174.
5. *Muntakhab-ul-Lubab*, pp. 651-52.
6. *Kalimat-i-Taiyyhat*, p. 115.
7. Hari Ram Gupta: *History of Sikh Gurus*, p. 249.
8. Bakhtawar Khan: *Mirat-e-Alam*, p. 159 as quoted by Hari Ram Gupta in *History of Sikhs*, Vol. I.

9. Sarkar, J.N.: *History of Aurangzeb.*
10. Abul Klam Azad, *Hijat-e-Sahidi*, pp. 52-53.
11. *Maasir-i-Alamgiri,* p. 120.
12. Bilgrami, Ghulam Ali Azad: *Khazan-e-Amira*, p. 328.
13. Khafi Khan: *Muntakhab-ul-Lubab II*, p. 213.
14. James Hastings: *Encyclopedia of Religion and Ethics*, p. 117.
15. *Anfasul-Arifin*, p. 9.
16. Rizvi, Sayyed Athar Abbas: *Muslim Revivalist Movements in Northern India,* p. 411, Agra University, 1965.
17. *Ibid.,* p. 412.
18. *Maasir-ul-Umara,* Vol. I, p. 237.
19. *Bachittar Natak*, Chapter VI, 1 to 28.
20. *Ibid.,* Chapter VI, p. 28.
21. Macauliffe, M.A.: *op. cit.,* Vol. V, p. 89.
22. Macauliffe, M.A.: Vol. V, pp. 322-23. About Guru's attitude towards *Masands*, also refer to Hukam Namas No. 46, 50, from the book *Hukam Name* by Dr. Ganda Singh.
23. Ganda Singh: *Hukam Name*; Hukam Nama No. 3 of Guru Hargobind, p. 67, Punjabi University.
24. Rose: *op. cit.,* Vol. III, p. 72.
25. Harji, Goshtan Guru Meharban—Gosht No. 30. Also refer to Sodhi Harji: *Jiwan Te Rachna* by Gurmohan Singh Ahluwalia, Punjabi University, 1985.
26. Ganda Singh: *Hukam Name,* Pbi. Uni., 1967, Hukam Nama No. 46.
27. *Ibid.* Hukam Namas No. 49 and 50, Macauliffe, M.A.: *Sikh Religion,* Vol. V, p. 95.
28. Certain Shias who renounced their allegiance to Zaid, grandson of Hussain.
29. Gandhi, S.S.: *History of the Sikh Gurus*, p. 429, Gurdas Kapur & Sons, 1978.
30. Var 41, Pauri 16.
31. *Takht Bahe Takhte Ke Laik Hoi.*
32. *Bachittar Natak Steek*, Fifth Chapter, Naraj Chhand, Stanza 7, 8, 9, 10, pp. 106, 107, Singh Brothers, Amritsar.
33. *Bachittar Natak Steek*, Chapter VI, Stanza 1, pp. 110, 111, 112, Singh Brothers, Amritsar, 1992.
34. Macauliffe, M.A.: *The Sikh Religion*, Vol. V, p. 91.
35. *Ibid.*
36. Harbans Singh: *The Heritage of the Sikhs*, p. 84, Manohar, Delhi, 1994.

37. The episode of the *Panj Pyaras*, their names and details of the preparation of Amrit have been recorded in *Gurbilas* Literature associated with Guru Gobind Singh. *See* Koer Singh's *Gurbilas Padshahi Dās* (1751) ed. Shamsher Singh Ashok, Punjabi Uni., Patiala, 1968, pp. 127-39. Sukha Singh's *Gurbilas Padshahi Dās* (1797 C.E.), pp. 90-92, Personal Library of Trilochan Singh.
38. *Jap ji* was composed by Guru Nanak, *Anand* by Guru Amar Das, *Jaap*, *Swayyas* and *Chaupai* by Guru Gobind Singh.
39. *Nishan-i-Sikhi Ast* In Panj Harf Hargiz Na Bashid; A Zin Panj Muaf Kara, Kard, Kangha Bi Dan Kesh Kachh Hech Ast Jumla Nishan (These five letters of K are emblems of Sikhism. These five are most incumbent and are steel bangle, big knife, shorts and comb and unshaven hair. Without unshaven hair, all others are of no significance.
40. Harbans Singh: *Heritage of Sikhism.*
41. Kapur Singh: *The Baisakhi of Guru Gobind Singh*, pp. 139-48.
42. Hari Ram Gupta: *History of the Sikhs,* Vol. I, pp. 274-75.
43. Harbans Singh: *Heritage of Sikhism*, p. 87, Manohar, Delhi, 1983.
44. Sarup Singh: *op. cit.,* 120-25.
45. *Ibid.*
46. Ahmed Shah Batala (*Twarikh-i-Hind*) and Ghulam Mohiyuddin (*Twarikh-i-Punjab*) specially mention twenty thousand persons accepting the new order, and in some of the modern works the number given is 80,000. These computations appear to be no more than a guess work. But it may be safely assumed that the number of persons present at Anandpur at this time ran into thousands and it was larger than the usual gathering on the Baisakhi days.
47. Sainapat: *op. cit.*, Chapter VI, 1/197.
48. Macauliffe, M.A.: *op. cit.,* Vol. V, p. 153: "The Guru said, 'Wine is bad, bhang destroyeth one generation, but tobacco destroyeth all generations'," Santokh Singh says that tobacco leaf resembles the ear of a cow, and so the Guru prohibited its use (*Suraj Parkash*, 5571).
49. Macauliffe, M.A.: *op. cit.,* Vol. V, p. 110.
50. The exact import of the term Khalsa provides an interesting study. Dr. Earnest Trumpp, the author of *Adi Granth* (1877) holds that it is an Arabic term meaning personal estate. The baptised Sikhs were the personal estate of the Guru. Cunningham writes that Khalsa is an Arabic derivation and has such original or secondary meaning as pure special five and Co. In the revenue records of the Sultans and the Mughals, Khalsa denoted the land as directly held by crown as distinguished from the land held by the tributary chiefs. The Khalsa, therefore, denotes either a kingdom of the Guru or that the Sikhs are pure chosen people. The Guru called his baptised Sikhs the Khalsa because they constituted the valued property of the Guru. They were not his paid soldiers but were a body of volunteers who were ever prepared to shed their blood for him.

51. Photostat copies appear in 'Hukamnamas' ed. by Dr. Ganda Singh on Serial Nos. 5 and 8.
52. Sainapat: *op. cit.*, p. 31.
53. *Ibid.*
54. *Ibid.*, p. 36.
55. Nand Lal: *Rahitnama* Gor Marhi Mat Bhool Na Jane (Worship not even by mistake a tomb or a relic of cremation).
56. The above address is based on the report of a news-writer sent to the Mughal court as it is recorded for by the Persian Historian Ghulam Mohi-ud-din in his work *Twarikh-i-Punjab*. The report is also contained in the book *Twarikh-i-Hind* written by Ahmed Shah Batalia.
57. For translation of the relevant portions of Guru Gobind Singh's compositions see the *Sikh Religion*, Vol. V, pp. 261-63, 306-10.
58. Sainapat: *op. cit.,* Chapter VII.
59. *Ibid.*
60. A literal translation of the Stanzas in *Sri Guru Sobha* by Sainapat, Chapter VII.
61. Koer Singh understands that the rise of the Jat power was the direct result of the creation of the Khalsa. A close study of the Chapter IX of *Gurbilas* makes it abundantly clear that the lower classes felt a sense of pride to join the new order and in a way, it found in it the augury of new era for themselves.
62. Cunningham: *History of the Sikhs*, pp. 375-76.
63. Macauliffe, M.A.: *Sikh Religion*, Vol. V, p. 312.
64. *Ibid.*, p. 31.
65. Bannerjee, I.B.: *Evolution of the Khalsa*, p. 118.
66. Teja Singh and Ganda Singh: *A Short History of the Sikhs*.
67. Malcolm, Sir John: *Sketch of the Sikhs*, p. 45.
68. Ashta Dharam Pal: *The Poetry of Dasam Granth*, p. 146. Trilochan Singh: *Guru Gobind Singh* (A Brief Life Sketch), Delhi, 1964, pp. 20-21.
69. Bal, S.S. & Grewal, U.S.: *Guru Gobind Singh*, p. 124.
70. McLeod, W.H.: *Evolution of the Sikh Community*, p. 13, Oxford University Press, Bombay, 1975.
71. *Ibid.*
72. *Ibid.*, 14.
73. Bannerjee, A.C.: *Sikh Gurus and Sikh Religion*, p. 300, Munshi Ram Manohar Lal, 1983.
74. Rose: *Glossary of Tribes and Castes of the Punjab and the North Western Frontier*, p. 318.
75. *Puratan Janam Sakhi*.

76. Macauliffe, M.A.: *The Sikh Religion*, Vol. V, p. 223.
77. *Ibid.*, 167.
78. *Samat Satarah Sai Bhai Barakh; Athasthan Bit Bhadon Sudi Pandras Bhaie Rachi Katha Kar Prit* (*Gur Sobha*, Chapter 1).
79. Cunningham, J.D.: *A History of the Sikhs*, reprint, S. Chand and Co., Delhi, 1955, p. 60.
80. Sarkar, J.N.: *History of Aurangzeb*, Vol. III, Calcutta, 1928, p. 314.
81. Narang Gokal Chand: *Transformation of Sikhism*, reprint, Ludhiana, 1989, p. 88.
82. *Akal Ustat.*
83. *Ibid.*
84. *Khulasat-ut-Twarikh*, Punjabi University, Patiala, 1972, p. 81.

13

KHALSA BATTLES AGAINST ISLAMIC IMPERIALISM AND HINDU CONSERVATISM

The immediate effect of the creation of Khalsa was that it brought the hostility of the hill chiefs in the open. They saw in the activities of the Guru a potent threat to their own religion and power.

The Guru, in fact, wanted peace for his new born Khalsa to grow and to organise, but the hill chiefs found in the Guru's mission and reforms something fundamentally different from what they had been taught to uphold. After presenting the model of civilisation known as Khalsa, one of the first acts of the Guru was that the Sikhs should be baptised according to new rites, and to this effect, he enjoined them to come to Anandpur. They responded enthusiastically. Ever mounting number of the baptised Sikhs surcharged with egalitarian spirit and disengaged from orthodox way of life, always ready to combat the evil, seriously alarmed the hill chiefs. It is, therefore, not surprising that the Guru's continued presence in their midst was considered a direct challenge to their feudal order and the value-system of Hindu civilisation.

Besides this, the hill chiefs, particularly Ajmer Chand of Kahlur had another grievance against the Guru. The ever increasing number of Sikhs who visited Anandpur created the problem of supplies. The Guru had no possessions besides Anandpur and its suburbs which he might call his own. For provisions, the Guru depended on the voluntary contributions of his followers which usually were sufficient for the need. But in the wake of the call of the Guru to immediately receive baptism, the number of the visitors to Anandpur increased manifold. At times, the supply of provisions did not match the demand with the result that it had to be supplemented from the neighbouring villages.[1] Since the hill Rajas, especially Ajmer Chand, the Raja of Kahlur state, in which Anandpur stood, had no love lost for the Guru for the reasons adumbrated above, they did not hesitate to create troubles by inciting the people in their favour. This fact in conjunction with others as referred to earlier so worked upon the Rajas that they made up their mind to restrain the Guru.

Two of them, Alim Chand and Balia Chand, chieftains[2] of certain rulers, finding their opportunity when the Guru with only a few Sikhs was sporting, fell on him. The Sikhs gave a determined fight, but because of enemy's large numbers, they started losing ground. Not long after, reinforcement under Uday Singh reached and the tables were turned. Alim Chand lost his right arm and left the field. Balia Chand was seriously wounded and his soldiers took to their heels. The Guru returned victorious.[3]

First Battle of Anandpur

The defeat of Alim Chand and Balia Chand unnerved the hill Rajas, who met in a council and decided to approach the Emperor for help. They represented to him through the Nawab of Sirhind that they had failed to restrain the Guru and if the Emperor did not deal with them instantaneously and firmly, he might later find the situation uncontrollable. According to M.A. Macauliffe, the Subedar of Delhi, under instructions from Aurangzeb who was at that time in the southern part of India despatched a force of ten thousand under his two able generals Painda Khan and Din Beg. The hill chiefs joined them at Ropar. The Guru met the combined forces near Anandpur. In a sanguinary battle Painda Khan was killed. Din Beg and hill Rajas fled away.[4] They were pursued by the Khalsa soldiers for some distance. A large booty consisting of horses, arms and baggage fell into the hands of the Sikhs.

Much chagrined and agonised, the hill Rajas now resolved to act against the Guru independently of the Mughals. They organised a federation and gave its leadership to Ajmer Chand[5], son of Bhim Chand of Bilaspur, who was the most knowledgeable among hill chiefs in regard to the Guru and his Sikhs because of the location of Guru's headquarter in his state. He sent a message to the Guru that he should either vacate Anandpur or pay the rent thereof as it lay in his territory. In case he did not respond appropriately, he would face Raja's wrath. The Guru downright rejected the demands of the Raja, and to counter his threat issued fiats to his followers to join him at Anandpur to participate in the war likely to be imposed on him. They responded in large numbers.[6] The hill Rajas besieged Anandpur. The Sikhs took positions in the forts of Anandpur, Fatehgarh and Kesgarh. On the first day (29th Bhadon, 1757 Bk), Ajmer Chand made a forceful attack on Taragarh near Anandgarh but was repulsed by Ajit Singh, the eldest son of the Guru. On the side of the Sikhs, Ishar Singh, Kalian Singh and Sangat Singh were killed among others.[7] A hill chieftain Raja Ghumand Chand suffered severe wounds in the battle.

Next day, Ajmer Chand again mounted fierce assault on the fort named Fatehgarh. He and his allies met with stout resistance and in the sallies organised by determined Sikhs under the wise command of experienced Bhagwan Singh, they suffered heavy casualties in a five hour battle. As the sun set in, the fighting stopped. Jawahar Singh and Bhagwan Singh received martyrdom.[8]

On the following day with the advent of dawn, fighting resumed. Ajmer Chand launched a vigorous attack, this time on Agamgarh, but failed miserably. The Sikhs lost their veterans, Bagh Singh and Gharbar Singh.[9]

Now Ajmer Chand called a conference of his allies in which stock of the situation was taken. It was decided that to begin with the fort of Lohgarh should be stormed to be followed by simultaneous attack on other sides of Anandpur. The command of the troops meant to storm the fort was given to a very brave chieftain, Kesri Chand Jaswania.[10] He meticulously planned his manoeuvres one of which was that a very highly intoxicated Prasadi elephant would be set against the door of Lohgarh to break it to make way for the hill forces to enter the fort. The plan though made in camera[11] leaked out to the Guru who forthwith took steps to counter it. The Guru wanted to appoint Duni Chand[12] considered to be very bold and iron-willed to face the elephant, but his spirit failed and he deserted the Guru.[13] Bachittar Singh, son of Bhai Mani Singh, lost not even a fraction of a second to offer his services to meet the challenge of the elephant. The Guru gave a pat and handed over a specially forged *Nagni* spear to face the intoxicated elephant.[14]

As the morning of 1st of Kartik month dawned, the hill forces, under the overall command of Ajmer Chand, positioned themselves near the fort of Lohgarh. From the front side rushed the forces led by Kesri Chand. They drove the intoxicated elephant to the main gate of the fort. When the furious animal advanced to strike the door with all its might, Bachittar Singh, having invoked the blessing of the Guru through prayer, struck it with his spear with such a force that it pierced through the plates covering its forehead to his brain making him lose his balance with the result that he turned back and ran pell-mell trampling everything in the way, including the hill soldiers. In the disorder thus caused, Uday Singh already astride his swift horse, sprang forward and challenged Kesri Chand. Kesri Chand seated on his horse-back attacked with his sword. Uday Singh swung aside and then hit him with his sword so strongly that his body was cleaved in twain.[15] Kesri Chand having met his nemesis, Ajmer Chand thought it appropriate to seek safety in retreat. Alam Singh son of Daria, Sucha Singh son of Rai Singh, Kaushal Singh son of Makkan Singh met martyrdom in the field.[16]

Fighting continued for four consecutive days but did not yield any result favourable to the hill Rajas; rather ignominy and demoralisation happened to be their lot. More failures in battle might have spelt disaster for them. These could have given opportunity to some disgruntled elements in their territories to defy them, besides being tempted to join the

Khalsa. Now to save face, the hill Rajas decided upon a stratagem at the suggestions of Parmanand, the family priest of Raja of Kahlur[17], well-known for his cunning. They sent Parmanand with a letter to Anandpur. He very cunningly and stealthily placed it at the gate of Anandgarh duly tied to an image of cow with *janeu* (sacred thread). In the letter, it was written that the Rajas sincerely regretted the losses on both sides and desired a settlement immediately so that the purposeless fighting might be stopped.[18] The letter also stated that a unilateral retreat on their part would be too humiliating and mortifying and if the Guru vacated Anandpur, the siege would be raised and then he could come back after some time, if he desired. According to Sainapat, they appealed to the Guru's sense of chivalry by requesting him to leave Anandpur to them as the "gao bhat"[19], that is the touch of the cow.

The Guru agreed thinking that the hill Rajas after all had realised the futility of waging war.

Battle of Nirmohgarh—1700 C.E.

The Guru came out in the open ground leaving Anandpur in the hands of some of his brave and trusted men and established himself at Nirmohgarh, a place four kilometres away from Anandpur.

The hill chiefs throwing their promise to the winds fell upon the Guru. The Sikhs resisted with all their might and the enemy had to retreat.[20]

In this battle, Dewan Sahib Singh and his band of one thousand Sikhs bore the brunt. The Dewan and some other eminent Sikhs such as Mathura Singh, Surat Singh, Deva Singh, Anup Singh and Sarup Singh were killed.[21] Then the Guru himself took the command and made so vigorous an assault that the hill forces had to lift the siege.

Ajmer Chand, now exasperated, decided to square up the issue with the Guru once for all. He decided to get aid from his suzerain, the Mughal government, and sent an envoy for the purpose.[22] It is not clear whether this appeal was made to Aurangzeb in the south or to Muazzam at Kabul or to the Mughal government at Delhi, whether directly or through the

Subedar of Sirhind. In any case, the Mughal contingents arrived shortly at Sirhind to collaborate with its Faujdar, who had been instructed to aid the chief of Bilaspur against the Guru.[23]

Ajmer Chand also succeeded instigating Gujjars and Rangars to fight against the Sikhs. Both these people were Muslims and inhabited in a number of villages around Anandpur in his state. They were organised into clans—each under one head. They were habituated to marauding and had often tried to plunder the Sikhs while they were on their way to Anandpur. Ajmer Chand played upon their communal feelings to enlist their co-operation against the Sikhs.

The Mughal army as well the army of the hill rajas joined together at Sirhind and then moved on to achieve the target. The Guru already abreast of circumstances made preparations. Apart from retaining some of the Khalsa who would normally come to have an audience, he had invited daring men of different *Sangats* from several towns and villages, given them arms and enlisted them as his soldiers.[24] The Guru's strategy was defensive while that of the enemy was offensive. The allied armies attacked Nirmohgarh from one side while Ajmer Chand attacked from the other. Their objective was to weaken the defences of the Guru. In Sainapat's simile[25] the enemy surrounded Nirmohgarh, 'as the stars surround the moon'. The contest lasted for about a day before the Khalsa could get respite from the enemy's vigorous attack. Ultimately, Guru was constrained to evacuate Nirmohgarh, probably because of the use of cannons of Mughal faujdar.[26] But before they could cross the river Sutlej, they were overtaken by the allies who were naturally keen in obstructing the passage.[27] The Khalsa fought desperately for four hours[28] and succeeded eventually in crossing the river and entering the territory of Raja Dharmapal[29], the chief of Jaswan, who was an admirer of the Guru. The Guru and the Khalsa marched towards the town of Basoli.

Battle of Basoli—1700 C.E.

The Guru had hardly left the place, when another engagement took place on the bank of river Sutlej. The Sikhs fought gallantly and forced the enemy to roll back. Sahib Singh, a notable Sikh general lost his life.

The combined forces of the hill rajas also crossed the river and attacked the Sikhs at Basoli. The Guru put up a formidable defence and once again the enemy was unable to subdue the Sikh forces. The battle is known as battle of Basoli.[30]

After this, the Mughal troops returned to Sirhind with doubtful satisfaction of having achieved although at a great cost, the limited objective of expelling the Khalsa from the territory of Kahlur on the eastern side of the Sutlej. The hill Rajas also went back to their respective territories.

The Guru and his family put up at the residence of the Raja while beautiful canopies made of cloth were pitched in the suburb of the town for accommodating the Khalsa soldiers.

The Guru stayed at Basoli for some days resting and enjoying hunting and other sports.[31] Soon, the Guru took initiative against Ajmer Chand leading incursions into his territory on the north of river Sutlej. He gradually moved towards Anandpur. At this time, the Gujjars and Rangars of the village Kamlot attacked a party of the Sikhs who had gone on hunting expedition. The Guru, on being informed, ordered the Khalsa to teach them a lesson with the result that Uday Singh, who headed the hunting party led an attack on the village. The Gujjars and Rangars were severely punished. Jiwan Singh[32], a notable general, got killed in this contest. His dead body was brought to Basoli where it was cremated with full honours.

Second Battle of Anandpur—1700 C.E. Skirmish at Bhadsoli

The Guru finding that Wazir Khan, the Subedar of Sirhind, had gone back, and the hill Rajas were satisfied that they had at long last got rid of the Guru, marched back to Anandpur[33] and lost no time to repair the forts and other buildings badly damaged by the hill forces. He also took prompt steps so that Anandpur functioned in full glory as the headquarter of the Khalsa. No wonder, the Sikhs in large numbers started surging to Anandpur to seek Guru's beneficence and also to offer their services. In the meanwhile news reached that *Sangat* of Darap region had been stripped of their belongings including their offerings for the Guru by Rangars of Bajrur. The Guru flew into moral rage and ordered Ajit Singh, his eldest son to at once proceed to Bajrur to punish the culprits. The order was obeyed and the Ajit Singh besieged the village. Chittu and Mitta, the leaders of the village were put to sword and the village was ransacked. People took lesson and never in future did they plunder or coerce the Sikh *Sangats*.[34]

Towards the end of 1700, the peace of Anandpur Sahib was disturbed by Wazir Khan, the Subedar of Sirhind, who made a surprise attack. The Sikhs had to vacate the city and proceeded to Bhadsoli 45 kilometres distant from Anandpur beyond Una across the river Swan. The Mughal forces went in pursuit and engaged the Guru's forces at Bhadsoli. In the hard contest, Sikhs came out victorious. Soon after, when the danger of the war diminished and tempers cooled down, the Guru returned to Anandpur[35], hopefully to renew ties with his Sikhs and to extend the area of Sikh influence.

The Guru obliged Sidh Shah, the ruler of Mandi, by paying a short visit to him in 1701.[36] He was accorded a very warm welcome by the Raja. At Mandi, the Guru interacted with other Rajas who had come there, seemingly in response to Sidh Shah's invitation. Consequently, the Rajas were convinced of the loftiness of the Guru's designs and in later years some of them played only a marginal role against the Guru while Raja of Mandi's role had been that of a follower and sincere admirer.

The Guru attended Rawalsar fair held every year on the first of Baisakhi. On this occasion the Raja begged the Guru for the perennial safety of his capital. The Guru granted the boon. The memory of this event is preserved in the tradition that the Guru got a small earthen vessel (*Handi* in Punjabi language) and threw it into the river Beas flowing by the side of Mandi. The vessel did not dissolve. The Guru uttered, "As my earthen vessel is safe so will remain safe your Mandi. When Mandi is plundered, heavenly balls will be fired."[37] It is believed that the town of Mandi continued to enjoy immunity from the Sikh intrusion till 1839, although it had long been a tributary to them from 1809 onward till the end of Ranjit Singh's rule because of the blessing of the Guru.

Third Battle of Anandpur—1702 C.E.

In 1702, Sayyad Beg and Alif Khan, two eminent commanders of Mughals, who were going to Delhi from Lahore, were tempted by Ajmer Chand to attack the Guru by offering them a huge sum. According to Hari Ram Gupta, they were promised the payment of one thousand rupees a day.[38] Both the commanders marched towards Anandpur, but after a few skirmishes, Sayyid Beg was so much impressed by the Guru's charismatic personality that he thought it appropriate to join the Guru.[39] Alif Khan had to retire in spite of his long-nursed desire to avenge his failure which he met earlier while fighting against the Guru in Kangra hills.[40]

Fourth and Fifth Battles of Anandpur—1703 C.E.

In 1703, the Guru had to face the attack twice. On both the occasions, Ajmer Chand was the architect of the attack. On the first occasion, he attacked in association with Rajas Bhup Chand, Wazir Singh and Dev Saran.[41] On the second occasion, he sought help from Mughal Subedar of Delhi and then attacked. On both the occasions, he suffered defeat[42] and the target remained elusive. Guru Gobind Singh's control over Anandpur[43] remained firm, to the disappointment and dismay of Ajmer Chand and his associate hill Rajas. The Mughal commanders were also non-plussed by the high morale of the Sikhs. In the second attack another remarkable thing happened. Maiman Khan, a Mughal commander, deserted his side and joined the Guru in response to the call of his conscience. The Guru blessed him and his entry into Guru's forces boosted the morale of Sikh soldiers. At this juncture, the Guru in exultation and exuberance uttered that "It is through them (Khalsa) that I have won my victories and have been able to grant gifts to others."[44] In the contest one hill chief and Sayyid Beg were killed. Enemy forces fought so hard that they drove the Sikhs out of Anandpur and plundered the town. Soon after, the Sikhs returned, fell upon heavily laden enemy troops, retrieved their position and recovered Anandpur.

After some time, the hostilities again started. The reasons were the same *viz.*, the increasing prestige of the Guru, dislike for the Sikh movement which championed values diametrically opposed to those held by the hill rulers.

Sixth Battle of Anandpur—1705 C.E.

Some hill Chiefs who could not tolerate the presence of the Khalsa at Anandpur arranged a formidable combination against the Guru and proceeded to attack Anandpur. They were met by the cannon shot from the fort of Anandgarh. They decided to lay siege to the town instead of suffering heavy losses in an attempt to capture it by a direct assault. In that plan also, they failed. They could not achieve any success against the sorties of the Khalsa cavalry whose shrewd tactics completely discomfited them. The hill chiefs were left with the immediate alternative of retreat. In spite of this, the hill Rajas never relented in their determination to drive out the Guru from their territory. They made preparations on a large scale. The Gujjars and Rangars were also incited to join the war against them. They harnessed their own resources with care and assiduity; they appealed to the Mughal authorities[45] and got the assistance of the troops from Sirhind and Lahore. The allied forces soon attacked Anandpur; but the Khalsa soldiers proved to be superior to them who were driven out of Anandpur. Then the allies encircled the Sikhs on all sides and the great siege of Anandpur began.

In this exigency, the Guru invited help from the Sikhs. He issued several letters to different *Sangats* to immediately reach Anandpur fully armed (1704 C.E. = 1761 Bk). One of such letters was sent to Bhai Mukhia, Bhai Parsa who were asked to come with "cavalries footmen gunners and daring youth".[46] The Guru divided his army into six contingents. He placed one each in five forts, while a detachment of 500 men, was kept in reserve. Anandgarh was in Guru's personal charge. Fatehgarh was entrusted to Uday Singh. Holgarh was in command of Mohkam Singh. Guru's eldest son Ajit Singh controlled Keshgarh. His other son Jujhar Singh held Lohgarh. Ajit Singh won great victory on the very first day by killing Jagatullah, leader of Rangars and Gujjars. Two heavy guns named *Baghan* (tigress) and *Vijay Ghosh*—victory warrant were mounted on Anandgarh. They wrought havoc among the enemy ranks. The siege of Anandpur started in Jeth 1762/May 1705 C.E. In the first day fight Wazir Khan lost nine hundred men.

The siege was conducted with great intensity and planned in such a manner that all ingress and egress for both goods and persons were completely blocked. All supplies being cut off, the Sikhs were put to great hardships. Food position became extremely serious and the Sikhs were driven to undertake some dangerous expedients. The Sikhs sallied out to snatch provisions from the besiegers but they met only a partial success and that too on a few occasions after which the allies collected their stores at one place and guarded them night and day. The Sikhs resorted to the direct assaults on the allies but they were worsted by them. A small hilly channel taken off from Charan Ganga which supplied water to Anandgarh was diverted by Kahlur Raja from its course.

Having suffered extreme hardships, the Sikhs besought the Guru to evacuate the fort, but the Guru counselled them patience for some time more. On perpetual insistence by some Sikhs the Guru declared them that everybody was free to leave whenever he/she wanted to.

When the enemy learnt of the distress in which the Sikhs and the Guru were placed at that time, they planned a different strategy to take advantage of the situation. They sent a message to the Guru suggesting that if he decided to abandon Anandpur, he would be allowed a safe passage. Their pledge of a safe passage was treacherous, since they had planned to draw out the Sikhs from within the shelter of the township and then attack them. The Guru sensed their ulterior motive when he received the message, and therefore did not accept the offer. But some of the *Masands* and the Sikhs who were under their influence insisted that the offer of the enemy be accepted and the Anandpur abandoned. Forty of them were so vehement in their demand that they became desperate and disclaimed Guru Gobind Singh as their Guru. At this juncture the Guru considered it sagacious to expose the hypocrisy of the enemy, as also to convince his followers of their folly.

The Guru ordered a number of bullocks to be laden with waste articles. When all preparations were complete, he informed messenger of the enemy that he had accepted their proposal. They were told that the Guru's treasure would leave the township to be followed after some time by him and his people. The enemy received this information with great joy. At the appointed hour of the night, the Guru called for the loaded bullocks, tied light torches to their horns and sent them out at mid-night, along with some Sikhs to accompany them. When the enemy saw the train bearing the treasure emerging from the township, they forgot all their pledges and fell upon the small party of the Sikhs to loot the treasure.[47] But their disappointment was great when they found that the treasure was made up of tatters and rubbish. After exposing the treachery of the enemy, the Guru according to Koer Singh, addressed his Sikhs in the following words:

> Never true to their words are these hill Rajas, you know not their deception. They are all big cheats unworthy of trust.[48] (Koer Singh in *Gurbilas*)

Wazir Khan expressed regret for the misconduct of some of his troops and delivered a letter to the Guru. This letter bearing the seal of Emperor Aurangzeb contained many assurances for the safe passage of the Sikhs out of Anandpur Sahib.[49] About this time, a letter from the Rajas of Kahlur and other states was also received to that effect (*Gur Pratap Suraj Granth*). The followers of Guru who were already anxious to leave the township became very vocal and active. They approached Mata Gujri and pleaded with her.[50] The Guru, however felt that the promises of the Mughals were simply the ploys to dupe the Sikhs. He had sufficient experience of double talk of the Mughals as well as of the hill chiefs.

But ultimately the Guru took a decision to evacuate the fort and the city, of course against his wishes and better judgement. Some scholars have wrongly surmised "that Guru's action smacked of acquiescence". In fact, the offer of safe passage was made by Wazir Khan and the hill Rajas with the full knowledge that the Guru would never surrender. And the Guru's decision was prompted more by his determination to die fighting than by the promise held out by the Mughals.

The Guru evacuated Anandgarh on 5/6 December, 1705 (6-7, Poh Samvat 1762 Bk). Just before this, the Guru distributed his treasures as well as arms among the Sikhs and when everything was ready, whatever could not be carried was put on fire.

According to Santokh Singh, the Guru was handed over another message of Aurangzeb through his envoy which stated:

> "I have sworn on The *Quran* not to harm thee. If I do, may I not find a place in God's court hereafter. Cease warfare and come to me. If thou desire not to come hither, then go wheresoever thou pleasest."

The Envoy who presented the letter added:

> "O Guru, all, who go to the Emperor's court praise thee. On that account the Emperor feeleth certain that an interview with you will add to his happiness. He has sworn by Muhammad and called God to witness that he will not harm thee. The hill Rajas have also sworn by the cow and called their idols to witness that they will allow thee safe conduct. Bear not in mind anything that hath occurred. The attack on thine oxen was not prompted by any Raja. The attackers have been spotted, and the ring-leaders are in prison. No one now, O, True Guru, dareth do thee any harm; wherefore evacuate the fort, at any rate for the present and come with me to the Emperor. Thou mayest afterwards do what thou pleasest."

The message was no more than a ploy to further tempt the Guru to be off guard. The moment the enemy got an inkling of the departure of the Sikhs, they forgot all about their vows[51] and set out in hot pursuit immediately. Skirmishes commenced from Kiratpur onwards. Realising the impending danger, Guru Gobind Singh assigned a band of 50 Sikhs to Bhai Udai Singh[52] and charged him with the responsibility of checking enemy's advance. Bhai Udai Singh fought at Shahi Tibbi a bloody battle with the enemy with a handful of his men; all of them perished fighting, covering themselves with immortal glory. The battle lasted for two and a half hours.[53]

When the battle of Shahi Tibbi was in progress, the rest of the caravan including Guru Gobind Singh had reached the bank of the Sarsa river. It was now almost daybreak. About this time the news arrived that a contingent of enemy troops was fast approaching. Bhai Jiwan Singh[54], a prominent Sikh, was assigned a band of 100 Sikhs and ordered to encounter the pursuers. With the rest of his people the Guru descended into the flooded waters of the Sarsa. The flood was so fierce that many of them were drowned and many more were swept away and separated including members of Guru Gobind Singh's own family. Besides, there was a heavy loss of valuable literature and property. It was here that the Guru's mother, Revered Mata Gujri and his two younger sons, Zorawar Singh and Fateh Singh, got separated and proceeded to Saheri, the village of their domestic servant—Gangu Brahman, who handed them over to the police at Morinda to be taken to Sirhind, where they were cruelly put to death by Wazir Khan, the governor of Sirhind in spite of the protests of the then Nawab of Malerkotla.[55] Mata Sundri and Mata Sahib Kaur were hurriedly led by Bhai Mani Singh to Delhi where they stayed in the house of Jawahar Singh.[56] As regards the Guru himself, he was able to reach, accompanied by his two elder sons and a band of veteran Sikhs, the village Ghanaula[57] on the other side of the river Sarsa. It was now planned to proceed further to Kotla Nihang Khan and pass the day safely in the residence of the Pathan Zamindar Nihang Khan, who being a sincere follower of the Guru, could be depended upon for help even in the critical situation such as this. Apprehending that the route ahead might be beset with danger, the Guru set apart a band of about 100 veterans including Sahibzada Ajit Singh under the command of Bhai Bachittar Singh and instructed them to march by the direct route whereas he along with some of his people preferred to take the longer path along the left bank of the Sutlej river. The Guru met no resistance on the way and reached Kotla Nihang Khan safely. Bachittar Singh and his men, however, had to fight their way through a cordon of the Rangars of Malikpur, a village on the way, and Pathans of Ropar. In the fierce fighting that took place on this occasion, majority of the Sikhs received martyrdom. The leader, Bachittar Singh, was mortally wounded and in that serious condition was carried to Kotla Nihang Khan by Sahibzada Ajit Singh.

The Guru did not want to stay at Kotla longer than was absolutely necessary. He decided to proceed further on the same day. His elder sons, Sahibzada Ajit Singh and Sahibzada Jujhar Singh, and 40 Sikhs were to accompany him. When the night fell the whole band set out on the onward journey. Nihang Khan detailed his son, Alam Khan, to guide them as to the route they were to follow.

When Guru Gobind Singh left Kotla Nihang Khan, his object, it seems, was to proceed to Machhiwara and Rai Kot. At the former place lived two Pathan brothers, Nabi Khan and Ghani Khan. They had many trade dealings with the Guru and eventually had become his followers. Moreover, they happened to be cousins of Nihang Khan and as such could be relied upon. The second place, Rai Kot, was under the control of Rai Kalla, whose daughter had been married to Alam Khan, the son of Nihang Khan. Besides, like Nabi Khan and Ghani Khan of Machhiwara, Rai Kalla also had become a follower of Guru Gobind Singh. Another reason for the Guru to select this route was that the sixth, seventh and ninth Gurus had already travelled across this area and attracted a good number of local people to the Sikhs faith.

Battle of Chamkaur, December 7, 1704 C.E.

After Kotla Nihang, the village, Bur Majra, became the halting place of Guru Gobind Singh and his men. Soon after their arrival there, the news was received that a large body of Sirhind troops were chasing them. Immediately, the Guru decided to face the enemy at Chamkaur. To this purpose he hurriedly reached the destination and encamped in a garden outside the village which belonged to Rai Jagat Singh, who was a local landlord. The Guru sent some of his disciples to him to request him to let him take shelter in his *haveli* (spacious walled house more like a garhi (mud fortress). He refused for fear of ruler's wrath. However, his younger brother, Rup Chand asserting his right as co-owner, very gladly handed over the same to the Guru. According to some chroniclers Bandhu Chand and Gharilu, who jointly owned the property offered the Haveli to the Guru. The Guru was well aware of the importance of this Haveli as he had fought a military engagement at this place in 1702.

Soon after, the army of the allies closed upon the place. The Guru's army comprised Forty men (exclusive of the Guru and his two sons), an infinitesimally small number in comparison to the huge army that had surrounded the fortress. His weapons of defence and offence were those which he and his men had managed to carry during fight from Anandpur. The allies' forces attacked the Garhi (mud fortress) by daybreak. The Guru organised all-round defence of the Sikhs. He himself occupied a position on the top storey to observe and direct the defence operation as also to shoot his arrows. Out of forty men about one fourth were deputed to defend the gate. An equal number was posted in the upper storey to keep a sharp watch on the enemy's movements. The rest look up their positions along the walls to keep vigil so that the enemy did not scale the walls. According to Inayat Khan the compiler of *Ahkam-i-Alamgiri*, the Garhi was attacked by 700 cavalrymen but the actual number appeared to be large.[58]

Imperial commanders, Khwaja Mohammad and Nahar Khan reconnoitred the Guru's arrangements and immediately started the psychological warfare. They sent their envoy to the Guru to remind him that he was to face not the paltry and indisciplined troops of the hill Rajas, but an invincible army of Aurangzeb, who was the king of kings, the asylum of the poor, the protector of the world, and it would be his sheer folly to attempt improbabilities. He should immediately renounce hostilities, make instant submission, embrace Islam and swerve infidelity.[59] The Guru's reaction to envoy's advice was that of gross indifference. Sahibzada Ajit Singh, however got provoked. He drew his scimitar and roared to the bearer of the message "Utter another word and I will slash your head off your body."[60] The envoy got infuriated though, yet he remained tight lipped. Soon he trudged back to his camp, agitated and perturbed.

The enemy then attacked the *Haveli* (a spacious building, some time called small fortress) with all the fury and might at their disposal. The Sikhs also gave them a hot welcome. They shot down arrows from all sides, from behind the walls, from the roofs, air holes and through every chink in the doors. Clad in black like a fly, the enemy made a sudden and concerted attack. The Guru at that juncture responded to it very swiftly. Every soldier who advanced from behind the wall was struck by an arrow and fell soaked in blood. Nahar Khan also tasted the pinch of the sharp-edged arrow of the Guru and found safety in flight. Many other Khans followed him betraying their cowardice. The Khawaja, seemingly the keyman of the Mughal forces, failed to muster courage to come into open and that really was the regret of Guru.[61] Many lives of the Sikhs were lost in the contest. The ammunition ran short two or three hours before the sunset. Now the Guru devised another stratagem. He divided his men into groups, each of whom went out and fought the enemy with their personal weapons *viz.* sabre, spear, sword and lance. These groups operated in different directions one after the other to keep the enemy guessing and themselves fighting on their chosen ground. The leitmotif was that the enemy should not be able to storm the *Garhi* that day. The Guru's sons, Ajit Singh (17 years) and Jujhar Singh (15 years) led vigorous attacks and received martyrdom in the process.[62]

By the night fall, thirty-five out of forty Sikhs and both the sons of Guru who were still in teens fell fighting. Only five Sikhs, Daya Singh, Dharam Singh, Man Singh, Sant Singh and Sangat Singh survived. They suddenly gathered in a group, deliberated on something in hushed tones and then resolved to enact the scene of Anandpur in which the Guru, five years earlier, had played a double role of being the Guru and disciple at one and the same time. They told the Guru that at the moment they were the Guru and he was a Khalsa. They ordered him to escape in the interest of the Panth.[63]

Daya Singh, Dharam Singh and Man Singh would accompany him. The remaining two Sant Singh and Sangat Singh would stay behind to continue the fight. The Guru refused to exit and resolved to die fighting to begin with, but then he left the fortress, for, he could not have refused the *Hukamnama* of *Panj Pyaras* (The Beloved five).

According to Sainapat Sant Singh was killed when the Guru and his party were on the verge of leaving the fortress. Sangat Singh alone had to hold the advancing enemy at bay till his last breath. He put on the dress including plume similar to that of the Guru and positioned himself in the upper storey which the Guru had occupied during the day time. From a distance, or to an observer who had not seen the Guru himself, it was well-nigh difficult to differentiate between the Guru and Sangat Singh because he was wearing the dress akin to that worn by the Guru. The latter resembled the Guru, almost. The enemy, therefore, concentrated their attention on him, mistaking him for the Guru, and, no wonder, they were jubilant when an arrow struck him dead. Historians have differed: whether it was Sant Singh or Sangat Singh or Jiwan Singh who put on the dress similar to that of Guru and successfully duped the enemy. Sant Singh could not be because Sainapat in his work *Sri Guru Sobha* says that Sant Singh was killed just when the Guru and his party made a move to abandon the fortress. He also informs us that the Guru got furious at the death of Sant Singh and very excitedly let fly arrows, causing havoc in the enemy ranks.

Bhai Jiwan Singh could also not masquerade as Guru because there is a positive evidence of Bhat Vahi declaring him to be a martyr in the battle on the bank of flooded River Sirsa.

Sangat Singh was the younger brother of Bhai Jaita, a day younger to Guru Gobind Singh. According to Kankan, a court poet of the Guru, he had enjoyed the privilege of being the Guru's companion at Patna, and even afterward.

He is mentioned as Bangesak by Koer Singh, Shamsher Singh Ashok, a modern writer, also supports him. Sukha Singh uses the expression Bangesh in the case of Sant Singh to convey that the latter used to live in Bengal. Since the time of Guru Gobind Singh, Patna where Sangat Singh played with Guru Gobind Singh, formed the headquarter of Suba of Bihar and not of Bengal, the usage of Bangesh to establish that Sangat Singh or Sant Singh belonged to Bengal does not carry conviction. The fact is that Bangsi or Bangesh both usages were meant to convey that Sangat Singh had connection with the people inhabiting the region called Bangesh. By the time Koer Singh wrote *Gur Bilas*, the Sikhs had over-run the region of Bangesh in the North-Western frontier of India and many of them had settled themselves there. Like other inhabitants of this region, they began to be called Bangesar *i.e.* to say they belonged to Bangesh region. This fact seemed to have impelled Bhai Sukha Singh to use this expression.

Now the three, namely, Daya Singh, Dharam Singh and Man Singh put on the dress of the Mughal soldiers and jumped down the outer wall of the *Garhi*. The rendezvous and its distance towards the north were decided with the help of a star. Since Anandpur was already captured and towards east was the town of Sirhind, a stronghold of the enemy and on the west lay the river Sutlej a formidable obstacle, it was therefore, decided to proceed towards the north.

All the three approached the enemy camps from three different directions, *i.e.* heading towards south, east and west, undetected. Just at the approach time which was co-ordinated, arrows from Garhi were discharged to extinguish torches of the enemy soldiers which had illuminated the Garhi, and its surrounding areas. While running past the enemy camp in the south, east and west, they individually raised loud cries warning that the Guru along with his soldiers was escaping. Since by now there was complete darkness, the allies' forces got confused and fell upon each other killing many of their own comrades. The allies' forces deployed towards the north of Garhi moved towards the east and west of Garhi to capture the Guru. At this moment when there was utter disorder, the Guru moved towards the north and escaped towards the already decided rendezvous.

The allies' force commanders unable to comprehend the motive behind the moves of the Sikhs delivered a forceful attack on the Garhi and had the satisfaction of having killed the Guru who was, in fact, Sangat Singh. Soon the reality dawned on them. The Garhi was captured. The Mughal forces' jubilance was unbounded as they were under the impression that the Guru had been killed. But shortly the euphoria evaporated when they came to know of the reality. It was not the Guru but his Sikh namely Sangat Singh, who was killed by their arrows.

The Guru had left the fortress under the very nose of the enemy. Similarly, Man Singh, Dharam Singh and Daya Singh effected their escape. Wazir Khan and his commanders had to face utter disappointment. They won the battle but gained nothing.

Thereafter, the Mughals employed all their resources to capture the Guru but in vain. The Guru had covered long distance during the night on unfamiliar tracks. According to one assessment, the Guru covered 16 kms. barefooted in unknown terrain full of thorny bushes by night in two hours and reached the predetermined meeting place before dawn.

When the Guru reached Jandsar, a Gujjar recognised him and raised an alarm but to no effect.[4] The Guru moved on and reached the village Behlolpur at a distance of three *Kos* to the west. From there he reached the wilds of Machhiwara. For days he had nothing to eat but only tender leaves of the *Akk* plant and had nothing but only a clod of earth to rest upon. The rough and thorny paths had lacerated his limbs. His feet were blistered and clothes torn. But he was unshaken. Reclining under a tree, in the lonely jungle, he sang:

> "Carry to the Beloved the message of His humble servant
> Soft beds are to him like a disease, if thou are not with him
> Living in the halls and mansions is like living among serpents, if thou art away
> Wine cups hurt him like the sword and things of comfort kill,

as does the butcher's knife, if thou art not with him
In the companionship of the friend, turf is superior to soft beds,
accursed really are the places if thou art away."

(*Shabad Hazare*)

At Machhiwara, he was joined by Dharam Singh, Man Singh and Daya Singh. But the situation was grave because the enemy was in hot pursuit. Realising this, one Gulaba, an old *masand* of Machhiwara, took the Guru and his three Sikhs to his residence, but soon the heart within him failed.

At this juncture, two Pathan brothers, Nabi Khan and Gani Khan, who used to visit Anandpur in connection with their horse-trade and had developed reverence for the Guru in the process waited upon the Guru. The Guru obliged them by agreeing to stay at their residence that was situated close to that of Gulaba at Machhiwara. Guru halted there for two days.

Fateh Nama

During this short period, the Guru wrote a letter popularly known as Fateh Nama which, in fact, was a admonitory letter.

In the first three couplets the Guru swore in the names of weapons, holy heroes of God and the Giver of Kingdom to Aurangzeb, the Granter of the privilege of shielding the faithful and the low.

Then in the next few stanzas the Guru seemed to be rebuking that Aurangzeb had been resorting to subterfuge and fraud in his dealings even with his father and brothers and how he had built an empire through loot, plunder and hypocrisy. In couplet 6, the Guru said: "The rosary, O King, is but a snare to entrap the people unaware. When thou maketh pretend to pray wistfully, thou watch the prey."

In certain other couplets, the Guru reminded the Emperor that retribution was sure to fall on him. His failure in southern campaigns and in Mewar were to be perceived in that context (couplet 1). He also made pointed reference to the killing of his two elder sons at Chamkaur. Through the cunning and craft holding in the same breath, he should not think that he had won (couplet 14). His Khalsa remains invincible and is in a position to deliver death blows to all his evil and aggressive designs.

In couplets 9 and 10, the Guru expressed that now under his loving care the people had received sacrament of steel and were determined to rid themselves of oppression, injustice and coercion.

If now Emperor dared to cast his covetous glances on Punjab, he would have to face so vehement an opposition that he would not be allowed to have a moment of respite, even a drop of water (couplet 13).

This time, the Khalsa would not take Emperor's words believable. He writes:

No more, in us, thy words inspire
The sort of faith thou doth desire
We 'll hence in arms correspond
The like of thee, to them, respond. (Couplet 17)

From couplet No. 18 through couplet No. 24, the Guru throws a challenge to the Emperor's military might as also to his personal bravery. Regarding his personal bravery, the Guru challenged Aurangzeb that he should come into the field personally instead of depending upon recruits. Guru brought a moral question in couplet No. 24.

Armed with sword and the shields,
Thou must personally take the field
It is cowardly to fire humanity
For thy evil aims and vanity.

The letter[65] contained 24 couplets in all. It was in Persian verse and is a unique example of epistolary poetry. In it the *masanvi* meter of Firdausi and Nizami had been employed and the choice of words was impeccable.

Bhai Daya Singh disguised himself as a Muslim Faquir while his companions, Dharam Singh, Man Singh, Nabi Khan and Gani Khan masqueraded as his attendants. He was then seated in a litter and taken out from Machhiwara. They told all the enquirers that they were escorting Uch-da-Pir or a high saint which by a pun would also mean the holy saint of Uch (a place near Bahawalpur—now in Pakistan). At the village named Lal, a military commander had certain doubts regarding the identity of the person seated in the litter, and he made searching queries. Considering the answers illusive and unsatisfactory, he sent for Qazi Pir Mohammad of village Saloh, from whom the Guru had studied Persian to identify the occupant of the litter. The Qazi certified that he was not Guru Gobind Singh. After that, Daya Singh was allowed to proceed further to his destination fixed by the Guru.

Wrongfully though, it has often been assumed that the Guru and not Bhai Daya Singh disguised himself as 'Uch-da-Pir'. The avowal is based on the information gleaned from Bhai Sukha Singh's *Gur Bilas* and *Suraj Parkash* by Bhai Santokh Singh. Regretfully, these celebrated works have not quoted any reliable historical source and have simply recorded the prevalent heresay while the authors of these should have taken into consideration the backdrop of the event, ideology of the person involved in the event before portraying the event. Guru Gobind Singh simply could not take recourse to a guise to escape from danger or conceal his creedal identity. He would not simulate or evade avowal of his identity, no matter how compelling the claims of expediency, for, to do so would belie his own teachings and assertion *Kahio Prabhu So Bhakh Hun, Kahio Prabhu So Main Karon* (I say whatever God orders, I do whatever God wishes).

In this connection, it must be remembered that only a day or so earlier in his predicament at Chamkaur, the Guru had stoutly refused to leave the mud walls of the Garhi without first throwing clear challenge to thousands of his enemies beleaguering him and trumpeting his defiance: "The Guru now comes forth from behind the mud-walls and let him who cares and dares to obstruct his progress advance and try."

It would be sheer travesty to assume that less than forty-eight hours afterwards, he would behave differently. The Guru was not a cyclothymic personality given to wavering will and vacillating creed and conviction. The Guru who taught

Joojh Maron Tau Saach Patije would never pretend to be *Pir-i-Ucha* under any circumstances whatsoever.

This statement by the Guru clinches the issue in the matter of his *Pir-i-Ucha* episode showing that although the Sikh chroniclers are correct in giving almost all the material details, they erred in equating the *Pir-i-Ucha* person with the Guru.[66]

There is another fact that militates against the literal acceptance of the chronicler's story. In the Islamic penal code, for six specific crimes, the punishment is fixed and punishment of apostasy which on the basis of Qiyyas includes false oath on the Koran by a Sayyad is death. In this, there is no discretion. Again to abet concealment and engineer escape of a rebel against the Islamic authority of the state is an act of high treason for which the punishment is death without discretion. Sayyad Pir Muhammad by dodging what he did according to Sikh chroniclers, should have earned death at the hands of the Mughal authorities when it was discovered that the Guru had escaped the Mughal forces, but by all available accounts, he enjoyed a natural span of life. Similarly, two Pathan brothers did not attract the attention of the state authorities for committing an act of high treason on account of having aided the escape of a dangerous and a powerful enemy of the state. From this, it becomes clear that the Mughal authorities as well as the politically sensitive Muslim populace were well aware that in the *Pir-i-Ucha* episode, Sayyad Pir Mohammad had testified and as such there was no such occurrence as Guru Gobind Singh's escape in disguise.

Guru Gobind Singh's own testimony on the point is quite conclusive. In his letter *Zafarnama* to Aurangzeb the Guru tells the Emperor that during his progress from Chamkaur to Bathinda desert (1705), he met no impediment or harm whatsoever. God led him safely out of the enemy's cordon without a scratch on his person.[67]

Closely connected with all this is a question who was the person seated in the litter if he was not Guru Gobind Singh? According to Sardar Kapur Singh, he was Daya Singh, who assumed the guise of a holy man and who was helped to escape local military vigilance in a manner normal and honourable in such a situation, and that Sayyad Pir Mohammad had rendered true testimony as enjoined by Koran when he solemnly testified that Bhai Daya Singh was not the Guru. Bhai Daya Singh had been entrusted with the task of delivering the letter personally to Aurangzeb and therefore he resorted to the stratagem of disguising himself.

Having been let off by the Mughal military commander, Bhai Daya Singh along with Nabi Khan, Gani Khan, Dharam Singh and Man Singh proceeded to Gulal where the Guru had already reached as per programme carefully chalked out by Gani Khan, Nabi Khan and Qazi Pir Muhammad. Here the Guru awarded the Qazi a Hukamnama acknowledging his services for him. The Qazi then returned to his place.

From Ghulal, the Guru visited Lal. Here he was served by a boy Bhag Mal who was an orphan. The Guru was so much pleased that he blessed him and uttered that he would be a 'person of immense fortune as his name suggested'. Next sojourns of the Guru were at Katani, Rampur and Kanech. At Kanech the *masand* named Fateh Chand avoided welcoming him as his spirit failed out of fear of Wazir Khan. He felt so much down-spirited that he did not part with his mare pretending that the same had been taken away by his son-in-law.[68]

From Kanech, the Guru reached Sahnewal whose Panchayat hesitated to pay respect to the Guru. When he was about to move on, the people including ladyfolk of the village came forward to offer apology. The Guru blessed them and went further to village Mohi near Jodhan, wherefrom he proceeded to Heira through village Silaoni. There lived Kirpal Das, a devoted disciple of *Udasi* Mahant of the same name, who had proved his mettle as a warrior in the battle of Bhangani. He accorded a hearty welcome to the Guru. On his request, the Guru decided to stay with him. Here he wrote a *Hukam Nama*—a letter commanding his followers always to hold Nabi Khan and Gani Khan in high esteem, for, they had rendered unto him selfless and altruistic service. The Pathan brothers thereafter returned to their homes, gratified and contented.

From this place, the Guru proceeded to village Lamma where the people, who had already embraced Sikhism, received the Guru with utmost courtesy.

From Lamma the Guru visited Rai Kot, the chief of which Raikala was Guru's devotee and a close relation of Nihang Khan. He knew the imperial orders that the Guru should be apprehended wherever he was, but he was not at all afraid. On the contrary when he heard all that the Guru had borne, the tears streamed down his eyes. According to Bhai Santokh Singh, he waited upon the Guru at Silaoni and requested him to visit Rai Kot. Now when the Guru visited Rai Kot, he left no stone unturned to provide comfort to him. The Guru granted Rai Kala an excellent sword in recognition of his selfless service. At the Guru's behest, he sent Nura Mahi to Sirhind to fetch news about what had happened to other members of his family.

Not long after, Mahi delivered the news of what had happened to the Guru's family members after he left Anandpur. He told that in the confusion that prevailed in the wake of Guru's departure from the city, Mata Gujri and his two grandsons Zorawar Singh and Fateh Singh, aged nine and seven respectively, had nowhere to go until their family cook Gangu, a Brahmin by caste, offered to take them to his own village, Sehri. They accompanied him to his house. Now he turned perfidious and deceitful, understandably to get some reward from the Mughals and also to possess valuables of Mata Gujri. He informed the Mughal officials Jani Khan and Mani Khan of Morinda that the Guru's mother and his two younger sons were staying at his place. The officials at once took them in their custody and passed them on to Sirhind, the headquarter of Nawab Wazir Khan. Gangu also went to Sirhind, where his services were appreciated.

Mata Gujri and her grandsons were imprisoned in a tower of the fort called *Thanda Burj* or the cold tower. It was extremely uncomfortable in the winter for 80-year-old lady and two children.

Wazir Khan, who was an inveterate foe of the Guru and was biting his lips for his failure to capture the Guru now found opportunity to settle scores with the Guru, albeit vicariously and unethically by exercising his authority on the little children.

On December 9, 1705, Zorawar Singh[69] and Fateh Singh were produced before Wazir Khan, who had just returned from the battle of Chamkaur. Wazir Khan tried to lure them to embrace Islam with promises of riches and honours, but they spurned the offer. He threatened them with death as an alternative to the acceptance of Islam but they remained unflinching. A death sentence was eventually awarded. Nawab Sher Muhammad of Malerkotla protested that it would be improper to harm the innocent children. Wazir Khan, however, ordered them to be bricked alive in a wall if they still refused conversion. They were kept in cold tower in that severe winter for another two days. On 11th December, they, under the orders of Wazir Khan began to be paved with bricks standing on the ground. However, as the masonry reached above chest height, it crumbled. On 12th December, 1705, the very next day the Sahibzadas (the sons of the Guru) were once again offered the choice of conversion to Islam or death. They chose the latter and fearlessly faced the executioner's sword. The aged Mata Gujri who had all along been confined in the cold tower only a little distance away breathed her last as the tragic news reached her ears. The dead bodies were kept for the night at a spot now called Bimangarh, just outside the fort wall and were cremated the following day by the Seth Todar Mal[70], a wealthy merchant of Sirhind who specially got the permission from Nawab Wazir Khan to perform the last rites of the Guru's sons and mother befittingly by offering as many gold Mohars as placed closely together would completely cover the spot for cremating the dead bodies.

Mahi also told how Revered Mata Sundri and Mata Sahib Kaur were escorted to Delhi by Bhai Mani Singh and lived secretly at a place where now is situated Mata Sundri Gurdwara in Delhi. Bhai Mani Singh escorted them.

A young and pretty girl Anup Kaur said to be a relative of revered Jito was captured by Sher Muhammad, the then ruler of Malerkotla. She was taken to Malerkotla, where she committed suicide instead of submitting to the carnal advances of the Nawab.

The Guru received the tragic news with amazing courage and equanimity. Mahi also told him that Wazir Khan's forces were on the move to apprehend the Guru.

Realising that the territory around Raikot was not a suitable place, strategically speaking, to put up a fight to the enemy, the Guru decided to move to Lakhi Jungle. The Guru is said to have stayed with Rai Kalla for sixteen days.

According to Ishar Singh Nara, the Guru's next sojourn was Lopogram, after which he stayed at a place[71] which is now called Alamgir. Nagahia Singh the brother of Bhai Mani Singh presented him with a beautiful horse. From this place the Guru proceeded towards Lakhi Jungle. On the way the Guru passed through villages of Manuke, Mehdeana, Chakkar, Takhtupura and Madhen, and reached Dina.

At Dina about 7 Kms. south-west of Takhtupura, a devoted Sikh Rama presented the Guru with a steed of a very high quality. The Guru accepted it and blessed Bhai Rama. The news of the Guru's arrival at this place soon spread and the Zamindars/peasants of the area started flocking to him, some to assure the Guru of their faith and some just to know of him and his mission. Some of the influential people who paid their obeisance here were Lakhmir and Shamir and Takht Mall (all the three were the grandsons of Jodha Rai who embraced Sikhism under the impact of the charismatic personality of Guru Hargobind), Param Singh and Dharam Singh, the sons of Bhai Rup Chand, *Mahant* Dayal Puri who came all the way from Sirhind. The Guru asked the *Mahant* to carry out the task of spreading Guru's message in the area around Sirhind, and in doing so, he should fear none. The Guru stayed there for quite some time.

The Guru around this time received a message from Aurangzeb, most probably as a reply to his letter (Fatehnama).

The original letter of invitation is not available in any of the collections of his Ruqat or Ahkam nor do we have any details of its contents. The twenty-eighth *Sakhi* of the *Sakhi Pothi* (book) (*Sau Sakhi* Ms 79) contains a brief summary of it. According to it, *Parwanas* were issued to the Guru saying, "There is only one kingdom. Seeing the *Parwana* you better immediately come here. Our religious sentiments are the same. If not I will come myself. The awe and superiority of saintliness will then have gone. You may live in kingdom as other saints and devotees live." To this, continues the Sakhi, were added some words of arrogance usual with the style of the royal *Parwanas* (letters) that the kingdom had been bestowed upon him by God.[72]

The Guru in response to the message wrote a letter bearing the title Zafarnama, in which he underlined the perjury of the Mughal officials and the urgency of his paying personal attention to his affairs.[73] The letter was taken to the Emperor by Bhai Daya Singh and Dharam Singh in the guise of a Muslim Darveshes. They came to Agra and from there proceeded to the south through Gwalior, Ujjain and the Malwa country till at last they reached Burhanpur. From there they finally reached Ahmadnagar via Aurangabad. Daya Singh went to the Sangat at Ahmadnagar and explained to the local Sikhs the object of his mission. He does not seem to have received any sincere assistance from the local Sikhs some of whom were openly critical of the Guru's policy and action. Then Daya Singh made an acquaintance with a Sikh who apparently had some influence in high quarters and arranged the delivery of the letter to Aurangzeb.

Zafar Nama (Epistle of Victory)[74]

Zafar Nama is a letter written by Guru Gobind Singh in reply to the oral and written communication of Aurangzeb, which the Guru received at village Dina through a Qazi sent by the Emperor in response to his earlier letter 'Fateh Nama'. This was composed in chaste Persian at Dina itself. The letter is an excellent literary piece replete with similes and metaphors superbly used to telling effect. It occupies a place of eminence in epistolary poetry of Persian. The following lines amply bear it out.

With limbs and skulls of warriors killed
The field was eminently filled
Like so many bats and balls to play
In the field, in heap, they lay. (*Zafar Nama*)

Besides being a tribute to the literary excellence, this letter is of great importance since it throws a flood of light on the Guru's approach to unethical issues, his concept of God and justice, his views regarding the duties and functions of a sovereign *vis-à-vis* his subjects, his outlook regarding the use of force and different historical events intimately connected with Guru's life.

In stanza 1 to stanza 12, the Guru's unshakeable faith in God is amply manifest. He extols Him as Eternal, Merciful, Bounteous, Benign, Dispenser of Justice, Holy Refuge, Guide, True King, Radiant, Sublime, Provider of livelihood, Wise, Caretaker of the humble, the low and the lost, Vanquisher of foe, Solution of all woes and troubles, Designer of supreme laws of nature and of the earth, Chastiser of foes[75], Fearless, True Emperor, Formless, Non-existent, Incomparable, Mightest of all[76] (stanza 72), Carefree[77] (stanza 71), Omnipresent, Omnipotent and Omniscient.

The Guru's invocation to such a God of myriad attributes and functions instil in him a moral spirit, always egging him on to function in the world without any fear, as also to advise and warn the people including even the Emperors to tread the righteous path.

He, therefore, makes bold to criticise Aurangzeb for his unethical conduct. He tells him frankly and fearlessly that he, his Diwans and Bakhshis (officials of the highest rung in Mughal bureaucracy) were liars, have no qualms and care a fig even for oaths on Koran, he himself is a defier of his religion, worshipper of mammon and a veritable pledge-breaker. He also pointed out that his pledged words on Koran, in fact, were snares to entrap the people. One such snare being his word that the Guru would not be harmed if he vacated Anandpur.

From stanza 19 to stanza 44, the Guru gave the account of the battle of Chamkaur, how he had to face a disproportionately large number of the Mughal troops and how he lost thirty-seven of his followers including his two elder sons Ajit Singh (17) and Jujhar Singh (14). In these stanzas it was also mentioned that the Guru killed Kehar Khan, a Mughal general and he and his Sikhs kept at bay the enemy for almost the whole day. Though the Mughal soldiers attired in black made furious charges shouting and shrieking like a swarm of bees, yet the Khalsa held them in check and the moment anyone left his defence in an attempt to commit offence, he was laid in the pool of blood by an arrow. But how Khalsa, only forty strong, tired and hungry, could hold against the countless number of the enemy, ultimately, except three all fell fighting. In the critical hours, God led the Guru out of the fort to a place of safety. Guru did not suffer even a scratch on his person in the process.

The Guru reminded in stanza 75 that no doubt Aurangzeb had claimed four tender lives (four children of the Guru), yet the spirit of the Guru was as high as ever, and the coiled cobra of deadly stings is very much alive in the form of Singhs. The Guru also warned him 'to be prepared for retributive justice on the Day of judgement for all the atrocious acts committed by him. His professions of adherence to the tenets of his faith was a mere fraud, because without the least qualms, he had broken the most solemn words pledged by him on *Quran*.'

To arouse his moral conscience, the Guru brought forth another fact which was that he sided with the crafty hill chieftains who were idolaters and fought against him who was an iconoclast (metaphorically speaking) like him. The Guru in his sweep clearly hinted at the real causes that caused confrontation between the hill Rajas and the Guru; he also tried to hammer into the mind of Aurangzeb his unethical unrighteousness and immoral conduct, simply to put him to shame, morally speaking. The Guru, while denouncing the immoral conduct of the king and his men for wanton repudiation of their own solemn words pledged by them voluntarily on their holy texts, said that if he had ever held out such solemn promises, he would have upheld their sanctity even at the cost of his life.

> Nothing could have led us astray from our self-chosen path. Had we sworn by the words we believe. Father? Never, our life be relieved.

Particular emphasis is, therefore, laid on the need for an upright and ethical conduct on the part of an individual embracing the entire gamut of his life. Aurangzeb was strongly condemned not only for his dastardly designs but also for the dishonest, unethical and immoral means that he invariably employed to wrest some advantage over his adversaries. In this strain the Guru spoke the following words:

> You (Aurangzeb) are not sincere in your affirmations to the tenets of your faith. A man who is not true to his words stands condemned and is rejected as a counterfeit coin by man and God both.

Guru Gobind Singh, therefore, raised ethical conduct to a sovereign status and made it as the true expression of the harmony of human personality with the will of God.

Living life ethically was the keynote of the teachings of Guru Gobind Singh and was a faith with him. Therefore, fully aware about the immoral acts of Aurangzeb, he wished that he should remould his life on ethical basis. He advised him to mend himself. In case he was willing to stand by his oral words and written note and his thinking and actions were in harmony, he was ready to negotiate with him. The Guru invited the Emperor to Kangar, (then outskirts of Dina) where all the contentious issues would be discussed and resolved[78] (stanza 58). The Guru also hinted that he would be welcomed appropriately and presented with a valuable steed. Alternative to this, the Guru left to him to find a way to know the real cause of the fight.[79]

All through the letter, not a trace of hatred could be felt or found; only there is a moral rage along with the very strong urge to reform Aurangzeb and to make him realise that whatever he had done towards him and his Khalsa was not in consonance with the will of God. The Guru took his essential stand on moral grounds and that is what formed the scarlet thread passing through the whole range of verses to impart coherence to them. The officials of Aurangzeb had forced an unjust war on Guru Gobind Singh and had broken their solemn vows and honourable conduct expected of a king of Aurangzeb's stature. If all this was done with the Emperor's approval, then the Emperor could not boast of being a believer in God. He should have really remembered the True Lord, if in the life hereafter, he wished Him to remember the Emperor. By ignoring the dictates of justice, Aurangzeb had shown himself to be a stranger to real statesmanship as well as to God. In possession of immense power, he should not have forgotten that power was entrusted to the ruler for protecting the innocent people and not for spilling their blood.

A very important undercurrent of *Zafar Nama* was that the righteous cause must be upheld and forces championing the unrighteousness must be resisted, even with the use of arms as a last resort. The sanction for the use of arms is embodied in the following oftquoted stanza of *Zafar Nama*.

> "When the affairs are past redemption,
> By all other means of peaceful intention,
> It is just to assert the right
> Through the sword and a righteous fight."

Unfortunately, it is not invariably understood in proper perspective. The message of the stanza is two-pronged; bloodshed should be avoided as far as possible, but at the same time cause should not be abandoned merely because, as a last resort, it warrants the use of force. The use of arms is allowed for a good cause of universal validity, after all other peaceful means for resolving the crisis have been completely exhausted. A very clear implication that, in such circumstances, the use of force, as an unavoidable ultimate necessity, must be limited to the bare minimum prominently pops out of these popular lines for all sensitive minds to take note of.

The *Zafar Nama* contains 111 stanzas and is written in chaste Persian. Bhai Daya Singh and Dharam Singh (according to *Gur Sobha* by Sainapat, Daya Singh and his five companions) were deputed to deliver the letter personally to Aurangzeb at Ahmadnagar. They reached Ahmadnagar after a considerable difficulty and succeeded in handing over the letter to the Emperor who seemed to have been much impressed by the contents of the letter. The fact is vouchsafed by a statement of Sainapat, in his treatise *Gur Sobha*. Mirza Inayat Ullah Khan in his compilation *Ahkam-i-Alamgiri* refers to a letter received from Guru Gobind Singh in which he had expressed his wish to meet the Emperor. Accordingly, Aurangzeb deputed a Gurzbardar and a Mansabdar, Mohammed Beg and Sheikh Yar Mohammad, to approach Guru Gobind Singh through Munim Khan and use all diplomatic skill in persuading him to go to Emperor; and if Guru Gobind Singh was to march through the territory of Sirhind, his safety was to be guaranteed and if he needed any money for his travel that was to be supplied from the properties seized from Guru himself. Dr. Anil Chander Bannerjee a renowned scholar of Sikhism, says: "There are reasons to think that the original text of the letter is no longer available. He based his conclusion on the grounds: firstly it is unusual to compose diplomatic communication in the style and form of *Zafar Nama*. *Zafar Nama* is written in a 'dramatic form' in verse in the meter in which the Persian Masnavis, as also the Shahnama, are composed. Diplomatic letters are not composed as such. Secondly, there are statements which can hardly be attributed to the Guru, as for example the epithet *Sarwar-i-ka-nat* applicable to God only, has been used with reference to Aurangzeb.

Both the grounds are flimsy, untenable and tenuous. *Zafar Nama* was not a diplomatic letter in the sense diplomacy is often understood. Had it been so, the Guru would have not called a spade a spade and peeled skin after skin of pretensions, fraud and hypocrisy of the Emperor, nor would he have asked him to look inwards to his own moral conscience and also ponder upon the inexorable laws of God, which always go against those who are unethical in the performance of duties. Further, it is not sound to base conclusion on a single expression. The referred expression seemed to have a distortion effected by a copyist or some vested interest, or a substitution for some other word. Anyway, any one stray expression cannot determine the tenor of any document.

In sum, Zafar Nama was a scathing exposure of the perfidy of the Emperor Aurangzeb, his unprincipled support to the hill Rajas, his wrong notion about sovereignty as well as about the conduct of public affairs, his distorted and smudged thinking about religion and his sadistic pleasure at the innocent killings, his hypocritical approach to God and his creations. At the same time, it was a testament of the assertion of the Guru that ethical principles were supreme in matters of public policy as well as of private behaviour that a sovereign must protect and promote righteousness instead of tyrannising the people; that sovereignty of morality both in the affairs of state as well as in the conduct of individual human beings should be upheld at all costs that absolute truthfulness should be adhered to equally by a sovereign and by an ordinary citizen, that people had inherent right to resort to force as a last resort against the forces of unrighteousness.

From Dina, the Guru occasionally went out and visited a few places in the neighbourhood. Two such places were Manan and Bhadaur.

The Guru in Lakhi Jungle

While yet at Dina the Guru came to learn that his whereabouts had become known to the Mughal government of Sirhind. From then onwards he started looking for some suitable place where he could best meet the challenge of the enemy.

The Guru left Dina and took to travelling from village to village. He visited Bander, Bargarhi, Saravan. At Saravan the Guru gave people a little practice in arrow-shooting. Next, he proceeded to Jaito. Therefrom, the Guru went to Kotha Maluk Das and Lambhawali wherefrom he made a dash to Kot Kapura situated 13 *Kos* in the north. It was situated on a promontory in a big pond and was admirably suited to stand a siege or an attack. Probably, the pursuing enemy forces had come too near by now. Chaudhri Kapura a Brar Jat and master of the fort welcomed the Guru who asked him to lend the use of his fort to him for a few days. Fearing the wrath of the Mughals, he politely refused to oblige the Guru.[80] From here the Guru proceeded to Dhilwan Sodhian, 3 *Kos* from Kot Kapura where Sodhi Kaul, a descendant of Prithi Chand, the elder brother of Guru Arjan Dev, received the Guru with great warmth and cordiality. It was here, as the tradition goes, the Guru took off his blue robes which he had been wearing ever since he left Machhiwara and tearing them off into small pieces consigned them, one by one, to fire. The historic words that he is said to have uttered on this occasion are memorable:

> "The blue robes have been torn off,
> And with that ends the rule of Turk-o-Pathans."[81]

Chaudhari Kapura, now repentant of his earlier disgraceful act, came to see the Guru and asked for his forgiveness. The Guru pardoned him and he provided the Guru with a good guide, Chaudhri Khana, under whose guidance the Guru marched westward in the direction of Dhab Khidrana. On the way, he passed through Ramiana, Mallan, Gauri, Sanghar and Kaoni.

Meanwhile hundreds of his followers had collected around the Guru. Among them were a large number of Majhails (people of the Majha region, the country lying between Beas and Ravi rivers), who came to the Guru to pay their respects and also to condole with him on the death of his sons and his mother.

The Guru received them warmly and counselled them to keep cool. Instead of being sad and anguished, they should learn to live in the Will of God.

The swarming of hundreds and thousands of the Sikhs to swim and sink along with the Guru transported the poet in the Guru to the realm of wonderment born out of his deep contemplation. He poured out his mind thus:

> Lakhī Jungle Khālsa Aye lagā,
> Didar Keeto Ne;
> Sun Ke Sad Mahī Dā

Mehi Pani Ghāh Muto Ne
Kise Nāl Nā Raliā Koi
Ih Kee Shauk Payo Ne
Gia Firak Milia Mahi
Tan Hi Shukar Kito Ne.[82]
"To Lakhi Jungle repaired the Khalsa
Resistless was the friend's call
They paused not for food and drink and rushed to the Guru like the buffaloes running to their master at his nod.
One waited not for another
Such eagerness swayed their hearts
Gone was the pangs of separation
Perfect Union prevailed
Overwhelming was their gratefulness."

According to Mohammad Latif, the number rallied around the Guru swelled to twelve thousand.[83]

BATTLE OF MUKTSAR—DECEMBER 29, 1705

In the meanwhile, when the forty Sikhs who had given up their discipleship of the Guru out of fear of death during the siege of Anandpur and in token thereof had handed over a signed disclaimer to the Guru, reached back their homes, deserting the Guru in his hour of difficulty, the Sikhs in general and especially those who lived in Majha region met in a convention at Patti and expressed their deep concern at the plight of the Guru as also at the perfidy of the Sikhs who signed *Bedawa* (a disclaimer). They decided to send their representatives to the Guru to offer their condolences at the sad demise of his four sons and to suggest that they could negotiate on his behalf to bring about reconciliation between the Guru and the Mughal Government.

The Forty Deserters

The public condemnation coupled with their own sense of remorse at their treacherous deeds impelled the Forty to do something to recompense for their infidelity and perjury. They, therefore, resolved to meet the Guru to offer their apology who at that time was in the jungle area of the Malwa. They and the Sikh representatives accordingly started their march towards the Guru. The Forty included Bhag Singh, Bhag Kaur's brother and her husband Nidhan Singh son of late Choudhari Des Raj of Patti. They met the Guru between Ramiana and Khidrana. After condoling the sad and untimely death of his sons, they offered to negotiate with the Mughal Government to effect compromise between the Guru and the Mughal Government.

The Guru replied, "Friends, you have come to advise me, thinking yourselves to be wiser than I. But I am not inclined to accept your advice. You have not rightly comprehended the real spirit of Sikhism. If you had, you would not be advising me, but seeking my advice and carrying out my orders. If you, had understood my ideals of life, you would have never thought of making peace between me and the tyrants. Rather, you would have joined my army and fought against them. You advise me to give up fighting and seek peace with the cruel bigoted tyrants. I cannot do that. Know ye not that I have no quarrel with, or personal grudge against any man? People are groaning under tyranny and oppression. It is to rescue them that I have taken up arms. My sword strikes at tyrants, not at meeks. It defends the weak against the strong. Come and join me in the holy task of liberating people. Your policy of cooperation and meek submission has only tightened the chains. What could you, or people like you do when Guru Arjan and Guru Tegh Bahadur were put to inhuman tortures and death respectively? The only sorrow that I feel springs from beholding my countrymen disunited and in chains. The only desire that sits ever alert in my heart is for the unification and liberation of the down-trodden people. If you are my Sikhs follow my advice. I am sorry I cannot concur with you or accept you as my instructors in this matter."

This statement of the Guru simply benumbed them. Preferring their safety to the Guru's cause, many of the advisers and the people retraced their steps to their homes. The Forty Sikhs who earlier had deserted the Guru at Anandpur refused to follow them. Now, they were changed persons, burning with the desire to regain discipleship of the Guru by displaying hundred per cent fidelity to his noble cause. Even Bhag Singh, one of the Forty, who faltered in the initial stages of conversation with the Guru displayed his determination to serve the cause of his Master at any cost. Mai Bhag Kaur seemed to have played a crucial role in keeping him on the right track. All the Forty Sikhs accompanied by Bhag Kaur decided to swim or sink for the cause of the Guru. They moved on towards the Guru who by then had proceeded further along with representatives of Majha region to select a strategically suitable place to give a fight to the advancing Mughal forces who were in hot pursuit of the Guru. These Forty were led by Mahan Singh of the village Sursinghwala in the district of Amritsar and included Nidhan Singh, husband of Mai Bhag Kaur. She herself was the Forty-first Sikh skilled in handling weapons and possessed of determination of steel.

The Guru apprehending the advance of Mughal forces crossed the Lakhi Jungle to reach a place known as Khidrana[84], which was famous for its water tank. The Guru planned the defence in such a way that it should not be easy for the enemy to capture the pool of water which was the one for the supply of water in that part of the country. He himself took up his position on the elevated mound and his Sikhs in bushes which lay around the maund and its adjoining pool of water.

The troops of Wazir Khan marched towards Khidrana striking fear and convulsion on the way.

As the Mughal forces reached near Khidrana, they were challenged by the Forty men of Majha region of the Punjab. They deemed it appropriate to block them on the eastern side just outside Khidrana. This happened on the 28th December, 1705 (Magh Vadi 10, 1762 Bk). In the battle that ensued these Forty led by Mahan Singh and inspired by revered Bhag Kaur (Bhag Kaur was in addition to the forty) fought heroically. In order that the enemy might not reach Khidrana, they resorted to subtle tactics. They spread loose cloth sheets on bushes to give impression to the enemy that a large force under the Guru lay encamped there. They took positions among the bushes and readied themselves to accord hot welcome to the enemy. When the enemy's troops came near, they assaulted on them so vigorously that they were simply amazed.

The clatter of arms and din and dust of the battlefield alerted the Guru who showered arrows from his position and when the enemy distanced itself from the farthest extent of the range of his arrow, he mounted the steed and moved hither and thither to aim his arrows successfully.

The Mughal soldiers got confused and bewildered. The Forty fought with rare valour and determination. Having exhausted their ammunition and queers of arrows, they were obliged to have recourse to their spears and swords. Small bands advanced, engaged the enemies in hand-to-hand fights, killed several times their own number, until they were completely overpowered and all of them were killed or mortally wounded[85] (only Bhag Kaur was seriously injured who recovered later on) but not long before they had shown the fire of their faith and their mettle as the toughest fighters whom the experienced Wazir Khan had ever known in his life. The Mughal forces were soon in great straits. They had already been fatigued in part caused by their long march and in part by the scarcity of provisions including water. But now when they found themselves face to face with determined Khalsa engaged in a pitched battle, they were further exhausted and exasperated. Another factor also tired their verve. The main body of the Khalsa under the command of the Guru was fresh with sufficient war materials and in possession of the only source of water that lay in the vicinity of Khidrana. Better positioned and better stationed, Khalsa force obviously constituted a psychological strain on Mughal soldiers. The net result of all this was that Wazir Khan decided not to pursue the Guru further. He thought it sagacious to feel satisfied that at least he had been successful in marginalising the Guru.

Wazir Khan's return to Sirhind without striking the main body of the Khalsa forces was considered a great victory among the Khalsa. The Guru's prestige and popularity increased manifold. His mission also received stimulus. According to Colonel Ravi Batra the Mughal forces numbered twenty thousand, while[86] the Khalsa forces numbered only two thousand including cavalry and irregulars.[87]

After the Mughal forces had left the field, the Guru visited the scene of actual battle and with a fatherly affection went about lifting the heads of the martyrs in the lap wiping their faces and blessing them one by one. When it was the turn of Bhai Mahan Singh to be thus caressed and blessed, the Master found that there was still some life in him. After a while, Bhai Mahan Singh opened his eyes and found himself in the lap of the Guru. He was filled with supreme joy. The Guru asked him if he had any desire to be fulfilled. Bhai Mahan Singh said, "No, Father, I have seen thee. What else or more could I desire? But if thou has taken compassion on us here, then tear off our disclaimer." The Guru at once acceded to his request and remarked, "You have saved the root of Sikhism in Majha. You and your companions, all Forty of you are 'Muktas' or the Emancipated Ones, delivered from the round of births and deaths for ever." Then the Guru went to the place where Bhag Kaur was lying senseless on account of her wounds. A little medical aid revived her. She told the Master the whole story of the repentant Forty. The Guru told her about the last deed of Mahan Singh how he made a request to tear off the paper bearing disclaimer.

The Guru was greatly pleased with Bhag Kaur for what she had done. She was removed from the battlefield and her wounds were tended. After her recovery, Bhag Kaur chose to stay with the Guru. She led the Sikh way of life in totality. After the Guru's death at Nander, she left for Bidar where she preached her Guru's teachings. Shortly after she breathed her last at Janwara 10 kms from Gurdwara Nanak Jhira.[88]

Khidrane-di-Dhab—Pool at Khidrana, also known as Ishar Sar was at that time renamed as Muktsar—Tank of Salvation. The event held out a great lesson and a sublime moral. Turning back on the Guru was a blasphemy, while turning towards the Guru was a pious and meritorious act. The event also held out hope to all those who would wish to reunite themselves to the Guru as he was an Eternal Forgiver.

The Guru renovated and enlarged the tank near the field of battle. It is believed that whosoever bathed in it would get salvation. Later on, a gurdwara was built at the site of the cremation of Forty Muktas. The area occupied by these shrines is called Tuti Ganddi Arena symbolising that the breach was healed and the lost were retrieved. A great fair is held there on the first of Magh every year in memory of the great event. The village also came to be known as Muktsar. It lies 50 Kms south-east of Firozpur.

NOTES AND REFERENCES

1. *Gurbilas* by Sukha Singh, XIII, 9, *Gur Sobha*, VIII 40, XI, 5, 6.
2. We have not been able to identify the hill states to which they belonged. Probably they were chieftains of some hill states.
3. Sarup Singh Kaushish: *Guru Kian Sakhian* edited by Piara Singh Padam Sakhi 64, p. 129, Singh Brothers, Amritsar, 1991.
4. M.A. Macauliffe: *The Sikh Religion,* V, pp. 124-26.
5. Raja Bhim Chand had abdicated in 1691 C.E. soon after he suffered reverses at Nadaun.
6. Macauliffe, M.A.: *op. cit.,* Vol. V, p. 126.
7. Sarup Singh Kaushish: *op. cit.,* p. 130, Sakhi 66, also see *Bhat Vahi Tumar Bijlautavi Ki* extract given by Piara Singh Padam in *Guru Kian Sakhian*, p. 130.
8. *Bhat Vahi: Jado basian Ki, Khata Bartie Kanau Ton Ka*—Also consult *Guru Kian Sakhian* by Sarup Singh Kaushish, p. 131.
9. *Bhat Vahi: Talaundha Pargana Jind, Khata Jalahne Puaron Ka.*
10. Sarup Singh Kaushish: *op. cit.,* p. 132.
11. *Ibid.,* p. 134.
12. He was the grandson of Bhai Salho. Refer to *Guru Pad Prem Parkash* by Bawa Sumer Singh, 1882; Sarup Singh Kaushish: *op. cit.,* p. 133.
13. Sarup Singh Kaushish: *op. cit.,* p. 135, Sakhi 67; Bawa Sumer Singh, *Guru Pad Prem Parkash*, p. 4 (1882 C.E.).
14. *Ibid.,* p. 135; also consult *Bhat Vahi Talaundha Pargana Jind*, Khata Jalhanon Ka.
15. Sarup Singh Kaushish: *op. cit.,* p. 136; also consult *Bhat Vahi Talaundha Pargana Jind*, Khata Jalhanon Ka.
16. *Ibid.*
17. *Ibid.,* p. 137.
18. *Ibid.*
19. Bannerjee, I.B.: *op. cit.,* II, 128, *Sri Gur Sobha*, 45.

20. Sarup Singh Kaushish: *op. cit.*, p. 137, Sakhi 69.
21. *Ibid.*, p. 138.
22. *Sri Guru Sobha* edited by Shamsher Singh Ashok, pp. 64-65, stanza 345.
23. The hill rajas wrote a letter to the Faujdar of Sirhind asking for his help against the Guru. Kartar Singh in *Life of Guru Gobind Singh*, p. 181; *Gur Sobha, op. cit.*, pp. 64-65, stanzas 345-51. According to Giani Gian Singh, Aurangzeb himself is said to have sent an order to Wazir Khan to proceed against the Guru. *Twarikh Guru Khalsa*, p. 915, Santokh Singh: *op. cit.*, pp. 2642-48.
24. Sainapat: *op. cit.* Chapter 9, p. 65, stanza 351.
25. Sainapat: *op. cit.*
26. Kartar Singh: *op. cit.* The use of canon by the Mughal troop is not improbable.
27. Sampat: *op. cit.*, 60.
28. *Ibid.*
29. *Ibid.*
30. Basoli fell in the territory of Jaswan.
31. Sainapat: *op. cit.*, p. 72, Chapter X, stanza 90.
32. He was the son of Prem Chand and grandson of Moola, *Bhat Vahi Talaundha Pargana Jind*, *Khata Jalhanon Ka*.
33. M.A. Macauliffe: *The Sikh Religion*, V, pp. 128-37, *Phir Basyo Anandpur Rajan Manian*.
34. Sarup Singh Kaushish: *Guru Kian Sakhian* edited by Piara Singh Padam, p. 142, Sakhi 72, Singh Brothers, Amritsar, 1995. The date of this event is given by Kaushish as *Chet Vadi Panchah Samvat* 1754 (1700 C.E.).
35. Sainapat: *Sri Gur Sobha*, ed. Harnam Singh, pp. 55-57, 62-65.
36. This date is given by Khazan Singh in his book *History and Philosophy of Sikhism*, Vol. I.
37. *Jaise Bache Meri Handi; Waise Bachegi Teri Handi; Mandi Ko Jab Lutenge; To Asmani Gole Chhutenge;* Lepel Griffin: *Rajas of the Punjab*, pp. 580-81. A Glossary of the Tribes & Castes of the Punjab and the N.W. Frontier Province.
38. Hari Ram Gupta: *History of the Sikhs*, Vol. I, p. 286.
39. M.A. Macauliffe: *Sikh Religion*, pp. 153-54. Sayyad Beg threw away his sword and vowed never to use it against the Sikhs again. See *Sakhi Pothi*, p. 59.
40. *Ibid.*, pp. 154-55.
41. *Ibid.*
42. M.A. Macauliffe: *The Sikh Religion*, V, p. 154.
43. *Ibid.*

44. Narain Singh: *Guru Gobind Singh Retold*, p. 229.
45. We are not sure whether direct representation was made, but it is fairly certain that the Emperor had sent orders to the Mughal official notably Wazir Khan, the Faujdar of Sirhind, Mirza Mohammed Harisi Ibratnama: S.H.R. 231, 66, 67, Ahmed Shah, *Tarikh-i-Hind*. S.H.R. 553, 158. Muhammad Qasim Ibrat Nama. Printed text pp. 133-46 (edited by Zahuruddin Ahmed, Lahore, 1977: "Honoured orders were issued from the Imperial court to Wazir Khan, Faujdar of Chakla Sirhind that if Guru lives like other recluses...., this would be better. But if he insists on actions that are against the regulation and does not shun them...he (Wazir Khan) should exert himself to the utmost to devastate the places under his control....
46. Ganda Singh: *Hukamname*, Punjabi University, p. 181, Hukamnama No. 60.
47. Macauliffe, M.A.: *op. cit.*, Vol. V, p. 175.
48. Koer Singh: *Gur Bilas*, pp. 155-56.
49. According to Hari Ram Gupta the letter was delivered by Wazir Khan himself; *History of the Sikhs*, Vol. I, p. 290; *Zafar Nama*, Verse 5, 13-15, Giani Gian Singh: *Twarikh Guru Khalsa*, p. 980, Language Department, Patiala. Santokh Singh: *op. cit.*, pp. 5843-44, 5852-53.
50. Santokh Singh: *op. cit.*, p. 5848.
51. *Gur Sobha*, VI, 64/467; Santokh Singh: *op. cit.*, 5855. The vows appear to have been most wantonly violated and to this we have poignant references in the *Zafar Nama*.
52. Bhai Udey Singh was the son of Bhai Mani Singh of Aliwal (*Shaheed Bilas Bhai Mani Singh* edited by Giani Girja Singh).
53. *Sri Gur Sobha*, XII, p. 84/479.
54. Bhai Jaita's name after baptism.
55. Inayat Ali Khan: *Description of the Principal Kotla Afghans*, pp. 13-14.
56. Lakshman Singh: *Guru Gobind Singh*, p. 105.
57. Santokh Singh: *op. cit.*, p. 5858, Chapter XI.
58. *Zafar Nama* 19-41. According to Zafar Nama the number was 10 lakhs.
59. Ganda Singh: *Makhiz-e-Twarikhe-Sikhan*, pp. 1-8. Also refer to Sayyad Muhammad Latif: *History of Punjab*.
60. *Zafarnama,* lines 19-41.
61. *Ibid.*
62. *Ibid.*; Hari Ram Gupta: *History of the Gurus*, p. 208, Manohar, Delhi.
63. Sukha Singh: *Gur Bilas Padshahi Dasvin*, Bhagat Lakshman Singh, *Sikh Martyrs*, p. 67; Macauliffe: *op. cit.*, Vol. V, p. 190.
64. *Guru Gobind Singh Marg*, edited by Dr. Fauja Singh, p. 44, Bhasha Vibhag, Punjab. According to Dr. Hari Ram Gupta there were two Gujjars, Ramzu and Kalu, who recognised the Guru.

65. Duggal, Devinder Singh: *Fateh Nama.*
66. That the Guru left Machhiwara in the guise of Uch-Da-Pir was not mentioned by *Sri Gur Sobha. Mehma Parkash* by Kirpal Singh (1798 Bk= 1731 C.E.); and *Bansavli Nama* by Kesar Singh Chhibber (1836 Bk= 1779 C.E.). The Uch-Da-Pir was first mentioned in *Gur Bilas* by Sukha Singh.
67. *Zafar Nama*, 44th stanza.
68. Ishar Singh Nara: *Safar Nama, Zafar Nama*, pp. 227, 228; *Guru Gobind Singh Marg*, Bhasha Vibhag, p. 40; Macauliffe, *op. cit.*, V, p. 193.
69. M.A. Macauliffe writes: "It is a general belief among the Sikhs that they were bricked into a wall and suffered to die in that position. The authors of *Suraj Parkash* and the *Gur Bilas* both state that the children were put to death in the order of their ages by the sword of a Ghalzai executor or Sainapat merely states that Zorawar gave a fitting reply which put the Nawab and his courtiers into extreme uneasiness and that the two boys chose the path of martyrdom for the sake of religion as their grandfather had done" (*Gur Sobha*, XI), see also Irvine, *Later Mughals*, Vol. 2, p. 88.
70. Hakim Ram Kishan: *Janam Sakhi Guru Gobind Singh*, p. 145.
71. Ishar Singh Nara: *op. cit.*, p. 236; Giani Gian Singh, *Twarikh Guru Khalsa.*
72. Avtar Singh: *Sakhi Pothi*, translated, printed and edited, pp. 60-61; 62-63; 112-13; Partap Singh Mehta ed. *Ibid.*, pp. 159-60.
73. *Zafar Nama*, Stanzas 53, 54, 56.
74. Translation by Macauliffe.
75. *Zafar Nama*, Stanza 44.
76. *Ibid.*, 72.
77. *Ibid.*, 71.
78. *Ibid.*, 58.
79. *Ibid.*, 52.
80. Giani Gian Singh: *Sri Guru Panth Parkash*, pp. 291-92.
81. The scholars have doubted the veracity of the tradition on the ground that Guru could not have uttered such words because he bore no enmity against the Muslims. Certainly, the Guru did not bear enmity against Muslims or Islam, but it is also not improbable that he would not wish the end of Turko-Pathan rule which was tyranous.
82. Koer Singh: *Gur Bilas Patshahi* X, p. 230.
83. Mohammad Latif: *History of the Punjab*, p. 266.
84. *Sri Gur Sobha*, edited by Shamsher Singh Ashok, p. 96; Sukhdial Singh: *Guru Gobind Singh, Ik Sarvekhan*, p. 92. According to a tradition, the owner of this place was Khidrana.
85. (1) Bhag Singh Jhubalia; (2) Dilbag Singh; (3) Gharbara Singh (Kandhara Singh); (4) Darbara Singh; (5) Ganda Singh (Ganga Singh); (6) Raj Singh Khairpuria; (7) Mahan Singh Khairpuria; (8) Sital Singh; (9) Sunder Singh

Jhallian; (10) Kirpal Singh; (11) Dayal Singh; (12) Nihal Singh; (13) Suhel Singh; (14) Kushal Singh; (15) Chamba Singh; (16) Sumir Singh; (17) Sarja Singh; (18) Garja Singh; (19) Boora Singh; (20) Sultan Singh Patti; (21) Mallan Singh; (22) Sobha Singh; (23) Joga Singh; (24) Hari Singh; (25) Karam Singh; (26) Dharam Singh; (27) Kala Singh (Kalla Singh); (28) Sant Singh; (29) Kirat Singh (Kehaj Singh); (30) Gulab Singh; (31) Jadho Singh; (32) Janga Singh (Sanga Singh); (33) Bhanga Singh; (34) Dhanna Singh; (35) Bhola Singh (Bhalla Singh); (36) Malla Singh; (37) Mann Singh; (38) Lachhman Singh; (39) Sadhu Singh; (40) Maiya Singh (Majja Singh).

86. Batra, Colonel Rai: *Leadership In Its Finest Mould: Guru Gobind Singh*, p. 58, SGPC, 1979.

87. Most of the troops at Khidrana were peasants and artisans.

88. L.S. Tandon: *The Sikh Review*, October, 1971, pp. 26-27.

14

DAMDAMA PERIOD

From Muktsar, the Guru moved to Rupana, Bhander, Gurusar and Thehri, Bambiha, Rohila and Jungiana, and Bhai Ka Kot which had been founded by Bhai Bhagtu. From there, he moved on to Chhatiana where Brars who had fought for him demanded the arrears of their pay under threat of blocking his onward march. But by God's Grace, it so happened that a devoted Sikh from the neighbouring area brought enough money about the same time which enabled the Guru to pay off all the arrears. The leader of the Brars Chaudhri Dana was extremely sorry for the insolence and impudence of his people and refused to get any payment for himself.

His act of self-abnegation greatly impressed the Guru who on his request immediately agreed to visit his native place, Mehma Swai. The journey lay through Ablu a place founded by his uncle, Dana. Reaching Mehma Swai, the Guru encamped at the place now called Lakhisar and from there made a visit to Dana's home and several other places around. After a few days at Lakhisar, the Guru decided to go to Talwandi Sabo at the request of Chaudhri Dalla. He took the same old route and once again passing through Chhatiana, Kot Sahib Chand and Kot Bhai arrived at Giddarbaha and then paying short visits to Rohilla, Jangiana, Bambiha, Bajak, Kaljhirani, Jassi Bagwali, Pakka Kalan and Chak Hira Singh reached Talwandi Sabo—renamed Damdama—a place of calm and tranquillity.

The place appealed to the Guru so much that he assumed a permanent residence there. The Guru reached here on January 17, 1706 and stayed up to October 30, 1706.[1] At this place Mata Sundri and Mata Sahib Kaur with Bhai Mani Singh came from Delhi. After obeisance and greetings Mata Sundri said: "Me Lord! Where are my sons? Where have they been left?" The Guru, ever equivable, consoled her and remarked, "The four sons have been offered as a sacrifice over the heads of these sons. What does it matter if we have lost four sons, while thousands like them are alive and are in thine lap and mine."

These words of the Guru had their instant effect. The mother's sadness vanished and new realisation dawned on her. Now she was altogether changed; she realised that death in the cause of righteousness is in fact a rejoicing in the *Hukam* of God.

The period at Damdama was put to best possible use by the Guru. The Guru utilised the time in laying abiding foundations of Sikhism in the Malwa tract. Many old and hereditary Sikhs were given Pahul and brought more thoroughly into the Khalsa. Dalla, the Chaudhri of Talwandi Sabo, Tiloka, the ancestor of the Nabha State and Rama, the ancestor of Patiala State, were outstanding examples. Besides, new converts were also made in large numbers. According to Trumpp their number swelled to one lakh twenty thousand.[2]

Talwandi Saboke attracted large crowds from far and near and presented the spectacle of a new Anandpur. The Sikh devotees and others who came to assemble here have been estimated at more than ten times the number of the people at Anandpur.[3] The Guru made a number of trips to important places. In one trip he visited Bhagi Bhander, 3 *Kos* north of Talwandi Sabo, Kot Shamir, 3 *Kos* further north and Chak Bhai Ke, about 10 *Kos* from Talwandi Sabo to the north. At the last named place, the Guru was given a warm reception by Rai Singh, grandson of Bhai Bhagtu. On another occasion, he went to Bathinda city and stayed there for seven days. While coming back to Talwandi, the Guru visited Mahima and Bhakri, both of them situated to the north of Bathinda. On some other occasion, he visited Tala Pind about 10 *Kos* to the south. At Kewal, Chaudhris, Rama and Tiloka waited upon him.

Guru Gobind Singh was equally awake to the spiritual needs of the people living at far off places. To this purpose, the Guru appointed preachers as for instance Bhai Pheru,[4] Sant Punjab Singh[5] and Rocha[6] after having been baptised at Bathinda were appointed to disseminate Sikhism in the areas such as Pothohar, Kashmir, district of Hazara and Muzaffarabad. They and their successors strove hard to awaken the people to the Khalsa way of life. All available records vouch the veracity of this fact. The Guru also made efforts to organise preaching work in Sind and Rajasthan. Bhai Kanhayya and his associates did wonderful work in Sind, presently a province in Pakistan.

Along with his work of administrating *Pahul* to the Sikhs the Guru spared no pains to transform the little culture which had gripped the minds of the people. It was exactly because of this that the Guru dwelt at length in his discourses to various *Sangats* on the futility of totems, esoteric practices, caste-distinctions as well as caste considerations, superstitions, grave-worship and many other prejudices. The Guru did all this to persuade the people to link themselves at mental level with better cultural roots.

To make the preaching effective and to keep it on the right track, it was found essential that a cadre should be raised to do the job and this thing necessitated the correct interpretation of the compositions enshrined in *Guru Granth Sahib*. The Guru interpreted the *Shabads* himself and asked some of his devoted disciples to understand its true meaning and import. According to Baisakha Singh,[7] Sixty persons acquired proficiency in the subjects, the most important of whom was Bhai Mani Singh. Besides this, the Guru created two Orders, one of the Nirmalas and the other of the Gianies. No doubt, the Guru, while at Paonta, sent eleven members to Benaras to learn Sanskrit and acquire knowledge in Hindu Philosophical systems and they were named '*Nirmal*—Pure; yet the order was set afloat at Talwandi Saboke. The purpose was to interpret

Indian religious thought and history in terms of basic tenets of Sikhism.

The Order of the Gianies also came into being under the direct inspiration of the Guru and that too at Talwandi Saboke. The underlying object was to raise a group of persons competent enough to interpret *Gurbani* rightly. Guru Gobind Singh interpreted the verses enshrined in *Adi Granth* and took steps so that a number of persons might acquire proficiency to do the same. Bhai Mani Singh was the most prominent person who received this training from the Guru. He laid the foundation of the order of Gianies. This class later on did a lot to ensure correct exposition of the Sikh scriptures as it was passed on to its head by the Guru himself. The two chief headquarters of his Order have been at Damdama and at Amritsar.

Another important and abiding contributions of the Guru during this period was to prepare afresh final recension of *Adi Granth*.[8] According to Giani Gian Singh, Mani Singh was appointed amanuensis. Everyday two watches of time were fixed for the purpose of preparing the Scripture. As the Guru dictated, so Bhai Mani Singh recorded. The project was completed in several months. A new volume of the original *Guru Granth* was prepared in this way. This is how that volume came to be known as *Damdami Bir*—Damdama Recension.[9]

The averment of certain scholars that the Granth was named so, because it was originally written at Talwandi Sabo, also known as Damdama is not correct.

Prior to Guru Gobind Singh, three recensions had gained currency and prevalence: Kartarpur Recension, Banno Recension and Lahore Recension. Kartarpur Recension was original and authentic as it was got written by Guru Arjan Dev in 1604. But because of certain extraneous influences and certain vested interests, Banno's Recension and Lahore Recension were prepared and each of them was passed on as the original. In Lahore recension the *Dhunis* which had been specified to be used while singing Vars in Kartarpur Recension were deleted because presumably its framers did not wish the Sikhs to be aroused under the impact of *Dhuni*-based Vars in view of the Mughal government's animosity towards the Sikhs.

Examination of the manuscript of the Lahore tradition has revealed that a significant number of them originated in the Kiratpur area during the period of Guru Har Rai (1644-1661 C.E.). This tradition continued to be popular in some section of the Panth right up to the beginning of the nineteenth century. The solitary and the only copy of the Lahore tradition that was written in the early nineteenth century is held at the British library in London.[10] This contains a solitary couplet attributed to Guru Har Rai. It comes after the Mundavani and as follows:

> Ik uṅkār gur parsād
>
> Slok Mohalla 7 Sri Har Rai jī da bolnā
>
> Jin kau satgurū daiyā kare tin rakh Charni laie
>
> Nanak tis balhārne Jin gurū dithā jai //[11]

The introductory formula in the beginning of this couplet (the voice of Sri Guru Har Rai) clearly shows that the Lahore Recension was quite different from the Kartarpur Recension and hence could not claim authenticity, originality and validity.

Likewise Banno Recension was also passed on as authentic, while it was not at all so. Firstly it contained spurious material, as for instance, Gosht Maler Nal, and Ratan Mala, a composition of 25 stanzas in Ram Kali. The alluded to apocryphal Sloks of Guru Nanak under both the headings have themes which have nothing to do with Sikh ideology. The first set of Sloks under the heading Gosht Maler Nal reflect discussions with a Muslim audience about creation while the stanzas of Ratan Mala give exposition of Nath Yoga technique which obviously cannot be the work of Guru Nanak.

Along with Lahore versions and Banno version, Kartarpur version was also prevalent. But different recensions had created a lot of confusion whose persistence was sure to provide pretexts for different vested interests to organise dissent or schism.

Guru Gobind Singh soon after the assumption of guruship took steps to set at rest any controversy or confusion caused or likely to be caused by vested interests including the Mughal government. He made an attempt to standardise the text of *Adi Granth* and thus correct the problem of the circulation of unauthentic Recensions. Although he approached Dhir Mal's descendants at Kartarpur to obtain the *Adi Bir*, he did not succeed in persuading them to part with the same. A number of copies of the Kartarpur text, however, were available at that time along with two other versions of *Adi Granth*. It was these he used to prepare the authorised and authentic version of *Adi Granth* at a resting place (Damdama) in Anandpur in the last quarter of the seventeenth century. He also included in it the *Bani* of Guru Tegh Bahadur as well as his own two lines (according to Trilochan Singh in his book *Hymns of Guru Tegh Bahadur*).

This Recension got lost or drowned in the flooded Sirsa rivulet when the Guru had to evacuate Anandgarh under unfavourable circumstances. Now at Talwandi Sabo, also called Damdama, the Guru got the authorised form re-prepared. The factors providing motivations to the Guru were the same, generally speaking, as for instance, to uphold the integrity of Guru *Bani*, to block the prevalence of spurious compositions of the Guru, to deprive schismatic groups to find their legitimacy in scriptural differences.

There was another factor that seemed to have had impact deeper than any other factor at this point of time. Since the emergence of *Adi Granth*, the Gurus had been emphasising that this was the embodiment of the 'Word' which God Himself, out of His grace, bestowed upon Guru Nanak and which each Guru passed on to his successor, thereby raising the person of each Guru to status of Guru. This implies that even the Guru was Guru because Word was enshrined in him. Various verses of Gurus very clearly vouch that Word is Guru.[12]

On account of this comprehension, the *Adi Granth* was without any doubt the Guru. The enlightened Sikhs regarded *Adi Granth* as such but this idea/belief had not yet been institutionalised formally and consequently many Sikhs were still in the grip of confusion. Hence the dire need of preparing authorised version of *Adi Granth*. In this connection, we must draw our attention to the hidden but nefarious designs of Dhir Mal's descendants, which also went a long way to motivate the Guru prepare the final form of *Adi Granth*. Finding that the Recension prepared at Damdama, at Anandpur had been lost during the turmoil raged after the evacuation of Anandgarh, they reckoned that now, because of strains and stresses besetting the Guru's future career, it would not be possible for him to prepare another Recension, and in that case it would be easier for them to lay their claim to Guruship because Kartarpur Recension, the authentic one, was with them. It was against this backdrop that the Guru sent his request through his special emissary to Dhir Mal to lend Kartarpur Recension, but he refused point blank to part with the same.

The Guru now decided to prepare the authorised version afresh and then to institutionalise it. Already on the momentous Baisakhi of 29th March, 1699, he had merged his physical personality in the Khalsa, thereby exalting the Khalsa equal to the Guru authorising it to operate in the world as per light of the Word.

Having raised Khalsa equal to the Guru to work in the world, it was only logical to institutionalise *Guru Granth Sahib* the embodiment of 'Word as the Guru Eternal'. And to do so it was imperative that the authorised version of *Adi Granth* could be prepared. The Guru, therefore, did the needful and installed it at Damdama (Talwandi Sabo). Bhai Mani Singh was asked to start a continuous reading of the sacred Book. The commencement hymn received by him is recorded in the *Guru Kian Sakhian*.[13] This was the Guru Arjan Dev's *Shabad* in measure Todi:

> "To Thy protection have I found my Lord
> Give me the gift of Thy name, of Thy praise
> So in harmony may I dwell,
> Easing the unease of mind.
> At Thy door have I at last thrown myself
> No other refuge do I know

Rescue this worthless one, O Lord,
Bring me not to account,
By this concession alone could I be saved
By Thy support are all sustained
Slave Nanak follows in the
footsteps of holy saints,
Liberate me, O Lord, here and now."

The recitation was concluded on the third day. Later *Karah Prasad* was distributed.

According to Ishar Singh Nahra,[14] the author of *Safar Nama* and *Zafar Nama*, the Guru dictated two copies, one to Bhai Mani Singh and the other to Bhai Gurdas (different from Bhai Gurdas). One was kept at Damdama Sahib (Talwandi Sabo Ki) and the other at Takht Sri Sach Khand Hazur Sahib. The finalisation of *Adi Granth* was celebrated with appropriate ceremony and thanks-givings. The Guru cast the ink and reeds used in transcribing into the pool close to the tent under which the work had been completed and uttered that Damdama would be 'Kashi of the Sikhs' and become famous as a seat of learning. Many, he foretold, would study here and become learned.

The Guru collected a galaxy of scholars, poets and men of parts at the place. Once again, literature began to be created to inspire the people to be awake to new realities. Literary meets were arranged to bring into focus the process of resurgence. Arrangements were also made to impart education to the people. Sukha Singh, the author of *Guru Bilas Padshahi Dasvin*, says that in addition to the extension of patronage to scholars of different disciplines, he encouraged the people to study at the *Ashram*. The tradition connected with *Likhan Sar* testifies to the ardent desire of the Guru to educate the masses of this area. It will not be wide of the mark that the Guru was doing all this under the conviction that literature being produced under Sikh inspiration would help the people to regain elan vital, so essential for any society to move further on the road to integrated progress. It is against this background that the Guru aspired to see 'Talwandi Saboo Ki' as a 'New Kashi' to symbolise aspirations of the new generation.

Side by side the above activities, the Guru continued to give military training to his followers and succeeded in rallying round himself a considerable number of armed disciples ever ready to lay down their lives for the ideals of the Khalsa without any desire of any pecuniary advantage. According to Dr. I.B. Bannerjee the Guru's strength seems to have increased to a great extent as besides regular followers he had also taken some Dogars and Brars in his service.[15] Koer Singh, the author of *Guru Bilas Padshahi 10*, also testifies to this fact. According to him, "everyday the Guru would distribute gold and silver coins and countless soldiers were attached to the Guru".[16]

Wazir Khan, the Subedar of Sirhind Sarkar, was all out in his efforts to snuff out the Khalsa movement and to arrest or kill the Guru. This attitude is clearly manifest in his two messages to Chaudhri Dalla. The gist of the messages was that Dalla should arrest the Guru, or else his territory would be plundered and he be punished severely. Dalla's reply was that of a person surcharged with the mission of translating the Khalsa ideals into reality. He said, "I will by no means have the Guru arrested to please thee. Nay, I will defend him with my life." Zabardast Khan, the Viceroy of Lahore was also averse to the Sikh cause. He never hesitated to plunder a party of Sikhs bound for making offerings to the Guru.

In the face of this attitude of the Mughal officials of Lahore province and of Sirhind Sarkar, the Guru intensified his military activities. He repeatedly made exhortations to the Sikhs to bear arms and diligently practise their use. The Guru said, "Now that the time had altered and the Sikhs were obliged to defend themselves. He had established Khalsa and whosoever desired to abide in it should not fear the clash of arms, but be ever ready for the combat and the defence of his faith." At the same time the realisation of Nām was still the chief object of the Sikh adoration.

Meanwhile, the Guru received tidings of Imperial emissaries deputed to convey Aurangzeb's willingness for a personal meeting with the Guru. Guru Gobind Singh's letter to Aurangzeb appears to have produced the desired effect. In *Ahkam-i-Alamgiri*, a collection of orders of Aurangzeb by

Inayat Ullah Khan Ismi (d. 1725), who served as Aurangzeb's secretary, there are four documents containing *farmans* relating to the Sikhs which occur in I.O.M.S. 3387, ff 204ab, 204b-205a, 243b and 245a-b. In the last two documents, the receipt of letter of Guru Gobind Singh has been acknowledged. Out of these two, the first one is addressed to Munim Khan, the deputy Governor of Lahore and the other to Wazir Khan, the Subedar of Sirhind Sarkar. These documents also reveal that Mohammed Beg, a mace bearer and Shaikh Yar Muhammad, a Mansabdar, were designated to carry the *farmans* (Orders) to be delivered to Munim Khan and Wazir Khan. The *farman* addressed to Munim Khan carried the instructions to him that he should ensure the safety and security of the Guru and depute some trustworthy person possessed of tact and vigilance to bring him to Aurangzeb's presence along with the mace bearer and Mansabdar. In the *farman* addressed to Wazir Khan, in addition to reference to the *farman* issued to Munim Khan, it was enjoined upon Wazir Khan that he would provide to the Guru escort to facilitate his movement in his jurisdiction. He was also asked to provide the expenses of the Guru's Journey in case he expressed the need. In case the Guru expressed some fears or doubts, he should be reassured. If he needed expenses for the journey, those should be given in accordance with his requirements (Document IV). Mace bearer and Mansabdar started their journey towards the north. Daya Singh and Dharam Singh were also with them.

That Aurangzeb was anxious to meet Guru Gobind Singh is evident from these documents, although it is not clear, why? Possibly, having perused Zafarnama, a new awareness dawned on him under whose impact he invited the Guru to find out enduring solution to the Sikh problem. The Guru, in his turn, also welcomed the opportunity and planned to move to Ahmednagar where Aurangzeb had been residing. The Guru left Talwandi on October 10, 1707 even before Daya Singh and Dharam Singh reached Talwandi Sabo Ki.

The tremendous success of the Guru in Bathinda area despite heavy odds was due to several causes. Among them the greatest importance may be attached to the Guru's decision to leave the hills and to come into the interior of the area which was the real base of his strength. Anandpur, notwithstanding its strong fortification, suffered from inherent weakness, for the population around, consisting mostly of the conservative and caste-ridden Rajputs, was hostile to the Sikhs and day in and day out caused harassment to them. On the other hand, when the Guru entered the Punjab plains, the people around were helpful and co-operative and were willing to rally under his banner, should the call come from him. This made all the difference. Closely allied to that was the second factor, the impact left by the previous Gurus on the people of these areas. The 6th, 7th and 9th Gurus had, one after the other, conducted extensive tours across this area and left a deep imprint on the minds of the people. Guru Gobind Singh's route through this area was dotted with the places which had already been visited by his predecessors, as for instance, Bur Majra, Ghulal, Lall Kalan, Katana, Bassian, Chakkar, Takhtupura, Patti Hira Singh, Bhagta Bhai Ka and Lambhawali, had all been sanctified by Sikh Gurus' visits previously. The third important factor was the valuable support provided by some of the influential Zamindars, prominent among them being Nihang Khan, Rai Kalla, Chaudhri Kapura, Chaudhri Dalla, Chaudhri Rama and Chaudhri Taloka. At that time the Mughal Empire was facing a serious agrarian crisis[17] as a result of which Zamindars were asserting themselves. The next important factor was the difficult terrain of the Jungle Desh. Last but not the least was the Guru's charismatic personality which could turn adversity into a fortune and discomfiture into a triumph. But for his powerful and towering personality, even the best of circumstances would have yielded no fruit.

NOTES AND REFERENCES

1. Gian Singh puts this period at 9 months and nine days. Another sources declares it 9 Months, 9 Days, 9 Pahars and 9 Gharis. C.F. *Punjab States Gazetteers*; XVII A, 1904, p. 75.
2. Trumpp: *Adi Granth*, p. XCII.
3. Dr. Fauja Singh: *Guru Gobind Singh Marg*, p. 217.
4. Baba Pheru Singh: received Pahul on the Baisakhi of 1699; preached Sikh religion in Kashmir and other hill areas around.

5. Punjab Singh: Birth 1672 at Nand Har Shahar, father's name Hari Ram Shah, a great scholar of Persian and Sanskrit, member of the band of preachers of Pheru Singh, received *Pahul* from Guru Gobind Singh at Damdama, nominated successor to Pheru Singh after his death in 1736. Preached in the areas of the Muzaffarbad, Poonch and Srinagar.
6. Rocha Singh: Birth in 1688 in village Kausa (Hazara district in Pakistan); received *Pahul* from Guru Gobind Singh. Preached in Hazara district, Kashmir.
7. Baisakha Singh: *Malwa Da Itihas*.
8. Some scholars aver that the Guru reproduced the *Adi Granth* from memory and completed it by adding hymns composed by his father that the hymns of ninth Guru were incorporated here is contradicted by the fact that there is a copy of Holy Granth at Patna bearing the date 1748 Bk (1691 C.E.), containing the hymns of Guru Teg Bahadur in their proper places. There is another such copy found at Dacca which was written in C.E. 1675, sixteen years earlier than 1691 C.E. 1675, in the first year of Guru Gobind Singh's accession.
9. Giani Kirpal Singh: *Sri Gur Panth Parkash*, Amritsar: Manmohan Singh Brar (1973), pp. 1678, 80.
10. British Library, 2748.
11. By the grace of the Eternal one, the true Guru slok Mahalla 7, *The Voice of Sri Guru Har Rai.* Those on whom the true Guru bestows his benevolence, they are kept in his refuge. I am devoted to those, Nanak, who go to have a glimpse of the Guru.
12. Guru Ram Das: *Guru Granth Sahib Rag Nat Narayan,* p. 982; *Rag Kanara,* p. 1310.
13. Sarup Singh Kaushish: *op. cit.*
14. Ishar Singh Nara: *Zafar Nama Safar Nama*, p. 307.
15. Bannerjee, I.B.: *op. cit.*, II, p. 138.
16. Koer Singh: *Everyday the Guru distributes gold and silver coins*, p. 307.
17. Irfan Habib: *Agrarian System in India*, Asia Publishing House, Delhi.

15

THROUGH RAJASTHAN, AGRA TO NANDER

The Guru left Damdama (Talwandi Sabo) for the Deccan on Kartik Sudi 5, 1763 Vikrami (October 30, 1760 C.E.). For some time he waited for Daya Singh's return at Talwandi Sabo whom he had sent to Aurangzeb at Ahmednagar to deliver his letter 'Zafar Nama' but he did not receive any communication from him or Dharam Singh. He, however, got wind that Daya Singh had to face a lot of difficulties caused by the obstructionist tactics of Subedar Wazir Khan's hired persons who were specially deputed to scuttle the attempts of Daya Singh to meet the Emperor to deliver the letter personally. The Subedar did so because he thought that if the Guru's letter and Daya Singh dialogue with the Emperor succeeded in arousing the moral conscience of the Emperor, a lot of harm was likely to accrue to him.

The Guru also got inkling that the letter had been delivered and its contents had moved the Emperor.

The Guru sensing change in the mood of Aurangzeb decided to move towards the Deccan even before Daya Singh could reach Damdama. The most important factor that impelled the Guru to take this decision was the fast failing health of the Emperor who was about ninety-one in 1706 and had been overtaken by illness. The Guru deemed it appropriate to go to Deccan himself and settle the affairs with the Emperor for which purpose Daya Singh had been sent with the letter.[1]

The exact number of those who accompanied the Guru is not known, yet, on the basis of accounts available to us, it is not difficult to surmise that the number was quite large. Among them, a few notables were Man Singh, Ram Singh and Fateh Singh of Bhagtu Family, Dharam Singh and Param Singh, the sons of Bhai Rupa. Rai Dalla also accompanied the Guru. As the Guru proceeded further, some of them went back to their homes, but even then the hard core was quite large and included Mani Singh, Bhupat Singh from Amritsar, Sodhi Kanwal Nain from Dhilwan, Udey Karan, Gurdas Singh from Sadhora, Ram Singh and Tilok Singh from Phul, Godaria Singh from Bhucho, Dan Singh with his son from Ablu, Ram Kaur from Ramdas.[2]

En route to Deccan, the first halt of Guru Gobind Singh was at village Kewal.[3] Then the Guru sojourned at village Jharori, wherefrom he proceeded to village Jhanda.[4] When the night fell, Fateh Singh and his brother Ram Singh left the Guru's camp. Rai Dalla placed his offerings comprising two gold bangles and one double-edged sword and slipped out of the Guru's camp and betook himself to his native place. These people did so because they could not shed their attachment with their people. Some others left the Guru fearing the difficulties of the arduous journey.

The Guru expressed surprise at the doings of Dalla particularly because he wished him to prepare himself for certain other jobs. When at dawn, the Guru asked where Dalla was, someone from amongst this followers told "There is no Dalla-Malla, there is only Allah and the Guru; the theme being that at that point of time, the Guru was all alone, determined to carry out his mission in spite of high risks involved in the process.

The Guru remained calm and continued to march towards his destination.

The Guru reached Sirsa[5] now in the state of Haryana which was a small town then. People expressed their regards for the Guru by serving him and his Sikhs. In the course of his stay, he was told that one goldsmith named Gulab Singh had been imprisoned in an underground cell by Nabi Bakhsh, the Chaudhri of the village, Khural. The reason was that he did not honour the order of the Chaudhri to offer his daughter to cater to his carnal fits. The Guru mounted his steed and taking five Sikhs with him marched to the place. He freed Gulab Singh and chided the Chaudhri who out of fear prostrated at the Guru's feet. The Guru forgave him and instructed him to stop tyrannising the people. The Guru having visited neighbouring places such as Gobindpur, came back to Sirsa. After this the Guru set out in the direction of Rajasthan en route to Ahmadnagar where the Emperor was encamped.

After passing through Haripur (Bad Tirath) the Guru reached Nauhar.[6] Here the people were the votaries of Jainism. Instead of practising the high ethical principles of their religion, their whole emphasis lay upon rejection of non-vegetarianism, which they thought was the only way to Bliss and social reconstruction. The Guru exposed the hollowness of their thinking and tried to make them understand the theory and practice and the ultimaticity of 'Non-violence'. Vegetarianism or non-vegetarianism are irrelevant to the process of building a good society as well as good individuals.

From Nauhar, the Guru proceeded to village Bhadra[7], where he was affectionately received by a Rajput family. The next halt of the Guru was at village Sahewa. During the course of travels, Dharam Singh and Param Singh carried the weapons and clothes of the Guru. They had taken a resolve to prepare a fresh cot for the Guru at his every halt.

Thencefrom the Guru proceeded to Bahaduran. There he gave horses, one each to Dharam Singh and Param Singh. Thereafter the Guru reached Sahena. From there he proceeded onwards to Madhu Singhnai. Bhai Ram Singh, a scion of Bhai Bhaktu, lost heart and beat a hasty retreat.

After this the Guru reached Pushkar Raj[8], a place of pilgrimage sacred to Brahma. The place earlier had been made hallowed by Guru Nanak. Pandit Chetan Misar who was the in-charge of the place fell at the Guru's feet and received *Pahul* to join the Khalsa fellowship.

After this, he Guru reached Naraina[9] also known as Dadudwara where the saint Dadu had lived. His shrine, by this time, had come under the charge of Mahant Jait Ram. One day the Guru saluted the sepulchre of Dadu by lifting an arrow to his head. The Khalsa took exception to it and demanded a *Tankhah* (religious punishment). One of them, Man Singh quoted the Guru's own verse *Gor Marhi Mat Bhūl Nā Mane* (worship not even by mistake cemeteries). The Guru at once confessed guilt of religious misconduct and paid a sum of Rs. 125/- part of which was spent on *Guru Ka Langar* and the rest on the purchase of a canopy to cover the place where food was served.

In the course of conversation, the Mahant raised certain pertinent questions. Was the living-style the Guru had adopted appropriate especially when according to Dadu, attachment with material world was futile and in no way helpful in the process of spiritual ascent? Was it justified to bear weapons? The Guru replied that materiality and spirituality are not exclusive to each other, rather they form the parts of the same whole. Both are to be developed if the individuals and world are to march ahead. God, man and the world are related to each other organically and certainly not antagonistically. God as the soul creator permeates everything, seen and unseen and hence material things are not to be discarded or looked down upon, rather utilised and harnessed properly. Resort to weapons is legitimate, if it is done to eliminate evil in emulation of God as a 'smasher of the wicked'. According to Dr. Hari Ram Gupta 'while sojourning at Naraina, the Guru asked the Mahant that he could secure help from the Rajput princes to eliminate the Mughal government. The Mahant replied that it was not possible'. There seems to be no plausibility in the statement of learned historian, for the Mahant being a recluse and indifferent to world affairs, had no worthwhile contacts with the Rajput princes. However, the Guru while travelling through Rajasthan, must have been disappointed at the political predilections of the Rajput princes. Except the Raja of Marwar, all other important princes such as Jai Singh of Mewar,

Mokam Singh of Nagaor, Jai Singh of Jaipur, were openly on the side of Aurangzeb.

From Naraina, the Guru reached Kalot via Lali and Maghroda. Bhai Daya Singh and Dharam Singh on way back from Deccan met the Guru and related to him their experiences in the Deccan. The Emperor's Gurj-Bardar and Mansabdar had gone ahead towards Delhi with the royal *farman* for Munim Khan while Daya Singh and Dharam Singh came to the Guru. After this, the Guru reached Bhagaur, the headquarter of a Parganah in the erstwhile Udaipur State about 70 miles north-east of Udaipur city. Here he heard the news of the death of Aurangzeb at Ahmednagar on February 20, 1707. The Guru decided to stop moving further towards the south. Aurangzeb being no more, march towards the South did not serve any purpose as now the Guru would not be able to build bridges of understanding between the Sikhs and the Mughal government nor could he arrange that the guilty Subedar Wazir Khan, was appropriately punished. He, therefore, decided to wait and watch and turn to Delhi where Revered Sundri and Sahib Kaur were living.

The war of succession had begun among the late emperor's sons. Prince Muazzam (Bahadur Shah) was in Jamraud, a few miles away from Peshawar when his father died. Azam Shah (Tara Azam) who was in Deccan with his father at the time of his death assumed command of the Imperial army and proclaimed himself as the next Emperor.

Bahadur Shah too marched from Jamraud to lay his claim to the throne. He left Jamraud in the last week of March, 1707, and reached Peshawar on the last day of the month. His trusted governor at Lahore, Munim Khan, had kept the troops in readiness for the long awaited war of succession and welcomed Muazzam who was formally declared Emperor Bahadur Shah before he entered Lahore. Collecting men and money from the officials of the Mughal government in that part of the empire, he reached Delhi in the end of May. Wazir Khan, the Faujdar of Sirhind, had contributed eight lakhs. Mohammad Muazzam left Delhi in the first week of June, took possession of treasures at Agra and moved toward

Dholpur to oppose Azam Shah, his rival claimant to the throne, who along with a huge army and his very intelligent and valorous son, Bidar Bakhat, was fast marching to this place.

On the way to Delhi, Muazzam, who had first hand knowledge of the Guru's valour and his influence in the Punjab, especially among the Sikhs, thought it appropriate to seek Guru's help, partly to avoid any Sikh trouble while he was busy in a civil war and partly to use the Sikhs in his cause. The Guru's contemporary Sainapat in *Sri Guru Sobha* says that the Guru was approached for help by Muazzam's emissaries. William Irvine writes in this connection "It seems certain that Gobind Singh met Bahadur Shah at some point when the prince was on his march down the country from Lahore to Agra to contest the throne with his brother Azam Shah."[10] Bhai Jodh Singh[11], in his work *Kalghi Dhar Hulas* says that the Prince Muazzam deputed Nand Lal to persuade the Guru to join with his Sikhs promising at the same time on behalf of Bahadur Shah that he would look into and redress any grievance, the Guru might have against his house. The Guru read the letter and also listened to the pleadings of Bhai Nand Lal. Though the Guru was not sure of Bahadur Shah keeping his word once victory was his, yet he decided to offer help to him.

While reaching this decision, the Guru seemed to have been actuated by certain considerations. First, Bahadur Shah was a generous, munificent and extremely good-natured prince. His tolerance and amiability were in great contrast to the bigotry and hypocrisy of his predecessor, Aurangzeb. The Guru had himself seen that in spite of his father's instructions, he had refused to molest the Guru in 1695. The Guru, therefore, thought that if he won the battle of succession, he would be more amenable to liberal influences, especially his own. Secondly, as per law of primogeniture, which was prevalent among the Mughal rulers, Bahadur Shah being the eldest of the three living brothers (Muazzam, Azam Shah and Kam Bux) had a legitimate right to the throne of his father. Thirdly, Nand Lal held out full assurance on behalf of the Prince. The

Guru thought in terms of influencing Bahadur Shah in the same way as he had envisaged a possible change of heart in the case of late Emperor, Aurangzeb.

According to the author of the book *Mulakat Da Parsang*[12], Bahadur Shah personally called upon the Guru at Delhi on May 20, 1707 to persuade him to assist him in his difficulty. The Guru agreed and deputed Kuldipak Singh as a Liaison Officer who remained with the Emperor upto the end of the battle of Jajau on June 8, 1707. He also decided to send two to three hundred Sikhs soldiers under the command of Dharam Singh to side with Bahadur Shah, as a token of his moral support.

The Guru at Delhi first stayed in a house lying at the back of Humayun's tomb. The site is now marked by the Gurdwara Damdama Sahib. As a token of love for the so-called low caste of Delhi on account of Bhai Jaita's valorous deeds, the Guru shifted to the colony of Shoe-makers, called Mochi Bagh. The cobblers (Mochis) served the Guru with great devotion. The Guru was so much impressed by their conduct that he changed the colony's name to Moti Bagh, the Garden of Pearls. A gurdwara stands at this place. It lies on the Ring Road now called Mahatma Gandhi Marg. When the Guru was in Delhi, a goldsmith supplicated for the boon of a son. He waited on the Guru a couple of times. One day the Guru was going to hunt in the neighbouring jungle, the goldsmith followed him along with the Sikhs. They had not gone far, when they saw a woman leaving a newly born male child in bushes. The Guru asked the goldsmith to adopt the child. Later, the child was adopted by Revered Sundri, the mother of the Khalsa who named him Ajit Singh.

The armies of Azam and Bahadur Shah clashed each other on June 8, 1707 at Jajau, situated between Agra and Dholpur. The fierce fire of joint armies of Bahadur Shah and of the Guru wrought terrible havoc in the ranks of Azam Shah and Bidar Bakht. Bidar Bakht was killed in action and immediately after, Azam also fell victim to an arrow.

Bhai Jodh Singh in *Kalghidhar Hulas* and Gian Singh in *Twarikh Guru Khalsa* hold that the Guru also reached the battlefield to assure Bahadur Shah's victory.[13] According to Jodh Singh, the Guru told the prince "Have faith, you will get victory."[14] Guru's word never goes in vain, the same author adds that the Guru pushed his horse near Azam's elephant and killed him with his arrows.[15]

Muazzam inquired whose arrow killed Azam Shah. The arrow was pulled out of Azam's dead body. It was found to be gold-tipped arrow of the Guru. After the defeat and death of Azam and his son, the Guru left for Delhi forthwith without even meeting the Emperor.

Bahadur Shah who now became the undisputed Emperor of India honoured the Sikhs who had taken part in the battle and gave each of them precious gifts. He sent Dharam Singh to Delhi with a letter expressing his gratitude to the Guru for the help which he had rendered in the battle. The emperor also invited him to Agra.

The residence of the Guru at Delhi became the focus of the Sikhs and non-Sikhs. The Guru held congregation of Sikhs twice daily. He often visited Gurdwara Sis Ganj Sahib in Chandni Chowk, where his father, Guru Tegh Bahadur, was martyred on November 11, 1675. The Guru also paid visits to the site of Gurdwara Rakab Ganj where Guru Tegh Bahadur's headless body had been cremated by Lakhi Shah Lubana by setting his house on fire. The Guru raised a gurdwara at that spot as a memorial to the supreme sacrifice of his father.

After about a month's stay at Delhi, the Guru made preparation to leave for Agra in response to the invitation of the Emperor. The Guru made appropriate arrangements for the stay of Mata Sundri at Delhi under the protection of the Sikhs. Sahib Kaur, however, importuned him to allow her to accompany him. The Guru yielded to her request, ultimately.

The Guru on the third day after his departure from Delhi arrived at Mathura and encamped at Suraj Kund on the bank of Yamuna.[16] He made a tour through Brindaban and visited all its famous places. Then he proceeded further on the road to Agra.[17] He established his camp 12 Kms from Agra and 6 Kms from Bahadur Shah's camp.

Shortly after, Khan-i-Khanan, Munim Khan the Prime Minister invited the Guru to his palace situated within a beautiful garden. The Guru along with his brave Sikh soldiers reached there. Munim Khan accorded the Guru a hearty welcome and received him with all the honour due to his position expressing, 'Guru ji' you have done a great favour to me by coming out to my palace to allow me an opportunity to have your sacred glimpse.[18] The same day the Guru came back and laid his camp nearby. On the fall of night, heavy rains poured. The next day, the Guru made a rapid survey of the area closeby and selected a garden, where he and his followers decided to stay.[19]

The life-style at the camp was that of a true Khalsa. Assemblies met twice a day where information of the Sikh creed was given. People in hordes from far and near visited the camp to receive instructions.

On July 23, 1707, Bahadur Shah invited the Guru to his court. The Guru and his Sikhs moved to the royal presence. He was accompanied by his soldiers, but at the gate of the place of the Emperor, he instructed them to stay back except one Sikh whom he took along with him to the place where the Emperor met him. The Guru was having an aigrette fixed to his turban and other weapons along with him. His face looked resplendent[20] and his personality radiant. The Emperor thanked the Guru for his help in the battle and offered valuable presents to the Guru. He distributed the presents to his Sikhs as well just as he did to his other generals. He honoured the Guru as a revered saint and requested him to continue to lend his company frequently.[21] The Guru was accompanied by two to three hundred horsemen and some more Sikhs on foot.[22] The Emperor, in token of his respect for the Guru, presented a robe of honour including a jewelled scarf, a Dhukh Dhukhi, and an aigrette worth sixty thousand rupees. The Guru did not, however, put it on his person there as it was the custom, but asked one of his Sikhs to carry it to his camp.[23] The Emperor did not mind this demeanour of the Guru, for he treated him as a holy saint and not as his servant or dependent.

According to Khazan Singh, another present of one Lakh of rupees was granted for Mata Sundri and sent to Delhi.[24]

The Guru stayed there for about five months. During this period he met the Emperor quite often, who sought solace from the Guru. The discussion often revolved around two points: religion and Sikh-Mughal relations.

What exactly transpired between the Guru and the Emperor during their meetings, we are not in a position to know; but even then circumstantial evidence and the Hukamnamas of the Guru help us to establish a few facts. The visit of the Guru first to Khan-i-Khanan, the Prime Minister, and then to the Emperor Bahadur Shah himself, had evidently a much greater significance than ordinary courtesy visits. The Guru had left the Punjab for the Deccan at the invitation of Aurangzeb for a personal interview. The only subject that could be discussed between them was the Mughal-Sikh relations—the causes of their estrangement, the ways and means of a peaceful solution of their problems and the implementation of the decisions arrived at between them. That alone again could be subject of Guru's talks with the Khan-i-Khanan and Emperor Bahadur Shah at Agra. The opportunity that had unfortunately been lost owning to the death of Aurangzeb, had presented itself under happier circumstances and interview with the Prime Minister and the Emperor had taken place in a very cordial atmosphere. Both were grateful to the Guru for his ungrudging response to their appeal for help in the struggle for the throne and were happy over the success in this context. Since no reliable details of discussions with them are available in any of the extant contemporary records, Persian or Punjabi, it cannot, therefore, be said with certainty as to what hopes were held out to the Guru by Bahadur Shah, but there is no denying the fact that the Guru was hopefully looking forward to a satisfactory conclusion of his negotiations with the Mughal Emperor and soon expected to return to Anandpur.

Regarding the Guru's objectives which the Guru had in his mind while negotiating with Bahadur Shah many illogical and flimsy conclusions have been drawn. According to M.A. Macauliffe, the Guru egged up by the spurt of revenge wanted

Wazir Khan to be sentenced to death as per Muslim law. Dr. Hari Ram Gupta[25] also opines like that and according to him, the Guru wanted Wazir Khan of Sirhind, Sucha Nand Diwan of Sirhind, Gangu Brahmin of Kheri, Jani and Mani of Morinda, Shamas Khan of Bajwara, Mukarram Khan of Jalandhar and Dilawar Khan of Lahore to be delivered to him.

Both the scholars have erred, and like a good historian, they have not cared to consider the mission of the Guru and his central tendency, nor have they based their conclusion on some reliable evidence. Harbouring revenge or taking resort to the revengeful act was in sharp contrast to the personality and mission of the Guru because revenge is an evil impulse and engenders hatred, and, secondly, it has never solved any problem—much less the problem of improving human material. From the perusal of *Zafar Nama* and other sayings of the Guru, it is almost certain that the Guru did not want anything more from Bahadur Shah than was normally required—that the unjust and the oppressors of the people be removed from office or transferred to distant places to create peaceful conditions in the country. It was fundamental to Sikh religion that punishment was no solution to reform the sinner. The Guru had brought about the change in Emperor Aurangzeb through his conduct and sacred words sent in the form of *Zafar Nama*, and now he had all hopes to change the attitude of Bahadur Shah who happily was made of nobler and sublimer stuff as compared to his father. In all likelihood, the issue of resettling at Anandpur was also broached by the Guru.

The Guru's point-of-view seemed to have a elicited affirmative response from the Emperor, but hill chiefs of Shivalik and Wazir Khan, the Faujdar of Sirhind, were not feeling comfortable at the development.

It is against the back drop of that the Guru issued instructions in the first week of October, 1707 to his Sikhs in the Punjab to join him fully armed on his arrival in Kahlur. For this, we have very reliable piece of documentary evidence in the Guru's own letter dated October 2, 1707 addressed from the neighbourhood of Agra to the Sikhs of Dhaul. Translated into English, the letter reads as follows:

From the Tenth Guru,

To the *Sangat* of Dhaul. You are my Khalsa. The Guru shall protect you. Repeat Guru Guru. With all happiness, we came to the Padshah. Dress of honour and a jewelled Dhukh Dhukhi worth sixty thousand was presented to us. With the Guru's grace the other things are also progressing (satisfactorily). In a few days, we are also coming. My instructions to the entire Khalsa *Sangat* are to remain united. When we arrive in Kahlur, the entire Khalsa should come to our presence fully armed. He who will come shall be happy...Sammat 1764[26], Kartik 1st.

The letter points to some other things, besides giving reference to the Guru's visit to Emperor Bahadur Shah, who presented to him a costly dress of honour. The other things could only be the friendly negotiations for a change in the century-old hostile attitude of the Mughals towards the Sikh Gurus. From the attitude of the Emperor during the interviews, the Guru seemed to have formed the impression that his negotiations would soon be concluded to his satisfaction, facilitating his early return to Anandpur. The only persons to be adversely affected, directly or indirectly, by the implementation of the peaceful settlement between the Emperor and the Guru were the hill Rajas of the Shivalik and Nawab Wazir Khan of Sirhind. To meet any emergency that might be created by them on his return to Anandpur in Kahlur state, the Guru asked Sikhs to join him fully armed. The irrefutable evidence of the letter also repudiates the conjecture that the Guru had left the Punjab either in despair or to arouse the Rajputs and Marathas against the Mughals. If the accidental changes in the circumstances, owing to the Prince Kam Bux's rebellion in Hyderabad, had not taken the Guru to the Deccan in company with the Emperor with whom the negotiations referred to above were then still in progress, in all probability, he would have returned to the Punjab.

From Agra to Nander

But the Guru's expectation of an early return to Anandpur, where he could pick up the old threads and continue with his mission, proved to be a wishful thinking. No doubt, the Emperor's gestures of goodwill towards the Guru were impressive, yet he was warys of agreeing to the demands of the Guru. With the issue of succession to Mughal throne not finally settled, he could ill-afford to annoy the Muslim fundamentalists' lobbies at the court by going against the interest of Wazir Khan who had the solid backing of the Naqshbandis, then led by Khalifa Saifud Din, and had contributed handsomely to the war fund of the Emperor for which he was given a stupendous raise in rank from 1500 zat 1700 sawar to 4500 zat and 4000 sawar (Akhbar-i-Mualla Dec. 1, 1707). At the same time, he could not afford to offend the Guru who had a considerable following of his devoted disciples, scattered all over the Punjab, possessed of the potential to disturb peace in the north-west. Nor could he vex the hill chiefs because they were also a potent political factor having the capacity for creating trouble. Therefore, he was sagacious enough to realise that Guru's presence near his court was preferable to his dangerous freedom in the Punjab. But simultaneously he was careful enough not to let his real calculations known to the Guru, atleast for the time being. His polite and kind demeanour towards the Guru was all the more impressive for its political, albeit negative advantage, to the new Emperor. To the Guru, he gave the impression that when the affairs of succession were settled, he would favourably consider his demands. Political conduct of the Emperor, generally speaking, portended *status quo* so far as the relations of the Mughals with non-Muslims were concerned. According to news-letter of December 7, 1707, he sent orders to the imperial kotwal of Delhi (Sarfraz Khan) to see that the Hindus should not ride in palanquins and ride on horses of Iraqi and Arab breeds. They should not visit the courts wearing emeralds in ears. They should also keep their heads shaved.[27] The realisation of *Jazia* and pilgrim tax continued as it was prevalent in the period of Aurangzeb.[28] The contemporary poet of Delhi, Mir Jafar Zatalli also condemned, although in different context, that to take up service under Shah-e-Muazzam was to lead the life of a beggar and disgrace.[29] Such conduct of the Emperor was indeed a malediction and much good could not be expected of him.

In view of all this, there was very little hope that Bahadur Shah would do something in favour of Guru.

The Guru had also smelt the rat, but still he did not break off with him. Perhaps, he was yet under the impression that after dealing with the disturbances, the Emperor would do the needful.

According to Dr. Hari Ram Gupta, 'The Guru's residence in the imperial camp was fatal mistake committed by the Guru. The entire Mughal court was anti-Hindu and anti-Sikh. The Guru was looked down upon as a rebel punishable with death. Wazir Khan was a hero for them, fit to be rewarded rather than punished. His representative was always in attendance at the court. He must have reported the matter to his master. The Guru's influence with the Emperor was looked down upon by one and all. Every courtier was alert to see that no harm came to Wazir Khan, while intrigues to harm the Guru were set afoot in right earnest.[30]

Dr. Gupta's portrayal of the scenario is sufficiently correct phenomenologically but the Guru was filled with the mission to bring about a change in the hearts of the fanaticised people and to give them a lesson in humanism as also to propel them to follow the course towards reconstruction of a society whose members were bound by the scarlet thread of love for each other, co-existing on the basis of mutual respect, equality and faith in 'Nām' permeating all things, living and non-living. The Guru had achieved some success in this direction, the proof of which lay in the admiration of a large number of Muslims including Pir Budhu Shah, Gani Khan and Nabi Khan *et al.* Even Aurangzeb, the arch-fundamentalist had to grow soft towards the Guru when he received his letter 'Zafarname' which was, in a way, an attempt to awaken divinity in Emperor. The Guru, therefore, was not discouraged, much less disappointed to work for his mission, even in the midst of hostile atmosphere. And the ray of hope there had always been, because Bahadur Shah respected and listened to him. If at the end, Bahadur Shah did not accede to the warrants of the Guru, that formed a story in itself with a moral of its own. In fact, Bahadur Shah could not extricate himself from the syndrome of Muslim fundamentalism in spite of the divinely inspired forces of humanism as symbolised by the Guru.

Nevertheless, the Guru's apostolic approach forbade him to leave Bahadur Shah in a huff.

Emperor Bahadur Shah lived at Agra in peace till November 12, 1797, when he had to go to Rajasthan as disturbances had broken out there.[31] The Emperor reached Amber (Rajasthan) on January 20, 1708. Raja Jai Singh Kachhwah had taken side of Azam Shah in the battle of Jajau and therefore had earned disfavour of the emperor. Now Bahadur Shah occupied Amber and confiscated the property and belongings of Raja Jai Singh. Then he made over the country of Amber to Bijal Singh, Jai Singh's younger brother, who had already served under Prince Muazzam when he was viceroy of Kabul.[32] After settling the affairs at Amber, Bahadur Shah advanced to Jodhpur via Ajmer. After a short sojourn at Ajmer during which he offered his prayers at the mausoleum of Khwaja Muinuddin Chisti, he proceeded towards his target Jodhpur, the capital of the State of the same name which, after the expiry of Aurangzeb, had been occupied by Ajit Singh, the posthumous son of Jaswant Singh who had been actively assisted by his faithful general and patron Durga Das.[33] The whole ethnic stock of Rathore Rajputs had rallied around Ajit Singh. After a lot of diplomatic exertions and show of strength, at long last Ajit Singh was prevailed upon to wait upon the Emperor and accept his suzerainty.[34]

The difficulty with Jodhpur being thus, to all appearance satisfactorily disposed of, the Emperor retraced his steps from Mairtha, a town nearby Jodhpur.[35]

On the 2nd April, 1708, the march was resumed in the direction of Chittor and Ujjain. On the 12th, the camp was not far from Hussainipur.

On the 14th April, 1708, Rana Amar Singh Sisodia sent a letter expressing reverence for the Emperor and an offering of twenty-seven gold coins. This gesture of the Rana assured the Emperor of the peaceful settlement of a large part of Mewar never accepting the legitimacy of the Mughal rule.

When the next day dawned, the Emperor was informed that the Rana had taken flight to the hills doubting the sincerity of the Emperor. Bahadur Shah felt much upset at the Rana's *volte-face*, but thought it politically expedient to first combat with his younger brother, Kam Bux, who had proclaimed his own sovereignty of the Mughal rule instead of acquiescing in that of Bahadur Shah.[36]

In Rajasthan, calm had been established, but it was uneasy. Sisodias, Rathores and Kachhawahs, the most important ethnic segments of Rajputs who had been smarting under the fundamentalistic rule of Aurangzeb, were in a mood to assert, and if possible, to assume independence. This type of mood was manifest when on 30th April, 1708, Bahadur Shah was at the town of Mandeshwar. Maharaja Ajit Singh, Raja Jai Singh Kachhawah and Durga Das Rathore, took to flight, throwing open challenge to the Mughal authority in Rajasthan which Bahadur Shah had recently established.[37]

The Guru did not immediately start his march along with Bahadur Shah when he left Agra. He stayed back and joined him at Ajmer between March 24 and April 2, along with his trusted Sikhs. He saw for himself how the Rajput princes reacted to the advances of Bahadur Shah and with what great difficulty the Emperor could secure superficial calm. He must have also noted how Aurangzeb's rabid fundamentalism had engendered innate hatred for the Mughal rule equally among the Rajput commonality and Rajput elites.

Even in the midst of mirk and dross, the Guru's nobility shone forth and its lustre enlightened whosoever came to his sublime presence, or to the assemblies of the Sikhs, held twice daily.

En route to Amber, the Guru visited village[38] Sanward seventy-two kilometres distant from Amber. He also visited

Udaipur Wati in the region of Sekhawati.[39] The Jagirdars as well as the people of these places showed utmost respect. It is said that one of the Jagirdars of Sanward was blessed with a copy of *Adi Granth*.[40] At Ajmer, the Guru encamped at a short distance from Mughal encampments. Tradition goes that the Guru paid a visit to the Masouleum of Khwaja Muinuddin[41] Chisti and honoured its custodians with Hukamnama (an epistle of benediction) (Piara Singh: *Sri Guru Gobind Singh Ji Di Rajasthan Yatra*).

On April 30, 1708, the Emperor was at Mandeshwar and sojourning at different places, he reached the bank of river Narbada in the second week of May, 1708.

While the imperial camp halted on the bank of Narbada river, a Muslim trooper killed Man Singh, one of the three devoted Sikhs, who escaped the battle of Chamkaur to swim and sink with the Guru even in his horrific predicament. The Guru was naturally much upset. The Emperor ordered that his murderer should be seized and handed over to the Guru for punishment.[42] The Guru forgave him and let him go scot-free, understandably to make him and all those of his ilk realise the Guru's house was incorrigibly merciful because mercy being the quality of God could engender vital forces in a sinner to shun committing sins again.

The Guru and the Emperor crossed river Narbada on May 17, 1708. During his halts en route, the Guru and the Emperor had their separate camps. According to Khafi Khan, the historian of the time, the Guru was proceeding towards southern India with Emperor Bahadur Shah at the head of two or three hundred horsemen and also infantry men armed with spears.[43]

Bahadur Shah reached Burhanpur situated on the river Tapti towards the end of June.[44] The Guru's camp also followed him. Where the Guru stayed, that place was known as Khooni Bhandar—the Bloody Spot—because at one time six cruel lions had been killed there.

The Guru was very warmly received here by the people. Sikhism had already made its niche in the psyche of a considerable section of its population.[45] At this place, a number of missionary centres of Suthre Shahis and Udasies were doing work of proselytisation for quite a long time.[46] Bhai Gurdas in his eleventh Var Pauri 30, had clearly referred to Bhai Tirath, Har Das and Dhir *et al.* engaged in missionary work at Burhanpur with the result that a large number of people had embraced Sikh religion.[47]

A Maratha writer, Sainapat, who is the author of *Sri Guru Sahai* says, "Guru came to this area for preaching to people of all shades and religious groups, who attended congregations." The Guru's holding of assemblies and imparting religious education has also been vouchsafed by *Tarikh-i-Bahadur Shahi*.[48]

All these witnesses prove beyond doubt that the Guru, while journeying along with the Emperor, did not lose sight of his central concern which was that humankind should be elevated spiritually and ethically to be ever humanistically dynamic.

The Guru stayed at Burhanpur for twenty days[49] during which period he, apart from meeting his Sikhs and non-Sikh devotees, stole time to visit Raj Ghat, a place on the bank of river Tapti, made sacred by Guru Nanak's visit earlier as also to have interface with other spiritual luminaries including Mahatma Jiwan Das, an aged holy personage who had chosen to be an 'Udasi' and had earlier met Guru Hargobind and Guru Tegh Bahadur.

The Guru also met Mahant Jait Ram of Dadu Dwara who per chance was there. Jogi Jiwan Das and Mahant told the Guru about one Bairagi Madho Das and his great occult power.[50]

The Emperor, who had left Burhanpur after a stay of one or two days, now wrote to the Guru to join him. According to Giani Ishar Singh Nara, Bahadur Shah did not want that the Guru's influence among the people should increase. The Guru being embodiment of transparent sincerity, uprightness, and truthfulness, did not doubt the Emperor and left Burhanpur. On the way, he sojourned at Jainabad, Balapur and Akola. Thereafter, he stayed first at Banera and then at Amravati.

From here the Guru proceeded to Hingoli. At some distance from this place, the Guru joined Bahadur Shah and held his camp at a distance of two three miles from Emperor's camp. Both Bahadur Shah and the Guru followed the route via Malikpur, crossed Ban Ganga on August 13, 1708[51] and in the beginning of September, 1708 both the camps halted at Nander, a place of pilgrimage on the river Godavari and about a hundred and fifty miles to the north-east of Hyderabad.

Throughout the journey from Agra to Nander, the Guru utilised his time for the propagation of his mission.[52] Dr. Ganda Singh writes that at times the Guru was not seen in either of the two camps for days together even for a whole week and was busy suffusing the people with Sikh religion.[53] On the way, he also acquired first-hand perception of men and matters around.

George Forster in his letter XI in *A Journey from Bengal to England* (Published, London, 1798, Vol. I, pp. 262-63) vouchsafes "He (Guru Gobind Singh) even received marks of favour from Bahadur Shah who being apprised of his military abilities gave him a charge in the army which marched into the Deccan to oppose the rebellion of Ram Buchish (Kam Bux)." Many of the later historians including Elphinstone, dittoed him. Elphinstone[54] asserted that Forster's account was confirmed by Khafi Khan. But this is not correct. Khafi Khan says that "Guru Gobind Singh accompanied Bahadur Shah with 200-300 horsemen carrying spears and some infantry.[55] His exact words were:

> Dar Ayam Ke Bahadur Shah Padshah
> Matwaju Haidrabad Gardindant
> Gobind Nam Az Sargrohan Aan Kaum
> Badnam Bahazur Rasida Ba
> Do Sad She Sad Sawar Neiza Dar Wa
> Piadah Dar Raqab Rafaqat Namud.

There is no ambiguity about the words 'Rafaqat namud' which only means accompanied and nothing more. The events in the life of the Guru do not lend any support to the aforesaid statement. At Agra, we find the Guru ordering the dress of honour presented to him by the Emperor to be carried away by a follower instead of carrying it according to court etiquette and practice in the royal presence. This was a rare privilege never allowed to officials or servants of the state. Again, during his southward march, Guru sometime separated himself from Bahadur Shah's camp for a number of days to carry on his missionary work. *Twarikh-i-Bahadur Shah* tells us that "Guru Gobind, one of the grandson's of Nanak, had come into these districts to travel and accompanied the royal camp. He was in the habit of constantly addressing assemblies of worldly persons, religious fanatics and all sorts of people."[56]

This could certainly not have been permitted to a servant of state especially when he was proceeding on a military expedition against a threatening rebellion. There is still another strong evidence against Forster's wrong conclusion. On the 5th Ramzan, 1121 H. (November 7, 1708) a month after death of the Guru, a report was made to the Emperor Bahadur Shah as to the disposal of movable property of the Guru Gobind Singh. It was of considerable value and according to rule (applicable to imperial officials and servants of the state) ought to be confiscated. The Emperor remarked that he was not in want of the goods of a Darvesh and ordered that the whole should be relinquished to the heirs.[57] The Akhbar-e-Darbar-i-Mualla (Rajasthan State Archives) has one entry on November, 1708, where the Emperor is reported to have said "The imperial treasury will not flourish with these goods, it is the property of Darveshain-Saints. It should not be interfered with." Here Emperor also did not consider the Guru as a state servant.

THE GURU AT NANDER

The Guru chose to stay at Nander and gave up the idea of accompanying Bahadur Shah. He selected for his residence a congenial spot overlooking the river. Soon a colony sprang up around his abode which began to be called 'Abchal Nagar', the city of the Eternal. The last days of his earthly life were spent here in all the wondrous glow of Sikh way of life as it began at Anandpur and had been kept undimmed all through. Anandpur was reproduced in Deccan.

Why did the Guru give up the idea of proceeding further with the Emperor? Why did the Guru select this place in particular? Contemporary evidence does not throw much light in regard to these questions. But circumstantial evidence does help us to reach some conclusions. The Guru was attached to Bahadur Shah from Agra to Nander over a period of about fifteen months (July 1707 to October 1708). Understandably, he was continuing old negotiations hoping that a satisfactory conclusion would soon reach but in the process he realised that it was not possible, because Bahadur Shah had shown marked amenability to come under the influence of Muslim orthodoxy, still spearheaded by Naqshbandis and Sayyids of Bārahas who were averse to any punishment of Wazir Khan, one of their coterie, or to any settlement between the Khalsa and the Mughal state. The Guru, therefore, thought it advisable to separate himself from Bahadur Shah.

Even then the Guru could choose some other place for his residence but he did not. The reason hitherto advanced is that the Guru wanted to see Banda in order to use him as his instrument to wage a war against the tyrannous Mughal rule, as also against the hill chiefs. This view is not plausible. Firstly, Banda was not personally known to the Guru. The Guru had only heard of him through the Mahant of Dadu Dwara[58], Guru could not be sure that he would give up his ascetic moorings and follow his mission. Secondly, the Guru's activities at Nander do not subscribe to this view as these aimed at establishing Sikh headquarter at that place to spread Sikh gospel in the whole of Deccan peninsula. The city of Nander, about 240 Kms distant from Hyderabad, was originally called *Nau Nand Dehra* because[59] it is said nine *Rishis* dwelt there in pre-historic times. It had assumed the status of an important pilgrimage centre, as apart from its associations with the Rishis, it was the abode of different Ashrams (camps) of Vaishnavites, Saivites, Lingayats and Bairagis *et al.* Further, the place was considered sanctimonious as it was touched by the water of the river Godavari considered primordial source of life in Hindu sacred texts. The Guru seemed to have considered it in the fitness of things to enter into dialogue with leaders of these holy camps to know their reactions and ultimately to convert them to his ideology, if possible.

The Guru started addressing congregations without much loss of time besides offering usual daily prayers.[60] The Guru soon became the focus of the people who thronged to him to have a glimpse of his divine personality and also to be suffused with his soulful ideology.

The Guru stayed at Nander for about a month during which period he was relentless in his pursuit of promoting the cause of Sikhism. Through his life-style and his vigorous preaching, he tried to awaken the people to enable them to discriminate between what was dross and what was vital. He organised hunting expeditions in the environs of the river Godavari to articulate the people to lead active and courageous life instead of drowsing in passivity and sloth. *Shikar Ghat Gurdwara* enshrines the memory of this aspect of Guru's activities.

He regularly attended and addressed the largely attended assemblies both in the morning and afternoon everyday. Thousands of people flocked to him. The Guru inculcated among them a new spirit through the recitation from *Adi Granth* and through sermons. Small Pothies (booklets containing hymns from *Adi Granth*) were got prepared under the overall supervision of Bhai Mani Singh and distributed among his disciples and seekers. Even copies of *Adi Granth* were prepared and given to the most deserving disciples/ seekers.

Of the many disciples who came to the Guru, Saeed Khan was one of the most important ones. He came all the way from Kangra hills to see the Master. One day in the full assembly of the disciples, a messenger arrived from the Punjab and gave a letter to Saeed Khan. He opened the letter and passed it on to the Guru. It was from his sister Nasiran; in it was a song, an epic telling how the Emperor's minions ransacked Sadhaura treating Pir Budhu Shah as a rebel. "Today Shah Sahib is gone to the heavenly land," Nasiran said. "And it is now my turn." These eyes had not seen the Beloved yet, but they have drunk of beauty in *Dhayānam*.

There is no sorrow. It is the inner joy blossoming up in the fullness of a willing death.[61]

As the letter was read, the Guru closed his eyes and blessed Nasiran. "The Guru never forgot his devotees, always inspired them with ideals which never allow a man to die even after the extinction of physical frame." Bhai Nand Lal, one of the counsellors of Bahadur Shah also attended upon the Guru. He enjoyed the blessing of the Guru's sacred presence. He told the Guru the Emperor's point-of-view but never went beyond his official duties.

The Guru in his resolve to propagate his mission fully utilised the service of *Dhadies*. Nath Mal was one such *Dhadi* out of the many in the Guru's court. He sang 'vars' to the accompaniment of Dhad to highlight the achievements of the Sikh Gurus and their Sikhs. Generally, he sang in Punjabi but at Nander all those who attended the congregations were not Punjabi-knowing people. Quite a large number of them particularly the Muslims understood and spoke Persian. To make them understand the Guru's mission, Nath Mal sang ballads (vars) in Persian also. One such ballad known as "Amar Nama" composed under the name of the Guru himself in the first person has come down to us through the son of Bhai Fatta, the seventh descendant of Nath Mal.[62]

A perusal of this ballad gives us, albeit, only an outline what constituted the essence of the Guru's teaching. Nath Mal says that the Guru pitched his camp in a graveyard which caused great tumult among the Muslims of the locality. The Guru's discreet silence and luminous personality overwhelmed and quietened them. This event underlined the point that the Guru attached no sanctity to the graves. Nath Mal further adds that the Guru killed goats on the day of solar eclipse, gave alms and rewards to the people irrespective of caste and professions *et al.*, issued injunction to the Sikhs not to seek guidance from Brahmans, threw the costly pearls given as an offering by Bahadur Shah into the river Godavari.

Urged by his success and the sense of mission, the Guru established apostolic seat of Sikhism in the south at Nander to organise the proselytising work in a better way. The ideal of setting up this apostolic seat first flashed across the Guru's mind when he was travelling in Malwa region of the Punjab. According to the Sakhi Pothi, when once the Guru expressed his desire to go to the south to establish the aforesaid seat, a Sikh sarcastically said why go to that hellish place which is Deccan. The Guru quipped "Don't speak in such a way about Deccan. It is dear to me and I have a work to do there." Anyway, the idea then was only in seed form; it sprouted when the Guru's proselytising activities met with success and that too in a remarkably short time.

Another notable feature of Nander activities was the Guru's unabated concern regarding the people who were suffering fresh wave of oppression and cruelty perpetrated by Wazir Khan and his orthodox henchmen, especially in the context of the indifference shown by Bahadur Shah towards the Guru's demand of persecuting him. Should Guru compromise with the oppression and the Sikh dispensation according to which evil must be fought at any risk and the wicked must be punished even with force, if all other means fail. The Guru decided never ever to relent and could not help thinking of the means to strike the oppressors. He had some infantry and two or three hundred cavalry equipped with lances. He had a great following in the Punjab and very influential and faithful batches of Sikhs. At this juncture, an event took place which proved very significant in the history of the Sikhs. Sometime after his arrival at Nander, the Guru repaired to Madho Das Bairagi's monastery on the bank of the river Godavari on September 3, 1708. It was a day of solar eclipse[63] considered sacred by the Hindus who spend it in performing ablutions, offering prayers and charities. Bairagi Madho Das too had gone to the river to have a wash and offer prayers.[64]

The Guru seated himself on his couch and waited for him, while the Sikhs killed a goat and started roasting meat. This act of the Sikhs was abhorrent to the disciples of Madho Das who were Vaishnavite vegetarians. They, therefore, became furious and informed Madho Das of all that had happened.

He deputed five of his disciples, known as *Birs*, to chastise the Sikhs for their acts of sacrilege. But to the Sikhs the solar eclipse was nothing more than a natural phenomenon and the cooking of meat in no way profane. There was, therefore, an unpleasant exchange of hot words and blows and the *Birs* were beaten back by the followers of the Guru. The Banda's disciples then worked upon the credulous Hindus to go to the Emperor to lodge a complaint against the Guru. The Emperor's response was that of indifference, because the complaint was frivolous. Madho Das then came to the Guru and entered into a dialogue with him.[65]

The same is recorded in Ahmed Shah Batalia's *Zikr-i-Guruan Wa-ibatida-i-Singhan Wa Mazab-i-Eshan*:

> Madho Das: Who are You?
> Guru Gobind Singh: He whom you know.
> Madho Das: What do I know?
> Guru Gobind Singh: Think it over in your mind.
> Madho Das (after a pause): So, you are Guru Gobind Singh.
> Guru Gobind Singh: Yes.
> Madho Das: What have you come here for?
> Guru Gobind Singh: I have come here so that I may convert you into disciple of mine.
> Madho Das: I accept it. I am your bonded slave.

Ahmed Shah Batalia wrote his treatise towards the end of the eighteenth century. Nowhere he quotes his source of the dialogue, probably the corpus of such a dialogue was a household talk in that part of the sub-continent of India where Banda spent his early life. Considering the folk talk as crucial for gauging the impact of Guru Gobind Singh on Banda, he presented the same in the form of a dialogue.

The dialogue is important as it explicitly states that there was a meeting between the Guru and Banda and the latter unreservedly surrendered to the Guru. It, however, does not throw any light what actually transpired between the Guru and Banda.

From its perusal, it appears as if the transformation of Madho Das was a miracle wrought by just the appearance of the Guru before Madho Das. Something difficult to swallow! There must have taken place between the Guru and Madho Das some dialogue the nature of which was very profound.

Banda's transformation underlined not only his repudiation of his earlier creed of asceticism but also marked his total break with the Indian tradition in which an ascetic is never to be shown as embracing the life in the world again for that marks his/her fall from his/her pedestal. As to taking up arms for the defence of Dharma, it was never to be conceived. Even a sage like Vishva Mitra who was born a king and was a great warrior did not destroy his tormentors—the demons. He had to ask Rama to do this job. The glory of Sikhism is that it differs with this view. Guru Gobind Singh in line with his predecessor Gurus reckoned that a true ascetic was an evolved soul and for that reason alone, he/she should lead the world to put an end to tyranny. Madho Das who was a firm ascetic and believed in retiring to places far away from the madding crowd in search of individual salvation joined the Guru in a point-counterpoint dialogue. The Guru satisfied him fully answering all his questions. Ultimately he realised that his path had not brought him peace while Guru's path had the potential to guarantee peace. Being a man of conviction and faith, he surrendered himself to the Guru calling himself as his Banda—a bonded slave. Now there was no duality left in his mind and he was ready to do anything at the bidding of the Guru. He discarded the path of resignation and self-abnegation and in response to the call of the Guru got ready to take part in Dharam Yudh—the battle of righteousness for the sake of righteousness.

The Guru perceived what was yet vital in the youthful ascetic and relumed it with promethean fire. He availed himself of this psychological moment, dressed him like a Sikh and administered to him the immortalising draught, the Amrit of the Khalsa. The ex-Bairagi was now given the new name of Banda Singh. Throughout his life and afterwards, he was popularly known and recorded by the historians by his self-conferred title of Banda[66] or Banda Bahadur. In an instant, he was a changed man. He was now no longer a Bairagi. He had now become a full-fledged Sikh, a disciple of Guru Gobind Singh, a member of the Khalsa Brotherhood. He had now found a true preceptor and saviour in Guru Gobind Singh who became the focus of all his religious devotion. His monastic establishment was at once dissolved and he followed the Guru to his camp to prepare for a new mission—a new life. Within days, he acquainted himself with the early history of Sikhism, the lofty ideals of the Gurus and their efforts to raise a nation of Saint-Warriors. He also heard how Guru Arjan Dev and Guru Tegh Bahadur fell prey to the injustice of the ruling class. The doleful tale of the cold blooded murder of the Guru's younger sons—Zorawar Singh and Fateh Singh—who were bricked up alive in a wall at Sirhind and were then mercilessly butchered to death for their refusal to abjure their faith, drew tears from his eyes and drove him into a sort of moral frenzy.

Finding Banda in a frame of mind to act to resist oppression and tyranny, the Guru gave him five arrows from his own quiver[67] as a token of victory. A council of five Pyaras, consisting of Bhai Binod Singh, Kahan Singh, Baj Singh, Daya Singh and Ram Singh was appointed to assist him and some twenty other Singhs were told to accompany him to the theatre of their future activities. A Nishan Sahib (flag) a Nagara and a robe were bestowed on him as emblems of temporal authority. The secret of his success lay, he was told, in personal purity and chastity and in the propitiation of the Khalsa who were to be regarded as the Guru's very self. Thus raised to the position of Jathedar or leader of the Khalsa and strengthened by the Guru's Hukamnamas or letters to the Sikhs all over the country to join in his expedition, Banda Singh Bahadur left for the Punjab to initiate and carry on the campaign against the cruelty and injustice of the Mughal government.

The commissioning of Banda on the part of the Guru to lead the Sikhs against the unjust rule of the Mughals in the Punjab was disliked by Bahadur Shah, who despite being in a hurry to go to Hyderabad to suppress the revolt of his brother,

Kam Bux, did not find if advisable to leave the Guru alone. He had the mistaken belief that the Guru's death would be a fatal blow to his scheme of brewing revolution in the Punjab. He, therefore, entered into a conspiracy with the two Pathans, Gul Khan alias Jamshed Khan and his brother Ata Ullah, already hired[68] and deputed by Wazir Khan to put an end to the fabulously rich life of the Guru.[69] Sainapat states that they paid several visits to the Guru and attended his prayer meetings, evidently to avoid suspicion and to look for a favourable opportunity to attack him. At last, one evening when the Guru was having a nap and his attendant happened to be drowsing, one of the Pathans surreptitiously crept to him and stabbed him on the left side a little below the heart, but before he could deal another blow, the Guru despatched him with his sword and his fleeing companion (Ata Allah) was put to death by the Sikhs.[70]

The Emperor in order to keep up his stance of a friend immediately sent expert surgeons to attend on Guru. One of them, it is said, was an English man called Cole. The injury got healed in a few days, although seemingly. Guru Gobind Singh resumed his task of addressing the congregations. There were rejoicing among the Khalsa at Nander that God had saved their beloved Guru. In a *Swayya* composed by the Guru, his gratitude to God for protecting his life is aptly expressed. Not even the innumerable weapons of all the enemies can inflict a fatal wound on those who seek refuge in God. But not long after, the Guru stretched a powerful bow causing healing wound to open and bleed profusely.[71]

A couple of days after, Sahib Kaur was sent back to Delhi to join Mata Sundri. Bhai Mani Singh was detailed to accompany her. On the 7th October, 1708, the Guru uttered a spirited 'Wahe Guru Ji Ka Khalsa, Wahe Guru Ji Ki Fateh' to bid his last farewell to the Sikhs whom he loved so much and who loved him above everything. As the Sikhs fervently responded with 'Wahe Guru Ji Ka Khalsa, Wahe Guru Ji Ki Fateh', he immersed himself in the Light. Thus passed from the earthly scene a great teacher, a great regenerator of mankind, the veritable messenger who revealed God's ways and will to the people and showed by personal example the ultimate possibilities of the human soul for compassionate as well as for heroic action and for suffering in vindication of the highest truth and values known to man. The Sikhs made preparations for the obsequies. The sacred body was placed on the pyre erected inside an enclosure formed of tent wall and the fire was lit amidst the chanting of the holy hymns. The Sohila was then recited and *Karah Prasad* was distributed. Bereft of the physical appearance of the Guru, the Sikhs felt an agonising emptiness, they had not known in the history beginning from Guru Nanak.[72] But they remembered the words of the Guru who had blended himself into Khalsa. The sense of the indwelling presence of the Guru through the Guru Granth and Guru Panth which meant the collective body of the Khalsa, gradually took hold of them and in course of time, permeated the collective consciousness of the community. This has been the Sikh living belief which has shaped the course of their history and led to one of the noblest endeavours in the annals of mankind in the cause of humanity, dignity and freedom.

A day before the end came, he asked for the sacred volume of *Adi Granth* to be brought before him. To quote Bhatt Vahi Bhadson Pargana Tanesar:

> 'Guru Gobind Singh Ji Mahal Dasam beta Teg Bahadurji ka pota Guru Hargobindji ka parpota Guru Arjanji ka bans Guru Ramdasji ki Surajbansi gosal gotra Sodhi Khatri Basi Anandpur pargana Kahlur Muqam Nander Godavari Des dakkan samvat satran Sai Painsath Katik mas ke chauth shukla pakhe budhwar ke dihun Bhai Daya Singh se bachan hoya Sri Granth Lai Ao. Guruji ne panj paise narial agey bheta rakh matha teka. Sarbat sangat se kaha mera hukam hai meri jagah Sri Granthji ko janana. Jo Sikh Janega tis ki ghal thaen paegi Guru tis ke bahuri karega Sat Kar Manana.'
>
> Guru Gobind Singh, the tenth Master son of Guru Tegh Bahadur, grandson of Guru Hargobind, great grandson of Guru Arjun, of the family of Guru Ram Das Surajbansi Gosal clan, Sodhi Khatri resident of Anandpur parganah Kahlur, now at Nander in the Godavari

> country in the Deccan asked Bhai Daya Singh on Wednesday, Katik Chauth, Shukla Pakh, Samvat 1765 Bk/October 6, 1708, to fetch Sri Damdama Sahib Wali Bir. In obeyance to his orders, Daya Singh brought the Granth Sahib. The Guru placed before it five paise and a coconut and bowed his head before it. He said to the *sangat*, "It is my commandment, own Sri Granth ji in my place. He who so acknowledges it will obtain his reward. The Guru will rescue him. Know this as the truth."

These utterances were unique and had far-reaching implications. The Guru pronounced an end to the institution of personal Guruship by asking the Sikhs to regard *Adi Granth* as their spiritual Guru after him. The Khalsa had already been invested with the status of Guru, now both Khalsa and *Adi Granth* were raised to the status of Guru.

Other documents authenticating this fact are a letter issued by Mata Sundri and Devraja Sharma's *Nanakacandrodya Mahakavyam*, an old Sanskrit manuscript which has been recently published by Hindu University, Varanasi. Even a cursory glance at the letter of Mata Sundri makes it clear how the Sikhs after Guru Gobind Singh believed that the Guruship had passed to the *Shabad*—Word, as contained in *Guru Granth Sahib*. "None in human form after the ten Gurus was to be acknowledged by the Sikhs as Guru. Those who like some Bandaie Singh's or Ajit Singh's followers called their leaders as Gurus, were committing a mortal sin. All other sins, says the letter, could be forgiven by repeating the Guru's Nām but not the sin of believing in a living Guru after the Ten Masters of the Sikh faith."[73]

The second document referred to above also records Guru's proclamation that Scripture would be the Guru after him. While the Master lays on his death bed, Nand Lal came forward and asked the following question. "Who shall be our teacher now? Whom shall we salute and see and what shall be the object of our discourses?" The Master replied, "The Granth which itself is the doctrine of the Guru shall be your teacher. This is what you should see; this is what you should honour; this is what should be the object of your discourses." The original in Sanskrit reads as follows:

> Nand Lalas Tada Prchhat Ko Asmakam Guruh Kam Namena Ca Pasyema Kasmai Varta, Vadema Ca Uce Gurustu Yusmakam Grantha Eva Gururmatah Tam Nameta Ca Pasyeta Tasmai Varta vedata Ca. (*Nanakacandrodya Mahakavyam* xxi, 227-29)

The personal guruship was thus ended by Guru Gobind Singh himself. Succession passed on to *Guru Granth Sahib* in perpetuity. This was the most significant development in the history of the community. According to Dr. Harbans Singh 'the finality of the Holy Book was a fact rich in religious and social implications. *Guru Granth Sahib* was acknowledged as the medium of the Divine revelation descended through the Gurus. It was for Sikhs the perpetual authority, spiritual as well as historical. They lived their religion in response to it. Through it they were able to observe their faith more fully, more vividly. It was central to all that subsequently happened in Sikh life. From it the community's ideals, institutions and rituals derived their meaning. It constituted the regulative principle for its aspiration and action, the integral focus of its psyche.[74]

Sainapat, writing within three years of the Guru's death gives us a simple account in the climax of the evolution of the Panth:

> "A day before his death, the Sikhs asked him as to the form he was adopting (or the person whom he was nominating to succeed him). In reply, he said that the Khalsa is his physical self and that to them he has granted his role and that the Eternal and limitless Word uttered with the Lord's light is the supreme Master (Sat Guru Hamara)."[75]

Bhai Nand Lal in his 'Rehatnama' elaborates this point. He quotes Guru Gobind Singh saying that the Guru had three forms (Roop): (1) Nirguna—(attributeless) *i.e.* the formless spirit of which the human soul was but a small part; (2) Guru *Shabad* i.e. the word of the Guru incorporated in the *Adi*

Granth; and (3) Sarguna, the visible Khalsa, absorbed in Gurbani.

Another close associate, Bhai Chaupa Singh records his 'Rehatnama' the Guru's commandment as follows:

> All the Sikhs are hereby commanded to obey the Granth as the Guru. The essence of the new system was that no individual would henceforth be recognised as the Guru; henceforth the Khalsa, inspired and guided by the Word (Gurbani incorporated in *Adi Granth*) would be the physical and spiritual controller of the Panth. According to Gian Singh, the Guru opened the holy book, placed five paisa and coconut before it, bowed before it, then went round the sacred scripture five times, bowed every time and declared it as the Guru for all times to come.[76]

The abolition of personal Guruship was anticipated but not accomplished at the Keshgarh Assembly in 1699. There the Guru accepted for himself only formal initiation into the Khalsa but also the discipline of the new fraternity. In this way, he merged his own personality in the Khalsa surrendering his high office. While hard-pressed in a mud fort of Chamkaur, the five Sikhs representing mystically the whole Khalsa asked the Guru to leave it to save his life. The Guru had to honour the verdict of the Khalsa, thereby affirming that the supremacy of the Khalsa Panth was unchangeable. This already established fact was openly canonised by the Guru on the 6th October, 1708 while he passed on the succession to the holy book, the *Guru Granth*. He declared to the Sikhs at the time of his death that the Word as embodied in Granth would be the Guru after him. 'The Guru Spirit' said he, 'will henceforth be in the Granth and the body in the Panth. Where there are any five Sikhs as representing the Khalsa, there Guru will be in body and with the Granth present, the Guru will be present in spirit.

The Khalsa accepted the change in obedience to the Guru's order. In the *Gur Bilas Chhevin Padshahi* by the poet Sohan, the prefix 'Guru' is invariably added to Granth and it is stated:

> "In the Kali age, the Guru Granth has assumed the form of Sri Guru. Recognise the Guru Granth to be veryself of the Ten Gurus."

What made the Guru Depart for the Deccan

The Guru's motives in going to the Deccan along with Bahadur Shah variously stated by different writers are as under:

(1) Bute Shah and Malcolm say that he went to Deccan because he despaired at terrible reverses and bereavement which had been his lot and wanted a change.

(2) Some writers say that the Guru joined the Mughal service. Cunningham says that the Guru received a military command in the valley of Godavari. According to Forster 'Bahadur Shah being apprised of his military qualities gave him a charge in the army which marched into the Deccan to oppose the rebellion of Kam Bux.[77] Irvine also thinks that the Guru joined the Mughal army.[78]

(3) Quite a few writers state that the Guru having found that it would be difficult to gather afresh an army strong enough to challenge and rout the Imperial forces decided to arouse the Rajputs and the Marhattas to fight against the Mughal tyranny.

Before arriving at definitive conclusion we will have to examine all the theories stated above. The view of Bute Shah and Malcolm that dejection overwhelmed the Guru, and he in order to have a change left for the South, is evidently unfounded, as it does not fit in with the Guru's demeanour in the face of severest losses. Indeed, his whole life is a lesson in fortitude, courage and high spirits. As a child of nine years, he lost his father and stood face to face with formidable Mughal Empire at its zenith; but that thing failed to have any depressing effect on his tiny, yet mighty heart. He saw his dearest Sikhs killed before his eyes, sent two eldest sons into the valley of death at Chamkaur; but these things could not plunge him into gloom. When his wife asked him where his four sons had gone, his reply was characteristic of his fundamental attitude to these things; he stated:

"What then if they four are gone?
They yet live, and shall ever live
Millions of our dear brave sons."

Certainly no trace of grief or despair in all this. Besides this, the tenor and tone of his letter "Zafarnama" testifies to the attitude of the Guru towards sufferings. In fact, he openly threatened the Emperor while he wrote, 'What though my four sons have been killed, my younger sons, the Khalsa, remains behind like a coiled snake. What bravery is it to quench a few sparks of life? Thou art merely stoking a raging fire still more.' Nowhere and at no time the Guru was despondent; he was always active in the pursuit of his ideals.

Thus in the presence of such unimpeachable evidence, it is absurd to repose faith in the dejection theory.

The second view that the Guru went to the Deccan in the capacity of an employee of Bahadur Shah is also far from truth. Cunningham who has given currency to this states that the Guru received military command in the valley of Godavari. He bases his version on the evidence of some Sikh writers as also on the writings of Khafi Khan and Forster. On examination of references cited by Cunningham, we ascertain that he had little or no acquaintance with original works of any Sikh writers. He alludes to *Bachittar Natak* and at another place *Gurbilas* of Bhai Sukha Singh. He also seems to have referred to Bhai Gurdas II, but all these accounts do not subscribe to the theory that the Guru took service with Bahadur Shah.

So far as the authorities such as Forster and Khafi Khan are concerned, a scrutiny of their writings also leads to the conclusion contrary to service theory. Forster writes that Guru Gobind Singh received marks of favour from Bahadur Shah who being apprised of military qualities gave him a charge in the army which marched into the Deccan to oppose rebellion of Kam Bux.[79] For this account, he relies on some historical record whose authors he names not. We have tried our best to discover those writers but we have failed, and we think that Foster might have made use of some distorted version of accounts of Khafi Khan or those of some detractors of the

Guru. Any way in the absence of some authentic information, it is difficult to maintain that the Guru had been in the employment of Bahadur Shah.

Khafi Khan too does not corroborate the view of Cunningham, although he, being a religious bigot, was in the habit of seeing everything through the religious myopic eyeballs. He regards the Guru not as a servant but a companion of Bahadur Shah. He uses for the Guru the word '*Rafaqat*' an abstract noun of Rafiq and means companionship or company according to Steingass's *Persian-English Dictionary*. Obviously, it does not connote any difference of status between the persons concerned. Thus the service theory finds no support from the statement of Khafi Khan. It appears that 'Service Theory' originated from the intentional or accidental mistranslation of Khafi Khan's passage.

A modern writer, Mohammed Latif while upholding the service theory, quotes Malcolm. But on perusal of Malcolm's book *Sketch of the Sikhs*, it has been found that Malcolm held a diametrically opposite opinion. He nowhere in his book lent credence to this theory. Hence Latif's view is without any foundation or at best an attempt to stain the unalloyed courage of the Guru.

'Service Theory' can also be rejected in the light of the ideology and ideals of the Guru. The memory of the wrong that had been inflicted on him and on his people were too fresh in him to have reconciled him joining the army of oppression. Nor, as Dr. G.C. Narang writes can the Service Theory be reconciled with the Guru's commission of Banda Bahadur to the leadership of the Punjab Khalsa.[80]

Similarly, the view that the Guru accompanied Bahadur Shah to Deccan because he wanted to arouse the Rajputs and the Marhattas to contribute their mite to end the Mughal tyranny, is at once, far-fetched and a mere figment of imagination. Had the Guru gone on this errand, he must have tried to see some groups of the Marhattas or of the Rajputs to gauge their strength and the will to combat the Mughal might. Since the Guru did not do anything of the sort, it is clear that he had no such purpose. No doubt in Khafi Khan's accounts one gathers that the Guru addressed to the assemblies of the people who gathered around him daily; but it does not seem probable that the Guru preached sedition or revolt against the Mughal government because in that case it was not possible for the Guru to spend so much time in the company of the Emperor.

Having negatived the oft-held views, the issue of the real motives of the Guru while accompanying Bahadur Shah to the Deccan still remains unsolved. We think that after his meeting with the new Emperor who had given him an honourable reception, the Guru wrote to his followers in the Punjab and conveyed his appreciation of what had passed between himself and the Emperor. In his letter, Guru Gobind Singh made a very significant allusion to the purpose of his meeting with Bahadur Shah. After receiving the jewelled scarf and the *Khillat* which the Emperor presented to him, the Guru expressed his satisfaction over the goings-on with the Emperor. He then informed the Khalsa that he would return to them in a few days, enjoined on the Sikhs to remain friendly with one another and come fully armed to his presence on his return to Kahlur.[81] The Guru seems to have believed that he would soon get justice or succeed in prevailing upon the Emperor to follow the liberal policies, to return Anandpur to him and to punish the Subedar of Sirhind for his excesses. The *Hukamnama* to this effect certainly epitomises a fresh approach to the problems. As a matter of fact, the Emperor throughout this period lived far away in the south at Ahmednagar, and it is possible that he might have not been kept fully informed regarding the affairs in the Punjab. Although the late Sikh records speak of frequent appeals to the Emperor on the part of hill chiefs and thus give the impression that the whole campaign was being conducted with the full knowledge of the Emperor, yet considering the distance of Emperor's stay from the Punjab and poor means of communications and transportations, their view may be considered with reservation. In this connection it is pertinent to note that no contemporary record makes mention of any representation from any party, whosoever.

Sainapat makes mention of an embassy to a Sultan only once, and it is doubtful whether even here the Emperor is meant.

In view of this, we may infer that the cause of the trouble was primarily the local officials including Wazir Khan, the Subedar of Sirhind, who did not brook the popularity of the Guru on account of religious as well as Imperial reasons. The crime of Wazir Khan in particular was so heinous and of so brutal a character that the Guru would have been false to himself and his ideals if he had not made efforts to get the accused punished promptly. He could not resort to armed conflict any longer because of his slender resources and hence the only way left to him was to resort to diplomacy. Thus, it is quite understandable that this was the purpose for which the Guru sought to see the Emperor. The death of Aurangzeb foiled him in his effort for a while, but he was consistent and persistent in the present course chalked out by him. It was this very purpose for which he extended his moral support to Bahadur Shah and kept himself in the Emperor's train.

The Sikh records, more or less, are definite that this was the object for the consummation of which, the Guru joined Bahadur Shah. This thing is also quite clear from the Guru's Hukam Nama (fiat) of October 2, 1707, wherein it is written 'old negotiations that had brought him so far, were then in progress and he soon expected to return to the Punjab.[82] But it appears that the negotiations had not yet culminated into any agreement. It appears that the Emperor started for Rajputana (12th November, 1707), the Guru had to accompany him. The Emperor, however, avoided the Guru under one pretext or the other. Soon after, the Guru discovered that his efforts had failed and the Emperor was not sincere in his overtures. He then commissioned Banda to achieve by force what he had failed to accomplish only on appeal to justice.

The Guru's Earthly Close

The Guru expired on 7th October, 1708 as a result of the wound caused by stabbing of the Guru by a certain Pathan. Various views have been expressed with regard to the circumstances of the assassination of Guru. Bhai Sukha Singh in his *Gur Bilas* states two Pathan youths, who were the sons of Painda Khan whom Guru Hargobind had killed in the battle of Kartarpur came to the Guru. One day the Guru gave one of them the sword which had been presented to him and said that a man who had sword in his hand and saw enemy of his father or grandfather before his eyes and yet failed to avenge the wrong had been born in vain. The youngman hesitated; but after a few days when he went to see the Guru he was again aroused. He struck the Guru, his third blow penetrated into the Guru's belly. Upon this there was a row and a Sikh came and cut off the Pathan's head. The wound was stitched up; but it could not be healed causing ultimately the death of the Guru.

The story, when put to critical analysis, falls flat on the ground. A son of Painda Khan who died in 1634 was by no means a young man in 1708. Moreover, first to arouse young Pathan to kill the Guru and then to see him being killed by the Sikhs is such an incongruity which is inexplicable by any norm of logic.

Another variant of the story has been given currency by Cunningham.[83] In this the name of Painda Khan has been dropped and we are introduced to a Pathan merchant who had sold horses to the Guru at Anandpur. One day, when the Guru was short of funds, the Pathan came and asked for immediate payment. The Guru asked him to come on some other day. He (the Pathan) used an angry gesture, and his utterings of violence provoked the Guru to strike him dead. The body of the slain Pathan was removed and buried, and his family seemed reconciled of the fate of his head. But his sons nursed revenge and availed an opportunity of fulfilling it. They succeeded in stealing upon the Guru's retirement and stabbed him mortally when asleep and unguarded. Other writers such as McGregor[84] state that the Guru shortly after realised his mistake and as a recompense for the fate of the victim, he showed special favours to the widow and brought up her son as a father would do. When the boy grew to manhood, he is said to have been incited by the Guru himself to strike him. The boy did it with fatal results for the Guru.

Trumpp also believes in this version and to give rationale to it states that the Guru had been disgusted with life and wanted to end it.

This version also cannot stand the test of historical scrutiny. The authors of the version unanimously state, the Pathan, the father of the assailant, was killed by the Guru after escaping from Chamkaur. The Guru's escape from Chamkaur took place in December, 1705. The Guru reached Nander in September, 1708. Obviously during this period of three years (approximately) the son of the Pathan who was a child as it is asserted could not grow into manhood fully trained in the use of arms, capable of attacking the Guru who was known for his physical strength and skill in the handling of arms. The assertion that the Guru who was in the grip of abject dejection invited the attack on himself is altogether absurd, because in that case, the Guru could not have properly sewn up his wounds and carefully attended to them. Moreover, if the Guru had lost all hopes and was completely disappointed, he could have not commissioned Banda Singh to do his job.

Furthermore, in recent years fresh light is thrown by a Hukamnama according to which no demand for immediate payment was put before the Guru. In fact a Pathan, who had certain claim on the Guru did meet him, but that not only did he make no demand for money, but actually refused to do so when reminded of it by the Guru. This fact is fully borne out by the Hukamnama[85] which the Guru granted to the Pathan appreciating his friendly overtures.

Another version of the story is given by M.A. Macauliffe: "More probable is the account given in *Twarikh-i-Bahadur Shah*.[86] The Guru was in the habit of constantly addressing assemblies of worldly persons, religious fanatics, and indeed all varieties of people. One day an Afghan who frequently attended these meetings was sitting listening to him. When certain expressions which were disagreeable to the ears of the faithful fell from the Guru's tongue, the Afghan was enraged and regardless of the Guru's dignity and importance stabbed him twice or thrice with a poniard."

This version also suffers from serious snags. There is implicit in the version that Guru spoke against Islam. This fact cannot be true because there is nothing in the life and writings of the Guru to show that he was the enemy of Islam. The story obviously is a concoction of a zealous and loyal Muhammedan. By inventing this story he has tried to smudge Guru's glory by depicting him as rash and indiscreet in his speech and inimical to Islam and has glorified the murderer by representing him as acting in wrath aroused by the Guru's words. He has also completely absolved the Emperor and Wazir Khan of having any hand in the affair.

The perusal of *Sri Gur Sobha* by Sainapat, one of the poets of Guru's court and Chatur Jugi the correct version has come to light. Sainapat states[87] that one Pathan came to the assembly that daily met around the Guru with murderous intentions. He could not have his chance because of many persons present there. He came again after two or three days. After this he came successively for several days. One evening he got his opportunity and struck the Guru with his dagger. He repeated his attack for the second time, but then he was despatched. The Guru then called out his Sikhs who hurried to him. Two confederates of his, who were waiting for him outside, fell under the swords of the Sikhs. The Guru's wound was immediately sewn up and in a few days, it appeared to have healed up. But when the Guru tried to raise himself, the thread broke. The wound was sewn up again but after three or four days *i.e.* to say on October 7, 1708, the Guru breathed his last.

No doubt Sainapat's account is sober and free from any inconsistency, but he does not disclose the identity of the person and the motive which prompted the Pathan to do the nefarious job. Here the author of Chatur Jugi as also Khushwaqt Rai and Bakht Mal come to our rescue. The man was a hireling of Wazir Khan of Sirhind who was the real instigator of the crime. As the Guru moved with Bahadur Shah, Wazir got apprehensive of the activities of the Guru. He knew what would happen to him if pact was made between the Mughals and the Sikhs. The Emperor had already shown inclination to help the Guru at the expense of Nawab. He had granted a *farman* in favour of the Guru directing Wazir Khan to make payment of Rs. 300/- a day. Wazir Khan was now in fear of his life and could not rest until he had got Guru Gobind Singh killed. Accordingly he deputed a young Pathan named Jamshed Khan, to murder the Guru, who having gathered necessary information from the Guru's wife at Delhi, proceeded to accomplish the assigned job.

Bhai Vir Singh says in *Kalgidhar Chamatkar* that Bahadur Shah was involved in the demise of the Guru. Our probe into the historical circumstances also leads to this very conclusion. The Emperor was enraged with the Guru for deputing Banda Singh to renew the struggle against the Mughal unrighteousness. He was also apprehensive that the Guru might join the Marathas in their struggle against the Mughals when the Emperor would be busy in warfare against his brother at Hyderabad. It was for this reason that though being in a hurry to reach Hyderabad as soon as possible to suppress the revolt of his brother Kam Bux, he was staying at Nander and was not leaving the Guru alone. Bahadur Shah had the mistaken belief that the Guru's death would be a fatal blow to his scheme of renewing the revolution in Punjab. He, therefore, entered into a conspiracy with two Pathans, Gul Khan alias Jamshed Khan and his brother Ata Ulla already deputed by Wazir Khan to put an end to the life of the Guru. The following historical facts testify to the involvement of Bahadur Shah in the conspiracy to kill Guru Gobind Singh.

On October 28, 1708, the Emperor ordered that a dress of mourning be presented to the son of Jamshed Khan Afghan who had been killed by Guru Gobind Singh. The imperial news-letter of Bahadur Shah's court records:

> Kih Guru Gobind Singh Rai Jamshed Khan Afghan Ra Bajan Kushtah Bud Khilat-e-Matami Bapisar-i-Khan Mazkur Mrahmat Shud.[88]

Jamshed Khan was not a Mansabdar or a high dignitary upon whom high honours were bestowed by the Emperor. He was a spy of Wazir Khan in the disguise of a soldier in attendance upon the Sayyad who was also deputed by the governor of Sirhind.

Two days after, on October 30, 1708, the Emperor ordered for the grant of a robe of mourning to Guru Gobind's family.

The news-letter of the court states "26 Shaban year 2, October 30, 1708 Hukam Shudki Bapisar Guru Gobind Singh Rao Nanak Panthi Khilat-e-Matami Pir Dar Badehand.[89]

It means that the Emperor treated Jamshed Khan and Guru Gobind Singh on equal footing, thereby confirming that Jamshed Khan enjoyed the patronage of the Emperor.

"On November 17, 1708 it was represented that the deceased Guru had left huge property."[90]

It was ordered that such chattels would not replete the Imperial treasury. This was the property of a Dervesh (saint). There should be no interference with it.

The Emperor's refusal to attach the property of the Guru against the wishes of his courtiers shows his diplomacy and cunning. It was purely an eye-wash of his complicity, a pious fraud.[91]

CULMINATION AND MIGHTY BEGINNING

The period of Guru Gobind Singh was atonce a period of culmination as well as beginnings. It marked the culmination because the concepts, organisational structure and goals of Sikhism became clear and concrete and elaborated to their logical end. This obviously brushes aside the views of some of scholars who hold that the tenth Guru stood away from Guru Nanak.

On conceptual plane, Guru Gobind Singh was monotheist of the type of Guru Nanak. As with all the Gurus, God with him was a living experience, a primal force to create, recreate and to take care of his creations; but in His social functions of God, the Guru regarded Him 'smasher of the tyrants, All steel, and the protector and saviour of the righteous'. This was obviously the logical development of the concept of God. Guru Nanak only once mentioned the God as "the killer of the unrighteous". This function of God continued to be hinted by Guru Arjan also; but it fell to the tenth Guru to express this thing clearly, explicitly and unequivocally. This function was not the result of thinking in an ivory tower, it was rooted in the social pattern which the Gurus were striving to finally emerge. A community of householders would ill-brook God who is unconnected with them and does not protect them against the disturbers of peace and destroyers of life and property.

Guru Gobind Singh in *Akal Ustat* says:

> "Thou art the Protector of life and the Giver of all prosperity
> Thou art the cure of all sorrows and sufferings
> I bow to Him
> Whom I see here as a warrior fully armed,
> and there as a scholar seeking pure knowledge."

That God helped and protected his dear ones or the good, and destroyed the evil was an old recognised strand of Sikh metaphysics. Guru Gobind Singh not only laid more emphasis on this strand than was the case before but also evolved the idea further. He envisaged God as a mighty, invisible warrior armed to the teeth and ever ready to use his powers in support of the good.

This institution of Guru also touched its culmination during the period of Guru Gobind Singh. 'Guru' had acquired a place of great importance in Sikh religion from the very beginning. The predominant personality of the Guru supplied a nucleus around which Sikh Panth could rally.

Still another respect in which the tenth Guru brought to completion development of an important old institution was the evolution of the Sikh scripture. Guru Arjan Dev had done a great job by authenticating the diverse compositions and preparing a single holy book for the benefit of his people. But since then, the work had remained where it was left. Guru Gobind Singh included in it the compositions of his father and put the seal of finality on it. Subsequently, this finalised version of *Adi Granth* was invested with Guruship.

Besides, he completed the evolution of institution known as *Sangat*. In the beginning, it was merely a religious gathering of devotees, functioning more or less in isolation. Gradually there was increase in its functions, and the isolation of one *Sangat* from the other was lessened by the forging of common links, such as building up certain religious centres, institution of *Manjis* and *Masands* as the agencies of the central leadership and the assertion of the principle of supremacy of the Guru. Guru Gobind Singh raised them to the state of Khalsa thereby investing them with the rights and powers of dealing with the Guru, directly instead of through some agency. With the foundation of the Khalsa, the network of semi-integrated *Sangat* was fully integrated. The investing of the Khalsa with the supreme powers marked the completion of the historical process long underway.

The institution of guruship also touched its culminating point under the direction of Guru Gobind Singh. Throughout the development of Sikhism in the pre-Gobind Singh period, the Guru had been assigned a place of predominance and significance. Guru Nanak regards the Guru as an absolute necessity. Guru Nanak in so many verses highlights this point. As a matter of fact in Guru Nanak's system, the Guru formed the pivot on which everything else hinged. The disciple was asked to walk in the path of God, to remain ever content within His will and to obey His commands. But in these matters, as in everything else, the Guru was to point out the right path, he was to interpret the will of God, and the commands of the Almighty were also to be issued forth through the medium of his ordainments. The Guru, therefore, was to be implicitly obeyed. In the *Guru Granth Sahib*, this fact was emphasised again and again. We can glean a large number of verses from the compositions of Guru Amar Das, Guru Ram Das and Guru Arjan Dev enjoining upon the Sikhs to obey the Guru in letter and spirit. Guru Ram Das says:

> "Sikhs of the 'Guru' and friends, walk in God's way.
> Faithfully obey what the Guru preacheth.
> Hear, servants of God and brethren, serve the Guru very promptly

Tie up service to the Guru as Thy travelling expenses to God.
Think not of today or tomorrow."

Sikh tradition is also eloquent on this point. Bhai Gurdas who lived in the late sixteenth century says in his exposition of the essence of the Sikh religion, "The Sikh who obeyeth the Guru's instruction is really a Sikh. To become a disciple must be like a purchased slave, fit to be yoked to any work which may serve his Guru. Love none but the Guru all other love is false."[92]

A natural consequence of such teaching was the unquestioning devotion of the disciples to their spiritual head. The author of *Dabistan* who had frequent meetings with Guru Har Gobind narrates a story how one of the Gurus praised a parrot and a Sikh immediately went to its owner and offered to barter his wife and daughter for the bird. This story and many others of this type which we cannot afford to narrate here on account of the paucity of space testify one thing atleast that the Sikhs had got utmost devotion for their Guru. Sujan Rai of Batala wrote in 1696, "The reliance which this sect (Sikhs) has on its leader is seldom found in other sects. If a wayfare arrived at midnight and takes the name of Baba Nanak, he was treated as a brother."[93]

The implicit faith in a common superior knit the Sikhs together like the members of a regiment. The predominant personality of the Guru supplied a nucleus around which the Sikh Panth could gradually arise. Under the leadership of Sikh Gurus, the Sikhs showed a sense of corporate unity which found expression through their behaviour and actions such as *Guru ka Langar* and *sangat*.

But what was the sense which the Guru came to hold upto the period of Guru Gobind Singh. The Guru was understood in three ways: The Guru was God, he was the voice of God and he was the 'Word', the Truth of God. A large number of verses can be quoted in support of the aforesaid three senses in which the Guru was held.

If we go deeper we will find complete identification of the apparently different senses. The following passage amply proves our point:

> The Word is Guru and the mind (which is focussed on it) continually is the disciple. By dwelling on the ineffable one, on Him the eternal Guru-Gopal, I remain detached. It is only through the Word that I dwell on Him and so through the Guru, the fire of *Haumai* is extinguished.[94] (*Sidh Ghost: G.G.S.*, p. 943)

The passage quoted above from Sidh Gosht brings out this identity not just with the pronouncement that the Word is the Guru but also with the reference to the Guru-Gopal. God Himself is Truth.

Closely connected with the above definition of the Guru is the question "were Gurus not Gurus?" They were Gurus but in the sense that they were the perfect personalities embodying "The Truth" and conveying only the truth; their persons, in themselves were not Gurus. This fact Gurus themselves brought home to the people by example and precept.

It is stated in the old *Janam Sakhi* that when Guru Nanak finally resolved to make Lehna his successor, he put five paisa before Guru Angad and fell down at his feet. In Tikki Di Var or the Coronation Ode we are told that "Guru Nanak in bowing to Guru Angad reversed the order of things. It shows that from the very beginning, the impersonal character of guruship was recognised. The personality of the Guru was detached from the spirit of guruship which was to be regarded as one indivisible and even continuous.

Further, the fact that the name Lehna was changed to Angad must be regarded as equally significant. Speaking of the nomination of Angad the Coronation Ode says, "He had the same light, the same ways." This idea is stressed again and again in the Sikh writings. The guruship was something apart from the personality of Guru and this would explain how the successive Gurus could be regarded identical. Mohsin Fani says, "They (the Sikhs) believe that when Nanak expired, his spirit became incarnated in the person of Angad. Angad at his death transmitted his soul into the body of Amar Das and Guru Amar Das, in the same manner, conveyed his spirit into the body of Ram Das; whose soul transmitted in the person of Arjan Mal; in short they believe that with the transfer of soul into Lehna (Angad), Nanak the first became Nanak the second and so on, to the fifth in the person of Arjan Mal. They say that whoever does not recognise in Arjan Mal the true Baba Nanak, is an unbeliever. In their hymns and compositions all the Gurus designated themselves as Nanak. Even in private correspondence they signed as 'Nanak'. This thing was even observed by the Bahadur Shah who called Guru Gobind Singh as 'Guru Gobind Nanak'.[95]

Guru Gobind Singh himself declares that all Gurus were one and that without understanding this vital aspect of hierarchy perfection could not be attained. Guru Gobind Singh says:

> Nanak assumed the body of Angad
> And made his religion current in the world
> Afterwards Nanak was called Amar Das
> As one lamp is lit from another
> The holy Nanak was revered as Angad
> Angad was recognised as Amar Das
> And Amar Das became Ram Das
> The pious saw this, but not the fools
> Who treated them all distinct
> But some rare persons recognised that they were all one.
> They who understood this obtained self-realisation.[96]

Guru Gobind Singh was not only fully conversant with the different stands of the concept of Guru but also subscribed to them.

For some time, the Guru did not effect any change. Then quite a few developments that had taken place prompted him to effect some change. One was the nature of relations between the Sikhs *vis-à-vis* the Guru. Dr. A.C. Bannerjee says, "The importance attached to the Guru did not, however, create a community depending on autocratic leadership. The ideal of brotherhood was an active principle from the very beginning. As a Sikh community was governed by principles of equality and democracy, the individual Sikh was exalted to a position almost equal to that of the Guru himself. Guru Ram Das says:

To those who obey the will of the Guru
I am sacrifice
I am ever a sacrifice to those who served the Guru.

Quite a large number of verses can be gleaned to prove the veracity of the aforesaid point.

The next important development was, that the unity of Sikhs was being disturbed by the emergence of the imposter Gurus of dissentient sects and the degenerate *Masands*. To keep unity among the Sikhs was the most important need of the time. This thing lurked in his mind when he took the momentous decision of making changes in the institution of the Guru. He, in 1699, on the day of Baisakhi made a pronouncement to the effect that henceforward, the Khalsa was his form, limb of his limb and breath of his breath. He invested the Khalsa with the dignity of guruship. In the Kesgarh assembly Guru received baptism from the Five Beloved. When they were astonished at his proposal, he said, "The Khalsa is the Guru and the Guru is the Khalsa. There is no difference between you and me. As Guru Nanak seated Guru Angad on the throne, so have I made you Guru."

The investing of guruship on the Khalsa was a step of great benefit to the Sikh community. It seems that the abolition of the guruship had a logical connection with the Guru's war against sectarianism within the Sikh community. The sects owed their origin to the ambition of the disappointed candidates for the guruship. It was not enough to boycott the existing sects; the emergence of the new sects must be prevented. The abolition of the guruship was obviously an efficacious remedy of the disease. Furthermore, to impart divinity to each individual of the Khalsa was to instil confidence, and establish democratic functioning of the Khalsa brotherhood.

But this development was the culmination of the process that had set in since the inception of Sikhism. The Guru could impart guruship to the Khalsa because essence of guruship being truth or Word was impersonal as well. And to the Khalsa he gave guruship because the Sikhs had already been exalted to be equal to the Guru. Guru Gobind Singh was able to transmit guruship to the Sikhs because there was no elective principle involved in the selection of the Guru. Each Guru was nominated by his predecessor. He could snap the human link but the idea of the new links had propounded and expounded by earlier Gurus.

Guru Gobind Singh effected another change in guruship on the eve of his death at Nander when he spoke to his disciples that they should regard *Guru Granth Sahib* as their Guru along with the Panth (Khalsa). The injunction that the Granth should also be considered as 'Guru' was also the culmination of the development under way. Word (*Shabad*) had already been given the status of Guru by all the Gurus. If the relative emphasis is a good guide to some conclusion, we can say that this point was more frequently stressed by Guru Arjan Dev. Guru Gobind Singh obviously comprehended the correct import and significance of this point. This being so, he completed *Adi Granth* by including the verses of Guru Tegh Bahadur in it and made a categorical statement investing 'Adi Granth' with guruship and the mystic identification of the Guru with the Word, the facts which were emphasised upon from the beginning of Sikh History.

Guru Gobind Singh also carried forward the social and religious revolutions inaugurated by Guru Nanak. The successors of Guru Nanak had guided these revolutions with great devotion and ability. Yet much more was needed to be done in this context. The creation of the Khalsa of Guru Gobind Singh was not merely an endeavour to integrate the members of his community, it was also a powerful bid to carry to completion his predecessor's resolutions in the fields of social and religious life. The code of conduct prescribed for the newly-created Khalsa was so devised as to impose a strict discipline on the Sikhs so as to ensure firm adherence on their part to the lofty ideals of Sikhism.

Theory of Struggle (Dharam Yudh)

The clear cut formulation of the DHARAM YUDH theory was also the work of Guru Gobind Singh. This theory can also be interpreted as the Theory of Progress. This theory in rudimentary form was already there. The Gurus preceding Guru Guru Gobind Singh followed it not only in their work-a-day life but also preached it through their sacred compositions. The vitriolic comments of Guru Nanak on the contemporary political and social systems are obviously indicative of some sort of struggle raging in his mind to establish new politico-social set-up.

The cheap and senseless imitation on peoples' part of their ruler's ways, with no other objective than that of placating them was exposed as an act of servility and submission to a tyrant and was dubbed as an act of shameful cowardice. Compromise with injustice or tyranny was thus shown as a great evil and fearlessness or heroism in resistance to a tyranny a great virtue. According to Guru Arjan Dev in the fight between good and evil, God's support would always be on the side of good, for, He is verily the smiter of the evil and the wicked and since times immemorial has been the unfailing protector of the good as against their enemies.[97] Guru Amar Das says: "In all Yugas he has been creating savants and in all Yugas has their honour been protected by Him. Harnaksh the tyrant was smashed by Him and Prehlad the victim saved. The arrogant and the foul-tongued were forsaken while favours were showered upon Namdev.[98] Guru Arjan depicts Sikh devotees as *Mal* or *Pehalwanra* (wrestler) in the wrestling bouts between good and evil.[99]

It was exactly to highlight this type of thinking that Guru Arjan Dev in his parting message to his son advised him to wear two swords; one symbolising *Shakti* and the other *Bhakti*. Guru Hargobind, on his part, addressed himself to the task of shaping the minds of the people to rise and fight against injustice and unrighteousness. He collected arms, trained his people in the technique of fighting by organising regular training exercises and roused them to imbibe the sense of fervent heroism by precept as well as by example. He also to evolve some sort of mechanism not only to salvage the society from the dross but also to make it dynamic enough to even move to progress through self-realisation fought a few successful military actions in which he and his men displayed marvels of valour. All this led to the building up of a glorious and never-to-be-forgotten traditions of heroism.

This tradition was further enriched by the ninth Guru. He, by his sacrifice, not only vindicated his faith in his stand, but also taught that oppression must be resisted. The sacrifice of the Guru blazed a new trail in so far as it was a commitment to an open struggle against the organised oppression of the state.

This, then, was the ideology which Guru Gobind Singh inherited. The Guru so modified it that it became a theory of struggle which would not only explain its aims but also boost the morale of the participants. He named this theory Dharam Yudh. The theory finalised by the Guru had the following adjuncts:

(i) that God was eternal protector of the good against the oppressors. He was also the mightiest warrior;

(ii) that it was morally justified to wage wars against the evil forces and tyranny;

(iii) that the use of force was justified against oppression and oppressors of all kinds.

This is why the Guru was motivated to raise the importance of weapons as they constituted the vehicle of success and power. Weapons were depicted as decorating the person of the Almighty Himself thus partaking of the attribute of divinity. In consequence they were entitled to all respect and veneration. The chief of them, the sword, was called *Khal Dal Khandan* (scatterer of the armies of the wicked), *Sukh Santa Karnan* (protector of the saints), *Durmat Darnam* (scourage of the evil), *Jagkaran* (creator), *Sant Ubharan* (saviour of the virtuous) and *Pratparan* (sustainer). Although the force was of primordial importance in Guru Gobind Singh's theory of Dharam Yudh, it should not be confused with militarism. In militarism force is employed for the sake of force, aggression and self-aggrandisement, but the Guru allowed its use only for a noble cause and that too as a remedy of the last resort.

It is the moral duty of the people to wage war against evil. Guru Gobind Singh professed openly that he had been ordained by God to extirpate the evil and uphold the good. In this context evidence of Bhai Nand Lal is of great importance. He says:

> Rakh-i-Adl O Insaf Afrokhta
> Dil-i-Jabar O Bedad Ra Sokhta
> Bina-i-Sitam Ra Bar Andikhta
> Sar-i-Ma Dalat Ra Bar Afrokhta.
>
> "He brightened up the force of equity and justice and burnt down the heart of tyranny and inequity. He uprooted the foundation of cruelty and lifted the head of justice."

The theory of Dharam Yudh of the Guru has been expressed very beautifully in the following excerpt from his composition 'Krishnavtar'.

> Glory to noble souls who on their earthly way
> Carry upon their lips the Name of the Lord
> And ever contemplate deep within hearts the good.
> Knowing that the body is a fleeting vesture,
> They make the Lord's song, they make Lord's Nām
> A boat to carry them over life's rough ocean
> They wear as a garment that is as a fortress serene
> detachment.
> Divine knowledge is the light of their minds
> Their cleaver's broom in their wise hands
> Is the broom of wisdom
> With it they sweep all cowardice and all falsehood.

The contemporary source such as *Sri Gur Sobha* also lends evidence to the theory of Dharam Yudh when he says:

> For this was the Khalsa created
> To fight the evil to smite the wicked
> And to get rid of crisis.

'Dharam Yudh' as preached by Guru Gobind Singh was 'not a fight to protect or promote the interest of a particular sect or creed and hence is to be distinguished from the Christian crusade of medieval period and the Muslim Jehad of the familiar variety. Nor was it a religious war in the usual sense of the term. It was a moral war waged for the victory of good over evil, for the triumph of righteousness over tyranny and oppression. His concept in traditional ethical terms was analogous to Goddess Durga's fight with the demons Mehkhasur, Sumbh and Misumbh, to Lord Rama's fight with Ravana of Lanka or to Lord Krishna's struggle with Kans. It was based on dynamic view of religion which in its essence is social catalyst. The Guru viewed religion as something committedly concerned with the problems of society and as it had a vital role to play in human affairs. It must work for healthy flow of social or collective life and must of necessity contend against the ills hampering the smooth and unhindered mainstream of its existence. But the revolutionary role that the Guru visualised for religion was not to be stunted in any way by harnessing it to the narrow interests of any particular religious creed or dogma; on the contrary, it was to be conducted with a view to promoting general good of the society.

Futhermore, the political and social ideals were concretised and institutionalised. Before Guru Gobind Singh it was not so; the Guru's credit is that he was forthright and clear in putting forth his views on social, political and cultural matters.

But the period of Guru Gobind Singh was not merely a period of culmination; it was also a period of beginning. By his reforms and under the impact of his dynamic leadership, the Sikh community was not only strengthened but also converted to a great vehicle of revolution.

Multi Splendoured Personality

When we picture to ourselves the whole gamut of the life and achievements of Guru Gobind Singh, he appears to us a gigantic personality having myriad layers—each layer unique and beautiful in its own way. The all-round impression that emerges is that he was perfect in all respects and in whatever capacity he was called upon to play his part, his was the pursuit for excellence. He was extremely handsome with sharp features and with well-proportioned body. His face sparkled like full moon. The general effect of his personality was that he was imposing, ever-decent, humane, sweet, responsive and tolerant. Straightforwardness, truthfulness and fearlessness were other hallmarks of his personality. He would never resort to underhand means, treachery and corruption for the achievement of his objects. Another important trait of the Guru's splendid personality was his equivableness. Nothing could ruffle him. He had to leave Anandpur, his hearth and home, he got separated from his companions and life-partners and his dear sons; he could with great difficulty save himself from the murderous fire of the Mughal artillery; his two younger sons were bricked up alive at Sirhind, but the did not lose the balance of mind.

To crown it all, he would not relent from his resolve. He took even the greatest difficulties as a part of the game. He recompiled the final Recension of *Adi Granth* after he had suffered a great loss in battles against the combined forces of the Mughals and the hill chiefs. Obviously he was 'Sthit Pragya' or equivable personality or perfect *Karam Yogi.*

Besides this, the Guru was fearless and courageous. 'Zafarnama' the letter written to Aurangzeb is a living testimony to his marrow-deep fearlessness. He wrote to Aurangzeb "I shall strike fire under the hoofs of your horses; will not let you drink the water of the Punjab—what use is it to put out a few sparks when you raise mighty flame instead. Not only this, the Guru in this letter calls the Emperor a crafty and deceitful fox.[100] He warns him of the nemesis which lay in store for him.

As a child, he aroused affection of his parents and elders. As a father and a householder, he showered filial kindness on his children in torrents. The innocent smiles of his children moved him and he felt thrilled when his children did something which was laudable. He did not miss anything which was essential for the sound growth of them. He cared for his household and made all possible arrangements for providing comforts to his family members. He always attended to his household duties. His family was an ideal one. He functioned his family unit not as a dictator but as a co-partner or as the first among the equals. His family was not patriarchal in the sense often understood, it was a unit suffused with spirit of harmony, equality and democracy. He believed in monogamy and advised his disciples to follow his advice. Polyandrous and polygamous families were contrary to his concept of family.

Similarly, as a general or as a leader he was unequalled. Such men are rarely born who can start from a scratch, and yet within such a short time can prepare such a formidable army which could challenge the mightiest of the Empires of his time. Dr. Indu Bhushan Bannerjee's expression at this point is worth-noting: "In the *Bachittar Natak* the Guru is rather modest with regard to his own performance and, as it is to be expected, attributes his successes to the Will of the Almighty, but from whatever little he says, it is not difficult to see what an accomplished archer he was and how unperturbed and dauntless he could be even in the midst of raining death. In forming an estimate of the military capabilities of Guru Gobind Singh, it must not be forgotten for a moment that there was a tremendous disparity in numbers and resources between himself and his enemies and the amazing thing is not that he lost but he could fight for so long. The defence that he extemporised at Chamkaur was excellent.[101] The Guru with only forty chosen companions kept at bay for several hours a whole host of the opposing troops, has hardly a parallel and the keen and discerning eye with which he chose the spot where the battle of Khidrana was fought and the army of Wazir Khan was compelled to retire leaves no doubt as to his tactical genius. The wisdom with which he raised forts at Anandpur and the quality of military training for which he made arrangement at the place bespeaks high of the standard of generalship the Guru provided. The Guru was a great military planner as well. In every battle, he fought with a definite plan and that was the reason that he put up a stout defence with only forty Sikhs against surging mass of human heads. No odds however heavy they might be, dampened his valour and resolve; no personal danger made him shirk his duty. Wounds only stirred him to greater exertion.

When he was called upon to assume the leadership, the circumstances were not congenial. The Government headed by Aurangzeb was not in a mood to tolerate any movement, much less the Sikh movement which was committed to usher in an era of liberalism in politics, social affairs and religious field. It was so much determined in its resolve that it did not feel hesitant even executing those who were liberal or who had sympathy for liberal movement. Sarmud and a score of Muslim Sufies and Guru Tegh Bahadur had to suffer execution because of their liberal views in the sphere of religion and social approach. The internal organisation of the Sikhs known as *Masand* system had also gone rotten and the *Masands* being corrupt and extremely selfish, were most ill-fit to knit the community into a compact socio-politico-religious group. The Hindu masses because of certain factors which had been operating since long, were completely demoralised and inept. Hill Rajas were more interested in their feudal interests than in their people. The Sikhs had yet to come out of the shock they had suffered in the wake of the unjust execution of Guru Tegh Bahadur. Besides this, the age factor also did not favour the Guru. The Indians long accustomed to holding the greybearded as wise and mature had to be convinced that ripeness had no perennial link with the age. Guru's own means, material as well as human, were also scanty.

It is really amazing that the Guru, notwithstanding all these adverse factors, succeeded to create his following and then to lead them in such a way that they became instrument of progress not only of the community to which they belonged but also of their country—even of whole mankind. In this process, he exhibited remarkable insight into the human nature, their psychological reactions and responses to different problems and challenges, and into the social mechanism then existing.

He exploited and harnessed all that was vital among the people. He employed theology, literature, poetry and photosophy to prepare the mind of the people to serve his purpose. He, through training and education, succeeded to transform the psyche of the people. This was the reason that the people who were considered to be the dregs of humanity were made to long for freedom and for doing brave deeds. As a matter of fact, the potentialities which lay dormant under the killing weight of the Mughal despotism and the outworn social system as recommended by Hinduism, were awakened and forged into a dynamic force to live and die for the sake of truth and righteousness.

Still the Guru did not allow his followers to develop narrow religious patriotism; he exhorted them to enlarge themselves to awaken to the ideal of establishing the rule of the virtue all over the world. In this context the Sikh movement was different from the Maratha Movement of revival. Sri Aurobindo Ghosh says, "The Marathas revival inspired by Ramdas's conception of the Maharashtra Dharma and cast into shape by Shivaji in spite of the genius of the Peshwas could only establish a military and political confederacy. Their endeavour to found a nation could not succeed because it was inspired by a religious patriotism that failed to enlarge itself beyond its own limit and awaken to the idea of united India." "The Sikh Khalsa, on the other hand, was an astonishingly original and novel creation and its face turned not to the past but to the future. 'His (Guru's) aim as a leader was not to lead the people in the context of contemporary circumstances but also to make them conscious of their role, even in the times to come.' He enjoined upon his followers that they were the soldiers of God (Akal Purakh Ki Fauj) and they should continue to strive to see that a society is established where there is no exploitation and no discrimination on the basis of caste, clime, wealth, birth and sex and there is freedom of expression of adopting any profession and where everyone has a right to hold his head high and where there is mutual love for each other."

The Guru was faced with a very difficult task. He was to give a suitable reply without resorting to atrocities and meanness. The Guru did give a suitable reply but he did it without leaving the road to moral values. Some scholars have given the name of crusade to the struggle of the Guru and his followers against the tyrannous contemporary rule; but it is incorrect. It would be an insult to give the name of crusade to wars of the Gurus. It was a sublime attempt, perhaps made for the first time in human history, to fight forces of evil without losing the human soul.

His contribution to the domain of thought was also of immense value. In fact, he was a creative thinker. He did not believe in the purely idealistic tradition of the country according to which it was held that the material world was unreality and the instruments of knowing it that is to say, perception and experience are also unreal. What we see, perceive or experience is either illusion or ignorance. These views were constantly and deliberately hammered by Indian philosophers, notable among them being Nagarjuna and Shankar. According to them, we, out of ignorance or illusion, consider natural things as real. They illustrate their point by giving the example of snake and rope. They hold that sometime rope is perceived as a snake. Just as illusion or ignorance creates the impression of rope being snake, similarly the natural things which are as unreal as rope-snake are illusory. This type of thinking when percolated among the people made them doubtful about their existences even and its social effect was to search reality somewhere else with the result that his philosophy, instead of bearing an imprint of progress, began to be used by the clever as a means to distract the attention of the people from the material world.

This type of working did not fit in the practical world. In one's practical life, one has to run for water when thirsty. He has to eat food and wear clothes. It is of no use laughing at all this as a banal talk. The real problem posed was a serious one. The evidence of practical life could not be overlooked. The snake perceived as the rope might not harm philosopher's contemplation but not so is the snake seen in the smoke.

The Guru was convinced that the tradition gripping tightly the minds of the people will not explain the things correctly and to the conviction of people. The evidence of practical life could not be just overlooked, and in fact on the basis of this evidence, it was not difficult for the Guru to surmise that the grand theoretical structure so laboriously built up by idealists would not be in a position to hold in the context of world.

He, therefore, did not accept it *in toto.* He accepted this much that the ultimate Reality was something—may be named as God—who is Formless, Deathless, Beyond space and time, Self-existent, all-Enlightenment; but he did not believe in the fact that all the things perceived, seen and experienced in this world are illusory because that would mean that God was not *Karta Purakh* (Person Creator). Illusion there is, but that is because of the faulty experience or faulty perception, not that the world—the whole world is illusion. From this it should not be concluded that the Guru began to believe in the other extreme *i.e.* to say that materiality is everything as it has been experienced and propounded by the Charvak School of thought or by the Marxist school of thought. The Guru did regard material things a reality and wanted the men should endeavour to improve their material world and for that matter the struggle of the Guru revolved round the establishment of the rule of the virtuous and the elimination of the evil-doers; but for Guru it was not everything. The Guru wanted his followers to struggle and strive to be Reality-like. He himself even in the midst of the material battles stole time to sit and mutter 'Thou art thou art'—the only reality. He preached genuine love for 'Reality', but unlike idealists, the Guru exploded the myth that the love for it was not a force, meant to be unsuccessful in this world. On the contrary he said that it was meant to be successful only in this world, for, outside it there was nothing except God. If a *Jivatma* emerges to get free of this vortex of life and death, straight it gets merged in the Lord. Thus love means nothing for that world where everything is merged in the Lord. Love was a force meant for this world *i.e.* to say that Dharam Khand. This was indeed a revolutionary idea for the practical world. By giving this idea, the Guru sought to win the earth back for the man. This is certainly one of the most important reasons that the Sikhs are not otherworldly. A Sikh looks upon the world as a genuine place to live, enjoy and to elevate himself. The social projection of this type of thinking on the part of the Guru was healthy and the Khalsa whom he created in his own image, became inspired group of men surcharged with the spirit of participating in the world to improve and ensure its progress. Besides, the Guru's idea of keeping up living separateness also exacts praise.

He asks his disciples to keep themselves in living separateness (as long as the Khalsa keeps up its living separateness, it will enjoy all my prestige). By living separateness, he meant that his disciples having raised themselves to the ideals he had set for them, should be conscious of it and be constantly vigilant that they were not swallowed up by the environment whose improvement was yet to be effected. This was a unique contribution, because it has been observed that the culture-pattern which gives up its living separateness and neglects its self-defence is prone to be swallowed up.

His ideas about religion were also striking and tinged with the revolutionary fervour. He repeatedly pointed out that his religion did not consist in turning increasingly towards the veiled stones, nor in approaching altars nor in throwing one self-prostrated on the ground, nor raising the hands before the gods, nor deluging the temples with the blood of the beasts, nor in heaping vows, but in beholding the height of God within a peaceful soul in dedicating one's mind, heart and soul to the service of humanity, which is the highest manifestation of the spirit of God.

> "Ascetics who eat dirty food are not better than filth eating swines.
> Yogis who pride in besmearing themselves with ashes
> Are no better than donkeys and elephants that bespatter themselves with dust.
> Recluses who retire to the grave-yards
> Are no better than jackals howling in the cemetery
> Monks who live in remote monasteries
> Are like owls living in deserted houses;
> Anchorites waste life in vows of silence;
> In what way are they better than the deer who lives and dies in silence in the forest.
>
> What avails giving five calls in the name of religion
> The jackal cries time and again in the bitter cold at night

Without enlightenment and divine knowledge
The fool sinks into the pit of hell
How can one attain divine wisdom
Without faith, love and devotion.

(Guru Gobind Singh: *Akal Ustat*)

It is an admitted fact that continuity in progress can be assured if the people at the helm of affairs of the society are not allowed to form a privileged class. It has been observed that such people are thrown up to lead a society by the society itself, then they become privileged and concentrate their energies to safeguard their privileges instead of identifying themselves with the interest of the people as a whole. Such people block the progress. The Guru correctly understood all this. In *Bachittar Natak* he exposes different saints and leaders coming up on the stage of the world and instead of leading it to a higher destination delimit their activities and form their respective coteries, caring little for the welfare of the human race as a whole. Guru bemoans that the truth (the Guru used the world 'Par Brahm'), is abjured and falsehood is followed (Par Brahm Kineh Na Pehchana). Humanity thus is not benefitted. The Guru constantly endeavoured to keep his action and teaching continuously linked with progress and turned his face against the privileged people. This he did before Rousseau wrote his 'social contract' and 150 years before Marx formulated his *Manifesto*. The Guru said:

All the battles I have won against tyranny
And I have fought with the devoted backing of these people.
Through them only have I been able to bestow gifts
Through their help I have escaped harm
The love and generosity of these Sikhs have enriched my heart and love;
Through their grace I have attained all learning
Through their help, in battles, I have slain many enemies.
I was born to serve them, through them I reached eminence.
What would I have been without their kind and ready help?
There are millions of insignificant creatures like me.

(Guru Gobind Singh: *Swayya*)

Guru Gobind Singh was the first prophet in world history to identify himself completely with the will and destiny of the people and to give them a place higher than the highest. By doing this, he made them creative. Lest they should become privileged class or vested interest themselves, he filled their minds with the spirit of cosmopolitanism. He uttered to them:

All men have the same human form
In all men blazes the same divine light.

(Guru Gobind Singh: *Akal Ustat*)

When the Order of the Khalsa was ushered in on the Baisakhi day, many Brahmans and Khatri followers murmured but all those people rejoiced who were considered low socially. The murmurs of the twice-born increased and many took their departure but Guru Gobind Singh exclaimed that the lowly should be raised and hereafter the so-called despised should dwell next to himself. The big ladder with which the Guru used to raise the people high was in the form of self-dignity of men. He effectively roused the dormant energies of vanquished people and filled them with a lofty although fitful longing for social freedom and national ascendancy, the proper adjuncts of that purity of worship which had been preached by Nanak.[102]

MISSION OF GURU GOBIND SINGH

The Guru, in *Bachittar Natak* tells that God spoke to him thus:

"I have cherished thee as My son
And created thee to extend my religion
Go and spread my religion there,
And restrain the world from senselessness."

"Understand this, ye hold men, in your souls
I assumed birth for the purpose of spreading the faith saving the saints
And extirpating all tyrants."[103]

From the reading of the above excerpt from *Bachittar Natak*, it emerges that Guru considers himself commissioned by God to spread God's religion, which was "to save the saints and to extirpate the tyrants".

The Guru throughout his life lived this mission. He never shirked upholding goodness even at the risk of his life. There is not even a single example of dichotomy between his mission and his action. Even in the field when the enemies were hell bent to destroy the Sikhs, he would not waver in upholding the principle of goodness and nobleness.

In fact, this thing was the central theme of Guru's actions. Battles he fought but did not occupy even an inch of territory—his purpose being only to teach a lesson to the unjust enemy. He used his sword and allowed his followers to use it but only for the protection of the poor and the helpless. All his wars were of the nature of 'Dharam Yudh', the fight for Dharam, righteousness. He never allowed the central content to disappear from his actions.

Bhai Kanhaiya gave water to a soldier belonging to the enemy's camp. The Sikhs got infuriated at him and reported the matter to the Guru. To the surprise of all, the Guru patted him and asserted that he had recognised the right path.

William Irvine and other scholars, mostly belonging to the 18th century state that the Guru's precepts prohibited all friendship with Muhammedans. This is wrong. The Guru perfectly understood that he was fighting against the Mughal empire which was unjust and had lately become tyrannous, and not against Muslims as such.

Amongst the best friends of Guru were the Muslims such as Pir Budhu Shah who sacrificed two of his four sons for the sake of the Guru. The Guru might have not been able to effect his escape from Machhiwara without the help of Ghani Khan and Nabi Khan. The Guru is absolutely right when he remarks that the Empire rather than Islam was the target of his strivings and exertions.

William Irvine and many other scholars have jumped to the wrong conclusion because in the circumstances of the eighteenth century, the fine distinction referred to above was difficult to maintain and it ceased to be valid for all practical purposes. The Mughal government had become rotten to the core and it was becoming futile any longer to expect any justice from its officials. One trouble led to another and the Sikhs soon found themselves in the midst of a never-ending discord with the Muhammedans. This struggle inevitably coloured the views of the later writers and inappropriate motives were attributed to the Guru, which find no support in his life writings.[104]

Nor did he fight for the protection of the Hindus. Bulleh Shah says in one of his couplets that if Guru Gobind Singh had not taken birth, most of the Hindus (particularly those of northern India) might have embraced Islam.

Similarly, Santokh Singh asserts "*Malechhas* would have flourished, and Hindus would have been ruined and the religion of the Vedas and Purans, would have been drowned, if Gobind Singh exalted like Brahma did not come down as an Avtar of Vishnu."

True that Hinduism was saved; but it happened as a part of bigger scheme of Guru Gobind Singh. Aurangzeb, with all his might, was determined to convert India into Dar-ul-Islam (the land of faithful). The Guru, by arming his disciples and arousing them to resist the Mughals, set an example that even the fear of Aurangzeb and the temptations of high offices failed to deflect them from their chosen path of resisting social and religious impositions.

It is, therefore, unfair to think that the Guru could have been the sworn enemy of a community or a class.

The Guru was cosmopolitan in outlook and approach and believed in the evolution of composite culture consisting of the best that was there in different types of traditions in this country or countries. The Guru spells out his point-of-view in the following lines:

> "The temple and the mosque are the same; the Hindu worship and the Musalman prayer are the same; all men are the same; it is through error they appear different. Musalmans and Hindus adopted their customary dress of their different countries. All men have the same eyes, the same ears, the same body, the same build, a compound of earth, air, fire and water."

"Alla and Abhakh are the same, the Purans and the Quran are the same; they are all alike; it is the one God who created all."

Another great thing in the Guru was, that he was a builder *par excellence*. He understood the exact nature of the challenges and fashioned suitable responses to them. The society was in tight grip of caste prejudices, feudalistic tendencies, economic inequities, injustice, particularism, obscurantism, despotic tendencies, Islamic imperialism and inter-religious-group tensions.

All these things had sapped the vitality of the people. The Guru fashioned a fitting response to these challenges. He made efforts to inculcate democratic ideas, spirit of social and economic equality, sense of justice, besides building the national will to fight and resist evil in any shape. A few half-hearted attempts had already been made by *Sufis* and *Bhaktas*, but the real beginning had been made only by the Sikh Gurus. Guru Gobind Singh brought about their culmination. He did not stop at preaching and setting his own example but he set afloat an organisation to preserve, perpetuate and consummate his programme. The organisation he evolved was the Khalsa.

The creation of the Khalsa speaks volumes of the organising genius of Guru. It was atonce a social pattern, an instrument to further the cause of Sikhism, a culmination of what the previous Gurus had thought and preached, a vision to be translated into reality in future. Nanak disengaged this little society of worshippers from Hindu idolatry and Mohammedans superstitions. Guru Amar Das preserved the infant community from reducing self into a sect of quietists or ascetics. Guru Arjan gave his increasing followers written rule of conduct and civil organisation. Guru Hargobind added to it the use of arms, and a military system. Guru Gobind Singh bestowed upon them a distinct political existence and inspired them with the desire of living socially free and naturally independent. But a mass of wax figures bearing the same hallmark and dressed up in a the same fashion could not form an effective machine. He, therefore, declared that the Sikhs were under the special protection of God and wherever five of them were present, God was present there also.

They were further impressed upon with the idea that they were born to conquer all evil-doers. The Guru was an embodiment of hope and confidence, and his followers were suffused with the same belief. The new salutation among the Sikhs was to be 'Waheguru Ji Ka Khalsa, Wahe Guru Ji Ki Fateh' (The Lord's is the Khalsa, the Lord's be the victory). A strong conviction of one's being the chosen instrument of God and the confidence it inspires, are the strongest guarantees of success and the Guru had given these guarantees to his followers.

They were asked to eschew caste and tribe-prejudices and entertain the ideal of democratic equality thereby enabling them to achieve unity which is the first step towards evolution of nationalism and cosmopolitanism and global society. He supplemented this moral force by some other ordinances which are as under:

1. All the Sikh names were to bear a common suffix of 'Singh' among the males and 'Kaur' in case of female.
2. All had to follow one form of salutation—Wahe Guru Ji Ka Khalsa, Wahe Guru Ji Ki Fateh.
3. There was to be no external object of homage except the revered *Guru Granth*.
4. The multiplicity of Hindu places of pilgrimage was too great to encourage nation's unity, so the Guru fixed upon Amritsar as the chief place of pilgrimage for the Sikhs; and that town has ever since been the Mecca of the followers of the Guru.
5. "The Guru was a philosopher" says Cunningham, "and understood fully how the imagination of men could be wrought upon". He thoroughly realised hypnotising power of certain external forms and symbols and knew that an inspiration, men often receive from a change in their outward appearances. He made it a rule that the Sikhs should keep five

"Kakārs" *i.e.* to say Kesh (Hair), Kangha (Comb), Kirpan (Sword), Kara (Steel Bracelet) and Kuchha.

According to G.C. Narang, "The observances at once singled out the genuine Sikhs from the mass of the lukewarm Hindus and produced a cohesion in the internal body of the Khalsa which was in a short time to make a strong Panth of them.[105]

Guru Gobind Singh's attempt and desire to make the masses creative, articulate and wide-awake led them to uphold democratic values. In fact, this tendency had been the fundamental theme of Sikhism since its inception and during the stewardship of Guru Gobind Singh, it was strengthened still more and instructions were issued not only to preserve it but also to make it the part of social consciousness of the people. The Guru abolished *Masand* system which in course of time had outlived its utility and *masands* had started impinging on the freedom of thinking and action of the people by acting in an authoritarian manner. By raising status of the Khalsa to that of the Guru, by impressing upon the people that they all were the creation of the Creator, by rejecting distinctions based of family, tribe, caste or class, birth or creed, and by regarding women as equal partners of men in the march of mankind towards progress, the Guru obviously clarified and demonstrated his stand for democracy and democratic values.

Thus, the Guru preached the principles of equality of men and women, of abolition of special privileges, of removal of caste prejudices of acting on Gurmata *et al.* These cannons upheld by Guru Gobind Singh are nothing else but the theory and practice of democracy. It shows that Sikhism of the Gurus is democratic both in essence and orientation. But the Guru's concept of democracy was slightly different from the modern concept. While it is correct that Sikhism is in its essence and orientation, democratic, it must be clearly understood that the basis of modern political democracy is essentially numerical, while the kind of democracy visualised by the Guru is qualitative, as depending upon the guidance of the people coming from the noble and the wise in spirit. Without this basis, the fabric of the Guru's vision cannot be erected.

FOOTNOTES

1. Sainapat: *Gur Sobha* XIV, 2-6; *Sakhi Pothi*, Sakhi No. 105, p. 116.
2. Sarup Singh Kaushish: *op. cit.*, p. 187.
3. Fauja Singh: *Travels of Guru Gobind Singh,* p. 18, Pbi. Uni., 1968.
4. Macauliffe, M.A.: *The Sikh Religion,* V, p. 226; Ishar Singh Nara: *op. cit.*, p. 8.
5. Fauja Singh: *Travels of Guru Gobind Singh*, p. 18, Pbi. Uni., 1968.
6. Macauliffe, M.A.: *The Sikh Religion*, V, p. 226; Fauja Singh: *op. cit.,* p. 18.
7. *Ibid.*
8. Macauliffe, M.A.: *op. cit.*, pp. 227-28.
9. *Ibid.*
10. Sainapat: *Sri Guru Sobha: Sikh History Research Board*, edited by Shamsher Singh Ashok, p. 114.
11. Jodh Singh: *Sri Kalghidhar Chamatkar Hulas*, pp. 203-05. William Irvine: *Later Mughals*, p. 89.
12. *Past and Present*. XVII-I, April 1983, *Guru Gobind Singh—The Last Phase* by Ganda Singh.
13. Gian Singh: *Twarikh Guru Khalsa,* Part I (Pbi.), pp. 1078, 1080.
14. *Ibid.,* pp. 1078, 1081.
15. *Ibid.*
16. Sainapat: ***Guru*** *Sobha* edited by Shamsher Singh Ashok, p. 118, Sikh History Research Board, Amritsar, 1967.
17. ***Ibid.***
18. ***Ibid.,*** p. 118.
19. ***Ibid.***
20. ***Ibid.,*** p. 112.
21. Sainapat: *op. cit.*, p. 121.
22. Khafi Khan: *Mantakhub-ul-Lubab*, p. 652.
23. Sainapat: *op. cit.,* 121; Ganda Singh: *Makhiz-e-Twarikh-Sikhan*, p. 82.
24. *A Newsletter of the Court of Bahadur Shah* dated July 24, 1707.
25. Hari Ram Gupta: *History of the Sikhs*, Vol. I, p. 319.
26. Dr. Ganda Singh: *Hukam Name*, p. 186, *Hukam Nama* No. 63.
27. *Akhbar-i-Durbari-Mualla* Dec. 7, 1707 C.E. Sunday (23 Ramzan, First Bahadur Shahi A.H. 1119).
28. V.S. Bhatnagar: *Life and Times of Sawai Jai Singh.*
29. Mir Jafar Ali Zatalli: *Kuliyat,* edited by Naim Ahmed, 1769, p. 27.
30. Cupta, Hari Ram: *A History of Sikh Gurus*, p. 317, Munshi Ram Manohar Lal, 1984.

31. *Hadiqat-ul-Aqalim* of Murtaza Hussain Bilgrami (p. 127-28). Imperial officers had for some time been clamouring for Jagirs and Bahadur Shah had very little money in the treasury at the time of his succession. At this juncture, Khan-i-Khanan Munim Khan suggested annexation of the territories of Kachhwa Rajputs.
32. William Irvine: *Later Mughals*, p. 46, Orient Books Reprint Corporation, 1971.
33. *Ibid.*, p. 47.
34. *Ibid.*, pp. 47-48.
35. William Irvine: *op. cit.*, p. 47.
36. *Ibid.*, p. 1708.
37. William Irvine: *op. cit.*, Vol. I, p. 48.
38. Abdu'r Rasul: *Nairang-i-Zamana* edited by Dr. Muhammad Bair and published from Lahore, 1960; Also see *Makhaz-i-Twarikh-e-Sikhan*, pp. 76-80.
39. Sainapat: *op. cit.*, XVII, p. 123.
40. Fauja Singh: *Atlast*, *Travels of Guru Gobind Singh*, p. 19.
41. Ganda Singh: *Makhiz-i-Twarikh-e-Sikhan*, I, p. 84.
42. Koer Singh: *Gurubilas*, pp. 49-51.
43. Ishar Singh Nara: *Zafar Nama and Safar Nama*, **pp. 404-06, Published** in 1971.
44. *Muntikhul-Twarikh* (ii), p. 618.
45. *Ibid.*, pp. 404-06.
46. Lakshar Bhai Tīrathā, Gulāri Har Das, **Bhava Pir** Ujjain **Wich Sadh Sangat** Gur Shabad Niwas.
47. Melā Waddā Burhānpur Sanmukh Sikh **Sehaj Parkāsh.**
48. Refer to *Indian History as Told by Own* **Historians, Elliot: p. 566.** Also refer to Muntakhab-ul-Lubab.
49. Gian Singh: *Panth Parkash*, p. 319.
50. Fauja Singh: *Travels of Guru Gobind Singh*, p. 20, Pbi. Uni. Patiala, 1968.
51. William Irvine: *Later Mughals*, p. 59.
52. He was in the habit out of constantly addressing assemblies of wordly persons, religious fanatics and all sorts of people. Elliot and Dawson: Vol. VII, p. 566.
53. *Tarikh-i-Bahadur Shah*: "Guru Gobind Singh, one of the descendants of Nanak, had come into the districts and accompanied the royal camp." *The Indian History As Told By Its Own Historians*. Elliot & Dawson: p. 566.
54. Elphinstone: *History of India* (Fifth Edition), p. 679.
55. Khafi Khan: *Muntakhab-ul-Lubab*, Asiatic Society (ii) p. 652. Also see the translation of Mutakhab-ul-Lubab by Khafi Khan in the *Indian History As*

Told By its Own Historians*, p. 413. Also consult Steingass's *Persian-English Dictionary*.

56. Elliot and Dawson: *History of India As Told By Its Own Historians,* VI, p. 566.
57. Bahadur Shah Nama: Irvine, *Later Mughals* (I), p. 90.
58. Mahant met the Guru at Dadu Dwara at Narayana, 14 miles to the west of Jaipur city.
59. Macauliffe, M.A.: *op. cit.,* V, p. 236. The author of Periplus of the Erythrean Sea identifies it with ancient city of Tagara. In the middle of the 4th century it was a capital of a small kingdom. Ruins of ancient edifices and dilapidated pillars of temples speak volumes of spiritual importance.
60. Sainapat: *op. cit.,* p. 128.
61. Puran Singh: *op. cit.*, p. 124.
62. Dr. Ganda Singh translated this ballad into Punjabi. This has been published by S.G.P.C., Amritsar. Piara Singh Padam's book titled *Zafar Nama* contains this ballad. This ballad, according to the author has two sections. He titles one as 'Safar Nama', and the other as 'Amar Nama'. It is believed that *Amar Nama* was put to black and white soon after the death of the Guru.
63. Nath Mal: *Amar Nama*, Edited by Ganda Singh and published by Sikh Itihas Board, S.G.P.C., Amritsar.
64. *Ibid.*
65. *Ibid.*
66. Ahmed Shah Butalia: p. 11; Ganesh Das, *Risalah-i-Sahib Nama*, pp. 186-87; Latif: *History of the Punjab*.
67. *Amar Nama*.
68. The view is supported by the 'Chatur Jugi' an old manuscript written by Bhagwan Singh and discovered by Dr. Bhai Vir Singh.
69. Ganda Singh: *A Short History of the Sikhs*, p. 74, Pbi. Uni. Patiala, 1989.
70. Sainapat: *Sri Gur Sobha*, Chapter XVIII, 8-18, 777-783, 128-29.
71. Sainapat: *Sri Gur Sobha*, Chapter XVIII, p. 131.
72. Sainapat: *op. cit.,* p. 131, verses 343, 35.
73. The letter is reproduced in the book *Heritage of the Sikhs* by Dr. Harbans Singh, pp. 97-98. "Dasam Patshahian Tak Jamai Paidhe Yarvin Barvin Chaubanda Ajita Vaghaira Te Aitkad Lai Auna Hatiya Hai. Hor Hatiya Guru Japan Nal Dur Hosan, Par Ih Hatiya Gunah Bakhshiaiga Nahi Jo Manukh Ke Jame Uper Aitkad Karenge." Extract from the original letter. The original letter is now in possession of Bhai Chet Singh of the village Rupa, to whose ancestors it was addressed.
74. Harbans Singh: *Heritage of the Sikhs*, pp. 110-11, Manohar, 1983.
75. Sainapat: *op. cit.,* Chapter XVIII, p. 132, verses 41 to 44.

76. Gyani Gian Singh: *Twarikh Guru Khalsa*, pp. 355-56, Bhasha Vibhag, Punjab, 1967.
77. Forster William: *A Journey from Bengal to England*, London, 1798, pp. 262-63.
78. William Irvine: *Later Mughals*, p. 90 edited by J.N. Sarkar, Orient Reprint Corporation, Delhi, 1971.
79. Gokul Chand Narang: *Transformation of Sikhism*, p. 97, New Book Society of India, 1954.
80. *The Indian History As Told By Its Own Historians*, Vol. VII, p. 413.
81. *Hukamnama to the Sangat of Dhaul*, dated Oct. 2, 1707; *Gur Sobha* xi 35.
82. Sukha Singh: *Gur Bilas Patshahi* 10, pp. 432-34, Bhasha Vibhag, Punjab, 1989.
83. Cunningham: *A History of the Sikhs*, p. 73, S. Chand and Co., Delhi, 1955.
84. Gregor: *History of Sikhs*, Vol. I, pp. 99-100.
85. Hukam Nama which the Guru granted to the Pathan for good behaviour, is still preserved by the descendants of the Pathan. Refer to *Life of Guru Gobind Singh*, p. 263 by Kartar Singh.
86. Tarikh-i-Bahadur Shahi as incorporated in the *History of India as Told By Its Own Historians* by Elliot and Dawson, pp. 566-67.
87. *Gur Sobha, op. cit.*, XVIII, 127, 35.
88. Akhbarat-i-Darbar-i-Mualla, dated 24 Shaba, second year of Bahadur Shah (October 28, 1708) quoted by Dr. Ganda Singh in *Makhiz-i-Twarikh-e-Sikhan*, p. 83.
89. Akhbarat-i-Darbar-i-Mualla, quoted in *Makhiz-i-Twarikh-e-Sikhan*, p. 83.
90. William Irvine: *Later Mughals*, p. 90.
91. H.R. Gupta: *A History of Sikh Gurus*, p. 330, Munshi Ram Manohar Lal, Delhi, 1984.
92. Macauliffe, M.A.: *History of India*, IV, pp. 244-63.
93. Moreland: *India of Aurangzeb*, p. 91.
94. Sidh Gosht: *Guru Granth Sahib*, p. 943.
95. William Irvine: *Later Mughal*, I, p. 90.
96. Bannerjee, *Anglo Sikh Relations*.
97. Guru Arjan Dev: *Var Gujri Adi Granth*, p. 517.
98. *Sakat Ninda Dusht Khin Mahe Bidariyan.* (He smites the evil-minded, the ill tongued and the wicked in a second.)
99. Mohalla 4, Chhant Ghar 4, *Adi Granth*, p. 451.
100. *Zafar Nama*, pp. 24-25.
101. Bannerjee, I.B.: *op. cit.*, VI, p. 159.
102. Cunningham, J.D.: *History of the Sikhs*, p. 75, S. Chand and Co., 1955.

103. *Bachittar Natak,* Chapter VI.
104. Macauliffe, M.A.: *Sikh Religion*, pp. 296-301.
105. Narang, Gokul Chand: *Transformation of Sikhism,* p. 82, Kalyani Publishers, 1989.

16

GURU GRANTH SAHIB—THE ETERNAL GURU

In 1708, at Nander, Guru Gobind Singh terminated human succession to the Guru and established instead the condominium of the Granth, the Book, and the Panth, the Order of the Khalsa, with the following declaration which ever since is recited at the conclusion of every congregational prayer—morning and evening and all occasions of public worship by the Sikhs:

> The Order of the Khalsa was established
> as was the command of God
> This is now the commandment for all the Sikhs
> Accept the Granth as the Guru.
> Know Guru Granth ji as the visible body of the Gurus
> He who hath a properly trained mind
> shall find confirmation thereof in
> the contents of the book itself.[1]

Ever since, the Sikhs have recognised no human successor to the Gurus and have spoken of Guru Granth with utmost reverence. They call it as "Guru Eternal", the Everliving, Everawake and Everpresent embodiment of the spirit of ten Gurus (from Guru Nanak to Guru Gobind Singh), the Fulfiller of wishes, Never-failing Protector here and hereafter.[2]

Such a high esteem held by the Sikhs for Guru Granth Sahib is due to the fact that it enshrines the holy utterances of their Gurus, called Gurbani in the Sikh parlance. Gurbani or Bani is the word revealed by God direct to the Gurus who were under His direct commission and who themselves had vouchsafed that it came directly from God.

"The utterance has come from the Primal Divine source. It has annulled all anxiety."[3]

God merged His Self in the Gurus through whom He revealed and dispensed His Word.[4] Guru Nanak Dev is categorical in his statement "Word of Lord descends on me, I make it known to the people."[5] The Sikhs are, therefore, bidden to accept the Revelation of true Guru as true for ever as it is God Himself who maketh the Guru utter it. According to Guru Arjan Dev "The Holy Granth is the dwelling place of God, for it is the embodiment of the perfect Divine wisdom." Guru Amar Das asserts "The revealed Word of the Guru is the Light of the World. God's Grace descends into human soul by means of it." Word is revelation. According to Guru Ram Das "Revelation is the Guru and the Guru is the revelation. Whosoever shall accept the revelation of the Guru shall behold the Guru himself." "The Holy Guru is the Holy Word. And the Holy Word is the Holy Guru himself, which shall lead one to the way of salvation." Another utterance of the Guru makes this point more lucid. The Guru declares that 'the Word that God had lodged in the True Guru, has been revealed by the True Guru.'[6] The Word is Brahm itself and union of God is achieved through it. Word is also a true 'knowledge'.[7] According to Guru Amar Das, 'It (Word) is the light of the world a formless[8] manifestation of God, incomparable, infinite, guarantee for salvation. It is the true preceptor and guide of great profundity and inscrutability'[9], the only medium of communication between God and human beings.[10] Word is the Guru and the Guru is in the word. All the nectars are contained in the Word. If the disciple obeys what the Word says, the Guru becomes manifest and saves him.[11] In fact, the Gurus are Gurus because they embodied the spirit, light or Shabad. It is, therefore, emphasised in a number of compositions of Guru Granth Sahib that *Shabad* (Word) was Guru, as well as the God and His manifestation. Since 'Word' was directly revealed to the Gurus, it was uniquely sacrosanct, worthy of reverence of one and all. It is from this perspective that the

Sikhs regard the Holy Granth the repository of the sacred Words and holy utterances, as the continuing manifestation in visible form of the mystic personality of their ten Divine Masters. It is this conception of the directly revealed (determinate) word distinguishable from the Hindu Sphota and the Neoplatonic logos that elevates Guru Granth to the status of eternal Guru expressing the Divine spirit that descended in history through the revelatory medium of Sikh Gurus.

Guru Granth Sahib has always commanded respect and reverence of not only the disciples but also of the Gurus themselves. In 1604, the task of compiling and editing of the Holy Granth was accomplished. The event was momentous and it was celebrated with fervour and devotion. The Granth was taken to Hari Mandir Sahib, the construction of which was completed three years earlier, in a colourful procession. Baba Budha (1506-1631) who was appointed its first Granthi carried it on this head and Guru Arjan Dev walked behind reverently waving the fly-whisk over it as a sign of great respect. It was ceremoniously installed on August 16, 1604 in the sanctum sanctorum. When Bhai Budha opened the volume to obtain *Vak* or *Hukam* for the inaugural as well as thanks-giving ceremony, Guru Arjan Dev stood behind in attendance. He thanked God and addressed the congregation. According to *Gur Bilas*, he uttered:

> "Listen you all to my directive
> And believe it as ever true.
> Accept the Granth as equal with the Guru
> And think no distinction between the two."[12]

Bhai Santokh Singh records "Sri Guru addressed them that God is incarnate in this sacred volume" (Sri Gurū Kahio prab darbārā/ granth parmesar ke avtārā).

These chronicles also inform us that when the Holy Granth was closed after the evening service, it was taken to its resting place where it was lodged on a bedstead covered our with splendid bedspread. Guru Arjan Dev himself slept by its side on the ground, betokening his profound reverence for the Word. The author of *Gur Bilas Chhevin Padshahi* vouches that Guru Arjan Dev made it a routine to sleep on the ground daily by its side after saying prayers.[13]

Guru Har Rai (1630-1661) observed "Whoever is our devotee or disciple, he must revere Gurbani with all his heart. Whoever does not revere the Guru's hymns know him not to be our Sikh."

The occasion which evoked this observation was when some Sikhs singing hymns from Guru Granth Sahib visited the Guru. At that time, the Guru was resting on a couch. On hearing the hymns, he atonce rose up. When asked the reason, he said "Hear, my beloved Sikhs, the Guru is embodied in compositions whose sanctity is immeasurable and unrivalled. The Guru's instruction is a raft to cross over the fiery oceans of the World. It conferreth happiness on true Guru's Sikhs and removeth sin from the hearts of the readers and reciters.... It produceth divine knowledge and dispelleth ignorance."

When Guru Harkrishan, the eighth in apostolic line, was on the verge of his final departure from the world, the prominent Sikhs present there asked, "How would we be able to see and serve you?" The Guru replied, "Gurus may die but their heart that is Granth Sahib, shall remain with you. It containeth instructions, divine knowledge, and the Guru's spell. It will satisfy all men's desires. Read it and act on its counsels and Guru Nanak will ever assist you."[14]

Thus, the Holy Word enshrined in Guru Granth Sahib was always cherished and revered not only by the disciples but also by the Gurus themselves. According to Professor Teja Singh, "From the very start, Guru Arjan Dev intended Granth Sahib to be not only the scripture of the Sikhs but more than that to take the place of a living Guru. Guru Arjan Dev himself had stated and so had his predecessors, that in reality it was the Word that was the Guru."[15] Guru Arjan Dev's successors also laid emphasis on this point. Guru Gobind Singh, the last Guru in human form declared Granth Sahib to be his successor a day before his final exit from this world. This happened on 6th October, 1708 C.E. Granth Sahib therefore, began to be reverently called as Guru Granth Sahib and the Word revealed to the Gurus and enshrined in Guru Granth Sahib would be the eternal Guru of the Sikhs. Guruship of Guru Granth Sahib must be understood in two senses. One, no human being or scripture other than Granth Sahib could claim to be the Guru of Sikhs and secondly and more importantly 'Word' being the message of God transmitted though the Gurus could not be but everlasting for the whole human race.

Ever since the Guru vested succession in Granth Sahib, the Sikhs have been reverencing it the way they reverenced their living Gurus. Guru Granth Sahib has been not only the focal point of their intense devotion but also the only object of their veneration. As the succession was passed on to it in perpetuity, the Sikhs accepted it as their Guru Eternal. This has been their complete understanding and inviolate conviction since the passing away of Guru Gobind Singh.

In their hard, exilic days soon afterward the death of their tenth Master, when they were outlawed and had to seek the safety on the hills and jungles, the Sikhs' most precious possession, which they cherished and defended at the cost of their lives, was the Guru Granth Sahib. In the time of Maharaja Ranjit Singh, who established sovereignty in the name of the Khalsa, personal devotion and court ceremonial centred upon the Guru Granth Sahib. As historical records testify Ranjit Singh began his day by making obeisance to the Guru Granth Sahib. On festive occasions of Baisakhi and Diwali he made pilgrimage to Amritsar to bow before Guru Granth Sahib. For the Sikhs, Guru Granth Sahib was the only focus of religious attachment. None other existed in either human form or symbolically. It was owned as the medium of revelation descended through the Gurus. Also it was for Sikhs the perpetual authority, spiritual as well as historical. They lived their religion in response to it. Through it, they were able to observe their faith more fully, more vividly. It was central to all that subsequently happened in Sikh life. It was the perpetual source of their intellectual and cultural activities and attainments. It moulded the Sikh concept of life. From it the community's ideals, institutions and rituals derived their meaning. Its role in ensuring community's integration and permanence and in determining the course of history has been crucial.[16]

It is a unique scripture, which is non-denominational and universal even as it is the Eternal Guru of the Sikhs. It contains utterances of 36 seers. Out of these only six are Sikh Gurus or prophet teachers; Guru Nanak, Guru Angad, Guru Amar Das, Guru Ram Das, Guru Arjan Dev and Guru Tegh Bahadur. Only one Dohra (couplet) included in the Slokas of Guru Tegh Bahadur is ascribed to the tenth Master Guru Gobind Singh. Hymns of fifteenth Bhaktas including Muslim Sufis and compositions of eleven Bards (Bhatts); the composition of Satta and Balwand and Sundar are also incorporated in the corpus of Guru Granth Sahib.

Among the Hindu saints while Bhagat Ravi Das (C.E. 1267—1335) was a cobbler and Bhagat Nam Dev (C.E. 1270—1350) was a calico printer and Bhagat Dhanna (C.E. 1415) was a peasant. Out of the rest, Bhagat Jai Dev (1142—1200), Rama Nand (C. 1366—1467), Parmanand (B. 1483) and Sur Das (B.C. 1529) were Brahmans. Bhagat Trilochan (C. 1267—1335) was Vaish and Bhagat Pipa (1408—1468) was a Rajput prince, Bhagat Sain (1390—1440) was a barber. Eleven Bhatts who contributed *Swayyas* to Guru Granth Sahib were all Brahmans.

Seven of the contributors were Muslims. Out of them Sheikh Farid (1173—1265) and Bhikhan (1480—1573) were Sufi mystics. Bhagat Kabir (1398—1448) born of Hindu parents and brought up by Muslim parents, was a weaver by profession while Sadna (of late thirteenth century) was a butcher by vocation. Bhai Mardana (1459—1534), Balwand and Satta were Mirasis (a caste of hereditary ministrels and genealogists) and had served the House of the Gurus as rebeck players, hence called Rababis. Except Sheikh Farid, all of them were from the so-called lower classes of society. The contributors hailed from different places situated in different regions of India and hence the 'scripture' was not any place or region specific.

The contributors being diverse in terms of religion, castes strata of society and regions the Holy scripture represented thoughts and expressions which were marked for transcendence and rendered it inter-communal, non-denominational and ecumenical.

It was this uniqueness, which distinguished it from other scriptures. According to Dr. Kirpal Singh, "No other scripture of any other religion of the world contains any kind of writings of any Holy person belonging to a faith caste or creed other than that of its own, much less of those who had been regarded and treated as outcastes and untouchables for centuries together." And this in spite of the fact that the Sikh Gurus and their disciples did not share their beliefs, as for instance, the Sikh Gurus did not believe in the incarnation of God, finality of prophethood, idol worship, caste exclusiveness, penances, tonsure of the Hindus and circumcision of the Muslims. To Guru Arjan, who compiled and edited the Holy Granth, the respective creeds, castes, places, callings, locales etc. were irrelevant. On the other hand, their message, its spiritual quintessence, universal spirit and truth alone were crucial. By doing so, Guru Granth Sahib struck an important note that truth is never the exclusive monopoly of any one individual, caste or creed; it could be realised and possessed by any one having sincere yearnings for it. In this perspective Radhakrishnan has observed very aptly, "A remarkable feature of the *Adi Granth* is that it contains the writings of the religious teachers of Hinduism, Islam etc." exhibiting thereby "respect for all religions, belief in the freedom of human spirit, virtue of toleration", and "noble quality of appreciation of whatever was valuable in other religious tradition."[17]

At places in Guru Granth Sahib, some hymns of certain Bhagtas express such views which differed from those of the Gurus. Sheikh Farid, for instance, curses himself for not going to a mosque five times a day for offering Namaz (the Muslim prayer):

> Farīdā beniwājā kutiā, eh nā bhalī rīt
> kabhī chal nā Aia, panje wakht masīt
> "O, Prayerless accursed Farid
> This is not good for you,

You have never gone to the mosque
at the five times of prayer."[18]

Obviously, Gurus consider such prayers a mere formality. Such examples can be culled in scores. But the Guru's point was something different about which Prof. Teja Singh's observation is worth noticing. He says, "We must know that these antithetical sayings are given an honoured place in *Adi Granth* which not only holds a scriptual position among the Sikhs but wields authority equal to that of the Gurus whose word is law. The Sikh Gurus ushered in a new era in the religious history of mankind, when they declared that the true religion consisted of two things only: love of God's Name and purity of conduct.[19] The Guru dispensed with all the formalities in favour of these two things, which are nowhere contradicted by any of the Saints/Bhagtas whose compositions are incorporated in the Guru Granth Sahib. They might be differing from the Gurus in their method of worship but in their aim they were not different and their aim was to love God and to do good. Their writings were included not for their doctrinal value but for their ability to create a stir of the Nām in one's heart.

As long as the aim of the Bhagtas was to foster love for God, in whichever form they conceived Him and as long as their writings had the effect of suppressing evil tendencies in men, the Gurus welcomed them and gave an honoured place to them as co-workers. Religion, according to the Gurus, is not a set of doctrines but a clean way of life dedicated to God.[20] Only such hymns of the Bhaktas were incorporated as conformed to the spirit of reform then in vogue.

Guru Granth Sahib has brought forth a new conception of Ultimate Reality, a new vision of universal man, and a new pattern of non-discriminatory society based on equalitarian and pluralistic concepts, as expressed, for instance, in its following verses:

God at first created His Light,
Then all the people were made from it.
As the entire world has come from that Light,
Then who are superior, who inferior?

O, brethren be not strayed by illusion.
For, the Creator is in the created
and the created in the Creator,
Who pervades all, everywhere.

(Bhagat Kabir, *Guru Granth Sahib,* p. 1349)

Arnold Toynbee has, therefore, aptly remarked that Guru Granth Sahib is "a part of mankind's common spiritual treasure". He stated "It is important that it should be brought within the direct reach of as many people as possible.... A book that has meant and means, so much to such a notable community as the Sikh Khalsa deserves close study from the rest of the world."[21] Toynbee also prophesied in 1960 "Mankind's religious future may be obscure, yet one thing can be foreseen. The living higher religions are going to influence each other, more than ever before in these days of increasing communication between all parts of the world and all branches of human race. In this coming debate the Sikh religion and its scripture, the *Adi Granth*, will have something of special value to say to the rest of the world.

The Guru's message is terse, lucid, unequivocal that it is irreligious to subscribe to differences on account of birth, caste, creed, calling, colour or country and instead it enjoins upon people to cultivate universal respect for all, regarding all as equal and respectable. Guru Nanak, highlighting this point, says:

Call everyone high (noble)
for none seems low (mean)
As God, the only potter (maker) has
fashioned all vessels alike
And it is His Light alone
that shines in all creation.

In the same vein Guru Arjan Dev threw further light underlining such a radical concept of unity, fraternity and universality:

Nā kō bēri nāhin bēgānā
Sāgāl sāng hum ko bān aie.[22]

Neither is anyone my foe
Nor am I enemy of anyone
I have made all and sundry my living friends,
And I am a friend of one and all. (*G.G.S.*, p. 1299)

Equality among people, races and nations as enjoined upon by Guru Eternal is not rooted in polemics of dialectical materialism nor was it the product of some social concepts based upon Humanism or theological formulations rather it was the product of the understanding of the Ultimate Reality and that of His creations the best part of which is Man. This being so the Guru repeatedly lays emphasis on the point that man must cultivate love for God, mutual love and understanding, truthful living and social responsibility. The Guru believes:

Jo rte seh apne
Tin bhāve sab koi.[23]

They who love God
love everybody.

"Cherishing long devotion to Him in humility is a guarantee to salvation"[24], a man or woman without true love is an empty shell which soon crumbles and is reduced to dust.[25]

Love must be expressed in altruistic service to humankind. The Guru's utterances are very pertinent at this point. He says, "All living beings are your own creatures but none can obtain any reward without rendering devoted service to you and to your created one." "A resting place at the Divine court can be found only through the devoted service of the people in this world."[26]

While envisioning and preaching social equality, altruistic service to the people of the world, social justice, love and harmony, the Guru very explicitly profiled that mankind must be freed from all kinds of bondages—mental, spiritual, social and political etc., so that it may realise its true self or Divine within. In the time of the Gurus as it is even now the people were/are enmeshed in labyrinths of formalism, oppressive political set-ups, creedal particularism, class and caste divisions, false beliefs, superstitions, divisive ideologies and this is one of the important reasons that they were unable to forge ahead to attain Self-realisation. Guru Arjan Dev's utterances in this respect are abundantly enlightening. He says:

> "The egg shell of doubt has shattered
> And the mind is illumined
> The Master has freed us from bondage
> by putting off fetters from our feet."[27]

This excerpt from Guru Granth Sahib is an explicit testimony to what the Guru cherished for the people.

Observance of fasting either by the Hindus or by the Muslims, ritual bathing, pilgrimages to Kaaba to perform Hajj or to Hardwar or any other place, performance of different rituals or ceremonies are of no avail as these are empty acts and induce hallucinations, illusions, confusions and false consciousness. These are, in no way, relevant to the realisation of God and remodelling of society as envisaged by the Guru Granth Sahib. The following utterances of the Guru-Eternal are at once cardinal and significant:

> "I neither observe fasting (like Hindus), nor keep the fast during Ramzan (like a Muslim), for, I serve only Him who saves at the last. The Gosain of the Hindus and Allah of the Muslims are one and the same to me for I have found release from the rituals of both. I neither go to Kaaba to perform the Hajj nor to Hindu pilgrim-stations for ritual bathing and worship, for, I serve only the one God, and no other. I neither worship in the Hindu way, nor say prayers like the Muslims, for I bow within my heart, only the one formless. We are neither Hindu nor Muslims, for our body and soul belong to one Supreme Being, who alone is both Rama and Allah for us."[28]

Guru Granth Sahib exhorts that religious exclusiveness dogmatism and egocentric individualism are anti-thesis of religion which is Truth, and nothing but the Truth. Expressing this conviction in very clear terms, it states:

> "He, who grasps the Truth
> realises that as the Creator is One

and ever the same age after age,
There is, therefore, one religion of all mankind."[29]

"The most exalted of all religions consists
of love of God's name and purity of conduct.
The highest of all actions lies in the
effacement of impure thinking in the
company of the holy."[30]

"And the true religion is within the reach of every one, low, high, Khatri, Brahman, Sud, Vaish, Jogis, Jattis, only they need loving devotion to the name of God and doing good deeds in all humility. In fact, the Guru Eternal heralds that there is no need of renunciating the world nor to practise asceticism as one can relish and celebrate beatific union between oneself and God while leading a full life of smiling, playfulness and cheerful enjoyment of wear and food."[31]

Man is further advised to uphold his firm faith in God's Will, and remain grateful to Him and be content with whatever He bestows on him in His wisdom and His Will. The Guru says:

Tu kāhe dole prānia | tudh rakhegā sirjan hār ||
Jin paidaish tu kiā | so deie adhār ||

(Guru Arjan Dev, *G.G.S.*, Rag Tilang, p. 724)

Why do you waver and fall into suspense
He, your creator, shall surely sustain you.
He, who has created this world,
Also takes care of it.

Guru Granth Sahib's vastness of vision envisions even specific religious/social group such as Jogis, Hindus, Muslims, farmers and traders holds out that Yoga consists not merely in talk or chatter. He, who looks upon all alike and regards all equal, may be acclaimed as a true Yogi.[32] Similarly, it tells the Hindus as well as Muslims to recognise the truth rather than remain sunk in formalism and rituals, ceremonies and sectarianism. For instance Hindus' attention is drawn to their performance of idol worship instead of the Primal God. The Guru warned that they would be doing a futile exercise. How can a stone which sinks, can ferry others across.[33] Muslims who had lost the true track were also advised to develop compassion, faith in righteousness modesty, uprightness if they intended to be a true Muslim instead of laying emphasis on mosque, prayer-mat, Koran, circumcision and fasting.[34] Likewise traders and farmers are made to realise that while pursuing their vocations the ultimate objective should not be forgotten. Let their actions be those of love and amity and of such nature that none of them should repent afterwards. The Guru in fact advises that never ever be particularistic, be universal, transcendental and humanistic.

The Eternal Guru is splendid—very splendid. It embodies in itself appeals and prayers invoking benediction of God for the whole mankind. It says:

"All creation is yours, O Lord,
And you are the only Master of all
Why are they visited, then, with your wrath.
In spite of your having wrath on them
They are still yours and you are theirs, O, Lord."

(*Guru Granth Sahib*, *Rag Siri*, p. 25)

"The World is in flames
Save it, O, God, out of your mercy,
Save it through whichever dispensation
It can be saved O, Lord."

(*Guru Amar Das, Rag Bilawal*, p. 858)

"Be Merciful, O Lord!
And keep all beings in your care.
Let grain and water be in plenty,
Shatter our suffering and penury,
And ferry us across the ocean of existence."

What a universal appeal, what a marvellous altruistic spirit, what a lofty attitude—seeking boons and blessings for the peace, prosperity and welfare of every human beings, irrespective of one's belief, faith, caste, creed, colour gender or status.

Again and again, with vehemence and deep concern, we find Guru Eternal tending counsels that seeker should salvage himself from ego or *Haumai*. Man's ego is the cause of most of his/her motivations and actions. Self-conceit or I-am-ness gives rise to five main vices: lust, greed, anger, attachment and pride. An egoist thinks only of oneself and one's own interest and does not care for others. Hence, exploitation, violence and wickedness. How can man be free from self-centredness? Guru Granth Sahib speaks of the cure:

> Self-centredness is to be replaced by centredness. Service to God is also service to man. Only then will man start to think more of his duties than of his rights. He who performs acts of charity and benefits others and improves links between God and himself.
>
> By shedding his ego, man may unite with God.
>
> (*G.G.S.*, p. 750)

To shed *Haumai* and reach the stage of Self-realisation, Guru Granth Sahib exhorts that a seeker should attend *Sangat*, an assembly of seekers of Truth. In numerous verses in Guru Granth Sahib, the importance of *Sangat* has been highlighted as a nursery of true human beings called 'Sachiar' or 'Gurmukh' as a raft to come nearer to God, as a guide to enable one to protect himself/herself from the evil forces from within or outside. Lest man should go astray and run after illusions or wrong goals, Guru Granth Sahib defines what liberation—Mukti really means. It is realising identification with God and then to work and strive to make his creation more beautiful, more lovable. It does not mean extinction of oneself or total absorption of oneself in God. Asceticism is thus rejected by the Guru Eternal as it negates life which is held very sacred by the Guru.

Guru Granth Sahib, highly esteemed by the Sikhs, is central within the structure of Sikh worship. But this centrality is much more than it can be understood in physical sense. All aspects of Sikh worship relate directly to it and practically the entire context of worship is drawn from it. The Sikhs have always cherished to accord the maximum respect to Guru Granth Sahib. Therefore, at physical level, they have kept it draped, normally in expensive cloth on a cot under a canopy (called 'chandni' in Sikh parlance) either at a gurdwara or at a

Sikh home. While it is undraped, it is usually protected by the use of a flywhisk.

Every gurdwara (Sikh temple) has Guru Granth Sahib opened in its congregational hall which is arranged as an oriental throne room, with the Guru Granth installed on the improvised throne. All this is done to show nothing more than the usual symbols of royalty, enjoying sovereign powers familiar to the East from time immemorial and in this case it is to indicate no more.

The whole scene and ceremonious atmosphere and conduct are scrupulously designed to indicate to all and sundry that the Order of the Khalsa claims to be sovereign, *sui generis* and that he who barters away this sovereignty is a traitor and he who assumes it, instead, is a usurper. To infer from this anything different, as many have done such as that the Sikhs worship their sacred book, or that the Sikhs are bibliolaters is wholly misconceived.

In this connection it would not be out of place to point out that Guru, while in human form, expressly disclaimed worship unto him insisting that worship was due to God alone. The human Guru is not to be worshipped, nor scripture in physical sense be accorded worship.

The language of Guru Granth Sahib is fluid and expansive. No geographical or regional barriers limit it. Moreover, there is a rather long time lapse between writings. Consequently, literary critics had a hard time labelling the language of Guru Granth Sahib. For instance, language of Guru Nanak's compositions is held by some as Punjabi, by some as Hindi, and by some the language of a traditional period. Guru Nanak had to pass on his dispensation to the multitude and not only to the learned, and he, therefore, made use of the vocabulary intelligible to his audience. His sermons therefore carried a mixture of Punjabi, which was the prime language of his writings. This was so in the compositions of his successors too who sought to echo his style, his manner of communication. Thus even though there is a mixture of different words from different linguistic sources, which each contributor from a different period and locale brought, the overall language of Guru Granth is Punjabi, whose script is Gurmukhi—the characters of which were developed and standardised by Guru Nanak and Guru Angad. Most of the elements, which seem to suggest a heterogeneous collection of linguistic forms are, in reality, closely related. There are certainly words from diverse languages as Sindhi, Arabic, Persian and Marathi but with very rare exceptions these produce no more than vocabulary problems and certainly there is nothing to contradict the fact that Guru Granth Sahib's language is Punjabi.

The words in Guru Granth Sahib, which in fact always form the stuff of any language are poetic meaning thereby, that their quality is full, dynamic, sensuous. Certainly, they are not uncouth paradoxes, obscurities that multiply and grow as human mind advances in the realm of philosophic speculation. In Guru Granth Sahib, 'poetic' words maintain their concreteness and vitality. For example, in the Guru Granth Sahib we very often read the word *dhan*. However, each time it has its own use because sometimes it can be understood as a native bride and at others as an erotic beauty of a respected mother or a woman having given up spiritual quest and so on. "Not once is *dhan* tritely conceived or abstracted under a philosophic designation."[35]

Nor the language of Guru Granth Sahib is a steno language in the sense that its meaning is rigidly fixed. "Engulfed in a aura of mystery, the words of Guru Granth Sahib are always open. Paradoxical though it may seem, in the openness of the words is their capacity to conceal. In fact, the words of Guru Granth Sahib conceal and unfold perennially. Does not the 'I' in the beginning of the creedal statement (*Mul Mantar*) in Guru Granth Sahib manifest the entire Guru Granth Sahib and yet hides as incredible amount too."[36]

Words from Punjabi, Hindi, Arabic, Persian plus various vernaculars merge into one another, presenting a kaleidoscope of images. According to Heidegers "the nature of image is to let something be seen". Surely the images in Guru Granth Sahib partake of such character. According to Dr. Gurvinder Kaur "poetic images as in the Guru Granth Sahib are imagings in a distinctive sense not mere fancies and illusions, they are imagings that are visible illusions of the alien in the sight of the familiar". "They seem to have an elastic force which impulse the imagination to an infinite loftiness, providing at the same time strong foundations beneath. The images of Guru Granth Sahib come from different contexts, natural scenery, economics, politics and domestic life *et al.*; and all of them, without exception, awaken us to visualise and face the unseen."

Metaphors, similes and symbols are extensively used in Guru Granth Sahib. The purpose was clear: (i) to make the people understand clearly through comparisons; (ii) to embellish the poetry; and (iii) to stir the imagination to look even beyond the obvious. When the Guru writes himself as 'humble bee, always thirsty', his intense longing, a deep psychological phenomenon, metamorphoses through the cool heat of the imagination into projecting a wanting so beautiful, so beautifully. "That the metamorphous is not distortion of actual experience but contrarily a verification and enlivening of the Guru's thirst is clear. The metaphor generates an energy, which moves one faculty into another—senses (sight—humble bee over the lotus, taste: the succulence of the lotus)—emotion (desire)—imagination (perceiving the affinity) never diminishing only expanding them." Such metaphors are used frequently and they not only lend charm and vitality to the language but also metamorphose.

So is the case of wide usage of similes in Guru Granth Sahib. These weave images and provoke or impulse one to reflect upon them to comprehend the theme—through which the Guru wanted his disciples to comprehend and imbibe.

Symbols, like metaphors and similes, flash forth beautiful images and deep thoughts. Going beyond themselves 'the symbols participate in reality of that which they represent'. For instance, there is the symbol of bridegroom coming to wed his wife (sajjan viahan aia) and is central to Guru Granth Sahib. The relation of the bridegroom is entirely from a physical world but as symbol, it has the capacity to evoke numerous religious emotions along with the love, the sentiment for bridegroom. Even after four centuries of its installations, the *Guru Granth Sahib* is still the only continuing spiritual and historical authority for the Sikhs, and shall ever remain as such, because it has become not only their religious guide, but also the greatest factor capable of shaping intellectual and cultural environment. In the present times when enlightened elites have started searching for the acceptable pattern of globalisation which they think is the most wanted because it can accrue a lot of benefits to the whole human race, *Guru Granth Sahib's* message is sure to attract their attention for its approach is universal and its embrace as vast as the whole humankind.

FOOTNOTES

1. Āgia Bhei akal ki tabe chalaeo Panth ||
   Sab Sikhan ko hukam hai Guru maneo Granth ||
   Guru Granth ko maneo pargat guran ki deh ||
   Ja ka hirda shud hai khoj shabad mein leh ||
2. Dusan padshian di jagdi jot hazra-hajur, jahra zahur, sarab *ichha purak*, halet palat de rakhe Sri Guru Granth Sahib ji.
3. Dhur ki Bani aie, Tin sagli chint metaie
4. Gur meh app samae, shabad vartaia ||
   Guru Nanak Dev: *G.G.S., Rag Malhar*, p. 1279.
5. Guru Nanak Dev: *Ibid.*, p. 308.
   Satgur ki bani sat sat kar janho
   Gursikho har karta app mohuhu kadhaie
   Mahalla 4, *G.G.S.* , p. 308.
   Pothi permeshar ka thān
   Sadh sang gaveh gun Gobind
   Puran brahm gian ||
   Guru Arjan Dev: *G.G.S.*, p. 1226.
6. Guru Nanak Dev: *G.G.S., Rag Malhar*, p. 1279.
7. Guru Amar Das: *G.G.S., Rag Sri*, p. 39.
8. Guru Amar Das: *Ibid., Rag Sri*, p. 67.
9. Guru Amar Das: *Ibid., Rag Gujri*, p. 515.
   Waho waho bani nirankar hei, tis jevad avar na koe ||
10. Guru Nanak Dev: *Ibid., Rag Sorath*, p. 653.
    Shabad Gur peera gaher gambhira.... ||
11. *Ibid.*, p. 58.
12. Sohan: *Gur Bilas Chhevin Padshahi*, Stanza 409.

13. *Ibid.*, Dohra, Stanza 41.
14. Macauliffe, M.A.: *The Sikh Religion,* Vol. IV, pp. 327-28.
15. Teja Singh, Prof.: *In the Sikh Review,* Calcutta, June, 1958.
16. Harbans Singh, Prof.: *Sikh Heritage*, p. 100.
17. Radhakrishnan: *Selections from the Sacred Writings of the Sikhs, op. cit.*, p. 17. There is another unique feature of Guru Granth Sahib. Among the saved scriptures of the world Sri Guru Granth Sahib is the only Scripture compiled and authenticated by the Guru himself and acquired scriptural and transcendental status of eternally living Guru by a formal investiture of spiritual authority at the hands of Guru Gobind Singh, whereas the holy books of other religions attained this distinction only gradually through building up of tradition in the long course of time.
18. Sheikh Farid: *Guru Granth Sahib, Slok* 70, p. 1381.
19. Guru Arjan Dev: *Guru Granth Sahib, Rag Gauri, Sukhmani*, p. 266.
20. Teja Singh: *The Holy Granth, op. cit.*, pp. xxiii, xxiv.
21. Toynbee, Arnold in his Foreword to Unesco's *Selections from the Sacred Writings of the Sikhs*, London, 1960, pp. 9-11.
22. *Rag Kanra, Guru Granth Sahib*, p. 1299.
23. *Ibid.*, p. 557.
24. *Ibid.*, p. 470.
25. *Ibid.*, p. 62.
26. Wich dunia sev kamie I ta dargeh besan paiai II
27. Guru Arjan Dev, *Guru Granth Sahib*, p. 1002.
28. *Ibid.*, p. 897.
29. Guru Nanak Dev: *Guru Granth Sahib*, p. 1188.
30. Guru Arjan Dev: *Ibid., Rag Gauri Stanza* 3, p. 266.
31. Guru Arjan Dev: *Rag Gujri, G.G.S.*, p. 522.
32. Guru Nanak Dev: *Guru Granth Sahib, Rag Suhi*, p. 730.
33. Guru Nanak Dev: *G.G.S., Rag Bihagra*, p. 556.
34. *Ibid. Rag Majh*, p. 140.
35. Gurvinder Kaur: *The Guru Granth Sahib*, p. 90.
36. *Ibid.*, p. 71.

17

SIKH RELIGIOUS ORDERS

Extraordinary potential inhered Guru's gospel. It illumined consciousness which in turn facilitated people's passage to a high level of consciousness. That stage enabled the people to better appraise their long-held concepts, notions, fancies and faiths and then build new metaphysical and social constructs along with requisite organisations which are often named sects, wrongly though because in Sikhism, there is no room of any sect or cult. These organisations at best can be appreciated as artifices to express the laudable teachings of the Gurus.

Sewa Panthis

The Sikh Gurus were humanists par excellence. They had put man in the centre and endeavoured hard to bring him solace and salvation. They not only tried to uplift man on religious plane but also endeavoured to improve the lot of man on political plane. Guru Gobind Singh addressed himself to man 'qua man' without the narrow distinctions and antagonisms of east and west, Hindu and Muslim, Masjid and Mandir. The west was not so prominent a factor of influence in India during the 17th century, yet the writings and teachings of the Gurus resounded with international humanitarian overtones, that there is no difference between man and man is clearly portrayed by the tenth Guru in the following words:

> One man by shaving his head to become a holy monk
> Another sets up as a yogi or some other kind of ascetic

Some call themselves Hindus: other call themselves Musalmans
Among these are the Shiahs, there are Sunnis also
And yet man is of one race in all the world.
God as Creator and God as Good
God in His Bounty and God in His Mercy
Is all one God. Even in our errors we should not separate God from God
Worship the one God, for all men the one Divine Teacher
All men have the same form
All men have the same soul.[1]

The discrimination between man and man is altogether excluded and the leitmotif of all the activities is welfare and upliftment of man.

This theme of the Gurus, on operational plane, found expressions in the Gurus' literary compositions and their actions. It also found its expression in the activities of the Order of the Seva Panthis—followers of Path of Service whose sole aim is to see to the welfare of human beings without cherishing any desire for fruit or reward in the mundane sense. They were in fact motivated by purely altruistic impulses.

The founder of this Order was Bhai Ghaniya, who belonged to Sodra, a village in Gujranwala district and was a *Dhamman*[2] *Kshatri*. Since his childhood, he had religious propensities and showed signs of transcending narrow-mindedness and egocentricity. When he was ten years old, he happened to go to Anandpur along with his father, and was much impressed by the towering personality of the ninth Guru. He again went to Anandpur at the age of sixteen. This time he felt so much attached with the Guru's mission that he decided to pass his life in serving the Guru and his cause. He was handsome, well-built and intelligent. His parents wanted him to marry but he chose to work for the Guru's cause which, in fact, was no other than the people's cause. In spite of the best efforts of his parents, he refused to marry not because he did not believe in this institution, but because he did not want to give divided attention to his mission.

All records show that Bhai ji engrossed himself in rendering service to the Guru, individuals and the people in general. He felt pleasure in rinsing utensils, cleansing campus of *Guru Ka Langar* (Guru's kitchen), bringing water for the kitchen as well as for the thirsty travellers and visitors. He slept very little, hardly four hours at night. All the time his attention was fixed on the wonderous God and His Creations. He would spare not even a second without doing something for the people. Bhai ji enjoyed the sweet utterances of the ninth Guru, and felt elevated by his sacred darshan and transported to Bliss by his sermous. He was lucky enough to accompany Guru Tegh Bahadur in his eastern tours. He drank deep at the fountain of *Gurbani*. He very unassumingly and steadily served the people irrespective of their beliefs, group affiliations and status.

His dress used to be made of home-spun coarse cloth, expressive of his simplicity and honest living. He was extremely humble. Humility was his root tendency. Sometimes when Guru Tegh Bahadur out of amusement told him that people had lodged complaints against him, he would at once say:

> We are stained by the sins which are numerous; only God can purify us.

Guru Tegh Bahadur was executed under orders of Aurangzeb on the 11th November, 1675. Bhai Ghaniya suffered a shock at the gruesome execution and could recover only after some time.

As time rolled on, Bhai ji's zeal for sewa (service) redoubled. Day in and day out, he was busy with assuaging the afflicted, dressing the wounded and comforting the comfortless.

In 1703 C.E., the battle of Anandpur ensued. The enemy forces comprising the armies of hill States, Srihind Sarkar and irregulars such as Ranghars and Gujjars. The Guru had also collected nearly ten thousand men. Although this number was insignificant as compared to the strength of the enemy, yet on the Guru's side there was will of the people to fight and die for their Master.

The Sikhs fought valiantly with the result that the enemy's hope for having easy victory was dashed to the ground.

One day complaints were made to the Guru that a Sikh, Ghaniya by name, had been serving water and rendering first aid not only to the Sikhs but to the wounded enemy. The Guru called Ghaniya and enquired if it was true. The humble Ghaniya replied that he had been serving those who fell in the battlefield. "My eyes could not distinguish between Sikhs and Mughals,[3] as I saw Guru's face in everyone." The Guru appreciated him and remarked that he had really understood his mission. As a mark of approval of his action, the Guru gave him a box of ointment with the remark that he should not serve water alone to the wounded in the battlefield but also ointment to the wounded to ensure their speedy recovery. According to Bhai Kahan Singh, the Guru, as a token of his pleasure for his humanitarian work, gave him a bed and a handkerchief.

The gifts from the Guru inspired him all the more and he collected round himself a band of the Sikhs, ever prepared to put in service for the people. Guru Gobind Singh evacuated Anandpur on the night of 5-6 December, 1705. The enemy forgot all about their pledges and set out in hot pursuit immediately. Realising the impending danger, Guru Gobind Singh gave a band of 50 men to Bhai Udai Singh and assigned to him the responsibility of checking the enemy's advancement. Bhai Udai Singh fought a bloody battle at Shahi Tibbi with the enemy with a handful of his men; all of them perished fighting covering themselves with imperishable glory.

When the battle of Shahi Tibbi was being fought, Guru Gobind Singh along with his men had reached the bank of the Sarsa River. It was now almost the day-break. About this time, the enemy forces mustered themselves to attack the Guru. The Guru ordered Jiwan Singh, a Ranghretta Sikh, to encounter the pursuers and himself with the rest of the people plunged into the flooded Sarsa River. There was confusion all-around. Many persons were swept to death by the fast moving water and many more were scattered. Bhai Ghaniya also lost track of the Guru. He moved about in the Malwa region of the Punjab till he reached some place near Jagraon. A Bairagi Sadhu who met him there told him the whereabouts of his Guru. Bhai ji felt overjoyed and lost no time to reach Talwandi Saboki where the Guru gave him an affectionate pat and told him to devote exclusively to the dissemination of Sikh tenets. Bhai ji stayed for some time with the Guru, but when the Guru departed for Deccan, he, along with his associates, undertook tours in different parts of the Punjab, acquainting the people with the Guru's faith and putting in service for the benefit of the people. He could persuade the people to put in joint effort to alleviate their difficulties. He could inspire them to sink wells or to dig tanks to overcome the need of water. On his part, he would march with vessels full of water laden on both sides of the humps of a string of camels so that he might provide relief to the areas suffering from the shortage of water. He would also provide spiritual balm to the tension-ridden minds of the people.

He established various *Dharamshalas* where he made arrangements for the propagation of Guru's views and philosophy. Having done a lot of work in Majha and Malwa, he left for the south-western Punjab and spread the Guru's Gospel in the villages of Jhang, Manghiana and Dera Ismail. He wanted to advance to the province of Sind as well, but he dropped this idea, probably he thought it more useful to convert Sewa Ram who was born at Hyderabad (India) and whose mother had died and father had left home in search of peace and had undertaken tour of different sacred places to find the way to bliss. When he came across Bhai Ghaniya, he felt peculiar placidity and requested Bhai ji to initiate him into his Order and give him instructions. Bhai ji then acquainted him with the teachings of the Gurus and the importance which the tenet of service enjoys in Sikhism. He said, "To provide comforts to all human beings irrespective of their forms and affiliations and to have faith in the teachings of the Gurus is our only advice."

After this, Bhai ji and Sewa Ram entered the province of Sind. They sojourned at Nurpur. Finding there is a scarcity of water, a programme of sinking well was launched. Sewa Ram took leading part in this work. Service was also rendered in the construction of the *Dharmshala* of Nurpur by Bhai ji and

Sewa Ram. A *Dharamshala* was also established at Lao Nagar which is situated near Jhang Manghiana. At this place, Bhai Ghaniya won over another disciple Addan Shah who had learnt Punjabi from an Udasi saint, Gurdas and who possessed religious bent of mind, saturated with love for one and all. In this way, many persons became Bhai ji's followers, and a separate Order emerged known in history, as Sewa Panth, the Path of Service. Bhai Ghaniya died but his Order carried on his work un-interruptedly. Wherever the members of this Order went, they preached human sympathy, selflessness, universal brotherhood and since they always evoked respect for themselves, they by implication endeared Sikhism among the people. In the later Mughal period if the commonality among the Musalmans did not dislike the Sikhs, and Sikhism was regarded as a balm for the afflicted humanity, much of the credit goes to them.

After Ghaniya's death (1718 C.E.) at Sodra the work was carried on under the over-all guidance of Sewa Ram. Sewa Ram's headquarter was at Nurpur (Sind) wherefrom he used to fan out in different directions to serve the people to make them realise the importance of truthful living.

After Bhai Sewa Ram, his disciple Bhai Santokh Singh took charge of the headquarter. Bhai Santokh Singh belonged to the village, Khari. During his lifetime, he had been instructed by Sewa Ram who said, "Recognise the light within every body, serve all and raise yourself above worldly attachments."

Bhai Santokh Singh was succeeded by Bhai Budhan Ram and Sahib Ram. Sewa Panthis from Nurpur headquarter had been rendering yeoman's service to the people.

Bhai Ghaniya's another disciple, Addan Shah also made a mark in rendering service to the people. He belonged to village Lao and often lived there. He stayed at Phagwara and Kartarpur also. He did a lot of travelling to sacred places. He had his admirers among big zamindars and masses alike. His charismatic personality won over quite a large number of disciples. He used to spin coarse yarn, prepare ink for his livelihood. He advised his disciples also to earn livelihood through honest earning, without becoming rich. In 1757, he expired at Jammu. This was the time when Punjab was suffering from political turmoil caused by Ahmed Shah Abdali's invasion.

After 1757, Sewa Panthis made a lot of progress in terms of general popularity and organisation. Many Dharamshalas were raised in different parts of the country. Bhai Aya Ram, Bhai Ranga ji, Bhai Daya Ram, Bhai Dayal, Bhai Soma, Bhai Paras Ram were the most important among many Sewa Panthis of the later Mughal period. Paras Ram being a *Pingla* could not walk easily, but still the zest for service which he showed was unsurpassed. The Dharamshala from where he operated still stands in the Jangi Shivala Bazar, Amritsar. He and his disciples did not allow the earthen lamp to extinguish in Hari Mandir during the times of Zakariya Khan when the government was bent upon destroying the Sikhs root and branch.

Many other Sewa Panthis served Sikhism. Bhai Jawahar Singh of Mitha Tiwana was another luminary of the galaxy of the line who served the people from 1900 to 1950. His disciple Sant Nischal Singh had been serving the people of Haryana from his headquarter at Jagadhari in the recent past.

The Sewa Panthi Order was just like the Servants of the People's Society or the Red Cross Society whose objective is to bring about consciousness among people to love one-another, to help one-another and to respect one-another. The members of this Order were committed to the aforesaid objectives and regarded service (Sewa) as the true path to salvation, for doing service unto others was possible only when one had transcended narrowself.

For their own sustenance, they did not like depending upon alms or collecting their requirements through begging. Unlike many orders of saints in India, they never roamed about begging the eatables or other requisite things. Bhai Aya Ram advised Bhai Dharam Das, "Never get offerings, Live upon the earning of your labour. Make ropes or strings out of hemp yarn, sell them and live by the earnings you get. Bhai Bhall Ram said to his disciples, "You should not keep more than five rupees with you. More wealth distracts one from social service." Addan Shah's advice was that his disciples should work honestly and diligently. He said, "The rope must be made nicely; the work should be done properly."

One can adopt any profession according to one's capacity and capability. If one did not know making ropes, one could cut grass and sell in the market. According to Dr. Balbir Singh, "Each Sewa Panthi must do some labour. If one cannot do hard labour, one can adopt such jobs which involve less labour; one could prepare ink or pens made of reed. Addan Shah himself wrote books."

Sewa Panthis were prohibited to get loans because they wanted to keep themselves at a safe distance from the implications which were bound to flow from money transactions. They believed in distributing their everything among the people. Bhai Ram Kishan never felt any hesitation while giving even his clothes and shoes to the needy.

Sewa Panthis did not believe in married life. They looked down upon woman and considered her 'a temptress'. When Bhai Bhall went to Nurpur to see Bhai Aya Ram, he got made a veil to be hung between him and the people around so that ladies should not come to him. It is recorded that henceforward ladies saluted him from outside only.

Sewa Panthis is an Order just like monastic order of the Christians in the medieval age. But whereas the Christian monastic order turned to be the hot-bed of intrigues and centre of corruption, Sewa Panthis could keep themselves above these things. The reasons probably were their emphasis on living through honest earnings and keeping needs to the bare minimum.

The source of inspiration of Sewa Panthis is ten Gurus and Guru Granth Sahib. Upto Addan Shah, they did not have any particular dress but after Addan Shah they began to wear simple cloth-made caps on their heads and an unstitched sheet of cloth around to cover the lower part of their bodies. Short shirts (Kurti) were used to cover the upper parts of their bodies. They were not particular about keeping long hair

(Keshas) although Bhai Ghaniya had grown them. Sewa Ram and Addan Shah had never shaved. They were fond of white clothes.

Nirmal Panth

The term 'Nirmal Panth' is as old as Sikhism itself. What is the etymology of term? The reply to this question is given by Kanwar Mrigindra Singh.[4] He says, "The religious order started by Guru Nanak was without any particular form and just comprised the teachings of Guru Nanak and righteous living taught by him to his pupils. But in the course of time, other schools found it necessary to refer to it by some name, for the name 'Sikh' was then ambiguous being used by the Buddhists, Yogis of Gorakh and the followers of all Hindu schools. Therefore, Guru Nanak's school with its emphasis on purity was referred to as Nirmal Panth (Pure Path) by others and later even by Guru Nanak's Sikhs in reference to themselves for their distinction." Bhai Gurdas refers to Guru Nanak's school Nirmal Panth (Pure Path). Similarly, Bhatts use this term in reference to Guru Amar Das and Guru Arjan Dev.

Upto Guru Gobind Singh's time no distinction was made between Nirmal Panth and other names 'Nanak Panth', 'Gurmukh Panth' and 'Guru Sikh Panth'.

But with Guru Gobind Singh, the annotation did not remain as wide as it was before; it began to be used in reference to a particular school committed to definite goals and programmes.

As it is well-known, Guru Gobind Singh matured and concretised most of his plans at Paonta. One of those plans was the propagation of Sikhism through the medium of literature throughout India. It was with this object that Guru Gobind Singh wanted to establish a special order of his Sikhs particularly to make comparative study of religions and also interpret classical Indian tradition in terms of the basic philosophy of Sikhism.

The project thus conceived had incidental advantages as well. Since times immemorial learning and teaching had been the exclusive privilege of Brahmans, Sanyasis or Vairagis (ascetics), but the project of the Guru was to give a strong blow to the idea of class learning and of missionaries belonging to a particular caste.

Since most of the classical Indian religious literature was available in Sanskrit, the Guru found it imperative to make arrangement for the teaching of Sanskrit to his followers. Accordingly, Guru Gobind Singh asked his court poet Pandit Raghu Nath to do the needful. The Pandit politely and very diplomatically replied that he was prohibited by convention to teach the language of gods (Deva Bhasha) and the holy scriptures to non-dvijas *i.e.* Shudras and women. Guru Gobind Singh admonished him for his ego and pride for his most unreasonable stand. The same day Guru Gobind Singh also invited the Udasis to assist him in seeing his plans through.

They also did not respond and were not ready to effect any change in their traditional outlook and approach.

Ultimately, the Guru selected about thirteen Sikhs from all classes, castes and creeds, and sent them to Benaras. Their names were (1) Pandit Karma Singh, (2) Pandit Rama Singh, (3) Pandit Ganda (Singh), (4) Pandit Vir (Singh), (5) Pandit Sobha Singh, (6) Dharam Singh, (7) Daya Singh, (8) Kesar Singh, (9) Muhkam Singh, (10) Gian Singh, (11) Gaja Singh, (12) Chanda Singh, (13) Saina Singh. All these chosen Sikhs studied under the guidance of Pandit Sadda Nand for six years. In the seventh year, they came back to the Guru who now had shifted to Anandpur.[5]

Guru Gobind Singh was much pleased to find that they had become really good scholars and allotted them different duties. Pandit Karma Singh was asked to give sermons on Guru Granth Sahib in the Guru's court in the morning.

He did his job meticulously and nicely. Having been deeply impressed by his exposition the Guru directed Bhai Mani Singh to become his student and learn six *darsanas*. Within a short time quite a few hundred scholars belonging to all castes were ready for missionary work.

As the number of Nirmalas increased, they were divided into two distinct branches: (i) Nirmala saints who wore the ascetic pink (Bhagva) robe given by the Guru and did not marry, (ii) the Nirmalas who put on white clothes. The latter were further split into two categories: the unmarried among them were referred to as 'saint' but the married were referred to as Giani (knowledged).

Nirmalas exerted a lot to disseminate Sikhism and to bring about general awakening among the people. In the lifetime of Guru Gobind Singh, by his orders, Bhai Punjab Singh Nirmala came to the Punjab, settled down at Khadur. He so identified himself with the cause of the people that they adored him and thought it a good luck to enter into Sikh fold. His grand pupil Rocha Singh Nirmala was responsible for conversion, on a large scale, in the predominant Muslim areas of Kashmir and Pothohar (West Punjab in Pakistan).

After the death of Guru Gobind Singh, the Nirmalas spared no pains to spread the message of the Guru. They acted not only as torch bearers of Sikhism but also as conscience keepers and political advisers of the Sikhs. When differences arose between Vinod Singh Trehan (in the seventh generation of Guru Angad Dev), Dharam Singh Nirmala advised him to leave Banda Singh Bahadur in the larger interest of the Sikhs. It was again Baba Dharam Singh who brought Vinod Singh in touch with Baba Dip Singh and Baba Ala Singh (the founder of Patiala State). Baba Ala Singh took Khande-ki-Pahul in which Baba Dharam Singh, Baba Vinod Singh and Baba Dip Singh acted as Piyaras (The beloved ones of the Guru). Baba Ala Singh so much appreciated the sagacity of Baba Dharam Singh that he gave him the land[6] where the ceremony was held to honour Baba Gurmukh Singh Nirmala, a pupil of Baba Dharam Singh Nirmala. One of the Panj Piyaras, Bhai Durgah Singh Nirmala, who settled down at Kankhal (two miles from Haridwar, U.P.). He was a great marks-man. He fought for Rai Ahmed of Najibabad against the Rohilas. Since Rai Ahmed of Najibabad was victorious, he offered a grant of land to Bhai Durgah Singh Nirmala on account of his dedicated service. Sant Nikka Singh was given a gift of thirty villages by Bibi Pradhan, the daughter of Baba Ala Singh. Sant ji refused to accept such a big grant for his maintenance and only kept one village, named Khudi near Barnala. Many other such gifts were given to the Nirmalas by the Khalsa for their much-needed services to them.[7]

Sardar Dhyan Singh of Shahbad willed his estate to Sant Karam Singh Nirmala (Chote). Sardar Ganda Singh of Bhangi Misl offered thirteen villages to Sant Jai Singh Nirmala who instead of keeping it for himself passed it on to Udasi Dera of Santokh Das. Similarly, Sardar Sadda Singh of Bahirwala gave a patta of seven villages to Sant Bhagat Singh Nirmala in the year A.D. 1766. The offer was declined by the Sant but the Patta is still available at Bunga of Mana Singh Wala, Amritsar. Sardar Jai Singh's daughter-in-law donated two villages in favour of the Nirmala Dera at Kankhal.

In the year 1796, Maharaja Ranjit Singh offered a written *sanad* to Sant Nihal Singh Nirmala. The Sant passed on the property to Udasi Akhara of Santokh Das.

In the years when there was comparative peace in the Punjab after the failure of Ahmed Shah Abdali in his invasions, Nirmalas stepped up their activities of proselytization. It was during this period that they started visiting different places at the time of the Hindu festivals to conduct their missionary work. This thing as well as the extensive patronage of the Sikh chiefs to the Nirmalas caused a lot of heart-burning among the Hindu sects of *Sannyasis* and *Vairagis* who had always thought that the gifts would be given only to them by the chiefs. The heart-burning led, not unoften, to serious quarrels.

In 1796 C.E.,[8] Nirmalas as well as Udasis had pitched their camps, hoisted their flags and started Akhand Path of Guru Granth Sahib three days before the Kumbh Mela at Haridwar. Naga Sadhus were given magisterial control of the fair both by the Maratha and the British and they charged every Hindu pilgrim eight Anna to one rupee. The Nirmalas and Udasis refused to give any money on the plea that they were not Hindus but Sikh missionaries. The Nagas attacked them and constrained them to stop the recitation of Guru Granth Sahib and very arrogantly burnt their flag. When the news reached the Sikh Sardars such as Rai Singh of Buria, Karam Singh

Maharaja of Patiala, Karam Singh of Shahbad, Dasaundha Singh of Sadhora, Bhagel Singh of Malaud, Jodh Singh of Kalsia and Rup Singh of Ropar, they rushed to the spot. The Udasis who had been killed were cremated, the flag was hoisted and the recitation of Guru Granth Sahib was completed under armed protection. On April 10, when the pilgrims melted away and Naga Sadhus were counting their collections, the Sikh Sardars attacked them with firing and killed everyone that came their way. From that day onward, the Nirmalas and Udasis were never taxed and were given special facilities for preaching the teachings of Guru Granth Sahib in Haridwar and Kurukshetra fairs.

In 1807, again a serious quarrel sparked. The occasion was Kumbh festival at Haridwar. There was a polemical discussion between the Nirmalas on oneside and Sannyasis and Bairagis on the other. The Nirmalas made such a great philosophical impact on the people showing the distinction between Guru Nanak's spiritual, temporal philosophy and other schools of socio-religious philosophy that both *Sannyasis* and *Vairagis* accepted that a Nirmala whatever be his caste and creed could enter any temple in India. One such controversy arose at Triambak, near Nasik in Maharashtra. The Brahmans objected to their having bath in *Kushavrat Sarovar* where only the Brahmans had the privilege to bathe. They also took exception to the Nirmalas taking along with them, allegedly low caste people, while visiting the Temple. Also they did not like the Nirmalas covering their heads with turban and wearing a kachheira (an undergarment) while entering the temple against the established custom of visiting the temple bare-headed and in unstiched clothes. The Brahmans challenged the Nirmalas to debate the issues. A heated discussion took place. Ultimately, the Brahmans had to realise the hollowness of their stand. Diwan Singh Thikriwala was the Nirmala representative to take part in the discussion. Such discussions took place at certain other places as well, but Nirmala scholars always came out victorious.

After this happening, the Nirmalas began to attend all the Kumbha Melas at Haridwar, Nasik, Ujjain and Triveni. Most of the Gurdwaras at such places owe their existence to them. The 'Gurdwara Pakki Sangat of Triveni' built to perpetuate the memory of Guru Teg Bahadur is with the Nirmalas even today.

It was through the sustained and consistent efforts of Nirmalas that many persons of the province of Sind (Now in Pakistan) came into the Sikh fold.

Nirmalas have done commendable work in the field of comparative study of classical philosophy and have written books of great value in this connection in Sanskrit, Braj, Hindi, Punjabi both in Gurmukhi script and Devnagri script. Sant Nikka Singh translated Yoga Vasishtha into Braj and wrote it in Punjabi script. Sant Nihal Singh Nirmala wrote a Sanskrit commentary on the 'Japu' of Guru Granth Sahib. Tara Singh Narotam also produced a few good books such as *Gurmat Nirnay Sagar* and *Guru Tirth Sangreh* etc. The Urdu Language was also enriched by them, as they produced a lot of literature in it for their missionary work.

Nirmala works can be broadly divided into two categories. One, they comprised translations of several Hindu scriptural and other texts from the original in Sanskrit to Sadh Bhasha in Gurumukhi script. Second, they dealt with 'Gurmat'. These works went a long way to familiarise the non-Sikh scholars and people residing at places like Varanasi, Haridwar, etc. with Sikh tenets. From the mid-eighteenth century onwards, the works produced by Nirmala scholars on Sikh religion were laden with Vedantic thought which showed that they had started interpreting Sikhism in the context of Vedantism with the result that they failed to highlight Sikhism as an independent and sovereign religion, and instead, in many of their exegetical works they seem be trying to superimpose vedantic viewpoint on Sikh theological and philosophical formulations.

Giani Gian Singh wrote *Panth Prakash* (1880) a versified history of the Sikhs in Braj, *Twarikh Guru Khalsa*, *Suraj Parkash Vartak* (an abridged version in prose of Bhai Santokh Singh's *Sri Gur Partap Suraj Granth*), *Ramayana Bhai Mani Singh Jidi*, *Twarikh Amritsar*, *Twarikh Lahore Patit Pawan*

Gurdham Sangrah. Sant Nihal Singh composed poetry, mostly in Braj. Three of his works are, *Akal Natak*, *Nirmal Prabhakar* and *Sikh Prabhakar*. Bhai Santokh Singh (b. 1780, d. 1843 C.E.) produced many a good works such as *Nam Kosh* (1821 C.E.), *Sri Guru Nanak Parkash* (1823 C.E.) and *Garb Ganjni Tika* which was a rejoinder to the Tika of Anandghan, an Udasi scholar. His another product, the most venerated and the most voluminous, was *Gur Pratap Suraj Granth* a versified history of the Gurus.

In order to share their learning and understanding about Sikhism, they started many schools/seminars. The Nirmal Sanskrit Vidyalas in Chetan Math and Sangat Lahore Tola have been among the pioneer Nirmala institutions. At Kankhal too, they raised a Sanskrit Mahavidyala. The *deras* of Dyal Singh Thakur and Baba Mishra Singh in Amritsar were also important centres to impart the knowledge of Sikh religion. Even in modern times the Nirmalas have established several colleges and schools in Punjab and other Indian States. They are also accredited for their commitment to preserving Sikh tradition by looking after several historical monuments and literary sources. For example, the gurdwara at Kainthal associated with the visits of the Sikh Gurus was maintained by a renowned Nirmala Dargah Singh. The role of Nirmalas in the management of Sikh shrines in the eighteenth century was also crucial, specially when it is juxtaposed with that of the Udasis who in the latter part of eighteenth century strived to treat them as their personal estates and without any compunction made hold to hinduise Sikh tenets and customs.

In 1862, Nirmalas set up their central organisation at Patiala to coordinate their activities. The organisation was named as Nirmal Panchayati Akhara or *Dharma Davaja* or Akhara Guru Gobind Singh. Its formal inauguration took place on 7th August, 1862 C.E. It was in this year that yellow flag of Guru Gobind Singh with Khanda superimposed was flown on the building known as *Dharam Davaja*.

At the time of setting up the aforesaid Akhara, it was also agreed upon to set up 'four wandering Akharas and each of them was put under the charge of a Mahant. The four

Mahants appointed at that time were Bhola Singh, Kahan Singh, Karam Singh and Nihal Singh. Thereafter many more centres of Nirmalas came to be established. According to *Encyclopedia of Sikhism*, Maharaja Narinder Singh of Patiala, Raja Bharpur Singh of Nabha and Raja Sarup Singh of Jind took active part in getting this organisation afloat. They placed Chanarthalian Di Haveli at the disposal of the organisation. An elaborate constitution called Dastur-ul-Amal was drawn up which was duly approved by the above-mentioned rulers. The first Mahant was Mehtab Singh who was very deeply respected among the Sikhs. The Dastur-ul-Amal aimed at smooth functioning of the organisation.

It (that signed by Phulkian states) has nine clauses. Clause one states that Bhai Mehtab Singh is the Chief of Akhara and after his death his successors will take-over. Clause two refers to the sum of Rs. 82,000 donated by Patiala state and to the manner of its use. Clause three declares that treasury of the Akhara will be under the charge of Mehtab Singh. Clause four authorises Bhai Mehtab Singh to make or change any other Mahants as he thought fit. Clause five puts the condition on all residing in the Akhara not to keep any money on their person. Clause six authorises Bhai Mehtab Singh to appoint anyone on a responsible position and punish those found violating the Code. According to Clause seven, if Mehtab Singh wants to appoint during his lifetime his successor, he must consult the three Phulkian states. Clause eight assigns honour to Phulkian states to replace any of the successors of Bhai Mehtab Singh if he is found wanting in his personal piety and character. Clause nine says that the functioning of Panchayati Akhara be carried as per the clauses of the document.

This organisation was in addition to the headquarter of the Nirmalas at Kankhal founded and developed by Bhai Durgah Singh on the land donated by Rai Ahmed, the local chief whom he helped during his fight against Rohillas. The organisation complemented the task of the headquarter.

The Nirmalas are the Khalsa, having full faith in Guru Granth Sahib and ten Gurus, five Kakārs *i.e.* to say sword, unshorn hair, a pair of shorts (Kachheira), comb, iron bracelet.

The name of all Nirmalas end with 'Singh'. They do not follow Udasis who keep knotted hair (Jatas) and whose names end with 'das'. Taking Khalsa baptism is not considered obligatory among them. As a distinguishing mark of the sect, they don at least one of the garments in ochre colour. They generally practise celibacy. They touch each other's feet as they meet to express their reverence for the other. Appending of gotra (sub-caste) to the names is 'a taboo' to them. They are absolutely free from caste-spirit and altogether reject caste system.

The future of Nirmalas does not seem to be bright, the foremost cause being their internal dissensions. They have divided themselves in two major groups: One, owing allegiance to Nirmal Panchayati Akhara, the second, flaunting their independence. The Nirmalas of both the groups have not shown any deep interest in promulgation of Khalsa point-of-view. Besides they have not updated and upgraded their learning to respond suitably to the present-day challenges. The squabbles, whether they are inter-groups or intra-groups, are often about property disputes or other petty issues which are only remotely religious or not religious. Recently, Mahant Ganesha Singh appointed a Committee to suggest ways and means so that Nirmala world-view might prevail. Nothing seems to have done so far. Notwithstanding this, we do hope that the Nirmalas with ample mental and material resources at their disposal would awake and shed vedantic or other extraneous influences and harness themselves in the cause of Sikh religion.

Udasi Order

Udasi, the missionary of the Sikhs, was set afloat by Sri Chand (1494-1629), the elder son of Guru Nanak.

The word 'Udasi' is derived from the Sanskrit word '*Udasin*' which means the one who is indifferent to or disregardful of worldly attachments, an ascetic or a mendicant. Taking cue from this, some scholars have ventured to trace the origin of Udasis back to the Puranic age, having intimate connections with the Hindu ascetic tradition; but historically speaking, Sri Chand (1494-1629), the elder son of Guru Nanak was the originator of Udasis. The authenticity of this fact has been amply vouchsafed not only by *Matra*, the sacred compositions attributed to Balu Hasna, wherein he records that Sri Chand received enlightenment from Guru Nanak and founded the Order after the passing away of the latter but also by the fact that in the whole range of the history of religious development in India, there is no mention of any sect or cult or Order bearing the name of Udasi.

Sri Chand was a devoted Sikh and a saintly person. He was a celibate with ascetic temperament and when he saw his father going on missionary tours in the dress of Udasis (recluses who renounce the world), he started training himself as an ideal Udasi and prospective successor to his father. Despite all this, Guru Nanak chose Guru Angad as his successor six months before his death and asked him to set up his pontific seat at Khadur. Kartarpur, where Guru Nanak had spent the last twenty years of life, was left to the exclusive control of his sons.

It was a surprise for Sri Chand. He could not believe that an outsider who had become a disciple of his father only during his last fifteen years of his life could know more about him than a religious minded person like him, who was a born celibate and whose self-control and ascetic habits and Yogic powers were well-known.

Much upset at such happenings, Sri Chand stopped taking interest even in management of Kartarpur establishment, the responsibility of which was exclusively taken over by his brother Lakhmi Das. He stayed at *Samadhi* which he built at the place where Guru Nanak was cremated. He disassociated himself from mundane affairs and led a life of a determined ascetic. He wore nothing but a loincloth and his friend from childhood-cum-his disciple used to burn during the extreme cold of winter cow-dung cakes in front of him to keep his body warm.

Subsequently, this Dhuni (lit. the small heap of burning cow-dung cakes) became a logo of the Udasi Order. After about ten years in 1605 Bk. (1548 C.E.), he quietly left for Bath, a village near Pathankot, and continued to live there upto his last.

All these days whether he was at Kartarpur or at Bath he preached religion of Guru Nanak as he perceived and understood. He had full faith in Guru Nanak and his successors as legitimate and rightful Gurus. He regarded their hymns as the voice of God transmitted through them to the people to enable them to elevate themselves both at individual and societal levels. He highly appreciated institutions of *Sangat* and *Guru Ka Langar*. He missed no opportunity to recite and sing Word. Despite all this, he preferred complete renunciation to the householders' life. In one of his hymns, Guru Nanak had instructed that God dwells everywhere, whether it is home or jungle or any other place. Therefore, home or outside home, both situations are alike. And one shall be Udasi in the sense that he/she can meditate on Him for self-realisation anywhere and everywhere. Guru Nanak says:

> "High above is the sky,
> Above the sky is God
> The protector of the World,
> Unfathomable, great Lord abides there;
> By Guru's instructions I deem alike both home and abroad
> Nanak has become such an Udasi."[9]

Sri Chand's fixation with asceticism was perhaps because of his faulty perception of the rationale of Guru Nanak's wearing of dresses which are often associated with ascetics while he undertook religious itineraries.

Guru Nanak never stuck to any one dress (*Bhekh*) nor held any one of them sacred. He wore such dresses as these were considered respectable by people in general and thus facilitated his preaching work. When the Guru decided to settle at Kartarpur, he gave up his Udasi dress and lived in ordinary Punjabi dress. Sri Chand could not catch the real point and thought it appropriate not only to wear the *Udasi*-ascetical dress but also to consider asceticism as an integral part of Guru

Nanak's mission. This being the perspective, his missionary Order began to be known as 'Udasi Order'. This Order does not qualify to be called a sect because its teachings did not substantially differ from those of Sikhism nor could it be designated as a cult because believers in it were not passionately attached with its leader. Sri Chand's personal piety, his prestigious lineage, close resemblance of his teachings with those of Sikhism, the innate tendency of Indian people to treat asceticism with respect engendered and buttressed from time immemorial by the belief that these were short cuts to self-realisation. All these elements combined together sustained and enhanced his popularity and prestige among the Sikhs as well as among people in general. Apprehensions arose that people might not form wrong impression about the configuration of Sikhism. This fact is borne out in the compositions of Guru Angad Dev as well as in the sayings and social actions of Guru Amar Das and Guru Ram Das. Guru Angad Dev says, "Eh Kinehi Āshqī Dujai Lagge Jaeh"[10] which implicitly hinted at the deviation of certain Sikhs from the true principles of Sikhism. Guru Amar Das too was obligated to point out the difference between Udasi teachings and genuine Sikh teachings for the benefit of the common Sikh as well as for saving genuine Sikhism from deformation/adulteration. According to Macauliffe circular letters were sent to the people enjoining upon them that asceticism was foreign to the creed of Guru Nanak. In this connection the author of *Mehma Parkash* relates that once a man named Gangu enquired from the Guru as to what was the correct path to self-realisation, the Guru told him that he should start business at Delhi, earn his livelihood through honest means and share a part of it with the needy. Bhai Randhir Singh, in his work *Udasi Sikhan Di Vithia* refers to an old recension of the Guru Granth Sahib, which contains a text entitled "Sakhi Guru Amar Das Ki Mehle 3".[11] Herein Guru Amar Das declared that a householder's life was better than that of a renunciant, and the Sikhs were warned in unambiguous words against becoming renunciants. Guru Ram Das also expressly and explicitly put it "Remain Udasi while still being a householder as lotus flower remains above the water." Except cautioning their followers and seekers that the mission of Guru Nanak did not recognise asceticism either as the right path to Bliss or progress, the Gurus always held Sri Chand and his followers in deep respect. Never any bitter word was spoken either by the Gurus for Sri Chand or by Sri Chand for the Gurus. It is on record that Guru Amar Das in 1609 Bk., Guru Ram Das in 1674 Bk., Guru Arjan Dev in 1656 and Guru Hargobind did their obeisance to Sri Chand at Bath[12] out of respect for him. According to Kesar Singh Chhibber, Sri Chand sent two turbans at the death of Guru Ram Das in C.E. 1581, one for Pirthi Chand, the eldest son of Guru Ram Das and the other for Guru Arjan Dev in recognition of his succession to guruship.

In 1629, Sri Chand asked Guru Hargobind to spare one of his sons to join him in his religious preaching. The Guru agreed and Baba Gurditta (1612-30), his eldest son was admitted to the Udasi Order. Baba Gurditta at that time was sixteen years old and had been married to revered Ananti alias Natti, daughter of Bhai Rama of Batala on April 17, 1629. Before his death, Sri Chand bestowed his mantle on him signifying that Udasi order was not a break-away group, rather a respectable missionary wing of Sikhism.

Baba Gurditta appointed four head preachers—Almast, Balu Hasna, Gobind (or Gonda) and Phul. He gave them smouldering embers from Baba Sri Chand's Dhuni (hearth) to be taken to prospective preaching centres. These prominent preachers set up from those embers new Dhunis preaching centres. In this way there came into existence four Dhunis or hearths. Each Dhuni came to be known after the name of its principal preacher. The Udasis proved to be zealous preachers and carried the message of Guru Nanak far and wide in India and abroad. They discovered places which had been visited by the Gurus and had fallen into obscurity with the passage of time. They established on such spots deras (camps) and *Sangats* and preached Gurbani.

Almast and Balu Hasna were brothers. Both of them were born in a Gaur Brahman family of Srinagar in Kashmir. Their parents were Bhai Hardatt and Mai Prabha. Almast's original name was Alu; he came to be called Almast (lit. intoxicated in a state of ecstasy) because of his mystical proclivities. He was also called Kambalia or Gedaria because he would normally be dressed in a ragged blanket (Kambal, in Punjabi), or a light quilt or padded sheet. At the age of 21, he came to Dera Baba Nanak and fell under the spell of Sri Chand. Since then he served at the *deora* (a memorial building) of Guru Nanak. For his livelihood he tended a flock of goats. Baba Gurditta deputed him to preach the message of Guru Nanak in the eastern provinces of India. He first went to Puri in Orissa where he raised a shrine to commemorate Guru Nanak's visit to the place. The shrine, better known as Gurdwara Mangu Math, is still in existence. In 1633, he visited Nanak Matta, formerly known as Gorakh Matta, where Guru Nanak had a discourse with the Nath Yogis under a peepal tree and where a shrine dedicated to the Guru had later been established. The place had been reoccupied by the Yogis who had demolished the Sikh temple. Almast solicited the help of Guru Hargobind who reached Nanak Matta in 1634, chastised the Nath intruders and restored the Sikh shrine to Almast. Bhai Almast spent the rest of his life at Nanak Matta wherefrom he sent eight of his disciples to preach in various districts of eastern India. These disciples established Sikh shrines at places visited by Guru Nanak during his first Udasi.

Almast had his headquarter at Nanak Matta which had its branches at several other places such as at Dhaka, Patna and Puri.

Balu Hasna (1564-1660) like Almast was also a man of pious disposition. He embraced Sikhism when he along with his brother came to Amritsar in 1604 and received instructions from Guru Arjan Dev. Thereafter, he dedicated himself to the Guru's cause. He served Guru Hargobind devotedly. He always bore smile on his face. The Guru gave him the appellation of Hasna (lit. the laughing one). Baba Gurditta deputed him to preach Sikh tenets in Pothohar region (North Western Punjab).

He passed away at Peshawar on December 2, 1660. His disciples carried on his work in western and southern Punjab, North Western Frontier Province and Sindh. Bhai Lal Das

Daryai and Bhai Jado Rai are said to have accompanied Guru Gobind Singh to the South. Bhai Lal Das took 'Pahul' and was renamed Prehlad Singh, who is said to have compiled one of the Rehat Namas—Sikh Code. Another of the followers of Balu Hasna, Udho Das served Mata Punjab Kaur, widow of Baba Ram Rai at Dehradun.

Bhai Govinda (1569-1649), like Almast and Balu Hasna, also belonged to Srinagar. He was born to a Khatri family and his parents were Bhai Jai Dev and Mai Subhadra. He turned a Sikh under the impact of the charismatic personality of Guru Arjan Dev. This happened in 1596 C.E. when he visited Punjab in quest of enlightenment.

On 11 September, 1637, he was made the head of a Dhuan. He preached mostly in Doaba region of the Punjab. He died in September, 1649 at Phillaur where a *Samadh* was constructed in his honour.

Phul (1574-1663), was the younger brother of Bhai Govind and like him embraced Sikh faith at Amritsar on 20 March, 1604. He donned the ochre robe at Kiratpur on 21 January, 1637 and was ordained by Baba Gurditta as head of the Dhuan. He preached in the Punjab for some time and then made an extensive tour to holy places throughout India. Finally, he settled down at Bahadurpur, now a part of Hoshiarpur town, where he established an Udasi centre. He died there on 17 May, 1663. The followers of this Dhuan later preached Sikhism in central India also where they established an Udasi centre at Chikhli in Maharashtra.

Besides the four Dhuans there came into existence another set of Udasi seats called *Bakhshishan*. These flourished during the time of Guru Har Rai, Guru Tegh Bahadur and Guru Gobind Singh. A Bakhshish (lit bounty) was a missionary assignment conferred upon an individual by the Guru. There were six prominent Bakhshishan *viz*. Bhagat Bhagvānie, Suthre Shāhīe, Saṅgat Sāhibīe, Miaṅ Sāhibīe or Mian Dasie, Bhat Mallie and Jit Mallie (followers of Jit Mal).

Bhagat Bhagvānei were the followers of Bhagat Bhagwan, who was a resident of Gaja and was a sanyasi to begin with.

Once he in the company of Sanyasi comrades came to Punjab. He learnt about the splendour of Guru Nanak and his successors. His quest for enlightenment urged him to have the sacred glimpse of Guru Har Rai, the seventh in succession to Guru Nanak. He listened to him and was totally changed. He fell at the feet of the Guru. The Master blessed him and he took to preaching of Master's word. In this process he had been greatly helped by Mehar Chand, the grandson of Baba Lakhmi Das whom he met at Kartarpur. He joined Udasi Order. Mehar Chand renamed him Bhagat Bhagwan. According to Randhir Singh, "Not only he but all his co-fellows whose number was three hundred and sixty turned[13] Udasi Sikhs." All of them including their disciples preached vigorously the gospel of the Guru in Bihar, Uttar Pradesh, Sind, and at various places in the Punjab.[14]

Suthre Shāhīes were the followers of Suthre Shah who was born at Brahampura near Bara Mula in a Nandi Khatri family. On birth he was found to be having black mark on his forehead and prematurely grown teeth. On this account his parents threw him outside their home considering him unlucky for the family. Just at the moment, Guru Hargobind who had been touring Jammu-Kashmir happened to pass that way. When he heard the cries of the child, he halted and got down his horse. He enquired why the child was crying. On being told that he was a cast-away of his family that considered him ill-fated. The Guru's heart melted and he took him under his care. He named the child, then called 'Kuthra' *i.e.* dirty ugly, as 'Suthra' which means pure or spotless. Among the Sikhs he came to be known as Suthra Shah, the suffix 'Shah' in Punjabi being the equivalent of English word 'Esquire'. Suthra Shah was reputed for his devotion to Guru Hargobind and for his humour and wit. Many anecdotes are still in currency highlighting this aspect of Suthra's personality. He was appointed by Guru Har Rai, Guru Hargobind's successor, to preach Sikhism in the hill-states of Punjab including Kashmir. He also preached the message of Guru Nanak in or around Delhi. His disciples lit the torch of Sikhism in Sindh, the western Punjab and Afghanistan as well. Suthre Shāhīe also visited Jaunpur and according to *Sri Guru Tirath Sangreh* by Tara Chand Narotam (p. 15), they established a Dharamshala at the spot in Jaunpur where Guru Nanak stayed during his first Udasi.

Sangat Sāhīe

They are the followers of Sangat Sahib, who was born in the family of Uppal Khatri at village Amba Mari in Lamma region of the Punjab in 1640 C.E. (1697 Bk.). When he came of age, he started earning his livelihood by marketing ghee at different places. He met Guru Har Rai when the latter happened to pass by his village while on a preaching tour in Malwa region. Overwhelmed by the Guru's charismatic personality, he decided to be a Sikh. The Guru blessed him and asked him to serve the people in a spirit of selflessness. Accordingly, he started serving in *Guru Ka Langar* alongside his profession of selling odd articles by hawking.

One day *Guru Ka Langar* ran short of cooking-oil (ghee). Sangat immediately supplied the same but refused to take payment even at the insistence of Bhai Bhagtu who supervised farming at Guru's fields at Kiratpur and who informed Sangat about the shortage. This fact was brought to the notice of the Guru. He was moved by his devotion. Bhai Bhagtu also spoke lyrically how devotedly and altruistically Sangat served in *Guru Ka Langar*.

One day the labourers who worked in Guru's fields at Kiratpur complained of the absence of ghee for their diet. Bhai Bhagtu, who was in-charge of agricultural operations, got non-plussed. Sangat came to his rescue. He atonce supplied the requisite quantity of ghee. He was asked by none but he did so of his own believing that *Guru Ka Langar*, being the kitchen of God Himself, should not face any shortage. Bhai Bhagtu made efforts to make payment but he silenced him by saying that he had simply done his duty. The news reached the Guru. The Guru called him to his presence. Sangat fell at his feet and cherished the desire to be initiated into the house beautiful of Sikhism. After interaction, he was given a new name Bhai Pheru, a 'Divine Wanderer' always delivering comforts to the comfortless and the desolate. He was blessed with honorific 'Lord of *Guru Ka Langar*'. Since then, he took pains to establish and run *Guru Ka Langar* wherever he happened to be. According to Randhir Singh, he was made in-charge of preaching in Nakka and Lamma regions.

In token of having invested him with the sacred duty of preaching he was given a *Pothi* (booklet) containing Guru's hymns, a *Mala* (rosary) a *Majithi* robe and the authority to initiate people into Sikh faith. He established his Dera—Camp near Mian[15] Ke Maur (now in the district of Lahore, Pakistan). Here he ran *Langar* for all twenty-four hours. His preaching was very effective and covered a vast spectrum of people. He earned a name in respect of his saintliness, honesty, selfless service and deep understanding of Sikhism.

When Guru Gobind Singh conducted investigation to locate corrupt and unscrupulous *Masands* to duly punish them, he found Sangat perfectly honest pious and totally committed to Guru's cause, and honoured him by suffixing 'Sahib' (Master or Lord) with his name and by calling him 'Sachi-Darhi'—Immaculately Truthful Beard. He expired at sufficiently advanced age[16] and was cremated near village Chunia on the outskirts of Lahore now in Pakistan.

Mian Sāhibīes or Mian Shāhīes

Bhai Mian was the founder of this Bakhshish (Preaching Centre). His real name was Ram Dev. His father was Nand Lal Sohna, a devotee of Khwaja and Jani, both Muslim devotees of Guru Hargobind. Like his two mentors he had fascination for Guru Hargobind, his striking personality and his ideology.[17] Once when he went to the Guru, the latter was impressed with his amiable disposition and handsomeness and bestowed upon him an epithet Sohina (The beautiful). Nand Lal wished his son to follow in his footsteps and took him to Guru Harkrishan whose sacred glimpse and divine innocence completely transformed him. Ram Dev decided to remain in attendance upon the Guru. He took upon himself the duty of carrying water for *Guru Ka Langar* and sprinkling water upon the ground where *Sangat* (holy assembly) met morning and evening. When Guru Tegh Bahadur set out on his travels through the Malwa region of Punjab in 1665 C.E., Bhai Ram Dev was in his retinue performing his usual chores. At every sojourn he would sprinkle the water on the dusty ground in such a way that it seemed as if gentle rain was pouring. According to *Mehma Parkash*, Guru Tegh Bahadur pleased at his service, nicknamed him Mihān (bringer of rain). The name stuck and Ram Dev began to be called Bhai Mihān.

While at Dhamtan, during the course of his preaching tour, Guru Tegh Bahadur bestowed upon him a drum and a banner as symbols of spiritual sovereignty and released him from his personal attendance enabling him to preach on his own. Ram Dev preached mainly in northern India. He also once waited upon Guru Gobind Singh. Guru Gobind Singh was so much pleased with his contribution to the spread of Sikh religion that he considered it appropriate to 'Suffix' Sahib (Master) with Mihān, the epithet with which he was earlier honoured by Guru Tegh Bahadur. From the time of Guru Gobind Singh, he began to be called as Mihān Sahib. He had a number of followers, who established Deras (Preaching Centres) in different parts of the country as far as Patna, Bhagalpur (in Bihar), Cuttuck (Orissa), Amravati, Kohlapur, Ujjain (Madhya Pradesh), Khan Gam, Band Rameshwar in Southern India, Sadhu Bela Sakhar (Sind in Pakistan), and Qandhar (Afghanistan). Mihān Sahib's most important disciples were Bhai Nanak Bakhsh, Bhai Manh Das, Bhai Sidkia, Bhai Gurdial, Bhai Tehal Das, Bhai Man Singh *et al.* Out of these Lakhmir, Mall ji, Surat Ram, Magni Ji, Bhola Das and Ram Das were the most distinguished and their preaching centres became very famous and influence-wielding. Their followers also established many Deras (Centres), the prominent among them being Dera Magni Ram at Patiala, Sadhu Bela, near Sakhar (now in Sind, Pakistan), Sangal Wala Akhara at Amritsar (established in 1795 C.E.). Bawa Pritam Das in cooperation with Santokh Das did two remarkable things: the first important thing was that he organised Panchayati Akhara at Triveni (Allahabad) in 1779 C.E., which, in due course, established its sub-centres at Kankhal (Hardwar), Kurukshetra,

Ujjain and Godavari river in South, secondly, he was responsible for digging out a small canal, known as Hansli from the river Ravi right upto Harimandir Sahib to supply water to the holy tank, known as Ram Sar or Amrit Sarovar.

Bakht Malias

These Udasis regarded Bakht Mal as their mentor. He belonged to Nakka region of the Punjab and was a devoted Sikh. In the time of Guru Hargobind, he was Masand at Kabul. According to 'Gar Udasin Mat Darpan', he embraced Sikhism in the time of Guru Har Rai. But the generally accepted view is that he was converted to be a Sikh under the impact of Guru Hargobind, but Bakhshish was conferred on him by Guru Gobind Singh. H.A. Rose, the author of *A Glossary*[18] *of the Tribes and Castes of the Punjab and N.W.F. Province*, writes:

> "Bhakht Mal—Sadhu, a Sikh sect founded by Bakht Mal. When Guru Gobind Singh destroyed Masands or tax gatherers, one of them, by name Bakht Mal, took refuge with Mata Gujar woman (Mata Gujri—Rose mis-stated, perhaps he could not understand Mata Gujri was a proper noun and was the name of mother of Guru Gobind Singh), who disguised him in a woman's clothes putting bangles on his wrist and a 'nath' or nose ring in his nose. This attire he adopted permanently and the Mahant of his Gaddi still wears bangles. His followers are said to be also called Bakhshish Sadh but this is open to doubt. The headquarter of the sect appears to be unknown."

Observation of H.A. Rose clearly supports at least this view that Bakht Mal was blessed with the duty to start preaching of Sikh religion by Guru Gobind Singh at the recommendation of the Guru's mother. From the account made available by Rose, it can also be surmised that he was a devoted Sikh holding the rank of Masand.

Bhai Randhir Singh, who launched a probe into the activities of Bakht Mal and his followers in fifties of the present century found their centres at Bahawalpur, Multan,

Karachi (Sind, Pakistan), Santal Rai in Uttar Pradesh. Bakht Mal's important followers were Balak Rai, Charan Das, Santokh Das.

With the passage of time this Order merged into the Order of Bhagat Bhagwan.

Jit Maliei

Jit Malieis trace their origin to Jit Mal who was a dedicated Sikh and held the rank of a *Masand*. When Guru Gobind Singh called *Masands* at Anandpur Sahib in 1754 Bk. = 1697 C.E. to chastise them for their dereliction of their assigned duties, he found Jit Mal immaculately pure and honest. He blessed him and allowed him to disseminate the message of Sikhism among the people and link them with the Guru directly.[19] Jit Mal felt happy and highly encouraged. He took *Pahul* and fanned to acquaint the people with the Guru's dispensation. His followers continued to tread the path shown by their mentor. Some time in the eighteenth century, Ajit Malieis merged their identity in the followers of Balu Hasna.[20]

Other Prominent Udasis

Besides the well-known Bakhshishan (preaching centres) there were some less known. Among them Giani Gian Singh has mentioned Gurdas Ke, Sodhi Dakhni Rai Ke, Sadhu Nand Lal Ke, Dewane, Hira Dasiei and Ram Dasiei. Ram Das Ke Udasis trace their origin to Bhai Gurditta, the grandson of Baba Budha of Ramdas, District Amritsar to spread the message of Guru Nanak. Ram Das Ke Udasis established their sub-centres at Naine Kot and Muradabad. To begin with, their headquarter was in the village Ramdas in Tahsil Ajnala, District Amritsar.[21] The Udasis, known as Sodhi Dakhni Rai Ke, consider Sodhi Dakhni Rai, a scion of Sodhi Meharban's family as their original mentor. They preached the message of the Gurus mostly in Malwa. Gharachon in Sangrur district was their main centre. Some of the Udasis of this order preached in Sindh, Sialkot district in Pakistan and Uttar Pradesh.

Dewaneis owe their existence to Baba Bhundar Das, originally a follower of Manohar Das Meharban (son of Prithi Chand). He met Guru Har Rai Sahib while he was on his tour in the Malwa region. Bhundar Das was in ecstasy. Guru Har Rai was highly pleased with him and honoured him with appellation of 'Dewan Sahib'. Bhundar now committed himself to preaching of Sikh ideology. He extricated himself from the influence of Meharban and became a devoted Sikh. His example was followed by his associates also. He and his followers established different preaching centres mostly in the Malwa (Punjab). In 1762-63 Bk. or 1705-06 C.E., Guru Gobind Singh visited people in Lakhi Jungle. A Dewana wanted to force his entry into the room where the Guru was sleeping. He was asked to wait but when he insisted, he was put to sword by a bodyguard of the Guru. Baba Gudda, a leading Dewana Udasi, incited fifty Dewanas to attack the Guru to avenge the death of their comrade. None but only two Dewana Udasis took courage to go near the Guru. Instead of attacking the Guru these two Dewanas sought solace and begged forgiveness from him. They played on their Sarangis (a musical instrument) and sang the greatness of the Guru demanding nothing except his benediction. Baba Gudda was shocked and unnerved but the Dewanas as a group preached Sikhism.[22] According to H.A. Rose "They are for the most part non-celibate. Outwardly these keep the hair uncut and wear a necklace of shells with a peacock feather in the turban. They follow the *Adi Granth* and repeat the true name. Their important centres were Patiala, Ambala, Raipur, Amritsar and Pirkot."

Hira Dasies were the followers of Hira Das. Hira Das was a cobbler by caste and lived at village Sursingh in the present District of Amritsar. During the period of Maharaja Ranjit Singh, they established a big preaching centre. Hira Das was a great preacher and a scholar. Quite a number of booklets containing Guru's hymns and handwritten by him and his followers are available.

On the basis of the history of different orders of Udasis it can safely be surmised that Udasis were a part of Sikh mainstream. They were much venerated and substantially helped by the Gurus. Their idiosyncrasies apart, they spread Sikhism far and wide. They highly respected Guru Granth

Sahib and placed it with decorum at their Deras (Preaching Centres). After the winding up of the Order of the *Masands* by Guru Gobind Singh on the eve of the creation of the Khalsa, their importance increased because they *suo moto* took up most of the duties of Masands. They went to the remote corners of India, established missionary centres at all places visited by Guru Nanak from Kabul to Dacca and from Nepal to Kanya Kumari and Rameshwaram. They learnt the languages of these regions, prepared copies of Guru Granth Sahib and installed them at different places. Besides they interpreted the sacred scriptures and acquainted the people with the achievements of their Gurus as best as they could.

When Guru Gobind Singh evacuated the fort of Anandgarh, an Udasi monk, Gurbakhsh Das undertook to look after the local shrines such as Sis Ganj and Kesgarh Sahib.

When the unscrupulous *masands* of Ram Rai cremated their mentor while he was still in his *Samadhi* and captured his *dera*, Guru Gobind Singh expelled these armed treacherous *masands* and installed Punjab Kaur the wife of Ram Rai to re-organise the dera on Udasi pattern. She adopted an Udasi youth as her spiritual son and lived upto 1744 C.E. to establish the Dehradun Dera exclusively on Udasi style. When after the death of Guru Gobind Singh, one Gulab Rai an imposter proclaimed himself Guru and tried to take possession of the shrines, Gurbakhsh Das thwarted his nefarious design. Gurbakhsh Das's successors continued to look after the Anandpur shrines, till their management was taken over in recent times by the Shiromani Gurdwara Parbandhak Committee. At Nander where Guru Gobind Singh passed away, *Mahant* Ishar Das Udasi performed the services at the Darbar and managed the shrine from 1765 Bk./1708 C.E. to 1782 Bk./1725 C.E. He was succeeded by his disciple Gopal Das Udasi, who remained in-charge of Darbar Hazur Sahib upto 1803 Bk./C.E. 1746. Gopal Das was succeeded by his disciple Saran Das Udasi, who served the shrine for a long period of thirty years. After Saran Das, the control of Durbar passed into the hands of the Sikhs who had, by that time, come from the Punjab in considerable numbers and settled in

Nander. In 1711 C.E., an Udasi Sadhu, Sant Gopal Das popularly known as Goddar Faqir was appointed Granthi at the Harimandir at Amritsar by Bhai Mani Singh whom Mata Sundri had deputed to serve as a custodian of Sri Harimandir Sahib, Amritsar. Gopal Das was later replaced by another Udasi Chanchal Singh a pious devoted Sikh.[23] According to a rough estimate nearly fifty per cent, if not more, nearly correct recensions of Guru Granth Sahib, Vars of Bhai Gurdas and works of Bhai Nand Lal were prepared by Udasi scribes and preserved in Sikhs Shrines supervised by Udasis.

As Udasis like Nirmalas and Sewa Panthi were organised by Gurus themselves, they were respected by the Sikhs as their indispensable part. Just as Khalsa had complete military responsibility for military activities, the Udasis were given equal and free participation in religious and cultural affairs. Over a hundred prominent Udasi saints and mystics are well-known for their missionary work in Kabul, Dacca, Gorakh Mata, Puri, Rameshwarm, Allahabad, Hardwar and a number of places in Punjab. Even in Aizerbaijan, Afghanistan, they reached and preached the gospel of Guru Nanak. This fact is eloquently vouchsafed by an inscription found on the gate of a temple, built long back by Zoroastrians.

As the time rolled on and the Sikhs entered eighteenth century, the Sikhs had to wage a struggle first against the Mughals and then against the Afghans. They succeeded in 1710 in ousting the Mughal government from a large part of the Punjab and established Khalsa sovereignty under the leadership of Banda Singh Bahadur. But it was short lived as it was put to an end in 1716 by the Mughal rulers. Banda Singh Bahadur was butchered at Delhi and orders were issued for the whole sale massacre of the Sikhs. The persecution thus started continued till about 1765 C.E. when the Sikhs occupied Sirhind Sarkar.

During this period the Udasis' role was admirable. They established themselves in different gurdwaras as Granthis. Since they were different from Khalsa in appearance, they were not targeted by either the Mughals or by the Afghans, with the vigour and ferocity the Sikhs were targetted. At times they felt afraid of the Mughal and Afghan rulers and found safety in leaving Punjab and settling elsewhere in India. Quite a number of them settled at different religious centres such as Hardwar, Allahabad, Nanak Mata *et al.* bringing themselves face to face with different religions and their ideologies. This thing affected their thinking and outlook. Dislodged from their original places, some of them felt desperate and took to identifying themselves with the mainstream religions prevalent in a particular area. This is one of the major reasons that Udasis started incorporating customs, mostly of Hindus in their programmes. Their counterparts in Punjab also got affected although not to the extent they were influenced. Hence they did not lose their closeness with the mainstream Sikhism.

How devoted and committed the Udasis were as Sikh missionaries, can be assessed from the following incident reported in Thomas Hardwicke's *Narrative of a Journey to Srinagar*.[24]

Udasis as well as Nirmalas had pitched their camps, hoisted their flags and started Akhand Path of Guru Granth Sahib three days before the Kumbh Mela at Hardwar. Naga Sadhus also called. Gosain Sannyasis were given magisterial control of the fair both by Maratha and the British and they charged every Hindu pilgrim eight annas to one rupee. They moved about flaunting their deadly weapons and would not hesitate from firing and flogging every one who did not fulfil their demand. Captain Hardwicke relates how these Nagas slavishly served British officers who were there by offering them special facilities.

The Udasis and Nirmalas refused to give any money on the plea that they were not Hindus but Sikh missionaries. Nagas at first threatened and then carried out their threats by stopping the recitation of Guru Granth Sahib and burning their flag. Nirmalas went away quietly but Udasis resisted. They were brutally attacked by all types of weapons and many of them were killed. The Guru Granth Sahib was chopped with axes. All pilgrims who had come for *Guru Ka Langar* were either killed or injured. The incident took place in April, 1796 C.E.

When the news reached the Sikh Sardars such as Rai Singh, Sher Singh and Maharaja of Patiala, they rushed to the spot. The Udasis who had been killed were cremated, their flag was hoisted and the recitation of Guru Granth Sahib was completed under armed protection. On April 10, when the pilgrims melted away and Naga Sadhus were counting their collections, the Sikh Sardars launched attack on them and killed every one that came their way. From that day onward, the Nirmalas and Udasi Saints were never taxed and were given special facilities for preaching the teachings of Guru Granth Sahib in Hardwar and Kurukshetra fairs.

The Sikh Sardars who had established their principalities in trans-Sutlej and Cis Sutlej Punjab towards the end of eighteeth century were very liberal when it came to sanctioning grants to religious places. Almost every prominent Sikh gurdwara or ashram got a sizable landed property attached to it. Udasi centres popularly known as Akharas were also granted huge properties with the result that their income grew handsomely, which made them greedy, morally corrupt and great derelicts in their duties. They started preserving and promoting their vested interest by delinking gurdwara from Sikh *Sangat* and managed it in such a way as if it were a temple. This thing indeed suited them because participation of *Sangat* in the affairs of gurdwaras clashed with their interest of being the sole master of the influence, offers and properties of gurdwara/ ashram. But all this they did with such finesse that they continued to be held in high esteem, generally speaking. In the mid-nineteenth century, the number of Udasi establishments that received state patronage and found mention in official record exceeded 250.[25] Of these most of Akharas were at the places either associated with or sanctified by the Gurus or where they found ready audience to preach their ideology. The revenue free grants of the patronised Udasi institutions amounted to about twelve lakh rupees a year forming nearly ten per cent of the total estimated *dharmarths* under the Sikh rule.

The tendencies of Udasis to deform or distort the message of the Guru got further strengthened during the reign of

Maharaja Ranjit Singh, although there was no open cleavage between the mainstream Sikhism and the Sikhs continued to look upon them as Sikh missionaries of Udasi establishments.[26]

Udasis' Orders have been open to all castes and professions. In religious practices, they differ from the Sikhs in certain respects. Their Ardas is different from that of Sikhs and they do not subscribe to the Sikh rites. Ringing of bells (ghanti or gharial), blowing of instruments (Narsingh or Singhi) form part of their religious service while it is non-existent in Sikh religious service. They do not hesitate to worship icons of Guru Nanak and Baba Sri Chand while icon worship is prohibited in mainstream Sikhism. Their salutations are Waheguru (Glory of God), Gajo ji Waheguru (Hail aloud the glorious Lord) or Alakh (Hail the unknowable). The Udasis believe that after gaining Matra one can attain Param Tatva (the highest truth) and achieve Mukti (release). The literal meaning of Matra is a measure or quantity which stands in prosody and grammar for the length of time required to pronounce a short vowel. But in Udasi tradition Matra has acquired a new meaning and it signifies an incantation or sacred text. According to *Encyclopaedia of Sikhism*[27] 'an Udasi Matra is the sacred formula addressed to the disciples as counsel and advice'. There are considerable number of these Matras attributed to Guru Nanak, Baba Sri Chand, Baba Gurditta, Almast and Balu Hasna. The Udasis without exception keep *Adi Granth* in their monasteries or Akharas and profess faith in all the Gurus from Nanak to Guru Gobind Singh, although side by side they show keen interest in the chain of succession which descended from Sri Chand down to the *Mahant* (superior) of the branch, they followed.

Udasis' dress is not uniform. Some of them wear white while others prefer green or red coloured garments. Some of them prefer to be naked, wearing nothing except a brass chain around their waist. Some wear matted or uncut hair, while some others prefer to be cleanshaven. Quite a number of Udasis used Tilak, wore the Janeu (sacred cord) and mālā (Rosary)[28] towards the end of the eighteenth century. Besides preaching Word of Guru Nanak, Udasi centres had been serving as seminaries of Sikh learning. Chelas *i.e.* disciples sat at the feet of the head of the monastery who instructed them in Sikh and other classical texts. Udasi centre at Amritsar, Brahm Buta Akhara ran a Gurmukhi School, which was renowned enough to attract a considerable number of pupils. Some Udasi centres imparted training in Indian system of medicines and physiology. One such seat was the Bunga of Pandit Sarup Das Udasi who was a great scholar as well as an authority on Charak Samhita.

In 1849, Punjab was occupied by the British. The gurdwara officials mostly Udasis began to care more for the interests of the government than for their duties. In this process, they went a step further. They made the most of the opportunity of fresh revenue assessment in the province to get the land endowments of the gurdwaras under their charge entered in their personal names with the specific purpose of turning gurdwara properties into private properties to be used or disposed of anyway they liked. They further claimed the right of their descendants to inherit this property and showed no hesitation in appointing their successors from amongst the members of their families. Their conduct too did not match their exalted status. Besides, they started presenting Hinduised version of Sikhism.

Such religious derelictions by the Udasis and other officients of gurdwaras and Akharas galled the reformers and spurred them not only to reform gurdwaras but also to wrest control of gurdwaras managements from Udasis. In the emergence of such resolve, motivations to use the moral and material resources of the gurdwaras both to make hegemonic the Singh identity and carve out politic-social entity also played a significant role. This being the perspective, Gurdwara Reform Movement was started to wrest the management and control of Sikh shrines. After a long struggle spanning over nearly five years, the movement succeeded and the ownership and management of historical shrines passed into the hands of a democratically elected apex body called 'Shromani Gurdwara Parbandhak Committee' by virtue of enactment of Sikh Gurdwara Act, 1925. Even then some of the Udasi incumbents of the Gurdwaras continued to occupy gurdwaras which were not historical but had considerable properties by declaring that these were not gurdwaras but their 'deras' (camps). They removed from such places Guru Granth Sahib as also monuments and documents which could testify that it was not dera but a gurdwara. The Udasis even succeeded in securing court decree—declaring themselves as Hindus. Since the jurisdiction of Sikh Gurdwara Act did not go beyond Punjab, Haryana and Chandigarh the Gurdwaras/deras existing outside the specified territories remained to be owned and controlled by the Udasis who till today spread the message of Guru Granth Sahib to the non-Sikhs in the regions in which they live even to this day, although they have reservation about Singh identity.

Akali/Nihang Order

The term Akali is originally from Akal, the timeless one. Guru Nanak (1469-1539) described God as Akal Murat, the Eternal form. It was used to name an order during the time of Guru Gobind Singh.

There are different accounts current about the origin of this order. One of these recalls an amusing prank by Guru Gobind Singh's child Fateh Singh (1699-1705). It is said that Fateh Singh once appeared in the Guru's presence dressed in a blue chola (loose short hanging skirt-like below the knees) fastened at the waist with a linen girdle and a large blue turban with a dumala (piece of cloth forming a plume). The Guru was pleased to see his son and remarked that such should be the dress of the soldiers of God. From this expression, Sikhs committed to the Guru's ideology and cause organised themselves into an Order known as Akali Order.

Another view is that Guru Gobind Singh, after his escape from Chamkaur, donned blue dress as a disguise, which he discarded and burnt upon reaching the village of Dhilwan near Kot Kapura in December, 1705. Man Singh, his zealous attendant, saved a piece of the blue garment and stuck it on the top of his turban. Those who followed Man Singh galvanised themselves into a band of committed soldiers of their Guru or God and assumed the name "Akali/Nihang".

These traditions are emphatic how the Akalis adopted the dress but do not convey explicitly why the Order was originated. In fact, the emergence of this Order was rooted in Sikh religion. Guru Gobind Singh through administering "Pahul" transformed the psyche of the Sikhs who now became fierce brotherhood of crusaders. Guru Gobind Singh did not mean to change the faith of Guru Nanak. The only change he brought about in the religion was to expose the other side of the coin. Whereas Guru Nanak had propagated goodness, Guru Gobind Singh condemned evil. One preached the love of one's neighbour the other the punishment of the transgressers. Nanak's God loved His saints; Guru Gobind Singh's God destroyed His enemies. The change of emphasis was made operative by the military brotherhood of zealots who came to be known as Akali-Nihangs.

Since each Akali was passionately committed to the cause of the Guru and was determined to work for its consummation—even at the cost of his/her life, he/she began to be called 'Nihang'—the name which in course of time began to be used in place of Akali or along with Akali. It was because of this that Akali Order assumed another name Nihang Order.

The origin of the term Nihang is traced back to Persian word Nihang (alligator, sword). The term seems to refer the reckless courage, members of the order possessed and displayed in battles. The term also visualised a modified form of Nihang, often used in Sikh scriptures to mean Nirlep (unsmeared, sinless, not attached to anything).

Whatever be the genesic root of the term, it signifies the characteristic qualities of the Akali/Nihang Order—its freedom from fear of danger or death, readiness for action and non-attachment to worldly possessions.[29]

Akalis/Nihangs have played a significant part all through the history of the Sikhs. In the eighteenth century, they had always been in the vanguard during the struggle of the Sikhs for survival and supremacy. Towards the end of the eighteenth century, when Misls established their hegemony over the large part of the Punjab and succumbed to mutual rivalries and recriminations, the Akali/Nihang bands (Nishanwalia Misl and Shahidi Misl to which they were affiliated) kept themselves aloof from race for power and prosperity. Their self-discipline and commitment to the Guru's cause earned them a lot of popularity—far more than their numerical strength. They were considered torch bearer and custodian of the conscience of the Khalsa brotherhood. Because of their lofty ideals and spirit of self-sacrifice, they were privileged to convene assemblies of the Khalsa at Sri Akal Takht Sahib in which momentous decisions were taken. They conducted such assemblies and kept record of their proceedings.[30]

In the time of Maharaja Ranjit Singh they maintained their independent existence. Their leader Akali Phula Singh Nihang, the custodian of Sri Akal Takht, was acclaimed as the moral voice of the Khalsa, and, at times, he censured and chastised even the Maharaja Ranjit Singh. The Maharaja valued their qualities of valour and persuaded them to join a special wing of his army. Nihang troops under the leadership of Akali Sadhu Singh and Akali Phula Singh played a crucial role in some of the toughest battles of the Maharaja, battles of Multan and Nowshehra (1823). Nihang bands took active part in the battle of Sabraon under the leadership of Hanuman Singh.

The Akali-Nihangs had been openly antagonistic towards the European officers of the state as also to the occasional embassies sent out to the Punjab by the British East India Company. When Lt. William Barr and his colleagues were in Lahore, the Nihang compared them to "a couple of pigs". They did not even spare the forty-two Firangees Ranjit Singh had employed to train his army. "One is reminded of the ordeal that August Theodar Shoefft, the Hungrarian painter had to bear while he was executing a panoramic view of the Golden temple commissioned by the Sikh court of Lahore. Engrossed in work while changing the paint brushes, he put one in his mouth. This the Nihangs noticed from a distance and imagined that he was smoking. The painter's life was barely saved by the timely intervention of the temple chief priest who explained how the unfortunate incident was the result of faulty observation.[31]

Apart from their distinguishable mode of dress, the Nihangs/Akalis have always tried to preserve the form and content of the Khalsa practice. All of them receive *Pahul*, recite daily compositions from *Guru Granth Sahib*, the *Dasam Granth* and *Sarb Loh Granth*. They attend *Sangat* (congregation) and listen to *Kirtan* (Hymn-singing) and *Katha*. They are fond of horse-riding and take special interest in learning traditional warfare. They are always ready to perform self-abnegating service. They are strict tee-totallers and will not stand smoking in their presence even by non-Sikhs. They, however, have developed habit of consuming Sukha, a potion of Indian hemp thoroughly crushed with heavy wooden pestle in a mortar. Mostly non-vegetarians, they would take meat only of those animals/birds whom they slaughter themselves in one stroke. "Faithful to the Sarb-Loh (all-steel) symbolism propounded by Guru Gobind Singh, all accoutrements of Nihangs, including their weapons and utensils are of steel. They reserve special veneration for *Sarb Loh Granth*, which depicts in primordial symbols, the eternal fight between good and evil—in this instance, between Sarb Loh and Brij Nath, the king of demons.[32]

Decline in their influence set in with the death of Maharaja Ranjit Singh. After the occupation of the Punjab by the British, policy of systematic suppression of them was followed and consequently their influence as well as their number diminished. In the 1892 census, only 1376 persons were returned as 'Sikh Akalis or Nihangs' and in 1901, this number further came down to a bare 431.

During the eighteenth century when the Mughals and the Afghan rulers were hell-bent to destroy the Sikhs roots and branch, Nihangs were the most fearless and courageous to challenge them. In the course of their resistance they underwent extreme hardships. But they remained steadfast and in high spirits. They made light of their adversity and coined special vocabulary both to sustain their own courage and to demoralise their enemy. Death was called an expedition of the Khalsa into the next world. One with empty stomach would call himself maddened with prosperity. Parched grams were called almonds, hunger intoxication, dying would be campaign while a unit of one would be described as one and a quarter hundred thousand. In a spirit of heroic manly humour, running away was described as becoming a stag and a limping man, Tamerlane.

The Nihangs are today divided into several groups or dals each with its own cantonment and a headman, but are loosely organised into two Dals—Budha Dal and Taruna Dal, names initially given to the two sections into which the Khalsa army was divided in 1733 C.E. The Budha Dal calling itself Chhianaven Karori Chalda Vahir (960 million-strong column ever on the move) has its headquarters at Talwandi Sabo in Bathinda district, while the principal headquarters of Taruna Dal is at Baba Bakala. Anandpur, the birth place of the Khalsa remains the main centre of Nihang congregation. Thousands gather here a day after Holi to celebrate Hola Mohalla. It is believed that Guru Gobind Singh ordained his Sikhs to assemble here on this day to perform mock battles and military exercises. This tradition with certain variations is staunchly followed by Nihang Singhs.

Giani Sampardai or Order

Giani, the Punjabi form of Sanskrit jnani from the root jna (to know) originally meant a scholar of high learning. In Sikh tradition a Giani is a learned man of pious character, competent to recite faultlessly, interpret and expound the Guru Granth Sahib and other Sikh texts. Sampardai denotes a school of thought of accredited standing.

This school of Gianis originated with Bhai Mani Singh (d. 1737) who had the privilege of receiving instructions from Guru Tegh Bahadur at Anandpur and from Guru Gobind Singh at Damdama. He was reverently called Giani—a knowledgeable personage. At Damdama upto the departure of Guru Gobind Singh towards the south and at Hari Mandir till his last breath, he made a practice of expounding a *Shabad* (hymn) with illustrations from the lives of the Gurus and their disciples. His art of scriptural explication and the content of his discourses in course of time became a distinctive tradition of scriptural interpretation. The fervent adherents of this tradition began to be called Gianis. Hence the emergence of Giani Sampardai. Originally, such people were known by the common name, Sikh honorific of Bhai or Sant.[33] Bhai Gurmukh Singh son of Bhai Sant Singh earned the Giani appellation for the first time from the Sardars in Sikh times.

Bhai ji was survived by three exceptionally brilliant pupils namely Dewan Singh, Bhai Gurdial Singh and Gurbakhsh Singh, who carried on the scholarly tradition he had initiated and established. They had their own pupils who in turn trained their own pupils. Through this chain of pupils, the Sampardai has lasted to this day.

At Damdama, Baba Deep Singh guided the Sampardai's work. In 1726 C.E., he prepared four copies of Guru Ganth Sahib to be sent each to Sri Akal Takht, Amritsar, Shri Kesgarh Sahib, Anandpur, Sri Hazoor Sahib, Nander and Sri Sach Khand, Patna Sahib. He also got prepared anthologies of those compositions from Guru Granth Sahib, which were to be recited daily. After his martyrdom, the work of Sampardai was carried on by his dedicated pupils as for instance Gurbakhsh Singh and Surat Singh and Bhai Gurdas etc. The two headquarters at Amritsar and Talwandi Sabo worked in tandem in perfect harmony and a lot of preaching was done in the Majha and Malwa regions.

The distinctive feature of Giani Sampardai has been its strict adherence to the tenets of the Sikh faith and to the discipline made incumbent upon the Sikhs by the Gurus. At initiation, they take the vows of the Khalsa as prescribed by Guru Gobind Singh. They preach neither celibacy nor asceticism as do the Udasis and Nirmalas. On the doctrinal level, they have kept their own course relying solely on the teachings of the Guru and the Sikh tradition, as it had autonomously evolved. They do not recommend any ritual or short cuts to the ultimate goal, and insist on the observance of Nām Japnā, Kirat Karnī, and Wand Chhaknā. They have been strong protagonists of Gurbani as a means of transforming the individuals as well as society.[34] For them, the Vedas were not authority for Gurus' compositions as it was with Nirmalas (generally speaking) nor the Gurus' word regarded as an extension of or interpretation of the Vedas.

The Gianis have made very valuable contribution to the exegetical literature on Sikhism. Bhai Mani Singh wrote: *Gian Ratnavli* and *Sikhan-di-Bhagat Mala*. Bhai Chanda Singh and Bhai Hazara Singh wrote *Prayai Guru Granth Sahib* and *Sri Guru Granth Kosh*, respectively. In relatively recent times, Bhai Bishan Singh Giani (d. 1936), Bhai Vir Singh (d. 1957) have produced complete or partial commentaries of Guru Granth Sahib. Dr. Ernest Trumpp and Mr. M.A. Macauliffe while translating into English certain portions of Guru Granth Sahib were guided and helped by the scholars of this school. Throughout, they have remained uncompromising in their stand and have never hesitated to preach unalloyed Sikhism. Their recent outstanding lights were Giani Gurbachan Singh Bhindranwala, Kartar Singh and Jarnail Singh.

FOOTNOTES

1. *Akal Ustat*.
2. Dhamman is a sub-caste of Kshatriyas.
3. *The Encyclopaedia of Sikhism*, Vol. III, pp. 423-24.
4. Research Paper 'Nirmal Panth by Kanwar Mrigindra Singh, published in Punjab History Conference Proceedings, March 9-10, 1969.
5. Gandhi, Surjit Singh: *History of Sikh Gurus*, p. 323, Gurdas Kapur and Sons, Delhi, 1978.
6. The Dera is now called Dera Thakar Tota Singh and is situated at Thikri Wala in Sangrur district.
7. Refer to Nirmal Panth Darshan by Mahant Dayal Singh.
8. Thomas Hardwicke: *Narrative of Journey to Sri Nagar*, p. 450.
9. *Guru Granth Sahib*, p. 999.
10. *Ibid.*, p. 474.
11. Bhai Randhir Singh came across a MSS of *Adi Granth* dated 1728 Bk. reverently kept in a Dharamsala at Rawalpindi.
12. *Punjabi Vishva Kosh*, p. 252.
13. Randhir Singh: *Udasi Sikhan Di Vithya*, pp. 187-88, SGPC, 1969.
14. The information has been gleaned from Randhir Singh's book, *Udasi Sikhan Di Vithya*, pp. 185-216.
15. Randhir Singh: *Udasi Sikhan Di Vithya*, p. 159, SGPC, 1969.

16. Thursday, Chet 1763 Bk.
17. *Mehma Parkash*, Sakhi 28.
18. *A Glossary of the Tribes and Castes of the Punjab and N.W.F. Provinces*, p. 40.
19. Randhir Singh: *Udasi Sikhan Di Vithya*, p. 486.
20. *Ibid.*, p. 487, SGPC, 1969.
21. H.A. Rose: *op. cit.*, Part III, p. 481.
22. H.A. Rose: *op. cit.*, Vol. II, p. 243.
23. *Encyclopaedia of Sikhism*, p. 378.
24. Thomas Hardwicke: *Narrative of a Journey to Sri Nagar*, p. 450.
25. Dharam Singh: *Sikhism—Norm and Form*, p. 47. Vision and Venture, Patiala, 1997.
26. Sulakhan Singh: State Patronage to the Udasi under Maharaja Ranjit Singh in *Maharaja Ranjit Singh and His Times* ed. J.S. Grewal and Indu Banga.
27. *Encyclopaedia of Sikhism*, Vol. IV, p. 578, Punjabi University, Patiala.
28. John Ancher: *The Sikhs*, p. 228.
29. *Encyclopaedia of Sikhism*, Vol. III, pp. 222-27.
30. Gandhi, Surjit Singh: *Struggle of the Sikhs for Sovereignty*; Malcolm: *Sketch of the Sikhs*, pp. 120-37.
31. Kanwar Pal Singh's *Article Nihang Brotherhood.*
32. *Encyclopaedia of Sikhism*, Vol. III, pp. 122-27.
33. *Ibid.*, II, pp. 78-79, Pbi. Uni. Patiala.
34. Gandhi, Surjit Singh: *Struggle of the Sikhs for Sovereignty*, GDK Publications, Delhi, 1980.

18

IMPORTANT SIKH STRUCTURES

GURU KA LANGAR

Guru Ka Langar is a unique institution of the Sikhs and it is as old as Sikhism itself. It is not only manifestative of the Sikh principles of equality and fraternity but it also provides a mechanism for Sikhism to operate in a work-a-day life. It aims at removing the distinctions of caste, creed, birth and status *et al.* It has developed among the Sikhs the spirit of discipline and service and the will to give away something in the cause of religion and humanity in a spirit of dedication to the Guru. In *Guru Ka Langar* people are ordained to partake of food while sitting in a row without any consideration of caste, creed, race, rank, wealth, birth and gender etc. *Guru Ka Langar* as its very name shows belongs to God and to no mortal. The provisions in the *Langar* are provided by the devotees not in a spirit of giving alms but in a spirit of performing religious duty unto God and His creation. Guru Nanak, the founder of Sikh religion prescribed a certain way of life for his followers whose cardinal principles are:

Kirt Karnā	(Earning livelihood by honest creative labour)
Vand Chhaknā	(Sharing the fruits of ones labour with ones fellow beings)
Nām Japnā	(Developing discipline of the NĀM).

To uphold and project such a code of life, the Guru established *Guru Ka Langar* and carefully nurtured it so that it might become an integral part of Sikh psyche and Sikh moral structure. Wherever Guru Nanak stayed during his travels, he exhorted his devotees to run *Guru Ka Langar*. The people who gathered to listen to him or to deliberate upon his Word were called *Sangat*, and while they dined together, they were called *Pangat*. Thus *Sangat* and *Pangat* formed necessary accompaniments of each other and were inseparable. The place where the Guru put up was named Dharamsal. Guru Nanak insisted upon his disciples to share meals with others, visitors, strangers, friends and foes alike. Every Sikh was expected to contribute liberally for the maintenance of *Guru Ka Langar*. It could be done by making an offering in cash, kind, personal labour in cleaning, cooking and serving meals. The last years of Guru Nanak's life were spent at Kartarpur on the bank of the river Ravi, now in Pakistan. His house served as a Dharamsal, a place of worship as well as a free mess (*Guru Ka Langar*).

Guru Nanak's example was followed by all his successors. Guru Angad opened *Guru Ka Langar* at Khadur where he established his headquarter. His wife, honourable Khivi, looked after its arrangement and personally served in the preparation and distribution of food. She often served a sweet dish of rice-milk, the coveted food of Punjabis. Guru Amar Das shifted his seat from Khadur to Goindwal. He converted the *Langar* into a regular institution making it a rule that every visitor should dine in *Langar* before seeing him. Even Emperor Akbar was asked to follow this practice which he cheerfully did. In Guru Amar Das's time, pudding or *Karah Prasad* which in course of time became their consecrated dish was also served in *Guru Ka Langar*. Satta and Balwand say:

'Nit Rasoī Terī Aai Gheo Maidā Khān'

(Every day in your kitchen was served pudding made of clarified butter, refined flour and sugar.)

Under Guru Ram Das, Amritsar became his headquarter which continued to be so under the 5th and 6th Gurus. *Guru*

Ka Langar was operated with utmost care and devotion. One day Guru Ram Das paid a visit to *Langar*, a Sikh named Handal was kneading flour in a huge pan. On seeing the Guru, he rushed to prostrate himself before him. As his hands were covered with wet flour, he put them on his back and fell flat at the Guru's feet. *The Guru was pleased with his devotion and blessed him.* The *Langar* was maintained by Guru Arjan Dev and Sri Guru Hargobind with equal zeal and zest. During the latter's lifetime, his son, Baba Attal, was in-charge of the *Langar* which worked day and night and even supplied food to those Sikhs who were quite afar but needed food. Even in the battlefield, *Guru Ka Langar* reached out to soldiers. His service and devotion impressed the people so much that an adage 'Baba Attal, Pakki Pakai Ghal' (Baba Attal is ever ready to supply cooked meals) grew very popular.

When Guru Hargobind settled at Kiratpur in the last phase of his life (1634-44), *Guru Ka Langar* ran with usual fervour and sincerity. Mohsin Fani, who lived at Kiratpur during this phase of Guru's life testifies to it.

The seventh Guru Har Rai preserved and further promoted this institution. It continued to be maintained during the time of Guru Harkrishan. As Guru Tegh Bahadur remained mostly on the move, a mobile *Langar* followed him.

Guru Gobind Singh not only maintained his own *Langar* but insisted that others should also run *Langar*. One day in disguise, he called at the *Langar* of his disciples rather at odd hours at Anandpur. He found most of them reticent to serve *Langar* before time. Bhai Nand Lal, however, served him as best as he could. The following day, the Guru narrated his experience in his *Durbar* and advised his disciples to offer something to eat to visitors even at odd hours. The Guru said: "There is nothing equal to the bestowal of food. Blessed is the person who giveth to the hungry. Let no one fix any time for the exercise of this virtue. It is not necessary to consider whether it is night or day, evening or morning, whether, the moon is dark or full, or if there is a particular anniversary. avoid all delay in such a matter. Of all gifts, this charity is the most highly valued.

Some scholars have averred that the *Guru Ka Langar* had resemblance with free messes run at Khanquahs of Sufis and Ashrams of Yogis and thus it was not originally set up by the Gurus. Their view is erroneous. Historically speaking, only some of the Khanquahs and Yogi Ashram had the free mess and that too was run without any specific regulations regarding its organisation and operations. Not unoften, the high profile religious and political elites were not obligated to sit side by side with others without any consideration of caste, creed, wealth or status. This was so because the institution of *Langar* at such places was meant only for those who attended it. On the other hand *Guru Ka Langar* had roots in Sikh ideology and functioned as one of the essential structures of Sikhism. In Sikhism the world is a dwelling place of God and all the human beings are cast in His image. The upkeep of human beings was considered religiously meritorious. *Guru Ka Langar* in this context was certainly vital and meaningful.

Other salients of Guru's teachings were perfect equality among people including females and sharing of the fruits of one's creative labour. Regarding equality and sharing, the Guru's ordainments are very clear. Said Guru Nanak in Sorath Rag that "It is one God who is all light and from it has emanated the world. None is inferior to any one." "God is Eternal giver, never tired of giving or sharing, implying thereby said that giving or sharing is a Divine quality." This being so, Prof. Puran Singh says "By giving, the sense of 'I' is lost and you come close to Him."

Towards these two objectives, the institution of *Langar* played a role of great significance. It contributed a lot to engender equality and love for all and penchant for sharing with others by obligating people of all ranks to sit together for taking food and also to contribute to it as a part of their religious duty. Prof. Puran Singh named this institution as 'Temple of Bread'. According to Webster's *Encyclopaedia* unbridged *Dictionary of the English Language*, 'temple is a place where worship of a deity is effected'. In Guru's scheme, the divinity had been ascribed to Bread. Bread was deemed sacred, esteemed and venerated; it was never, scorned and avoided as it was the case in certain religious orders as for instance Yogism and Sannyasism.

In view of the unique role played by the *Langar* institution in the field of Sikhism as well as in Sikh society, it provided sinews for various very important formulations. *Degh* (Langar) began to symbolise socio-physical wants of man. These were to be satisfied as primary needs, as a pre-condition for spiritual progress. To secure it was the motive behind the revolutionary action, the principle of *Tegh*. *Tegh* stood for the use of force in fighting against and securing the overthrow of the adversaries intent upon depriving the people opportunities to fulfil their basic needs. Guru Gobind Singh devised the *Degh* and *Tegh* almost an aphorism or an epigrammatic statement for which he possessed a characteristic genius. The three Persian words 'Degh', 'Tegh', 'Fateh' that together make up the trenchant phrase denote the social aims of the Sikh movement in times of Guru Gobind Singh and means of their realisation as envisaged by him.

> "Let the pot (Degh) and the sword (Tegh) flourish in this world." (Guru Gobind Singh)

Degh stood for equality, fraternity and economic well-being for all. In short it beckoned a new social order. And Sword (Tegh) denoted the principled rebellion against the upholders of the iniquitous and unjust social Order as also the determination to establish a new Order based on righteousness. In a way, two words, *Degh* and *Tegh* taken together form a complete social philosophy that envisaged the destruction of all that was unrighteous and building a new social order guaranteeing complete social equality, inter-personal harmony, freedom from fear and freedom of expression and worship.

> "O God, in Your Will, let good come to all without exception."

Envisioning key role of 'sword' in his philosophy, the Guru bursts forth in his compositions *Bachittar Natak*—'The Wondrous Drama' to pay his homage to the Sword, calling the 'Almighty weapon', a 'comforter of the good', 'grinder of the evil and destroyer of all troubles and pains'. He goes further and equalises it with God Almighty. Not only this, God himself has been addressed by him as the 'Sword' 'Sabre'—Sword-armed, All steel.

The *Degh* philosophy became the cornerstones of various politico-socio-economic structures. It was this philosophy which impelled Banda Singh Bahadur to transfer the ownership of land to actual tillers and to base his political apparatus on it. During the regime of Banda Bahadur care was taken that the principles of equality, non-exploitation and non-discrimination were not flouted. He himself set an example of regarding himself first among the equals instead of bandying himself as a king or a dictator. He did not sit on a throne nor did he wear crown, understandably to emphasise this point.

From 1716 till 1765, the *Degh* philosophy at political level could not be given due consideration because sovereignty rested with the Mughals or Afghans. In the wake of the occupation of Lahore by the Sikhs in 1765, the whole of Punjab, by and large, came under Khalsa sovereignty and there is abundant evidence to testify that the Sardars of various principalities did take care of the Sikh principles, though the *Degh* philosophy was not galvanised into a comprehensive philosophy to take in its embrace all aspects of life. In Ranjit Singh's rule, *Degh* philosophy commanded respect, though, yet it could not become the basis of the polity of the Maharaja.

As a sentiment, it exists and will continue to exist, always cogitating the Sikhs. Small wonder, the Sikhs everywhere in the world run *Guru Ka Langar* which in its turn stimulates them to ponder upon their glorious heritage and also to strive to build a new world Order on the basis of *Degh* philosophy.

SANGAT AND GURDWARA

Sangat has always been given a place of importance in Sikh religion. The word *Sangat* literally means an assembly. In Sikhism, it denotes an assembly of seekers of truth. According to Guru Nanak it is the society where the praises of the Supreme Lord alone are expounded.

It has always played a key role in the development of Sikhism. Its emergence was a socio-religious and metaphysical event. It provided opportunity to the people to gather, to receive, to ponder upon and to practise the Sikh ideals, and to take decisions in regard to various subjects touching a wide range. Such gatherings in course of time galvanised themselves into a distinct socio-religious groups determined to educate themselves and all others who would so desire, as per instructions of the Guru. It was essentially because of this peculiar quality of *Sangat* that group-centred and group-oriented institutions such as *Guru Ka Langar* came into being and operated as an integral part of *Sangat*. Hence it is needless to remark that in Sikh conceptual vocabulary *Sangat* and *Pangat* (files of men sitting together to partake of food together), are used in special sense.

With common conceptual goals, the individuals constituting *Sangat* began to shed ego-centricity and all those thoughts and feelings which whipped up the individualistic tendencies and selfishness.

Guru Arjan Dev says in Gauri Sukhmani Mahalla V, Ashtpadi 7, "in the company of saints one gets rid of mine-ness", and instead, "God, Nām and Guru's *shabad*, taste sweet to him". Guru Amar Das explains that "One in the company of saints sheds all jealousies and feels that he is now enemy of none and no one in the world is stranger to him. He is friend of all the people."

As a matter of fact, *Sangat* socialises the ego-inhering a man, of course naturally by making him sit along with others and to concentrate upon Guru's 'Shabad' (sacred words) and to take decision in the light of that with a mind atonce clear and suffused with truthful feelings, thereby providing atmosphere and catalysts for the individual ego to transform itself into social conscience. Looked from this point of view, it can be surmised that this institution played a marked role in developing the macro-approach among the Sikhs.

This single factor of 'Macro-approach' and concentration on Guru's Gospel by all irrespective of any distinction, gave a stunning blow to the invidious distinctions based on deep-rooted caste-feelings. In fact, these distinctions are the anti-thesis of the very concept of *Sangat*, a congregation of the seekers of truth to develop the vision of looking upon everyone as an equal and a friend. This being so, *Sangat* initiates as well as champions the process of the fraternization of the people of all castes, all creeds and all walks of life on the bases of social equality and freedom to forge ahead and progress.

Sangat, besides conferring upon its members and all those coming under its influence, different advantages in social sense, was considered an academy wherein one could progress spiritually. Guru Ram Das says: "The true company is an academy of the true Guru where the teachings in the merits of God are imparted to the disciples." Bhai Nand Lal says: "My dear, if you are able to enjoy the company of the noble and the virtuous, you will require imperishable wealth thereby. Through the influence of the good company, I have seen particle of dust being exalted to the rank of a world-illuminating sun." Guru Gobind Singh's court poet Sainapat writes in his book *Gur Sobha*, that when the seekers assemble in *dharamsala, Parbrahm* is seen there. Guru Ram Das utters: "How and why and what way can I attain my own Lord. I may be instructed in the merits and messages of Lord's blessings within the true congregation. God's presence is felt and with the association of saints His merits are known. It has been my great and good fortune to have company of the true congregation. I meet Guru and my Lord. In view of all this, it can be inferred that *Sangat*, besides socialising the ego of a man and fraternising different people, also operated as an instrument to spiritualise man and society.

Sangat, as it has .delineated in the preceding paragraphs, appears to be a socio-religious institution, but it assumed another character also which was that of metaphysical. It became a metaphysical event and reality. To Guru Arjan Dev, it was an ideal company in which the spirit of True Guru resides. It was considered no less than the Guru. In Sikh hagiographical literature 'Sangat' was considered to be carrying more weight than the Guru. To express the idea in the words of Bhai Gurdas, if Guru's view scored 20 points, that of *Sangat* twenty-one points. When Guru Gobind Singh ordered that after him Guru Granth—Panth will be the Guru, then *Sangat* which is panth on a small scale acquired yet greater status. This was the reason that people sought solace not only in social and physical sense, but also in metaphysical and spiritual senses. Urged by the later sense, the people supplicated it to be blessed with such things as birth of an issue or prosperous family life, or any other advantage and facility.

Gurdwara

The place where *Sangat* congregated was known as Dharamsal. Since *Sangat* was held in high esteem, the Sikhs cherished that home of each one of them should function like a Dharamsal. When Guru Nanak settled at Kartarpur, a special Dharamsal was erected for Sikh gatherings. Likewise Guru Angad established a Dharamsal at Khadur. Guru Amar Das too raised a Dharamsal at Goindwal. Satta and Balwand recited Kirtan daily in the morning and evening. People in large numbers were attracted to listen to Kirtan and the instructions of the Guru. *Guru Ka Langar* (Guru's free mess) also functioned side by side as an integral part of Dharamsal.

By the time of Guru Hargobind, the number of *Sangats* increased considerably and some of them had also got copies of the Pothi (*Adi Granth*) compiled and edited by Guru Arjan Dev which they kept in their respective dharamsals. Such places then began to be called 'gurdwara' which implied 'Guru's Abode' or the gate through which one could reach the Guru. Gurdwara acquired a special status and sanctity when Guru Gobind Singh on the 7th October, 1708 proclaimed that hereafter the guruship would vest in *Adi Granth* and Panth subsequently designated as Guru Granth and Guru Panth.

Gurdwara being the lodge of Guru Granth and Guru Panth became very special, and, little wonder, it acquired a sort of sacredotal authority.

At Gurdwara, the *Sangat*, apart from reciting Gurbani and the compositions of Bhai Gurdas and Bhai Nand Lal, and pondering over their heritage, could discuss any matter, concerning them and the world around in a spirit of truth. It therefore, presented at once the focal point of Sikh activities—

political, social and spiritual as also ideal pattern of conduct, to be followed by the Sikhs both individually and collectively. The frequency with which the Dharamsala is mentioned in Janam Sakhis and hagiographical literature also indicâtes that Gurdwara occupied a central position in the life of the community.

Right from the times of Guru Nanak gurdwaras had been raised with devotion and enthusiasm by the Sikhs. Most of them were associated with one or another of the galaxy of the ten Gurus. The Guru period lasted for over 200 years and during this span a large number of sacred centres grew up bearing associations with the Gurus and representing places of worship for the Sikh community. Some of the Gurdwaras were raised to commemorate the sacred memory of the Sikh heroes who suffered martyrdom in the course of history.

Besides this, there were many other gurdwaras which the local Sangats raised, though former category of gurdwaras was held in special reverence, yet the function of the different gurdwaras were the same. In the Sikh psyche the gurdwaras were identified with notional identity. According to a modern writer's observation, "The freedom of their (Sikhs') temples has been the measure of their religious purity. They have their religion in their temples which are not only places of worship but also training grounds of social science, public administration and other kinds of practical religion as well."

Late professor Teja Singh's views regarding Gurdwaras' role in the build-up of the Sikh life and Sikh style are pertinent. He gave his remarks while evaluating 'Prayer' of the Sikhs. He says, "The Sikh prayer, in which the most stirring events of the Sikh History are recounted, grows most eloquent when reference is made to the brave heroes who suffered martyrdom for the sake of temples. Much of the daily religious discourse turns on the labours of the devout Sikhs, like Bhai Budha, Bhai Bhagtu, Bhai Bahlo, Bhai Kalyana and thousands of others in connection with the excavation of sacred tanks or the collection of material for the repairing of temples or it expatiates on the sufferings by the Sikhs, like Bhai Mahtab Singh and Baba Deep Singh, in their attempts to rescue their temples from the rulers or the immoral priests. Sometimes it is a Massa Ranghar and sometimes a Sarbrah, but the story is always the same. To tell the truth, the freedom of their temples has always been the measure of the Sikh freedom and prosperity."

The building aspect of Gurdwara also reflected and embodied the spirit of Sikhism. Gurdwara often consisted of a hall with four doors, a kitchen and a shoe-place with a wash-basin nearby. Besides, there was in the hall, a special place reserved for the holy Granth Sahib—high post with unfurled yellow or dark blue flag surmounted with a double-edged sword. The four doors of the hall were symbolic of the free and unrestricted access of anybody and everybody to the Gurdwara. No distinction of caste, creed or colour, it is God's place meant for the use of God's men. Women enjoyed the same privileges as men. There was to be no distinction between rich and poor and all people are to be seated alike with affection and regard. The Gurdwara was the meeting place of equals in every respect. Another significance of four doors of the hall is that God is not to be found in a particular direction. Whereas big hall provided accommodation to a large number of people sitting together at gurdwara, it also beckoned the way of conducting religious and social duties which was congregational or collective in its nature and content.

The flag post of Gurdwara was always embossed at the top by a double-edged sword. It could be seen from a distance. Both the edges of Khanda signify a two-fold duty of every member of the *Sangat*. It beckoned him to come under it in the hour of need and it also beckoned others to go out to help the needy. As a symbol of Shakti, it emboldened the Khalsa to be Shaktiman (strong) and help Shakti-heen (the weak). The *Khanda* symbolised God's power. Those who came under it could not remain powerless. A glance through the history of the Sikhs reveals that after offering an *Ardas* in a gurdwara, the Khalsa felt so much inspired that they won battles even where all odds were against them. More than once a desperate attempt was made to deprive the Khalsa of their gurdwaras so that they could become weak and defeated, and exactly in the same frequency and many a time with more intensity, the Sikhs struggled to get back their gurdwaras.

In view of what we have detailed in preceding paragraphs regarding the unique part which gurdwara had been playing in the development of Sikhism, the Sikhs felt emotionally attached to gurdwaras, and whenever they found time and resources, they would atonce repair, renovate or build new ones.

The Hari Mandir was destroyed by the Afghans thrice; but no sooner did Sikhs find opportunity, they rebuilt it. After the conquest of Sirhind (January 14, 1764), the Khalsa spread a sheet of cloth at the ruins of the temple and collected offerings amounting to nine lakhs of rupees. The amount was deposited with famous bankers of Amritsar such as Mohan Lal Lamba, Shyam Bhabra and Kalyan Pasi. Bhai Des Raj a Khatri of village Sur Singh, district Amritsar known for honesty and truthfulness was made in-charge of the finances of the project and was entrusted with the job of reconstructing the building of the temple and the tank should be completed as per plan. Bhai Des Raj was granted a seal 'Guru di Mohar' and a 'Hukamnama' from Sri Akal Takht by Sarbat Khalsa. The building work was started under the supervision of Des Raj. This time, the launching of the new construction of the building and the tank was laid by Sardar Jassa Singh Ahluwalia on 11 Baisakh, Samvat 1821 Bk. (A.D. 1764). With the joint effort of the Khalsa, the construction of Amrit Sarovar, the Hari Mandir, the bridge and Darshani Darwaza was completed in A.D. 1776. The construction of Parkarma (Circumambulatory Path) and religious places around the tank was completed by A.D. 1786. In the same way the amount was collected and the building of Anandgarh was constructed anew.

The management of the Gurdwara upto the time of the tenth Guru was done by the Sikh congregation. The central point involved in the management was to keep continuous rapport with the Gurus. The Sikh Gurus well aware of the problem strove hard to keep rapport with them through various means such as appointing their deputies known as

Masands, sending Meoras or special messengers to them and despatching 'Hukamnamas'—sacred fiats. The *Masands* acquired great importance in the time of the fifth and sixth Gurus. In the beginning these *Masands* were men of noble character and there was no problem of mis-management of the local gurdwaras. But as time went on, they acquired more and more following and consequently became more and more wealthy. This introduced an element of corruption in the management of local gurdwaras. Guru Hargobind was the first to sense the danger and he introduced some reforms to show the *Masands* their proper place. But after him, there was again a spurt in the undesirable activities of the *Masands*—so much so that the ninth Guru, Guru Tegh Bahadur, was put to considerable inconvenience by these *Masands*. Guru Gobind Singh, the tenth and the last Guru of the Sikhs, clearly saw through their nefarious activities and abolished the very institution of *Masands* thereby releasing the *Sangats* from the iron grip of the *Masands* and bringing them into direct relationship with the Guru himself. Now the management passed on to the *Sangats* who, for day-to-day administration of gurdwara selected out of them a number of persons, often unanimously and five in number known as Panj Pyaras.

After the death of Guru Gobind Singh, the Sikhs had to pass through a period of titanic struggle first against the Mughals and then against the Afghans. After Banda Bahadur, most of the Khalsa had to take refuge in the hills of Shivalik or in local jungles or in the deserts of Bikaner or at any other place where they could seek safe refuge. The military needs and the extension of the Khalsa influence shifted the Panth's primary interests away from *Sangat* towards the 'jatha' and later the Misl. Naturally during this period, they could not take direct interest in the management of their gurdwaras. However the respect in their minds for the gurdwaras remained as intense as it was ever.

The shift in interest does not mean that gurdwara as an institution had lost its importance; on the other hand, it was the only institution which worked at the level of masses and provided cement to bring about some sort of compactness among them. The gurdwaras developed a definite code of discipline. The services in gurdwaras started at 4 o'clock in the morning. If, somehow, the Misls could have maintained permanent liaison with the gurdwaras and taken lively interest in them the masses would have been Khalsised to a great extent, and to that extent the cause of the Khalsa must have been promoted. But alas! the Misls could not rise upto the occasion and failed to evolve suitable organisation to do the needful with the result that the Management of Gurdwaras passed into the hands of the Udasis and Nirmalas.

The Udasis were members of the Sikh monastic order which had been founded by Sri Chand, elder son of Guru Nanak. The Order of the Nirmalas had been created by Guru Gobind Singh. As the Sikhs had been outlawed by the Government, the Udasis with their clean-shaven heads and Hindu appearance did them a yeomen's service by managing the gurdwaras on their behalf. Of course these were difficult times and even the Udasis found it difficult to manage the gurdwaras. All the same, they managed the gurdwaras fairly efficiently. Nirmalas also conducted themselves very creditably. Hindu priests simply managed the gurdwaras but did nothing to promote Sikhism.

As the eighteenth century advanced, all the aforesaid three types of in-charges of Gurdwara began to act independent of Panth and Panthic ideology, and reverted to old Hindu religious practices. In fact, the Hindu religious practices and its framework so suited their vested interests that they reverted to them; they began to function the Gurdwara as if it were a Hindu temple. They did not encourage—rather discouraged the participation of *Sangats* in the affairs of gurdwaras as this thing went contrary to their own interests because they wished to be the sole master of the influence and the offerings which gurdwara wielded.

With establishment of the Sikh Misls in the Punjab this tendency was still more strengthened because Sikh Misaldars granted lands to the gurdwaras for their upkeep and hence placed at the hands of the priests a good source of income. The vast increase in the sources of income was also responsible for the introduction of element of corruption in the gurdwara management and for the degradation of the personal character of the priests. This thing also led them not to associate *Sangat* with gurdwara management because they apprehended criticism from the people constituting *Sangat*. This was one of the major causes that *Sangat* did not play any significant role in the later half of the eighteenth century. Thus the process of Sangat-i-sation of the people came to a halt at the level of the people.

No doubt, the Guru Granth Sahib was recited in gurdwaras and a definite code of its functioning was evolved; but all this began to be done in a Hindu way. Guru Granth Sahib began to be made out as the fifth Vedas or something to be worshipped as an idol, this, in spite of the dictum that the sacred Word enshrined in *Adi Granth*, was to be considered as "living Guru". The ten Gurus began to be presented as the incarnations of Vishnu. Money offerings were encouraged along with the repeated emphasis on the performance of various ceremonies such as placing of a coconut and an earthen pitcher filled with water and robed in a red piece of cloth during 'Akhand Path'.[1] Paths as for instance Sampat Path and Akhand Path were propagated to be the sure way to attain beatitude. The priests also resorted to spreading various types of superstitions such as sale of Talisman as life-saving gadgets etc. The landed property of gurdwaras donated by the devotees began to be treated as personal acquisition. The income through offerings was also treated likewise. *Sangat* was relegated to the background both in spiritual and temporal matters. In view of this, it can be surmised that the process of Sangatisation (Khalsisation) of the whole Sikh people gave place to Sanatanisation. These priests commonly known as *Mahants* made no pretence of observing Khalsa discipline. It was on account of this that authors of *Ludhiana District Gazetteer*, p. 73 recorded "Hindus and Sikhs except Kukas are greatly ruled by Brahmans. Everyone has a *prohit* or priest for everyday life, and a Panda or Superior Priest who must be a learned man, able to read the scriptures for marriage and other celebrations. Whatever observances a Brahman enjoins must be preformed and there is often a good deal of tyranny, hard penance, being ordered by trifling faults." The census report 1881, Vol. 1, p. 112 also bears evidence to the same effect "nearly all the Sikh villagers reverence and make use of the Brahmans almost as freely as do their Hindu neighbours".

Even the historical shrines with singular exception of Hari Mandir and Kesgarh began to be run on Hindu lines with dire consequences for the Sikh religion. In some of the gurdwaras Udasis and Nirmalas acted as priests but even their conduct was far from satisfactory. Udasis with a few exceptions, ran the gurdwaras as if they were monasteries. During the last few decades of the eighteenth century, they worked as a sect, more interested in sectarian interests than those of the Khalsa, and they seemed to have forgotten the role assigned to them by Baba Sri Chand. Nirmalas too did not come upto the expected standard. They being honoured scholars of Sikhism were expected to bring before the people the uniqueness and distinctness of Sikh religion; but as it happened, instead they gave Vedantic interpretation of Sikhism with the effect that impression gained strength that Sikhism had no distinct philosophy of stance. No doubt the Gurdwaras in their hands provided arrangement for imparting knowledge of Gurmukhi alphabet and of Sikh scriptures and to this extent benefitted the Sikhs; but hereto, the advantage was limited because the curriculum laid more emphasis on learning of Sanskrit and the books of Hindu philosophy.

In view of all this, Gurdwara ceased to serve a radiating centre of Sikh culture—much less, the school to educate the masses, although in terms of religious piety, the Gurdwara still provided strong bond of Panthic unity. The effects were not very happy. The Sikh masses were in a way delinked from their cultural sources and as a result they fell victim to the irrelevant doctrines and practices. Similarly, the Sikh ruling class had been thoroughly brain-washed upto the end of the 18th century (exceptions were undoubtedly there); they took interest in the chanting of mantras, went on pilgrimage to Hardwar and Benaras and forced their widows to perform Sati. Such was also the state of affairs during the reign of the superstitions Brahman-ridden Maharaja Ranjit Singh (1780-1839).

The sordid state of gurdwaras pricked the conscience of the Sikhs especially when they had been articulated to regenerate themselves under the impact of Singh Sabha Movement, whose main thrust was to bring about an awareness among the Sikhs regarding the true nature of Sikh religion, its institutions and its distinctive identity. Their anguish intensified when the officients of gurdwaras did not listen to them and conspired with the colonial government to stifle their voice. Determined to achieve their one-point objective of reforming gurdwara management, they launched struggle for gurdwara reform under the aegis of Shiromani Gurdwara Parbandhak Committee and its sister organisation, Shiromani Akali Dal in 1920. It lasted upto the passage of Sikh Gurdwaras Act in 1925, according to which central management and ownership of historical gurdwaras along with their properties passed on to the Shiromani Gurdwara Parbandhak Committee, an apex body of the Sikhs elected by all the Sikh adults, males and females.

At present, the gurdwaras from the point of administration can be placed in four categories. In the first category come those gurdwaras which are managed by the S.G.P.C. The second category comprises those gurdwaras which are managed by local *Sangats* through their elected or selected representatives. The third type of gurdwaras are those which are historically important and are managed by different bodies brought into being by different acts as for instance historical gurdwaras in Jammu and Kashmir are managed as per Jammu Sikh Gurdwaras and Religious Endowment Act, 1973 and the affairs of Takht Patna Sahib are regulated by Religious Endowments Act of 1863. The fourth category of gurdwaras is of those which are under the control of individuals such as so-called saints. The first category of gurdwaras conform to some standard. Regular religious service is observed. Granthies (Scripture reciters) recite from Guru Granth Sahib daily. *Kirtan* is performed regularly. *Guru Ka Langar* is distributed irrespective of caste and creed etc. The second category of gurdwaras has also a role to play as these are owned and managed by *Sangats*. These provide an atmosphere essential for the people to imbibe Sikh values. The third category of gurdwaras cannot be called gurdwaras in the right sense of term because in the Sikh perceptions and Sikh literature gurdwara is the abode of *Sangat* and Guru Granth Sahib. This being so, it cannot be managed by any agency other than *Sangat*. But gurdwaras in this category are controlled by the bodies which are not constituted by *Sangat*, either through election or selection, rather these are nominated bodies of the government. The last category of gurdwaras is acutely dangerous as far as the promotion of Sikhism is concerned, as the so-called saints who as individuals manage them and perform religious service often have cultish propensities and are interested more in projecting their own personalities rather than the greatness of the Gurus or Sikh religion.

SIKH RITUALS

Sikh religion like other religions has rituals which in many respects bear resemblance with those of others. For example, these involve prescribed action, express in symbolic form belief and values which are accepted in a particular society, serve as a means whereby such beliefs are transmitted from one generation to successor generations.

However, resemblance does not go far enough to obscure distinctiveness of Sikh rituals.

Sikh ritual has uniqueness of its own. It is grounded and nurtured in the religion which has its own stance and considers rituals as its sub-structure in the sense the latter promotes the former's intensity and deepens its impact. Certainly, it is not understood in the sense that it by re-enacting the cosmos and its activities can help the performer of the ritual establish links with ultimate Reality nor in the sense that certain bodily gestures including dance and music *et al.* associated with it have the potential to attract benefactions of Heaven as it is believed in a swath of the Hindus or arouses heaven's ire against the enemies of the performer of the ritual, nor in the sense that it is purificatory, salvic or condemnatory. The ritual of circumcision among the Muslims is believed to be auspicious for its performers and it not only assures purification of either sex, but also facilitates the passage of the one from one stage to the other. Similarly there is a popular rite among the Hindus that offering of three rice balls to the three preceding ancestors would guarantee the union of the deceased with his forbears. The funeral rite of the Hindus are considered propitiatory because these have the potential to enable the deceased to feel united with the Almighty.

Such salvic or condemnatory rites are unacceptable in Sikh religion because in it God/Supreme power can be approached through devotion directly without mediation of any person/agency—much less a ritual which is positively rejected as a way of realisation of God unlike Hinduism which regards its ritual-system as the appropriate means to realise God. This point can be better grasped if we juxtapose Hindu thought with Sikh thought.

The Hindu conception of rituals has at its core the vedic notion of RTA as the all-embracing cosmic universal Order to which even the gods are subject and subservient. In its essence the vedic RTA is a logical Order of causation in which the effect emerges from the cause with the logical necessity and inevitability. What is RTA at the cosmic level is a ritual at the societal level seen as DHARMA, which helps the society to be in order just as RTA is the principle that helps the cosmos to be in order. As such, ritual is, in fact, the compliance with DHARMA that in turn is identification with the cosmic order. According to Dr. J.S. Ahluwalia, "through the idea of Satya, the vedic notion of RTA and rite is co-related to the vedic conception of BRAHAM. Satya is a principle of Self-sameness of being in all times. So the Braham. Accordingly RTA comes out to be seen as manifestation of Braham. As vedic rite is grounded in RTA, the performance of ritual is not only identification with the cosmic Order, but also realisation of the Braham (Absolute). Hence the Hindu conception of realisation is a way of God." "Sikhism does not accept Hindu view of ritual—the notion of RTA, the nature of the absolute as immanent being the ideal of undifferentiated immediacy with Brahman. The Sikh religion envisages God as transcendental being having determinate personal relationship, with the Man (The concept of Akal in the Sikh *Mul Mantra* refers to the time transcendence of God and not to the divinity such as characteristic of the Vedic Braham). The ideal of life thus turns out to be a relation of communion with the Divine and not that of the undifferentiated immediacy.

And Communion in Sikhism means realising of the *Shabad*. This stage is blissful and it should be better called sacrament, an act which automatically is blessed with Divine grace.

Since God in Sikhism is transcendent as well as immanent and in His immanent aspect, His most important characteristic is mercifulness, His Grace is assured and flows spontaneously. The Sikh ritual, therefore, cannot be either propitiatory or expiatory. The direct communion with God through Karm Kand is considered both redundant and irrelevant.

In spite of Sikh ritual being repetitive in certain cases and to be performed meticulously, no specific individual or class of person is recognised as special or the repository of certain supernatural powers which make them particularly eligible to conduct rituals. In certain religions more specifically in Hindu Religion what is considered sacred is ritualised, thereby giving rise to the belief that whatever is ritualised is *ipso facto* considered sacred. This is how ritualised moral code and social norms become absolutised by the mechanism of ritual. In Sikhism ritual is not considered either as a determinant of sacredness or as an absolutising factor. It is considered a process evolved over time to make the seekers realise the Holy and His Grace, through Shabad. The Sikh rites—baptism, child naming and Anand Marriage—partake of the nature of such rites.

SOME SIKH RITUALS

Khande Da Amrit—Rite of Baptism

Most outstanding ritual is 'Khande Da Amrit'. The administering of 'Amrit' to the seekers is not a mechanical ritual rather a process to enable the seekers to reach a numinous state of mind through Shabad that is recited during the preparation of Amrit. Shabad here should not be taken as a *Mantra* recited during the performance of Hindu rituals during the initiation ceremony prevalent in certain religious sects such as Radhaswamis and Namdharis, because *Mantra* is considered as injecting certain indwelling qualities into the sacramental water whose mere intake would create a magical or mysterious effect on the recipient while the Shabad is solely a Divine Testament. Recitation of the Divine Word creates a numinous state of mind in which the recipient drinking the nectar comes to partake of the Divine qualities that elevate him to a higher state of spiritual enlightenment, moral consciousness and social responsibility.

Thus the ritual of baptism marks the entry of recipients into the Order of the Khalsa and their total commitment to the discipline of the Order both at individual and corporate levels. It is an act of Grace by the Divine Being towards man: it is not a result of the human efforts. In this context, Guru Granth Sahib says:

> "The Nectar yearned for by gods,
> Sages and men was received by
> The Grace of Guru (God)."

Recipients of Amrit at once realise that they are in communion with the Lord and are in covenanted relationship with God symbolised by the expression: Waheguru Ji Ka Khalsa, Waheguru Ji Ki Fateh.

On the historic Baisakhi day (29 March, 1699), Guru Gobind Singh made a call to the Sikhs to offer heads to his sword. Only five came forward, one after another. The Guru took each one to an adjoining enclosure. After some time, all the five were brought back by the Guru to the congregation—all dressed neatly, exuding spiritual exuberance. The Guru lovingly called them 'Five Beloved Ones'.

The Five Beloved after their complete surrender to the Guru and after partaking of Amrit were reborn into the newly created Khalsa, and in this way, their resurrection took place. No wonder a Sikh receiving Amrit by the Five Sikhs the Beloved Ones feels that his initiation is in essence a resurrection, a resetting with Waheguru. He/she is fully transformed and enters into a new stage, leaving behind his past *sanskars*.

Birth and Naming Rite

Birth and naming ceremonies are also not rituals in the sense these are generally made out. Mother along with the child and her relatives reach a gurdwara: hymns of thanks-giving are sung in the presence of Sri Guru Granth Sahib. Then a Shabad selected at random is read out of Guru Granth Sahib. From the first letter of the first word of that hymn, the congregation is requested to coin a name of the child. Several names may be suggested but the one that is ultimately approved by *Sangat* is announced. To a boy's name the word 'Singh' and to a girl's name the word 'Kaur' is suffixed. After reciting Anand and Ardas, the *Karah Prasad* is distributed.

All through the ceremony, the Shabad is recited as a Divine testament of numinous state of mind. Naming of child is regarded as an identity or entity of the whole made sanctimonious by the Grace of God. In this context, Guru Granth Sahib's utterance is significant:

'Sat Gur Sache Dia Bhej'

No specific priest is involved to conduct the ceremonies.

Anand Rite

Guru Amar Das initiated the Sikh Anand marriage rite which required the recitation of the 'Anand Sahib' for the marriage of his daughter Bhani to Bhai Jetha in 1553. Later on when a "Sikh complained to Guru Ram Das that a Brahman had refused to solemnise the marriage of his daughter as he could not afford to pay him a high fee, the Guru composed 'Lawan' (Wedding song) and made it a part of the Sikh ceremony. The purpose of this type of marriage is to make the couple realise that they should cast their relations in spiritual frame of mind.

The couple is expected to sit in *Gur Sangat* before Guru Granth Sahib in all humility and listen to the recitation of Lawan—four hymns, one after another. Each time when the recitation of a hymn is finished, the groom and the bride circumambulate Sri Guru Granth Sahib while the same hymn is sung by the musicians. The first hymn commits one to the life of a householder and its duties to be performed as per instructions of the Lord. In the second hymn gradually the Lord's all-powerfulness and all-pervadingness is realised thereby making Lord's fear the only legitimate fear. All other fears then seem to be unreal. The seeker is united to the noble qualities. The third hymn of the marriage ceremony depicts the higher state of the couple in their joy and their attitude towards the world. With the third hymn the mind is free from passion (vairag) and experiences the pure joy. The fourth "hymn" marks the completion of the transformation from the hectic aimless wanderings of the individual into a new union which is both social and spiritual. A new householder family thus comes into being under the comforting umbrella of the spiritual preceptor and the Lord. It marks the beginning of a new spiritual mission lived in the worldly surroundings. Nothing is given up and everything acquires a new meaning and significance. At this stage polarities of sex, wealth and ethnicity *et al.* vanish and the couple feels Anand—Absolute Bliss. Although marriage signifies a physical relation but the ideal embodied into it goes beyond a mere sensory experience.

Death Rite

Death rites also are, in fact, attempts to realise *Shabad* to feel the Grace of God, even at the moment which otherwise is generally considered ominous or inauspicious. Death rites make people feel that a deceased person is transported to another kind of eternity as part of a larger Cosmic Order. The seeming eternity of one's immediate desires and wishes are given up for an eternity mediated through the Divine Word (Shabad).

FOOTNOTE

1. Continuous reading of the whole *Guru Granth Sahib* within forty-eight hours.

19

SIKH POLITY

Before determining the pattern of Sikh Polity, we will have to find answers to certain important questions: (i) Did politics fall within the jurisdiction of Sikh religion; (ii) Did the Gurus take interest in political affairs; (iii) Did political power or basic moral issues form the fulcrum of the interest of the Gurus?

So far as the first question is concerned, our reply is that politics fell within the jurisdiction of the religion of the Gurus. This fact can be supported by adducing moral as well as historical arguments. The Gurus, as it is ascertained from their utterances, wanted to establish an Order where goodness should prevail and unrighteousness be eliminated, and where people should have absolute faith in the oneness of God. To make the people righteous, the Guru laid emphasis on the discipline of the individuals as also of the groups. In 'Jap' Guru Nanak spells out the steps which one should take to regenerate one-self. It is also mentioned that the regenerate should endeavour to make the society righteous.

The regenerate persons are variously known in Sikh religious literature. Guru Nanak calls them Gurmukhs, Guru Arjan Dev Brahm Giani and Guru Gobind Singh Khalsa. Now what is righteousness? The Guru somewhere explicitly and somewhere implicitly, explains that what is not based on justice, fellow-feeling, liberty and equality is unrighteous. But how to ensure righteousness. Obviously some agency is needed and in fact since the inception of the civilised society, the need has continuously been felt.

It was this need to which state and politics owe their existence. As a matter of fact, need to translate certain moral issues have always been the determinant of the nature and the pattern of the political power. In tribal society the panchayats or patriarch of a tribe was the symbol of power. When the society transcended that stage, the oligarchy became the wielder of the power. Oligarchy gave place to monarchy when the former outlived its advantage. The changes in the society on moral and social planes always effected corresponding changes in the polity or the agency to wield political power.

The Sikh Gurus who were committed to certain moral issues which formed the basis of the society of their concept could not help take interest in politics. But their interest was not simply an expression of their anguish for the political unrighteousness but it had a moral dimension also. For a proper appreciation of Guru Nanak's response to the events in question, the Babar Vani verses must be considered together. In these, Guru Nanak mentions the sufferings caused by war and explains that all this has happened because of the people's blind pursuit of wealth and riches. Because of wealth, it went hard with many. Wealth cannot be amassed without sins and it does not accompany the dead. Indeed, "He who is destroyed is first deprived of his virtue."[1]

It is thus clear that Guru Nanak's response to war and to sufferings caused by war is not only an expression of his rage but also involved a moral issue, the issue of the importance of virtue in the nation's healthy growth and stance.

Historical references in Guru Granth Sahib also go to prove that political affairs were not alien to the Guru's religion. Guru Nanak's familiarity, even interest in contemporary politics, may be inferred from his various expressions such as Sultan, Patshah, Shah-i-Alam, takht, taj, *hukam, mālik, shiqdār, Qāzī, chaudharī, muqqadam, raiyat,* Darbār, palaces, royal canopy, elephants, armour, cavalry trumpets, treasury, coins, mint, salary, taxes and revenue-free land.[2] In one of his hymns, Guru Nanak, in a general reference, called the Rajas as 'blood-suckers'.

> "The *rajas* are lions and the *muqqadams* dogs;
> They fall upon the *raiyat* day and night.
> Their agents inflict wounds with claws (of power)
> And the dogs lick blood and relish the liver."[3]

A condemnation of contemporary rule is unmistakably here. It may be pointed out, however, that Guru Nanak's attack is not directed against the rulers as 'Muslims' or as 'Hindus'. In fact, the bracketing of the *Muqqadams* (who mostly were non-Muslims) with the *rajas* strongly suggests that Guru Nanak adopts the standpoint of common people, the raiyat, as against rulers and their subordinates or agents. In another verse, Guru Nanak appears to have identified close connections between the holders of political power and those holding status in their faith; he also notices 'discrimination' against those who do not belong to their faith. Guru Nanak says:

> 'The *Aad Purkh* is called Allah,
> Now that the turn of the Shaikhs has come;
> The gods and their temples are taxed
> Such is now the custom.'[4]

The successors of Nanak also had full knowledge of contemporary political affairs. As Guru Arjan assumed pontificate and took some steps to consolidate Sikhism, Jahangir began to view him with suspicion. Perceiving the reaction that his activities had evoked in government circles, the Guru embarked upon the course of preparing his people to face the challenges, polemical as well as physical, with determination and wisdom. On the eve of his departure to Lahore in response to the summons of Jahangir, Guru Arjan left a message for his son, Guru Hargobind, that he should sit manfully on the throne and maintain as much army as he could afford. The message was an epitome of the active interest of fifth Guru in politics. A little earlier than the moment referred to above, the fifth Guru advised Bidhi Chand and Pairana to join the personal staff of Hargobind and hinted that their martial qualities would be utilised fully in the period of his son, Guru Hargobind whose policy of *Piri* and *Miri* left absolutely no doubt that the political affairs were not extraneous to the teachings of the Sikh Gurus. So is the case of Guru Harkrishan as well as Guru Har Rai. Guru Har Rai's keen interest in the welfare of Dara bears out the aforesaid assertion. Guru Tegh Bahadur's execution and Guru Gobind Singh's wars against the Mughals and Hill rajas also point to the conclusion that the Gurus were as much alive to the contemporary political happenings as to their moral and spiritual objectives. In *Bachittar Natak* XIII, 9-10, Guru Gobind Singh writes:

> "Those of Baba (Nanak) and those of Babar
> God Himself makes them both know the former thus;
> as the king of Religion.
> Guess the latter then as worldly king.
> They who fail to render that
> what is due to the (House of) Baba
> The minions of Babar seize them and make exactions upon them
> And inflict severe punishments upon such defaulter;
> In addition, their worldly goods and property are looted and taken away."

In these lines the Guru says in unambiguous terms that there are two forces which claim allegiance of men's souls on earth, the Truth and Morality as Religion, and the state as embodiment of mere utilitarianism and secular politics. The primary allegiance of man is to the truth and morality, and those who fail in this allegiance, suffer under the subjugation of worldly state, unnourished by the courage and hope which is born through unswerving adherence to the primary allegiance. In this perpetual struggle between the state and the church, for exclusive possession of the soul of man, a man of culture and religion, shall not lose sight ever of his primary allegiance and he who does so, he does it at his own peril, for, by doing so, he helps give birth to times in which every thing is force, politics, utility and poverty. The Guru does not assert that his perpetual dichotomy and antagonism of the church and the state must be resolved, or even that is capable of being resolved, by the suppression or subjugation of the one by the other; rather, he appears to recognise their eternal antagonism and character and in this antagonism sees the hope and glory of man, the social and political context in which the Sikh way of life is to be practised. The church must perpetually correct and influence the state without aiming to destroy or absorb it, as the history shows the attempt of the one to oust the other meets no lasting success and each of the two antagonistic entities arise again after having been crushed in vain and both appear as if bound together. This is what the Guru means when he declares in the Text, that the house of Baba Nanak and the house of Babar, God maketh both of them and those who repudiate their allegiance to the house of Nanak suffer grievously, without hope at the hands of the state. Obviously the Guru's corpus of thought includes also the matters which are essentially political.

Origin of Sovereign Power

Having decided that the Guru's moral order does not exclude political matters, the next question which arises is "Did the Gurus have some definite idea of polity?"

The Gurus were not political philosophers in the sense Plato and Rousseau were and hence we do not find any particular political thesis in their writings or utterances. All the same, there are hints scattered in their different writings which give quite distinct picture of the polity visualised by the Gurus. The cornerstone of the polity was that the sovereignty resided in the people. The Gurus say "The Guru's sovereignty is full of twenty measures, but that of the *Sangat*, as the mouth piece of the people, is of over-riding paramountcy, of twenty-one measure. This dictum repeatedly occurs throughout the Sikh literature from the earliest times as the basic principle of organisation and exercise of power in the Sikh society. Guru Nanak, in the sixteenth cant (Pauri) of 'Jap' says the 'Panch' must be recognised in the organisation of power (literally in the court). The Panches alone are fit to occupy seats of supreme authority for exercise of power.

The 'Panch' here cannotes 'people of five directions, meaning thereby people of the four directions of the compass and the people residing at the centre, the venue of the assembly'. It was in exegesis of this text of Guru Granth Sahib apparently, that Guru Gobind Singh while glorifying the Panj Pyaras declared, "I am ever present unseen, in the collective deliberations of the Panchas and there is no higher guidance on earth besides. According to Guru Gobind Singh, "the spirit of the people is the spirit of the God. When anyone causes suffering to the people, God's wrath falls on him".[5] Once when a very prominent Brahman, Kesho Datt, visited Anandpur, he felt insulted for not being given privileged treatment. He condemned outright and cursed what he called the low-caste crowd of the Sikhs who were treated better than the Brahmans and Kshatriyas.

Guru Gobind Singh calmly replied, "Do not blame me for ignoring you, for all are equal in my eyes. I will send you bedding and other things you need, but do not say a word against my inspired disciples."[6] Then glorifying the people, who were condemned by the Brahmans, the Guru said:

> All the battles I have won against tyranny
> I have fought with the devoted backing of these people
> Through them only have I been able to bestow gifts
> Through their help I have escaped
> The love and generosity of the Sikhs
> Have enriched my heart and home
> Through their grace I have attained all learning
> Through their help in battle, I have slain my enemies
> I was born to serve them, through them I reached eminence
> What would I have been without their kind and ready help?
> There are millions of insignificant people like me
> True service is the service of these people
> I am not inclined to serve others of higher castes
> Charity will bear fruit in this and the next world
> If given to such worthy people as these
> All other sacrifices and charity is profitless

From head to foot, whatever I call my own
All I possess or carry, dedicate to these people.[7]
(*Dasam Granth*)

Guru Gobind Singh wrote this unique 'song of the people' glorifying their innate strength and power merely sixty years before Rousseau wrote his 'Social contract' and about 150 years before Marx formulated his manifesto. For the Gurus, the people were the prophets of future, they were the first to point out in world history that the fate of future civilisation was not in the hands of mighty individuals but in the hands of the morally and spiritually awake people.

By people, the Gurus do not mean people of a particular society, religious group or social organisation rather the people in general, the people of the whole world, the whole mankind. According to Dr. Trilochan Singh 'the concept of society is found in two senses in the writings of the Sikh Gurus. It is generally synonymous with human society. It is also used in a limited sense for religious groups. When, for example, Guru Nanak criticises the dirty practices of the Jains, he does not condemn the religion but only the social aspect of this religious society. When Guru Nanak says, "The age is a drawn sword, the kings are butchers, goodness hath taken wings and flown; in the dark night of falsehood, I see not the moon of Truth anywhere", he is not speaking about the rulers of any particular state or country but of the world situation at that time. In his writings, Guru Gobind Singh addresses the whole human society, even if he refers to a particular person or group, the lesson is for the whole mankind.

Even the national cultures which divide people are regarded by the Gurus as superficial and artificial. The reasons assigned for such differences by Guru Gobind Singh are: *Nyāre, nayāre, desan ko prabhāo hai:* (different social customs, environments and manners of different countries have created these differences).

Prof. J.S. Bains, in his article 'Political Ideals of Guru Gobind Singh', says that "In conformity with the teachings of Guru Nanak, the tenth Guru had argued that authority in every sphere ultimately derives its validity from God and not from any human source." In support of his thesis the learned professor writes, "In the Zafar Nama which was addressed to Aurangzeb, the Guru had mentioned that the God is the true Emperor of earth and heaven and that He is the Master of both the worlds." He (the Guru) dilated on this point with more clarity when he said:

> The successors of both Baba Nanak and Babar
> Were created by God Himself
> Recognise the former as spiritual
> And the latter as a temporal ruler.

According to the learned professor, a similar idea was portrayed by the Gurus when they uttered the following words:

> "By His (God) *hukam* are all things formed
> Not one is blessed save by His hukam
> By his hukam alone nature doth run her course
> All serve under his hukam and none may act without it
> Under thy hukam, O God, hath all been done
> and naught of itself alone."

We, however, do not agree with the Professor who, in our view, has not been able to correctly interpret the verses of Guru Gobind Singh. The original text nowhere says, explicitly or by implication that the church and the state 'both derive authority from God Himself'. It only says 'God maketh them both' as the instruments of His will. The word in the text, 'kare' neither literally, nor here can be interpreted to mean 'authorised'; it simply means made by or maketh. Similarly, the world 'pehchano' does not mean in the sense of a commandment thou shalt recognise. It means, know, identify, understand, perceive. The House of Baba means the true religion on earth, and the text says, understand the term to mean thus as such. Likewise, Unmano (understand) cannot and does not mean 'recognise' and 'accept'. It literally and here in the text means understand, see, guess, infer, that the house of Babar means, the secular worldly state.

That the people were held to be the wielder of sovereign powers in Sikh Polity can be seen from the examples of the

Gurus. Once the Guru saluted the shrine of Dadu situated in Rajasthan. The Sikhs objected to this act of the Guru on the ground that it was not in conformity with the fundamental Sikh tenets and did not hesitate fining the Guru. The classic example of the high esteem in which the Guru held the Sikhs was when after selecting the 'five loved ones', he drank the holy water at their hands, thereby giving the Khalsa the pride of having selected their leader. This emphasis on popular basis of sovereignty and its equation with divine mandate was a unique idea and may be considered as a distinct contribution to democratic theory.[9]

The next issue before us is this as to how the sovereignty should operate? The Gurus seemed to be aware of this problem. They evolved various organisations for the people's sovereignty to be exercised.

Sangat

The most important among them is the institution of 'Sangat'. *Sangat* means an assembly, a union of men, a gathering. One of the main teachings of the Guru to all those who reposed faith in them was to form Sangats. Wherever Guru Nanak went, the Sikhs built a gurdwara and met every day and formed a regular *Sangat*. When the Sidhas asked Guru Nanak to show them miracles, the Guru replied, "I have no power for miracles. I derive all my power from the word (Bani), and the Sangat. Away from sangat, there is not a mole to support me." Anyone irrespective of caste, creed and clime can become the member of the Sangat. All services can be performed by the Sikh and non-Sikh devotees except the functions of baptism which can be performed by the ordained Khalsa who has lived up to the ideals. Sangat is not merely a gathering of worshippers nor is it just a forum for seeking personal salvation and blessedness, but it has stood for the total re-orientation of life of the individuals and society towards a creative purposeful existence. This being so, all the discussions concerning different aspects of man's life—from fair dealings in business and from disputes to inner conflicts of the soul were referred to *Sangat*. *Sangat* was considered to be so important that even the Gurus used to submit to the decisions of it. Guru Arjan Dev did not marry his son in the family of Chandu because Sangat had decided otherwise.

In fact, the decisions of Sangats have always been considered something based on reason, dispassionate and unbiased deliberations, the verdicts of a composite higher self, subordinating the petty considerations of the lower self (*Man Niwan Mat Uchee Mat Pat Ka Rakha Wahe Guru*). Such decisions are considered to be decisions of God who guides men's reason which are not overcome by personal or emotional considerations. Such an atmosphere prevails among the members of the Sangat sitting at a place which has assumed the name 'gurdwara', the door of the Guru.

The idea of Sangat is very old in India and in terms of its etymology, it was grounded in the polity of the early Indo-Aryans. There is a mention of Samiti, or a folk assembly in Rig Veda where there is a prayer for a common assembly and a common policy. In Atharva Veda also, the aforesaid assembly has been spoken of. The Atharva declares that 'this *samiti*, the Sikh equivalent of which is the Sangat, is a daughter of God'. The institution of Sangat continued to serve the society till it got smothered under the weight of monarchical institutions.

As regards the composition of Sangat, it may be said that it is composed of the people, sincere, truthful and honest, dedicated to the Guru's cause which is no other than the cause of the whole people. Sangat, like the Sangh of the Buddhist and the Samiti or Sabha of Indo-Aryans, is no Sangat if its members are not well-meaning and honest. The members who do not speak and act bonafides, are no honest members, and the honest and well-meaning members are those who are not swayed by bias or fervour and who speak out truthfully and fearlessly and are always guided by the guru-spirit enshrined in Shabad—Word.

So far as the mode of functioning of Sangat is concerned, it is very simple and straight. There is always a congregation in the presence of Guru-person or Eternal Guru, Guru Granth Sahib. At the end of the prayer the aggrieved person would stand up with his hands folded and submit his complaint to the gathering or he could make a report to the granthi (reciter of scripture) of gurdwara who would arrange to convey it to the Sangat. The Sangat may take a snap decision or may decide upon some other procedure to satisfy the complainant. Mohsin Fani, a contemporary of the sixth Guru, and a traveller from Iran, was wonder-struck at the amount and intensity of one's faith in the Sangat. He found that a Sikh would stand up and submit with his folded hands to the Sangat that he is sinful and the Sangat should pray to God, the Guru, to pardon and forgive his misdeeds and grant him salvation. His inner conflicts were removed and he enjoyed peace of mind. If he lived the remaining life with caution, he was sure to die a happy man.

Sangat's working is a two-way game. Every member of the Sangat should have a faith in it and every person who sits in the Sangat should be a disciplined citizen of the Guru's kingdom. Thus there should be perfect rapport between the complainant and the collective will of the Sangat. The complainant should feel that his own voice is also a part of the people's voice and the Sangat is not only his own self, enlarged and widened, but because of its nature of collectivity, it has gained a high degree of divinity and hence its decision will be just and true.

Next to Sangat, at local level, there were regional or circle Sangats. During the time of Guru Tegh Bahadur, there was a Bari Sangat at Dacca whose duty was to guide the local Sangats and to devise plans to ensure that the Guru's message is escalated and problems coming up on the way were solved.

No account of the operation of sovereignty is complete without reference to the institution of Panth.

Panth

Panth from Sanskrit Patha, Pathin or Patham means literally a way, passage or path and figuratively, a way of life, religious creed or culture. In Sikh terminology word 'Panth' stands for Sikh faith as well as the Sikh people as a whole. It represents the invisible mystic body composing all those who profess Sikhism as their faith and encompassing lesser bodies, religious as well as political, claiming to represent the whole of the Sikh population or any section of it. Panth for the Sikhs is the supreme earthly glory having full claim on their allegiance. It transcends any of its components and functional agencies.

A further dimension to the concept of Panth was brought about by Guru Gobind Singh. He introduced the initiation by double-edged sword and to repeat a line from Gurdas's Kabit 'transformed Sangat into Khalsa'. The Panth was now identified with the Guru himself, "The Khalsa is my life and soul." The Panth, now called Khalsa Panth, was the Guru Panth. Guru Gobind Singh at the time of his death declared *Adi Granth* as the Guru Everlasting for the Sikhs. The line of living Gurus came to an end and the Guru Panth became its own leader under the guidance of Guru Granth. By virtue of this status the concept as well as the fact that Panth as a corporate being was a sovereign power got further strength and affirmation.

The occasional Meets of the whole Panth is a long-standing tradition in the history of the Khalsa. In the days of the Gurus, Sikh Sangat in small representative Jathas used to come from all the Sikh centres and listened to the Guru's Word for some days. At these annual conclaves the Guru also gave instructions about the propagation of the Sikh way of life. When Guru Gobind Singh passed guruship on to *Adi Granth* and Panth, the institution of Panth acquired unique importance and no wonder the Sikhs began to look upon the institution as the apex organisati 1.

After the defeat of Banda Singh Bahadur, the Mughal rulers began persecution of the Sikhs with vengeance. The Sikhs organised themselves into Jathas and fled to local or far-off jungles, hills or deserts of Bikaner. Irrespective of blockade by the enemy, the Sikhs would come to Amritsar at least two times a year on Diwali and Baisakhi days. Such conclaves began to be known as Panthic congregations. It is well-known that in these conclaves very important decisions were taken which played a significant role in the history of the Sikhs.

Gurmata

The decision of the Panth taken in the presence of the Guru (after Guru Gobind Singh, Guru Granth and Guru

Panth), was called Gurmata. The first Gurmata is said to have taken place during the term of Guru Hargobind. Sohan Kavi, for example, uses the term 'Mata' in his work *Gurbilas Padshahi Chhevin* in the sense of a resolution. It related to the resolve of the Sikhs to fight against the Mughal troops detailed from Lahore to stop the activities of the Guru Hargobind which the Mughal Subedar considered an incipient threat to Mughal government. The prefix Guru to Mata was not fixed at that time, although it was much revered and respected and also regarded as Guru's decision because since the inception of Sikhism, it had been embedded in the Sikh psyche that Sangat is the abode of the Guru. Sainapat, who was a court poet of Guru Gobind Singh, has left an eye witness account of the activities of the Guru in his work 'Shri Gur Sobha'; refers to a Mata arrived at by Panches of a certain locality where the Sikhs of the locality were asked to receive Khande-ki-Pahul. Although he does not prefix 'Guru' to Mata but his narrative implies the same thing. In C.E. 1705 at Chamkaur, the five Sikhs symbolically representing the authority of the Panth, adopted a Mata ordering Guru Gobind Singh to vacate the mud fortress of Chamkaur and save his life to further carry on his mission. The Guru who was initially reluctant to vacate simply acquiesced in what the Panj Pyaras did. At Naraina, when the Guru saluted sepulchre of Dadu by pointing his arrow at it, the Khalsa objected and took a decision to award religious punishment to Guru for doing an act which was violative of Sikh doctrines. The Guru most willingly presented himself for punishment and admired his disciples for their right thinking and courage of conviction.

The Guru all along especially after the creation of Khalsa endeavoured hard to project the Khalsa Panth and Panj Pyaras as a source of authority. This he made clear whenever he found opportunity. When the Guru was about to expire, he reaffirmed that all the affairs of the Panth would be regulated by the council of five beloved ones chosen by the committed Khalsa in the presence of Guru Granth Sahib. The verdict was to be called Gurmata. It was to be adopted by the assembly of the Khalsa unanimously. Its implementation was binding on the whole Panth. Any infringement was to be considered a sacrilege.

Some scholars especially non-Indians have stumbled on the facts and have drawn wrong conclusion regarding the meeting of Gurmata as the 'General Council' of the Sikhs. James Brown used the term 'Grand Diet' for gurmata and Forster referred to gurmata as the 'Grand convention of Sikhs'.

All these views betray ignorance or faulty perception of the facts. Historical evidence is available in abundance to testify that Gurmata was a decision or a resolution adopted by the body of the Khalsa present at one time at a given place. The statement of the Ratan Singh Bhangu and later its endorsement by scholars such as Dr. N.K. Sinha and Dr. Ganda Singh have finally settled the issue that Gurmata was a decision taken unanimously by the assembly of the Khalsa in the presence of Guru Granth Sahib and it was called so because the tenth Guru vested the guruship jointly in Khalsa Panth and *Adi Granth*.

Usually, Gurmatas were passed at Sri Akal Takht but under special circumstances, these could be passed anywhere—the essential condition being the assemblage of the Sikhs in the presence of Guru Granth Sahib.

Panj Pyaras

Panj Pyaras, literally 'the five beloved', the name given to the five Sikhs, Bhai Daya Singh, Bhai Himmat Singh, Bhai Dharam Singh, Bhai Mohkam Singh, Bhai Sahib Singh, who were so designated by Guru Gobind Singh on March 29, 1699 at the historic *dewan* (congregation) at Anandpur Sahib, and formed the nucleus of the Khalsa as the first batch to receive at his hands Khande-Di-Pahul after they had proved their total commitment to the Guru-Person, Guru Gobind Singh, his ideology and his cause. The Guru sought baptism from them whom he had just then baptised. The event symbolised the equation of the Guru with them and the Khalsa whom they represented. Earlier, only the Guru and his nominated *Masands* could initiate one into the faith through the ceremony of Charan Pahul but now the Guru as well as the Khalsa could do so through administering Pahul. These chosen five in fact acted on behalf of the Guru in the latter's physical absence and enjoyed all powers. It is this equation between the two which Bhai Gurdas II highlights when he proclaims that great is Guru Gobind Singh who is both Guru and disciple.

The event signalled many things. It signified that the Guru and the Panj Pyaras, and, for that matter, the whole of the Khalsa, were one in spirit and hence coequal in terms of authority, ideology and cause. Implied in this was the motivation provided to the Khalsa to initiate people into the Order of the Khalsa and do other things on Guru's behalf. Following their example any five baptised Sikhs could constitute Panj Pyaras at any place any time. In fact, the institution of Panj Pyaras was neither fixed nor exclusive. It was believed that Guru was present among them and their collective wisdom implied the Guru's wish. The Guru, in fact, created a very viable alternative for the institution of Person-Guru. Understandably, the Panj Pyaras became the cynosure of the Sikhs, a symbol of authority, temporal as well as spiritual, an institution to project and radiate Sikh values, a mechanism to operate affairs in the light of the Guru-spirit. Panj Pyaras have collectively acted as supreme authority representing the Guru-Panth.

In C.E. 1705, the Guru, his two sons and forty Sikhs, put up stout resistance to the Mughal forces whose number was manifold than the Guru's soldiers. The Guru's ranks thinned and if the resistance had been continued, the Guru might have suffered grave consequences. At this juncture, five Sikhs waited upon the Guru in the form of Panj Pyaras and told him to leave the Mud fortress of Chamkaur for some safe place. The Guru had to submit to the decision of the Pyaras. By doing this, the Guru reiterated the doctrine of collegial leadership in the direction of state policies. The collegiality of leadership means that all party matters are accomplished by all party members directly or through representatives who all are subject to same rules. The collegial leadership now is popularly known as Panch Pardhani. It does not mean that the five can appropriate unto themselves the power, the authority, the temporal sovereignty of the Guru Panth; it can have significance in the sense of *Sangat* attuned to the Divine in the holy presence of Guru Granth Sahib spontaneously choosing five Gur Sikhs, deliberating upon or resolving some issue but without acting as autocrats.

According to Dr. Sher Singh, when mutual discussion persuasion or understanding each other's point of view did not help the assembly—the *Sangat* or the Panchayat to arrive at some definite decision then the Five were selected unanimously to give their decision after giving proper hearing and giving due thought. At Panthic Meet, even when there was no consensus of opinion, Panj Pyaras were selected to give judgement which was considered sacred and morally binding on the parties.

Form of Government

Having given the main features of the Sikh polity as developed up to Guru Gobind Singh, we have reached the stage where it is not very difficult to judge the form of government as envisaged by the Gurus.

Monarchical political structure does not fit in Sikh polity of the concepts of the Gurus. When the Sikh religion was being evolved, there were Hindu monarchs as well as the Muslim monarchs. The institution of the Hindu monarchy is very old. In the Rig Veda, the monarchy appears as the only and the normal form of government. In the Aitreya Brahmana, supplement of the Rig Veda, it is asserted that the law can never overpower lawlessness except through a monarch. "The devas and asuras were at war and asuras were victorious, defeated the devas. The devas said it is on account of our having no king that asuras defeat us. Let us have a king. To this all agreed." Rig Vedic tradition accorded divine sanction, for, in the *Manav Dharm Sastra*, it is laid down that God Himself created the king to protect people from lawlessness. Since the King ruled by divine right, he was a god, unamenable to the control or opinions of the people as far as the theory goes and therefore, "Even as in fact king must not be despised, as through a mere mortal, for he is a great god in human form."

The king to be formally invested with god-head must, however, be anointed with the Abhiseka ceremony by the Brahman priest, for an unanointed king is an unlawful king whom the gods do not favour. An unanointed king is a term of contempt in Hindu politics and it is declared that such barbarous customs are the hallmark of dirty Westerners and foreigners. According to Arthshastra of Kautalya 'a single wheel cannot turn and so government is possible only with assistance'. In this way Arthshastra recommends that a king should appoint ministers and listen to their advice.

Elaborating the concept of the Hindu monarchy, Sardar Kapur Singh says, "This is the eternal triangle of Hindu monarch; the god king, the priestly Brahmans and the ministers by royal choice. Here is a king who has no legislative powers and whose function is to uphold the social structure of varan ashram dharma as laid down in the Brahmanical sacred texts, whose formal installation is dependent upon the approval and goodwill of the hereditary priestly class of Brahmans, and who is constantly surrounded by a clique of ministers of his own creation, who tend to usurp powers and replace him. This Hindu polity ensures a static conservative society which abhors social progress and change as intrinsically undesirable and dangerous, for the *Manav Dharma Sastra* bids a citizen 'to walk in that path of good and virtuous people which his father and grandfather followed; while he walks in that, he will not suffer harm. It further ensures that this society is upheld by an autocratic king, who rules only by divine right but as a divine being, answerable to no mortal on earth, as far the theory goes. As a necessary consequence this form of government ensures the intellectual leadership of the Hindu society to the priestly Brahmans who are exhypothesis wedded to the varan ashram dharma, the four-fold fixed economic-political structure of the Hindu social pyramid."

Obviously, the Hindu monarchy as postulated above is alien to Sikh polity, according to which the ruler is divine in the sense it is a part of the Divine. He/She is not divine in the sense that he/she is infallible. Sovereignty does not reside in one man, rather it belongs to people as it emerges out of them.

The Sikh polity does not recognise any exclusive priestly class to anoint the king. According to the Gurus, there can be no loyalty to supra-individual state if there is no rule of law or no permanent civil service. Moreover, the four-fold economico-political structure of the Hindu society has no place in the Sikh political scheme. The Sikhs throughout their formative period from Guru Nanak to Guru Gobind Singh were continuously made to realise that they formed the microcosm of macrocosm and if they regenerated themselves and practised the programme as laid down by the Gurus, they were very honourable, and collectively they were as good as the Guru himself. By passing on physical guruship to the Panth, the Sikhs were made fully responsible and divine. Such people fully awakened to their inherent potentialities and responsibility could not but afford the democratic spirit. The idea of deifying any individual or glorification of any person which might lead to the growth of personality cult was rejected as irrelevant to the Sikh way of governance. The institution of Langar, Sangat and the Khalsa all have nourished and sustained democratic ideals. The Sikhs for the greater part of the eighteenth century were zealous about holding the democratic ideals aloft. The author of Fatu-hat-Nama-i-Samadi avers that Banda Singh was not unhampered while taking important decisions at crucial moments. He bowed to the majority decisions of the Sikhs while deciding about the offer of a negotiated settlement made to them by Abdus Samad Khan.

Islamic monarchy was also in no way better than Hindu monarchy. In the Islamic monarchy as it existed in India contemporaneous of the Gurus, the king assumes the status of the Mohammad's apostle instead of that of god, though by no means less exalted, as is apparent from the claim, which the Mughal Emperors made for themselves of being Zill-i-Ilahi, the shadow of God on earth. The laws of the static conservative society which he is required to uphold are derived from the Koran and the Hadith, instead of the Vedas and the Dharamshastras and the hereditary intellectual leadership of the Brahmans is replaced by the arrogant presumptions and prerogatives of the Ulemas. Likewise the Islamic monarch has his ministers selected and appointed by royal arbitration who are absolutely subservient to him.

Muslim type of monarchy also did not fit in the framework of the polity of the Sikh Gurus for those very reasons which did not qualify Hindu monarchy to be recognized in Sikhism.

The Gurus presaged new form of government to which Guru Gobind Singh gave the name of Khalsa Raj—Divine Kingdom. It will be run by the five beloved ones, inhering transcendental wisdom, ecumenical in approach, righteous in actions, and committed to the cohesion and upliftment of the people of the whole world. Such a government will guarantee autonomy of spirit and its free play, subject, of course, to the general interest of the people. All collectivities including religious and ritual types shall be given due recognition as each one is a reality in the context of space and time. Expressed otherwise government of Sikh concept will not only honour multiculturism, but also pursue such policies that would encourage co-existence and cooperation between different people. The Sikh government will be participatory aiming at inter-regional and inter-racial unity.

Sikh Polity being rooted in Sikh metaphysics and Sikh Ethics, the impression emerges that it is committed to defray the following obligations:

(1) It shall strive, propagate, uphold and make it a basic that there is inviolable sovereignty of the human person. If God is the true sovereign (Sacha Padshah) in the spiritual and temporal realms then as a creation of God, man/woman partakes of the sovereignty of the Divine.

(2) In consonance with this, man/woman is entitled to freedom of worship, freedom of expression, freedom from fear, and freedom to pursue any profession.

The martyrdom of Guru Tegh Bahadur was symbolic of the assertion of the fundamental right of freedom of conscience with the correlative freedom of religious belief and practice both at individual and corporate levels. With the Guru, freedom was not an empirical expediency in religiously heterogeneous society, but a transcendent value described by Guru Gobind Singh as Dharam in *Bachittar Natak*, characteristic of multi-religious, multicultural and multiethnic society that Sikhism sought to evolve as the composite integrated Indian or global society based on religion and political pluralism.

(3) It shall restructure society on equalitarian bases. It shall reject the concept of hierarchical fixity as the tradition-honoured principle of social organisation reflected in caste system which in its turn had to follow the orthodox law of Karma. It shall also discountenance other differences based on creed, wealth, race *et al.*, and instead, it would lend full recognition to worth and merit of each individual who is viewed in Sikhism as the very microcosm of God.

(4) It shall respect and promote pluralism, religious as well as social, for Sikh Polity is not only grounded in Sikhism but also sprouted and nourished by it. In this connection, we quote rather extensively from Dr. J.S. Ahluwalia's lecture which he delivered at University of California to illustrate our point. He says, "Different revelations of the spirit (God-Spirit) are like the variety of different seasons which refer back the same sun."[10]

For Sikh religion, all revelations of God are equally co-valid, having been given to man relative to the variables of time and place. This rules out any room for dogmatic assertion of fullness and finality of any single religious revelation as well as religious totalitarianism. All revelations being relatively valid, no 'ISM', religious or secular, can claim to be the sole way to God, the exclusive path to salvation. Guru Amar Das utters, "The world is ablaze O Lord! Shower your benediction. Through whichever door it can be delivered."

"The conception of religious pluralism envisaged in Sikhism provides a positive basis not only for co-validity and co-existence of different faiths in dynamic interaction with each other, but also for co-equality and co-existence of different religions and their co-participation in the national body-politic of their respective countries which partakes of the divinity of God. Sikh religion, therefore, is not a ethnicity-specific or region-specific or community-specific."

(5) Next important feature of the Khalsa Republic was to assume that every individual must engage himself/herself in honest productive labour and there shall be no exploitation of man by man with capital that is to say the accumulated wealth shall not be employed as the instrument of exploitation and there shall be no priviligentia based on the white collar and gift of gab.

'Khalsa Republic is expected to achieve all this not through coercion and imposition but through transformation possible through genuine religion only of the basic attitudes of the individuals, which transformation progressively destroys narrow selfishness. This is the moral imperative for the Khalsa state, it is not a supra individual identity as Hegel thought, to which obedience of an individual is due and for which an individual may be sacrificed.'

It shall not be, as it cannot be a theocratic state. One, in Sikhism, there is no canonised priestly class. Second, the source and sanction of secular law lies in the people-hood expressed through the will of the people. Third, Sikhism does not discriminate against individual or group on ground of creed or any other ground. All are equally entitled to a place in *Sach Khand* via any religious path. Sikh polity is neither communal nor unitarian in character. This being so, religious unitarianism as well as religious totalitarianism is violative of the spirit of Sikhism. Nor shall it assume the character of communitarian state. For it goes against the multi-religious, multi-communitarian, pluralistic society which finds validity and sanctification in Sikhism. Besides, "The Khalsa baptised by Guru Gobind Singh symbolises a generic sociological category representing the full-fledged sovereign people-hood, and not any particular sect or group."

FOOTNOTES

1. *Guru Granth Sahib*, pp. 417-18.
2. The relevant verses occur in Sri Rag (Astpadian), Rag Gauri (Astpadian), Rag Asa, Japji, Rag Wad-Hans (Chhant and Alahnian), Var Majh *et al.*
3. *Guru Granth Sahib,* p. 1288, Var Malhar.
4. Kapur Singh: *Prasar Prasna*, p. 349.
5. Khalak Khalak Ki Jankai, Khalak Dukkhavai Nah: (Tankhahnama).
6. *Sikhism and Indian Society*, Indian Institute of Advanced Studies.
7. Guru Gobind Singh: *Dasam Granth*, as translated by Dr. Trilochan Singh.
8. Dr. Trilochan Singh: *Social Philosophy of Guru Gobind Singh*—Article published in Transaction of the Indian Institute of Advanced Studies, Vol. IV, 1967.
9. S. Kapur Singh: *Prasar Prasna*, p. 324.
10. "Numerous are the seasons emanating from the one sun
    Numerous are the guises in which the creator appears."

20

SIKH SOCIAL ETHICS

A close study of the lives of the Gurus, their precepts and their utterances would lead us to the conclusion that the Sikh social ethics has four pronounced ingredients, namely social equality, universal brotherhood, seeking good of all (altruism) and social service. These ingredients are inter-related and interact. Altruism and social service are, in fact, practical measures to realise universal-brotherhood, the actualisation of which in its turn depends on the extent to which the principles of social equality is realised in the conduct of those who form the social fabric. The concept of social equality which is rooted in the belief that the whole matter is a unity and the moral world is that where this principle is crystallised in work-a-day life. The Gurus' concern for this unity was very acute and had been so vital a motivating force that they were very vocal and copious in their comments upon the contemporary social institutions which instead of unifying mankind on the principle of social equality propped up the inequitable and iniquitous social organisation and social ethics. In the process they made critical examination of the contemporary historical condition in India with a view to highlighting the problem of social equality in all its aspects in the contemporary contexts as also to suggest certain formulations to establish social equality.

The social organisation of the Hindus, in terms of the caste, which is described by Shri S.K. Maitra as the objective morality of the Hindus is completely rejected in Sikhism. "Complete equality among men is declared by the Sikh Gurus to be the fundamental moral principle required to regulate the social relations and communication." In Sikh scriptures, the *Rahit Namas* and in the utterances of the Gurus, one can trace the following flash-points which invalidate the caste philosophy and dismantle the social edifice built thereon.

There is no fundamental difference among men in terms of physical constitution. In a polemical discussion with the Brahmans Kabir enquires: "How are you Brahman and I a low caste? Is it that I have blood in my veins and you have milk?"[1] In this way he exposed the hollowness and absurdity of the superior claims of the so-called superior castes over so-called inferior castes in terms of differences in physical constitution. There is another reference in Guru Granth Sahib, which conveys that if the Brahmans are different from others why they did not appear in the world by means other than the biological process.

The second point of criticism against the caste system is on empirical ground. Guru Nanak points out that laws of nature do not act differently in respect of higher-caste-men. God makes no discrimination in favour of those who call themselves twice-born and hence the myth of caste-superiority is clearly to be seen as man-made. Guru Nanak, vehemently contends 'what merit is the caste'? and he himself answers 'This is the real truth that he who tasteth the poison will die.'[2] Guru Amar Das regards caste as an abnormality and a brazen perversity. He points out in his characteristic argumentative vigour mixed with sweet flavour of this diction. 'Every one says, there are four castes but it is from God that everyone comes. The same is the clay which fashions the whole world; the same clay the potter moulds into vessels of all kinds. The five elements make up the body's form, and who can say who has less of these or more?'[3]

The third point of criticism against the caste system is that men have emanated from the Primordial Being. According to Guru Nanak, 'There is one God who is all light and from it has emanated the whole world. None is inferior to anyone.

God of the Sikhs is self-existent—all hearts are illumined by the light of Lord.'[4] At another place in Guru Granth Sahib, Guru Nanak declares, 'You ought to see the light within all, and not look up for caste as the caste is of no consequence.'

Sikhism does not harbour the belief that caste has been prevalent since the beginning. In the primordial state 'no man of caste or birth, high or low, could be seen—there was no distinction of colour or coat or of the Brahman and the Kshatriya'. The view that different parts of the Primordial Being gave rise to different castes has been repudiated by the Sikh Gurus, and Sikhism, in harmony with its universalism, refuses to accredit the caste institution in social ethics and its seers, on the basis of their direct intuitive experience deny God having favoured a few by bringing them out from the higher parts of His body.

Finally, Sikhism holds that caste is of no consequence in the process of the realisation of the highest ideal. Men of the so-called low caste need not wait to be born again in the next higher caste for the attainment of liberation and spiritual realisation. Not birth but deeds must determine the purity of life. Kabir declares, 'I am a weaver by caste but a patient in mind. And so I utter the Lord's praise in a state of utter poise.' Guru Nanak in order to bear witness to the viracity of the statement identifies himself with "the lowest of the low, the humblest of the humble". Addressing himself to God he says, 'Thy mercy falls on the spots wherein the meek and the humble are cherished.' Speaking elsewhere on caste as the accepted channel of spiritual merit, the Guru expresses the view that not caste, which is only an accident of birth but deeds determine purity or merit. Sri Guru Nanak says:

> "Vain is the pride of caste, vain the pride of glory
> God alone gives shade to all."

(*Guru Granth Sahib*, p. 83)

Bhai Gurdas illustrates clearly the aforesaid stand-point of Sikhism in one of his compositions. He says, 'As the nature of the utensil has no bearing on the purity of the butter-fat, in the same way castes have no meaning for the holy men.' He then enumerates the cases of those saints who were born in the so-called low castes and yet reached the highest stage of perfection. The type of slant in favour of the low castes is seen in the utterances of all the Gurus. Guru Nanak says:

> "One who serves the higher castes is of great merit indeed
> But one who serves those of humble castes
> He may indeed wear shoes made from my body."
>
> (*Guru Granth Sahib*, p. 1256)

Convinced of the invalidity of the caste system, Guru Gobind Singh decries caste system and declares caste a taboo in the Order of the Khalsa. Guru Gobind Singh says in categorical terms, 'There is no consideration of caste or membership of varunas. He is all sympathy for the low, the down-trodden and the low caste people.' He hints out:

> "True service is the service of these people, I am not inclined to serve others of higher castes; charity will bear fruit, in this and the next world, if given to such worthy people as these." "From top to toe whatever I call my own, all I possess or carry I dedicate to these people."

Equality Among Classes in Sikhism

In the society contemporary to Nanak and other Sikh Gurus, wealth and rank were also the causes of its divisions as much as the birth was in the case of caste system, though the nature of the divisions in both the cases was different because in the former case classification could not be rigid because wealth is concrete and separable whereas in the latter case, the classification based on birth was rigid and inflexible.

Sikhism rejects the notion of superiority of the economically better placed class over the others. Bhai Gurdas while hailing the advent of Guru Nanak in this world exclaims that Nanak taught "Equality of a king and a commoner (*Raja-Runk Brabari*)." The age-old superstition that the poor are poor because of their past Karmas and hence poverty is ordained by God is repudiated in Sikhism, which avers that the higher classes are not governed by any separate code of ethics. The king and the poorest of the poor are governed by the same set of ethical and social rules and ideas. Sardar Kapur Singh, in his book *Baisakhi of the Sikhs* remarks, 'though men are not equal in ability, they are entitled to equal judgement and social equality'. The Gurus appear to presume that the notion of the superiority of man over man on the basis of wealth or rank is preposterous and arise when one forgets that one's life is rather short and death would level the so-called superiority of the classes. Thus, 'the ephemeral nature of human life is sought to be made the postulate of the declaration that any pride in the superiority of the classes is futile'. The classification of the society on the basis of wealth or rank is also rejected in terms of the ultimate objective of Sikhism which is that one should be *Brahm Gyani*—moral person—one who looks upon creation alike. The moral is exemplified from an anecdote from Guru Nanak's biography.

Guru Nanak is reported to have refused the partaking of the Brahm Bhoj of Malik Bhago in favour of the coarse food of Bhai Lalo. When asked by Malik for the reason, Guru Nanak replied that he thought it prudent and advisable to have food with Bhai Lalo because he earned his livelihood through honest means and was bereft of any pride-sense while his methods of earning money were objectionable and he was filled with pride. In fact, the Guru wanted to impress upon the people, that all ought to be treated as equals irrespective of the rank and richness. The superiority claimed on the basis of rank is also not recognised by the Sikh Gurus. In the vision which Guru Nanak brought to the people, contempt was cast on earthly potentates, whose power stemmed from aggression. The rule of God alone is eternal. "Thy kingdom is indestructible" (*Guru Granth Sahib*, p. 567). As he sang in Sri Rag, no form of earthly glory, the splendour of royal power even, was worth-having as against devotion to God, the fountain of all true values. Earthly monarchs and chiefs, as he expressed, in numerous contexts and with deep passion in the hymns pertaining to Babar's invasion would rule as long as God is on their side—in other words, if they have some moral principle to sustain them. Virtue and truthfulness alone is the prop of power. 'Mighty things', says the Guru in Jap 'hold not the worth of a worm in whom is not lodged the love of God'. And where dwells the love of God, egoity is automatically obliterated because if the human body is filled with ambrosia of love of God, no other thing can have any room in it.

Equality in Terms of Preceptor-Disciple Relations

On March 30, 1699 C.E., on the Baisakhi day, the tenth Guru established the Order of the Khalsa. After administering Amrit to the Five Pyaras—dear ones, he himself partook of the same 'Amrit' which was administered by the Five Dear Ones to him, thereby affixing his seal to the dictum that the Guru was Guru and disciple both rolled in himself. In this way Guru-disciple relationship was proclaimed to be based on equality. This was something novel and unique when it is juxtaposed with Indian tradition. Its social ramifications strengthened the democratic spirit.

Equality in Terms of Different Religions and Nationalities

When Guru Nanak addressed himself to the task of shaping society as per his conceptions, many religions such as Hinduism, Islam, Christianity, Jainism *et al.* were prevalent in the country. Religion, as we understand, is an attempt to instill harmony among the people coupled with constructive dynamism to enable them to improve their living as also to understand the secrets of the creation *vis-à-vis* God and his human beings. All religions, in fact, at the time of their birth or rise project the *modus operandi* as stated above, but as time passes, they fall victim to the parochialism of spirit or the narrow social political views. It was because of this that in Gurus' times, the religious groups were at logger-heads with one another. The followers of Islam, especially the Sunnis were committed to safeguard the interest of their own group and they felt pleasure in torturing the votaries of other religious groups particularly the Hindus. The ideal of Dar-ul-Harb is indicative of this fanatical attitude. The Hindus, in their turn, fared no better. They did not appreciate the good points of Islam and Islamic culture—rather they branded the Muslims as *Malechhas*—the demons. There were a few persons both among the Hindus and Muslims known as Sufis and saints who understood the real role of religions but their voice was not heard in the din and noise of the communal clamour. If there were no riots on the large scale, it was either because of the passivity of the Hindus or out of their fear of imperial Muslims or because of the fact that Muslims were satisfied with what they had achieved. Christianity and other religions also did not prepare the psyche so as to enable the people to appreciate and respect diverse religio-cultural paths. But the need of the people was the development of the attitude which might respect all religions and religious groups along with their social and cultural projections and ramifications. The profile of the response could be visualised in the teachings of Bhaktas particularly of the 14th to 16th centuries but their expression was not forthright and their views were not categorical.

It fell to Nanak to show the right path to the people lost in the vertex of religious squabbles and group ferocities. He preached openly that he believed in multi-national and multi-cultural society. All religions have fundamental unity in the sense that they aimed at the regeneration of man and the harmonious relations between man and man. An ideal Muslim is not different from an ideal Hindu. Similarly, an ideal Sikh is a Hindu, a Christian and a Buddhist at one and the same time. Nanak does not believe in the superstitious accretions of different religions and all those man-made postulates or practices which have deflected man from the pathway to the harmony of mankind. Discussing about the merit of men professing different religions, Guru Gobind Singh holds 'One may be a Hindu or Muslim, all human beings belong to one brotherhood of mankind. In consonance with the spirit of ethical universalism, the tenth Guru proclaimed:

> "The Hindus and the Muslims are all one though they may have different habits under the influence of different environments. They are also compounded of the same four elements, earth, air, fire and water. The Quran and the Purana praise the same God. They are all of one form and one God had made them all." (*Akal Ustat*)

These categorical and unambiguous remarks leave no doubt that men of all nationalities and religions are equal. Bhai

Gurdas very amply remarks, "There are in the world many Sunnis, Christians, Musais, Rafzis and those who have no faith in doomsday. Numberless are the Ferangis, Armenians, Romans, Africans, Sayyads, Turks, Mughals and Pathans. But wherever they may be, their merit and demerit cannot remain undiscovered."[5] According to Dr. Avtar Singh, "The attempt is thus made to transcend the creed labels and the geographical considerations to assert the fundamental equality in terms of the ethical perfection. The learned writer of the *Prem Sumarg* says, "When someone belonging to other religions and names comes to the house of Sikh, it is his/her duty to accord full respect and cordiality as this would make a Sikh perfect."[6]

According to Kapur Singh, "Sikhism fully recognises that the search for a fundamental unity of religions and the attempts at the religious rapprochement have their limitations, for, there are fundamental differences in the conceptions of Reality and attitudes towards the world, permanently impending a real and lasting synthesis between basically incompatible elements, preaches frank and unreserved dialogue between various religions and the human groups that owe allegiance to these religions so as to arrive at the experience that transcends religious particularism and realises a base of identity underneath all modes of religious expression. As a corollary thereof Sikhism favours a plural, free, open and progressive human society, God-oriented, non-aggressive but firm and ever-ready to combat rise and growth of evil through organised resistance and forwarding yet non-ambitious." This belief being posited in Sikhism led the Gurus as early as the medieval age to plead for and to practise inter-faith dialogue, not to emphasise differences but to highlight the commonness of religious experience which is essentially transcendental and all-embracing.

EQUALITY IN TERMS OF GENDER

Status of Woman

In Sikhism the issue of the status of woman has been tackled from many angles. Scriptural support has been extended in favour of woman that she is not at all inferior to man. Guru Nanak says:

> "From the woman is our birth, in the woman's womb, we are shaped. To the woman are we engaged and to the woman are we wedded. Woman is our friend and from woman is the family. If one woman dies, we seek another. The women are the bonds of the world. Why call woman evil who gives birth to kings. From the woman is the woman, without the woman there is none." (Asa Di Var)

Again he says:

> "That it is God and God the Creator alone who is independent of woman because he is unborn. Verily, society the home and the country where there is a true woman of divine virtues, are honoured, and become dignified and exalted in the Durbar of the True one."
>
> (Asa Di Var)

From this scriptural authority, it is clear that woman was assigned the status, in no way inferior to man. In fact home, society and the country are honoured only if woman is held in esteem.

The Gurus in their compositions address themselves as woman in relation to God. God Himself acts as a woman. Metaphysical argument is also harnessed to impress upon the people that woman occupies equal status to man. It is held that since all mankind is emanation of God, it is only ridiculous to deny equality to woman. Guru Arjan says: 'Thou art my father, thou art my mother.' He does not make use of *Mata*—mother in feminine gender, thereby pointing out—that physical differences also have no meaning in determining the status of woman.

Against the background of spiritual-cum-metaphysical thought *vis-à-vis* woman as detailed above, the Gurus discussed further the status of woman. The Gurus do not regard 'woman' as hurdle or obstruction on the path to the ultimate goal of Eternal Bliss. This being so, they reject asceticism or renunciation as the requisite pathway and regard householder's life if it is led in a righteous manner superior to that of an ascetic and is not contradictory to the moral Order the Gurus wanted to establish in this world. In fact, the moral Order means nothing if it is not to be realised in this world. To regard woman a 'temptress' or 'seductress' or 'unclean' is preposterous in the eyes of the Gurus. The Guru by bringing this type of vision to the people expects that she would be given honourable status in every social segment of the society.

Family being the smallest but the most important social unit was sure to draw the attention of the Gurus. A close study of the utterances of the Gurus would show that the Guru recognised this institution as the most fundamental salient of our social structure but the Guru wanted a change in its conceptual structure and in the relations between different members of the family. The Gurus never viewed this institution either as a patriarchal unit or a matriarchal unit because they reject the supreme authority of the eldest male member or the eldest female member in a family. They, on the other hand, wanted harmonious relations among the members of the family on equal footing.

In their views, the principle of division of work and responsibilities should form the basis of relationship among different members of the family, and it should be recognised that family, being one integrated whole, its each member is as important as the other. Father is father if he performs the duty of a father, and mother is mother if she functions as a mother. From the point of procreation either sex is equal, and in fact, it is the co-operative combined effort of both the sexes that procreation takes place, and in no case, either sex, individually or co-jointly with the opposite sex can create anything which is the miracle of God alone. In this context, Guru Nanak in prayerful mood designates God both as mother and father and to make himself more clear addresses God as mother in the same gender as he does when he addresses God as father. The Gurus regard progeny of the pair as brothers and sisters and wish that they function as such. But certainly they do not recognise the superiority of the one over the other. They should function as the important adjuncts of the family under the guidance of the superior talent of their parents but not as a slave of the family. From this point of view, the Gurus condemn all those parents who are not considerate to the susceptibilities of their wards and wittingly or unwittingly force them to conform to their whims and views. This tendency of the parents impedes the growth of creative harmony in the family, which instead of becoming the vehicle of progress retards it.

The institution of family is very closely knit with the marriage, which to a great extent, is the fulcrum of family as also its adhesive. This is why at all places where people began to make conscious efforts to grow as a civilised groups, marriage was considered to be a sacrament. Indians were no exception to it. Sikhism also recognises the fact and regards marriage very sacred. It is solemnised in the presence of Guru Granth Sahib and the four hymns from Guru Granth Sahib (*Lawan*) are recited on this occasion, the purpose being that marriage is a benefaction and hence hallowed and divine. It is indeed an irony that bridegrooms regard themselves superior to their brides, and do not feel abashed at their demands of dowry and such other things. The Gurus have condemned this attitude of the males and have regarded both of them two sparks of the same light (*Ek Jot Doe Moorti*). The variegated customs which have grown around marriage are meaningless accretions and have no spiritual or social functions. Sex, of course, is the natural basis of husband-wife relationship but to treat sexual gratification the chief object of marriage is to reduce oneself to the animal level. The Guru says that the marriage should not be a union of bodies. If it is so, then this union may break at any level. Bodies go on changing and the effect of the passage of time results in the deterioration of physical beauty and physical appearance. Devotion to sensuality and sexuality will, in course of time, lead to mutual contempt and discontent. Therefore, the Guru says that marriage instead of being a union of bodies should be a union of souls, of minds, leading to love of each other's qualities and care for each other's well-being (Var Maru III). It is only in this context, which is at once moral and spiritual that marriage ceremony has been called 'Anand'. Anand is different from pleasure. Although marriage signifies a physical relation, yet the ideal embodied into it goes beyond a mere sensory experience. The word 'Anand' indicates a physical immanent as well as spiritual transcendent. The withdrawal from the physical by the ascetic monk was substituted by the realisation of transcendence of Anand. The fulfilment was thus more meaningful and more valuable. By calling marriage 'Anand' the Guru conceived in this unit of society a partial realisation of God, as in the establishment of the Khalsa he had conceived a total realisation of the Supreme Being. All the social units in the Khalsa Order are really the evolutionary stages of the manifestation of God, of the Sargunisation of the Nirgun. The first step and a last step is the intimately fastened tie of man and woman in marriage. We saw that God manifested in this universe through the principle of His will which appeared in opposites: *Haumai* and *Nām*—individuation and universalism. This bio-polar nature of reality continues till we reach moral man as the highest achievement. The combination of man and woman in the highest moral order is the unity of bio-polarity, the first achievement of ultimate Anand. Mating is a universal characteristic but mating in the moral order is possible only in man. Hence Anand. This marriage has a metaphysical, moral and spiritual bases.

It is against this background, the Gurus rejected polygamy. Social argument has also been adduced by the Gurus in favour of their views. The polygamous or polyandrous marriages would run counter to the spirit of equality between the sexes. Only monogamous marriages fit in the conceptual and operational framework of the institution of family.

Gay marriages are inconceivable in Sikhism as these are unnatural, unprocreative and incapable of bringing into existence a family—the fundamental unit of Sikh social structure.

Female Infanticide

The practice of female infanticide has been denounced in Sikhism as it negates the ethical norms, spiritual and social equality of human beings. The origin of this practice has been traced to various causes. A scholar suggests that 'in Rome, Greece, Arabia, India and China, women of the upper classes relieved by the males of the harder tasks of both as an effort to keep them young and as a sign of rank became an economic burden and consequently infanticide fell mainly on the females. It is also held that the necessity of finding a dowry for daughters contributed to the selection of female children for infanticide in China and India. The origin of this custom is also traced to the Ancestor Cults.

According to A.M. Hocard "The ancestor cults in Greece, Rome, India and China could be transmitted only through the males and this also resulted in the destruction of girl infants."

Obviously, all the causes itemised above have either originated in the perverted human mind or in the appropriation of privileges by males or in the deep-rooted superstitions. The Gurus do not give credence to any of the causes and aver that infanticide is immoral and hence undesirable. Guru Gobind Singh in one of his fiats to the Khalsa made it an unpardonable sin and enjoined upon his followers not to regard the persons indulging in it as a Sikh. In *Rehat Nama* by Prahlad Singh it is stated "He who is a Sikh and deals with one indulging in female infanticide would be led to disaster ultimately."

Various steps on mundane level were also suggested to eradicate this evil. In order to overcome the difficulty in terms of the requirement of dowry to be offered by the bride's father, it is laid down in Sikhism that no dowry ought to be accepted from the bride's parents and in arranging her marriage, social help is required to be offered to the parents of the girl who may experience difficulty in finding matches for their children.

Status of Woman in terms of the Custom of Sati

Sati whose literal meaning is chaste denotes a custom of immolation on the part of women along with the dead bodies of their husbands. The practice is horrible but it was there in India when Sikhism emerged. What were the causes of its rise and prevalence and what social purpose did it serve, little is known. However, it appears that the custom was the outcome of the vagaries of emotion, the working of the mind of the males on conscious or unconscious levels to preserve their superiority and privileges. It did not serve any social purpose in positive or progressive sense.

Even the scriptural authority was appropriated to scaffold the contention that self-immolation on the funeral pyre of her husband was the only meritorious course that a virtuous woman could follow. "Not only would Sati enjoy eternal bliss in heaven along with her husband but her action would expiate the sins of three generations of her husband's family both on his father's and mother's sides." Thus the element of hope and encouragement were used to induce women for self-immolation to obtain the posthumous title of the virtuous woman (Sati).

The Sikh Gurus did not approve of the practice. Guru Amar Das declares that "Sati is one who lives contented and embellishes herself with good conduct and cherishes the Lord ever and calls on Him." Since the advice of the Guru is for all, it is only reasonable to arrive at the conclusion that the Guru required widows to conduct themselves as all others do. According to Dr. Avtar Singh[7] "The view is expressed by the Guru that in order to be known as virtuous, woman ought to maintain families knit by love. The separation on death also should be a matter of feelings. On the whole, according to the Guru, the virtues of the housewife are to be in terms of her role in the family and not in terms of self-immolation." The Guru says, "The women burn themselves on the pyres of their husbands; but if they love their spouses well, they suffer the pangs of separation even otherwise."[8]

The Gurus not only have indulged in moral and spiritual dialectics to reject the immoral custom of Sati but have suggested practical steps to eradicate this evil. Giani Lal Singh, a great scholar of Bhasaur School of Thought, quotes from Guru Nanak's composition in Rag Gaudi in Guru Granth Sahib in this connection. It is pointed out by him that the widow ought to have the right to exercise her option for re-marriage whenever she wants it exactly as the males have been allowed to do. In social sphere, in Sikhism no restrictions have been put on woman and she has been considered equal to man in all respects. The Gurus' view of society is neither male-specific nor female-specific, it is a universal brotherhood of man based on social equality rooted in the dignity of labour and saturated with *Nām,* the divine spirit. The society of this concept is obviously free from taboos and prejudices born out of sex. Any restriction on women is unethical and runs contrary to the Sikh principles. Guru Nanak while commenting upon the cause of the degeneration of Indian society in the fifteenth and early part of the sixteenth centuries deplores that "woman had become coward and wretched". By implication he meant that women should rid themselves of the role they had been constrained to play. They should participate as equal partners of men in the drama of life. Woman can adopt any profession and there should be no bar on her in this respect. Revered Khivi the wife of Guru Angad personally looked after *Guru Ka Langar*. During Guru Amar Das, several ladies were appointed to head the bishoprics (Manjis). Bibi Bhani's role in the development of Sikhism is too well-known to need any elucidation. The part played by Mata Gujri following the death of her husband will go down in history as the ever shining beacon of courage. The Order of the Khalsa as inaugurated by the tenth Guru also makes no distinction between male and female and in fact anyone entering this Order was named Khalsa, no separate name was assigned to woman seeking entry into this Order. Guru Gobind Singh, in his struggle for Dharma, did not regard woman in any way inferior to man. Sahib Kaur and Mai Bhago took part in political as well as religious affairs and their example was followed later on, with the zeal born of a regenerative process as initiated by the Gurus.

All these ladies proved beyond doubt that women, if allowed to play their role in society, can show their worth, in no way less than men. The Gurus in view of all this, denounced the Pardah System that had plagued the society since long. It is laid down in *Rehat Namas* that women ought not to wear veils. Whatever be the historical reasons for the practice, it being emblematic of the bondage of women and denial of equality to them has not been accredited in Sikhism. Women should not experience any inequality in matters of education, rather they should be free to attain education, unhampered by any crippling taboos. They should be free to learn language, literature, religious scriptures, music and science. Woman should not be confined within the four walls. She should not be treated as an island sequestered from man. She, being as much a part of God as man, has the inherent capacity and capability to contribute to the general society in measures equal to man. The Gurus, therefore, advocate forcefully that women are equal partners of men in their struggle to discover truth and realise it in the world to enable it to conform to the moral order as the Gurus perceived and preached. Women should be treated as integrated human beings and not the weaker vessel—the inferior sex which is often wrapped in hypocritical phrases like the 'fair sex'.

Social Equality *vis-à-vis* Professions or Occupations

In Sikhism one can adopt any profession—farming, trading and so-called menial professions. His love for us is not wanting provided we are truthful and honest. In Nanak's view, it is tantamount to committing sins if we look down upon those persons, who have adopted the professions of sweepers and scavengers *et al.* The Master says, "There is no intrinsic merit in professions. All are alike." Guru Arjan enjoins upon us:

> "Thou mayest do any work
> But it must be done in a righteous manner.
> Thou must not earn by living through corrupt means
> Thou must not claim what belongs to you not
> Let such rightful earning be shared with the children of God
> Thus wise will thy life become pure."

The Gurus do not consider it to be correct that 'Karma' activity, leads to the bondage of '*Jiva*'. According to Indian concept of metaphysics, God, in his true and real form is '*Nirgun Brahm*' who is *Satya-Chit-Anand* and is actionless. When *Nirankar* willed He became manifest (*Sargun*). It was willing or acting which brought formless God into form and shape. *Jiva* was also created in the same process. If '*Jiva*' wants to merge into the *Satya-Chit Anand Brahm,* it must also become *Akrai* (Actionless). Hence started the School of Thought which pleaded resignation from the field of activity in order to become '*Akrai*' because the belief was that every act of man leaves behind its '*Sanskar*'—impressions or traces which remain attached to 'Jiva' and determine its births and rebirths. The Guru redefines the theory of *Karma.* According to Guru Nanak "'*Karma*' theory does not operate in a mechanical way. *Jiva* can be made to realise that it is microcosm of macrocosm. It should not worry about the success and failure of its actions. Every activity is God's activity and every success or failure is His. He can, through efforts, transcend self and liberates himself from the chain of *Sanskaras.* The liberated soul is always in tune with the ultimate Reality." In Granthic hymns, this stage is known as the stage of *Nām.*

Thus a true Sikh works because that is the way of His worship. The more he works honestly, the more he worships. A hard and honest work takes him into the presence of God where he finds God's will all-around. Working for others is better because in this case, you rise above the narrow limits of self. Hence the social inequality on the basis of work or professions has no meaning.

Universal Brotherhood

The ideal of social equality is not the ultimate aim of the ethics of Sikhism. The equality may be maintained without feeling any affection or regard for the person who is held to be equal but such bare equality would not be enough because it does not conform to the ideal humanistic morality. Hence it is essential that it must be saturated with idea of spiritual unity of mankind. Thus the material content to the social ethics in Sikhism is provided from the same premises of spiritual unity which was used for providing human equality. Guru Gobind Singh's ideas in this regard are very expressive. He says, "As out of a single fire millions of spark arise, arise in separation but come together again when they fall back in the fire. As from a heap of dust, grains of dust are swept up and fill the air, and filling it fall in a heap of dust. As out of single stream countless waves rise up, and being water, fall back in the water again. So from God's form emerge alive and inanimate things and since they arise from Him, they shall fall in Him again." The Guru in this statement asserts that everyone ought to treat everyone as member of the same human brotherhood. To lend support to this idea, Guru Arjan says, "Thou art our only father, we are all thy children." The same Guru is much pained at the attitude of 'otherness' on the part of people and he says, "Meeting with the Guru I have abandoned the sense of otherness." In fact the Guru equates the meeting of the Guru with the demolition of the walls of the instinct of 'otherness'. The 'other' is not an 'other' but a co-sharer of the same source of emanation and a part of the same spiritual Order. The universal brotherhood is thus linked together by bonds deeper than family or national affirmities. This being so, Guru Gobind Singh declares "Recognise all humanity as one in spirit." According to Professor Avtar Singh, "The argument of the Guru seems to be that brotherhood is a reality but it is not visible because of the pall of ego or *Haumai* (individuation). Once this partitioning pall is removed, the relationship should be visible clearly. As a matter of fact, the whole of social ethics of the Sikhs is oriented towards the demolition of this wall of separation, and the realisation of wider and still wider identification is indicative of the progressive realisation of the ideal.

The greatest hindrances to the realisation of the ideal of universal brotherhood are slander and enmity. So far slander is concerned, the Gurus are profuse in their utterances against this evil. The Gurus regard 'Nindak' as the person who does not find peace here and hereafter.[9] Slandering others amounts to putting filth into ones own mouth.[10] Slanderer's fate is sealed forever[11] and he can never earn respect.[12] Slanderer's friends are undone because he is considered "a useless person for the people and is condemned to eternal bondage".[13] He cannot earn spiritual merit even if he pays visit to sixty eighty sacred places of pilgrimage.[14] He is given no place in the presence of True Lord.[15]

Slander, therefore, has been condemned both on spiritual as well as on social grounds. This evil causes mutual distrust and suspicion among the smaller social groups but may also poison the social relations among much larger groups. Social values of the slanderer is negative as he is not considered trustworthy. He is, in fact, a sick member of the society. In one of Guru Arjan Dev's hymns, this negative role of slanderer is very beautifully crystallised. He says, "I have abandoned the companionship of ego and now the friend and the foe are alike to me.[16] Viewed from this point of view, the conduct of slanderer is immoral and anti-social and definitely a great hurdle on the way to the universal brotherhood.

The second great hurdle on the way to the realisation of the goal of universal brotherhood is the 'enmity' towards others. Enmity is the desire to cause harm and pain to others. Guru Arjan Dev says, "Why to entertain enmity, God pervades everywhere." It is the duty of everyone that the feeling of enmity should be eradicated. These utterances of the Guru lead us to the conclusion that enmity hinders the spiritual growth and does not allow one to realise God who pervades everywhere. Bhai Gurdas discusses this evil on social level. He says, "It is common practice that men return good for good done unto them, but I am sacrifice unto those who return good even for evil or who are good and kind even to the evil-doers." Thus, persons are required not to retaliate to evil with evil but to return it with good. Only thus wise can a fellow being turned into enemy be won over. Even when evil has to be fought, it is to be done without any feeling of enmity towards the other person. "Love of one's enemy provides the acid test of whether one's love is a perfect love like God's or is restricted to those whom it is easy to love." Evil must be resisted without saturating one's self with a feeling of hatred for the evil-doers. This type of attitude would help the realisation of the goal referred to above. Bhai Nand Lal says, "If any man is injured it is the Creator who would be injured. The creator is the soul and life of creation." One ought, therefore, to eradicate completely any feeling of enmity and also guard against its development at any stage in life.

Selfless Services—Altruism

In Sikhism, another social ideal is the welfare and happiness of others. This ideal in modern parleys is known as altruism. The Gurus aver that the eradication of desires of enmity and slander is not sought for the complete realisation of human brotherhood, it must be realised positively by altruistic activities. And, in fact, this thing has been made as the test in terms of which a person professing Sikhism is evaluated. Bhai Gurdas says, "The test of good man is that he seeks always the welfare of others. The bad man is selfish, he does not do good to others."[17] There are hazards of altruism as well. It sometimes degenerates itself into a sort of social pity, at times it gives rise to pride which is an evil in itself. In view of all this, the altruist is required to regard his altruism as an opportunity for receiving divine sanctification since the Creator is there in creation. It was against the background of this type of altruism, that the Gurus and Sikhs made supreme sacrifices. The Guru lay stress on *par-upkar* (service of others) and in keeping with this, the compilers of Sikh moral codes enjoin upon the Sikhs. "When the food is ready, pray for some needy person to come and share your food so that your food may be sanctified." Bhai Chopa Singh, in consonance with this strain, requires the Sikhs to consider help to the needy as 'rendition unto the Guru'[18] and decries the hoarding of one's possession while his fellow-beings may be in great distress. Guru Hargobind calls the mouth of the poor and needy as the chest of the Guru, and scolded the Sikh in possession of honey (which he wanted to offer to the Guru) for not giving the same to his fellow-being named Kattu who suffered a sudden attack of asthma and needed honey for cure. Altruism is, indeed, the holiest spark in the life of human soul. Bhai Daya Singh and Bhai Nand Lal also express similar views when they come to discuss the attributes of the '*par-upkar*' (Service unto others).

Bhai Mani Singh, in his book 'Bhakat Ratnavali' divides the '*Gurmukh—Par-upkari Jiv*' into three categories, as he divides the evil persons into three categories. The *sine-qua-non* is altruism. The three levels of *par-upkari jiv* are (i) *Gurmukh*, (ii) *Gurmukhtar*, (iii) *Gurmukhtam*. *Gurmukh* is he "who does good unto those who do good unto him and returns evil for evil. *Gurmukhtar* is one "who has turned his back on evil deeds and his face is towards the teachings of the Guru. If someone does even a single act of goodness unto him, the *Gurmukhtar* would always do good to him. He never takes pride for the good he does unto others." *Gurmukhtam* is "the finest specimen of altruism. He seeks good of others even if they do evil to him. His altruism is spontaneous without any discrimination of friend or foe."

Of the three categories of the evil persons, the first is of the *manmukhs* who do not remember the good done to them but never forget the evil done to them. *Manmukhtar* forms the second category of evil persons. They are, in the moral scale, lower than the *manmukhs*. They always return evil in return both for the good as well as the evil done to them. In the third category come the *manmukhtam*, the persons who always return evil for any act of good done to them. They have no faith in the spiritual word. They invariably would argue that the spiritual word and the good of others is not fruitful for them, while the evil done by them to others leads to their own good. Such persons are perennially condemned ones.[19]

From the evidence of Bhai Mani Singh, it is also clear that altruism is the quality that was much-loved by the Guru. To lend another dimension to this virtue the Gurus say that persons saturated with altruism help others, achieve salvation. In this context *Gurmukhtar* plays the role of Bhodhisatva, and leads countless beings to Nirvana. In the words of Guru Nanak, *"Nanak Te Mukh Ujjale Keti Chhuti Nal"* testifies to the aforesaid role of *Gurmukhtar*. Guru Angad puts his seal to this view when he repeats the words of Nanak with solitary addition of the 'Hor'.[20]

FOOTNOTES

1. *Guru Granth Sahib*, Gaudi Kabir ji, p. 324.
2. *Ibid*., Var Majh Slok M. 1 (Paudi), p. 142.
3. Rag Bhairon M. 3, Chaupadas (1 to 4-1), p. 1128.

4. Sorath M. 1, p. 597.
5. Bhai Gurdas, Vars—Stanza 16 Var 8.
6. *Prem Sumarg* ed. Kahan Singh: *Gurmat Sudhakar*, para 835.
7. Dr. Avtar Singh: *Ethics of the Sikhs*, p. 181.
8. *Adi Granth*, Var of Rag Suhi, M. 3 (3-6), p. 787.
9. Aasa, M. 5 (4-10), p. 373.
10. Par Ninda Par Mai Mukh Sudhi Agan Krodh Chandal.
11. Jan Ka Aap Sahayee Hoa Nindak Bhage Haar.
12. Nindak Ka Mukh Kala Hoa, Deen Duniya De Darbar.
13. Aasa M. 5, p. 373.
14. Gaund Ravidas, p. 875.
15. Moonh Kale Tina Nindkan Tit Sache Darbar, *Guru Granth Sahib*, p. 649.
16. Prathme Chhodi Prayee Ninda, Utar Gayee Sab Man Ki Chinda (Bhairon M. 5 (4-27, p. 1147).
17. Bhai Gurdas, Vars—Stanza 12 Var 20.
18. Chopa Singh: *Rehat Nama*.
19. Bhai Kahan Singh: *Gurmat Sudhakar*, para 673.
20. Nanak Te Mukh Ujjle Hor Keti Chhuti Nāl.

21

SOME EMINENT SIKHS OF THE GURU

Baba Budha

Baba Budha, whose original name was Burha, was born on October 22, 1506 CE. His father's name was Sugha and mother's Gauran. They lived in Kathu Nangal, a village in present-day Amritsar district. Later, they shifted to Dhalla village not far from the river Ravi opposite Kartarpur.

When Guru Nanak was returning to Kartarpur, he saw a boy grazing cattle in the fields nearby. The boy rushed to him, paid obeisance and enquired if he could render any service to him. The Guru was much impressed by the demeanour and civility of the boy, who with passage of time, became more and more attached to the Guru.

The next morning Burha, taking a pot of butter-milk with butter floating in it, went to the Guru and presented it with reverence and humility. He listened to the Guru's sermons with the devotion of a true seeker. Then he beseeched the Guru to tell him the way to the state of bliss. Burha's questions were so deep and relevant that the Guru remarked that Burha was young in age but old in wisdom, and that he was not Burha but Budha, an awakened being. From then on Burha came to be known as Bhai Budha and later Baba Budha. He became a devotee of the Guru, spending most of his time with him. Thus Baba Budha entered into discipleship of the Guru at the age of ten.

Baba Budha always looked after the welfare of the Sikhs, and spared no pains to spread the Sikh faith among the people. Whenever a crisis loomed over the *Panth*, he was always there to help find a solution to save the situation.

On Guru Nanak's death in 1539 CE, Guru Angad left Kartarpur and established his seat at Khadur near the river Beas. Sri Chand, the elder son of Guru Nanak, was not happy at being overlooked in favour of Angad. Guru Angad, to avoid open clash with the son of Guru Nanak, retired to the house of an old Sikh, Bibi Bhirai, of village Sanghar. Baba Budha came all the way from Kartarpur to Khadur, and prevailed upon the Guru to grant audience to the Sikhs. At the time of Amar Das's nomination to guruship, similar crisis gripped the Sikhs. Guru Amar Das, because of his deep regard for Guru Angad, did not want to annoy his son, Baba Datu, who burned with jealousy at the succession of Amar Das to *gurgaddi*. He, therefore, retired to a hut in the jungle near Basarke village, with instructions that he should not be disturbed. It was again Baba Budha who persuaded the Guru to attend to his Sikhs who were regularly calling at Goindwal. Exercising his influence, Baba Budha was able to assuage Baba Datu also.

On ascendance of Guru Arjan to *gurgaddi*, Pirthi Chand, who himself wanted to be the Guru, entered into collusive arrangement with the *masands*, and pretended that he was the real Guru. Baba Budha was one of those disciples who with resoluteness denounced Pirthi Chand, and foiled his cunning attempts to usurp the *gurgaddi*. It was primarily due to the lead provided by Baba Budha and Bhai Gurdas that Pirthi Chand did not succeed in bringing about schism among the Sikhs, although he had tried hard. Guru Arjan held Baba Budha in high esteem.

Baba Budha was a great mystic and a great teacher. Though records do not speak much as to how he received his education, yet it is reasonable to surmise that he received his education at Kartarpur at the feet of Guru Nanak. He was well-versed in the sacred hymns of Guru Nanak and other Gurus, and would quote these profusely during his talks.

When Guru Angad decided to popularise Gurmukhi script and Punjabi language, he assigned the task of teaching it to Baba Budha. He also tutored Hargobind.

Guru Tegh Bahadur was also taught by Baba Budha. Guru Hargobind personally took him (Tegh Bahadur) to Baba Budha, the wisest among teachers and said:

> You were kind enough to be my teacher, O Enlightened One, accept my son also as your pupil.

Tegh Bahadur bowed before the sage who blessed him and accepted him as his student. Baba Budha taught him Punjabi, and passed on to him the deep spiritual experience which he had gained. Besides this, he made arrangements for his education in subjects such as languages, history and arithmetic. At an older age, he was taught the elements of Buddhism, Jainism, Nathism, Vaishnavism and Islamic creeds.

Baba Budha was an activist, and took part in almost all important projects initiated by the Gurus. When Guru Ram Das started the excavation of the *sarovar* at Amritsar, Baba Budha took upon himself the responsibility of supervising the digging operations. It was under his fostering care that the *sarovar* (tank) was completed. Again, during Guru Arjun's time, he was the person who oversaw the raising of Harmandar Sahib in the midst of the *amritsar* (pool of immortality). The construction of bricked steps around the pool was done under his supervision. Kaulsar was also excavated under his supervision. The emergence of the city of Amritsar as a thriving centre of commerce also owed much to his sagacious advice and the devotion with which he set about the task to convince people in the neighbouring areas to settle there.

When *Adi Granth* was installed at Darbar Sahib, Baba Budha was assigned the duty of reading from it in the morning and evening. Having placed the bound copy of *Adi Granth* on a cot, Baba Budha carried it on his head barefooted to Harmandir Sahib followed by Guru Arjan, also barefooted, waving a fan of peacock feathers over the sacred scripture. Bhai Gurdas was the third to follow at the head of the barefooted *sangat*. The first recitation was done by Bhai

Gurdas. As the head-priest of Harmandar Sahib, Baba Budha laid down the procedure to be followed meticulously in Harmandar Sahib. He was always aware of the exigencies of the circumstances and lost no time to take the required steps. When Guru Hargobind was imprisoned in the fort, he himself went to Gwalior to bring the news about the Guru.

The greatest contribution of Baba Budha was to render the much-needed help to the *sangat* in making explicit the policy of *miri* and *piri*, which meant that the political as well as spiritual sovereignty vested in the Guru. Guru Arjan trained Guru Hargobind in the philosophy of this dual responsibility. This fact is corroborated by Bhai Mani Singh in his book *Bhagat Ratnavali*. He says:

> Bhai Sigaru and Bhai Jaita were great warriors and philanthropists. They were asked to live in the service of Guru Hargobind. Guru Arjan said to them, 'The House of the Guru will take up arms under Hargobind. The dark age prevails. After learning the use of weapons, the Sikhs will wrest political power from the rulers and through the love of Divine Word (*Shabad*) they will acquire the spiritual wisdom of Divine Teachers. Abide with Hargobind.'

Baba Budha, following the advice of Guru Arjan, asked Guru Hargobind to don two swords, one as the symbol of *miri* (temporal sovereignty) and the other as the symbol of *piri* (spiritual sovereignty), when the sixth Nanak ascended the *gurgaddi*. This explicit pronouncement caused a furore among the Sikhs. Some of them, incapable of grasping the import of the Sikh movement in all its aspects, began to entertain doubts regarding the validity and desirability of the policy. Baba Budha not only helped clear the misgivings of such people, but also made them understand the perspective which was responsible for the enunciation of such a policy.

The great sage passed his last days in meditation at Jhanda Ram Das, or simply called Ramdas, where the family had shifted from its native village, Kathu Nangal. As the end came on 16th November, 1631 CE, Guru Hargobind was at his bedside. The Guru, as says *Gurbilas Patshahi Chhevin*, gave his shoulder to his bier, and performed the last rites. Bhai Gurdas, started a reading of the *Adi Granth* in memory of the deceased. Two shrines stand in Ramdas commemorating Baba Budha, Gurdwara Tap Asthan Baba Budha ji, where the family lived on the southern edge of the village, and Gurdwara Samadhan, where he was cremated.

Bhai Mardana

Bhai Mardana was the closest associate and the first disciple of Guru Nanak. According to Manohar Das Meharban, Mardana had been the companion of Guru Nanak since childhood. Both Bhai Mardana and Guru Nanak were born at Talwandi Rai Bhoi Ki, Bhai Mardana in 1459 CE and Guru Nanak in 1469 CE. Mardana's original name was Dana. Mardana was the name conferred on him by Guru Nanak. The names of Dana's father and mother were Bhai Badrew and Bibi Lakho. According to Bhai Kahn Singh, Mardana breathed his last in 1534 CE and Guru Nanak himself performed his last rites.

Badrew and Mardana called every morning at the houses of local residents and obtained alms, generally in kind. Both would sing to the accompaniment of the *rabab*, and receiving alms, would move next door. According to Professor Satbir Singh:

> Nanak and Mardana first came into contact in 1480 CE at Talwandi, while, once lying under a tree, the sound of someone's playing on the *rabab* reached his (Guru Nanak's) ears. He rose, approached the man playing on the *rabab*, and asked his name. He answered, 'Sir, Mirassi (bard) people call me by the name Dana.'
>
> Hearing this, Baba appreciated his fine playing on the *rabab* and his excellent understanding of *raags*. Baba asked Mardana to accompany him to play the *rabab* and sing the *shabad* with him, so that he would get the better of both the worlds. To this Dana replied, 'We hardly make our both ends meet by singing *raags* before the rich. In case we follow you, our families would starve, we shall miss our prayer (*Namaz*) even, and thus,

> we might stand condemned in both the worlds. How do you plan to liberate me?' Guru Nanak said, 'O Dana! You are ignorant. God protects and feeds us all. *Namaz* (prayer) and *roza* (fast) are benedictions bestowed by God. God's abode is the heart of the saints. At the final judgement, none shall come to the rescue.' Guru Nanak further emphasised, 'Dana, in case you now turn to be *Mardana* (brave) and play *rabab* along with singing the Word of God (*Shabad*) you will gain in both the worlds.' Now Mardana set out with Guru Nanak to enlighten the people living in this world. Mardana played on the *rabab* and Guru Nanak sang the *shabad*. Often Mardana would accompany the Guru in singing the divine Word. Thus the *kirtan* originated among Sikhs.[1]

In the course of time, Nanak left Talwandi, and went to Sultanpur Lodhi, where he was employed in the service of Daulat Khan Lodhi, the governor of Jalandhar Doab. Nanak, after some time, sent for Bhai Mardana from Talwandi. He came in response to Guru Nanak's call, and began to reside at Sultanpur with him.

After the divine experience at Sultanpur, the Guru decided to awaken the people to the Reality by undertaking long and arduous journeys in the four directions. To begin with, he proceeded to the eastern part of the subcontinent, and also covered places in the south including Ceylon (Sri Lanka).

All the time, during these travels, Mardana was with Guru Nanak. *Janamsakhis* are replete with anecdotes portraying the wit and wisdom of Mardana. Barring a few episodes which are either concocted or associated purposely with the fair name of Bhai Mardana, possibly to emphasise that the Guru had the unique power of transforming brass into gold, all other stories touch the deepest chords of human heart as also the root problems of the world which hamper human progress. Hunger, thirst, family problems, poverty, insecurity, etc., were some of the things, which often tormented Mardana, as much as any other human being, but he did not allow himself to be given to them, and with sustained effort reached the stage of identification with the Guru. At the end of the first itinerary, when Mardana reached Talwandi, his wife and children tried to stop him from going again with Nanak, but he did not agree. Now he was awakened. So, he again accompanied Nanak on his journey to west Asia.

Nanak and Mardana sailed for Saudi Arabia along with other *hajis*. Having visited Mecca and Medina, they reached Baghdad, the capital of the caliph of Islam. As usual, they stayed outside the town near a graveyard. Nanak's visit to Baghdad is recorded in the *Vars* of Bhai Gurdas:

> Baba went to Baghdad, and put up outside the city. The Immortal personified Baba was accompanied by the *rabab*-player Mardana.[2]

On the roadside, Nanak began to sing hymns in praise of God, and Mardana played a symphonic strain on his *rabab*. Although people could not understand the language of the hymns, yet the melodious voice and the emotion with which the hymns were sung, produced a soothing effect on their minds.

Guru Nanak passed the last two decades of his life at Kartarpur. Mardana also came to settle at this place. His wife and two sons, Shahzada and Raizada also joined him. Daily he played *Rabab* while the Guru sang the celestial songs, sometime in solitude, sometime in congregations morning and evening, some at such times as the Guru or Mardana deemed appropriate. Guru Nanak loved Mardana and Mardana reverenced Guru Nanak. Mardana played in *Rabab* in such a fine way that its tunes and sound matched with the singing of the hymns by Guru Nanak. Its result was that Mardana imbibed the essence of *Shabad*, thereby enabling himself to feel oneness with *Shabad* or Guru or God. Now he felt elevated always enjoying bliss like a true mystic.

In 1534 CE, Mardana fell ill. He grew increasingly weak, and there was little hope of recovery. Visualising the approaching end of Mardana, Guru Nanak asked if his body after death might be let into water like Brahmans, or it might be cremated like Khatris, or it might be thrown to the winds like one of the

Parsis or it may be buried like that of a Muslim. Mardana answered:

> "Well, Baba! You are talking of the body. By the grace of your teachings, I have entirely forgotten about it. Now, I regard my soul as the sole guardian of my body."

Again Guru Nanak said:

> "Do you wish to be made famous by having a suitable tomb constructed in your memory?"

Mardana replied:

> "When my soul has been separated from its bodily tomb why shut it up in a stone sepulchre."

Baba stepped forward, took Mardana in his embrace and declared:

> "Mardana, you have realised the Infinite."

The following morning, a watch before day-break, Mardana passed away.

Mardana was a master *rabab* player. He improved the old form of the instrument by fixing four to six strings to a hollow base so as to produce a deep and mellow resonance.

Mardana composed verses also. Two sloks in the name of Mardana are included in the *Adi Granth* in *Bihagre ki Var*. In the first *slok*, Bhai Mardana calls the modern age a vessel filled with the wine of sexual desires.

> With egotism acting as the server, the mind uses anger as the cup, fills it with the wine of emotional attachment and drinks it. When one keeps the company of falsehood and greed, the result is total ruin.[3]

Mardana goes on to say that one should "make the distillery of one's good deeds using Truth as molasses and thus make the True Wine".[4]

In the second *slok*, Mardana compares the body with a vessel of conceit, and the wine with desires of all kinds, acting as our buddies in drinking. He calls the fabled messenger of death, the server of this wine. But he suggests that one should make spiritual wisdom the molasses, praise of *Waheguru* the bread, and Fear of God the meat.[5]

Bhai Gurdas

A brilliant scholar, a great poet, a devoted Sikh, a zealous missionary, an astute organiser and a great visionary, Bhai Gurdas was born in 1551 CE. He was son of Ishwar Das, who was the son of Chander Bhan, an uncle of Guru Amar Das. Thus, Bhai Gurdas was the nephew of Guru Amar Das. His mother's name was Jeoni. He was thus, the first cousin of Bibi Bhani, who was a daughter of Guru Amar Das, wife of Guru Ram Das and mother of Guru Arjan. His parents belonged to village Basarke, but later migrated to Goindwal, the headquarters of Guru Amar Das. Since his childhood Gurdas had fascination for Sikh *sangat*. His father died when he was three years old and his mother when he was twelve. According to Hari Ram Gupta:

> He possessed a sweet and melodious voice, and enthusiastically participated in singing hymns. He developed great love and affection for the Guru's teachings. He picked up Gurmukhi and learnt by heart *Gurbani*. He seldom missed any divine service.[6]

According to *Mahankosh*, Bhai Gurdas adopted Sikhism through the blessings of Guru Ram Das, the fourth Nanak, and did an in-depth study of *gurmat* (Sikh religion) under the guidance of Guru Arjan. Very soon he became proficient in the languages of contemporary use, particularly Punjabi, Sanskrit, Braj and Persian as well as the ideology of Sikhism, Islam and Hinduism, and science of music.

He remained in close association with the third, fourth, fifth and sixth Gurus from 1579 CE to 1637 CE for about fifty-eight years. Naturally, his stance and psyche bore the stamp of their teachings. His devotion to the Gurus knew no bounds.

When Guru Ram Das started building the city of Amritsar, he called Bhai Gurdas and asked him to look after the development of the new township, and to persuade people from the neighbourhood to settle there. On the ascending of

Guru Arjan to *gurgaddi*, Guru Ram Das' eldest son, Pirthi Chand, became hostile to his brother. He started collecting offerings from *sangat* in the name of the Guru, and would usurp these himself. Thus, the offerings reaching the Guru became a trickle. Bhai Gurdas, with the active help of Baba Budha, successfully countered the false propaganda of Pirthi Chand, and warned the Sikh *sangat* against his designs. The financial crisis was solved by asking the Guru to allow him to introduce the *daswandh* system among the Sikhs. *Daswandh* means one tenth of the income of a *gursikh*, for the treasury of the Guru. The *masands*, who would bring the money thus kept apart by the Sikhs to the Guru at regular in intervals.

Being an erudite scholar, he was chosen as the scribe when Guru Arjan decided to compile the *Adi Granth*. The Guru selected a site two kilometres to the east of the *sarovar* in a grove of *Beri* trees (*Ziziphus Jujuba*) on the bank of another *sarovar*, called Ramsar. For four hours every day the Guru would give dictation and Bhai Gurdas would continue writing without a pause. The *Granth* was written in the Gurmukhi script.[4] Bhai Gurdas' own writings, although not included in it, were described by the Guru as 'the key' to understanding of the philosophy propounded in *Gurbani*.

When Emperor Akbar was on a visit to Lahore, he stayed at Batala for some time. Pirthi Chand is believed to have complained to the Emperor that Guru Arjan in the *Adi Granth* had denounced both Hinduism and Islam. The Emperor ordered that the complaint be checked. The Guru sent the *Adi Granth* under the custody of Bhai Gurdas and Baba Budha to Batala. Akbar asked Bhai Gurdas to read at a certain place. Bhai Gurdas at once complied, but the Emperor found nothing offensive to Muslim susceptibilities. Then Akbar asked his clerk Munshi Sarb Dayal who could decipher Gurmukhi script to again read sacred Granth from some other page. Now it was read to be as under:

> Koi Bole Ram Ram, Koi Khodae (some call Him Ram Ram others Khodae)

The Emperor was pleased as the readings echoed his feelings. He made an offering of 51 gold mohars to *Adi Granth* and awarded robes of honour to its two bearers and a khilat for the Guru.

Bhai ji suffered from extreme mental agony when Guru Arjan was executed. He was present in the congress of the important Sikhs held at the instance of the Guru on the eve of his departure to Lahore in 1606 CE. He was amongst those who listened to the parting message of the Guru.

Bhai Gurdas played a vital role in bringing forth the essence of the doctrine of *miri-piri*, whereby the Guru was seen as the sovereign of both spirituality as well as temporality.

Bhai Gurdas will ever be remembered for his compositions, known as *vars*, in which he explained the main tenets of Sikhism apart from giving general information regarding men and matters of his times. He wrote 39 *vars*, and 675 *kabits* (in Braj). These compositions contain several references to persons and events which are of great importance to historians of today.

There are a number of passages in 39 *vars*, which deserve particular attention from a historian's point of view, viz.:

Var 1	:	*pauris* 17-48.
Var 11	:	gives the names of important Sikhs, who lived during the time of Guru Nanak to Guru Hargobind.
Var 21	:	*pauris* 13-31.
Var 24	:	*pauris* 1-25.
Var 3	:	*pauri* 12.
Var 20	:	*pauri* 1.
Var 38	:	*pauri* 20.

It is really surprising that Bhai Gurdas did not write anything about the compilation of the *Adi Granth* and the martyrdom of Guru Arjan. The reference to the martyrdom of the fifth Guru is indirect and vague. He writes:

> The Guru hath taken his abode in the river among the fish, as moths that see the flame fall upon it and merge their light with His Light, as deers hear the sound of a distant drum and run to it without a care of doom, as

> butterflies settle on the lotus and die in it during the night.
>
> The Guru's teachings we forget not, and like the monsoon birds, are ever calling, the good have peace, the nectar of love and the company of the gentle.
>
> Thus is my life a sacrifice to Guru Arjan."

Bhai Gurdas' compositions are a key to understanding of the Sikh doctrines, organisation, cosmology, metaphysics and theology. He dwelt on the disciple-preceptor relationship, and the spirit that the Gurus were. His compositions provide perspective, which enables the reader to grasp the true import of the theme. He saw the Gurus as benefactors, redeemers and prophets. He regarded *sangat* as a school for spiritualisation, soul culturalisation and socialisation of the individuals. Moreover, he spelt very methodically the process of regeneration of the degenerate man. He also explained in depth what is meant by Universal Brotherhood in Sikhism. Bhai Gurdas apart from being a great amanuensis and a far-sighted person possessed of high-class managerial skill was a great philosopher as well. His comments on Vedas, six schools of Indian philosophy are eloquent testimony to his superb analytical skill. In the process, he dwelt at length on the uniqueness, even of the superiority of Sikh religion. He presented the exposition of Sikhism so artfully that one has to admit that he was a veritable philosopher. According to Dr. Jodh Singh "In his varan though at places he comes forward as a devoted theologian having bubbling missionary zeal in his heart and mind, yet, his terse comments and his own postulates about Vedas and Shastras stand him apart as a philosopher. However, he is not a philosopher dealing in abstractions and making confused people more confused."

Bhai Gurdas chose to remain celibate throughout his life. He was, however, no advocate of the asceticism. On the contrary he rated a householder's life as highest among the *dharmas*. In the *Kabit* number 376, Bhai Gurdas expounds:

> Among the lakes the ocean is great, among the mountains Sumer is the highest, among the trees the sandal tree is

> the finest, golden swan among the birds and lion among the animals are great, among stones the philosopher's stone and among the musical measures, *Sri Raag* is the chief one...likewise, among all the *dharams*, performance of the duties of household life is the greatest.

Bhai Gurdas breathed his last in early 1632 CE, having lived a life as an ideal for the Sikhs of his time and the Sikhs to come after him.[7]

Bidhi Chand

Bidhi Chand was a great warrior as well as preacher of the time of Guru Hargobind. He belonged to village Sur Singh, 34 kilometres south of Amritsar. His father's name was Vassan and his grandfather's, Bhikki. His mother was from Sarhali, another village in the same district. In his youth, he fell into bad company and took to banditry. He was known for his daring and ruthlessness. One day, a pious Sikh, Bhai Adali of the village Chohla, led him to Guru Arjan. The Master's glimpse metamorphosed him, and he now confined his activities to punishing the evil-doers and the tyrannous officials of the government. For this reason, he was labelled as 'Robinhood of Majha' by Dr. Trilochan Singh in his scholarly treatise on Guru Tegh Bahadur. Soon he learned what Sikhism stood for in religious as well as temporal domains. For his dedication Guru Arjan loved him much and included him among the five Sikhs whom the Guru selected to accompany him to Lahore in 1606 CE.

He was a witness to how the fifth Guru was tortured to death and how serene and calm he remained up to the last. He also observed the donning of two swords, one symbolising *piri* (spirituality), and the other *miri* (secular authority) by Guru Hargobind, proclaiming that these domains were not exclusive to each other, but rather interconnected and complementary and essential for the integrated development of mankind. He also participated as a trainer in the military exercises and camps which the Guru organised to impart training to his Sikhs in martial arts. The Guru also chose him to be one of the commanders of the armed forces.

As a commander and a soldier, he displayed great feats of valour in the battles the Guru Hargobind had to fight against the Mughal imperialists.

When Tegh Bahadur, the youngest son of the sixth Nanak, crossed his childhood, he was put under the charge of Bidhi Chand for military training as well as to grasp the import of Sikh heroism. According to Dr. Trilochan Singh:

> Amongst the sage disciples of Guru Hargobind, Bidhi Chand along with Bhai Budha and Bhai Gurdas deeply influenced Tegh Bahadur.

Once, Emperor Shahjahan and Guru Hargobind were hunting in the same forest. Guru Hargobind's hunting party pursued a hawk, which apparently belonged to the Emperor. Guru's party cleverly captured it with the help of their own hawk. At this the leader of the Imperial party demanded the same for the Emperor. The Sikhs refused because according to the rules of the hunting the hawk belonged to the man who captured it. There was a clash between the two parties. The Imperial party was led by Faujdar Ghulam Rasul Khan while Bidhi Chand was the leader of the Sikh party. In the skirmish, the leader of the Imperial party was wounded and two of his men were killed.

Feeling insulted at the defeat of the Imperial party, the Lahore governor, probably at the nod of Shahjahan, sent a detachment of troops under Mukhlis Khan.

About this time, the Guru was to solemnise the marriage of his only daughter, Bibi Viro with Bhai Sadhu of Malla village. He immediately sent a messenger to the bridegroom's father that the marriage party should wait at village Jhabal. The onslaught of the Imperial army was met at Lohgarh, built around 1609 CE, where twenty-five brave Sikhs fought to the last man. They used wooden cannons and prevented the Mughal army from entering the city till the evacuation of women, children and other non-combatants was complete. Among the leading commanders of the army was Bhai Bidhi Chand, who fought with great valour. Bidhi Chand won great accolades from the Guru for his determination and excellent generalship.

The Mughal government was enraged at the victory of the Guru, who being aware of this fact decided to retire to the semi-desert wastelands of Bathinda to avoid immediate clash. About this time, the Guru had sent one of his devoted Sikhs to purchase horses in Central Asia. The Sikh, Bhai Sadh, went to Balkh, but found no suitable horses. From Balkh, he went to Baghdad, and purchased three horses of the finest breed. On his return journey, he was joined by Mohsin Fani at Kabul, where he was waiting for a caravan on its way to India.

At Lahore, Khalil Beg, governor of the Punjab, along with his son, visited the caravan in which the merchandise was opened for sale. They were fascinated at the sight of Bhai Sadh's horses. They asked for their price. Sadh told them that they were not for sale. The son of Khalil Beg forcibly took possession of two horses. Sadh tried to reason with them but to no avail. Exasperated, Sadh managed to ride the third horse to Guru Hargobind, who at that time was camping at village Rupa. Mohsin Fani records:

> Eventually, he brought three Iraqi horses. The brutal Khalil Beg saw them and carried them off. The horses did not prove lucky for him. Within a year, his son who was responsible for that act, died and the governor himself fell into disgrace and degradation.[8]

The seizure of the horses was taken very seriously by the Sikhs, who regarded this as a challenge to their ideology of sovereignty, which was very dear to them. It was against this background that Bidhi Chand undertook the responsibility to recover the horses at all costs. The task was no doubt difficult, but still more difficult was to compromise with the wanton high-handedness of the Mughal high-profile mandarins.

Bidhi Chand went to Lahore to achieve his mission of recovering the horses. He contacted one Bhai Jiwan, who was a Sikh by conviction and a carpenter by profession, and was equally interested in getting the horses back. Bhai Jiwan provided him a *Khurpa*, a hand tool with sharp-edged blade of iron fixed with a wooden handle, for grubbing up grass. With this in hand, Bidhi Chand posed as a grubber. Soon he gained access to Sondha Khan, the stable-keeper, and so managed things that he was appointed to supply grass to the steeds, which were special to the upper echelons of the Mughal bureaucracy. Bidhi Chand worked hard for some days during which he won the admiration of the officials and his equals alike. One night, finding the official watchman lying in slumber, he placed the saddle on one of the horses seized from Bhai Sadh, and struck it with a whip. The horse which had never previously been struck, on receiving a cut with a whip, roused himself at the unusual summons, gathered his strength, set his limbs, and on Bidhi Chand's command cleared without hesitation the high battlement and plunged with his rider into the river. Bidhi Chand, well skilled in horsemanship, steadied the animal in the water and guided him safely to the shore, and then to village Bhai Rupa, where the Guru was camping at that time. In the morning, when Sondha Khan came to know about the disappearance of one of the two favourite steeds of the Emperor, he felt much perturbed. The trackers were sent all-around, but no clue could be found.

Bhai Bidhi Chand was not fully satisfied. He resolved to recover the second horse also. He, therefore, went to Lahore and declared that he was an experienced tracker and astrologer and could trace anything that had been lost. Soon he attracted the attention of the stable-keeper who entreated him to locate where the horse was.

Bidhi Chand examined the place, visited the stable, and caressed the second horse, who responded with low neighing. Then he sat in meditation. After a while, he said he would ride the horse in the compound to see if it could jump up as high as the fort wall. Just at that very place he mounted the horse, jumped over the high battlements, and plunged with it into the river. He made haste for the Guru's camp and produced it before him. The Guru was highly pleased, and took Bidhi Chand in his embrace.

Emperor Shahjahan was enraged when the news of the horses missing from the royal stables reached him. At his nod, Mughal forces were ordered under the command of Qamar Beg and Lala Beg to confront the Guru. A tough battle was fought in 1634 CE (17th *Poh*, *Samat* 1691) between the Mughal forces and the Sikhs at Lehira Beg on Bathinda-Barnala road. The Mughal commanders were slain and the remnants of their army retreated to Lahore. Bidhi Chand was one of the three (the other two being Jati Mal and Raj Jodha) who were specially honoured by the Guru for their bravery and military skill.

In the battle of Kartarpur, which was fought between the Mughal forces under the command of Kale Khan, the brother of Mukhlis Khan, who had been killed in the battle of Amritsar by the Sikhs. Bidhi Chand's valour exacted praise from one and all. Kale Khan was killed in this battle. Painde Khan, originally a devotee of the Guru, joined the enemy camp and was put to the sword by the Guru.

Besides being a brave warrior, Bidhi Chand was well-versed in Sikh lore and tenets. From Kiratpur, the Guru sent him to eastern provinces of the Indian subcontinent to enlighten people about the Guru's creed. It speaks volumes of the all-round development of Sikh character that a warrior could be sent out as a missionary. At Deonagar in the Gangetic plains, he met Pir Budhan Shah's disciple, Pir Sundar Shah. A deep bond of spiritual affection was established between the two. At the death of Pir Budhan Shah, Sundar Shah came to Kiratpur to pay homage to his Master. Sundar Shah urged Bidhi Chand to once more visit his place. Bidhi Chand could not think of leaving the Guru, because he wished to serve him to the last, but he promised to come a month before his death. Sundar Shah was very happy and assured him that they would leave their earthly vesture together. In September 1638 CE, Bidhi Chand felt that his end was near. He sought the Guru's leave to go to his friend Sundar Shah at Deonagar.

Guru Hargobind praised the services of Bidhi Chand and called him one of the rarest gems amongst his disciples. Bidhi Chand received all the blessings from the Guru, and when he touched the feet of the Master, Guru Hargobind hugged him and praised him to the congregation.

Bidhi Chand went to Deonagar, and it is said that both he and his Muslim friend, Pir Sundar Shah, sat in meditation and departed from this earth on the same day, 14th August, 1640 CE. Sundar Shah's disciples buried their Master's body in accordance with Muslim rites and cremated Bidhi Chand's body in accordance with Sikh rites, and raised shrines in their honour. Some time later, his son, Lal Chand, brought from the site of his shrine at Deonagar some earth over which he build a memorial in his ancestral village, Sur Singh.

Bhai Mani Singh

Bhai Mani Singh was born on March 10, 1644 CE at Alipur in Muzaffargarh district (Pakistan). His father's name was Mai Das and Mother's Mudri Bai. Not much is known about his childhood except that his sensibilities were shaped by the environment which was essentially Sikh because of the deep faith of his parents and brothers in Sikhism. According to *Bhat Vahi Talauda*, Bhai Mani Singh's grandfather, Bhai Ballu, had died in 1634 CE in the battle of Amritsar between the Sikhs and Mughals. In 1654 CE, he got the chance to have first contact with Sikh movement when he was brought by his father to Guru Har Rai at Kiratpur. The Guru's hallowed personality instantly inspired in him deep admiration and devotion.

At the death of Guru Har Rai, Bhai Mani Singh decided to stay on at Kiratpur so serve Guru Harkrishan. According to the author of *Shaheed Bilas*, he was one of the privileged few who accompanied Guru Harkrishan to Delhi.

Bhai ji went to Bakala along with Mata Sulakhni, the mother of the eighth Nanak, to hand over the legacy of the predecessor Gurus to the ninth Nanak, Guru Tegh Bahadur. When Guru Tegh Bahadur was executed at Delhi in 1675 CE, Bhai ji was at Anandpur with Guru Gobind Singh.

Guru Gobind Singh assigned Bhai Ji such tasks as involved high degree of responsibility. At the age of thirty-five, Bhai ji emerged as a great scholar, possessing the requisite acumen to undertake the important job of preparing copies of *Adi Granth*.

Bhai Mani Singh accompanied Guru Gobind Singh to Nahan in 1687 CE.

Bhai ji had the privilege of accompanying Guru Gobind Singh when he went to Dehradun after the death of Baba Ram Rai to condole with Panjab Kaur, wife of Baba Ram Rai. In the battle of Bhangani in 1688 CE, Bhai Ji fought valorously.

In 1691 CE, Guru Gobind Singh appointed him as his *Diwan*, in which capacity he had to attend to multifarious duties.

All through his long life, Bhai Mani Singh regularly discoursed on the meaning of the hymns of the Gurus. It appears that his method of transmission of words of the Guru was so effective that in the course of time a school of Sikh thought, popularly known as Giani *Sampardai* (Giani School of Thought), emerged. In 1699 CE, on the occasion of creation of the Khalsa, Bhai Mani Singh also received *amrit*-initiation from the *Panj Piare*. Bhai ji's five sons were also initiated into the order of the Khalsa.

When in 1699 CE, Guru Gobind Singh sent out several batches of Sikhs to preach the Khalsa way, Bhai Mani Singh was commissioned to take charge of Harmandar Sahib. He reached Amritsar accompanied by Gulzar Singh, Bhupat Singh, Kair Singh Chandra, Dan Singh, and Kirat Singh whom the Guru had specially chosen. Bhai Ji abolished all anti-*gurmat* practices that had been introduced in Harmandar Sahib by the rival Sodhis to strengthen their own cause. He stopped circulation of the literature that had been specially prepared by these pretenders to propagate a creed wherein Pirthi Chand, Meharban and Harji were accorded the status of guru.

Mani Singh used to come to Anandpur off and on along with the *sangat* for guidance and instructions by the tenth Nanak himself. On the eve of the first battle of Anandpur (1st September, 1700 CE), Mani Singh was with the Guru and took part in the battle. His sons Bachittar Singh and Udey Singh also fought in this battle. Vir Singh Bal says that the Guru called Bhai ji, gave him a sword, shield and arrows and sent him to the battlefield.[9] In this battle, Bhai ji, as also his three sons, showed remarkable valour.

Bhai Mani Singh's sons also participated in the battle at Nirmohgarh when the hill chiefs Bhim Chand and Wazir Chand attacked the Guru. The Guru was pleased at their bravery and valour and honoured them by awarding a *Hukamnama*.[10]

At the time of evacuation of Anandpur by Guru Gobind Singh in December 1704 CE, Mani Singh followed the Guru. When on the bank of the river Sarsa, the Khalsa was suddenly attacked at night by Mughal forces and all were scattered in different directions. The Guru's mother and his two youngest sons went in one direction. The Guru's wives, Mata Sundar Kaur and Mata Sahib Kaur, followed in the company of Bhai Mani Singh who managed to escort them to safety in Delhi in the guise of peasant women.

When he got wind of the Guru's station at Talwandi Sabo, now called Damdama Sahib, he along with the Guru's wives reached there and contributed his best to the process of the re-organisation of the Khalsa as also to making copies of the *Adi Granth* at the instance of the Guru himself.

Having spent a year and a half at Damdama, the Guru decided to leave for the Deccan to have a meeting with Aurangzeb. Bhai Mani Singh was one of the Sikhs who accompanied the Guru on this journey.

At Baghaur the Guru learnt that the Emperor was no more. He changed his programme and turned towards Delhi. He joined the new Emperor, Bahadur Shah, at Agra in July 1707 CE. Mata Sundar Kaur remained in Delhi, while Mata Sahib Kaur accompanied him. Bhai Mani Singh remained in attendance upon the Guru.

Guru Gobind Singh passed away at Nanded on October 17, 1708 CE. Bhai Mani Singh was present there. He escorted Mata Sahib Kaur to Delhi where both the Guru's wives lived for the rest of their lives.

Shortly afterwards, Bhai ji returned to Amritsar with the specific purpose of further strengthening the organisational mechanism which the Guru had put in place to continue the mission of Guru Nanak. On the Vaisakhi day in 1709 CE,

Bhai ji convened a huge gathering of Sikhs by issuing letters far and wide to apprise them of the latest developments.

After the execution of Banda Singh, Sikhs became divided on the issue of control over Harmandar Sahib in Amritsar. The situation was explosive and could lead to open hostilities between the two groups. Bhai Mani Singh was then in-charge of Harmandar Sahib. He was respected by all. He handled the situation tactfully, so that the control remained with the mainstream Sikhs or the *Tat* Khalsa. It was Bhai Mani Singh's personality and farsightedness that a major clash in the *Panth* was averted.

The Mughal Government of Lahore had issued strict instructions forbidding Sikhs from visiting Amritsar and bathe in the *sarovar*. On all sides of the city, strong contingents were posted to arrest Sikhs approaching Harmandar Sahib.

In October 1734 CE, just before *Diwali*, Bhai Mani Singh applied to the Governor for permission to Sikhs to hold a fair at Amritsar on Bandi Chhor day for a tribute of five thousand rupees. Permission was granted, but the real object of the Government was to destroy the Sikhs *en masse*. Bhai Mani Singh had sent messages all over the Punjab inviting Sikhs to collect at Harmandar Sahib. When, however, he sensed the nefarious designs of the Government, he cancelled the meet and asked the Sikhs not to come to Amritsar on the Bandi Chhor day.

No fair was thus held and no offerings came. So, Bhai Mani Singh who had planned to pay five thousand rupees out of the offerings could not do so, nor had he any other source of income to make payment. The Government demanded the stipulated fee. Mani Singh blamed the Government for not allowing the Sikhs to assemble. The Government arrested him in 1734 CE and took him to Lahore. The Qazi pronounced the judgement that he was to be cut to pieces limb by limb. On the site of his martyrdom in Lahore stood Gurdwara Shaheed Ganj until the partition of Punjab in 1947 CE.

Bhai Mani Singh's achievements in the literary sphere are numerous. To him are attributed two works in prose—*Gian*

Ratnavali, an account in traditional style of the life of Guru Nanak, and *Bhagat Mala*, an illustrative commentary in anecdotal style on Bhai Gurdas' *Var* XI. The author of *Gurbilas Patsahi Chhevin* also claims that his work is based upon discourses given by Bhai Mani Singh.

Koir Singh, the author of *Gurbilas Patsahi Dasvin*, also acknowledges his huge debt of gratitude to Bhai Mani Singh for vital information on the life of the tenth Guru, which he gathered from his friend who was on security duty in the Lahore jail where Bhai ji had been clamped.

Bhai Nand Lal

Bhai Nand Lal was one of those blessed Sikhs who had the good fortune of receiving the patronage and guidance of Guru Gobind Singh. He was born in 1633 CE at Agra. His father was Diwan Chhajju Ram who, because of his erudite scholarship in Persian and Arabic, was much liked by Dara Shikoh. When Dara was sent to Qandhar to subjugate it, he took Chhajju Ram along with him, appointing him his Chief Secretary (Mir Munshi). Dara Shikoh returned to Agra but Chhajju Ram chose to remain at Ghazni working as Mir Munshi of the Governor of Ghazni.

Bhai Nand Lal's father made all possible arrangements to ensure good education for the boy. Chhajju Ram himself spared time to give lessons to his son. Shortly, Nand Lal acquired efficiency in Persian and Arabic and could compose verses in Persian at the age of twelve.

Diwan Chhajju Ram was a staunch *Vaishnavite*. Nand Lal was nourished on the religious views of his father. There was another element that entered into his psyche. During those days, the Sikhs all over the subcontinent and Afghanistan had established their *sangats* where they used to pray and discuss spiritual as well as social views of the Gurus. Bhai Nand Lal came into contact with these *sangats* and could not resist the impact of Sikhism.

When Bhai ji was sixteen years of age, his mother died. Three years after, his father also breathed his last. Bhai Nand Lal, as per custom, expected the post of his father to be given to him. He even tried for it but the Governor of Ghazni was not willing to oblige him and instead offered him the petty post of a clerk. Bhai ji declined the offer because he did not consider this post commensurate with his ability and the status of his family.

Thus finding himself helpless, Nand Lal decided to leave Ghazni. He sold the property which he had inherited and reached Multan along with his two brothers and two loyal Pathan caretakers. He selected Multan for his residence. This was the right choice since Multan was a great centre of trade and possessed great political importance. He built a house there outside Delhi Gate.

Shortly after his arrival at Multan, the fame of the scholarship of Nand Lal began to spread. Nawab Wassaf Khan, much impressed by Bhai ji's integrity and learning, appointed him to the post of *munshi* in which capacity he worked with distinction and won approbation from all quarters.

After this, he was put in charge of the fort at Bhakkar. He collected the arrears of revenue from the *zamindars* of the area and remitted the same to the Multan treasury. Soon after, he was made *Nazim* of Dina, Kehror, Fatehpur and Pargana Mahayyuddin Pur. He acquitted himself with distinction even at this post. The next post which he held was that of *Naib Subedar* (Deputy Governor) of Multan. About the period of his deputy governorship, no reliable source throws any light on his performance or achievements in that capacity.

According to *Dastur-ul-Insha*, the book written by Bhai ji himself, he, as *Nazim*, made his mark as a military general also. He led a punitive expedition against a notorious dacoit, Sahu, who had a seven hundred member group to support him in his nefarious activities. Sahu was arrested and nearly half of his followers were slain.

According to Dr. Ganda Singh, Bhai ji served the state in different capacities for about thirty years. He also got the chance of serving Prince Salim and Prince Mohammed Akbar (1678-79 CE).

During the regime of Aurangzeb, Bhai ji was turned out of Government service. The exact reasons for his dismissal are not known, but the conjecture is that he had to quit because of his father's good relations with Dara Shikoh, the fact which was uncondonable for Aurangzeb.

All the same, subsequent period of his life was fruitful to him in another way. He discovered himself. He came into contact with Guru Gobind Singh who wrought a transformation of his psyche. Bhai Nand Lal saw new height and new horizons. His poetry found new stimuli, and symbolised new ideas. The fulcrum of his activities became Guru Gobind Singh, the never-failing protector of the oppressed humanity.

He went to Anandpur, the seat of Guru Gobind Singh, leaving his family at Multan. He saw for himself the Guru's multifarious activities, operating with finesse to bring about new awakening among the people and endeavouring to shape new values to fit in the general framework of the society of his ideas. His intellect quickened, his sensibility sharpened, his self responded to his generous gestures and he became beau ideal of a Sikh, embodying the Sikh ethos in its totality.

Admiring the Guru's cause, Bhai ji decided to stay at the court of the Guru.

In 1695 CE, Bhai ji went to Agra where he got the post of *Mir Munshi* of Prince Muazzam, who had, just after his release from the prison, assumed the charge of *subedar* of the province of Agra. However, Bhai ji was not destined to work at this post for long.

It is said that once Aurangzeb asked the interpretation of a certain excerpt from *Al-Quran*. Various interpretations were presented to the Emperor, but the version forwarded by Prince Muazzam was considered to be the most appropriate by Aurangzeb. On further probe, he came to know that it was Bhai Nand Lal who had interpreted it. Aurangzeb felt upset because he did not like a *kafir's* mastery (*kafir* literally means blasphemous and orthodox Muslims recognised non Muslims as kafirs) over the sacred text. He suggested that such a man of learning should be converted to Islam. In a public Darbar, Nand Lal was awarded a robe of honour and a cash prize of Rs. 500.

When Aurangzeb's ulterior motive came to Bhai Nand Lal's knowledge, he felt perturbed. There were only two courses left for him. He could either embrace Islam or leave his present position. The former option was rejected by him forthwith because he had, to all intents and purposes, entered the Sikh fold. The second course seemed more practical to him. He at once packed up, begged leave of the Prince and reached Lahore. Here he met his pupil, Ghias-ud-din, the *Darogha* of Agra who had come on leave to this place. Both of them reached Anandpur. Ghias-ud-din returned to Lahore after some time, but Bhai Nand Lal prolonged his stay at Anandpur till 1705 CE.

During this period Bhai Nand Lal drank deep in the fountain of Sikh spiritual thought as enshrined in *Adi Granth*. He listened to the enlightening discourses of the Guru. He keenly observed the Sikh way of life and understood the ultimate goal of the Sikh movement. The inauguration of the Order of the Khalsa was also noted by him.

All those things and the splendid personality of Guru Gobind Singh constituted an environment wherein Nand Lal's poetic genius quickened and flowered. Bhai ji produced books of Persian poetry. The first book of poetry which he presented to the Guru bore the title '*Bandgi Nama*' which was changed to '*Zindgi Nama*' by Guru Gobind Singh. The Guru wrote the following verse at the end of the book:

> Ab-e-hai-van pur shud, chun jam-e-o
> *Zindgi Namah shud, Bandgi Namah-e-o*
> (When his goblet was filled with the water of life,
> His *Bandgi Namah* became *Zindgi Namah*.)

When the Mughal forces in combination with the hill forces attacked the Khalsa on the bank of the river Sarsa, Bhai ji, as also many other Sikhs, got separated from Guru Gobind Singh.

How he passed the year of 1706, no one knows but this much is certain that in 1707 CE after the death of Aurangzeb,

Bhai ji went to Prince Muazzam who by this time had occupied the Mughal throne at Agra and had assumed the title Bahadur Shah.

Even after occupying the throne, Bahadur Shah was not feeling comfortable because Prince Azam was threatening to overthrow him and was advancing at the head of a force from the Deccan to Delhi. At this critical juncture, Bhai Nand Lal approached Guru Gobind Singh for active assistance for Bahadur Shah. Guru Gobind Singh acceded to the request and sent three hundred Sikhs to fight on the side of Bahadur Shah whose right to the throne was considered legitimate. Some scholars are puzzled at this gesture of the Guru, for they cannot find any rationale for Guru's sympathy towards Bahadur Shah whose father was responsible for the death of Guru Teg Bahadur and so much hardship the Guru himself. But if they keep in view the mission of the Guru and then try to appraise the policy of the Guru *vis-à-vis* Bahadur Shah, they would see no contradiction whatsoever. The Guru's mission was to uphold righteousness and to see that crookedness did not flourish. Since Bahadur Shah was not a bigot in his religious policy and was right in his stand, the Guru helped him.

Shortly after, Bahadur Shah had to attend to the revolt of the Kachhwaha Rajputs of Rajputana. When he had just started operations against the Rajputs, he got the news of the open revolt of his brother Kambakhsh. He at once marched to square up with him.

All the time, Bhai Nand Lal was with Bahadur Shah. Dhadhi Nath Mal writes:

> Nand Lal was one of the councillors of the Emperor. He had the privilege of being a very close associate of the very fortunate Emperor.[11]

Bhai ji must have tried his best to influence the emperor *vis-à-vis* Sikh principles. The Emperor's intransigence must have caused disappointment to him. However, he continued to serve the Emperor up to the latter's death at Lahore. In 1710 CE when the Emperor was given the news of Banda's anti-Mughal campaigns in the Punjab, he lost no time in marching towards Punjab. Bhai ji was in the Emperor's camp and reached Lahore along with the Emperor. Bahadur Shah expired in 1712 CE and Bhai ji forthwith left for Multan.

After this, Bhai ji lived only for a year, but this period of his life by no means lacked activity. He established a school in which he himself imparted higher education in Persian and Arabic. This school continued to serve the people even after his death, and when in 1849 CE Multan came under the occupation of the British, the school was being run by his descendants. Bhai ji expired in 1713 CE.

Bhai Nand Lal wrote ten volumes. As is clear from the diction and thought of these books, it is not difficult to surmise that he wrote under the deep impact of Guru Gobind Singh and the Sikh philosophy. He composed verses under the pen-name of 'Goya' and 'Lal'. Listed below are some of his writings:[12]

Zindgi Nama

As explained earlier, this was the first compilation of Bhai ji. The subject of this book is love for God and devotion for the Guru. For thoughts and perspective, Bhai ji copiously refers to the hymns of the Guru. It contains 719 verses.

Ghazaliat

This volume is a good attempt to interpret the Guru's compositions. From the point of view of style, thought and diction, this composition is superb.

Tosifo-Sana and Khatima

Except *Khatima*, which is in poetry, the whole composition is in Persian prose. Its style is marked for its difficult diction. It contains no historical information, and is purely literary in content.

Ganj Nama

This composition is in prose as well as in poetry. In it one comes across the devotion for the Gurus with which the author seems to be saturated. It is a panegyrical discourse on all the ten Gurus individually.

Jot Bigas (Persian)

This composition explains at full length the doctrine of Unity in the plurality of the Gurus. The first Guru had categorically rejected the doctrine of incarnation, *i.e.*, the appearance of God on earth in human form, but had studiously advocated by practical illustration the doctrine of blending his spirit with the next and so on. It is in this volume that we find Bhai Nand Lal using epithets such as *Badshah Darvesh*—king saint, *Puran Manukh*—perfect man, etc., for Guru Gobind Singh. This book is a great aid to scholars engaged in the study of the personality of Guru Gobind Singh.

Jot Bigas (Punjabi)

This book is not a translation of the former book, although its subject matter and title are the same.

Rahit Nama and Tankhahnama

According to Sardar Attar Singh of Bhadaur, both these compositions are the creations of Bhai ji, although Bhai Kahn Singh does not agree. *Rahitnama* articulates the code of discipline to be followed by the Sikhs. This book was written on December 4-5, 1695, and hence referred to the code which was required to be observed before the creation of the Khalsa. *Tankhahnama* was written after the creation of the Khalsa and it lists some of the do's and don't's which the Khalsa should observe in their day-to-day life.

Dastur-Ul-Insha (Persian Prose)

The book provides valuable information on social, economic and political condition contemporaneous to Guru Gobind Singh. It is a collection of letters in Persian prose to Nand Lal's relatives and friends.

Arzul-Alfaz (Persian Poetry)

It provides abundant information regarding the spiritual currents which Sikhism had caused. In it, Bhai ji is profuse in his praise of God and the Gurus. The Persian and Arabic words which Bhai ji had used manifest profusely of Bhai ji's overflowing devotion for the Guru and his own scholarship.

MAI BHAG KAUR

Guru Arjan Dev was a vigorous preacher, besides being a great organiser and a creative genius. It was because of his proselytising campaigns that most of the Majha people shed their old beliefs and embraced Sikhism. One of them was Langah, son of Abul Khair who was a staunch devotee of Sakhi Sarvar. As chance would have it, his friends happened to be Sikhs under whose influence he visited Amritsar and saw Guru Arjan Dev for himself. The illuminating personality of the Guru wrought transformation of his mind and he entered the fold of Sikhism. By degrees, through his devotion and selfless service, he rose in the estimation of the Guru who began to involve him in the tasks of far-reaching importance for the nascent Sikh community. His brother Pero Shah and his nephew Malo Shah also grew to be devout Sikhs. Malo Shah was much loved by Guru Hargobind.

Mai Bhag Kaur was Malo Shah's daughter and was born at Jhabbal (Distt. Amritsar). She was brought up in an atmosphere which was suffused with Sikh ethos and culture. Admittedly, Bhag Kaur was imbued with Sikh ideals and her psyche shaped accordingly. She got the chance to have a glimpse of Guru Tegh Bahadur when she was taken to Anandpur by her parents. Again she was lucky enough to be present along with other members of her family on the occasion of 1699 CE when the Khalsa was created at Anandpur. Her family members were among those who received initiation of the double-edged sword. She was married to Nidhan Singh of Patti.

Immediately after the inauguration of the Order of the Khalsa, people on large scale were administered *Khande-ki-Pahul.* Bhag Kaur also was among them.

In 1701 CE, fighting ensued between the Guru on one side and the hill chiefs and the Mughal Government on the other. The hostilities continued up to 1705 CE.

When the news of the excesses of the hill chiefs and the Mughal subedar of Sirhind reached the Sikhs of Amritsar, they were enraged. The grandsons of Duni Chand, Sardar Anup

Singh and Sardar Sarup Singh got ready to participate in the war on behalf of the Guru. Mai Bhag Kaur's brothers too rushed to Anandpur to render the much needed assistance to the Guru. Many more people did the same. Though the enemy had taken precautions to stop the Sikhs from reaching Anandpur, yet they managed to reach somehow at great personal risk. Bhag Kaur was a witness to all this.

In 1705 CE, the final battle of Anandpur took place. The Sikhs fought gallantly. The siege lasted for more than seven months. The strategy of the enemy during the siege was to force the Sikhs to surrender by completely barring their access to food and water. The effects of the strategy began to be felt as the days passed and supplies started dwindling.

The situation deteriorated to the extent that the Sikhs did not have anything to live upon. When the enemy learnt of the distress of the Sikhs, they planned a different strategy to take advantage of the situation. They sent a message to the Guru suggesting that if he decided to abandon Anandpur, he would be allowed a safe passage. The Guru sensed a trap and did not accept the suggestion. At this some Sikhs persisted that the offer of the enemy should be accepted. When the Guru did not listen to them, some of them disclaimed the Guru and left for their homes.

The Guru, ultimately, had to evacuate Anandpur on 5-6 December, 1705 CE. The moment the enemy got an inkling of the departure of the Sikhs, they forgot all about their pledges and set out in hot pursuit. The Guru suffered a lot, but wended his way to Chamkaur where he gave battle to the enemy. In this battle the Guru had only forty odd soldiers while the enemy commanded a force running into *lakhs* (according to *Zafarnama*). All the Guru's soldiers, except three suffered martyrdom. Most prominent among the Sikh martyrs were *Sahibzadas* Ajit Singh and Jujhar Singh and three of the *Panj Piaras* (Beloved ones).

After this, the Guru had to move from place to place for regrouping the Khalsa. While at Dina, the Guru received definite information about the determination of the Sirhind authorities to send another body of troops against him. This news also reached the Majha area of the Punjab. The self-respecting Khalsa was cut to the quick. Bhag Kaur told her husband that time had come to prove their commitment to the cause of the Guru. Her husband assured her of his steadfastness and readiness to make any sacrifice in this connection.

Bhag Kaur, greatly heartened at her husband's gesture, drew her sword out of the scabbard, alighted a horse and called upon all those who had love for the Guru's cause to come forward and march to the Malwa region of the Punjab to forestall the nefarious designs of Wazir Khan. Her exhortations were specially directed at those forty persons who had come back to their homes by signing a disclaimer (*bedawa*).

Bhag Kaur's call had a magical effect. She led a band of Sikhs to the *Khidrana ki Dhab* where the Guru had planned to give a fight to the Mughal forces. On the way, she was joined by a large number of Sikhs. Some leading men from Lahore who had thought they had some influence in the Mughal *Durbar* also joined them.

The party met the Master between Ramiana and Khidrana. The deserters begged the Guru's pardon. The leading men from Lahore advised him to give up fighting and make peace with the Emperor. They offered to act as negotiators. The Guru spurned their advice saying that it was not possible for him to make peace with tyrants. They acquiesced in quietude, and returned to their homes. The Guru continued his advance to his destination.

The rest of the party headed by Bhag Kaur and Mahan Singh of village Sur Singh Wala followed Guru Gobind Singh.

On reaching Khidrana, they found the tank dry. The Master had for that reason moved on from the place. Bhai Mahan Singh proposed to engage the enemy there and to allow time to the Guru to reach a place of safety. Big white sheets of *khaddar* (hand-woven coarse cotton cloth) were spread on the shrubs so that the enemy might think that the Sikhs were encamping there in large numbers. Soon the Mughal army arrived.

The Sikhs under Mai Bhag Kaur and Bhai Mahan Singh bore the brunt of the enemy's attack. All the Sikh soldiers fought with unparalleled courage and strength. The Mughal soldiers did their best to overpower the Sikhs and advance towards the Guru who from a place of elevation was aiming arrows on the generals of the enemy forces. Mai Bhag Kaur's leadership was not only heartening to the soldiers but also manifestative of the resurgence of women, which had taken place under the Sikh Gurus and their ideology.

The Sikhs, having exhausted their ammunition and quivers of arrows, were obliged to have recourse to their spears and swords. Small bands advanced, engaged the enemy in hand to hand fights, killed several times their number, until many of them were killed or seriously injured and were incapacitated to carry on the fight. They did not win the battle nor were they fighting for it. Their aim was the vindication of their faith in the Guru's cause and to win over the pleasure of the Guru. All the same, they did succeed in constraining the Mughal forces to retrace their steps to their headquarters at Sirhind.

After the enemy had been repulsed, the Guru came down to the field of battle, and with fatherly affection went about looking for the injured. When he came to Bhai Mahan Singh, the Master found that there was still some life in him. After a while, Bhai Mahan Singh opened his eyes, and seeing the Guru was filled with supreme joy. The Guru asked him if he had any desire to be fulfilled. Bhai Mahan Singh said, "No, true father. I have seen thee. What more could I desire? But if thou has taken compassion on us here, then kindly tear off our disclaimer." The Guru at once acceded to his request and remarked, "You have saved the root of Sikhism in the Majha. You and your companions, all forty of you are *Muktas*, the saved ones, delivered from the bonds of birth and death for ever." Then the Guru went to the place where Bhag Kaur was lying unconscious. She had not been severely wounded but had fallen down out of utter exhaustion. With a little medical aid she regained consciousness.

The Guru was greatly pleased with Mai Bhag Kaur for what she had done. He got her removed from the battlefield and arranged for her treatment. Soon she recovered completely.

After her recovery, Bhag Kaur chose to join the entourage of the Guru.

Bhag Kaur combined in herself virtues both of a saint and a warrior. She was strong in character, firm in faith and unflinching in her determination. In view of these qualities, the Guru allowed her inclusion in the guard of ten Sikhs, meant to remain close to the Guru. She used to dress in male attire and remained with the Guru at Talwandi Sabo. She was also in the camp of the Guru when he marched along with Bahadur Shah first to Rajasthan and then to the Deccan. She observed for herself the parleys that took place between the Guru and Bahadur Shah and how Banda was converted to Sikhism.

After the death of Guru Gobind Singh at Nanded in 1708 CE, Bhag Kaur retired further south. She settled down at Jinwara, eleven kilometres from Bidar in Karnataka, where immersed in meditation she continued to stay for the rest of her life. Her hut in Jinwara has now been converted into Gurdwara Tap Asthan Mai Bhago. At Nanded, too, a hall within the compound of Takht Sachkhand Sri Hazur Sahib marking the site of her residence is known as Bunga Mai Bhago. As long as she lived, she served the cause of the Guru. Her example was that of a person embodying all the virtues of a good Sikh as also those of an ideal Sikh woman alive to her duties as much as to her rights, believing in perfect gender equality and discarding the common view that woman was primarily an appendage of man. Her performance, both in the battlefield and the sphere of preaching speaks volumes about the regenerating process that Sikhism, since its inception, had set in motion. Her achievements were enduring, her character and conduct flawless, her leadership stimulating, her faith unflinching and her demeanour striking. No wonder, she has been a perennial source of inspiration to the Sikhs to keep their head high and dignity aloft.

Bhai Jaita

The Sikh religion up to the time of Guru Gobind Singh had caught the imagination of the masses. The downtrodden section of the people, which is always the biggest one in the feudal social structure, was especially attracted towards it because of its emphasis on ameliorating their condition both at social and economic planes. It can be safely surmised that the people whom the Guru met or about whom he spoke were mostly the poor, the downtrodden and the so-called low caste people. The Guru's focus on the uplift and empowerment of these people made them his staunchest supporters.

When the Guru made the declaration, "The Rangretta (tanner) is the son of the Guru", he was not only reaffirming what his predecessors had preached but also stressing that Jaita and all the downtrodden are Guru's sons and daughters. This singular act was a sign beckoning the emergence of a new society repudiating distinctions on grounds of caste, birth, wealth etc. and basing itself on a new-value pattern.

Sada Nand, son of Ram Jas and grandson of Sukh Bhan, came to Delhi along with his father from Mathura which was his original habitat. Sukh Bhan was a musician of renown and being a disciple of a famous musician of the court of Akbar, Hardas, was much respected. In 1680, when Akbar started the Order of Din-e-Illahi, he joined it. After the death of Akbar, he had to leave Delhi because of the strong dislike of the orthodox Muslims. Hindus looked upon him as an apostate and their being no provision in Hindu religion for re-admitting the one who leaves it, he could not rejoin the Hindu society. Understandably, to save himself from the taunts of his erstwhile brethren, he moved to Kathu Nangal wherefrom the family shifted first to Gago Mohal and then to Ram Das Pur (all these villages are in the Punjab).

Sada Nand's elder brother Saju did not move to Punjab, and remained at Rai Saina in Delhi at or near the place where now Rakab Ganj Gurdwara is situated. Sada Nand used to pay occasional visits to his brother.

Sada Nand became a great musician like his father and grandfather. As his fame increased, Lajwanti, daughter of Shiv Narain and herself a great musician, expressed her attraction towards him. Soon Sada Nand was captivated. To begin with Pandit Shiv Narain expressed willingness but then declined to marry his daughter to him, even being aware of the love between Sada Nand and his daughter. So stubborn he became in his stand that he along with his family left for his ancestral abode, Aligarh (at that time called Koil).

Sada Nand became disconsolate. He visited Kiratpur in search of peace of mind.

He attended Sikh congregation and listened to the Guru's *Shabads* (hymṇs) being sung melodiously.

Recently, an entry discovered in *Bhatt Vahi Multani Sindhi* records that Bhai Jaita's father's name was Agya Ram, who was the resident of Mohalla Dilwali Sikhan, Delhi. In view of this evidence, conclusion may be drawn that Bhai Jaita belonged to Delhi and his father was not Sada but some other man, but a little probe into matter will bring into relief the reality. Bhai Agya, after the death of his wife, began to live a life of resignation, becoming self-absorbed and disinterested in the world around. People often unable to penetrate into the real self of the man began to call him 'Sada', a simpleton.

The musician in him urged him to take part in the *Kirtan*. Soon he became a musician of Guru Darbar. Sada Nand found solace and his depression vanished. Now he was in the House of Nanak, where there was freedom from temptations, uncalled-for restrictions and fear. Baba Tegh Bahadur contacted Shiv Narain and successfully prevailed upon him to marry his daughter to Sada Nand. The marriage was solemnised in March 1656 at Koil[13] and the couple returned to Kiratpur wherefrom marriage party had gone. Pandit Shiv Narain also came to settle at Kiratpur to save himself from the jibe of his caste people.

Sada Nand was much loved by Baba Tegh Bahadur, who included him in his entourage which he took along with him on his preaching tours in the eastern part of India. *En route*, the Guru stayed for some time at Banaras where a son was born to Sada Nand and his wife Lajwanti, renamed as Premo by Mata Nanaki and Mata Gujri. The child was named Jaita.

According to Naranjan Arfi, the date of birth of Jaita was 5th *Sawan*, 1714 Bk.[14] Two months after, on the occasion of *Diwali*, Baba Tegh Bahadur and his whole entourage came back to Kiratpur. Sada Nand and his wife made obeisance to Guru Har Rai and sought his blessings for their son. Guru Har Rai is said to have uttered that Jaita would be a great person, always eager to do good to others, even at the risk of his own life.

Sada Nand's whole life was a saga of his unselfish service to the Guru's cause. He came to Bakala and stayed there singing *Gurbani* and doing sundry jobs for Guru Tegh Bahadur. In 1661 CE, he worked as a preacher at Benaras. This duty was assigned to him by Guru Har Rai. Even after the assumption of guruship by Tegh Bahadur, Sada Nand remained with him, serving in various capacities.

According to Dr Fauja Singh, in the *hukamnamas* that Guru Tegh Bahadur addressed to the Sikhs of Patna, Dacca and Mughair, the name of Sada Nand was conspicuous.[15] From this it may be inferred that Sada Nand stayed in Patna and other places nearabout doing preaching and organisational work and was considered an eminent Sikh of the Guru.

Jaita, therefore, was lucky enough to pass the early years of his childhood at Banaras, Bakala, Chak Nanaki and Patna. Jaita could not escape the osmotic effect of the environment. He became acquainted not only with Sikh religion but also with other religious dispensations, such as Islam, Buddhism, Jainism, Brahmanism and cults of different persuasions. His fondness for knowledge being very intense, he soon acquired proficiency in explication of the Guru's compositions. By the age of twelve, Jaita had become a renowned man of letters.

At Patna he received training in weaponry of different kinds and learnt the art of warfare besides horse-riding, swimming, music and *Kirtan*.[16] He became famous for his boldness, strategic skill, organising capacity and handling of weapons—especially guns. Ratan Bhagwan Singh says, "Jiwan Singh Rangretta was a known *Bandookchi* (gunner)." Bhai Santokh Singh, the author of *Suraj Parkash Granth* records, "When Bhai Jiwan Singh (the name which Jaita was given after receiving *Pahul*) fired his gun, none could escape his aim. The enemy, therefore, often thought it appropriate not to come in the range of his gun." According to the author of *Gur Katha*, "Jaita and his brother Sangat enjoyed the company of child Gobind Rai and were treated as they were of the Guru's family."[17] Mata Gujri, Mata Nanaki, Bhai Kirpal and Bhai Dyala—all showered affection on him.

In 1671 CE, Guru Tegh Bahadur started his journey back to Nanaki Chak after undertaking tours to different places in the east of India. Sada Nand and his sons, Jaita and Sangat, were with him. *En route* when they reached Delhi, it seems that Sada Nand decided to settle along with his family at Mohalla Dilwali. Bhai Jaita took to preaching the Guru's teachings like his father and soon shot into prominence among the Sikhs. It was at this time that he developed close acquaintance with Lakhi Shah and his family.

Bhai Jaita used to come to Anandpur off and on to keep himself abreast of the latest instructions of the Guru and when Guru Tegh Bahadur was arrested and taken to Delhi, Bhai Jaita came to Anandpur to pay his homage to Guru Gobind Singh and also to apprise him of the situation and the mind-set of the Mughal government. Whether Guru Gobind Singh gave him certain instructions or not, one thing is clear that he went back to Delhi, fully inspired and determined to do his best to serve the cause of the Guru.

The fateful day came on November 11, 1675, and executioner's sword decapitated the Guru. The body and the head lay in front of Kotwali in the Chandni Chowk, which used to be the most crowded place in the city. The plan of the Government was to cut the body into four pieces and to quarter them on all sides of Delhi. Bhai Jaita could not withstand all this. Bhai Nanu, another Sikh, also of Dilwali Gate, felt just like Jaita. Both of them met each other. Bhai Sada Nand also took part in the deliberations. According to *Bansavalinama* and *Bhat Vahis*, Bhai Nanu picked up the head, went home and asked Bhai Jaita to take it to the Guru. Jaita wrapped the head in a piece of cloth, put the same in a basket and covered it with flowers. He, regardless of the danger of the Mughal pursuers and caring little for physical inconvenience, ran towards Anandpur. He was accompanied by his father and Bhai Nanu. On the way, he stopped at four places, *viz.*, Sonepat, Ambala, Nadha (near Chandigarh) and Kiratpur. At Kiratpur, Guru Gobind Singh received the hallowed head of his father, took it with all reverence to Anandpur where it was consigned to fire. Guru Gobind Singh was so much moved at the courage and devotion of Bhai Jaita that he took him in his embrace and announced, '*Rangretta Guru ka Beta*', i.e., 'Bhai Jaita is the son of the Guru'. From then on Bhai Jaita started living at Anandpur. The Guru was all affection for him, and had full faith in him.

Bhai Jaita was married to Bibi Rajkumari, the daughter of Sujan Singh, a Sikh of Patti, who had settled at Anandpur. It is believed that on the request of the mother of Jaita, the Guru asked the *sangat* to find a suitable match for Jaita. Sujan Singh stood up and offered his daughter in marriage. Accordingly, *Anand* ceremony was performed by the Guru and the couple was blessed. The wedding transcended caste considerations and symbolised union of two souls. According to Shamsher Singh Ashok, Jaita fathered four sons—Gurdial Singh, Gujar Singh, Sukha Singh and Sewa Singh.[18]

Bhai Jaita witnessed variegated activities of Guru Gobind Singh at Paonta and possibly it was here that he became an adept in the art of archery, gunnery, swordsmanship and horsemanship. He also composed heroic poetry, but alas, that is lost for ever.

In the battle of Bhangani, Nadaun and Hussaini (Anandpur), which the Guru fought, Jaita played his part well. In the battle of Bhangani, he acted as the commander of a unit. Similarly his role was crucial in the battle of Nadaun and in the battle of Hussaini. When the Mughal and hill forces made a joint attack on Anandpur in 1704 CE, he was in-charge of one of the forts.

On March 29, 1699 CE, when Guru Gobind Singh inaugurated the Order of the Khalsa, he took *Khande-di-Pahul* and was given a new name, Jiwan Singh.[19]

At Anandpur, there is a building known as Tap Asthan, 'place of meditation', of Bhai Jaita, very close to Guru Gobind

Singh's dwelling place. No other Sikh had his house so near as Bhai Jaita's. This leads us to conclude that Guru Gobind Singh had special regard for Jaita. Tradition says that Bhai Jaita not only used to meditate and reflect on the Guru's word but also gave lessons in Sikhism to people. '*Tap Asthan*' in Sikh context does not mean a place of an ascetic, rather by this is meant the place where Sikh culture is imbibed and steps are taken to inculcate it among the people.

Guru Gobind Singh evacuated Anandpur on the night of 6-7 Poh, Sammat 1762 Bk (5th-6th December, 1705 CE). The moment the enemy got wind of the departure of the Sikhs, they forgot all about their pledges and set out in hot pursuit immediately. Skirmishes commenced from Kiratpur onwards. Realising the impending danger, Guru Gobind Singh gave a band of 50 men to Bhai Udey Singh and charged him with the responsibility of checking the enemy's advance. Bhai Udey Singh fought at Shahi Tibbi with the enemy with a handful of men; all of them perished fighting covering themselves with eternal glory.

When the battle of Shahi Tibbi was in progress, Guru Gobind Singh, along with the rest of the caravan reached the bank of Sarsa river. Bhai Jaita was with the Guru, advancing and planning.

About this time, the news was received that a contingent of enemy troops was fast approaching and was likely to launch an attack in a short time. The river was in spate at that time, and it was apprehended that in the eventuality of an attack from the enemy, it would become very difficult to cross it. Under the circumstances, it was considered imperative by the Guru to set apart some Sikhs for checking the further advance of the enemy. The choice of the leadership of the *Jatha* fell on Bhai Jiwan Singh, who proved himself worthy of the trust reposed in him by the Master. Bhai ji and his 100 brave companions offered a stout and stubborn resistance to the enemy and all of them embraced martyrdom. Sarup Singh Kaushish, the author of *Guru Kian Sakhian*, records as under:

> A momentous battle was fought on the bank of Sarsa, the arrows of Bhai Jiwan Singh wrought havoc upon the

enemy. All the Sikhs fought gallantly with a total disregard for their lives. A large number of the Turks were killed in the battlefield. A hard contest took place between the two parties for one and a half *pahar* (four and a half hours). Then suddenly as a result of a volley of matchlocks, Jiwan Singh was shot in his forehead. His departing words were '*Waheguru ji ki Fateh*'. By sunrise, all the Sikhs had lost their lives.[20]

Makhan Shah

Makhan Shah, son of Naik Dase Shah, hailed from Mota Tanda in the present-day Muzaffarabad district of Jammu and Kashmir. He was a wealthy trader, and belonged to the tribe of Lobanas[21] who, according to W. Crooke, "acknowledge one God and look on Guru Nanak as the Supreme Teacher".[22]

According to J.H. Hutton,[23] their main profession was supplying and transporting provisions and other necessities of life to far off places on pack animals, such as oxen and mules, etc., or through boats. Makhan Shah, from his childhood had evinced keen interest in the dispensation of Guru Nanak about which his father often talked.

According to *Bhat Vahi Talauda Pargana Jind*, Guru Har Rai reached Srinagar via Galotian, Sialkot, in 1660 CE, and stayed in Hap Bazar. Makhan Shah, along with some other Sikhs, came to the Guru to pay obeisance. Among them was Arure Ram, father of Kirpa Ram Dutt, who later led to the presence of Guru Tegh Bahadur a group of Kashmiri *Pandits*, driven to dire distress by State persecution. The Guru blessed Makhan Shah, praising him for diligently following the Sikh discipline on the high road to self-illumination.

Responding to the request of Makhan Shah, the Guru, some time after visiting Mattan and Martand, visited Mota Tanda, to which Makhan Shah belonged, and which had become a centre of Sikh activities. The Guru was pleased to see Makhan Shah, and his dedication to the Sikh way of life.

Makhan Shah was a splendid personality. Stalwart, brawny, broad shouldered, he had the demeanour of a leader from his appearance, and looked like an aristocrat from his princely robes and dress. Through land, sea, and river routes, his convoys and ships provided provisions to the Mughal army, wherever it would travel for imperialistic exploits. He had a roaring trade and a packed schedule. Even then he could steal time to contemplate on *Shabad* as well as to persuade others to do the same. In a way, he acted in his moments of leisure as a missionary of Sikhism.[24]

About 1664 CE, a ship carrying his goods was caught up in a storm. His life and goods were in great danger. So helpless was he, that he knelt down and prayed to the Guru for help. He vowed that if by the grace of the Guru, he landed at the nearest port safely, he would make an offering of 101 Mohars to the Guru.[25]

Makhan Shah's ship steered safely out of the wild storm. He felt overwhelmed by the grace of the Guru. Therefore, the first thing he decided to do was to fulfil his vow. He first went to Delhi[26] where he learnt of the distressing news that Guru Harkrishan had passed away. He also came to know that the new Guru was at Bakala.

He travelled to Bakala with his wife Soliji. He was bewildered to see twenty-two persons, each posing as the ninth Guru of the Sikhs. Being a disciple of Guru Har Rai, well-versed in Sikh tradition and history of its leadership, he knew that only one Guru could succeed Guru Harkrishan. So he decided that it would be a mistake to believe them all as the real successors. He, therefore, made up his mind to put them all to test. He decided to offer only two mohars to everyone, who posed to be Guru Harkrishan's successor. He was sure that the real Guru would demand the exact amount he had vowed, and that it would not be possible for the impostor gurus to divine the exact purpose of his visit.

Makhan Shah, thus, decided to visit about four or five claimants everyday, make the offering of two mohars each, discuss theological problems, and study their response. Makhan Shah, first of all, paid a visit to Dhir Mal, who was then sitting on a raised platform with the original recension of *Adi Granth* on his right side. He bowed before him, placing before him two mohars. Dhir Mal blessed him, and offered him a robe of honour.[27] Dhir Mal acted like an inspired prophet as artfully as he could, but his talk in his own praise and his abusive reflections on others convinced Makhan Shah that he could not be the rightful successor.

Makhan Shah visited all the claimants, which convinced him that they were devoid of higher vision of life. Neither their talk nor their demeanour reflected any spirituality or enlightenment. Their hypocrisy, hollowness and pretensions were too glaring to be ignored by a devout and discerning Sikh like Makhan Shah, who was well disciplined in the true spirit and traditions of Sikhism.

Convinced of the falsity of the pretenders, he enquired if there was any other Baba in Bakala whom he had not met as yet. A lad of fifteen among the crowd came forward, and said that there was one more Baba who kept a low profile, remained absorbed in meditation and was called Baba Tegh Bahadur.[28] This piece of information gave a ray of hope to Makhan Shah as it was coming from an innocent boy of the village, and not from an agent of some impostor.

Makhan Shah forthwith proceeded to the house of Baba Tegh Bahadur. Mata Nanaki greeted him. He bowed reverently and touched her feet. In the courtyard, Makhan Shah recognised Diwan Durgah Mal and Bhai Gurditta, whom he had met at the court of Guru Har Rai. He then entered the basement where Guru Tegh Bahadur was sitting, resplendent in the joy of supreme enlightenment. Deeply moved, but without saying a word, he stepped down, and after placing two *dinars* before the Guru, bowed low in humble reverence. Guru Tegh Bahadur gave him his blessings pointing out at the same time that his offering was considerably short of the promised five hundred. Makhan Shah's[29] heart leapt with joy and he forthwith made good the difference. Bhai Santokh Singh writes:

> He was so delighted, ...his face blossomed like the flower opening up at the sight of the sun. This was like a beggar striking a treasure.[30]

Makhan Shah ran upstairs and began shouting from the roof top, "*Guru Ladho re* ! *Guru Ladho re* !"—I have found the Guru ! I have found the Guru.[31] Sikhs flocked to the house, greatly excited on beholding the true Master.

Makhan Shah's announcement dispirited the impostors, but nothing could assuage the jealousy of Dhir Mal. His *masands* fanned his ambitions. Together, they conspired to harm the Guru, so much so that he was waylaid on the outskirts of the town when he was returning to his house. Muskets were fired but they missed the target.[32] Dhir Mal's men ransacked Guru Tegh Bahadur's house. The Guru remained calm and composed.

Makhan Shah and Kirpal (the brother of Guru Tegh Bahadur's wife) attacked Dhir Mal's house in retaliation.[33] They not only recovered the things plundered from the Guru's house, but also carried away some of Dhir Mal's belongings, including the copy of the *Adi Granth* lying with Dhir Mal. Dhir Mal and Shihan were handcuffed. The Guru in his magnanimity forgave them, and ordered the Sikhs to return the articles looted from Dhir Mal's house. The Sikhs returned everything but the copy of *Adi Granth* which they considered to be the property of the Sikhs and not a private belonging of Dhir Mal. Later, when Guru Tegh Bahadur came to know of it, he asked the Sikhs to return the same also forthwith. The Sikhs obeyed and gave the original recension back to Dhir Mal.

Makhan Shah, however, warned Dhir Mal that he should refrain from such tactics in future. Immediately after, Dhir Mal left for Kartarpur.

One day Makhan Shah expressed his wish to visit Darbar Sahib, Amritsar, and felt elated when he came to know that the Guru also planned to go there. As they reached Amritsar on *Maghar Purnmashi* 1721 Bk (22nd November, 1664 CE), the custodians of Harmandar Sahib barred their entry. The Guru encamped at a nearby place, which now-a-days is called *Thamb Sahib*—the Pillar of Patience. These custodians were followers of Prithi Chand, his son Meharban and his grandson Harji, and were called *Minas*. They had installed their own copy of the *Granth* in which not only had they corrupted the compositions of earlier Gurus but included their own as well.

They propagated that Guru Arjan was succeeded by Prithi Chand, Meharban and Harji in that order. They refused to accept Guru Tegh Bahadur as the ninth Guru. They feared that once Guru Tegh Bahadur and his disciples entered Harmandar Sahib, they would take control of it, and drive out the *Minas* and their *masands*, just as they had driven out Dhir Mal from Bakala.

Extremely annoyed at the behaviour of the *Minas*, Makhan Shah beseeched the Guru to allow him to teach them a lesson so that they might not corrupt the Sikh doctrine.[34]

The Guru asked Makhan Shah to keep patience. The Guru uttered:

> "Actually they (*Minas*) live and burn in the flame of greed and lust for wealth. In these flames, they will be scorched and extinguished."
>
> "Their days are numbered. Their misdeeds will bring about their fall."
>
> "A day will come, when they will reap what they are sowing now. No Sikh will allow them to enter the door of his house."[35]

From Amritsar, the Guru journeyed northwards and stopped for the night at the village of Walla in response to the entreaties of a Sikh named Bibi Harian.

Immediately after the Guru left Amritsar, the *Mina masands* had to open the doors of Harmandar Sahib under the pressure of womenfolk of Amritsar who displayed courage of conviction by going *en masse* to Harmandar Sahib to protest against the shabby behaviour of *Mina masands* towards Guru Tegh Bahadur. At this juncture, Makhan Shah, who lay in wait for an opportunity to enter Harmandar Sahib and pay his obeisance at the sacred shrine, acted promptly. He admonished *Mina* priests for showing disrespect to Guru Tegh Bahadur and for misrepresenting the religion of Guru Nanak. He told them that if they did not mend their ways, they would have to repent bitterly all their lives.

Leaving Walla, Guru Tegh Bahadur decided to spend some time touring the *Majha* and *Malwa* regions of Punjab. On the occasion of *Vaisakhi* (1765 CE), the Guru reached Dhamtan in the heart of Bangar area which is in fact the extension of *Malwa*. The Guru reached Kiratpur in May 1765 CE. All the time Makhan Shah was in attendance. He was a witness to the laying of foundation of Chak Nanaki by Baba Gurditta, son of Baba Budha, on June 19, 1665 CE, which, in the course of time, grew to be the beautiful town of Anandpur.

Makhan Shah was uncompromising in his convictions, and vigorous and assertive in executing his plans. He was an inspired Sikh, creative in his vision, always humble before God and the Guru. He spent all his time, money and energy in the labour of love, his only target was to provide relief to the suffering humanity. One day, one of his men reminded him that the rainy season was drawing near and it was high time that they attended to the trade commitments. With a heavy heart, he asked his men to get ready and with folded hands he addressed to the Guru, "The rainy season is drawing near. My home is far away. As the streams get flooded, travel will become arduous. May I take my leave, Gurudev? Pray, do not ever forget this servant of yours." Guru Tegh Bahadur blessed him in these words:

> You have taken refuge in Truth. Ever contemplate the divine Word which shines like a diamond in your soul and ever live in the peace of your spiritual enlightenment. You are the noblest example of a Sikh, and like a true Sikh you live unbroken spiritual communion with the Guru. When you are so deeply and eternally united with me in the life of the spirit, the temporary separation in the physical world is no separation. You have achieved the perfect self-illumination of Nirvana in the light of which neither joy nor sorrow, neither pleasure nor pain will ever disturb your peace. You are Jiwan Mukta, the liberated soul.[36]

Makhan Shah clasped the Guru's feet. Tears rolled down as he left Kiratpur.

Ever since his departure from Chak Nanki, the recorded history is silent about his activities, although in oral tradition which has come down to us, he had always been a proactive Sikh ever-ready to do anything for the cause of Sikhism. His son, Jawand Singh, sacrificed his life in the battle of Chamkaur.[37]

NOTES AND REFERENCES

1. Taken from the article *Guru Nanak's Life-long Companion—Rababi Mardana* by Satbir Singh.
2. Bhai Gurdas: *Varan*, 1:35:
   ਬਾਬਾ ਗਿਆ ਬਗਦਾਦ ਨੂੰ ਬਾਹਰ ਜਾਇ ਕੀਆ ਅਸਥਾਨਾ ।
   ਇਕ ਬਾਬਾ ਅਕਾਲ ਰੂਪ ਦੂਜਾ ਰਬਾਬੀ ਮਰਦਾਨਾ।
3. Guru Granth Sahib, *Bihagrhe ki Var*, p. 553.
4. *Ibid.*, p. 553.
5. *Ibid.*, p. 553.
6. Gupta, Hari Ram: *History of the Sikhs*, Vol. I, Delhi, reprint 1994, p. 368.
7. Different historians give different dates of the death of Bhai Gurdas. *Gurbilas Patshahi Chhevin* gives *Samat* 1686 Bk (1629 CE). Sant Sampuran Singh gives *Samat* 1687 Bk (1630 CE). These dates cannot be accepted because Bhai Gurdas was alive on these dates. *Mahan Kosh* gives *Samat* 1694 Bk (1637 CE). This date also needs further research because during this year Guru Hargobind was at Kiratpur while Bhai Gurdas passed away before Guru Sahib went to Kiratpur. We have taken the probable last year of Bhai Gurdas' life as 1631 CE, after the death of Baba Budha. Or he died in early part of the year 1632 CE.
8. Fani, Mohsin: *Dabistan-i-Mazahib*.
9. Bal, Vir Singh: *Singh Sagar*, Chapter 11.
10. The *Hukamnama* is in the custody of Giani Garja Singh. According to *Shaheed Bilas* by Sewa Singh, Bhai ji returned to Amritsar from Baghaur.
11. Nath Mal, Dhadhi: *Amarnama*, Sikh History Society, Amritsar, 1953. Translation by Gurtej Singh, *Abstracts of Sikh Studies*, January 1995, p. 92.
12. For greater detail refer to *Bhai Nand Lal Granthavali*, edited by Dr. Ganda Singh, p. 12, 1968.
13. Arfi, Niranjan: *Rangretian da Itihas*, Literature House, Putli Ghar, Amritsar, 1993.
14. *Ibid.*
15. Fauja Singh: *Hukamnamé*, Punjabi University, Patiala.
16. Arfi, Niranjan: *op. cit.*, pp. 238-39.
17. *Gur Katha*, p. 55. This composition has been edited by Dr. Gurmukh Singh and published by Raghubir Rachna Parkashan.
18. Ashok, Shamsher Singh: *Mazhabi Sikhan da Itihas*, p. 151.
19. *Ibid.*, p. 71.

20. ਜੀਵਨ ਸਿੰਘ ਬੇਟਾ ਆਗਿਆ ਕਾ, ਪੋਤਾ ਦੂਲੂ ਕਾ, ਬਾਸੀ ਦਿੱਲੀ, ਮਹਲਾ ਦਿਲਵਾਲੀ ਸੌ ਸਿੱਖੋਂ ਕੋ ਗ਼ੈਲ ਲੈ ਸੰਬਤ ਸਤ੍ਰਾ ਸੈ ਬਾਸਠ ਪਖੋਂ ਮਾਸੈ ਸੁਦੀ ਦੂਜ ਵੀਰਵਾਰ ਕੇ ਦਿਹੁੰ, ਸਰਸਾ ਨਦੀ ਦੇ ਤੀਰ ਰਾਜਾ ਅਜਮੇਰ ਚੰਦ ਬੇਟਾ ਭੀਮ ਚੰਦ ਕਾ, ਪੋਤਾ ਦੀਪ ਚੰਦ ਕਾ, ਪੜਪੋਤਾ ਤਾਰਾ ਚੰਦ ਕਾ, ਬੰਸ ਕਲਿਆਣ ਚੰਦ, ਚੰਦੇਲ ਗੋਤਰ ਰਾਣੈ ਕੀ ਫੌਜ ਗ਼ੈਲ ਦਸ ਘਰੀਆਂ ਜੁਝ ਕੇ ਸਾਮ੍ਹੇ ਮਾਥੇ ਸ਼ਹਾਦਤ ਪਾਈ। ਆਗੇ ਗੁਰੂ ਭਾਣੇ ਦਾ ਖੀਵੰਦ, ਗੁਰੂ ਗਤਿ ਜਾਣੇ ਗੁਰੂ ਜਪਣਾ ਜਨਮ ਸਉਰੇਗਾ।

21. Rose, H.A.: *A Glossary of the Tribes and Castes of the Punjab and North Western Frontier Province*, Vol. III, Bhasha Vibhag, Punjab, Patiala, 1970 (reprint). "The term Lubana has been derived from Lavan, a Sanskrit word which means salt." According to Crooke, "Lubana tribe of Banjaras took their name from the business of carting salt (*lavan*)." *Tribes and Castes of North Western India*, Vol. I, Cosmo Publications, Delhi, 1974 (reprint).

22. Crooke, W.: *Tribes and Castes of North Western India*, Vol. I, p. 154.

23. Hutton, J.H.: *Tribes and Castes of North Western India*, p. 21, 1896 CE.

24. It is perhaps because of this that a Sikh wrote that Makhan Shah was a *masand* in-charge of some part of Gujarat region of this subcontinent.

25. *Guru kian Sakhian* mentions 101 gold *muhars*. *Bhat Vahi Tomar Binjlaunton ki* gives the same figure. However, popular tradition refers to 500 *muhars*. Gian Singh and Gulab Singh aver that Makhan Shah had vowed 1000 *muhars*. All records, however, are unanimous in saying that Makhan Shah got into difficulty while traversing trade-routes.

26. Sukha Singh: *Gurbilas Patshahi Dasvin*, p. 11.

27. Bhalla, Sarup Das: *Mehma Parkash*.

    Le Puja Khushi Sikh ko kini,
    Siro pao Pagdi Tis dini.

28. Sukha Singh: *Gurbilas Patshahi Dasvin*, Bhasha Vibhag, Pṇnjab, Patiala, 1989, p. 8.

29. *Ibid.*, pp. 10-11.

30. Santokh Singh: *Gurpartap Suraj Granth*, Vol. X, p. 4003.

31. *Ibid.*

32. There is a difference of opinion on this point. The author of *Suraj Parkash* mentions that the bullet caused the injury to the head, while Gian Singh in his *Twarikh Guru Khalsa* writes that the bullet did not cause any injury to the Guru, but killed a disciple, who was standing beside him. Some other accounts refer to shoulder injury. Anyhow, the injury does not seem to have been serious as the Guru soon after left for Amritsar.

33. Sukha Singh: *op. cit.*, p. 11.

    Also see, *Gurpartap Suraj Granth*, *Ras* 11, *Ansu* 18.

34. *Suraj Parkash*, *Ras* 11, *Ansu* 21.

35. *Ibid.*, *Ras* 11, *Ansu* 22.

36. *Ibid.*, *Ras* 11, *Ansu* 28. Translated by Trilochan Singh in his book, *Guru*

Tegh Bahadur, published by Delhi Gurdwara Parbandhak Committee, Delhi.

37. Kaushish, Sarup Singh: *Guru kian Sakhian*, Singh Brothers, Amritsar.

ਜਵੰਦ ਸਿੰਘ ਬੇਟਾ ਮੁ਼ਖਣ ਸ਼ਾਹ ਕਾ ਪੋਤਾ ਦਾਸੇ ਸ਼ਾਹ ਕਾ ਪੜਪੋਤਾ ਬਨੇ ਕਾ ਉਲਾਦ ਬਹੋਣ ਸ਼ਾਹ ਪੇਲੀਆ ਗੋਤ੍ਰਾ ਬਨਜਾਰਾ । ਬਾਸੀ ਟਾਂਡਾ ਪੁਹਾਂਨਾ ਦੇਸ਼ ਮਜਫਰਾਬਾਦ ਦੇਸ਼ ।

22

MUSLIM DEVOTEES OF THE GURUS

Pir Budhu Shah

Guru Gobind Singh's personality was as fascinating as his teaching were soul-stirring. He transformed human beings into a race imbibing a tradition of fire and steel, sacrifice and death, ever ready to do anything for the uplift of mankind irrespective of caste, creed, clime or social status. All right-thinking persons loved the Guru and admired his teachings. These included people of all religions, castes and political affiliations. One such person was Pir Budhu Shah, a Muslim saint of Sadhaura in Ambala district in the present province of Haryana, India. His piety and holiness had made him the cynosure of all people—Hindu, Muslim, rich and poor, old and young. His original name was Badruddin. He was born on June 13, 1641 CE, and was the scion of a Sayyed family of Sadhaura and enjoyed not only a high religious status by virtue of being one of the descendants of Prophet Muhammad but also held a respectable political position.

He was serene and meditative. His interest lay more in realisation of the self than in surface knowledge or in materialistic things of the world. He studied Al-Quran and other religious books of Islam with a penchant for the inner meaning of the message of the Prophet. A man of contemplation as he was, he was not much communicative and was thus misunderstood by the people who began to call him a *Budhu*, meaning stupid—the nickname that stuck to him throughout his life. He never reacted to this apparently uncomplimentary nomenclature. On the other hand, he engulfed everybody, even those who decried and ridiculed him, with his innate love and affection.

As he reached manhood, the reality dawned upon people and they began to call him *Pir* in reverence and thus he came to be known as Pir Budhu Shah.

He was married to Bibi Nasiran, younger sister of Sayyed Khan, who later became a renowned general of Aurangzeb. He had four sons by her—Muhammad Ashraf, Muhammad Bakhsh, Muhammad Shah and Shah Hussain.

Pir Budhu Shah saw for himself the swing in the religious policy of Shahjahan towards orthodoxy. During the reign of Aurangzeb, it was firmly in the Imperial saddle and, therefore, policies towards non-Muslims, particularly the Hindus, were palpably fanatical; their temples were demolished; their religious books were burnt; their entry into public service was restricted; rewards were offered for conversion to Islam and punishments awarded for refusal. Guru Tegh Bahadur was a victim of this fanatical policy of the Mughal government. Unlike many of the Muslims high officials or *Mansabdars* who rejoiced at the fanatical policy of Aurangzeb, Pir Budhu Shah's mind was tormented and anguished. His understanding of Islam was different from that of the orthodox Muslim *ulema*. He was a devout Muslim but Islam of his conviction did not discriminate between man and man on grounds of faith and beliefs. His understanding of *jehad* was a crusade against evil and not against the non-Muslims.

When Guru Gobind Singh was at Paonta in Sirmour state, only 16 kilometres north of Sadhaura, Pir Budhu Shah called upon him and expressed his sincerest condolences. After expressing his grief at the execution of the Guru's father, he conversed with him on matters spiritual and moral. The Pir enquired as to how one could meet God. The Guru replied as night meets day. The Pir quipped that in that case night would disappear. The Guru replied that this is what is desired. When self merges in Him to become a part of the whole, falsehood disappears, only truth remains. Therefore, attempts are to be made to realise self to feel that it is part of the Self. Attachment of family, life, wealth, power, prestige and fame has to be curbed and self-realisation achieved only by conquering ego, resigning completely to the will of God. An extraordinary calmness descended on Pir Budhu Shah and his face exuded sublime serenity. He could clearly see the greatness of the Guru.

One of the most important features of the Guru's activities at Paonta was that he imparted military training to his followers to prepare them to face the challenges from the orthodox Hindu hill chieftains as well as from Aurangzeb, who had launched a coercive policy to convert non-Muslims to Islam. He needed trained military personnel to accomplish his mission.

Five Pathan leaders of village Damla in Tehsil Jagadhari, not far from Paonta, had their own contingents of troops, each roughly consisting of one hundred men. As they were unemployed, they approached the Pir to recommend them to the Guru for service. The Pir took them to the Guru who employed them on daily wages, each group leader was to get five rupees and a soldier one rupee. In September 1688 CE, the battle of Bhangani or clash with the hill chiefs led by Fateh Chand of Garhwal was imminent. A few days before the actual battle, four out of the five Pathan leaders deserted the Guru, lured by the promises of the hill chiefs that not only would they be paid higher wages but also given permission to plunder the Guru's camp and the city of Paonta. The Guru promptly took measures to offset the setback of their desertion. Pir Budhu Shah too came quickly to know of what had happened.

The perfidy of the Pathans whom he had recommended for employment was too much for the Pir to digest. He made a clarion call to his disciples to meet him. Within no time, they reached Sadhaura. The Pir told them about his dilemma—how a man of God had been betrayed by the Pathans and why he wanted them to support him. Out of his disciples, he selected seven hundred whom he placed under the command of his two sons and two brothers. All of them marched to Paonta and Pir Budhu Shah also accompanied them to join the Guru's camp.

According to Dr. Hari Ram Gupta's findings, the Pir's sons and brothers were designated as *Risaldars* at Rs. 150 per month, while soldiers received Rs. 30 as monthly emolument.

Pir's men fought with dogged determination. In the hard contested battle, Pir's two sons, Sayyed Muhammad Ashraf and Sayyed Muhammad Shah, his brother Bhure Shah, and many of his followers lost their lives. The Pir's timely help was one of the major causes of the victory of the Guru. The Guru expressed his deepest gratitude to Pir Budhu Shah for his singular contribution at the most critical juncture. He blessed him and as a token thereof, conferred a robe of honour on him and issued a *Hukamnama* to the Sikhs to always honour him and his family.

Pir Budhu Shah bore the loss with calmness and fortitude, but for his wife, Nasiran, it was not easy to resign to the Will of God. Fully aware, the Guru paid a visit to Sadhaura to personally console her, immediately after. He did his utmost to alleviate her grief and told her that we all should learn to live in the Will of God. The participation of Pir in the battle was a response to his inner conviction that the Guru's cause was righteous and that he was unjustly attacked by the hill chiefs. It did not signify anything else. No politics was involved. And very rightly, the Mughal government did not take any notice of Pir Budhu Shah. Nor did the hill *rajas* become raucous against the Pir, probably because Sadhaura did not fall in their jurisdictions. Sixteen years passed, nothing happened to the Pir who preached his *Sufi* doctrines freely and successfully thereby blunting the communal and particularistic angularities of fanatic people.

Wazir Khan of Sirhind as well as the fundamentalist Naqshbandis never approved of Budhu Shah's role. Wazir Khan was a sworn enemy of the Guru, and wanted to capture him dead or alive. However, he did not succeed. The Guru, fighting all the way from Anandpur, reached the safety of

Malwa region. This infuriated Wazir Khan. Maddened by anger, he ordered Usman Khan, the *Daroga* of Sadhaura, to destroy the Pir and his family. They were killed in cold blood on March 25, 1705 CE.

Mia Mir Hazrat (1550-1635)

A well-known Sufi saint of the Qadiriyah order, a contemporary of Guru Arjan Dev and Guru Hargobind (1595-1644). His real name was Sheikh Mir Muhammed. He was born the son of Qazi Sayandanah (Sai Dutta according to some chroniclers) bin Qazi Qalandhar Faruqui in 957 AH/ CE 1550 at Sahvan (also called Sevasyan) in the present Dadu district of Sind in Pakistan. His mother was Bibi Fatima, daughter of Qazi Qazan. His family claimed descent from Hazrat Umar Faruq, the second Caliph successor to Prophet Muhammed. His father died when he was a young boy and it was his mother who put him under Shaikh Khizr Sevastani for study of Qadiri silsila (school) of Sufi thought. Soon he acquired proficiency and began to be recognised as a great Sufi mystic. At the age of twenty-five, he shifted to Lahore. There he joined the school of Maulana Said Ullah and subsequently of Maulana Niamat Ullah and Mufti Abdus-Salah to study traditional and rational philosophies. Soon he became known as a distinguished Alam (scholar). Even as he engaged in temporal affairs, he found time to meditate. He was averse to publicity and preferred to spend his time in contemplation in solitude. Perhaps for this reason, he left Lahore and went to stay at Sirhind, a very important Islamic centre. There too, he could not feel comfortable, probably because of the preachings of Naqshbandi Order of the Sufis which did not conform to his own convictions about Islam. Shortly, he decided to once again to return to Lahore. He resided in the suburbs of the city, then known as Begampura. Now the area is known as Mian Mir after his name.

During this period, he developed regards for Guru Arjan Dev in whom he found a man, truly spiritual. According to Dr. Hari Ram Gupta, Guru Arjan often visited Lahore to see the birth place of his father as also to meet his relatives. On one such occasion he met Mian Mir. Both became enamoured of each other. Bonds of eternal friendship developed as both found each other as committed to building a new humanity, fully harmonised on basis of love for one another.

In 1589, Guru Arjan Dev planned to build a temple in the centre of the holy tank called Amritsar (tank of nectar). As it was to be the symbol of humanistic cosmopolitanism, transcendence, and universalism, the Guru considered it appropriate to invite Mian Mir to lay its foundation for his humaneness and his belief in oneness of the whole mankind. He came to Amritsar wearing a religious mendicant's long cloak made up of patches of coarse wool and a cone cap of a number of gores with a rose flower on top.

He was accorded a tumultuous welcome and was explained the purpose of raising Harimandir. The Guru pointed out that there were temples either of the Hindus or of the Muslims or of Zoroastrians or of the Christians but there was no temple of God. And exactly this would be Harimandir, open to all irrespective of any temporal or religious label and praying for the welfare of all including even those who harbour hatred for others or have a brutalised conscience. Mian Mir liked the concept as well as the project of giving it shape at physical level. Mian Mir's gesture not only affected his followers but also attracted the attention of other Sufi orders operating in the Punjab. Gradually, many of the Sufis started admiring the Guru. According to some observers, quite a number of Sufis contemporaneous of Guru Arjan Dev were favourably inclined to the Guru. It was this development that was repugnant to the Muslim orthodoxy and was responsible for persuading the state power to unleash terror on liberal, and non-orthodox people even among Muslims.

In 1606, Guru Arjan Dev was implicated in the affair of Khusro, the rebel son of Jahangir. He was imprisoned in the Lahore Jail and was executed under the law of Yasa. While in prison, Mian Mir came to see the Guru and suggested that he might he allowed to intercede on his behalf with Emperor Jahangir. The Guru forbade him saying that God's Will must have its course unchecked as it was not proper to interfere with its working. He only asked for the Hazrat's blessings for his son, Guru Hargobind. When after the martyrdom of Guru Arjan Dev, Guru Hargobind was interned in Gwalior Fort in 1609, Mian Mir used his influence to get him released from the fort in 1612.

Shortly after his release, Guru Hargobind called on Mian Mir at Lahore at his Khanqah. Mian Mir welcomed him and paced forward to hold the reins of his horse as a mark of respect. The Guru at once alighted and made obeisance to Mian Mir saying, "No royal visitor ever dares ride a horse while Bala pir (Mian Mir) was on foot."

They embraced each other. It was the embrace of two gods vowed to a life of friendship and love. Hand in hand they moved on to the Khanqah, where Mian Mir introduced all his eminent disciples including a young beautiful girl Kaulan. She was the daughter of Rustam Khan, Qazi of Lahore. Being religious-minded since her childhood, she became a disciple of Mian Mir. She had made up her mind to ever stay in Khanqah. Since in Qadiri Order the stay of a lady at Khanqah after attaining her puberty was prohibited, Mian Mir refused to oblige her. In the meanwhile when she listened to Hargobind who was engaged in illuminating discussion with Mian Mir, she was much impressed. She expressed her admiration about the Guru at home to her father, who was shocked and became wild with sage. To him Guru Hargobind was a Kafir and her admiration was nothing short of blasphemy. Already an altercation had taken place between him and the Guru's disciple about the transaction of some horses. He now could not tolerate his daughter speaking so highly of the Guru.

At this critical moment Mian Mir sent her to Amritsar under the care of his disciple Abdulla. According to another version, Guru Hargobind personally went to Lahore along with five Sikhs to escort her safely to Amritsar.

Kaulan was given a separate house and some women attendants. Complete arrangements were made for her comforts and life of solitude and prayer. She enjoyed the calm and serenity of Mian Mir's Khanqah. Her life of meditation and spiritual communion with God now began to flower and no wonder her sight became ennobling and his words soothing. Guru Hargobind had complete faith in her noble character and in her never-failing intuition and her spiritual destiny. Guru Hargobind immortalised her by constructing a tank which he named Kaulsar, the tank of lotus symbolising purity even amidst impurities. She shifted to Kartarpur when certain evil-minded persons started spreading rumours that the relations between Kaulan and Guru were other than spiritual. After this incident she left for her heavenly abode. It is said that at this moment Mian Mir in a special message admired Guru Hargobind for taking care of Kaulan.

Mian Mir was equally esteemed by people as well as political elites. Jahangir in *Tazuk-i-Jahangir* writes:

> The great man is unique today in his unblemished spiritualism and purity of heart. I go to him and he enriches me with religious and worldly guidance. I wanted to present some cash but he does not accept it from anybody. I, therefore, did send the prayer-mat made of stag's skin which he has very kindly agreed to accept and then left for Lahore. (Akhlaq Hussain Delvi: *The Sikh Review*, July 1980, p. 46)

Jahangir was highly impressed with Mian Mir's discourse. Once he asked him for any service. Mian Mir replied "Then I request you not to disturb me again."

Mulla Abdul Hamid Lahori in his dissertation 'Badshah Nama' says that Emperor Shahjahan paid his respectful visits to Mian Mir a number of times. The author of 'Shahjahan Nama' records that Shahjahan waited upon Mian Mir on his way to Kashmir and on his return journey. When Shahjahan came to Lahore in 1628, he met the sage. As he knew that he did not accept my cash he made the offering of a rosary and a white turban which he accepted and then gave his blessings, Shahjahan's daughter Nidira Begam and his eldest son Dara Shikoh were the disciples of Mian Mir. Once Dara fell ill. There was almost no hope of his survival. He was taken to Mian Mir. The Saint held the prince's hands and he immediately recovered. Dara went to him barefooted. He hugged him and Dara felt relieved and elevated. All this happened when Dara was nearly twenty. Thereafter he became a disciple of his and wrote many a treatises on spirituality.

In the year 1635 CE Guru Hargobind received the news of the departure of great Saint Mian Mir for his heavenly abode. He spoke with feeling about the spiritual greatness of Mian Mir and his historic association with the house of the Guru. He was in fact the golden bond bridging the gulf between the aggressive and bigoted force of Mughal Imperialism and the progressive and resurgent force of Sikh faith. He was buried at village Hashimpur.

Saifud-din Mahmud

Saifud-din Mahmud, popularly known as Saif Khan (d. 1685) which was in fact the title which Aurangzeb conferred on him. He was a man of religious disposition and on account of this he earned popular epithet Faquirullah meaning a holy man of God. In some of the contemporary and a semi-contemporary records, Nawab has been added as prefix to his name. As it was practice in the 17th and 18th centuries, the word Nawab appears to have been added to his name to indicate his eminence.

His father Tarbiat Khan had been Bakhshi in the court of Shahjahan and his elder brother Fidai Khan was Aurangzeb's foster brother. During the war of succession he fought against the forces of Aurangzeb but after the defeat of Dara's forces, Aurangzeb won him over and raised him to the rank of 2500 Zat and 1500 sowars and conferred upon him the title of Saif Khan.

He was also made governor of Agra. Relieved of his post later, Saif Khan returned to his main fief in Sirhind Sarkar where he founded in 1666-67 a fortified habitation named Saifabad, now known as Bahadurgarh near Patiala. He held the post of governor of Kashmir twice that is to say in 1665-68 and in 1669-71.

In 1671 he quit the post and turned a hermit. He was restored his title and rank at the end of 1675 and made Subedar of Bihar in 1678.

Saif Khan had great qualities of head and heart. He was humble, disciplined, God-fearing and possessed of carefree manners (*Maasar-Ul-Umra*, vol. II). He was a great soldier and a good administrator. As a soldier, he displayed his acumen in the war of succession (1858) and then while he was conquering Ladakh. For this admirable job, he was specially recognised by his master, Aurangzeb. He was a Sufi in his religious views and had a rare knack to keep himself detached while living amidst the mundane world. He was a patron of men of letters. Nasir Ali Sirhindi a renowned poet of Sirhind enjoyed his bounteous patronage. In a couplet he paid him the highest compliments:

> "Just as talk parried by parrot is inspired by a mirror similarly one's life breath is inspired by Saif Khan."

Saif Khan was very fond of music. He wrote 'Rag Darpan' a treatise on music which delineated 'divisions and rules' of various 'Ragas'.

His humanitarian nature and love for music and poetry made him special, and naturally he was attracted towards Guru Tegh Bahadur who on his own part was a great poet and musicologist and fervently engaged in the service of mankind.

Saif Khan had very cordial relation with Guru Tegh Bahadur. They exchanged views regarding matters concerning a vast spectrum of problems both spiritual and socio-political. In one of the 'Hukamnamas' preserved in Hari Mandir at Patna, the Guru had instructed the congregation of Patna to procure for him five pieces of fine pottery viz. five earthen jars and mugs and send them to Bhai Kalyana's Dharamsala, Delhi for gifting Nawab Saif Khan. Evidently the letter indicated Guru's great regard for Saifud-din. According to Dr. Kirpal Singh "This Hukamnama was probably written when the Guru was in Assam with Raja Ram Singh and had decided to return to Punjab via Patna in 1669. According to *Bhatvahi Taluda Pargana Jind*, Saif Khan met the Guru at Delhi in 1670. At that time Saif Khan was Governor of Kashmir for the second time.

The Guru seemed to have been in touch with him through correspondence or through emissaries. Both liked each other and both had shared the same values. According to *Guru Kian Sakhian,* a published Punjabi Source (1790), the Guru first visited Saifabad in 1665 CE when he was returning to Dhamtan (Modern District Hissar, Haryana) after founding Nanki Chak and stayed at Saifabad for the night and the next day he set on for Dhamtan. For the second time, the Guru visited Saifabad in 1672 CE after Saif Khan had met the Guru at Delhi on June 20, 1670 as already mentioned. According to *Guru Kian Sakhian*, the Guru stayed there for three days and then returned to see his brother-in-law.

Saif Khan accorded utmost respect to the Guru. The author of *Sakhi Pothi* gives the following details:

> Saif Khan received the Guru in his garden (which was laid by Saif Khan in 1669) thanked him for his visit and offered him dry fruit. After stay of some days, the Guru was invited to reside in the fort. The Guru entered the fort on horseback and his wife was in palanquin and Saif Khan himself walked on foot as a mark of respect. When the Guru entered the fort, he found a building and enquired what it was? He was told that it was a Masque, the house of God. When the Guru reached the residence of Saif Khan, the latter offered him gold Mohars and clothes. The wife of Saif Khan paid her respect to the Guru's wife. The total stay of the Guru was three months. At the time of departure, Saif Khan made the offering of gifts to the Guru comprising a number of camels, a fine horse and a chariot for use of Guru's wife.

An old gurdwara across the road from Bahadurgarh Fort now marks the site where Guru Tegh Bahadur had stayed as Saif Khan's guest. Saif Khan died in 1685 CE. His tomb is located near the fort. People including Sikhs still remember him with reverence as Saifa Baba and visit the tomb, especially on Thursdays.

APPENDICES

APPENDIX-I

IMPORTANT PLACES VISITED BY GURU HARGOBIND SAHIB

District Bathinda

1. Wadi Mehraj, 2. Phul, 3. Dhapali, 4. Gill Kalan, 5. Bhundar, 6. Lehra Muhabbat, 7. Jaimal Singh Wala, 8. Nathana, 9. Mari Karla Patti, 10. Chhota Mehraj, 11. Mari, 12. Bhai Rupa, 13. Kale Bagh, 14. Gumti Kalan, 15. Dyalpur Bhaika, 16. Kangar, 17. Draj, 18. Maur.

District Sangrur

1. Bhadaur, 2. Bhadalwad, 3. Thulli Wal, 4. Nanki, 5. Bhotna, 6. Gehal, 7. Khurana, 8. Sangrur, 9. Akoi, 10. Kanjhla, 11. Ghanaur, 12. Baur-hia, 13. Dhaler Kalan, 14. Kamalpur Kale Ke, 15. Sehna.

District Faridkot

1. Himmatpura, 2. Navan Machhike, 3. Lopo, 4. Daughar, 5. Madoke, 6. Bagha Purana, 7. Doad, 8. Lambwali, 9. Malha, 10. Baja Khana, 11. Fatehgarh Chabri Khan, 12. Sahoke, 13. Laldhaike, 14. Chandpurana, 15. Salhine, 16. Ghal Kalan, 17. Wada Ghar, 18. Kaunke, 19. Matwani, 20. Kokri Kalan, 21. Rode, 22. Ajit Singh Wala, 23. Nhande-ana, 24. Takhtupura, 25. Patto Hira Singh, 26. Daroli Bhai.

District Ludhiana

1. Hathoor, 2. Lakha, 3. Chakkar, 4. Gurusar Chakkar, 5. Sodhi Wala, 6. Sidhwan Kalan, 7. Burj Kularan, 8. Bilaspur, 9. Hera, 10. Sudhar, 11. Rakba, 12. Rahune, 13. Ludhiana, 14. Doraha, 15. Katana Sahib, 16. Lall Kalan, 17. Ghulal, 18. Kotan, 19. Dhamot, 20. Kudhani Kalan, 21. Gidri, 22. Rara Sahib, 23. Aluana, 24. Bhagruana, 25. Jaghera Jhingar, 26. Jandali Khurd, 27. Ghungrana, 28. Delhon, 29. Jassar, 30. Ayyali Kalan, 31. Sangrana Sahib, 32. Gujjarwal, 33. Narangwal, 34. Pul Wala, 35. Kailey, 36. Littar, 37. Jatpur Lamme, 38. Phillaur, 39. Iko Laha, 40. Chakohi, 41. Eesru, 42. Jandali, 43. Seora, 44. Bhurthala Mander, 45. Jarg.

District Amritsar

1. Bhai-ki-Darauli, 2. Amritsar, 3. Khairabad, 4. Khiala, 5. Madoke Brar, 6. Satlani Sahib, 7. Khara, 8. Chahal, 9. Neshta, 10. Pucca Pind Neshta, 11. Kakkar, 12. Bhindian Aulakh, 13. Ramdas, 14. Mattewal, 15. Mehta, 16. Vairo Nangal, 17. Udoke, 18. Baba Bakala, 19. Sathiala, 20. Butala, 21. Thande, 22. Takhtu Chak, 23. Gajal, 24. Khem Karan, 25. Kot Budha, 26. Harike Pattan, 27. Chheharta, 28. Goindwal, 29. Jhubal, 30. Tarn Taran, 31. Chabewal, 32. Dhand, 33. Gang Bhuha, 34. Dobli, 35. Chorasti Attari, 36. Gur Singh Wala, 37. Malhian.

District Jalandhar

1. Gurplah Soter, 2. Poonia, 3. Gobindpur, 4. Jalandhar, 5. Kartarpur, 6. Dalla, 7. Jandhu Singhan.

District Kapurthala

1. Jindowal, 2. Ganeshpur, 3. Gondpur, 4. Pul Pukhta, 5. Bodal, 6. Purheeran, 7. Moonak Kalan, 8. Phagwara, 9. Nadala, 10. Dumeli, 11. Bhogpur, 12. Balher.

District Fatehgarh Sahib

1. Mandi Gobindgarh, 2. Saunti, 3. Salana.

District Firozpur

1. Gada Singh Wala.

District Roop Nagar

1. Kiratpur, 2. Bharatpur, 3. Manguwal, 4. Pehal Khurd, 5. Behloo, 6. Roop Nagar.

Uttar Pradesh

1. Nanak Matta, 2. Mathura, 3. Agra, 4. Pilibhit.

Haryana

1. Cheeka, 2. Ambala, 3. Pehoa, 4. Kurukshetra.

Jammu & Kashmir

1. Bara Mula, 2. Kalampura, 3. Tahli Sahib, 4. Naushera, 5. Rajouri.

Rajasthan: Dhaulpur

Delhi

Madhya Pradesh: Gwalior

Pakistan

1. Chukalha (Lahore), 2. Muzang (Lahore), 3. Nankana Sahib, 4. Hudiara Sahib, 5. Wazirabad, 6. Narali (Rawalpindi), 7. Gujrat, 8. Ghalotian (Sialkot), 9. Gujranwala, 10. Matte Bhaike (Gujranwala), 11. Hafizabad, 12. Guru Mangar (Lahore), 13. Amar Siddu (Lahore), 14. Dhilwan (Lahore), 15. Padhana.

APPENDIX-II

MARTYRS OF CHAMKAUR SAHIB

In the battle of Chamkaur, Guru Gobind Singh had only forty brave Sikhs with him. All of them, with the exception of Daya Singh, Dharam Singh and Mann Singh died martyrs in the battlefield. No single source gives the names of all of these thirty-seven martyrs. But on the basis of the information gleaned from various Granths the following list of martyrs has been prepared:

1. Kirpa Singh : son of Arhu Ram, grandson of Narain Das, resident of Kashmir.
2. Anak Singh : son of Bhai Mani Singh, grandson of Mai Dass, great grandson of Balu and brother of Bhai Bachittar Singh.
3. Sanmukh Singh : real brother of Kirpa Singh (No. l).
4. Ajab Singh : real brother of Anak Singh (No. 2).
5. Ajaib Singh : real brother of Anak Singh (No. 2).
6. Alim Singh : son of Durga Dass, grandson of Padma, great grandson of Kauna, resident of Daburji, Pargana Sohdara of Chander Bansi Gotra, Chaheman (Chauhan).
7. Dan Singh : son of Mai Das, grandson of Mul Chand, Chander Bansi Bhardwaj and of Pawar Gotra.
8. Tula Singh : son of Dhuma, grandson of Kana, resident of Ladwa, Pargana Thanesar.
9. Mula Singh : son of Dhuma, grandson of Kana, resident of Ladwa, Pargana Thanesar.
10. Jawand Singh : son of Makhan Shah, great grandson of Bana, descendant of Bahorh Shah and of Pelia Gotra Banjara, resident of Mota Tanda, Pargana Muzaffarabad in Kashmir.
11. Bakhshish Singh : Kalal, Rahtia caste, resident of village Pairowal.

12. Bakhshish Singh : Kalal, Rahtia caste, resident of village Pairowal.
13. Sher Singh
14. Nahar Singh
15. Hukam Singh
16. Mohkam Singh
17. Sahib Singh
18. Himmat Singh
19. Deva Singh
20. Ram Singh
21. Tehl Singh
22. Ishar Singh
23. Fateh Singh
24. Dhian Singh
25. Dhanna Singh
26. Siam Singh
27. Mohar Singh
28. Bir Singh
29. Sukha Singh
30. Sant Singh
31. Kotha Singh (Mazhbi)
32. Madan Singh (Ravidasia)
33. Kirat Singh
34. Anand Singh
35. Lal Singh
36. Kesara Singh
37. Amolak Singh
38. Jawahar Singh
39. Sangat Singh

Note: (i) No details are as yet available regarding Nos. 13 to 39.

(ii) The total number of these martyrs ought to be 37. It is quite possible that a couple of these persons might have borne more than one name, due to which the number has exceeded by 2. In all probability 8 & 9 stand for one person; so do 11 & 12.

APPENDIX-III

POETS, WRITERS AND MEN OF PARTS OF THE DARBAR OF GURU GOBIND SINGH

1. Bhai Mani Singh Diwan
2. Bhai Nand Lal Goya
3. Bhai Chaupa Singh
4. Bhai Daya Singh
5. Pandit Kirpa Ram
6. Nanuan Vairagi
7. Bhai Ram Kumar
8. Devi Das
9. Lakhan Rai
10. Bhoj Raj
11. Tansukh Lahori
12. Chandersain Sainapat
13. Kanshi Ram
14. Prehlad Rai
15. Amrit Rai Lahori
16. Mangal Rai
17. Hans Ram Bahjpai
18. Kunvresh
19. Tehkan Das
20. Chand
21. Ani Rai
22. Sukhdev
23. Brind
24. Girdhar Lal
25. Alam Shah
26. Nand Ram
27. Hari Das
28. Gopal
29. Dharam Singh
30. Gurdas Singh
31. Gurdas Guni
32. Bhai Pheru
33. Brahm Bhatt
34. Heer Bhatt
35. Sunder
36. Sharda
37. Sudama
38. Hussain Ali
39. Chandan
40. Dhanna Singh
41. Ram Das
42. Brij Lal
43. Mir Chhabila
44. Mir Mushki
45. Kesho Bhatt
46. Desa Singh Bhatt
47. Narbad Singh Bhatt
48. Kirat Singh
49. Nihchal Fakir
50. Pindi Lal
51. Nand Lal
52. Mallu
53. Kallua
54. Ballu
55. Ballabh
56. Allu
57. Madhu
58. Udai Rai
59. Thakkur
60. Man Das Vairagi

61. Ishar Das
62. Mathra Das
63. Ram Chander
64. Madan Gir
65. Rai Singh
66. Sukha Singh
67. Mahan Singh
68. Harjas Rai Hazoori
69. Pandit Raghunath
70. Pandit Mithu
71. Madan Singh
72. Dhian Singh
73. Mala Singh
74. Bidhi Chand
75. Khan Chand
76. Brikha
77. Rawal
78. Shaikh
79. Sahib Chand
80. Dharam Chand
81. Alam Singh
82. Nanu Rai
83. Nand Chand
84. Daya Ram Prohit
85. Ram Singh
86. Karam Singh
87. Ganda Singh
88. Vir Singh
89. Shobha Singh
90. Deva Singh
91. Tehal Singh
92. Ishar Singh
93. Fateh Singh
94. Daya Singh
95. Dharam Singh
96. Himmat Singh
97. Mohkam Singh
98. Sahib Singh
99. Bihari
100. Lal Das Ghiali
101. Aadha
102. Jado Rai
103. Phat Mal
104. Kesho Guni
105. Bhagtu

Munshi & Mussadi

106. Asa Singh Mussadi
107. Saina Singh
108. Mani Singh Mussadi
109. Bal Gobind
110. Fateh Chand
111. Nihala
112. Bala
113. Darbari Singh Chhota
114. Gharbari Singh
115. Darbari Singh
116. Hari Das
117. Ram Rai
118. Sital Singh Bahurupia
119. Roshan Singh
120. Pakhar Mal
121. Shihan Singh
122. Ram Singh
123. Chhauna Singh
124. Bulaka Singh
125. Sahib Singh

APPENDIX-IV

SERMON GIVEN BY GURU GOBIND SINGH ON THE BAISAKHI OF 1699

Guru Gobind Singh delivered a very inspiring speech while addressing the mammoth gathering at Anandpur Sahib on the Baisakhi day of 1699. Mr. Max Arthur Macauliffe (1837-1913) attributed the source of this information to the report of a contemporary news-writer of the Mughal court and for this, he depended upon Ghulam Muhai-ul-Din's book *Tarikh-i-Punjab* written in 1848. According to Dr. Ganda Singh, the report was first inscribed in *Tarikh-i-Hind* written by Ahmed Shah Batalia in 1818.

We reproduce here below the original text in Persian and its transcription in Gurmukhi script along with its English translation by Dr. Harnam Singh Shah.

Original Text in Persian Script

همه هادر یک مذهب درآید
که دُوئی از درمیاں برخیزد۔
وار چهار برنے قوم هنود
از برهمن و چهتری وشُودر و وَیش۔
که هر یکے را دهرم شاستر دین علیحده مقرر است۔
آں را ترک داده بریک طریق سلوک نمائند
وهمه برابرند
ویکے خُود رابر دیگرے ترجیح نه دهند۔
وآں عملے کیش از میاں برداشته۔
ترقی بیابند۔

همہ ہادر یک مذہب درآید
آں کہ در وید و شاستر تعلیمے آں ہا
تاکید مزید رفتہ است
از خاطر بدر کند۔
و سِوائے از گورو نانک و خلیفائے اُو
بردِ گراز سنادیدے ہنُود
مثل رام کشن و برہما دیوی وغیرہ
اعتقاد نہ نمائند۔
و پاھلے من گرِفتہ
مردمانِ ہر چہار برن
در یک ظرف بخرند و از یک دیگر اصلاح برند۔

ہم چنیں سخُنہائے بسیار گفتند۔
چوں مردماں بشنیدند
بسیار از برہمناں و چھتریاں برخاستند و گفتند
کہ ما مذہب کہ گورو نانک و ہمہ گوروان بداں قایل نہ شُد باشند۔
و مذہب کہ مخالفِ وید و شاستر بود ہرگز قبول نمے کنیم۔
و مذہبے کہنا را کہ پیشینہ نگاں اقدام نمُودہ اند۔
بگفتہ کودکے از دست نہ دہیم ایں گفتہ برخاستند۔

مگر بست ہزار کس رضا دادند
و مطابقت بر زباں آوردند۔

Original Text in Gurmukhi Script

"ਹਮਹ ਹਾਦਰ ਯਕ ਮਜ਼ਹਬ ਦਰਆਇਦ
ਕਿ ਦੂਈ ਅਜ਼ ਦਰਮਿਆਂ ਬਰਖਜ਼ਦ।
ਵਾਰ ਚਹਾਰ ਬਰਨੇ ਕੌਮ ਹਨੂਦ,
ਅਜ਼ ਬ੍ਰਹਮਨ ਵ ਛੱਤ੍ਰੀ ਵ ਸ਼ੂਦ੍ਰ ਵ ਵੈਸ਼

ਕਿ ਹਰ ਯਕੇ ਰਾ ਧਰਮ-ਸ਼ਾਸਤ੍ਰ ਦੀਨ ਅਲਹਿਦਾ ਮੁਕਰਰ ਅਸਤ।
ਆਂ ਰਾ ਤਰਕ ਦਾਦਹ
ਬਰ ਯਕ ਤਰੀਕ ਸਲੂਕ ਨੁਮਾਇੰਦ।

ਵ ਹਮਹ ਬਰਾਬਰੰਦ
ਵ ਯਕੇ ਖ਼ੁਦ ਰਾ ਬਰ ਦੀਗਰੇ ਤਰਜੀਹ ਨ ਦਿਹੰਦ।
ਵ ਆਂ ਅਮਲੇ ਕੇਸ਼ ਅਜ਼ ਮੀਆਂ ਬਰਦਾਸ਼ਤਹ,
ਤਰੱਕੀ ਬਯਾਬੰਦ।
ਹਮਾ ਹਾਦਿਰ ਯਕ ਮਜ਼ਹਬ ਦਰਾਇਦ
ਆਂ ਕਿ ਦਰ ਵੇਦ ਵ ਸ਼ਾਸਤ੍ਰ ਤਾਲੀਮੇ ਆਂ ਹਾ,
ਤਾਕੀਦੇ ਮਜ਼ੀਦ ਰਫਤਹ ਅਸਤ,
ਅਜ਼ ਖ਼ਾਤਿਰ ਬਦਰ ਕੁਨੱਦ।
ਵ ਸਿਵਾਏ ਅਜ਼ ਗੁਰੂ ਨਾਨਕ ਵ ਖ਼ਲੀਫ਼ਾਇ ਊ
ਬਰ ਦਿਗਰ ਅਜ਼ ਸਨਾ ਦੀਦੇ ਹਨੂਦ
ਮਸਲ ਰਾਮ ਕਿਸ਼ਨ ਵ ਬ੍ਰਹਮਾ ਦੇਵੀ ਵਗ਼ੈਰਾ
ਇਅਤਕਾਦ ਨਾ ਨਮਾਇੰਦ।
ਵ ਪਾਹੁਲੇ ਮਨ ਗ੍ਰਿਫ਼ਤਹ
ਮਰਦੁਮਾਨੇ ਹਰ ਚਹਾਰ ਬਰਨ
ਦਰ ਯਕ ਜ਼ਰਫ਼ ਬਿਖੁਰੰਦ।
ਵ ਅਜ਼ ਯਕ ਦਿਗਰ ਇਸਲਾਹ ਬਰੰਦ।"

ਹਮ ਚਿਨੀਂ ਸੁਖਨਹਾਇ ਬਿਸਯਾਰ ਗੁਫਤੰਦ।
ਚੂੰ ਮਰਦੁਮਾਂ ਬ ਸ਼ਨੀਦੰਦ
ਬਿਸਯਾਰੇ ਅਜ਼ ਬ੍ਰਹਮਨਾ ਵ ਛੱਤ੍ਰੀਆਂ ਬਰਖ਼ਾਸਤੰਦ ਵ ਗੁਫਤੰਦ,
"ਕਿ ਮਾ ਮਜ਼ਹਬੇ ਕਿ ਗੁਰੂ ਨਾਨਕ
ਵਾ ਹਮਹ ਗੁਰੂਆਂ ਬਦਾਂ ਕਾਯਲ ਨਾ ਸ਼ੁਦ ਬਾਸ਼ੰਦ।
ਵ ਮਜ਼ਹਬੇ ਕਿ ਮੁਖਾਲਿਫੇ ਵੇਦ ਸ਼ਾਸਤ੍ਰ ਬਵੱਦ,
ਹਰਗਿਜ਼ ਕਬੂਲ ਨਮੇ ਕੁਨੇਮ।
ਵ ਮਜ਼ਹਬੇ ਕਹਨਾ ਰਾ ਕਿ ਪੇਸ਼ੀਨਾ ਨਿਗਾਂ ਇਕਦਾਮ ਨਮੂਦਹ ਅੰਦ,
ਬਗੁਫਤਹ ਕੋਦਕੇ ਅਜ਼ ਦਸਤ ਨ ਦਿਹੇਮ।"

ਈਂ ਗੁਫਤਾ ਬਰਖ਼ਾਸਤੰਦ,
ਮਗਰ ਬਸਤ ਹਜ਼ਾਰ ਕਸ ਰਜ਼ਾ ਦਾਦੰਦ,
ਵ ਮੁਤਾਬਕਤ ਬਰ ਜ਼ੁਬਾਂ ਆਵੁਰਦੰਦ।

Its Translation into English

"All should come into the fold of one creed
so that the difference among them may disappear.
And all the four castes of Hindus,
(viz. the Brahmans, Chhatris, Vaishas and Shudras)

for each of whom the *Ved, Shastras,*
should abandon those altogether;
follow one path and
adopt one form of adoration (of God).
They should consider one another as equals;
and no one should think himself preferable to another.
They should leave aside all those rites and customs,
and be progressive in their pursuits.
The notion about pilgrimages, like that to the Ganges etc.,
which are enjoined and emphasised in the *Vedas* and
Shastras, should be removed from the mind.
With the exception of Guru Nanak and his spiritual
successors,
none of the Hindu deities,
Such as Rama, Krishna, Brahma and Devi, etc.,
are to be adored.
After receiving my *Pahul* (Baptism of the Double-edged
sword),
men of all the four castes
should eat out of the same vessel
and reform one another."

He (Guru Gobind Singh) said
many more such things.
When the people heard those,
many of the Brahmans and Chhatris got up and said:
"They would never accept the religion
which Guru Nanak and the other Gurus did not adopt,
and which was opposed to the teachings of *Vedas* and
Shastras
On the other hand
they would not give up the ancient religion
which their ancestors had believed in,
at the bidding of just a boy."

Saying this, they left.
In spite of that, twenty thousand men
accepted the Guru's gospel
and pledged to act upon it.

APPENDIX-V

PLACES VISITED BY GURU TEGH BAHADUR

Uptil now one hundred and thirteen places have been identified, which were hollowed by the Guru's visit. According to Dr. Sukhdial Singh, out of them, six places, Baba Bakala, Anandpur, Bahadurgarh, Damdama, Talwandi Sabo, Dhilwan (Sangrur district), were such places where the Guru sojourned for a bit longer period. The following is the list of places visited by the Guru in chronological order:

(1) Baba Bakala, (2) Sathiala, (3) Kaleke, (4) Amritsar, (5) Verka, (6) Valla, (7) Ghookewali, (8) Khemkaran, (9) Chohla Sahib, (10) Kartarpur, (11) Plahi Nagar, (12) Chak Guru, (13) Hakimpur, (14) Durgapur, (15) Nawan Shehar, (16) Kiratpur Sahib, (17) Anandpur Sahib, (18) Bharat Garh, (19) Malikpur Ranghran, (20) Ropar, (21) Dugri, (22) Kotli, (23) Kurali, (24) Manpur, (25) Gharooan, (26) Nandpur Kalaur, (27) Raillo, (28) Baher, (29) Railly, (30) Bassi Pathana, (31) Makaropur, (32) Bhagrana, (33) Ugani, (34) Bahadurgarh, (35) Mehmadpur, (36) Raipur, (37) Seel, (38) Sheikhupur, (39) Harpalpur, (40) Kaboolpur Hasanapur, (41) Nanheri, (42) Bibipur Khurd, (43) Magar Sahib, (44) Budhmur, (45) Karhali, (46) Patiala, (47) Tehalpur, (48) Khandauli, (49) Naulakha, (50) Lang, (51) Aakar, (52) Seembro, (53) Dhangera, (54) Agaul, (55) Rohta, (56) Thuhi, (57) Ramgarh Bauran, (58) Guni-ke, (59) Aaloarkh, (60) Bhawanigarh, (61) Phaguwala, (62) Gharachon, (63) Nagra, (64) Tal-Ghanaur Jattan, (65) Samana, (66) Dodra, (67) Kamalpur, (68) Dirba, (69) Nanhera, (70) Behar Jakh, (71) Moonak, (72) Makror Sahib (Damdama Sahib), (73) Gurney Kalan, (74) Lehal Kalan, (75) Gaga, (76) Sanghreri, (77) Gobindpur, (78) Barhe, (79) Kot Dharmoo, (80) Talwandi Sabo, (81) Tahla Sahib, (82) Maur, (83) Mysar Khana, (84) Bhaini Bagha, (85) Dikh, (86) Khiala Kalan, (87) Joga, (88) Bhupal, (89) Bhikhi, (90) Dhalewan, (91) Smaian, (92) Kanakwal Kalan, (93) Gandhuan, (94) Bachho-ana, (95) Khiva Kalan, (96) Alisher, (97) Pandher, (98) Hiron Kalan, (99) Shahpur, (100) Kattu, (101) Dhaula, (102) Handiaya, (103) Sohiwal, (104) Roore Kalan, (105) Dullami Ki, (106) Dhilwan, (107) Pharwahi, (108) Sekha, (109) Jahangir Pura, (110) Babbanpur, (111) Rajomajra, (112) Moolowal, (113) Bhaini Mehraj.

APPENDIX-VI

SIKHS OF THE GURUS AS RECORDED BY BHAI GURDAS

Some Eminent Sikhs of the Gurus as Recorded by Bhai Gurdas in Var XI

Pauri 13 (Inventory of the Names of the Sikhs of Guru Nanak)

From the very childhood detached natured Taru, a Sikh of *Popat* clan, was liberated (by Guru Nanak). One Mula of a wonderful nature was there; he would conduct as the servant of the servants of Guru. Pirtha and Kheda of *Soiri* clan also got merged in equipoise because of the shelter at the feet of Guru. Mardana, the bard and witty person, and a good player of *rabab* in assemblies, was a disciple of Guru Nanak. Pirthi Mal of *Sehgal* clan and Rama, the devotee of *Didi* clan were of detached nature. Daulat Khan of *Lodhi* clan was a nice person who later on came to be known as living *pir*, the spiritualist. Malo and Manga were two Sikhs who would remain always absorbed in the joy of *Gurbani,* the holy hymns. Kalu, having many wishes and desires in his heart, came to the Guru and under the influence of *Gurbani,* was honoured in the court of the Lord. The wisdom of the Guru, *i.e.*, the *Gurmat*, spread the loving devotion all-around.

Pauri 14 (Sikh Name Listing)

A devotee named Bhagata of *Obari* clan and Bhagat of Japu family were two Sikhs who would always go on serving (the Guru). Sihan of *Uppal* clan, and another devotee of *Uppal* clan were very dear to the true Guru. One Bhagirath of Malsihan town was there who earlier was a devotee of Kali, the mythic goddess. Jita of *Randhawa* clan was also a fine Sikh and Bhai Budha whose earlier name was Burha, would remember the Lord with single-minded devotion. Bhai Phirana of *Khaira* clan, Jodha and Jiva always remained absorbed in the service of Guru. One Sikh named Gujjar, blacksmith by profession, was there who would preach Sikhism to the Sikhs of Guru. Dhinga, the barber, serving the Guru got his whole family liberated. Thy *gurmukhs* having sight of the Lord themselves, make others also to have the same glimpse.

Pauri 15 (Sikhs of the Second Guru)

A Sikh of high achievement, Bhai Paro was there of *Julka* clan, on whom the Guru showered grace. A Sikh named Mallu was very brave and Bhai Kedara was a great devotee. I am a sacrifice unto Bhai Dev, Bhai Narayan Das, Bhai Bula and Bhai Dipa. Bhai Lalu, Bhai Durga and Jivanda were gems among the wise men, and all the three were altruists. Jagga was of *Dharani* clan, and Sansaru was one with the Formless Lord. Khanu and Mayya were father and son and Govind of *Bhandari* clan was an appreciator of the meritorious ones. Jodha, the cook, served the Guru, and crossed the ocean of life. The perfect Guru protected their honour.

Pauri 16 (Dalla Sangat of the Third Guru)

Pirthi Mal, Tulasa Bhalla and Malhan were devoted to the service of the Guru. Ramu, Dipa, Ugarsain, Nagori would concentrate upon the word of the Guru. Mohan, Roop, Mehta, Amaru and Gopi had eased their sense of ego. To Saharu and Gangu of *Bhalla* clan, and to Bhagu, the devotee, the devotion of the Lord was very dear. Khanu, Chhura, Taru had swum (across the ocean of life). Many courtiers of the Guru's court such as *Mallia, Saharu, Bhallas* and calico-printers have appeared. Pandha and Bula are known as the singer and scribe of the hymns of the Guru. Grand was the assemblage of Dalla inhabitants.

Pauri 17 (Sabharwal Sikhs of the Fourth Guru)

Bhai Tirtha was the leader among all the Sikhs of the *Sabharwal* clan. Bhai Puro, Manik Chand and Bisan Das have become foundation of the whole family, *i.e.*, they have got liberated the whole family, Taru, Bharu Das, the Sikhs at the door of the Guru are held as ideals for all the Sikhs. Mahanand is a great man and Bidhi Chand has a pious wisdom. Brahm Das is of *Khota* clan and Dungar Das is known as *Bhalla*. Others are Dipa, Jetha, Tiratha, Saisaru and Bula whose conduct is truthful. Maia, Japa and Naia are known to have come from *Khullar* clan. Tulasa Bohra is known as inspired by the teachings of the Guru. The true Guru alone chisels one and all.

Pauri 18 (Sikhs of the Fifth Guru)

Bhai Puria, Chaudhari Chuhar, Bhai Paira and Durga Das are known for their charitable nature. Bala and Kisna of *Jhingran* clan, and Pandit Rai adore the assemblies of Sikhs. Brave is Tiloka of *Suhar* clan, and Samunda, another Sikh, always remains in attendance of the Guru. Bhai Kulla and Bhai Bhulla of *Jhanjhi* clan, and Bhai Bhagirath of *Soini* clan maintain a truthful conduct. Lalu and Balu are *Vij* clan members, and Haridas remains always happy. Nihalu and Tulsia are forbearing, and Bula Chandia is full of many virtues. Toda, Tota and Maddu from *Mehta* family of Gokha city are contemplators of the word of the Guru. Jhanjhu, Mukand and Kedara perform *kirtan* of *Gurbani* before the Guru. The grandeur of the holy congregation is manifest.

Pauri 19 (Other Sikhs of the Fifth Guru)

Gangu is Nau and Rama, Dharma, Uda are brothers belonging to *Sehgal* clan. Bhai Jattu, Bhattu, Banta and Phirana are brothers belonging to *Sud* clan and love each other very much. Bholu, Bhattu and Tiwari give happiness to others and are known as the Sikhs of the court of the Guru. Dalla, Bhagi, Japu and Nivala have come to the shelter of the Guru. Mula, Suja of *Dhavan* clan and Chandu of *Chaujhar* clan have served (in the Guru-court). The fishermen Bisanu, Bibara and Sundar presenting themselves before the Guru, have adopted the teachings of the Guru. Great is the grandeur of the holy congregation.

Pauri 20 (List of Sikhs)

Along with Nihala, Jattu, Bhanu and Tiratha of *Chaddha* clan love the Guru very dearly, and they are servants always in attendance of the Guru. Nau and Bhullu are known as sadhus of *Sekhar* clan, and are the Sikhs of good conduct. Jattu of Bhiva clan and the greatman Mula along with his family are the Sikhs of the Guru. Chatur Das and Mula are *Kapur* clansmen, and Haru and Garu belong to *Vij* clan. A Sikh named Phirana is of *Bahal* clan, and Bhai Jetha is a good-hearted liberator of the family. Vissa, Gopi, Tulasia, *et al.*, all belong to *Bhardwaj* clan and always remain with the Guru. Bhaiara and Govind are devotees belonging to *Ghai* clan. They remain at the door of the Guru. The perfect Guru has fetched them across (the ocean of life).

Pauri 21 (Sikhs from Sultanpur)

Bhai Kalu, Chau, Bammi and Bhai Mula love the word of the Guru. Along with Homa, the cotton trader, Gobind of *Ghai* clan was also taken across by the Guru. Bhikkha and Todi both were *Bhatts,* and Dharu Sud had a large mansion. Gurmukh of *Kohli* clan and Ramu along with Nihalu are also serving there. Chhaju was *Bhalla* and Mai Ditta was a humble *sadhu*. Devotee Tulasa is of *Vohra* clan, and I am sacrifice unto Damodar and Akul. Bhana, Vigah Mal and Buddho, the calico-printer, have also come to the court of the Guru. Sultanpur is the warehouse of devotion (and devotees).

Pauri 22 (Masand Sikhs)

An obedient Sikh named Dipa of *Kasara* clan was like a lamp at the door of the Guru. In the town of Patti, Bhai Lal and Bhai Langah of *Dhillon* clan are well placed. Ajab, Ajaib and Umar belonging to *Sangha* clan are the servants *(masands)* of the Guru. Paira is of *Chhajal* clan, and Kandu belongs to *Sanghar* clan. They meet everybody with smiling face. Kapur Dev, along with his son gets blossomed, when he meets the Sikhs. In Shahbazpur, Saman takes care of the Sikhs. Jodha and Jalan are in Tulaspur, and Mohan lives in Alam Ganj. These big *masands* surpass one another.

Pauri 23 (Very Close Sikhs)

Bhai Dhesi and Bhai Jodha belong to the Husang clan of Brahmans and Bhai Goind and Gola meet with smiling faces. Mohan is said to be *Kuk* clan and Jodha and Jama adorn Dhutta village. Manjh, the blest one and Pirana *et al.*, conduct in the will of the Guru. Bhai Hamaja, said to be Jaja, and Bala of *Marvaha* clan, behave delightfully. Nano Ohari is of pure mind and along with him remains Suri, the *chaudhri.* Inhabitants of mountains are Bhai Kala and Mehara and with them Bhai Nihalu also serves. Wheatish complexioned Kalu is brave and Ram Das belonging to *Kad* clan is obeyer of the words of the Guru. Rich person Subhaga resides in Chuhania town and with him are Bhag Mal and Ugvanda, the *Arora* clansmen. All these devotees vie with one another.

Pauri 24 (Sikhs of Punjab Only)

Paira of *Chandali* clan and Jetha of *Sethi* clan are engaged in service of the Guru. Bhai Latakan, Ghura and Gurditta are fellow students of *Gurmat*. Bhai Katara is a jeweller, and Bhai Bhagwan Das is of devotional nature. Inhabitant of Rohtas village and belonging to *Dhavan* clan, a Sikh named Murari has sought shelter of the Guru. Adit, the brave, belonging to *Soin* clan, and Chuhar and Sain Das also have sought the shelter of the Guru. Along with Nihal, Lala (Lalu) also knows how to merge consciousness in Word. Rama is said to be of *Jhanjhi* clan. Hemu also has adopted the wisdom of the Guru. Jattu Bhandari is a good Sikh and this whole congregation lives in Shahdara (Lahore) happily. Glory of the house of the Guru is manifest in the Punjab.

Pauri 25 (The Sangat of Lahore - Mujang)

In Lahore, from the family of *Sodhis,* the elderly uncle *(taia)* Sahari Mal is a close Sikh of the Guru. Sain Ditta of *Jhanjhi* clan and Saido, the *Jat,* meditate on the word of the Guru. From the family of potters Sadhu Mehta is known to be a devotee of the Formless. From among the Patolis, Bhai Lakhu and Bhai Ladha are the altruists. Bhai Kalu and Bhai Nano, both masons, and from among the *Kohlis,* Bhai Hari are grand Sikhs. Kalyana *Sud* is the brave one and Bhanu, the devotee is meditates on the Guru's word. Mula of *Beri* clan, Tirtha and Mukand are also well-known Sikhs. A devotee from Mujang is known by the name of Kisana, and I am sacrifice unto Mangina, the wealthy person. A goldsmith named Nihalu along with his family is ever in attendance of the Guru. Service gives them all comfort.

Pauri 26 (The Sikhs from Country and Abroad)

Bhana Malhan and Rekh Rao, the fellow disciples of the Guru residing in Kabul are well-known. Madho *Sodhi* introduced the Sikh tradition in Kashmir. The truly devoted and close Sikhs are Bhai Bhiva, Sih Chand and Rup Chand (of Sirhind). Bhai Partapu is a brave Sikh and *Vithar* clansman Bhai Nand also serve the Guru. Bhai Sami Das of *Vachher* clan inspired the congregation of Thanesar towards the house of the Guru. Gopi, a *Mehta* Sikh, is well-known, and Tirath and Natha have also come in the shelter of the Guru. Bhai Bhau, Mokal, Bhai Dhilli and Bhai Mandal have also been initiated into the *Gurmat*. Bhai Jivanda, Bhai Jagasi and Tiloka have served well at Fatehpur. Great is the glory of the true Guru.

Pauri 27 (Agra Congregation)

Saktu Mehta and Nihalu Chaddha of Agra have been blessed. Bhai Garhial and Mathara Das and their families are said to be dyed in the love for the Guru. Ganga belonging to *Sehgal* clan is brave, and Harbans, the hermit, serves in the *dharamsal,* the inn for the pilgrims. Murari of *Anand* clan is a saint of high order, and Kalyana is a house of love and pure like lotus. Bhai Nano, Bhai Latakan and Bind Rao have served the congregation with full commitment and love. Alam Chand Handa and Sainsara Talvar are the Sikhs who live in happiness. Jagana and Nanda both are *sadhus,* and Bhana of *Suhar* clan is competent like swan to discern the real from false. These disciples of the Guru are like the jewels on a necklace.

Pauri 28 (The Sikhs in Attendance)

Sigaru and Jaita are nice and brave with an altruistic bent of mind. Bhai Jaita, Nanda and Piraga have accepted Word as basic to everything. Tiloka Pathak is the glorious mark who considers holy congregation and its service as benevolent. Tota Mehta is a great man and like *gurmukhs* loves delightful fruit of the Word. The whole of the family of Bhai Sain Das is like invaluable diamonds and jewels. Noble Paira, the *Kohli,* is the store-keeper of the court of the Guru. Mian Jamal is blessed, and Bhagtu is immersed in devotion. The behaviour of the perfect Guru with the Sikhs is also perfect.

Pauri 29 (Names of the Sikhs of the Sixth Guru)

Ananta and Kuko are good persons, who adorn the occasions. Ita Arora, Naval and Nihalu meditate on the Word. Takhatu is serious and serene, and Dargahu Tuli is always absorbed in remembering the formless Lord. Mansadhar is profound and Tirath Uppal serves all the time. Kisana Jhanjhi and Pammu Puri are also dear to the Guru. Dhingar and Maddu are carpenters and are very noble persons. I am sacrifice unto Banvari and Paras Ram who are experts in paediatrics. The supreme Lord sets right the wrongs done to the devotees.

Pauri 30 (Other Sikhs of the Sixth Guru)

Bhai Tiratha is from Laskar and Hari Das Soini belongs to Gwalior. Bhava Dhir comes from Ujjain and is devoted to the Word and the holy congregation. Famous are the Sikhs of Burhanpur who love one another and live in a state of equipoise. Bhaia Bhagvan Das is a devotee, and with him is a Sikh named Bodala, who lives in his home fully detached. Kataru, the noble one, and the physician Pirthimal are especially well-known personalities. Devotee Chhura and Dallu are inhabitants of Rihana (Haryana). Sundar and Swami Das both promote the tradition of Sikhism and live always like a blossomed lotus. Bhikhari, Bhabara and Sulas are Gujarati Sikhs. Loving devotion is their way of life.

Pauri 31 (Sikhs of the Sixth Guru)

In village Suhanda is Bhai Maia of *Lamb* clan who sings the holy hymns in the holy congregation. Chuhar of *Chaujhar* clan from Lucknow is *gurmukh* who remembers Lord day and night. Bhai Bhana of Prayag is a close Sikh who works hard to earn his livelihood. Jattu and Tapa, the residents of Jaunpur have served in accordance with *Gurmat* with a stable mind. In Patna, Bhai Naval, and among *Sabharwals* Nihala are pious persons. One wealthy person is known by the name of Jaita who likes nothing except service to the Guru of Rajmahal city of Bhanu Bahal whose mind is absorbed in the wisdom of the Guru and the loving devotion. Badali Sodhi and Gopal are rich persons, and understand the gurmat. Sundar Chadda of Agra and Bhai Mohan, a resident of Dhaka are ever engaged in service.

BIBLIOGRAPHY

PERSIAN

Abdul Rasul Maulvi: *Twarikh-i-Muazzam*, Rampur Library, M.S.

Abul Fazal: *Akbar Nama*, English Translation by M. Beveridge.

Abdul Qadir Badauni: *Muntakkh-ut-Twarikh*, English Translation S.A. Ranking.

Ahmed Shah Batalvi: *Twarikh-i-Punjab,* Tr. By Gurbakhsh Singh Pb. Uni. Patiala.

Ahmed Sirhindi Sheikh: *Maktuqat-i-Imam Rabbani*, Punjabi University, Patiala.

Akbar Nama, Eng. trans. by A.H. Beveridge, Calcutta, 1897-1903.

Aqail Das: *Halat-i-Aurangzeb*.

Akhbarat-i-Darbare Mualla, preserved in the old Historical Record, Jaipur.

Babur, Nūr-ud-dīn Muhammad: *Babur Nama*, Tr. by A.S. Beveridge in 1921 from the original text.

Bakhat Mal: *Twarikh-i-Sikhan*.

Bhandari, Sujan Rai: *Khulasat-ut-Twarikh,* completed in C.E. 1696/A.H. 1107.

Bhim Sen: *Nuskha-i-Dilkhusha*, 1708.

Bilgrami, Murtza Hussain, *Hadiqat-al-Aqālin*.

Bilgrami, Ghulam Ali Azad, *Khazan-i-Amira.*

Bute Shah: *Twarikh-i-Punjab* (Persian).

Chaturman: *Chahar Gulshan* completed in 1759.

Dara Shikoh: *Sakinat-ul-Auliya.*

Dhadi, Nath Mal: *Amar Nama,* 1708, Tr. by Dr. Ganda Singh.

Ganesh Das: *Char Bagh-i-Punjab,* ed. Kirpal Singh.

Gobind Singh, Guru: *Zafarnama.*

Gulam Hussain Khan: *Siyar-ul-Mutakhirin,*1785, English tr. by Briggs, London, 1832.

Inayat Ulla Mirza: *Ahkam-i-Alamgiri,* 1703-1707.

Jahangir, Nur-u-din: *Tuzk-i-Jahangiri.*

Kanahya Lal: *Twarikh-i-Punjab.* Tr. by Jit Singh Sital, Pbi. Uni., Patiala.

Kamvar Khan: *Tazkirat-us-Salatine Chughtaiya.*

Khushwaqt Rai: *Twarikhe Sikhan.* M.S. dated 1869. Sikh History Research Deptt., Khalsa College, Amritsar.

Khafi Khan: *Muntakhab-ul-Lubab,* completed in 1731, printed in 1860-74.

Mohsin Fani: *Dabistan-i-Mazahib*, Eng. tr. by Umrao Singh Shergill.

Muhammad Qasim: *Ibrat Nama*, written in 1723 C.E.

Nand Lal, Bhai: *Granthavli* edited by Dr. Ganda Singh.

Nur Muhammad Qazi: *Jang Nama* completed in 1765.

Saqi Mustad: *Maasar-i-Alamgiri* completed in 1710 C.E., Tr. by Fauja Singh, Pbi. Uni., Patiala.

Sarup Lal: *Twarikh-i-Sikhan va Dastur-ul-Amal,* M.S. 1855 C.E.

Unknown: *Twarikh-i-Bahadur Shahi*, completed in 1747 C.E.

Shahnawaz Khan, Nawab, *Másirul Umara*, Asiatic Society, Calcutta, 1888-91.

Suri, Sohan Lal: *Umadat-ut-Twarikh*, Daftar Awall, Arya Press, Lahore, 1885.

English

Ahluwalia, Jasbir Singh: *Metaphysical Postulates of Sikhism*, Godwin Publishers, Chandigarh, 1976.

Ahluwalia, Jasbir Singh: *Sikhism Today*, Guru Gobind Singh Foundation, Chandigarh, 1987.

Archer J. Clark: *The Sikhs in Relation to Hindus, Muslims, Christian and Ahmadyas*, Princeton University Press, 1996.

Ashta Dharampal: *The Poetry of Dasam Granth*, 1959.

Ashraf, K.M.: *Life and Condition of the People of Hindustan*, Manohar, Reprint 1970.

Athar Ali: *The Apparatus of Empire*, Aligarh Muslim University, 1985.

Attar Singh: *Travels of Guru Tegh Bahadur and Guru Gobind Singh*, English translation of *Sakhi Pothi*.

Avtar Singh: *Ethics of the Sikhs*, Punjabi University, Patiala, 1970.

Bamzai, P.N.K.: *A History of Kashmir*, Metropolitan Book Co., New Delhi, 1973.

Bandyopodayaya, N.C.: *Development of Hindu Polity and Political Theories*, Calcutta, 1938.

Bannerjee, A.C.: *The Sikh Gurus and the Sikh Religion*, Munshi Ram Manohar Lal, Delhi.

Bannerjee, Indu Bhushan: *Evolution of the Khalsa,* 2 Vols., Calcutta, 1947.

Bannerjee, A.C.: *Guru Nanak to Guru Gobind Singh*, Rajesh Publications, Delhi.

Batra, Colonel Rai: *Leadership in its Finest Mould: Guru Gobind Singh*, SGPC, 1979.

Cunningham, Josheph Dev: *A History of the Sikhs*, Reprint, S. Chand & Co., Delhi, 1955.

Dardi, Gopal Singh: *Sri Guru Granth Sahib*, Tr. World Sikh Uni. Press, Delhi.

Dardi, Gopal Singh: *Guru Gobind Singh*, National Book Trust, India, 1966.

Dhillon, Balbir Singh & Bhullar: *Battles of Guru Gobind Singh*, Deep & Deep Publications, Delhi, 1990.

Dhillon, Balwant Singh: *Early Sikh Scriptural Tradition*, Singh Brothers, Amritsar, 1999.

District and State Gazetteers of the Undivided Punjab, Four Volumes bound in two, Low Price Publications, Delhi, Reprint in 1993.

Elliot and Dawson: *History of India as told by its own Historians*, 1866-67, Vol. II & VII.

Fauja Singh, Gurbachan Singh Talib: *Guru Tegh Bahadur, Martyr and Teacher*, Punjab University, Patiala.

Fauja Singh: *Hukam Name Shri Guru Tegh Bahadur*, Pbi. Uni., Patiala.

Foster George: *A Journey from Bengal to England*, 2 Vols., R. Faulder, London, 1978.

Ganda Singh: *Makhz-i-Twarikh-i-Sikhan*, Amritsar.

Ganda Singh: *Hukam Name*, Punjabi University, Patiala, 1967.

Gandhi, Surjit Singh: *Sikhs in the 18th Century*, Singh Brothers, Amritsar, 1999.

Gazetteer of Bilaspur.

Gordin, J.H.: *The Sikhs*, London, 1904, Reprint in 1970, Language Deptt., Patiala.

Grewal, J.S.: *Guru Nanak in History*, Pbi. University, Patiala, 1963.

Gupta, Hari Ram: *History of the Sikh Gurus*, New Delhi, 1973.

Gurmukh Singh: *Historical Sikh Shrines*, Singh Brothers, Amritsar.

Guru Gobind Singh: *Dasam Granth.*

Guru Gobind Singh Marg: Language Department, Patiala.

Habib Irfan: *Agrarian System of the Mughals*, Asia Publications, Delhi.

Habib Irfan: *Evidence for the Sixteenth Century Agrarian Condition in the Guru Granth Sahib in the Indian Economic and Social History Review,* Vol. II, No. 3, January-March, 1964.

Harbans Singh Editor-in-Chief: *The Encyclopedia of Sikhism,* Vol. I to Vol. IV, Punjabi University, Patiala.

Harbans Singh: *Degh Tegh Fateh*, Hazoor Printing Press, Chandigarh, 1986.

Harbans Singh: *Guru Tegh Bahadur*, Manohar, Delhi.

McLeod, W.H.: *Sikhism*, Penguine Books, 1997.

Hugel, Baron Charles: *Travels in Kashmir.*

Hans Surjit: *A Reconstruction of Sikh History from Sikh Literature*, ABS Publications, 1988.

Hutchinson and Vogel, J.P.: *History of Hill States*, 2 Vols., Govt. Printing Press, Lahore, Reprint, 1982.

Jodh Singh and Dharam Singh: *Sri Dasam Granth* Text and Translation into English Vol. I and Vol. II, Gurdwara Board, Takht Sach Khand Sri Hazur Sahib, Nander, 1999.

Jodh Singh: *Varan Bhai Gurdas*, Text tr. Vol. I and Vol. II, Vision & Venture, 1998.

J.S. Grewal and S.S. Bal: *Guru Gobind Singh*, Panjab University, Chandigarh, 1967.

I.H. Qureshi: *A Short History of Pakistan*, Uni. of Karachi, Reprint 1985.

Irfan, Habib: *An Atlas of the Mughal Empire*, Oxford Uni. Press, 1982.

Irvine William: *Later Mughals*, Vol. I, II, Oriental Books, Reprint Corporation, New Delhi.

Kapur Singh: *Parsar Prasan—Baisakhi of the Sikhs*, Guru Nanak Dev University, Amritsar.

Kapur, Prithipal and Dharam Singh: *The Khalsa*, Punjabi Uni., Patiala, 1999.

Kharak Singh and Others: *Fundamental Issues in Sikh Studies*, 1992.

Khushwant Singh: *A History of the Sikhs,* Vol. I, Oxford Press.

Latif, S.M.: *History of Lahore.*

Lakshman Singh Bhagat: *A Short Sketch of the Life and Work of Guru Gobind Singh*, 1919.

Latif Sayyad Mohammad: *History of the Punjab*, 1889 C.E.

Macauliffe, M.A.: *The Sikh Religion,* Vol. I to Vol. VI, Reprint S. Chand & Co., Delhi, 1963.

Malcolm, Sir John: *Sketch of the Sikhs*, London, John Murray, 1912.

Marenc Ethnek: *The Transformation of Sikh Society*, Heritage Publications, Delhi, 1976.

McLeod, W.H.: *The Evolution of the Sikh Community*, Oxford Uni. Press, 1975.

Muhammad Akbar: *Lahore-Past and Present*, Punjab Uni. Press, 1952.

Muhammad Akbar: *The Punjab under the Mughals*. Idarah-i-Adabyat-i-Delhi, Reprint 1974.

Narang, Gokul Chand: *Transformation of Sikhism.*

Nayyar, Gurbachan Singh: *Sikh Polity and Political Institutio*-- Oriental Publishers and Distributors, New Delhi, 1979.

Nikky, Gurvinder Kaur: *The Feminine Principle in the Sikh Vision of the Transcendent*, Cambridge University Press, 1983.

Nur-ul-Hassan: *Sayyad Sheikh Ahmed Sirhindi and Mughal Politics*. Proceedings, Indian History Congress.

Pashaura Singh, *N. Gerald Barrier*: *Sikh Identity*, Manohar, 1999.

Puran Singh, Prof.: *Spirit of the Sikh*, Part II, Punjabi Uni., Patiala, Reprint 1980.

Puran Singh: *Guru Gobind Singh*, Guru Gobind Singh Foundation, Chandigarh.

Puran Singh: *The Book of Ten Masters*, Singh Brothers, Amritsar.

Rizvi Sayyad Athar Abbas: *Muslim Revivalist Movements in Northern India in the 16th and 17th Centuries.*

Rose, H.A.: *Glossary of Punjab Tribes and Castes.*

Sarkar, Sir Jadu Nath: *A Short History of Aurangzeb*, M.C. Sarkar and Sons, 1930.

Sharma, Sri Ram: *Religious Policy of the Mughal Emperors.*

Sher Singh: *Social and Political Philosophy of Guru Gobind Singh.*

Sikh Religious and Human Civilization ed. by Dr. Jodh Singh, Punjabi University, Patiala, 1999.

Singh, G.B.: *Sikh Relics in Eastern Bengal.*

Singh, Patwant: *The Sikhs*, Hopper Collins Publishers India, 1999.

Sarkar, J.N. Sir: *Assam and the Ahoms.*

Sarkar, J.N. Sir: *Anecdotes of Aurangzeb.*

Sarkar, J.N. Sir: *History of Aurangzeb* Vol. III Orient Longman, First Edition 1928, Delhi.

Teja Singh: *Sikhism, Its Ideals and Institutions*, Lahore Book Shop, Lahore, 1944.

Talib, Gurbachan Singh: *The Impact of Guru Gobind Singh on Indian Society*, Guru Gobind Singh Foundation, Chandigarh, 1966.

Trilochan Singh: *Ernest Trumpp and W.H. McLeod as Scholars of History, Religion and Culture*, International Centre of Sikh Studies, Chandigarh.

T.W. Beale: *An Oriental Biographical Dictionary.*

Vasvani, T.L.: *In the Sikh Sanctuary*, Madras, 1922.

W.H. McLeod: *Guru Nanak and the Sikh Religion*, Oxford, 1968.

William, G.R.C.: *Historical and Statistical Memories of Dehra Doon*, Roorkee, 1874.

Yusaf Hussain: *Glimpses of Medieval Indian Culture*, Bombay, 1957.

Punjabi

Arif Naranjan: *Rangretian Da Itihas*, Literature House, Amritsar, 1993.

Bhalla, Sarup Das: *Mehma Parkash* (*Punjabi*), Bhasha Vibhag, Patiala, 1971, written in C.E. 1776.

Bhalla, Kirpal Singh: *Mehma Parkash Vartak,* written in C.E. 1739.

Bhat Vahi Jadobansian, Punjabi University, Patiala.

Bhat Vahi Multani Sindhi, Punjabi University, Patiala.

Bhat Vahi Talauda Pargana Punjabi University, Patiala.

Bhat Vahi Purbi Dakhni, Punjabi University, Patiala.

Bhat Vahi Tumar Bijlautavi Ki, Punjabi University, Patiala.

Bhangoo, R.S.: *Prachin Panth Parkash* (Punjabi).

Chhibber, Kesar Singh: *Bansavli Nama Dasam Padshahian.*

Daulat Ram: *Guru Gobind Singh*, Lahore 1918, Reprint by Singh Brothers, Amritsar, 1997.

Giani Gian Singh: *Sri Guru Panth Parkash,* Bhasha Vibhag, Punjab, 1970.

Gurdas, Bhai: *Vaaran.*

Guru Gobind Singh: *Fateh Nama*, English tr. by Devinder Singh Duggal.

Ishar Singh, Giani: *Safar Nama Te Zafar Nama*, 1979.

Janam Sakhi: Puratan edited by Bhai Vir Singh.

Janam Sakhi Meharban.

Janam Sakhi; Bhai Bala.

Janam Sakhi Gyan Ratnavli (Mani Singh Bhai's *Janam Sakhi*).

Kahan Singh Nabha: *Guru Shabad Ratnakar*, Mahan Kosh (Punjabi).

Kankan Das: *Gur Katha*, Khalsa College, Amritsar, 1967.

Karam Singh Historian: *Amritsar Dī Twarikh.*

Kirpal Singh: *Janam Sakhi Parampara*, Punjabi University, Patiala, 1969.

Koir Singh: *Gurbilas Patshahi* 10, Punjabi University, Patiala, 1968.

Narotam, Pandit Tara Singh: *Guru Tirath Sangreh.*

Padam, Piara Singh: *Dasam Granth Darshan*, Singh Brothers, Amritsar, 1998.

Pothi Punjab Sakhian (M.S. Punjabi).

Randhir Singh: *Udasi Sikhan Di Vithya*, S.G.P.C.

Randhir Singh: *Itihasik Pattar*, 1953-54, Sikh History Society, Amritsar.

Randhir Singh, Bhai: *Shabad Murat*, S.G.P.C.

Sainapat: *Sri Guru Gobind Singh*, ed. by Ganda Singh, Pbi. Uni., Patiala, 1969.

Santokh Singh: *Sri Gurpartap Suraj Granth*.

Sewa Singh: *Shaheed Bilas* ed. by Garja Singh, Punjab Sahitya Academy, Ludhiana.

Shabdaarth Dasam Granth Sahib, Punjabi University, Patiala, 1973.

Sohan Kavi: *Gur Bilas Padshahi Chhevin*.

Sukha Singh: *Gur Bilas Padshahi* 10, Bhasha Vibhag, Patiala.

Tara Singh: *Gurmat Nirnai Sagar*.

Tek Singh, *Chatar Jugi, Bhai Vir Singh*, Personal Collections, Amritsar.

Titus Murray, T.: *Islam in India and Pakistan*, Madras, 1959.

Toynbee, Arnold: *A Historian's Approach to Religion*.

Trumpp, Ernest: *The Adi Granth*, London, 1877.

Ved Prakash: *The Sikhs in Bihar*.

Urdu Sources

Gian Singh, Giani: *Twarikhi Guru Khalsa*, Wazir Hind Press.

Kanahiya Lal: *Tarikh-i-Punjab*, New Imperial Press, 1887.

Khalifa Saiyad, Muhammad Hussain: *Tarikh-i-Patiala*, 1878.

Gazetteers

Dehradun Gazetteer.

Gujranwala Gazetteer.

Hoshiarpur District Gazetteer, Lahore, 1904.

Imperial Gazetteer of India, Oxford, 1908.

Mandi State Gazetteer

Punjab State Gazetteer

Sylhet District Gazetteer

Settlement Reports Pertaining to Punjab.

Translation and Exegeses of Guru Granth Sahib

English translation, 4 Volumes, Gopal Singh, World Bank Centre, Delhi, 1960.

English translation, 4 Volumes Gurbachan Singh Talib, Pbi. University, Patiala, 1988.

Punjabi translation Exegesis, 10 Volumes Bhai Sahib Singh, Raj Brothers, Jalandhar.

Journals and Periodicals

Abstracts of Sikh Studies, Institute of Sikh Studies, Chandigarh.

The Journal of Sikh Studies, Guru Nanak Dev University, Amritsar, (Pb.).

The Punjab—Past and Present

The Spokesman

The Punjab Journal of Politics.

Sikh Review, Calcutta.

The Journal of Religious Studies, Pbi. Uni., Patiala.

INDEX

E

F

G

K

L

M